A Place to Call My Jewish Home

Memories of
The Liberal Jewish Synagogue
1911–2011

Pam Fox

This edition first published in 2011 by
The Liberal Jewish Synagogue
28 St John's Wood Road
London NW8 7HA

British Library in Publication Data
A catalogue record for this book is available from the British Library

Copy-edited and proofread by Amanda Kay, Copsewood Editorial Services Ltd
www.editorial.copsewood.net

Layout and design by Hope Services (Abingdon) Ltd, www.hopeservices.co.uk

Indexing by Vivien Rose, and Read Indexing, www.readindexing.co.uk

Printed in England by CPI Antony Rowe, Chippenham, Wiltshire

ISBN 978-0-907443-09-4 Paperback

Note about the title of the book: *A Place to Call My Jewish Home* is taken from an article in the *Jewish Chronicle* in which Michael Grade talked about his sadness at the death of Rabbi John Rayner, former Senior Rabbi at The Liberal Jewish Synagogue, and his commitment to the synagogue (see the *Jewish Chronicle*, 3 March 2006).

In memory of **Rosemary Lazarus** (1935–2009)
who gave so much to the LJS and was loved by so many.

Rosemary Lazarus (née Levy), 1935–2009.
(undated, c. 1955)

Foreword

Memories and hopes, these are the staple diet of the Jewish spirit. There is perhaps no people on earth that remembers more faithfully or looks forward more fervently. Past and Future, these are the twin poles around which, it seems, all our thoughts and emotions revolve … The Past is the source of our strength, the Future is the purpose of our endeavours. But it is in the Present, and only the Present, that life can and must be lived. Abraham Geiger used to say: Aus der Vergangenheit schöpfen, in der Gegenwart leben, für die Zukunft wirken, 'We must learn from the Past, live in the Present and work for the Future.'

John Rayner, *An Understanding of Judaism*, 1997

THE MEMORIES of my own childhood and adult life, like many of those who have contributed to this book, are bound up with certain episodes in the history of the congregation of The Liberal Jewish Synagogue, whose stories have been meticulously researched and presented in these pages.

The LJS was born into an era of great uncertainty and change, but also out of a measure of optimism and hope. The 'Three Ms', whose names are inextricably linked with the founding of the synagogue, Claude Montefiore, Lily Montagu and Rabbi Dr Israel Mattuck, infused the new congregation with their love of scholarship, their passion for Judaism and their ability to unify and integrate these qualities with the day to day lives of those – young and old – who became members of the synagogue.

Sincerity in worship and service to others, combined with an awareness of the prophetic obligations of justice and compassion, characterise the first stage of the history of the LJS. And these timeless principles remained at the heart of the work of the synagogue before and during the Second World War, when the congregation rose to the challenge of accepting responsibility and care for those who were fleeing Nazi-occupied Europe. This period of displacement and tragedy affected the congregation deeply, as it did the rest of the Jewish world.

By the late 1960s and 1970s, as the synagogue continued to grow and change, its membership was learning to challenge the classical models of faith that had set their seal on the theology and prayerbooks of the first fifty years of Liberal Judaism. There was an urgent need to re-structure and re-configure progressive Judaism in response to new social expectations and freedoms.

This is the story of how a synagogue has not only survived, but flourished in a century of extraordinary social change. In many ways, its members led the changes – intellectually and socially – unafraid of confronting the issues of gender equality, human rights, refugee and asylum issues, homosexuality, mixed-faith relationships and many others.

That drive for social change, for inclusiveness and equality, has not diminished, although it is perhaps tempered by the cynicism and dishonesty of our own age.

One hundred years after the founding of the LJS, we find ourselves caught between the growing and often militant secularism of British society, and the recognition that humanity cannot live without the external expressions of faith, without the aesthetic and uplifting nature of ritual, music, symbols and language. The Liberal Jew, rightly, eschews the identification of image, symbol or ritual with the place and presence of God, but recognises that our lives require the integration of reason and intuition and a 'divine discontent' that encourages us to know ourselves more deeply and to search for greater connection and meaning in past and present.

The voices that are heard through the pages of this book are a testament to all those who have remained loyal to, and inspired by, the LJS. In her history of the LJS, Pam Fox tells the story of a remarkable and enduring institution. In the interviews, we glimpse the encounter between the individual and synagogue and the way our lives, through design or accident, can be touched by the power of community, friendship and faith.

The book is an important milestone in our ground-laying work for the next century and a reminder that the story of the LJS is not complete, for we, its authors, are still required to write the next chapters of its life.

לֹא עָלֶיךָ הַמְּלָאכָה לִגְמוֹר, וְלֹא אַתָּה בֶן חוֹרִין לְהִבָּטֵל מִמֶּנָּה.

(Avot 2:16)

R Tarfon said:

You are not required to complete the task,
but neither are you at liberty to abstain from it.

Alexandra Wright
Tammuz 5771/July 2011

Preface

THIS BOOK IS a social history of The Liberal Jewish Synagogue in St John's Wood Road, London. It charts the development of the synagogue from its inception in 1911 until the present day when it is celebrating its centenary.

Although the book records important events in the development of the synagogue, its main emphasis is on the people of the LJS and the part that they have played in its evolution. It is intended that this will not only make the account of the synagogue's history more interesting, but it will also make the book consistent with a main tenet of Liberal Judaism – the belief that Judaism should be a dynamic religion, evolving over time to reflect changes in society and the developing needs and aspirations of Jewish people.

As far as possible, the history of the LJS is told through the eyes and in the words of LJS members and those closely associated with the synagogue. The book is largely based on interviews with a variety of people – congregants, spiritual and lay leaders and professional staff – carried out over the last two decades. However, information has also been drawn from other sources in which people have recorded their views and experiences about the LJS, including transcripts of talks, speeches and lectures, quotes in the media, articles in newsletters, letters, and autobiographical and biographical accounts. Secondary sources have been used only to a limited extent for the purpose of helping to interpret the oral history materials.[†]

I have tried to ensure that the material included in the book is as accurate as possible, while being aware that it would not be possible to achieve either 100 per cent accuracy or consistency. People's memories are sometimes fallible and they remember things differently. I did not see this as a problem, but a reflection of the richness of the materials with which I have been working.

Similarly, this history of the LJS is neither comprehensive nor definitive. Despite extensive research, I know that some topics and developments have been given more coverage than others and that there are some gaps. Again this is a result of the nature of oral history – people talk or write about what is of interest and importance to them.

These disclaimers aside, I hope that I have produced a book that people will enjoy reading as much as I have enjoyed compiling – it has been a joy, a labour of love and a voyage of discovery. I have learned a lot and met some simply wonderful people.

The book is arranged in three parts. Part One is a chronological history of the LJS covering the main historical events and developments, but also seeking to capture less tangible cultural changes. Part Two draws out themes and issues that span the history of the synagogue, such as the development of educational activities, the changing nature of the rabbinic and lay leadership of the congregation, the evolution of forms of worship and the consistent commitment to social action. Part Three of the book presents the

---

[†] See Appendix 1 for more information on the materials used in the book.

memories of a cross-section of people, covering not just their involvement in the LJS, but also their lives in general. Space did not allow me to include everybody's memories, as I would have liked to have done, but I have tried to ensure that as many voices as possible appear in other parts of the book. The book concludes with some reflections on the LJS in its centenary year.

Pam Fox
July 2011

Contents

Photographs

All photographs are from LJS archives unless otherwise stated. The photographer is named where they are known.

See note on photographs used in the book in Appendix One.

While every effort has been made to ensure the accuracy of the information about the photographs, total accuracy cannot be guaranteed.

Acknowledgements

I WOULD LIKE to thank Vivien Rose and Carolyn Simon for their help during the early stages of the 'Centenary Book Project'. Without Vivien and Carolyn, the book would never have got off the ground.

I was very fortunate to be able to draw on a number of interviews that had already been carried out by the LJS's Honorary Archivist, Bryan Diamond, and by Neil Levitt. Bryan and Neil continued to conduct interviews as the project progressed, and I am very grateful to them. Nearly all of the interviews Bryan and Neil tape recorded were painstakingly transcribed by Janet Ramsay, to whom thanks are also due. In addition, I thank Trixi Blaire, who carried out several interviews.

Bryan Diamond helped me to find photos and documents in the LJS archives, and Neil Levitt was a mine of information on the subject of the LJS building.

Jane Rayner read early drafts of the book and provided insights and encouragement. Bob and Ann Kirk generously shared their editorial expertise along with their knowledge of the LJS. I am particularly grateful for their help in editing the memories in Part Three of the book.

Rabbi David Goldberg and Rabbi Alexandra Wright advised on matters of style, particularly with regard to transliterations of Hebrew terms, and on religious content. Both rabbis also read drafts of the book and provided helpful feedback.

Throughout the process of producing the book Rosita Rosenberg made an invaluable contribution. In the early stages she commented on accuracy and content and, in later stages, she suggested really helpful editorial changes. Having produced a book herself, Rosita was also extremely helpful in providing general support and guidance. She devoted a great deal of time to the whole project and I am very grateful to her.

Thank you also to Judith King, for her editorial advice, and to my husband Michael Hart for editing a number of the interviews, reading drafts and keeping me sane when the going got tough! Several people advised on specialist topics covered in the book. They are too numerous to mention, but I do thank them.

I also want to say thank you to Amanda Kay who not only did a first class job in copy-editing and proofreading the book but also gave a lot of additional helpful advice – I learned a lot and I am indebted to her!

I would like thank Vivien Rose for her work on the index, and Jane Read of Read Indexing. Geoff Fisher at CPI Antony Rowe was unbelievably patient, and Mark Harvey and Sally Grimwood at Hope Services did a great job in designing and typesetting the book in a really short space of time.

I would like to thank everybody in the LJS office for their assistance, particularly Michael Burrnan for printing numerous versions of the book.

Finally, thank you to all those congregants who agreed to be interviewed, or who provided written reminiscences, and to Rita Adler for supporting the project from when it was just the seed of an idea.

Pam Fox
July 2011

PART ONE

A chronological history of The Liberal Jewish Synagogue

A chronological history of
The Liberal Jewish Synagogue

The founding of Liberal Judaism

THE ORIGINS OF the LJS lie in the movement to modernise Judaism that started in northern Germany in the early nineteenth century. Led by Israel Jacobson, the movement was a response to the era of emancipation ushered in by the French Revolution. The reformers were seeking changes, such as the shortening of the liturgy, the omission of prayers for the return to Zion, the introduction of choral singing and the reciting of some prayers in German rather than in Hebrew.

The movement spread quickly, if unevenly, across Germany and, by the 1840s, had reached America. In Britain, however, the reform of Judaism was slower to develop. In the face of bitter opposition, repeated attempts to introduce changes failed. These sporadic attempts included the holding of Sabbath afternoon services in Hampstead between 1890 and 1893 by the Rev. Morris Joseph. He was assisted by the philosopher, scholar and theologian, Dr Claude Goldsmid Montefiore.[1]

It was not until the very end of the nineteenth century that developments occurred which enabled what became known as Liberal Judaism to establish its roots. The main catalyst for change was an article, 'Spiritual Possibilities of Judaism To-day', written by 25-year-old Lily Montagu,[2] daughter of a strictly Orthodox Jew, Samuel Montagu, who later became Baron Swaythling.

> The little paper seems trite enough today, but coming as it did from an ordinary Jewish girl, brought up in an Orthodox home, it surprised many people so much that they paused to think, and in many instances, they remained to sympathise.
>
> Lily Montagu[3]

The article, which appeared in the *Jewish Quarterly Review* in January 1899, articulated the problem that was concerning certain quarters of Anglo-Jewry at the time – the apathy and lack of spiritual awareness amongst Jewish people resulting from Jewish emancipation, anglicisation and secular education, referred to by Lily Montagu as Anglo-Jewry's 'spiritual degeneration'.[4] She argued that changes should be made to Jewish worship to 'lift Judaism from its desolate position'.

---

[1] See photographs 2, 6, and 14.
[2] See photographs 3, 14, 17, 18 and 70.
[3] The Hon. Lily H Montagu, 'In the Beginning', in *The First Fifty Years, A Record of Liberal Judaism in England, 1900–1950,* published by the Younger Members' Organisation and the Alumni Society of the LJS (March 1950).
[4] The Hon. Lily H Montagu, 'Spiritual Possibilities of Judaism Today', *The Jewish Quarterly Review*, 11 January, 1899.

The views that Lily Montagu expressed in her article aroused an enthusiastic response. She was encouraged by Nathan Joseph,[5] a prominent member of the New West End Synagogue in St Petersburg Place attended by Lily Montagu's family, to approach leading members of Anglo-Jewry who might be sympathetic to her cause for modernising Judaism. Many of those she approached were close family friends or relatives of the Montagus.

Lily Montagu's efforts resulted in the bringing together, in November 1901, of a group of people who decided to form a society to organise services for adults and children as a means of adapting 'the ancient faith to the progressive needs of our contemporaries'.[6] The society was named the Jewish Religious Union (JRU) to indicate its commitment to Judaism, to religious faith and to the unity of the Anglo-Jewish community. The members of the JRU did not at that time see themselves as a breakaway movement. While they recognised that Jewish people of a liberal inclination might find it difficult to pray in existing synagogues, they hoped to liberalise both Orthodox and Reform synagogues by changing them from within.

The first open meeting of the JRU was held on 16 February 1902 at the home of Henrietta (known as Netta) Franklin, Lily Montagu's eldest sister.[7] It was attended by eighty-five people from a variety of Jewish backgrounds, but who were united in their commitment to revivify Judaism by making it responsive to the modern world. They wanted more English to be used in services, men and women to sit together, organ music to be used to accompany a mixed choir, and greater congregational participation in worship. These ideas were, at the time, both radical and contentious.

The first leadership committee of the JRU included Lily Montagu, who became Vice-President. Claude Montefiore, who had been a significant influence on Lily Montagu's developing liberal views, became President after much persuasion by her. The JRU Committee also included a number of established ministers[8] and others who were both well informed and influential in Jewish affairs.[9]

---

[5] He became a founding member of the JRU and was the father of Ernest Joseph, the LJS's long-standing Honorary Architect and a leading Council member.

[6] Quoted by David Goldberg in *To merge or not to merge?*, three talks by Rabbi David Goldberg and Rabbi John D Rayner on the historical background of, and the issues involved in, the current discussions about a possible unification of the Union of Liberal and Progressive Synagogues and the Reform Synagogues of Great Britain, given in February 1984.

[7] She was married to her cousin, Ernest Franklin.

[8] At this time, rabbis in Britain were ordained as 'ministers' rather than as 'rabbis'. The ministers involved in the JRU were Simeon Singer, Minister at the New West End Synagogue who also became a Vice-President; A A Green from Hampstead Synagogue; J F Stern from the East London Synagogue in Stepney; Morris Joseph, Senior Minister at West London Synagogue.

[9] Lily H Montagu, 'Pioneer Personalities of the JRU', undated draft of article in LJS archives. The prominent members of the JRU included: Dr Israel Abrahams, Reader in Rabbinics at Cambridge University and joint editor with Claude Montefiore of *The Jewish Quarterly Review*; Harry S Lewis, a Sephardi scholar and social worker at Toynbee Hall; Felix Davis, Honorary Treasurer at the United Synagogue and Secretary to the Norwood Orphanage; Alfred Jessel, an honorary officer of the United Synagogue and cousin of Lily Montagu, the JRU's third Vice-President; F H Harvey Samuel, Secretary and Treasurer at West London Synagogue and Honorary Secretary of the Jews' Temporary Shelter; Sir Isidore Spieleman, art lover, President of the Jewish Historical Society, an ex-warden of the New West London Synagogue and another cousin of Lily Montagu.

2. *Claude Montefiore, LJS President 1913–38. (1925)*

3. *Young Lily Montagu. (undated, c. 1902)*

The first JRU services

The first Sabbath service organised by the JRU was held in the Wharncliffe Rooms at the Great Central Hotel, Marylebone Road, London (now the Landmark Hotel) at 3.30 p.m. on 18 October 1902. The service, which was attended by over 300 people, was conducted by the Orthodox minister, the Rev. Simeon Singer. The sermon was given by Claude Montefiore.

In accordance with decisions taken by the recently formed JRU Services and Music Subcommittees, the service was mostly in English, men and women sat and prayed together, men had their heads covered and a mixed choir was accompanied by a harmonium. Algernon Henry Lindo had been appointed by the Music Subcommittee as Choirmaster, and was given the authority to appoint paid choristers if necessary.[10]

---

[10] Programme for 'A Tea to Celebrate the First Hundred Years of Liberal Judaism', held on Saturday 19 October, 2002 at the Landmark Hotel, Marylebone.

Since the JRU services were not seen as the prelude to the setting up of a separate denomination within Anglo-Jewry, the JRU approached the then Chief Rabbi, Herman Adler, to discuss holding services in a United Synagogue. This overture was rejected and the JRU denounced. Later, sufficient pressure was placed on the JRU members who were Orthodox ministers to force them to resign from its Committee.

After the first service, the JRU accepted an invitation from the West London Synagogue to discuss the possibility of services being held there. However, the stipulations made by the synagogue, such as the right to veto the content of services and the refusal to allow men and women to sit together, were unacceptable to the JRU.

In the decade that followed, the first Liberal prayerbooks were written, publications issued (including the widely circulated series *Papers for Jewish People*), lectures were organised and children's religion classes were established in Hampstead.[11] Contact was made with other Liberal and Progressive congregations in Europe and the USA. Services continued to be held at the Great Central Hotel, in various halls in the West End, and also in the East End of London (an East End branch of the JRU had been formed in 1903). Mr (later Dr) M Epstein was appointed to give addresses and to encourage attendance of services. He was not given the status of a minister, but was referred to as the 'curate'.[12]

> We were told to go slowly and offend nobody. But that was not the way chosen by the JRU from its initiation. With Claude Montefiore as our leader, we were unafraid. We met in committee and in small groups. We held propaganda meetings all over London and had the assistance, as speakers, of distinguished American religious leaders as well as rabbis from Germany and France.
>
> Lily Montagu[13]

The JRU found itself faced with fierce opposition, including from Lily Montagu's own father, who described the JRU as 'a menace to Judaism'.[14] It was widely seen as being schismatic in intent and it encountered a highly critical press.

> Some of our leaders and adherents lost their positions of trust because of their 'heresy'. Some were socially ostracised by the set to which they belonged; family quarrels were not infrequent and they were fraught with genuine pain.
>
> Lily Montagu[15]

Although personally wounding to JRU members, this opposition had a unifying impact, drew attention to JRU's activities and, in the end, helped to ensure its success. Attendance at services gradually increased and the JRU attracted back to Judaism a number of non-observant Jewish people.

---

[11] The first classes were held at the home of Mr and Mrs Ben Strauss in Daleham Gardens, London NW3.

[12] Lawrence Rigal and Rosita Rosenberg, *Liberal Judaism: The First Hundred Years*, Liberal Judaism (2004).

[13] 'Introductory Address at the Central Jubilee Service by Lily Montagu', *Liberal Jewish Monthly, Golden Jubilee Supplement*, November 1952.

[14] Cited in Edward Kessler (ed.), *A Reader of Early Liberal Judaism*, (2004).

[15] 'Introductory Address at the Central Jubilee Service by Lily Montagu'.

The setting up of The Liberal Jewish Synagogue

However, by 1907 the impetus behind the JRU was waning.

> But the novelty of our services began to wear off. Our attendances dwindled and again and again we discussed the necessity of closing down. But because we believed that our message contained the promise of ultimate success, we would not admit to defeat.
>
> Lily Montagu[16]

Divisions within the leadership became apparent. Initially the movement had mainly concentrated its attention on forms of service rather than on articulating the beliefs that underpinned the changes that were being introduced. This avoided potentially divisive differences of opinion being aired but, as time progressed, it was no longer possible to ignore a discussion of beliefs.

At a conference held in November 1908, it was acknowledged openly for the first time that the beliefs of the JRU differed from those of both Orthodox and Reform synagogues and that the only means for ensuring the survival of a liberal view of Judaism was to establish a separate Liberal Jewish movement. This acceptance was influenced by several speakers attending the conference who talked about developments in other countries, especially in Germany and France, where independent Liberal congregations were being formed.

In January 1909 the JRU decided that the time had come to set up a Liberal synagogue in Britain, even though this was expressly excluded under the JRU's original charter. The new synagogue would have its own rabbi, building and facilities for life-cycle events.

This proved to be a step too far for those holding more traditional beliefs who, as a result, left the JRU Committee. Committee members who remained committed to the JRU came under pressure to relinquish their positions elsewhere. Claude Montefiore was forced to resign from the Jewish Religious Education Board and Lily Montagu was asked to stop conducting children's services at the New West End Synagogue.

Despite these setbacks, the JRU pressed ahead with plans to establish a new congregation to be called The Liberal Jewish Synagogue (LJS). The JRU published a 'manifesto' written by Claude Montefiore, together with a pamphlet, *The Jewish Religious Union – Its Principles and Its Future*. These publications created a great deal of interest and, by the autumn of 1909, applications for membership of the proposed new synagogue, together with the annual subscriptions promised, were sufficient for a viable congregation to be formed.[17]

A public meeting was called at which the JRU changed its name to the Jewish Religious Union for the Advancement of Liberal Judaism to signal its new status as a separate movement. It was at this point that Lily Montagu resigned from her role as Vice-President to avoid angering her father even further.[18]

---

[16] Ibid.

[17] The minutes of the JRU for 1909 note that 110 applications for membership of the new synagogue had been made.

[18] Ellen M Umansky, 'Lily H. Montagu: Religious Leader, Organizer and Prophet' in *Conservative Judaism*, Vol. 34, July/August 1981.

The schism was now complete and the new movement, facing severe criticism and often the vilest of abuse, went bravely on its way.

Eric Conrad[19]

In March 1910 premises for a synagogue were acquired in Hill Street,[20] Marylebone[21] in a building which had previously been a Mount Zion Baptist Chapel. Described by Marjorie Moos who became a teacher at the LJS, as 'that little synagogue, so hidden from view and difficult to find',[22] it had seating for 232 on the ground floor and a further 192 in the gallery. Seats were initially allocated to those who paid an annual fee, a few at the front being retained for older people and those with a hearing impairment.

4. Exterior of Hill Street building. (undated, c. 1920)

An Ark was installed and inscriptions were made on the walls around it in both Hebrew and English. One scroll was presented to the synagogue by Professor Charles Singer (son of the Rev. Simeon Singer) and the JRU purchased a second scroll. The curtains for the Ark and the mantles for the scroll were provided and subsequently cared for by the women of the new congregation under the auspices of a Ladies' Committee which had been set up

---

[19] Eric V Conrad, *Lily H. Montagu – Prophet of Living Judaism*, National Federation of Temple Sisterhoods, (1953).

[20] See also photograph 78.

[21] Hill Street no longer exists. The disused chapel was located close to what is now Rossmore Court, London, NW1.

[22] Talk by Marjorie Moos to the LJS Women's Society in the 1980s, tape recording in LJS archives.

in 1910. The conversion of the chapel was overseen by Ernest Joseph,[23] Honorary Architect to the JRU. He and his wife became founder members of the new synagogue.

The first service of The Liberal Jewish Synagogue was held on 4 February 1911. It was led by Israel Abrahams and the sermon was given by Claude Montefiore.

The early years at Hill Street

One of the first tasks facing the leaders of the LJS was to find a rabbi. The person appointed was 28-year-old Rabbi Israel Mattuck.[24] Born in Sirvintos, Lithuania (then part of the Russian Empire), Rabbi Mattuck had graduated from the Hebrew Union College in Cincinnati in 1910.[25] He was serving a congregation in Far Rockaway, New Jersey when he was head-hunted by Claude Montefiore and Charles Singer. They had made a month-long journey to America after previous attempts to identify a suitable minister for the LJS closer to home had failed.[26]

5. *Rabbi Israel Mattuck, Senior Minister 1912–48, Rabbi Emeritus 1948–54. (1927)*

The impression that Rabbi Mattuck made on Claude Montefiore and Charles Singer matched the glowing testimonials that they had already received about him. When they

---

[23] See photograph 82.
[24] See photographs 5, 14, 18, and 63.
[25] See Part Two for more detailed biography.
[26] While in America, Claude Montefiore considered several possibilities for a suitable rabbi including Charles Fleischer, a rabbi in Boston. Cited in 'A Question of Backbone: Contrasting Christian Influences upon the Origins of Reform and Liberal Judaism in England', Manchester Journal for Jewish Studies 2004; 3:1–47.

returned to England with news of their 'discovery', Lily Montagu likened it to another momentous occasion:

> [It was] ... as great as that of Christopher Columbus and for us as full of promise.
>
> Lily Montagu[27]

Rabbi Mattuck was invited to preach at the LJS on 17 June 1911. The next day he addressed a members' meeting at the Great Central Hotel and on the following Saturday he conducted a children's service. He made such a positive impression that the JRU Committee agreed unanimously to invite him to become the Minister (as he was then referred to) of the LJS.

> [He] spoke to us on 'Faith'. I well remember that first sermon and the serious ardent face of the young man who delivered it.
>
> Lily Montagu[28]

Rabbi Mattuck was given a five-year contract which was renewed 'as a matter of course' in 1916[29] and he was inducted into the LJS by Claude Montefiore on 20 January 1912. In his inaugural sermon, entitled 'The Aim of Liberal Judaism', he articulated a vision from which he never wavered. He made an immediate impact as an exceptionally powerful speaker. This was welcomed by Claude Montefiore who was aware his own limitations in drawing a crowd and holding its attention.[30]

> The first service I heard Dr Mattuck preach at was the weekend of the Titanic disaster, and very soon I began to attend his lessons and became a member of the Alumni Youth Group.
>
> Marjorie Moos[31]

It was also quickly apparent that Rabbi Mattuck had a forceful personality. This proved to be essential as his early years at the synagogue were not always easy. As the first Liberal minister in Britain, he experienced considerable difficulty in establishing his credibility as a rabbi. The level of antipathy directed against him personally came as a great surprise as he had not encountered such opposition when working as a Progressive rabbi in America.[32]

> Dr Mattuck opened a door to intellectual thinking that I had never found before then. He was a wonderful orator and really reached out to all types of Jew. He was very much lampooned by the Orthodox for his rather flamboyant style of speaking. But he was an American and he didn't have the same reserve as the English rabbis. In those days, most of the rabbis in England came from Poland or Lithuania and they had that indefinable sort of Yiddish feel to them. Anglo-Jewry wanted something different, something with which they could empathise.
>
> Ruth Ive (Pt. 3)

[27] Lily Montagu, 'Dr Montefiore's Discovery', quoted *in Liberal Jewish Monthly*, March 1949 from her speech at a reception held in honour of Rabbi Mattuck on 26 January 1949.

[28] 'In Memoriam of Israel I Mattuck', *Liberal Jewish Monthly*, June 1954.

[29] LJS Annual Report, 1917.

[30] 'Very large congregation today. They do like M[attuck]'. Letter from Claude Montefiore to Lucy Cohen, 30 March 1928. L Cohen *Some Recollections of Claude Goldsmid Montefiore 1858–1938*, (1940).

[31] Talk by Marjorie Moos to the LJS Women's Society.

[32] Rabbi Dr I Mattuck, 'Liberal Judaism in Great Britain' in *The First Fifty Years*.

In retrospect, it was recognised what a momentous decision Rabbi Mattuck and his wife, Edna, had taken in coming to the LJS.

> Since my visit to the USA I realise a little better something of what the decision must have cost our friends. Big synagogues, great congregations, with all their vitalising influence; a multitude of friends; recognised leadership; a youthful and enthusiastic country; and we asked them to leave all this.
>
> Lily Montagu[33]

> It was a great challenge to take charge of a newly founded congregation, the first of its kind, and therefore of uncertain future, in a distant country, but Israel Mattuck accepted it in the spirit of our *Haftarah.*
>
> John Rayner[34]

Rabbi Mattuck also experienced difficulties within the LJS with its powerful lay leaders who had become accustomed to taking all the decisions relating to the movement. On occasions, Rabbi Mattuck found it necessary to exert his rabbinic authority. For example, in 1913, he pointed out firmly that matters of conversion should be dealt with by him as a rabbi, rather than by a committee of lay people.[35]

> [B]y the sheer force of his personality and vision, Rabbi Mattuck led the Council of the LJS.
>
> David Goldberg[36]

Rabbi Mattuck was a good organiser and was pivotal in helping to consolidate the embryonic LJS congregation. One of his first tasks was to create a prayerbook, as those previously produced for Saturday afternoon and children's services were not appropriate for a synagogue with an Ark or for a service with a scroll reading. The new prayerbook produced by Rabbi Mattuck, *The Liberal Jewish Prayer Book,* contained a cycle of six Saturday afternoon services and was widely welcomed by the congregation.[37]

In consolidating the congregation, Rabbi Mattuck worked very closely with Lily Montagu and Claude Montefiore, for both of whom he developed an immense respect.

> Among the factors which promoted the growth of the synagogue as an important place has to be given to personal ones, such as Mr Montefiore's guidance and influence, and Miss Montagu's devoted and untiring zeal.
>
> Israel Mattuck[38]

Together, Israel Mattuck, Lily Montagu and Claude Montefiore became known retrospectively as the 'Three Ms'. They were very different from each other, but they had a common vision for the development of the LJS. As a result, the synagogue went from strength to strength and, in 1913, it was necessary to employ a paid secretary (Mr Duparc) to manage its affairs. Mr Duparc[39] replaced A Lindo Henry who had been carrying out

---

[33] Lily Montagu, 'Dr Montefiore's Discovery'.
[34] 'The Spirit of Israel Mattuck', sermon by Rabbi John Rayner at the LJS, 25 January 1992.
[35] Lawrence Rigal and Rosita Rosenberg, *Liberal Judaism: The First Hundred Years.*
[36] Rabbi David Goldberg, 'Mattuck the Boss', in *LJS News,* December 1991.
[37] First LJS Annual Report, 1913.
[38] Rabbi Dr I Mattuck, 'Liberal Judaism in Great Britain' in *The First Fifty Years.*
[39] See photographs 10 and 74.

the role on a voluntary basis, but who was now finding the burden too heavy. Shortly afterwards, the LJS appointed a Beadle (Isaac Nathan).[40]

In 1913 the synagogue was registered to conduct marriages and, after a long search for a suitable site, a cemetery was established in Pound Lane, Willesden. It was a two-acre site designed to provide 1,500 grave spaces. Until that time, burial spaces were provided by West London Synagogue. The Pound Lane (Willesden) Jewish Cemetery Company was formed to administer the cemetery. As well as functioning as a prayer hall, the cemetery had a columbarium[41] where ashes could be scattered and there was also the facility for ashes to be buried under a rose bush, both of which were a major break with Jewish tradition. Isaac Nathan acted as the Sexton for the cemetery and Mr W Brady was appointed to act as the Superintendent, a role he held for thirty-eight years until retiring in 1945.

6. *Tree planting by LJS President, Claude Montefiore, at newly established LJS cemetery, Walm Lane, Willesden. Photograph also shows Marjorie Moos (above Montefiore's left shoulder) and Julian Simon (to Claude Montefiore's right). (1914)*

By 1915 membership of the synagogue had increased so dramatically that there were no longer enough seats for those who wanted to join. A waiting list was therefore introduced and the practice of having named seats was abandoned. In 1916 attendance at LJS High Holyday services was so large that they had to be held at the Bechstein Hall (subsequently the Wigmore Hall) and, the following year, held in the Kingsway Hall in Holborn. One Passover service had to be held in a cinema because no other accommodation was available.[42] In the same year it was decided that the Sephardi pronunciation should be used by the congregation.

---

[40] Further information on the early synagogue appointments can be found in Part Two, Section Five, The people and the place.

[41] A columbarium is a wall with niches into which ashes can be placed. The niches are covered with plaques with an inscription.

[42] Introduction to *The First Fifty Years*.

At this time, the main Sabbath services were still held on Saturday afternoons because many people were working a five-and-a-half-day week. Rabbi Mattuck was assisted by a number of laymen[43] and visiting rabbis, mainly from America. Mr Duparc also conducted afternoon services when Rabbi Mattuck was unavailable.

> The first years I was the Secretary, we only had one Minister, Dr Mattuck, and, during his holidays each August, I ran the Saturday afternoon services, wearing a top hat and morning dress, including reading from the scroll and sermons written by Dr Mattuck before he went away… I used to memorise the sermon before each service, so that I didn't have to read it from a paper.
>
> Michael Duparc[44]

In January 1916 Rabbi Mattuck also started to invite distinguished speakers to give lectures at the synagogue on Sunday afternoons, events which commanded large audiences.

As its membership grew, the LJS found itself under attack from the Anglo-Jewish establishment, including from the Chief Rabbi, Joseph H Hertz, who referred to Liberal Judaism as 'The moving staircase out of Judaism into Christianity'.[45] The LJS experienced difficulty in being seen as a *bone fide* synagogue within the Jewish world. Parents forbade their children to attend services at the LJS and communal organisations shunned the synagogue.[46]

> [W]hen my father joined the new movement, most of our relatives refused to have anything to do with us. They regarded us as worse than heretics; we were in their eyes positive traitors.
>
> Leslie Edgar[47]

However, early congregants were not deterred by the antagonism. Instead the congregation developed a sense of being at the forefront of a new movement. The leadership of the LJS persisted and the synagogue gradually established itself as a recognised part of Anglo-Jewry.

> I can assure you that our survival as a Movement was by no means then an accepted fact in Anglo-Jewish life, but perseverance and, above all, the unquenchable belief in the rightness of our presentation of Judaism in the twentieth century slowly but certainly overcame the hostility which many of our co-religionists felt and vigorously expressed about our alleged deviation.
>
> Louis Gluckstein[48]

Nor were early members discouraged by the uncomfortable conditions at Hill Street.

> The interior of the Synagogue had been most dignifiedly converted, but the general exterior of the Synagogue and the Religion School seemed to me very run-down indeed. The entry

---

[43] The laymen included Claude Montefiore, Israel Abrahams, Lionel Jacob (Vice-President of the synagogue), Sydney Mendelssohn (one of the Treasurers), Sir Philip Hartog, A Lindo Henry and Sir John de Villiers.

[44] Pamela Fletcher Jones, 'Mr Duparc remembers', special edition of *ULPS Focus* to celebrate the first seventy-five years of Liberal Judaism, Autumn 1977.

[45] Rabbi Dr I Mattuck, 'Liberal Judaism in Great Britain' in *The First Fifty Years*.

[46] Ibid.

[47] Rabbi Dr Leslie I Edgar, *Some Memories of My Ministry*, Liberal Jewish Synagogue, (1985).

[48] Sir Louis Gluckstein 'Sixty Years of L.J.S. History', *LJS News*, November 1972.

passage … was the least prepossessing of all. The buildings backed on to a railway goods yard and to get to the Synagogue and Religion School, one had to go up the 'ramp' by which the dray horses drew the carts into the railway goods yard. It was sordid and often dirty. Only the spirit of the congregation, and above all, the superlative leadership could have overcome these dowdy and – not to say rather unpleasant – surroundings.

Leslie Edgar[49]

[B]ecause Hill Street was so tiny and rough, it encouraged you and made you feel loyal; it certainly didn't make you complain.

Maxwell Stern[50]

7. *View from Hill Street window. (1925)*

8. *Interior of synagogue building at Hill Street. The staircase led up to the offices. (undated, c. 1925)*

As the congregation grew, so did the size of its Religion School (or the Sunday School as it was then known), which was set up on Rabbi Mattuck's arrival. Nine children were initially enrolled in the Religion School but, by 1916, there were 108 young people, the children of both members and non-members.[51] To start with, the children were taught on a voluntary basis by Rose Solomon. However, Rabbi Mattuck remained very involved in teaching activities.

---

[49] Rabbi Dr Leslie I Edgar, *Some Memories of My Ministry.*
[50] ULPS Oral History Project, interview with Maxwell Stern. See Appendix 1.
[51] First LJS Annual Report, 1913.

I went to Religion School first run by Dr Mattuck who knew every child by name. He was quite wonderful.

Denise Franklin

The Hill Street building was unsuitable for the LJS's educational activities. Children had to be taught in every conceivable corner.

My particular class was held in the choir loft and in the front of the synagogue. At the same time, a younger class was being taught by Miss Rose Solomon in the front pews. I don't think there was a class in the pulpit, but it wouldn't have surprised me! There were certainly classes, one or more, in the adjoining hall, another one on the stage in the hall, another one in the vestry and further ones held up the rickety staircase in the Secretary's office.

Dorothy Edgar[52]

The pressure on space for teaching was eased a little in 1917 when the Beadle moved from the house next to the synagogue to other accommodation, thereby making a few extra rooms available for the Religion School.[53]

Early pupils at the Religion School included Rabbi Mattuck's daughter, Dorothy, who was taught by Leslie Edgar. He subsequently became her husband and Assistant Minister (later Senior Minister) at the LJS.

Young people graduated from the Religion School at the age of sixteen with what were called Confirmation ceremonies. Introduced from America by Rabbi Mattuck, these were the first such ceremonies in Anglo-Jewish history.

At the Confirmation service, perhaps the most moving moment was when the rabbi gathered the confirmees around him for a private talk and prayer and then raised his hands in the priestly benediction. The congregation always found this impressive.

Dorothy Edgar[54]

The ceremonies included both boys and girls. There were no *B'nei Mitzvah,* since the strong feeling of the LJS's early leaders was that, at the age of thirteen, children were too young to commit themselves to Judaism.

A number of the families who joined the new synagogue had children at boarding schools. Correspondence classes for these young people were started in 1912. They were run by Cecile Coopman until 1921 when Samuel (Sam) Rich, by then a teacher in the school, took over.

1912 also saw the initiation of various forms of social welfare, especially programmes working with disadvantaged children, which were to become a key feature of the LJS. A Social Service Guild was established to oversee and encourage these activities. Following a talk given at the synagogue in November 1913 by Basil Henriques, a prominent LJS member, on his work in the East End of London, members of the Guild started to help run a Boys' Club in St George's-in-the East, which Henriques was setting up.

---

[52] ULPS Oral History Project, interview with Dorothy Edgar. See Appendix 1.
[53] LJS Annual report, 1917.
[54] ULPS Oral History Project, interview with Dorothy Edgar. See Appendix 1.

9. *Samuel (Sam) Rich, teacher at LJS Religion School.*
Photograph by Topical Press. (undated, c. 1940)

Then we went out in procession, and Mattuck started his speech which lasted nearly a quarter of an hour. I can't remember a single word of it, for I simply couldn't listen to it. At last it was my turn, (it is a boast in this diary, but for three-quarters of an hour, during which I made my first speech, there was not a sound to be heard), and the applause which greeted me at the end made me think that it had gone well. Afterwards I went down to the audience and had congratulations simply showered on me.

Basil Henriques[55]

It was a signal of how far the synagogue had progressed that it was approached in 1915 to nominate a representative to the Board of Deputies for British Jews. However, the synagogue felt unable to accept this offer as, at that time, the Board was not prepared to change its constitution to allow women members of the LJS to vote for a representative to the Board. This was an important point of principle for the LJS, and it was not until 1922 when the Board changed its constitution, that the synagogue was willing to join it.

The Council of the LJS began to consider the issue of vacating the Hill Street premises early in 1914, but the advent of the First World War delayed serious exploration of the possibility. The war also disrupted the religious life of the synagogue. Having been in existence for only four years, the LJS congregation was depleted as many of its younger members left to serve in the Armed Forces, including some of those holding key positions: the Choirmaster and several members of the choir, the Sexton and the Honorary Secretary.

Towards the end of the war, Rabbi Mattuck set up the synagogue's first youth group, the Alumni Society. After a slow start it became an integral part of the LJS and a novel aspect of synagogue life in England. The first Alumni Society meeting was held on

---

[55] Taken from the diary of Sir Basil Henriques, quoted in introduction to Henriques Music Archive produced by Sally Civval, 2011.

10. *Young people with Mr Duparc at Hill Street. (undated, c. 1920)*

13 January 1918, when twenty-six young people met to discuss 'The Conscription of Women'. Shortly afterwards, the society began to publish its own magazine, the *Alumni Gazette* (subsequently the *Alumni Digest*).[56]

On Rabbi Mattuck's recommendation, Lily Montagu became the first woman to speak from the pulpit at the LJS. On 15 January 1918 she gave her first sermon to an adult audience. The subject of her sermon was 'Kinship with God'.[57]

> It was an innovation when Miss Montagu first preached. I remember very well the outcry there was in the *Jewish Chronicle* that a woman would have dared to preach in a synagogue.
>
> Hannah Feldman

Two years later it was decided that women synagogue members should also be given the right to read prayers in services.

The interwar years

Rabbi Mattuck devoted a great deal of effort to rebuilding the congregation after the First World War.

> It says much for our Leader that he has known how to work with good and marked effect amid all of these difficulties [referring to the war]. It says much for his power, his eloquence, his insight, his religious sincerity and tenacity that he has … made and kept many men and women staunch and faithful believers … who would otherwise have drifted away.
>
> Claude Montefiore[58]

---

[56] Lawrence Rigal and Rosita Rosenberg, *Liberal Judaism: The First Hundred Years*.
[57] Lily Montagu, *History of the Jewish Religious Union*, pamphlet in LJS archives, (1927).
[58] Quoted in unattributed article, 'Israel I Mattuck – His life and work'.

As a result, membership of the synagogue rose rapidly and, by 1919, the LJS had one of the largest congregations in England. Its membership was more than double the number of seats available in the synagogue[59] and its services were regularly attended by visitors from all over the world. On one Saturday morning in 1920, for example, the congregation included people from America, Canada, New Zealand and Russia.[60] A move to larger premises became a priority and a Building Committee was set up to conduct the search.

This took some time, and the tenancy on the Hill Street building, which had been due to expire in 1920, had to be extended on an annual basis while the search continued. Attempts to find a building that could be converted into a synagogue were fruitless. The LJS Council therefore decided that it was necessary to construct purpose-built premises. A site was acquired on the corner of Upper Gloucester Place and Park Road, but this eventually proved unviable because of the number of sitting tenants on the site. It was therefore sold and a new site identified in St John's Wood Road opposite the Grace Gates of Lord's Cricket Ground.[61]

Although he was diffident about fundraising, Rabbi Mattuck spearheaded a building appeal amongst the synagogue's membership, which raised enough money within a year to finance most of the new building.

> We were all very excited over that for years. We did enormous amounts of work to collect the money. My father, of course, was the prime mover in all of this; he almost worked himself to death over collecting the money for it.
>
> Dorothy Edgar[62]

Both the Women's Society, which had been set up in 1923 to encourage more women to become active in the life of the synagogue, and the Alumni Society were involved in fundraising for the new building. The Women's Society set up a Sacrifice Fund and the Alumni Society donated the proceeds of a concert it had organised.[63]

The imposing synagogue[64] erected during 1924 was designed by Ernest Joseph, now Honorary Architect of the LJS and a leading Council member. The portico of the new synagogue consisted of six ionic columns donated by Bernhard Baron, a well-known philanthropist and synagogue member.[65] Inside there was seating for 1,350 people and a communal hall, named the Montefiore Hall, which could accommodate an additional 500 people. Upstairs there were several classrooms. The erection of this large and beautiful building was a major achievement for a congregation which had begun with 145 members only thirteen years previously.

There are many memories of the digging of the first piece of turf and of the laying of the first bricks for the new synagogue.

---

[59] 'The Years Between 1911–1951', LJS exhibition catalogue produced in connection with the re-consecration of the main synagogue in 1951 by the LJS Younger Members' Organisation.

[60] LJS Annual Report, 1920.

[61] Once it was established in its new location, the Rev. A A Green, Minister at Hampstead Synagogue, used to quip, 'The Liberal Synagogue is in St John's Wood Road, but not on the Lord's side'.

[62] ULPS Oral History Project, interview with Dorothy Edgar. See Appendix 1.

[63] LJS Annual Report, 1923.

[64] See photographs 11, 12, 13, 79, and 80.

[65] Bernhard Baron also provided the finance for a new building for the St George's Settlement in the East End founded by Basil Henriques with the support of the LJS and West London Synagogue.

There then came the surprising and exciting message for me to meet with other people opposite Lord's. When we got down there we saw a green thatched hut with a few bushes and one tree. There were seven of us: Dr Mattuck, Dr Montefiore, Miss Montagu, Lionel Jacobs, Michael Green, Mr Duparc and myself as Youth Representative.

Marjorie Moos[66]

I recall also the thrill when, as a very young Religion School teacher myself, I took my class to St John's Wood Road for the symbolic laying of bricks for a wall of the great new synagogue which was soon to arise.

Leslie Edgar[67]

11. *Laying of the first bricks for the new synagogue in St John's Wood Road by an unknown member of the Religion School. (1924)*

However, there were mixed feelings about leaving Hill Street.

A lot of the members said they would be sorry to be moving. They felt that it [Hill Street] was more intimate, there were smaller groups and you knew your minister.

Hannah Feldman

By the early 1920s, a full Sabbath service was being held on a Saturday morning, but afternoon services were still held for those working on a Saturday morning. Once the LJS was established in its new building, Rabbi Mattuck introduced additional Sunday morning services at the synagogue.

The synagogue quickly became an outstanding institution in Anglo-Jewry, and even to no small extent, in the religious life of the nation, owing to the eloquent preaching of Rabbi Mattuck, especially at Sunday Services ... where he dealt with contemporary issues, drew large congregations and was widely reported.

Leslie Edgar[68]

---

[66] Talk by Marjorie Moos to the LJS Women's Society.
[67] Rabbi Leslie Edgar, 'The Early Days and the Formation of the LJS' in Diamond Jubilee Celebration concert programme, 19 November 1972.
[68] Rabbi Leslie Edgar, 'The Early Days and the Formation of the LJS'.

12. *Work in progress on new synagogue in St John's Wood Road. (1925)*

13. *Exterior of first synagogue building sited at 28 St John's Wood Road. (undated)*

The Sunday morning talks were advertised, so they were really a public forum, and the meetings were packed. Dr Mattuck always spoke on very controversial subjects. We used to have question-and-answer sessions; people would write questions on slips, and runners – myself included – would take these to Dr Mattuck.

Ruth Ive (Pt. 3)

In 1925 the Hebrew Union College of Cincinnati conferred on Rabbi Mattuck an honorary degree of Doctor of Hebrew Law and the interwar years saw a number of other important developments in the ministerial leadership of the LJS. In 1921, Austrian-born Maurice Perlzweig was appointed to assist Rabbi Mattuck. He had been leading the newly formed North London Progressive Synagogue, which he continued to do while he completed his studies at Cambridge. It was not until 1925 that he was able to work more than occasionally at the LJS.[69]

As the congregation continued to grow, the Rev. Perlzweig and Rabbi Mattuck were joined in 1928 by the American rabbi, Solomon Starrels,[70] who also served at the West Central Synagogue recently established by Lily Montagu. In 1931, Leslie Edgar,[71] Rabbi Mattuck's soon-to-be son-in-law, was appointed as Assistant Minister. His role was largely to work with the younger members of the synagogue. Together with Sam Rich, Leslie Edgar managed the Religion School and started early morning Sabbath services for young people.[72]

In 1924 members of the synagogue organised a conference of Jews and Christians, which led in 1927 to the founding of the London Society of Jews and Christians, the first interfaith organisation of its kind. It was co-chaired by Rabbi Mattuck and W R Matthews, Dean of Saint Paul's Cathedral.

Building on her successful work in fostering a Liberal community in India, in 1926 Lily Montagu organised the first international conference of Liberal and Reform Jews, which was held at the LJS. At this conference, the World Union for Progressive Judaism (WUPJ) was founded. It has continued to hold conferences biennially ever since, except during wartime. Lily Montagu was elected as the Union's first Honorary Secretary, Claude Montefiore as its President and Rabbi Mattuck as its Chairman.[73]

In 1926, too, the first World Union garden party was held at our home with all the world-wide figures of the Progressive movement.

Dorothy Edgar[74]

The philanthropic and social welfare activities of the synagogue continued after the First World War. In 1919, the St George's Jewish Settlement was established by Basil Henriques with the support of the LJS working in co-operation with the West London Synagogue.

---

[69] LJS Annual Report, 1921.
[70] Rabbi Starrels trained at Hebrew Union College in Cincinnati and religiously was comparatively left-wing. He left the LJS in 1933 to become the rabbi at the North Western Reform Synagogue in Alyth Gardens.
[71] See photographs 15, 18, 35, 63, and 64.
[72] Rabbi Dr Leslie I Edgar, *Some Memories of My Ministry*.
[73] Until 1960, when it moved to New York in America (and in 1973 to Israel), the World Union had its headquarters at Red Lodge, Bayswater, the home of Lily Montagu and her sister, Marian. The European Region of WUPJ (now the European Union for Progressive Judaism) continued to be run from Red Lodge for many years.
[74] ULPS Oral History Project, interview with Dorothy Edgar. See Appendix 1.

14. *Participants in conference held at LJS in 1926 at which the World Union for Progressive Judaism was founded. Seated far left, Rabbi Israel Mattuck, Lily Montagu, seated centre and Claude Montefiore, standing right. (1926)*

The LJS's charitable activities in the East End and elsewhere were supported by the Women's Society under the chairmanship of Lady Sassoon. Similarly, when the Younger Members' Organisation (YMO) was set up in 1933 to co-ordinate activities for young people in their twenties, its members also became involved in social welfare and social action.

At the urging of its leaders, in the 1920s the congregation became increasingly involved in contemporary social issues. In 1932 Leslie Edgar set up a club for unemployed men which, despite some initial objections from the LJS Council and an uncertain start, was soon used by several hundred men five days a week.[75]

> Before my time, in the early 1930s, the synagogue had opened a soup kitchen for the unemployed. We had a dreadful depression in the early 1930s ... I think it was held once or twice a week; a hot lunch was served to the unemployed. Anybody that wanted to come could. I think there was a Labour Exchange on the Edgware Road and the men used to come from there.
>
> Ruth Ive (Pt. 3)

> A canteen was formed and a member of the Synagogue, a noted restaurateur, came personally to shew [sic] the men how to make a cheap but nourishing meal. Another member gave a complete cobbling outfit so that the men could mend their own and their family's shoes.
>
> Leslie Edgar[76]

---

[75] Rabbi Dr Leslie I Edgar, *Some Memories of My Ministry.*
[76] Ibid.

A Social Issues Committee, also led by Leslie Edgar, was set up. Made up of men and women experienced in public affairs, the Committee drew up reports informed by relevant experts on topical issues.

The synagogue's other major involvement during the interwar years was supporting refugees from Nazi persecution. Many refugees had a progressive religious background and therefore joined Liberal and Reform synagogues in England, including the LJS, despite being discouraged from doing so by those from Orthodox congregations. The refugees included a number of trained rabbis who helped at Progressive synagogues. Among them was Rabbi Jakob Kokotek, who assisted at the LJS during the 1930s and became a rabbi at the synagogue in 1941.[77]

Rabbi Mattuck worked tirelessly to raise large sums of money to enable German refugees, especially young people and children, to come to Britain.[78]

> The conditions in Germany from 1933 gradually worsened for the Jewish population, from petty restrictions to Jews losing all their civic rights, culminating in *Kristallnacht* on 9 November 1938. After *Kristallnacht*, the British government agreed to allow 10,000 unaccompanied Jewish children into this country provided the Jewish community made itself responsible for their upkeep. Dr Mattuck, who was the Senior Rabbi at the LJS, preached a sermon in which he asked the congregation to really think seriously about providing a home for a child from the *Kindertransport*.
>
> Ann Kirk (Pt. 3)

The synagogue was successful in arranging for 156 refugees to be settled in the country before the Second World War broke out.[79]

> I had met Jo in 1947 at the London School of Economics (LSE), where we were both evening class students. Jo studied Economics and Sociology, and I studied Commerce. Jo also had a connection with the LJS because she was sponsored by members of the synagogue on a *Kindertransport*.
>
> Willie Kessler (Pt. 3)

Although the reception they were given by the community at large was often hostile, the refugees were warmly greeted by the LJS. They were welcomed into the homes of LJS leaders and introduced to prominent members of the congregation.

> Lily Montagu also introduced me to her social circle and asked me to her house. She had a big family and introduced me to the Franklins, the Samuels and the Montefiores.
>
> Eric Conrad (Pt 3)

> My main memory of that period is about the sermons, but I do recall comments being made about the situation in Germany before 1939. My parents had a young man to dinner who had concentration camp markings on his hand, so they were aware of what was happening there.
>
> George Rigal (Pt. 3)

---

[77] Rabbi Kokotek went on to become involved in other Liberal synagogues, notably in Liverpool and in the New Liberal Jewish congregation, which became Belsize Square Synagogue.
[78] Rabbi Leslie Edgar, 'The Early Days and the Formation of the LJS'.
[79] Rabbi Dr Leslie I Edgar, *Some Memories of My Ministry*.

In 1933 young German Jewish refugees began to meet informally each Thursday evening at the synagogue. They were entertained and introduced to English friends by members of the Alumni Society and the newly formed Younger Members' Organisation. In 1938, these informal sessions were placed on a more formal footing when Bruno Woyda[80] formed a Friendship Club for German and English young people, which was soon catering for gatherings of up to 250. The club subsequently became a separate organisation, the New Liberal Jewish Association, which was initially chaired by Lily Montagu. The Association eventually founded the congregation that became the New Liberal Synagogue in Belsize Square.[81]

During the interwar years, the LJS's leaders worked hard to support the new Liberal and Progressive congregations they had been instrumental in founding in London and elsewhere. By the outbreak of war, Liberal and Progressive synagogues had been founded in North London (1921), West Central (1928), Liverpool (1928), South London (1929), Birmingham (1935), and Brighton and Hove (1935).

Despite these endeavours, there was still time for social activities and celebrations. During the 1930s, the LJS celebrated both the 5th and the 10th anniversary of the opening of the new building in St John's Wood Road.

> We have a wonderful photo of a grand LJS dinner at the Savoy in 1930, celebrating the 5th anniversary of the laying of the cornerstone of the new building. The four young Edgars are in the foreground. Leslie, of course, went on to become Rabbi Leslie Edgar and my great-uncle.
>
> Carolyn Simon (Pt. 3)

In 1937 a Thanksgiving Service was held at the LJS to celebrate the 25th anniversary of Rabbi Mattuck's ministry. All the congregations of the JRU participated in the service.[82]

Although the Anglo-Jewish establishment remained generally hostile to the LJS, by the 1930s there were some signs of rapprochement. For example, in 1934 the LJS applied to the Board of Deputies for certification as a congregation authorised to perform marriages under the Marriage Act of 1936. This was granted with the acquiescence of the Chief Rabbi. In 1937 Rabbi Mattuck and Claude Montefiore were invited to participate in a communal service held in the Great Synagogue to celebrate the coronation of King George VI. This was the first time that representatives of the LJS had been asked to attend a service alongside Orthodox sections of the Anglo-Jewish community.

However, relations with West London Synagogue deteriorated. In 1928 Rabbi Harold Reinhart had been appointed as Senior Minister there. Like Rabbi Mattuck, Rabbi Reinhart was a graduate of the Hebrew Union College in America, but relations between the two rabbis were 'at best coldly formal'.[83] The tensions between them set the tone for interaction between the two synagogues for the remainder of the interwar years. In 1936 Rabbis Mattuck and Reinhart attempted to put aside their mutual antipathy and sought

---

[80] Father of Walter Woyda whose memories are included in Part Three of the book.

[81] For many years the New Liberal Synagogue was the largest user of the cemetery in Pound Lane. This accounts for the predominance of German surnames on headstones at the cemetery. See George Rigal, 'Gone but not forgotten', *LJS News*, June 2002.

[82] LJS Annual Report, 1937.

[83] David Goldberg in *To merge or not to merge?*

to bring about closer co-operation between Liberal and Reform synagogues but, after a few meetings, the attempt was abandoned.

During the interwar years, two of the LJS's first leaders died – Israel Abrahams in 1924, and Claude Montefiore shortly after his 80th birthday in 1938. In 1938, the Assistant Minister, Maurice Perlzweig, left the LJS to join the North Western Reform Synagogue in Alyth Gardens.[84]

The LJS during the Second World War

The war years were a testing time for the LJS. It took a great deal of effort by Rabbi Mattuck to keep in touch with synagogue members serving in the Armed Forces, with the children who had been evacuated, and with the many families who had moved out of London, while at the same time holding together the congregation remaining in the capital.

He produced a weekly circular for the congregation and a monthly newsletter for members in the Armed Forces. He encouraged those living in different parts of London to meet together to discuss religious practices and sent out copies of his sermons to those living elsewhere.[85] The Alumni Society produced its own wartime *Gazette* and there was a twice-yearly Religion School magazine. One of those who maintained his contact with the LJS because of Rabbi Mattuck's efforts was John Rayner, who was later to be a rabbi at the synagogue.

> I joined the Army and during my four years there I, like a number of people here, was a regular recipient of Rabbi Mattuck's famous LJS Forces newsletter. It was an amazing thing that he did. He produced it every now and then, monthly perhaps, I cannot remember now. It was a duplicated newsletter, which ran to twenty or thirty pages or so, containing news about the LJS, about Judaism, general news about the war, new poetry that had been published and ideas about philosophy. He kept us in touch, not only with the world of Judaism, but the intellectual world and it played, I am sure, a large part not just for me but many other people too, in keeping us in touch with our spiritual headquarters in St John's Wood, which we might easily have lost otherwise.
>
> John Rayner[86]

Although he was recruited as the first Liberal Jewish Chaplain to the British Forces, Leslie Edgar was also involved in keeping in touch with LJS members. Despite these efforts, the size of the congregation decreased. In 1939 the LJS had 1,700 members. By 1946 membership had fallen to 1,300 notwithstanding the arrival of increasing numbers of German Jewish refugees.[87]

As the war progressed, synagogue life was disrupted more and more. Part of the building was taken over by the St Marylebone Borough Council as a public air raid

---

[84] Now commonly referred to as Alyth Gardens Synagogue.

[85] See LJS newsletters for 1941. These 'Sermons for Country Members' were still being sent out for a while after the war ended – see newsletters for 1945/6.

[86] Transcript of talk by John Rayner (undated) in LJS archives.

[87] Sir Louis Gluckstein, 'Sixty Years of LJS History'.

15. *Rabbi Leslie Edgar as wartime Army Chaplain. (undated, c. 1940)*

shelter and part of the basement became an Air Raid Precautions (ARP) Post.[88] When the war started, services were staggered to limit the number of people in the building. However, normal arrangements were restored within a few months in spite of a few scares.[89]

> [T]here had been one or two minor incidents in the form of incendiary bombs and an unexploded high explosive bomb had gone to earth just by the front entrance.
>
> Michael Duparc[90]

After the first air raids, the synagogue housed for several days 300 people from West Ham, who had been bombed out of their homes and placed there temporarily by the LCC while more permanent accommodation was found for them.[91]

The synagogue became a hive of industry in support of the war effort. The Women's Society was particularly active in helping evacuated children, the Armed Forces and refugees. Towards the end of the war, the Women's Society gathered goods and supplies to be sent to the women and children liberated from the Belsen Concentration Camp and displaced families.[92]

---

[88] 'The Years Between 1911–1951', LJS exhibition catalogue.
[89] J M Duparc, 'Our Congregations', *Liberal Jewish Monthly*, October 1949.
[90] Ibid.
[91] See Rabbi Mattuck's 'News Letter for members in the Forces', No. 1, November 1940.
[92] See Part Two for further information on the wartime activities of the Women's Society.

The exigencies of war encouraged co-operation between the LJS and Reform synagogues which had proved difficult in pre-war years. Reform and Progressive synagogues worked together to provide educational and other support for evacuees.

On the night of 1 November 1940, a 1,000 lb bomb fell on the synagogue. The building was seriously damaged, but seventy people sheltering in the air raid shelter in the basement were unharmed.[93]

> One Saturday, I left home as usual and went to the service and when I reached St John's Wood Road there was a policeman in the middle of the road who told me I couldn't go down there. I said I had to and when he said, 'What for?' I said I was going to the service and he never said another single word to me and I proceeded. I went on down the road only to get to see the terrible sight of smoke and fire and damage that the bomb had caused the previous night. Dr Mattuck and Miss Montagu had been warned about this. They had tried to warn me, but I left home too early. As we stood shocked and forlornly there, out from Lord's came Sir Pelham Warner, Captain of All England and he insisted that Dr Mattuck and all of us should hold our service in the Members' Room [services were held in the Oak Room, not the Members' Room] at Lord's. And so we did for a week or so.
>
> Marjorie Moos[94]

Subsequent services were held in a nearby church hall and sometimes in people's houses while temporary repairs were made to Montefiore Hall. The Hall was then used for religious activities until the synagogue was restored and redecorated.[95] The classrooms were destroyed, but the Religion School met each Sunday. The *sukkah* was used for social activities.

> The Montefiore Hall was just useable, but the whole building was in great danger of being condemned as unsafe by the District Surveyor, and therefore liable to being completely demolished. Thanks to the efforts of Mr Ernest Joseph our architect, and my own acquaintance with the then Minister of Works, who inspected the building, a stay of execution was granted, and the west side, which gaped wide open, was securely propped up for the remainder of the war.
>
> Louis Gluckstein[96]

In 1941, because of the limited accommodation available, two or sometimes three consecutive services were held on festivals and High Holydays. In 1942 services for festivals and High Holydays were held at the Friends' Meeting House in Euston Road[97] and the Communal *Seder* took place in the restaurant at Lord's Cricket Ground.

Shortage of materials and the various licences required by the Ministry of Works and the War Damage Commission meant that it took some time for the synagogue to be repaired.

> I remember that, before the badly bombed synagogue was rebuilt, it became infested with pigeons. My father, being eminently practical, gave an air gun to my brother Roy (a good shot), and told him to dispatch the pigeons that were flying about the building. Although

---

[93] See photograph 81.
[94] Talk by Marjorie Moos to the LJS Women's Society.
[95] Unattributed article, 'Israel I Mattuck – His Life and Work'.
[96] Sir Louis Gluckstein, 'The Work of Our Hands'.
[97] Now called Friends' House.

he managed to hit quite a few, Roy told me that they were so tough he doubted any of them had actually been killed!

Jean Jaffa (Pt. 3)

In April 1941 the West Central Club and Jewish Settlement in Alfred Place founded by Lily Montagu were completely destroyed, and for a time, the Settlement services were held at the LJS. When enemy bombing increased in 1944, Religion School classes were sometimes held under the stairway of the synagogue to avoid flying glass, and services were conducted against the background noise of sirens and bombs dropping.[98]

Religious education continued via correspondence courses led by Rabbi Kokotek, Marjorie Moos, Sam Rich, Rose Solomon and Bessie Hayes.

I went on to Confirmation during the Second World War. My family lived in Barton-on-Sea on the south coast. It was some way from London, and although we had the odd bomb, it wasn't too bad. I took the correspondence course organised by Miss Moos and came up to London for my Confirmation on 8 April 1942. My uncle who was living here took us out for lunch. The Confirmation service took place in the Montefiore Hall and was a low key affair. When I arrived, Alfred and Lilly Loebl asked me: 'Have you got the prayer that you were going to read?' I said 'I don't know anything about a prayer.' They then asked: 'Which passage were you going to read?' I said I hadn't been told about this. I was handed something and told: 'This is it' so I went up onto the *bimah* and read it. I have not kept in touch with any of the other confirmands. Of the names on the flier that I have kept from the service, the only one I recognise is Peter Lazarus.

Eva Feldman (Pt. 3)

I was told that Marjorie [Moos] was a firewatcher during World War Two and wrote many of her lessons sitting on a roof drinking poor quality coffee.

Sharon Lewison

Despite the fact that much of the synagogue remained out of use, a number of wartime weddings took place in the partially restored Montefiore Hall.

16. *Wartime wedding of Joan (née Rubenstein) and Eric Abrahams. Photograph owned by Jenny Nathan (née Abrahams). (1940)*

---

[98] Talk by Marjorie Moos to the LJS Women's Society.

At the end of the war, two services were held at the LJS on 8 May 1945, the Day of National Thanksgiving. A marquee was erected alongside Montefiore Hall to accommodate the congregation. Rabbi Mattuck preached on 'The Meaning of Victory'. On 19 August that year, two services were also held to mark the end of the war with Japan.[99]

Several members of the synagogue were honoured for their work during the war, including Phyllis Gerson, who was awarded an MBE in recognition of her services in connection with relief work in Europe and Sir Ian Heilbron, who was awarded the American Medal of Freedom. Both Colonel Louis Gluckstein and Pilot Officer Alan Rubinstein were Mentioned in Dispatches.

Post-war developments

The post-war years were a time of rapid expansion for the LJS as those who had served in the war came home and started families and as evacuees returned to London. Many people who might otherwise have left the congregation felt that, after the Holocaust, it was essential to maintain their Jewish affiliations.

> I was very smitten with Judaism after the War. I'd had a bad experience with a rabbi at religion school in Germany and I swore then that when I left the LJS Religion School and was confirmed, I would never enter a synagogue again. But I changed my mind.
>
> Eva Feldman (Pt. 3)

In addition to catering for the needs of an expanded congregation, the LJS also sought to play its part in rebuilding Progressive Judaism in the countries affected by the Holocaust and in supporting the new communities established by refugees and survivors in various parts of the world. The organisation through which the LJS played this role was the World Union for Progressive Judaism, which gained new importance when the internationally famous Rabbi Leo Baeck, himself a Holocaust survivor, was appointed as its revered President.

17. *Leo Baeck (left), Lily Montagu (centre) and Martin Buber (right) at the LJS after the World Union for Progressive Judaism Conference in 1947. Photograph by E H Emanuel. (1947)*

[99] LJS Annual Report, 1945.

In 1946 a Reconstruction Appeal was launched under the leadership of Ernest Joseph to raise funds to bridge the gap between the amount recoverable from the War Damage Commission and the sum required to repair the damage to the synagogue.[100]

The repair works commenced the following year and advanced stage by stage.

> At that time, the Sanctuary had not yet been repaired following extensive war damage, and so we were married in the Montefiore Hall of the old building on 21 May 1950. The Hall was temporarily furnished with the pews from the Sanctuary, where they were later reinstated. As a result, the gangways were extremely narrow and the bride had to sidle up the aisle.
>
> Bob Kirk (Pt. 3)

During 1947 there were two significant developments which helped to raise the profile of the LJS. The first of these was a broadcast by Rabbi Mattuck on the BBC Home Service on 22 July, when he spoke on 'What I Believe'. Later that year, Rabbi Mattuck published his latest book, '*The Essentials of Liberal Judaism*', which was based on his experience of preparing confirmation candidates for the previous thirty-five years.

By 1948 sufficient progress had been made on the renovation of the synagogue to enable the Communal *Seder* to be held in the synagogue for the first time since the bombing. There were three services: one in the annexe, one in the *sukkah* and one in the Montefiore Hall. In 1949 the *bimah* was restored with new desks and seats for the ministers. A bronze grille was installed in front of the choir gallery, and the organ was rebuilt by its original makers. By 1951 the work was complete. The synagogue was reconsecrated and a stone commemorating its restoration was unveiled on 23 September 1951. Two Services of Thanksgiving had to be held because so many people wanted to be present.

The first of the two services commenced with the ceremonial unlocking of the Ark by Ernest Joseph, with a golden key brought to the *bimah* by Bernard Lawton, Chairman of the Alumni Society. The Ark was opened by Sir Edward Baron and Rabbi Reinhart, Senior Minister at West London Synagogue. The six Scrolls of Law were then processed into the synagogue by Rabbi Dr Leo Baeck, Basil Henriques, Bernard Davidson, Ronald Simon, Michael Duparc, and John Cross, Chairman of the Younger Members' Organisation. The introductory address was given by Rabbi Leslie Edgar and after prayers had been said by Lily Montagu and the Assistant Minister, Philip Cohen, the *ner tamid* was lit by LJS President, Louis Gluckstein.[101]

> I also remember the rededication service that was held in 1951 when the synagogue was re-opened. It was an important service and part of it was broadcast on the radio. There were only enough tickets for adults to go and I can remember sitting at home by the radio trying to get the right spot to hear the little bit from our synagogue – that was very exciting.
>
> Jenny Nathan (Pt. 3)

Although his health was failing, Rabbi Mattuck gave a stirring main address.

---

[100] 'The Years Between 1911–1951', LJS exhibition catalogue.
[101] *Liberal Jewish Monthly. Re-Consecration of The Liberal Jewish Synagogue, Commemorative Number*, November 1951.

18. *Service of Reconsecration after the repair of the synagogue, 23 September 1951. On the bimah from left: Rabbi Mattuck, two unknown people, Sir Louis Gluckstein, Rabbi Leslie Edgar, Basil Henriques, the Rev. Philip Cohen and Lily Montagu. (1951)*

Particularly moving was Dr Mattuck's thanking, in his Address, the MCC, represented at the Service by Sir Pelham Warner, for their generosity in coming over from Lord's to offer us a room for holding our Sabbath Service on the day the synagogue was bombed. Unforgettable was the moment when that venerable and impressive figure of the internationally famed Jew, Rabbi Leo Baeck, carried the first scroll into the Reconsecration Service of the restored synagogue.

Leslie Edgar[102]

Less than an hour later, the synagogue was again crowded for the second service, which was a special service for children and young people. It opened with a procession of children from the Religion School who presented two reading desks to the synagogue. The main address was given by (now) Rabbi Leslie Edgar and a message of faith by Marjorie Moos.[103]

With the war over, friction between Reform and Liberal synagogues re-emerged as the two movements vied for the leadership of the new congregations establishing themselves in various parts of the country as part of the post-war 'bulge'. However, these tensions were less apparent amongst younger congregants, many of whom were prominent in

---

[102] Rabbi Leslie Edgar , 'The Early Days and the Formation of the LJS'.

[103] *Liberal Jewish Monthly. Re-Consecration of The Liberal Jewish Synagogue, Commemorative Number*, November 1951.

helping to establish the Youth Section of the World Union for Progressive Judaism in 1951.

> The Federation of Liberal and Progressive Jewish Youth Groups [FLPJYG] organised monthly discussions, for example, on Israel and intermarriage. I attended these meetings in different synagogues, thus becoming familiar with other clubs. There was also an annual drama competition held in the Montefiore Hall at the LJS. I attended the annual conference in April at Dorking and appear in photographs, such as one that was used for the centenary history of the Liberal movement. At the request of Rabbi David Goldstein, in 1958 I became the Treasurer of the World Union for Progressive Judaism Youth Section conference held in Italy.
>
> Bryan Diamond (Pt. 3)

By this stage the synagogue had become very well known and had begun to attract nationwide attention through the media:

> So my first knowledge of The Liberal Jewish Synagogue was when, having listened to either the rugby or the cricket on the radio, the news would come on and if there was anything of importance to be said about the views of Judaism in this country, the BBC would say, 'At The Liberal Jewish Synagogue in St. John's Wood today, Rabbi Israel Mattuck said...' and that was the authentic view of Judaism to the British public in those days and that was my first introduction.
>
> Robert Greenberg

Following the end of the war, Rabbi Mattuck took six months' leave of absence from the synagogue to tour America, but the war years had taken its toll on his health. In 1948, he retired as Senior Minister and became Minister Emeritus, leaving Rabbi Edgar to take over his role.

> Dr Mattuck had made such great and continuous efforts to keep in touch by writing to the scattered members of the Synagogue and had worked so hard ... that he was clearly worn out ... Not only did he need, and had, several months of rest, but from this time unfortunately he was an increasingly ill man and I had to take on much larger responsibilities than I had expected.
>
> Leslie Edgar[104]

The reconsecration of the synagogue described above had been due to take place in April 1951, but was deferred for several months because of Rabbi Mattuck's illness.[105] In January 1952 a special service was held to mark the 40th anniversary of Rabbi Mattuck's induction to the LJS. However, he was too ill to celebrate publicly his 70th birthday in December 1953. He died in April 1954. His death was widely reported and elicited widespread tributes. A special memorial issue of the *Liberal Jewish Monthly* was published to commemorate his contribution.

> In April 1954 Rabbi Israel Mattuck died. I felt his death as a great personal bereavement. I had spent many long hours with him at his house in Hampstead ('Wildwood', behind the Old Bull and Bush), and at his country cottage in Long Crendon near Thame.
>
> John Rayner[106]

---

[104] Rabbi Dr Leslie I Edgar, *Some Memories of My Ministry*.
[105] Unattributed introduction to 'The Years Between 1911–1951', exhibition catalogue.
[106] John Rayner, *Before I forget*, unpublished autobiography (1999).

Despite this great sadness, the 1950s were a time of many celebrations for the LJS. October 1952 saw the Golden Jubilee of the Union of Liberal and Progressive Synagogues (formerly the JRU). The thirteen Liberal synagogues now operating in various parts of the country each held their own celebrations, but the central service was held at the LJS where the *bimah* was occupied by sixteen ministers and lay ministers. At the reception held after the service, speeches were given by two ministers in training, one of whom was John Rayner,[107] who spoke of how he had been inspired by Rabbi Mattuck and Lily Montagu.[108]

In 1953 Louis Gluckstein, President of the synagogue since 1944, received a knighthood in the Coronation Honours list, and in 1954 Lily Montagu, now eighty, was elected President of the World Union in succession to Rabbi Leo Baeck. By this time, the synagogue's congregation had risen to 2,600 and the LJS had a high profile with many of its activities being covered in the national media.

In 1956 the LJS celebrated Rabbi Edgar's 25th anniversary as a minister at the synagogue.

> About 600 people, including many representatives of Jewish communal organisations and of interfaith bodies attended and I was presented with a most beautiful Georgian silver tankard (in which I said that I would drink to the Congregation 'for having put up with me for so long').
>
> Leslie Edgar[109]

After the end of the war, the synagogue organised a range of activities to deal with its aftermath, such as helping displaced families and those freed from concentration camps, but by the early 1950s it was resuming its involvement in social welfare activities more locally. Members of the synagogue continued to work in the East End of London. The Women's Society Sewing Guild made clothes for children at the Alice Model Nursery and several LJS members were social workers.

> I was a student until 1953 and then I had a job for a year at the Jewish Welfare Board in the East End. It was in Petticoat Lane, so I picked up quite a few Yiddish words. I did a lot of home visits, mainly alone. There were one or two roads where we would say, 'I am going down Cable Street today, so if you don't hear any more of me…'.
>
> Margaret Rigal (Pt 3)

In the pre-war years, the main LJS services had been well attended, but in the post-war years, attendance was much lower. This was partly due to the fact that many members, especially younger people, were more intent on socialising, but also because many of the families who had made up the initial congregation had moved out of London during the war and tended to come to the synagogue only for special occasions and the major festivals.

Following the departure of Philip Cohen after twelve years of service at the LJS, Rabbi Edgar was joined in 1957 by John Rayner as Assistant Minister, who in turn became Senior Rabbi at the synagogue in 1961 when Rabbi Edgar retired early.

---

[107] See photographs 20, 23, 44, 58, 65, and 68
[108] *Liberal Jewish Monthly*, Golden Jubilee Supplement, November 1952.
[109] Rabbi Dr Leslie I Edgar, *Some Memories of My Ministry*.

Rabbi Edgar felt weighed down by his responsibilities so that his health suffered, and in the autumn of 1961, although he was only 56, he wrote a letter to all members of the LJS informing them that, on medical grounds, he had been strongly advised to reduce his work load, and that it had therefore been agreed with the Synagogue Council that, with effect from 1 October, he would become Minister Emeritus, and I would succeed him as Senior Minister.

John Rayner[110]

By this time, Liberal synagogues had won the right to appoint their own marriage secretaries.[111] This was largely achieved through unremitting efforts on the part of LJS President, Sir Louis Gluckstein:[112]

The large increase in our membership and the improvement of our status was not, however, achieved without unhappy conflict within the Anglo-Jewish community, a conflict that was certainly not of our seeking. We found, however, that the discrimination of the Board of Deputies against the appointment by our synagogues of marriage secretaries had grown so serious that we withdrew our representative from the Board. Thereafter attempts were made to obtain by legislation permission for Liberal Synagogues to appoint marriage secretaries in their own right and without reference to the Board of Deputies. This was finally achieved in 1959 through the good offices of Sir Keith Joseph MP (one of our members).

Louis Gluckstein[113]

In 1960 the synagogue was closed for four months to allow it to be redecorated. At the same time, a panelled sycamore screen was installed on the wall of the choir gallery. It was gifted to the synagogue by the family of its long-standing Honorary Architect, Ernest Joseph, who had died earlier that year.

As Assistant Minister, John Rayner set about increasing the synagogue's educational activities. The Religion School was expanded, with classes being held on Saturdays as well as Sundays. He was also very prominent in the moves that were made in the 1950s and 1960s to establish a college for training rabbis, teachers and youth leaders.[114]

In 1961 Rabbi Sidney Brichto, a recent graduate of the New York branch of the Hebrew Union College, arrived to study in London. Before his arrival, he had accepted a part-time role at the LJS, which helped to relieve the pressure of work at the synagogue. In 1963 Rabbi Chaim Stern, another American rabbi (and a cousin of Sidney Brichto), who had joined the synagogue a year earlier, temporarily took over ministerial leadership of the LJS while John Rayner took a two-year sabbatical to complete his rabbinic studies at the Hebrew Union College in Cincinnati.

When we went to America on the Queen Elizabeth, our cabin was filled with flowers, chocolates and books and toys for our three young children from Louis and Dora Wolchover.

Jane Rayner

1963 was also the year in which Lily Montagu died.

---

[110] John Rayner, *Before I forget.*
[111] The Marriage (Secretaries of Synagogues) Act received Royal Assent in 1959.
[112] Sefton D Temkin, 'An Old Controversy', *The Jewish Chronicle*, 20 January 1959.
[113] Sir Louis Gluckstein, 'The Work of Our Hands'.
[114] See Part Two for further information on the LJS's educational activities.

On January 23 1963, at the age of 89, Lily Montagu died: the last of the 'Three Ms', all giants of the spirit, who had created the Liberal Jewish movement in Britain ... Her death marked the end of the chapter, and in a sermon entitled, *The Next Chapter* at the LJS on 2 February, I made an impassioned plea for an updated ideology backed up by greater learning and observance.

John Rayner[115]

A new wing of the LJS[116] was consecrated in Lily Montagu's honour following the launch of an appeal the previous year under the joint chairmanship of Robert Hermann and Dora Wolchover to mark the Golden Jubilee of the foundation of the synagogue. £50,000 was raised to build the new wing.[117]

[W]e were enabled to build our new small synagogue, four much needed excellent class rooms for our Religion School, a new and more suitable sukkah, and best of all a room dedicated to Dr Mattuck which is now used for Council meetings.

Louis Gluckstein[118]

The new small synagogue, which could hold 130 people, was used for *Shabbat* services when there were no Religion School classes.

Shortly before Rabbi Chaim Stern's return to America in 1965, Rabbi Dr David Goldstein,[119] previously the Minister of the South London Liberal Synagogue, was appointed as Associate Rabbi. He stayed with the synagogue for eleven years before taking up a research appointment at the British Library. However, he continued his association with the synagogue by teaching in the Religion School, leading the proselyte class and taking Friday evening services.

In 1965 (now) Rabbi John Rayner and Rabbi David Goldstein were joined by an American rabbi, Roger Herst, who stayed with the synagogue for three years and led many activities for younger people. The rabbinic team was supported for three years by rabbinic student, David Goldberg.

I married David [Goldberg] when he was the student Rabbi at the LJS and found the whole experience of being introduced to the congregation pretty terrifying. I was not used to 'public life' and was rather shy. Each time I was 'produced' I used to worry whether I had ladders in my stockings! I remember David's surprise in discovering that he was not as good a teacher as he had thought. The week after our engagement was announced only two men returned to the large adult education course he was teaching at the synagogue; all the single women had departed!

Carole Goldberg

At this time, Rabbi Rayner was completing the editing of a new prayerbook for the ULPS to replace those produced many years previously by Rabbi Mattuck. He did this in a transatlantic partnership with Rabbi Chaim Stern. The new prayerbook, *Service of the Heart* (which had been commissioned by the ULPS for use across its member synagogues), was introduced for LJS services in 1967 and in 1973 the new High Holyday prayerbook, *Gate of Repentance*, again edited by John Rayner and Chaim Stern, was used for the High Holydays.

---

[115] John Rayner, *Before I forget*.
[116] See photograph 83.
[117] Sir Louis Gluckstein, 'Sixty Years of L.J.S. History'.
[118] Sir Louis Gluckstein, 'The Work of Our Hands'.
[119] See photograph 66.

Between 1971 and 1974, Rabbi Alan Mann served part-time as Associate Rabbi.[120] Rabbi David Goldstein was succeeded in 1975 by Rabbi David Goldberg (previously rabbi of the then Wembley Liberal Synagogue).

In 1971 Margaret Rigal, a prominent member of the LJS congregation, formed with Rita Eker the Women's Campaign for Soviet Jewry known as 'The 35s'.[121] The group campaigned for persecuted Soviet Jews who had been forbidden to leave the USSR (the 'refuseniks'). Political lobbying had proved effective, but the group realised that more support was needed to ensure the safety and future of the refuseniks. The synagogue set up its own Soviet Jewry Committee in 1978 and many members of the synagogue became involved in its work, which continued until the latter part of the 1990s, by which time the main focus had shifted to supporting Russian Jews who had emigrated to Israel.

The LJS had been part of a united Jewish front that had supported Israel during the Six Day War and the *Yom Kippur* War. However, during the latter part of the 1970s, Rabbis John Rayner and David Goldberg started to challenge the policies of the right-wing government of Israel. They took a critical stance on Israel's continued occupation of the West Bank and its subsequent invasion of Lebanon in 1982. Their opinions were widely condemned, including by other Liberal congregations, but the two rabbis remained resolute.

During this period there was a notable expansion in the synagogue's congregational welfare activities. In 1967 Restaurant Tuesday was set up to provide cooked meals once a month for older members of the congregation and in 1978 Peggy Lang House, a home for the elderly, opened in Willesden.[122]

Towards the latter part of the 1970s, attendance at services began to decline. By then, most *Shabbat* services were usually attended by no more than a hundred people. Some members were also leaving the synagogue. In the mid-1970s there were 3,000 members of the LJS, but by the mid-1980s membership had fallen to 2,300.[123] This was partly due to the fact that people were moving out to the suburbs and were either joining or founding new communities there, such as the ones at Pinner (now Northwood and Pinner Liberal Synagogue), and in Stanmore (now the Liberal Synagogue, Elstree). However, membership also declined because some people were now looking for more traditional approaches to worship than those at the LJS, including the introduction of *B'nei Mitzvah*. Although most other Liberal congregations had introduced *B'nei Mitzvah* by this time, there was significant resistance to doing so at the LJS.

However, after much deliberation, in 1981 the LJS Council eventually took the decision to introduce these ceremonies, subject to an agreement that the young people would continue their education in the Religion School until their Confirmation, and that there would be equality for boys and girls.[124] The first *Bar Mitzvah* was celebrated for thirteen-year-old Jonathan Schwartz in November 1981.[125]

---

[120] He also worked part-time with the Hertsmere Progressive community (now The Liberal Synagogue, Elstree).

[121] See Part Two for further information on the refuseniks.

[122] See Part Two for further information on these welfare activities.

[123] The reduction was also partly explained by the fact that a number of people were taken off the membership list following a review of LJS records which showed that the list was very out of date.

[124] See Part Two for further details of the debate surrounding the introduction of *B'nei Mitvah*.

[125] LJS Annual Report, 1981.

The LJS celebrated the 75th anniversary of its founding during 1986/7. The celebrations included a wide range of cultural and religious events.

> In 1986 I had the pleasure of masterminding the celebrations for the 75th Anniversary of the synagogue, with a great deal of hard work by Dorothy Moncrieff, who mounted an extremely interesting exhibition, and Prue Baker.
>
> Bob Kirk (Pt. 3)

By this time, the synagogue had started to become less austere. There began to be more socialising between congregants before and after services, and works of art began to be introduced to the building, such as the *chanukkiah* designed by the Israeli artist Frank Meisler, which was donated in 1973. Murals by William Uttermohlen depicting the Pilgrimage Festivals were donated by Irvine Sellar and unveiled by Norman St John-Stevas (then Minister for the Arts) in 1981. In 1983 the Women's Society introduced the serving of coffee in the Mattuck Room before Saturday morning services and food began to be served after services at *Kiddush* on a more regular basis.

The LJS in recent years

The main development of the last twenty-five years is the building of the new synagogue. Although the synagogue was repaired following the bomb damage of 1940, the discovery of serious structural defects in 1984 prompted the LJS Council to rebuild the synagogue completely on the same site. This difficult decision (referred to as 'The Challenge of Change'), was taken despite the reservations of some long-standing members of the LJS who would have preferred to repair the much-loved building. There were also suggestions that the synagogue should be relocated since a large proportion of its congregation now lived in other parts of London.

> It took one of the first lady members of Council, Toni Assersohn, to suggest that we rebuild. Staid members of the Council were aghast but structural surveys showed that the existing building had deteriorated to a point where it was uneconomic to contemplate only repairs and maintenance. As a result a decision was made that we would redevelop.
>
> Neil Levitt

A farewell service was held in the old synagogue on 30 April 1988. Whilst the rebuilding was taking place, the congregation relocated to a deconsecrated church and church hall in Loudoun Road near Swiss Cottage.

After the synagogue moved out of the St John's Wood Road building, Sabbath services were initially held in the hall of St John's Wood Church (referred to by the congregation as 'the church on the roundabout'), but subsequently took place in the Loudoun Road premises. However, the High Holyday services could not be accommodated at Loudoun Road. They were held in the Central Hall Westminster on two occasions, and once in the Camden Community Centre. During this period, the Religion School was based in a school in Abercorn Road.

A rebuilding appeal was launched in January 1989 and, within just a few months, the sum pledged by members and friends of the synagogue had reached £1 million. The right to build flats above the new synagogue was sold to a developer to help subsidise the project.

The rebuilding of the synagogue was a major undertaking and its success owed much to the leadership of Sir Peter Lazarus, Chairman of the LJS, and Rabbi David Goldberg.

> A new committee called the Design and Use Committee was formed, and I was asked to chair it during the whole period of the construction of the synagogue. This involved meetings nearly every fortnight at 8.00 a.m. with the architect, builders and other technicians, together with Trevor Moross and Prue Baker who brilliantly ran the organisational side on behalf of the synagogue. As well as these, the Design and Use Committee met every month in the synagogue's temporary home in the church in Loudoun Road. Every member was dedicated to ensure that nothing was excluded and, under the continuous eye of Sir Peter, every organisation was approached to ensure that nothing was missed.
>
> Neil Levitt

On 14 November 1989 a group of synagogue members, led by the actress, Janet Suzman, placed a time-capsule[126] under one of the stones in the portico wall to the left of the foundation stone marked simply with the date. The items included in the canister were suggested by LJS members and the final choice was made by Rabbi John Rayner and Brenda Nathanson, then Chair of the Education Committee.[127]

A final Sabbath service was held in Loudoun Road on 12 January 1991 and, the following day, a Service of Dedication was held in the new building. The *ner tamid* was lit by Daphne Nathan representing the Religion School. She received the taper from Sharon Moross (now Lewison) and Louis Steinman, who had in turn received it from Marjorie Moos. The scrolls were carried back into the synagogue by Tim Simon, Willie Kessler, Les Koski, Theo Rubin, Raymon Benedyk and Prue Baker, who had all played a major role in the rebuilding project.

> When the doors opened I just held my breath. I was so worried that people might say something like they didn't like the skirting boards. But they just loved it!
>
> Prue Baker

A Service of Thanksgiving to celebrate the rebuilding of the synagogue on 16 March 1991 was attended by many dignitaries. The following year the synagogue was reconsecrated.[128]

---

[126] A time capsule had also been buried under the old building but this was remembered too late to save it from the bulldozers when the building was demolished. Interview with Prue Baker, 1 August 2010.

[127] The items placed in the capsule were: photos of the original LJS, Loudoun Road, and social activities; original 1902 photocopy of membership list; current membership list; service sheet for last service at 28 St John's Wood Road, service sheet from foundation stone dedication; Annual Report 1988; appeal brochure; LJS newsletter; a copy of *ULPS News*; pamphlets on history of Progressive Judaism; copy of *Service of the Heart* and the Passover *Haggadah*; copy of *Gate of Repentance*; copy of *Judaism for Today* by Rabbi John D Rayner and Rabbi Bernard Hooker; copy of *The Jewish People – Their History and Their Religion* by Rabbi David J Goldberg and Rabbi John D Rayner; sermons by Rabbi John D Rayner and Rabbi Alexandra Wright; message to finder from Rabbi David J Goldberg and from Richard Moross on behalf of the children of the Religion School; a miniature *kiddush* cup and *kiddush* wine.

[128] See photograph 84.

19. *Relighting of the ner tamid, 13 January 1991.*
Sharon Moross (now Lewison) with children from
the LJS Religion School. (1991)

20. *The scrolls being brought into the new synagogue 13 January 1991. Carrying the scrolls are*
Raymon Benedyk, Les Koski and Willie Kessler (to the left of the bimah, from front to the rear)
and Tim Simon, Prue Baker and Theo Rubin (to the right of the bimah, from front to the rear).
To the left of the bimah are Rabbi John Rayner, Rabbi David Goldberg (at the reading desk),
Rita Adler and Neil Levitt (by the Ark doors). To the right of the bimah are Trevor Moross and
Bob Beral (by the Ark doors), Bob Kirk and Rabbi Helen Freeman.
Photograph by Michael S Goldhill. (1991)

I wrote a special piece for the last service in Loudoun Road and the two special services in the new synagogue. Attendances were huge so I had something of a captive audience for three performances of my anthem, *Kumu Sharim* ('Rise up, O singers').

Yakov Paul

In 1994 Ruth Gledhill, Religious Correspondent for *The Times*, attended a *Shabbat* service. In her subsequent article she described the experience as a 'spiritual high' and awarded five stars for the architecture of the new building. The warmer atmosphere of the new building helped to increase the trend towards greater informality in the synagogue. This has been welcomed by some, but regarded as a mixed blessing by others.

> But I think we have lost out slightly in that, before a High Holyday or Saturday morning service, people tend to chat because it is such a friendly building. It upsets me that they don't listen to our outstanding organist, Tim Farrell, when he is playing music beforehand and don't get into a reflective mood for the service. I think there is perhaps a bit too much informality now. On the other hand, it is a building which does buzz, especially when there are kids around. I like that.

David Goldberg (Pt. 3)

During the 1990s, the synagogue, with its attractive new building, became 'the place' to be married. When demographic surveys were showing a marked drop in Jewish marriages, the number of weddings taking place at the LJS increased significantly. In 1995 there were twenty-six marriages at the synagogue.[129]

> The last wedding I did was in fact the rather famous one of Simon and Santa Sebag-Montefiore. Prince Charles was one of the witnesses to the wedding documents. When he was about to use his pen I said, 'I would be obliged if you would use my pen,' to which he replied, 'Why do you want me to use your pen?' I said, 'Because mine has ink in it which won't fade.' He said, 'But my pen has ink in it which won't fade,' to which I responded, 'Nevertheless, I would prefer you to use my pen!' So he put his pen away and used mine. I dined off that incident for months, but maybe it cost me my knighthood.

Raymon Benedyk

Because of the increase in the number of marriages, two further Marriage Secretaries were appointed – Bob Kirk and Michael Salmon.

The last twenty-five years have seen some notable advances for women. In 1986 the synagogue appointed its first woman rabbi, Rabbi Alexandra Wright who, as Alexandra Levitt, had grown up at the LJS. When Alexandra Wright became the rabbi at Radlett and Bushey Reform Synagogue in 1990, she was succeeded by Rabbi Helen Freeman who served as Associate Rabbi until 1999 when she moved to West London Synagogue. In 2000 Rabbi Kathleen de Magtige-Middleton joined the rabbinic team. She remained at the LJS for eight years, before going on to become the rabbi of her own congregation at Middlesex New Synagogue. On her return to the congregation in 2004, Rabbi Wright became the first female Senior Rabbi of a major congregation.

There have been similar developments in the lay leadership of the synagogue. In 1992 Rita Adler was the first woman to become Chairman of the synagogue. She held this position until 1998 and was Chairman again from 2007 to 2011. Ellen Schmidt was Chairman between 2004 and 2007.

---

[129] Bob Kirk, 'LJS Bucks the Trend', *LJS News,* January 1995.

These leadership appointments were mirrored by the wider involvement of women generally in the life of the synagogue. In 1991 the Women's Society was disbanded. This was partly due to the fact that it had become increasingly difficult to involve women in meetings as they were working, but also because it was now widely recognised that it was no longer appropriate for women to be largely confined to stereotypical activities.

> I have seen the role of women in the synagogue change through the years. They were always involved in volunteering and 'good works', and there have been some very powerful women who have had very influential roles, such as Margaret Rigal's involvement with the refuseniks. Some women, like Jo Kessler, Ann Kirk, Ann Hart and others, were very active in the community and some of them still are. The committees used to be quite male-dominated, but now women are very involved in decision-making, and take on more roles beyond those relating to education and welfare. Ironically, it is now quite hard to recruit men to take an active role in synagogue committees and on the Council.
>
> Ellen Schmidt (Pt. 3)

In 1989 Rabbi John Rayner formally retired and became Rabbi Emeritus and David Goldberg took over as Senior Rabbi. Under his leadership the LJS developed further its interfaith work,[130] its work with refugees, and became even more inclusive. In 1991 the first Open House service attended by non-Jewish people and interested religious leaders was held. Blessings for mixed-faith marriages were introduced, non-Jewish partners of members were now able to become 'Friends' of the synagogue, and non-Jewish parents were able to take part in *B'nei Mitzvah*.

> As far as I know, I did the first mixed-faith wedding blessing in this country. I also instituted the category of 'Friends of the Congregation'. The idea is commonplace now, but I remember it was quite daring then and made front page headlines in the JC when we announced it. People have their own good reasons for not wishing to convert, but if they are sympathetic to our aims and wish to support them, they should feel part of the community. In addition, I initiated the participation of non-Jewish parents in *Bar* and *Bat Mitzvahs* (they had previously not been allowed on the *bimah*).
>
> David Goldberg (Pt. 3)

Rabbi Wright has taken forward Rabbi David Goldberg's interfaith work as did Mark Solomon, who was rabbi at the LJS from 2000 until 2009. On 21 July 2005, a Multi-Faith Service of Remembrance and Hope was held at the LJS to commemorate those who died and were injured as a result of the London bombings on 7 July that year.

> The LJS held a service of reflection and reconciliation, together with St John's Wood Church and the London Central Mosque. Coming together so soon after this tragedy, and on the day when there was another, this time attempted bombing, was very moving and powerful. From that service emerged Pathways, the local clergy group which has become a place of great friendships and influence in the local community.
>
> Alexandra Wright (Pt. 3)

The congregation was much saddened by the death of Rabbi John Rayner in September 2005. His life and work were remembered at a special Service of Celebration held at the LJS on 27 October 2005.

---

[130] See Part Two for further information on the development of the LJS's interfaith activities.

At the Service of Celebration for Rabbi Rayner there were many beautiful and moving tributes paid to John as rabbi, teacher, colleague and mentor. But perhaps the most memorable insight was that given by Michael Stannard, the son of the Church of England vicar who had taken John into his family when John arrived, aged fifteen, on the *Kindertransport* in August 1939. He recalled the serious theological debates between his father and John and that when John was ordained, his father, who was by then a bishop, was privileged to be present and gave him his *tallit*. Probably a unique event.

Vivien Rose

The trend towards ever-greater inclusivity continued. In 2006, the synagogue introduced same-sex commitment ceremonies, which were welcomed by many and which attracted new members to the synagogue.

Rabbi Mark Solomon, who, at the time, was Associate Rabbi at the LJS, was the perfect bridge for us to LJS membership. He told us at a JGLG gathering that we would be welcomed as a family at LJS. We therefore joined the synagogue as members in April 2003, partly because we wanted a community to be a constant feature in [her daughter] Lily's life that was accepting of her and her family.

Karen Newman (Pt. 3)

Externally, the synagogue has also maintained its involvement in social welfare and social action, although the nature of its interventions has changed to reflect changes in the political scene at home and abroad. A Social Action Committee was set up in the early 1990s to co-ordinate this work, which has included the twinning of the synagogue with the Progressive Jewish community of Vinnitsa in the Ukraine, support for the Bayswater Family Centre for asylum seekers and refugees, and organising annual Mitzvah Day activities at the O2 Centre in Swiss Cottage. In 1991 a multi-faith Bosnian Support Group was set up under the leadership of Barbara Brandenburger to respond to the 'ethnic cleansing' taking place in Bosnia. Many synagogue members were involved in its fundraising activities and its work in supporting its adopted refugee camp in Hrastnik, Slovenia.

Although the Women's Society was disbanded in 1991, there has been an expansion in the synagogue's welfare activities. This is a reflection of the fact that an increasing number of LJS members, as in society generally, are elderly and in of need care. In 1991 a Keep in Touch (KIT) group was set up and in 2003 a professional Community Care Co-ordinator, Liz Crossick, was appointed. A number of welfare activities, such as Restaurant Tuesday, have now been maintained over several decades.

When one looks back on the past we see that the social, caring and catering sides of the synagogue are much more active than ever before, despite the fact there is now no Women's Society. We still have Tuesday Lunches and we serve coffee and biscuits before the service on Saturday, as well as *Kiddush* afterwards. We have members welcoming visitors at services and a professional Community Care Co-ordinator. Previously, this work used to be done by the rabbis in their pastoral role with help from the Women's Society.

Rita Adler (Pt. 3)

The other aspect of synagogue life that has become more prominent and placed on a professional footing, is the LJS's education activities. By the 1990s the Religion School had become a major undertaking and it was therefore agreed that the time had come to appoint a paid Director of Education to manage its affairs and also to develop the synagogue's educational provision for all age groups. In 1999 Jan Roseman was appointed as the synagogue's Director of Education and, after eleven years, she was succeeded by Dov Softi who became Head of the Religion School.

Following lengthy discussions with Westminster City Council, in 2004 a Nursery School was set up under the headship of Caroline Villiers. The first class of three-year-olds started in September of that year. Since then three further classes have been added and the Nursery School has gone from strength to strength. It is open to both members and non-members of the LJS and the children attending its classes come from very diverse backgrounds, attracted by the high quality of education provided at the school and its emphasis on interfaith activities.

> The synagogue is now a much busier place than it was. If you went into the building during the week it used to be very quiet, but now there is always something happening. The Nursery School in particular has brought it alive during the day.
>
> Ellen Schmidt (Pt. 3)

PART TWO

Themes and issues spanning the synagogue's hundred-year history

Section One: A place of worship – the spiritual life of the synagogue

Chapter One: Services and worship

THE FOUNDERS OF the LJS stressed that ceremonial observances were primarily a means to an end – to enable Jewish people to be conscious of God and to give them a sense of unity – rather than an end in themselves. They therefore commended the ceremonies which they saw as strengthening people's attachment to Jewish beliefs and ideals, but they modified or omitted those observances they believed were no longer relevant to modern life, those which had lost their power to inspire, or those which implied beliefs that the founders thought were no longer widely held or tenable.

As a result, the early services organised by the JRU in the Wharncliffe Rooms were very different from services in Orthodox synagogues. Men and women sat together, hymns were sung (mainly in English) and very little Hebrew was used in the prayers. The aim was to make the services as simple and as devoid of ritual as possible.

Early synagogue services

Early LJS services were very similar to those held in the Wharncliffe Rooms except for the addition of a short reading from the scroll selected to illustrate the theme of the sermon.[131] The format of the main Sabbath services continued largely unchanged for several years; however, in 1916 it was decided that the Sephardi[132] pronunciation of Hebrew should be adopted. There were no regular sermons or a choir during the summer months.[133]

> With little Hebrew, and hymns with rousing tunes to involve the congregation, we were stimulated by the poetry of the readings.
>
> Michael Nathan (Pt. 3)

> Regarding early services at the LJS, with which I became most familiar from 1922, they were of course chiefly in English as were the hymns, except for the concluding hymns, such as the *Adon Olam* and part of the *Shema*.
>
> Dorothy Edgar[134]

The scroll was simply dressed with very little or no embroidery. *Tallitot* were only worn on the *bimah* when they were worn folded, never draped over the shoulders. Lay and spiritual leaders encouraged the wearing of head coverings only for those leading services. The first LJS spiritual leaders wore birettas similar to those worn by Christian clerics, but

---

[131] Lily Montagu, *The Jewish Religious Union and Its Beginnings*, JRU, (1927).
[132] See Glossary for explanation of this term.
[133] LJS Annual Report, 1914.
[134] ULPS Oral History Project, interview with Dorothy Edgar. See Appendix 1.

with the point at the side. Claude Montefiore wore a skullcap and Lily Montagu wore her own clothes until much later when she invented a type of uniform.[135]

LJS leaders, particularly Rabbi Mattuck, emphasised the need for decorum during services. He disapproved of the wearing of jewellery or furs and other ostentatious displays of wealth. Members were also discouraged from talking before and during services and the proceedings were quite formal.

> The best story, of course, is the one about the Rev. A A Green, the Minister of Hampstead Synagogue who attended one of our services and by chance found himself sitting behind two of his own members. They were talking quite loudly and he patted them on the back and said, 'Members, friends, do remember you are not in an Orthodox synagogue now.'
>
> Maxwell Stern[136]

> We used to be accused of being rather 'cold' – possibly 'reserved' would have been a better description – a feeling perhaps not helped by the beautiful but nevertheless somewhat austere appearance of the Sanctuary, with its subdued colour scheme and impressive carved mahogany Ark screen.
>
> Bob Kirk (Pt. 3)

Experimentation with services

To begin with, the main Sabbath services were held on Saturday afternoons to accommodate those who worked five-and-a-half days a week. However, by 1922 a full Sabbath service was also being held on Saturday mornings, a move that began in 1916 when the synagogue started to encourage its members to attend the Saturday morning children's services. The format of the service was varied to include a sermon to attract all age groups.

The Saturday afternoon services continued but in a changed form. They were merged with the services of the West End Central Section of the JRU before being phased out in the 1930s.

In 1920 Rabbi Mattuck started to hold additional Sunday morning services in the Mortimer Hall,[137] which became a regular feature of the religious activity of the synagogue in November 1925. They were very informal.

> Some people said, 'Ah, now the Orthodox will say that they have just moved the Sabbath to Sunday.' But that wasn't it. The services were for the many people who could not get to the Saturday morning services, and to give people a chance to expand their knowledge of Judaism and of contemporary and religious subjects, but there was no reading from the scroll.
>
> Ruth Ive (Pt. 3)

The Sunday services included very little liturgy and consisted mainly of biblical readings chosen to complement the speech following the service. There was neither music, nor a choir, and the Ark was not opened. Rabbi Mattuck took off his gown and hat before

---

[135] Ibid.

[136] ULPS Oral History Project, interview with Maxwell Stern. See Appendix 1.

[137] Mortimer Hall no longer exists. It was located near Queen's Hall, east of Regent Street, halfway between Oxford Circus and the Broadcasting House.

answering written questions posed by congregants.[138] Well-known people, some of whom were not Jewish, were often invited to speak after the Sunday services on ethical, religious and political topics. The services and talks proved very popular, on occasion attracting audiences of over 1,000 people.

Initially, the Sunday services were held only in the winter months and collections were made after the services to help meet their cost, but they were mostly financed by a donation by the philanthropist and LJS member Bernhard Baron.[139] They continued, albeit on an increasingly intermittent basis, into the 1940s.

There were, over the years, various experiments with holding services for particular groups. In 1924 Rabbi Mattuck introduced special monthly services for business people on a Saturday afternoon. They were soon discontinued since they were not well attended.[140] In 1933 special Sabbath services were introduced for university students and these ran for a number of years. In 1935 Rabbi Mattuck tried again with services for businessmen, this time held on Wednesday lunchtimes at the Memorial Hall in Farringdon. However, they lasted for only a few months as the venue was not close enough to where people worked and an alternative venue could not be found.[141]

From 1936 Wednesday evening services were held once a month at the synagogue, which continued until the outbreak of the Second World War.

The re-adoption of traditional practices

During the early days of the LJS, services were established in a way that served the wishes of the congregants, but for those who joined the synagogue during the 1930s and 1940s as refugees from Europe, the services seemed very strange indeed.

> After all the emigration procedures were completed, I finally arrived in England on 21 April 1939, and the very first Saturday that I was in this country, the 'aunts' – that is what I was told to call the Misses Levy – took me to the LJS. Well, my first impression really was that I was going to a church. Men and women were sitting together, the men wore no *kippot*, no *tallit*, and there was very, very little Hebrew. As far as I remember, it was only the *Shema* and the *Kaddish*, which is Aramaic (although I didn't know that at the time). I do remember Leslie Edgar, who was then the Associate Minister, coming down from the *bimah* when it was time for the sermon and, taking me by the hand, leading me out for the children's talk. I wrote to my parents for reassurance: Were these ladies Jewish? Was I taken to a Jewish synagogue? They replied that, yes, the Misses Levy were indeed Jewish, and this was a modern form of Judaism.
>
> Ann Kirk (Pt. 3)

> After our experience of Liberal synagogues in Germany, the LJS seemed very 'stiff' and very anglicised. John Rayner understood our background and helped us to adjust.
>
> Ludwig Spiro

---

[138] ULPS Oral History project, interview with Maxwell Stern. See Appendix 1.
[139] LJS Annual Report, 1925.
[140] LJS Annual Report, 1924.
[141] Lawrence Rigal and Rosita Rosenberg, *Liberal Judaism: The First Hundred Years*.

Those joining the synagogue having previously belonged to an Orthodox synagogue experienced a similar 'culture shock'.

> It was through my husband, Leonard, that I became involved with the LJS. Leonard had earlier joined the LJS with his mother and brother because of the sympathy and kindness shown to them on the death of his father. I still remember the culture shock I experienced when I joined Leonard in 1952, hearing for the first time an organ in a synagogue and female voices in the choir! But I was thoroughly impressed by the unfamiliar decorum, and the wonderful experience of a service conducted almost entirely in English. At last I could follow, understand and participate in all those beautiful prayers.
>
> Louise Golding (Pt. 3)

Over the years, there has been a gradual re-introduction of some of the traditional rituals and forms of worship abandoned by the synagogue's early leaders. During 1935 a series of experimental Sabbath services were held to test out the congregation's reaction to the inclusion of more traditional elements, but it was soon decided that the existing format of services should be maintained.[142] However, after the Second World War there was a more discernible trend towards readopting traditional practices, starting with the conducting of *Kiddush* for the first time. It was introduced by the Rev. Philip Cohen and was held in the *sukkah*.

These changes have been attributed, in part, to the increasing numbers of refugees who joined the synagogue during the 1930s and 1940s who had different traditions. However, the Holocaust and the setting up of the State of Israel in 1948 provided a greater impetus towards more traditional forms of worship. After these two momentous events, there was a much stronger desire for people to be in touch with their Jewish identity rather than the wish to be 'more English than the English' that had been the predominant desire amongst early LJS congregants.[143]

However, there remained a tendency within the congregation to adhere to the type of service established in 1911. For many years, services remained very formal affairs.

> All in all it was necessary to dress formally in those days, and we always had to wear a jacket and tie, even as children. It is something of a wonder that I was not put off religion for life.
>
> Tim Simon[144]

The trend towards more traditional forms of observance became even more evident with the arrival at the LJS of John Rayner as Assistant Minister. With his European background, he had a vision that differed somewhat from that of Rabbis Mattuck and Edgar. More Hebrew began to be used in services and fewer English hymns were sung.

> In the 1970s there were some moves to make the services a little more traditional ... There was occasional experimentation with processing the scrolls around the synagogue, but this stopped after a while, because the congregation didn't like it. John wrote or preached about these changes, setting out the pros and cons and why he recommended a particular view.
>
> Michael Hart (Pt. 3)

---

[142] LJS Annual report, 1935.
[143] Lawrence Rigal and Rosita Rosenberg, *Liberal Judaism: The First Hundred Years.*
[144] 'Anniversaries: Milestones in Liberal Judaism' *LJS News* December 2001/January 2002.

During the 1970s and 1980s, with the encouragement of Rabbi Rayner and then Rabbi Goldberg, an increasing number of men began to wear *kippot* and women stopped wearing the dress hats which had been commonly worn in the early years of the LJS.

> Once John Rayner started to express the opinion that, although hats were perfectly acceptable, they were not a religious object, the wearing of *kippot* came in. Sir Louis Gluckstein traditionally read *Jonah* wearing a top hat but, out of respect for John Rayner, even he switched to a *kippah*. The wearing of hats by ladies has now dropped off entirely, except for the occasional reader and at the High Holydays. This has made it much easier to see the *bimah*, without the ladies' hats in front of you, but it took a long while for this to happen.
>
> George Rigal (Pt. 3)

It was some time before women started to wear *kippot* and *tallitot,* even when they were participating in the service on the *bimah*. One of the first women members of the LJS to wear a *tallit* on the *bimah* was Anita Schwartz.

> The occasion was the service to mark the end of the Women's Society, in 1991. Ann Kirk rang me up and asked me if I'd wear one. I thought, 'Why not?' We all wore one, except for two members of the Committee, who didn't want to. Before the service I said to Louis Steinman, 'I don't know how to put it on,' so he helped me. It felt good – lovely and warm. I don't feel quite right wearing one though; I was brought up Orthodox. The only time I wear one now is when Alex Wright puts one round my shoulders if I'm carrying a scroll at *Simchat Torah.*
>
> Anita Schwartz

Pressure for change mounted. In 1974 a Services Committee chaired by Bob Kirk was set up to review forms of service and other matters relating to worship and rituals. However, there remained some strong resistance to change, particularly from the powerful President, Sir Louis Gluckstein, who was wedded to the simple style of services established by Rabbi Mattuck. Consequently, some of the newer Liberal synagogues established in the post-war years began to re-adopt traditional practices at a significantly earlier date than the LJS.

Once Sir Louis Gluckstein retired as Chairman in 1963, the re-adoption of traditional forms of worship began to occur more quickly. Some members of the synagogue have welcomed the changes while others, largely the longer-standing members of the synagogue, have not.

> I feel we have moved away from the liturgy of the Liberal movement, and the services are not as they used to – I am not happy with the amount of Hebrew. However, I know I should not complain and I have come to accept it. I am happy that the sermons are still built on the ethics of the movement.
>
> Walter Woyda (Pt. 3)

Some congregants like a balance between tradition and modernism in services. Others, while not wholly welcoming the changes introduced over the years, have understood the reasons for the evolution of services.

> The balance is not right with everyone who comes here, just as it is not right for everyone who goes to an Orthodox synagogue. I don't want it to become too Anglican. I want to come in here and get the smell and the taste of Jews. As Spencer Tracy said in one of his

films, *Vive la Différence*, and I don't want to miss that. On the other hand, I don't want it to be all like the Orthodox synagogue where I couldn't understand what was going on and they were mumbling away to the left and the right of me and I tried to look over and see what page they were on.

Lee Montague

There is now much more Hebrew during services, and although I can read Hebrew, I am not proficient enough to read it at speed let alone understand it. I must say, I preferred the past when more of the service was in English. However, many new members seem to like the form of the service now, and so one must embrace change and follow the swing of the pendulum. Sincerity of belief and action are more important than outward form.

Rita Adler (Pt. 3)

I have absorbed many changes in the services over the years. I think it has a lot to do with the fact that my background is partly Orthodox. When my father left the Orthodox synagogue and came to the LJS, he liked the fact that we included more Hebrew because that seemed more familiar to him. I think the changes in the services are part of Liberal Judaism which is about effecting change.

Jenny Nathan (Pt. 3)

Rabbi Mark Solomon attempted to allay concerns about the chanting of the *Torah* by writing a piece in the *LJS News* explaining the origins of the tradition of cantillating. He described the different chanting styles used for different kinds of text from the declamatory style used for the *Purim Megillah* to the mournful tone of the Book of Lamentations.[145] As a result, there are now signs of greater acceptance of this practice.

Perhaps a small and heartening illustration of our approach to the future is the enjoyment now felt by the congregation (at first shocked by its instigation) when the *Torah* is chanted at some services. And even more encouraging is the feeling of support for those *Bar and Bat Mitzvah* candidates who chant their portion with such brio.

Susan Bilmes[146]

One of the most controversial changes has been regarding the reading of the *Torah* portion. In the synagogue's early days, readings during services were chosen at random and were designed to be uplifting. No blessings were recited before and after them. Over the years, there has been a phased move towards reading the traditional portion after which each *Shabbat* is named. Rabbi John Rayner reintroduced the annual cycle of scroll readings, but omitted those he considered to be unsuitable. However, since the arrival of the current generation of rabbis, a wider selection of *Torah* portions have been read, including those that would have previously been seen as 'un-Liberal'.

This trend has been the subject of lively debate. In 2005 there was a heated discussion about whether the *Torah* portion for the week should be read. In an article in the *LJS News*, Rabbi Mark Solomon argued that the relevant portion should be read as a general rule.[147] This article resulted in a response from Rabbi Emeritus, David Goldberg, who held the view that something more uplifting should be substituted on those weeks when the set portion was something likely to be regarded as particularly offensive.

---

[145] *LJS News*, October 2001.
[146] 'Anniversaries: Milestones in Liberal Judaism'.
[147] *LJS News*, May 2005.

[U]nder my stewardship and that of Rabbis Rayner, Edgar and Mattuck before me it was *always* the practice to choose what we called 'a timeless passage' rather than set before the congregation a litany of laws about animal sacrifice, skin infections, ritual purification and the like.

David Goldberg[148]

This elicited a number of letters from congregants taking a variety of positions. In the end it was decided that the set portion would be used unless it meant that a particularly inappropriate portion would be read by *B'nei Mitzvah* students.

Service length and participation in services

To begin with, Sabbath services tended to be comparatively short.

> Sermon lengths were around fifteen minutes, and the whole service around seventy-five minutes. CGM [Claude Montefiore] took much longer. No one dared to tell him to make things shorter!
>
> Dorothy Edgar[149]

Rabbi John Rayner remembered that, during his first ten years at the synagogue, the whole of the Sabbath morning service rarely exceeded an hour, even though sermons were sometimes up to twenty minutes long and the anthem was nearly always after the service.[150] However, by 1970 services were between an hour and twenty minutes and an hour and a half long.

> We came [the Religion School] out of the service when the scroll was returned to the Ark at about 11.40. Services must have been shorter because that usually happens at about 12 noon now. This was probably because the liturgy was not so long, there was no special theme and the introduction to the scroll reading was brief.
>
> Michael Hart (Pt. 3)

From the outset, members of the LJS congregation were involved in many aspects of the Sabbath services.

> Ark openers were chosen by the LJS Beadle from the laity, some just prior to the service, including Sir Louis Gluckstein.
>
> Dorothy Edgar[151]

> I was deeply impressed with my first Sabbath morning service at the LJS. From then on, I never missed a morning service on Saturdays and, very soon, was drawn into the service. I was asked to read from time to time and, almost every Saturday, I was called up to help open and close the Ark and with undressing and dressing the scroll.
>
> Eric Conrad (Pt. 3)

Over the years, services became even more participative, especially from the early 1960s when LJS members began to be invited to read the *Haftarah*.

---

[148] *LJS News*, June 2005.
[149] ULPS Oral History Project, interview with Dorothy Edgar. See Appendix 1.
[150] Email from Rabbi John Rayner to Bryan Diamond, LJS Honorary Archivist, 1 September 2003, LJS archives.
[151] ULPS Oral History Project, interview with Dorothy Edgar. See Appendix 1.

Ann [his future wife] introduced me to the LJS at an *Erev Shabbat* service run by the Alumni. It was a real eye-opener to find laymen thoroughly involved, including delivering the sermon – on that occasion by the Society's Chairman, Bernard Lawton, later a long-serving Chairman of the House Committee and Chief Steward.

Bob Kirk (Pt. 3)

I was constantly being asked to act as Ark opener because, in those days, there were very few male members in the congregation physically able to lift the scrolls. It was not a large congregation then, so I regularly used to do a double act with Mr Klementaski.

George Rigal (Pt. 3)

A greater variety of people, including young people, also became involved in contributing to services.

When I look back, one of the great changes was when Louis Steinman left and a team of *shammashim* took over. It made for a very different atmosphere in the synagogue because they all had their different ways of doing things, and therefore we had a much wider variety of people who were given *mitzvot*.

George Rigal (Pt. 3)

Friday night services

In 1945 the LJS introduced Friday evening services. They were held on the first Friday of each month and were organised with the help of the Younger Members' Organisation and Alumni Society. These services represented a real departure in LJS practice because, until then, there had been no Sabbath eve services (later referred to as *Erev Shabbat* services) as Rabbi Mattuck firmly believed that a good Jew should spend Friday nights at home with their family.[152]

A feature of the *Erev Shabbat* services was cantorial singing by Rabbi Kokotek, again something new to the synagogue. After the services, young people were invited to the rabbis' studies for informal discussions around the Sabbath candles.[153] A few years later, the Alumni Society established its own Friday night services on the third Friday of the month under the guidance of the Rev. Philip Cohen, to which well-known personalities were invited.

With the arrival of John Rayner, Friday night services followed by communal meals were held more frequently.

As well as attending Religion School, we went to the *Onegei Shabbat,* which used to be organised by the Women's Society on Friday nights. There were lots of people at them and they had a lovely feeling. I enjoyed being able to go into the kitchen and getting involved in the preparations. It felt very special to be able to do that.

Ellen Schmidt (Pt. 3)

Rosa Mintz was the *shammash* on Friday evenings for a many years. She decided who lit the candles and who opened the Ark for the *Shema*. She had no hesitation in walking up

---

[152] ULPS Oral History Project, interview with John Rayner. See Appendix 1.
[153] LJS Annual Report, 1945.

to someone whom she did not recognise with the greeting: 'Hello, I'm Rosa, are you Jewish?' She was eventually replaced by Bernie Bulkin who was *shammash* every Friday evening for about five years until a rota was created.

The custom for tea to be available before the service and at *Kiddush* afterwards was begun. Once *Kiddush* had been said, the rabbi and those congregants who wished to stay would gather around the table for a short *Oneg* discussion.

> When I first came to the LJS these were random topics. Later, David Goldberg had the idea of going through great Jews of all time alphabetically. We did this for a year. As I led Friday evening services from time to time, I recall doing the *Oneg* on Bialik and, later in the year, on Miriam. Alexandra Wright later changed this *Oneg*.
>
> Bernie Bulkin (Pt. 3)

Chavurot (communal meals) after Friday night services continue to be held once a month but have, from time to time, been under threat.

> On the first Friday of the month we have a *Chavurah* supper. Everyone brings a non-meat dish to share and there is a short programme of some sort. When I first arrived, these arrangements had been suspended by Rabbi Goldberg because the suppers had begun to attract a large number of people who ate a lot and contributed little or no food. One woman regularly turned up with two small pots of yoghurt and, if they were not eaten, she took them back home with her.
>
> Bernie Bulkin (Pt. 3)

The Friday evening service is generally regarded as being a gentle, meditative way to end the week. The Sanctuary can be lit so that it is dim at the back, and those gathering at the front feel part of an intimate congregation. Many visitors come to Friday evening services, from all over the world.

Continuing innovation

In keeping with Liberal Judaism's emphasis on progress, a number of innovations have been tried at various times, such as the daily evening services trialled for a year in the early 1980s. Some innovations have become part of the mainstream operation of the synagogue; others have had a mixed reception.

> Other developments over the years seem much more positive, such as the inclusion of baby blessings in the *Shabbat* service rather than as a separate event afterwards, the availability of the *Torah* and *Haftarah* readings within the service sheets rather than needing to take a Bible or *Chumash* into services, and the now generally accepted gender-inclusive language.
>
> Michael Hart (Pt. 3)

In recent years one striking innovation was the first 'Crystal Clear' service, which took place in the Montefiore Hall on *Shabbat* 15 July 2006. It was the brainchild of Alex Cowan who had been closely involved with the Disability *Shabbat*. The LJS worked with the Jewish Deaf Association in planning the service conducted by Rabbis Alexandra Wright and Kathleen de Magtige-Middleton and a number of congregants. More than fifty people attended, of whom twenty were deaf- or hearing-impaired. They were able to follow the service through sign language interpreters and a lip-speaker. A second similar service, this time held in the Sanctuary, took place in December of the same year.

On the *Shabbat* that followed the terrorist attacks of 11 September 2001, many Americans were stranded in London because of the ban on flights. In recognition of the large American contingent amongst its congregation, the LJS choir sang *America the Beautiful* as an anthem and there was an extended *Kiddush* after the service.

Services for children and young people

When it was first set up, the LJS introduced short Saturday morning services alongside the main afternoon services. Conducted mainly by lay readers, these services were primarily intended for children (of both members and non-members of the synagogue), and were run along the lines of those previously led by some of the founding members of the JRU. As part of the new Religion School's activities, assemblies for children were also held on a Sunday morning.

> We had an assembly on Sunday mornings, at which we had what were considered to be suitable hymns for children and we all had to recite a proverb. We preferred to choose the shortest one that we knew. That continued certainly until we were at no. 28 St John's Wood Road.
>
> Dorothy Edgar[154]

When adults first started to attend Saturday morning services at the synagogue, children left the service during the sermons that had been introduced. A less formal sermon was given for them in the Montefiore Hall attached to the synagogue. Once the main Sabbath services began to be held on a Saturday morning, arrangements were made to hold special services for children and young people, which have continued in various forms until the present day.

During the 1920s, the format of the Saturday morning service was adapted once a month to attract young people and in 1932 dedicated services for young people were reintroduced by Leslie Edgar early on a Saturday morning. The running of these services was taken over by the Younger Members' Organisation which varied the services between Saturday mornings and Friday evenings before moving them to a more regular time on Saturday afternoons in 1936. They were a combination of an informal service and discussions.

In 1935 the synagogue also reintroduced services for younger children to run at the same time as the main Sabbath morning service, after which the children attended a class run by Mrs Cowen.

> I first went to the LJS in 1936 when I was seven years old. My mother took me to a children's service, which was conducted by Rabbi Leslie Edgar. At the time I was utterly entranced. The building was most impressive and Rabbi Edgar held me spellbound as he explained the meaning of the Ark, the scrolls and the *ner tamid* over the course of a number of services.
>
> Michael Salmon[155]

---

[154] ULPS Oral History Project, interview with Dorothy Edgar. See Appendix 1.
[155] 'Anniversaries: Milestones in Liberal Judaism'.

From about this time, once a year children from the LJS Religion School also attended a combined service for all Liberal and Progressive schools run by JRU/ULPS congregations, an arrangement which continued over several decades.

After a gap during the Second World War, regular services for children were initiated in the autumn of 1952 but by the 1960s these services were being held less frequently. However, at that time children attending the Religion School also frequently joined the main Sabbath service.

> The format of the Religion School was that we had one lesson lasting forty minutes, after which we went down to the Montefiore Hall and lined up for a Children's *Kiddush*, when we said the blessings over the wine and the bread. We were allowed to let off steam, running round the hall before lining up again in our classes to go into the first part of the main synagogue service. Bob Kirk and the other teachers sat behind us to keep us in order, to check we were following the service and, sometimes, to tell us to be quiet.
>
> Michael Hart (Pt. 3)

The special children's services held at that time were sometimes run by the Religion School teachers such as Bob Kirk, Michael Cross, Michael Alpert and Celia Rapp, but one of the rabbis also often led the services. The Israeli teachers by now working in the Religion School were able to assist with the Hebrew.

> I remember when we took services as children we were instructed to speak at the same speed as Mrs Rapp, but it was impossible because she always waited so she was a minute behind. She sang very loudly and was wonderful with young children – one of those teachers you never forget.
>
> Jane Kessler

> Once or twice a term the pattern changed and we had a short children's service instead of joining the main service, where one of the rabbis, often Rabbi David Goldstein, gave a short talk. I still remember one of these in which David likened all of those present to links in a chain, passing on Judaism from generation to generation and stressing what would happen if the links broke. The teachers taught us the importance of speaking slowly and projecting our voices when reading at the children's service. I also remember being shown by Bob Kirk how to undress and dress the scroll, and how to lift it correctly from the reading desk.
>
> Michael Hart (Pt. 3)

The Religion School assemblies and the special services were held in the new small synagogue which had been opened in 1963. During the school holidays when there was no Religion School, many children attended the main services with arrangements being made for them elsewhere in the synagogue during the sermon.

> When my children were old enough to attend services, I used to organise quizzes for them during the sermons, particularly during the summer holidays. We took the view that you didn't go to synagogue only during term time, so we always took our children during holiday periods as well. The quizzes were to make the sermon times more child-friendly. They weren't just for my children, but for any children in the congregation. They would be announced and I would take the children out. As an incentive for regular attendance, I used to organise cumulative quizzes so the children could carry scores forward from one service to the next.
>
> George Rigal (Pt. 3)

On several occasions during the 1960s, parents with children under seven years of age were invited to bring them to the synagogue before the Sabbath service so that they could be given an insight into its rituals. However, children attending services were not always made welcome.

> In my day, children at the LJS were still expected not to make a sound. If you brought a baby even to a children's service and it gurgled, somebody near you would say 'Shush!' It happened to me at a *Chanukkah* Service. So we didn't bring children to the synagogue much until they started Religion School, which by then was on Saturdays rather than Sundays. I was left at home with the babies.
>
> Margaret Rigal (Pt. 3)

Even today when children who accompany their parents are generally given a warmer welcome, some would prefer children to attend only the special Family Services, which are now held on a quarterly basis. Until very recently, these Family Services have involved children making a variety of contributions supported by the Director of Education, but the aim now is to make the services more inter-generational. In 2006, Rabbi Kathleen de Magtige-Middleton instigated 'Tiny Tots Services' for under fives, their parents and grandparents. These monthly services mainly consist of stories and singing to guitar music provided by Thea Daum, but also include the recitation of the *Shema*.

Chapter Two: Festivals and High Holydays

Festivals

WHEN THE SYNAGOGUE was established, it was agreed that the LJS would celebrate all of the main Jewish festivals of the Pentateuch and all of the High Holydays. Until the 1960s, these were generally referred to by their English rather than by their Hebrew names (that is, the Day of Memorial, the Day of Atonement, Passover, Pentecost and Tabernacles rather than *Rosh Hashanah, Yom Kippur, Pesach, Shavu'ot* and *Sukkot*).

The service for Tabernacles was soon established as a major event, with a great deal of involvement from the congregation in preparing for it. In the early days of the LJS, the *sukkah* was decorated by the Women's Society, assisted by the caretaker up a ladder.[156] Gifts of fruit and sheaves of corn were solicited by letters handwritten by Dorothy Edgar and her mother, Edna Mattuck, and later on, by Jane Rayner.

> At that time, the massive sheaves of corn for the *sukkah* and the Sanctuary were provided by our great friend and 'gentleman farmer', Arthur Simon. (They were grown in a field set aside for that purpose.) Later on Cedric Rigal provided the sheaves. The centrepiece, a huge loaf of bread in the shape of a wheatsheaf, was donated annually by Dora Wolchover.
>
> Jane Rayner

---

[156] ULPS Oral History Project, interview with Dorothy Edgar. See Appendix 1.

It has long been a tradition that at *Sukkot* children from the Religion School process into the synagogue while the *Hallel* is sung.

> We lined up in the Montefiore Hall before the synagogue doors were thrown open and we marched in either side and merged rather like at the Royal Tournament, and laid flowers along the front of the *bimah*. All this was painstakingly rehearsed by Bob Kirk.
>
> > Edward Cross

During the 1950s and 1960s, children carried plants into the service and placed them on the *bimah* in specially designed boxes commissioned by Marjorie Moos and therefore referred to as 'Marjorie's Boxes'.[157]

Passover services were also an important event in the LJS calendar. The first Communal *Seder* was held in 1916.[158] The Women's Society catered for the *sedarim*.

> Rosemary Lazarus, who was Chairman of the Women's Society, said: 'Why don't you come along to a meeting and see what help you can give?' In those days, the Women's Society did visiting, cooking and catering. It catered for the Communal *Seder* and I remember a recipe starting with, 'Take 12 lbs of apples...'.
>
> > Rita Adler (Pt. 3)

But Passover (or *Pesach*) was also celebrated outside the synagogue. It was a time for large gatherings of families and friends.

> One of these extended families always had a Passover picnic of about fifty-strong. I saw a photograph album of one of these picnics at the home of Violet and Lewis Levy, a past chairman, and Rosemary Lazarus's father. It was obviously something they all loved being part of.
>
> > Carole Goldberg

In 1952 the synagogue took the decision to move the Communal *Seder* to the second night of *Pesach* to enable family celebrations to take place on the first night. Morning services on the first day of *Pesach* continued to attract sizeable congregations, including large numbers of children, many of whom took part in the reading of the service.[159] However, by the 1980s attendance at *Pesach* services had declined significantly as fewer congregants were able to take the day off work.

The festivals celebrated at the LJS remained relatively unchanged for the first fifty years of its existence. However, when John Rayner became Senior Rabbi he gradually increased the number of festivals and observances celebrated by the congregation to include *Yom ha-Atz-ma'ut* (Israel Independence Day), *Yom ha-Sho'ah* (to commemorate the Holocaust), *Tisha B'Av* (to commemorate the destruction of the Temple) and *Selichot*[160] services. He also introduced *Tu bi Sh'vat* (a celebration of the new year for trees) and *Tikkun Leyl Shavu'ot*, a special service and all-night study session for *Shavu'ot*.

---

[157] Information provided by Bob and Ann Kirk 1 December 2010.
[158] LJS Annual Report, 1916.
[159] LJS Annual report, 1953.
[160] Late night service held on the Saturday before *Rosh Hashanah* as preparation for the High Holydays.

21. *Festival of Tu bi Sh'vat, February 2004.*
Rabbi Kathleen de Magtige-Middleton in centre
of the photograph. (2004)

Not everybody, I know, has been or is happy with all these changes. Some may regard them as irrelevant or even retrogressive. But it can hardly be denied that, in their totality, they have planted us more deeply in the soil of our Jewish past and bonded us more closely with our fellow Jews in the present.

John Rayner[161]

Many of the new festivals and celebrations were introduced on an experimental basis before they were formally adopted. They were supported by relevant entries in the new generation of prayerbooks that were introduced in 1967 and 1973 (see below).

The early leaders of the LJS rejected the celebration of *Purim* because of what they felt was the unsuitable content of the Book of Esther which is read at *Purim*. In recent years this festival has been re-established in the calendar of events at the LJS (and in other Liberal and Progressive Synagogues), although this is mainly as an occasion for light-hearted celebration. However, there remains certain ambivalence to celebrating *Purim*.

A question which I was asked at my initial interview really introduced me to the LJS as it was. That question was: 'What is your opinion about *Purim?*' As this my first ever interview, I didn't know quite what questions to expect, but I definitely never expected a question like that! And I realised that at The LJS traditional Liberalism was not a thing of the past – that the 'Three Ms' and their ethos, their theology were not part of the historical development of the LJS, but still very much part of its outlook, its self-definition and even its praxis. Coming from a much more traditional background (albeit also called 'Liberal') I had to get used to the polite 'tut tut' when the name Haman was uttered, and it took a couple of years, a bit of hard work and, but most importantly, a good bottle of Vodka until *Purim* at the LJS started to sound bit more like *Purim* ought to sound.

Kathleen de Magtige-Middleton

---

[161] Sermon by John Rayner on 21 June 2003 to mark the 50th anniversary of his ordination.

Similarly, in the early years of the LJS, the festival of *Simchat Torah*, which follows the festival of *Sukkot,* was given relatively little attention, but there is now an energetic parading of the scroll.

> The way we celebrate *Simchat Torah* – the jollity, the exuberance – that was absolutely undreamed of by our founders, who had a very austere, ethical, rather Quaker kind of Judaism.
>
> David Goldberg[162]

High Holydays

High Holydays have always attracted large congregations of between 800 and 1,500 people[163] and, during the synagogue's history, a variety of arrangements have had to be made to accommodate those attending High Holyday services. When the LJS was located in Hill Street, High Holyday services were held in both the morning and the evening in various locations.

> Well, what happened when it came to the High Holydays? The congregation was growing and the chapel [in Hill Street] would not hold the congregants. So for these occasions the Kingsway Hall in Holborn became our place of worship, and I can remember that some later ones were held in the Marble Arch Cinema opposite The Cumberland and close to the Park Lane corner of Oxford Street.
>
> Ruth Hadley[164]

The service on the eve of *Yom Kippur* in 1917 at the Wigmore Hall was only partly read in the Hall. An air raid warning was given part way through the service, which therefore had to be transferred to the basement to shelter from possible Zeppelin attack.[165] For the first few years, special children's services were held on *Yom Kippur* by the JRU in the vestry room of the synagogue.[166]

When the synagogue moved to its larger building in St John's Wood Road, simultaneous High Holyday services were held in the synagogue and in the adjacent Montefiore Hall, with the choral and organ music being relayed from the synagogue to the Hall. This created logistic challenges in ensuring that the services were synchronised.

> When we had parallel High Holyday services in the synagogue and Montefiore Hall, with the choir relayed from the former to the latter, we also had what we called a 'whisperer', i.e. a sort of loudspeaker turned on very softly to enable the person conducting the service in the Hall (but nobody else) just to hear how far they had got in the synagogue so as to keep in synchronisation with it and switch on the choir at the right moments. It was something of a nightmare because it meant that the reader in the Hall had to concentrate simultaneously on his own reading and listen to what was going on in the synagogue. On one occasion I

---

[162] Quoted in Stephen Brook, *The Club: The Jews of Modern Britain*, (1989).
[163] The LJS Annual report for 1922 reported that 1,700 people had attended the *Yom Kippur* service and the LJS Annual Report for 1924 reported an attendance of 2,000.
[164] Letter from Ruth Hadley to Rabbis Rayner, Goldstein and Goldberg dated *Rosh Hashanah*, 1977 in LJS archives.
[165] LJS Annual Report, 1917.
[166] Annual Report, 1912.

read and translated the *Torah* portion in the hall paragraph by paragraph whereas Leslie Edgar in the synagogue read it from beginning to end before translating it, so it was touch and go as to whether we would finish at the same time. Luckily, we did.

John Rayner[167]

The atmosphere on High Holydays during the 1920s is captured by a foreign visitor attending the *Kol Nidre* service just after the opening of the new building in 1925.

In common with hundreds of others we drove to the new synagogue, which from the outside is a beautiful and imposing building. Our car had to take its place in the queue that was being directed by two policemen. Up and down the street were hundreds of magnificently appointed cars parked on both sides of the streets, waiting for the conclusion of the service to take their owners home!

Yehudah[168]

When membership of the LJS reached around 3,000 in the 1960s, the arrangements for simultaneous services were not sufficient to accommodate the increased congregations on High Holydays. Additional High Holyday services were therefore held initially in the Friends' Meeting House in Euston Road and then at the Porchester Hall near Paddington Station to where rabbis and lay readers had to commute from St John's Wood.[169]

There was a ticketing system for High Holyday services. Only long-standing members of the LJS were able to get a seat downstairs in the main synagogue. Others had to go to the overspill services held at Porchester Hall. We felt like second-class citizens and it took some time to graduate even to sitting upstairs in the gallery at the synagogue, let alone downstairs.

Ellen Schmidt (Pt. 3)

When there were two services, at St John's Wood Road and at the Porchester Hall, the rabbis delivered the sermon at the service on the morning of *Yom Kippur* in one venue and then repeated it in the other venue in the afternoon. One year, my father realised that he was a lay reader for the morning service in Porchester Hall and also for the afternoon service at St John's Wood. He mentioned this to Rabbi John Rayner, who looked disconcerted and replied that he'd now have to write two sermons. My father immediately replied, 'Don't worry, John, I always sleep through the sermons anyway.'

Nicholas Feldman

A crèche was provided by the Women's Society and, for many years, Miss Moos gave an address at the special services held for children on High Holydays.

The size of the LJS congregation decreased significantly during the 1970s and it was no longer necessary to continue using the Porchester Hall. Simultaneous High Holyday services were re-established at St John's Wood Road using the small synagogue that had been opened in 1963.

---

[167] ULPS Oral History Project, interview with John Rayner. See Appendix 1.
[168] Letter from 'Yehudah' in *Ivri Onouchi*, 1 November 1925 (newspaper in Johannesburg), photocopy in LJS archives.
[169] In 1974 the synagogue overlooked the need to book the Porchester Hall and the 'overflow' service had to be held instead at Lord's Cricket Ground.

> I remember going to High Holyday services as a child, and looking down from the balcony at the congregation below. Given the family precedents, I wondered whether my future husband was sitting down there somewhere. At the end of the service Uncle Leslie, in black robes and biretta, would, with fatherly presence, stretch out his arms to bless the congregation.
>
> Carolyn Simon (Pt. 3)

In more recent years, the parallel service held in Montefiore Hall has had a different content from that held in the Sanctuary. In 1999 Rabbi Helen Freeman introduced an 'alternative' *Kol Nidre* service, which provided a smaller and more intimate setting for prayer and reflection. Subsequently, Rabbi Mark Solomon conducted a cantorial service in Montefiore Hall on *Kol Nidre* where almost all the service was sung.

The morning services on both *Rosh Hashanah* and *Yom Kippur* held in Montefiore Hall have sometimes had their own special liturgy, designed for and largely conducted by children and younger synagogue members, such as the dramatisation of the Jonah story by members of the *Kabbalat Torah* class.

In the early years, the High Holydays were very formal affairs with prominent roles being played by the lay leaders of the congregation. Claude Montefiore established the tradition of the LJS President reading the Book of Jonah in the afternoon service of *Yom Kippur*, a tradition which continued after his death. During the periods when there has been no President, the Book of Jonah has been read by another leading member of the Council, or by one of the rabbis.

> On the High Holydays we would attend a children's service taken by the redoubtable and lovable Marjorie Moos, but we were always allowed back in the main synagogue to hear my father read the Book of Jonah on the Day of Atonement, for which a silk hat was *de rigueur*! In fact hats played quite a big part. I recall that Lily Montagu had a rather jaunty black velvet number, and my grandfather, who had been a founding member at Hill Street, sported a rather dapper grey trilby.
>
> Tim Simon[170]

Another important tradition is the blowing of the *shofar*. To begin with, it was blown but the different blasts were not called.

> The Day of Atonement Service was being held there [in the synagogue] when air raid sirens sounded throughout the day and the 'all clear' was heard as the *shofar* was being blown at its conclusion.
>
> Israel Mattuck[171]

The LJS has had some noted *shofar* blowers including Louis Steinman, the long-standing synagogue Beadle, and Norman Noah.

> Having started as an Orthodox Eastern Sephardi Jew, my father joined the LJS with his sons after the tragic death of his first wife. It was quite a sight to see this diminutive man, scarcely five foot high, with asthma, blow the *shofar* every year.
>
> Jack Noah[172]

---

[170] 'Anniversaries: Milestones in Liberal Judaism'.
[171] Rabbi Mattuck quoted in 'An Historic Service at The Liberal Jewish Synagogue', *Liberal Jewish Monthly*, October 1947.
[172] Memory submitted by Jack Noah, document in LJS archives.

Even now I still think about Louis Steinman when I hear the *shofar*. It once took me six breaths when he did *tekiah gadolah*.

Jane Kessler

22. *Louis Steinman, LJS Beadle, with the shofar. (undated)*

Chapter Three: The liturgy of the LJS

T HE GRADUAL RE-ADOPTION of more traditional practices at the LJS is reflected in the different generations of prayerbooks, each of which built on the liturgies that had gone before it.

When the JRU was preparing for the first services at the Wharncliffe Rooms, it set up a committee to produce a prayerbook to be used at these services.[173] A *Selection of Prayers, Psalms and Other Spiritual Passages and Hymns for Use at Services of the Jewish Religious Union* appeared in 1902, first as an 'experimental edition' and then as a longer 'provisional edition'. Alongside traditional Jewish prayers, these books included English prayers that had been used at Hampstead Sabbath Afternoon Services in the 1890s,[174] together with some newly written ones. The book did not include set services, but did have a series of prayers that could be used in rotation.

> We had, as a committee, been preparing for many months and had produced a book bound in red covers containing an order of service ... It was the humble ancestor of our present prayerbook with its many complete forms of service.
>
> Lily Montagu[175]

---

[173] The committee was made up of the Rev. Simon Singer, the Rev. A A Green, Dr Claude Montefiore, Dr Israel Abrahams, H R Lewis, F H Harvey-Samuel, Oswald Simon and Lily Montagu. See Lawrence Rigal and Rosita Rosenberg, *Liberal Judaism: The First Hundred Years*.

[174] Ibid.

[175] Lily H. Montagu, 'The First Service of the Jewish Religious Union', typed article in LJS archives to celebrate the 50th anniversary of the founding of the JRU in 1952.

While the early prayerbooks had proved adequate for the public JRU services, they were less appropriate for a synagogue with its own scroll and Ark. A JRU Liturgy Subcommittee was therefore set up in 1910 to start work on a new prayerbook.[176] Completion of the work was delayed until the arrival of Rabbi Mattuck from America in 1912 so that he could help shape the liturgy.

The first prayerbook produced by Rabbi Mattuck appeared in 1912, a second edition appeared in 1916 and a third in 1926. This series of prayerbooks was revised in 1937 to include more services. They were used at the LJS (and by other ULPS congregations) until 1967. They owed much to Rabbi Mattuck's inspired literary style, as well as to the influence of American Reform Judaism, but particularly to Rabbi Dr David Einhorn's *Olat Tamid*.[177]

> His prayerbooks were radical compilations that combined a drastically pruned, traditional liturgy with material from the Bible, the Apocrypha, later Jewish literature, English poetry, and many of Mattuck's own compositions.
>
> David Goldberg[178]

> The old prayerbook had a Shakespearean sonnet in the Day of Atonement service. As a child I certainly remember singing the hymn 'Abide with Me', omitting the inconvenient verses.
>
> Maxwell Stern[179]

Rabbi Mattuck's prayerbooks seemed very 'foreign' to the European refugees who joined the LJS in the 1930s and 1940s.

> At the time I arrived at the LJS, we were using the 1937 edition of the *Liberal Jewish Prayerbook*, written largely by Rabbi Dr Israel Mattuck. That was quite a culture shock. Hebrew usage was at a minimum and, coming from an Orthodox background, I was greatly struck by the very different format of the liturgy.
>
> Bob Kirk (Pt. 3)

They also became increasingly difficult to follow for young people because of the archaic language in which they were written.

> My memory of that time is of taking the boys up into the balcony of the old synagogue. Very often we sat right at the back so we couldn't be heard. We were then using the Mattuck prayerbook, which I needed to translate into modern English for David and Barry as it was quite archaic.
>
> George Rigal (Pt. 3)

During the 1950s, John Rayner worked with John Rich of South London Liberal Synagogue on the production of a new *Haggadah* for the ULPS. Until then, the *Haggadah* consisted of just twenty black and white pages. The new version, which was published in 1962, consisted of over fifty pages. An illustrated edition was published in 1968. Most of the English passages had been written or rewritten for this edition.[180]

---

[176] Ibid.

[177] Charles Middleburgh, 'Birth of a dynamic new liturgy', *LJ Today*, May/June 2010.

[178] Rabbi David Goldberg, entry in the *Oxford Dictionary of National Biography*, written in 2004.

[179] ULPS Oral History Project, interview with Maxwell Stern. See Appendix 1.

[180] The 1962 *Haggadah* was succeeded by a new version in 1981, which was also edited by Rabbi John Rayner in

John Rayner then moved on to producing a replacement for Rabbi Mattuck's prayerbooks. The new prayerbook, *Service of the Heart*, was commissioned by the Ministers' Conference (subsequently the Rabbinic Conference) of the ULPS for general use in Liberal and Progressive synagogues.

> There were electricity strikes while I was typing the draft of the new prayerbook so I had to type much of it by candlelight.
>
> Jane Rayner

In producing the new prayerbook, John Rayner worked in partnership with Rabbi Chaim Stern, a graduate of the New York branch of the Hebrew Union College with a keen interest in liturgy. Peggy Lang, Publications Officer for ULPS, was the Technical Editor. Rabbi Rayner, Rabbi Stern and Peggy Lang subsequently worked together on editing *Gate of Repentance*, the prayerbook for High Holydays published in 1973.

> Well, while the prayerbook was in the midst of being edited by John, he went off to the States [to complete his studies], and Chaim [Stern] came on the scene. Chaim had an enormous love of Jewish liturgy, and he just became part of it. It became obvious that his talent should be used. He got on with it in John's absence. Due to a good relationship with John Rayner across the seas, they did communicate and they did come together, and there was good partnership. They each had a special gift which they both contributed, which made *Service of the Heart* and the subsequent *Gate of Repentance* two such wonderful books.
>
> Sidney Brichto[181]

Like *Service of the Heart, Gate of Repentance* sought to strike a balance between traditional and modern liturgical materials.

> In the early years of my ministry I soon became aware of the fact that there was something of a polarisation going on in the movement, in that the older establishments like the LJS seemed to be happy enough to carry on essentially in the same way as before, but an increasing number of suburban congregations began to feel the need for a more traditional kind of service and also a more Zionist kind of ideology. I was worried that this might lead to the break-up of the ULPS ... This explains why a new prayerbook was needed for a movement between the traditional and the radical ones.
>
> John Rayner[182]

Many people were involved in the production of the new prayerbook, but John Rayner had very clear vision for the content.

> One of the highlights of being at the LJS during that period was serving on the Editorial Committee for the new prayerbook, *Siddur Lev Chadash*. John Rayner's scholarship was formidable and we immersed ourselves in the history, variety and development of the liturgy. We all contributed to the prayerbook, but John was very firm about what he wanted. I remember submitting a draft of a special theme and he almost completely rewrote it, but generously attributed parts of it to me.
>
> Alexandra Wright (Pt. 3)

---

collaboration with Rabbi Chaim Stern and with illustrations selected by Rabbi Lawrence Rigal. There were optional versions of this edition – either opening right to left or left to right. The 1962 *Haggadah* was used until 2009 when a new one, produced by Rabbis Andrew Goldstein and Pete Tobias, was published.

181 ULPS Oral History Project, interview with Sidney Brichto. See Appendix 1.
182 ULPS Oral History Project, interview with John Rayner. See Appendix 1.

23. *Rabbi John Rayner and Peggy Lang being presented with Encyclopaedia Britannica by Rabbi Sidney Brichto after the launch of Gate of Repentance. Photograph by Harvey Johns. (1973)*

I am quite proud of the fact that I was invited to be a member of the lay consultancy panel for both the *Siddur* and the *Machzor*. I had frequently attended study sessions with the rabbis, particularly with John Rayner, but this was quite different. John's meticulous preparation, with many pages of background on the history and text of prayers, with reasons why he favoured a particular formulation, was an educational experience like no other. These prayerbooks, together with more accessible music and greater use of lay readers, have done much to improve participation in services.

Bob Kirk (Pt. 3)

Both new prayerbooks were generally welcomed by LJS congregants.

It was more modern and accessible than the previous ones by Rabbi Mattuck, which had included lots of different services and hymns that were sung in English. The new prayerbook also contained several very meaningful readings and poems in the 'special themes' section. Above all, it was comfortable to hold and a much friendlier book to use than anything before or after it. I always remember, for example, that we had to turn to page 364 for the *Aleynu*, which I associated with being one number less than the days in the year. *Service of the Heart* was a definite step forward.

Michael Hart (Pt. 3)

However, not everybody was comfortable with the new prayerbooks. As with changes in forms of worship, LJS President, Sir Louis Gluckstein, objected strongly to modernisation of the liturgy and studiously used the old prayerbook when he read the Book of Jonah on *Yom Kippur*.

At that time, it seemed to some people very revolutionary and we had some powerful opponents of the idea, not least Gluckstein, and no doubt there are still some people who think that we should have stuck to 'thou' and 'thee', but I think that they are now in a small minority.

John Rayner[183]

Service of the Heart was succeeded by *Siddur Lev Chadash* in 1995, which was again edited by Rabbis Rayner and Stern. Although Rabbi Rayner also played a role in the editing of and contributing to *Machzor Ruach Chadash*, the new prayerbook for High Holydays introduced in 2003, the leading editors were Rabbi Dr Andrew Goldstein and Rabbi Dr Charles Middleburgh. The technical editing for this generation of prayerbooks was undertaken by Ann Kirk.

The two newer prayerbooks, which are still in use at the LJS, made an even greater attempt to modernise the language of the liturgy including, after some debate, gender-neutral language for God and humanity. Like traditional prayerbooks, but unlike their Liberal predecessors, they were paginated from right to left. Again they had a mixed reception, particularly in respect of the gender-neutral language, which had been encouraged by a new generation of women student rabbis studying at Leo Baeck College, especially Sheila Shulman and Elli Sarah, and by Rabbi Rayner's daughter, Susan.[184]

I didn't like the new gender-inclusive translation of *Avinu Malkeynu*. I prefer saying 'Our Father, Our King' to 'Our Creator, Our Sovereign'. To me it's a bit like changing the Hebrew words written thousands of years ago. Not everything has to be 21st century.

Julie Carlin-Sasaki[185]

[T]he world as portrayed in the [previous] prayerbooks – all male and focussed on the welfare of Jews – always set my teeth on edge. I was delighted when the daily prayerbook was rewritten and Sarah, Rebekah, Rachel and Leah burst onto the scene. But that made the High Holyday prayerbook seem even more out of touch. When on this *Rosh Hashanah* I found myself in a world where men weren't in charge of everything and there were more opportunities to pray for the welfare of all, I could do it with real enthusiasm!

Marlene Winfield[186]

When ULPS decided it was time for a new prayerbook to replace *Service of the Heart*, I was invited to join the lay consultancy panel. This certainly wasn't on account of my Hebrew scholarship, more likely because of my pedantic eye for ensuring commas and apostrophes are in the right place. However, I was passionately committed to the cause of gender-inclusive language, and remember standing up to Sidney Brichto on this matter during one of our meetings. In *Siddur Lev Chadash*, 'Lord' became 'the Eternal One'; 'Mankind' became 'Humanity' and we sang of 'how good it is, and how pleasant, when brothers *and sisters* live together in unity'. The prayerbook was used for the first time at the ULPS biennial conference in April 1995. After so many centuries, women were no longer marginalised in our liturgy! I was so moved by this momentous breakthrough that I sobbed uncontrollably throughout the service. Michael [her husband] and I were newly married at this time. He stood next to me, uncertain whether to hold my hand or turn a blind eye.

Carolyn Simon

---

[183] ULPS Oral History Project, interview with John Rayner. See Appendix 1.
[184] Information from Jane Rayner.
[185] *LJS News*, November 2003.
[186] Ibid.

One striking feature of *Siddur Lev Chadash* is the collection of special themes devised by Rabbi John Rayner, each one linked to the theme of the *Torah* portion of the week. These include extracts from a diverse range of sources, both ancient and contemporary rabbinic thought as well as secular material, such as from Kalil Gibran's *The Prophet*.

Both *Service of the Heart* and its successor, *Siddur Lev Chadash*, gave those leading services more choice on forms of service and on the use of Hebrew.

> We noticed a change in the language of the services from 90 per cent English to more Hebrew under John Rayner's leadership. It occurred very gradually but, once *Service of the Heart* was introduced, it was very evident. It is left to the leader of the congregation to choose what will be read in Hebrew or English. They take a measure of the congregation and decide how to proceed. If there are a lot of non-Jewish visitors, they might do more English.
>
> Ann Kirk (Pt. 3)

The modern prayerbooks, which were strongly influenced by Rabbi John Rayner, were used as a model for a new generation of prayerbooks for the Reform movement in America edited by Rabbi Chaim Stern, and also in various European countries.

> For me the epitome of the fine creative writing in our Liberal liturgies was John Rayner's piece for private confession in the morning service of *Yom Kippur*. It is a testimony both to his genius as a liturgist and the honesty and approachability that are the hallmarks of the prayerbooks that play such an important role in our Jewish lives.
>
> Charles Middleburgh[187]

Chapter Four: Music in services

THE FIRST SERVICE organised by the JRU in the Wharncliffe Rooms included music provided by a mixed choir accompanied by a harmonium.[188] Choral singing and organ music were subsequently established as an integral part of JRU services and, when it was established in 1911, of services at the LJS.

Choirmasters and Directors of Music

In the early days of the LJS, music mainly provided an accompaniment to hymns, but has been developed significantly in its role and style by successive Choirmasters and Directors of Music: Ivor Warren 1910–49, Israel Hoffman 1949 until 1976, Yakov Paul[189] 1977 until 1996, and Cathy Heller-Jones[190] from 1996 onwards.

---

[187] Charles Middleburgh, 'Birth of a dynamic new liturgy'.
[188] The music included the pieces 'Unto the hills I lift mine eyes' (Psalm 121) and 'God of Grace' – see programme for concert held to celebrate a hundred years of liturgical music used in Liberal synagogues, held at the LJS 11 November 2001.
[189] See photographs 25 and 55.
[190] See photograph 27.

24. *Ivor Warren, first LJS Choirmaster, 1910–49. (undated, c. 1920)*

Ivor Warren was the fourteenth son of the cantor and composer Chaim Wasserzug. After graduating from the Royal College of Music, he started work as a singer with the Sadler's Wells Opera Company. In 1904 he joined the JRU choir and in 1909 he succeeded the JRU's first Choirmaster, Alegernon Henry Lindo. He went on to be appointed as the Choirmaster at the LJS when it opened in 1911.

Rabbi Mattuck was able to draw on the music used by the American Reform movement to accompany the materials he incorporated into his prayer books from earlier American liturgy. He also used music from the West London Synagogue, which had a well-established musical repertoire. However, Ivor Warren enriched much of the American music with his own harmonies, and he also wrote music himself to accompany the modern materials included in the prayerbooks. Many of his compositions, such as *Kedushah* and his setting of *Yismechu*, remain in use today.

> His compositions really arose from necessity rather than choice, as it was part of his job to provide the music for the various services and if he couldn't find anything suitable already in existence, he just sat down at the piano and wrote it himself ... When the synagogue was bombed in the early hours of one Saturday morning [in 1940], my father arrived at the usual time to prepare for the morning service. When he saw the devastation he unobtrusively found a ladder and climbed up into the wrecked choir gallery to rescue his precious music.
>
> Harold Warren[191]

Israel Hoffman, Ivor Warren's successor, started his career as a concert pianist but, after the Second World War, he became a school teacher, a career which he combined with directing music at the LJS. He wrote music for the new ULPS prayerbooks *Service of the Heart* and *Gate of Repentence*. He also updated and rearranged many traditional melodies from Eastern Europe and Israel, and composed many works in his own style such as his haunting setting of *Shelach Orecha*.

---

[191] Letter from Harold Warren in LJS archives.

A Choirmaster not to be crossed, he is still respectfully (and perhaps somewhat fearfully) remembered by choristers who sang with him all those years ago.

Cathy Heller Jones[192]

He wrote many compositions, many of which I think are superb and far too little known, let alone appreciated, outside the LJS, not even within the ULPS. There was a tape recording of his own compositions done by the choir before he died. I also remember when *Gate of Repentance* came out we put together a programme of readings and music which we performed on television for which Israel Hoffman wrote some instrumental music as well as some further vocal compositions. The cellist was the world-famous Stephen Isserlis, only seventeen years old then.

John Rayner[193]

He was very meticulous in the setting of music to *ivrit*, which pleased John Rayner very much!

Tim Farrell[194]

Yakov Paul also combined school teaching with directing the music of the LJS, having previously worked in the same way for Middlesex New Synagogue and Harrow and Wembley Progressive Synagogue.

I first worked with Yakov at the LJS one Sunday afternoon some 20 years ago ... On this particular Sunday, Yakov (as Director of Music-in-waiting), was to observe a wedding conducted by Israel Hoffman, the retiring Director of Music. None of us knew, until the last minute, that Israel had been rushed into hospital following a motoring accident. As would be expected, Yakov rose to the occasion, and this was the start of what [was] a truly memorable era of music.

Tim Farrell[195]

I arrived at no. 28 in a state of dress befitting the DIY enthusiast. I was in the middle of home decorating, only to be informed that Mr Hoffman was unable to take the service. Would I direct the choir at the wedding due to take place? Fully exposed, I well remember feeling like a swimmer jumping off a diving board – and I can't swim!

Yakov Paul[196]

Yakov Paul spent long hours building up an extensive and unique Jewish liturgical music library and knew a large number of experienced artistes whom he could approach. With the increasing use of Hebrew in the liturgy, he had the painstaking task of resetting many of Ivor Warren's English compositions to the original Hebrew text. Within three months of his arrival at the LJS, he had arranged, compiled and edited the music for the third generation of ULPS prayer books.

It was no small task modifying the music for all the Sarah, Rebecca, Rachel and Leahs in our gender-inclusive texts. Many special themes also needed corresponding music, which Yakov, I am reliably told, tossed off on his tube journeys to St John's Wood.

Cathy Heller Jones[197]

---

[192] Writing in service sheet for special service to celebrate the music of the LJS Directors of Music held on 2 April 2011 in honour of the centenary year.
[193] ULPS Oral History Project, interview with John Rayner. See Appendix 1.
[194] *Chavorah* talk at LJS on 1 April 2011 given by Tim Farrell.
[195] *LJS News*, October 1996.
[196] Copy of article (undated) in LJS archives.
[197] Writing in service sheet for special service to celebrate the music of the LJS Directors of Music held on 2 April 2011 in honour of the centenary year.

Like his predecessors, Yakov composed special anthems, including his setting of *Mah Tovu*, which was used at the reopening of the synagogue in 1991.

> It is a measure of the affection in which he [Yakov Paul] is held by his singers that they were even prepared to forgive him on those occasions when his warm heart runs away with his cool head and he cannot restrain himself from all too audibly reinforcing the tenor line.
>
> Desmond Feldman[198]

Cathy Heller Jones came to Britain from New York to study at the Guildhall School of Music. She became involved in the LJS initially as a member of the Professional Choir (see below) for High Holyday services.

> Listening to the inspired and provocative sermons of Rabbis John Rayner and David Goldberg from the concealed choir loft led to me becoming a member of the LJS congregation.
>
> Cathy Heller Jones

Cathy Heller Jones was later appointed as the *Shabbat* evening vocal soloist before becoming Director of Music. She has significantly developed the synagogue's musical repertoire which, as a result, is now very varied.

> As for the music, I think that our high standards have been maintained because of the work of Cathy Heller Jones and Yakov Paul before her, whom I brought with me from Wembley. They have been eclectic in their musical choices and would rather go for a John Rutter setting of 'The Lord bless you and keep you' than some mediocre Jewish setting that you can strum on a guitar.
>
> David Goldberg (Pt. 3)

Musical traditions

Drawing on the synagogue's roots in nineteenth-century European Reform Judaism, classical settings of the liturgy by Louis Lewandowski and Salomon Sulzer continue to be sung in the LJS and western-style choral writing is combined with age-old traditional chants sung by a soloist. Composers from Europe and the United States such as Bloch, Janowski, Mombach, Schalit and Schlesinger also feature in services, as do more contemporary Israeli and American-style folk tunes, mostly non-liturgical in their origin, by composers such as Debbie Friedman, Klepper and Carlebach. *Dodi Li*, 'My Beloved Is Mine' and *Tasim (Nasim) shalom* are prime examples of this type of modern music used at the LJS.

> John [Rayner] loved singing *Adon Olam* to as many contemporary tunes as possible, sometimes with very amusing results. He produced a song book of Jewish songs both traditional and modern.
>
> Jane Rayner

The congregation of the LJS is very proud of the synagogue's musical tradition and, from time to time, congregants have expressed clear views about the introduction of new tunes

---

[198] 'Yakov Paul at 70', in *LJS News*, July/August 1995.

for well-known prayers as well as on the question of whether particular prayers are sung in English or Hebrew.

> The introduction of a Hebrew rendering of 'At the Dawn I Seek You' on *Shabbat* mornings was met with strong protest as was the substitution of *Adon Olam* for 'All the World Shall Come to Serve You' at the end of the *Rosh Hashanah* service. Similarly, views on the singing of 'I Vow to Thee My Country' as an Anthem on Remembrance *Shabbat* in November or singing *Adon Olam* to the tune of 'Yankee Doodle Dandy' were definitely mixed.
>
> Vivien Rose

One enduring feature of service music at the LJS is the opening of the *Kol Nidre* service with a cello playing Bruch's *Kol Nidre* at the beginning of the service.

> Over the years we have been fortunate enough to have had world-class players which have included cellists Steven Isserlis, Raphael Wallfisch, Natalie Clein, Gemma Rosefield and Andrea Hess. We have also had the eminent double bass player, Gary Kerr, and the viola player, Rivka Golani. Cellists in the 'alternate' *Kol Nidre* services have included various students from the Yehudi Menuhin School and, more recently, the cellist, Rachel Sanders-Hewett.
>
> Cathy Heller Jones

> An emotional and spiritual highlight of the year for me is the opening of the *Kol Nidre* service. Often it is a real struggle to get to the LJS in time for the start of the service – leaving work early, grinding through traffic when the whole of North London seems to be on the move means I am often quite frazzled by the time I take my seat before the service. The Sanctuary is filled almost to capacity and there is a great deal of buzzing and fidgeting before the service starts as people find their places and greet friends. But once the cello sounds out with that plaintive, ancient/modern motif the whole place gradually quietens down and there is a collective sigh as the music reaches its crescendo. By the end of the piece, the Sanctuary is completely still and everyone is in a contemplative mood ready for the challenge of the *Yom Kippur* day.
>
> Vivien Rose

LJS choirs

Since its inception, the LJS has always had a Professional Choir that has included both male and female choristers. To begin with, the choir was quite small but by 1950 had gradually increased to twelve choristers. However, it subsequently became smaller again and, for a number of years, it has consisted of five choristers – two sopranos, one contralto, one tenor and one bass.

The current choir includes professional singers, some of whom perform with London opera companies. It is involved in Saturday morning services, except when the Members' Choir sings (see below). The choice of a man or woman to perform a particular solo is determined purely by musical considerations.

The size of the choir is increased to nine or ten for High Holydays and other special occasions. Extra choristers were brought in to sing on High Holydays when services were held at both St John's Wood Road and the Porchester Hall.

For many years Paul Weaver was the tenor with the Professional Choir. He composed many pieces of music for the LJS, such as his settings of *Yih'yu l'ratson* and *Rom'mu*.

25. LJS professional choir conducted by Yakov Paul, LJS Choirmaster, 1977–1996.
Photograph by David Gluckstein. (undated, c. 1980)

Despite the importance attached to musical accompaniment in services, the early synagogue leaders felt the need for some degree of separation between the choir and the congregation. The choir originally sat out of sight in a specially constructed console either side of the organ.

> The choir were in the loft. The organist had to empathise with readers unusually well. Sometimes he would look around the curtain to see the *bimah*. Then the choir became visible. There was a query therefore whether they should wear hats.
>
> John Rayner[199]

It was not until comparatively recently that the LJS choir has sat amongst congregants, having been encouraged to move out of the choir loft by the Members' Choir.

In its early years, the LJS had a Volunteer Choir of Ladies. It was led by Miss Theodora Davis who sang and played the organ at the children's services held on a Saturday morning, and who organised a weekly choral practice after the service. Members of the congregation also sang alongside professional singers at the Saturday afternoon services.[200]

A Members' Choir (initially called the Choral Society) was set up in 1974 at the instigation of Pamela Cross. Pamela soon passed on her leadership role to her son, Edward, who had acquired a passion for the music of the LJS as a child. He not only directed the Members' Choir but also composed music for it.

> My earliest memory of the LJS is of going to a children's service when I was about four. I remember standing on the *bimah* and being blessed by Leslie Edgar, although I was most interested in the ornate rug under my feet. I was most thrilled by the music so afterwards my father took me upstairs to the choir loft where the organist, Paul Lichtenstern, played 'Pop Goes the Weasel' for me.
>
> Edward Cross

[199] Email from John Rayner to Bryan Diamond, copy in LJS archives.
[200] See LJS Annual Reports.

26. *Members' Choir rehearsal. From left: Maureen Roe, Susan Levitt, Rosemary Lazarus, Valerie Gaynor, Fleur Castro, Ann Kirk, unknown, Bob Kirk, William Falk. (1993)*

Edward Cross was succeeded by Norman Lazarus who conducted the Members' Choir for twenty-five years before the role was taken over by William Falk in May 2002.

Although those involved with the Members' Choir have always been very enthusiastic about its role, it was not universally welcomed in its early days.

> Israel Hoffman didn't really want a Members' Choir as well as his Professional Choir and he was very scathing about us. We were very new and our voices were probably not at all brilliant. He would try to warm us up with 'Baa Baa Black Sheep'.
>
> Ann Kirk

27. *Kiddush for Norman Lazarus retiring from leading the Members' Choir, 25 May 2002. From left: Norman Lazarus, Cathy Heller Jones, Rosemary Lazarus, and William Falk. (2002)*

It is now an established practice for the Members' Choir to sing at the *Shabbat* service held on the first Saturday of each month. It rehearses on alternative Monday evenings supported by organist, Martin Sanders-Hewett. The Members' Choir also sings on the morning of *Rosh Hashanah* and on *Yom Kippur* at the parallel services and also at the main service on *Yom Kippur* afternoon. As the music is complex, the choir starts rehearsing for the High Holyday services over the summer months.

The Members' Choir became involved in a variety of communal activities.

> Our standard improved considerably, and we also sang at weddings and old people's homes. I recall that we went all the way to Nightingale House in Clapham as well as singing at Sunridge Court, a Blind Club, and to the Out and About Club.
>
> Norman Lazarus (Pt. 3)

> The Members' Choir used to entertain the Out and About Club. Bob and I were the 'comic turns', performing songs like 'Mud, Mud, Glorious Mud', miming and hamming up to the choir singing. We also recited comic poems. We used to disappear into the store room at the back of the Montefiore Hall and re-emerge in costume, much to the audience's amusement. Perhaps our best effort was 'We're a Couple of Swells'.
>
> Ann Kirk

The LJS choirs were part of the BBC Radio 3 celebration of Mendelssohn's bicentenary celebration in 2009.

> Mendelssohn's 'Oh for the Wings of a Dove' was sung by an enlarged choir in the service and featured Max Loble as the solo treble voice. Max, with his twin brother, Harry, have made an invaluable contribution to the musical richness of our services, both with their beautiful treble voices as well as Harry's organ playing. They are both in the interview which was aired as part of the Radio 3 programme, 'The Choir'.
>
> Cathy Heller Jones

The nurturing of young musicians and singers has always been a high priority at the LJS. A Children's Choir (sometimes referred to as the 'Junior Choir') was first established in 1921 and sang at Saturday morning services. It ran intermittently until 1967 when it was revived by Edward Cross, who directed the Children's Choir with the help of Mike Beral (and later Susan Guth). It rehearsed in the Montefiore Hall and sang regularly at children's services.

> One of those involved was a young Alexandra Levitt and her friend Ruth Steinman, daughter of the Beadle, Louis Steinman. They were extremely naughty and always baiting me. Alexandra tied my shoe laces together. I wonder what happened to her.[201]
>
> Edward Cross

The Children's Choir lapsed for some time, but was re-established at the instigation of Rabbi Mark Solomon on the arrival of Cathy Heller Jones in 1996 who met with them monthly before Friday night services. Nowadays, the choir, known as the Children's Music Group, meets most Saturday mornings before Religion School classes commence. The children lead the singing at family and festival services. They also sing with the adult choirs for special occasions and at other communal events.

---

[201] Now Alexandra Wright, she is Senior Rabbi at the LJS.

At the LJS, I was involved in the Junior Choir for a number of years, having always loved singing. In the Junior Choir we met once a month to practice and sing in the Friday night service. We also performed in a Gala concert, where I sang one of the parts for the duet of ABBA's 'I Have a Dream'. I also sang my *Bat Mitzvah* portion, having received a lot of support and lessons from Rabbi Solomon. For two of the years that I was involved, I was given a singing part in the *Purim Spiel*.

Rachel Brouwer

In the past, the LJS had one regular cantorial soloist for Friday night (*Erev Shabbat*) services. Toby Mundy and then Cathy Heller Jones both performed this role for many years before a rota system was introduced whereby various professional singers from the choir alternate in their leading of the music for *Erev Shabbat* services.

During his tenure as rabbi at the LJS, Mark Solomon made a major contribution with his cantorial singing during services, as well as his energetic leadership of *chavurot* suppers and *Pesach sedarim*.

His knowledge of synagogue music, cantorial chant and melodies was inexhaustible. His expertise in the chanting of the *Torah* graced our services on numerous occasions, as well as inspiring our younger children to chant their portions.

Cathy Heller Jones

In 2007 music sung for LJS services was recorded by singers from the Professional Choir, Tim Farrell and Rabbi Mark Solomon, and produced onto a CD. A *Musical Companion to Siddur Lev Chadash* was also published.

The congregation has always been invited to sing along with the choir, but in the old building in St John's Wood Road, the acoustics were poor which discouraged congregational singing. When the synagogue was refurbished in the 1970s, ceiling tiles were installed to reduce an echo which made it difficult to hear people speaking on the *bimah*. Unfortunately the tiles had the side effect of absorbing sound and deadening the musical acoustics.

Another change over the fifty years I have been coming to the LJS is the singing. The shape of the old synagogue made it quite impossible to hear other people singing. The choir in those days were concealed in an organ loft above the *bimah*, and however much noise the congregation made when joining in, you couldn't hear it. The acoustics were so poor that you always felt you were on your own, so there was much less congregational participation.

George Rigal (Pt. 3)

Organs and organists

In the LJS's first premises at Hill Street the synagogue had its own organ to provide an accompaniment to the Professional Choir.

The organ at Hill Street was worked by a bellows which, of course, as children kept us entertained and was liable to considerable temperament.

Dorothy Edgar[202]

---

[202] ULPS Oral History Project, interview with Dorothy Edgar. See Appendix 1.

The Hill Street organ was replaced by a much grander organ when the synagogue moved into its new premises in St John's Wood Road in 1925. Following a visit to the cinema by a Council member, where he had heard an organ accompanying the film, it was decided that what the LJS needed was an English cinema organ, but that it had to be invisible. Eventually the Council selected a four-manual organ built by the John Compton Organ Company in 1926. It had 1,500 pipes which were installed in two rooms behind the *bimah* and beneath the choir loft. To enable the organ music to be projected upwards, holes were cut in the ceilings of the two rooms and the acoustics were further helped by a high-curved baffle.

The purchase of the Compton organ not only enhanced the reputation of the firm which built the organ, but also increased the profile of the LJS. It was sometimes used for making recordings.

> The music of the LJS in the 1920s and 1930s apparently had a wonderful reputation. Some people joined the synagogue because of the music. My great-aunt, Rosa Rosenstein said, 'I really came for the music.'
>
> Edward Cross

When the synagogue was bombed during the Second World War, the Compton organ sustained significant damage and had to be restored by its original builders. The initial intention was to retain this organ when the synagogue was rebuilt in the 1980s. However, due to difficulties in accommodating it, a new four-manual Copeman Hart electronic instrument was installed. While the LJS was based in the deconsecrated church at Loudoun Road, the organ from the small synagogue was transferred for use in the temporary premises, where it had the unnerving habit of sometimes picking up BBC Radio 2.

Over the course of its history, the LJS has had a number of organists. The first was W J McLean, who by the 1920s was supported by a number of assistant organists. He was replaced during the Second World War by Alfred Harris, but continued as organist until he was succeeded by Paul Lichtenstern (1941–75) and Tim Farrell.

The son of professional musicians, Tim Farrell grew up in Cape Town and was already playing the piano by the age of three. He won scholarships to the Royal College of Music in London and to the Worshipful Company of Musicians. After a brief period as assistant organist at St Paul's Cathedral, he was appointed Sub-Organist at Westminster Abbey. In 1974, he became Organist, Choirmaster and Composer to her Majesty the Queen at the Chapels Royal. In the following year, Kenneth Tudor, a Lay Vicar at Westminster Abbey, who also sang bass in the LJS's choir, told Tim Farrell that there was a vacancy for the position of organist at the LJS. He has held the position since 1975.

> Tim would arrive just before the service after playing at the BBC and jumping in a cab. He sight-read anything and used a shaving mirror to follow the conducting from a distant gallery while transposing at sight and playing a tasteful and supportive accompaniment for the amateur and children's choirs. He was a real pro.
>
> Edward Cross

28. *Tim Farrell, LJS organist since 1975, showing Compton organ. (undated, c. 1980)*

We tend to overlook the fact that Tim Farrell is composing original music at every service. He skilfully improvises a short composition, usually after the sermon, always complementary and sensitive to the mood which the sermon has set.

Cathy Heller Jones[203]

Tim Farrell married Jane Emmanuel, who was a soprano soloist with the LJS choir for a number of years.

I remember one *Shavu'ot* morning service soon after I joined the LJS, Jane Emmanuel sang a solo setting of 'The Song of Songs' by Max Heffman, accompanied by Tim. I thought it was the most beautiful and moving thing I had ever heard and I thought at that time that if I ever got married at the LJS I would ask Jane to sing it at my wedding. Many years later when Bernie and I got married, Jane did indeed agree to sing it when we were standing under the floating *chuppah* in the Sanctuary. It was an absolutely magical moment in the service.

Vivien Rose

Michael Foley (Organist and Choirmaster at St Alban's Holborn) played the organ at LJS High Holyday Services when Paul Lichtenstern was conducting at the Porchester Hall. He also stood in for Tim Farrell during his sabbatical.

He brought energy and style to his playing which was unique in the synagogue. He showed what the organ could really do and the feelings it could evoke. He brought something extra to it. In his prime he was a thrilling musician.

Edward Cross

Martin Sanders-Hewett now plays the organ at some of the High Holyday services.

---

[203] Writing in service sheet for special service to celebrate the music of the LJS's Directors of Music held on 2 April 2011 in honour of the centenary year.

Section Two: A place of meeting – the community life of the synagogue

Chapter One: The Women's Society

E̲VEN WHEN THE LJS was accommodated in the cramped conditions of Hill Street, attempts were made to foster the community life of the synagogue. As early as 1912, a Ladies' Needlework Guild was set up. Its main purpose was to look after the synagogue's robes and linens, but it was also seen as a means for involving women in the life of the community. Over the next ten years, the activities of the Needlework Guild (later renamed the Sewing Guild) were expanded to include making clothes for the first Jewish crèche in the East End of London set up by Alice Model, a dedicated social worker and early member of the synagogue.[204] This involvement continued until the Sewing Guild ended over seventy years later.

In 1923 the Ladies' Needlework Guild came under the aegis of the newly established Women's Society.

> I know that my grandmother, Florence, was involved in the Women's Society at the synagogue because, a short time ago, I helped Rita Adler in finding a cleaner for an embroidered tablecloth. The names of all the women involved were embroidered on the back, and one of them was Florence Simon.
>
> Tim Simon (Pt. 3)

The Women's Society[205] had two main purposes: 'to deepen the corporate life of the community by promoting a spirit of fellowship amongst its members and to undertake such tasks in connection with the synagogue itself, or in connection with any social work that might be promoted, as fell naturally within the scope of women's activities'.[206] Its first Chairman was Lady Sassoon. Mrs J H Simon was its Honorary Treasurer, and Mrs I M Gluckstein its Honorary Secretary.

During the 1920s, the Women's Society provided the catering for some key events, such as the reception held for the opening of the Montefiore Hall in the new synagogue in St John's Wood Road, the 1926 conference at which the World Union for Progressive

---

[204] Alice Model, Chairman of the Women's Society during the 1930s, had set up a day nursery for Jewish Children (later the Alice Model Nursery) for the children of working mothers in Stepney in 1897, which was supported over many years by the LJS's Women's Society. Alice Model had made a name for herself by successfully starting the Sick Room Helps Society at Underwood Street and a maternity home. At the beginning of the war, the nursery was evacuated and closed down. Phyllis Gerson, a relation of Alice Model's, and another prominent LJS member, started a wartime emergency school at the Beaumont Hall. When the older children were relocated Phyllis Gerson found that she was left with a lot of younger children, so she started the Beaumont Hall War Nursery which was later renamed the Alice Model Nursery. The new nursery was not therefore directly connected to the original Alice Model Nursery. Information provided by Joan Salter.

[205] The writing of this section was greatly assisted by the invaluable work carried out by George and Margaret Rigal. They read through back copies of LJS newsletters and produced a précis of the activities of the Women's Society.

[206] 'The Years Between 1911–1951', LJS exhibition catalogue.

Judaism was founded, and a congregational reception to mark Claude Montefiore's 70th birthday in 1928. They also did the catering for the main festivals.

> It did all sorts of things – I remember they did all the catering – they did it on a grand scale. For example, for the *seder* supper, we asked the entire congregation to bring pieces of fried fish and they all turned up in the morning, for my mother and Mrs Mattuck, with all different sizes of bits of fish from large bits of whole cod to sardines. It was a terrible failure and they decided they could never go through that again, sorting out all the fish! They also did the *matzah* balls with a huge batch of fish stock which one of the cooks had made. They had that on the boil and people were asked to bring along their matzah balls and apparently Ma stood and lobbed them in – *matzah* balls varying from the size of a pinhead to almost the size of cannon balls. They varied in texture too. They had to bring the fish and the balls in the morning so they could sort it all out. So it was a wonderful feeling of togetherness which I rather miss now – whose bit of fish had you got, some burnt and some not burnt. But my mother said she would never do it again because it gave her backache. The Women's Society bought the food themselves as their contribution.
>
> Ruth Ive[207]

In addition to holding regular monthly luncheons for its members, the Women's Society organised lectures, discussions, concerts, 'At Homes', and decorated the *sukkah* and the synagogue at *Chanukkah*. In the society's early years, garden parties were held at the homes of Lady Sassoon, Mrs Mattuck and Mrs Salmon. The society became affiliated to the Union of Jewish Women and to the National Federation of Temple Sisterhoods in America.

29. *LJS garden party. (1926)*

---

[207] This quote is taken from an interview conducted with Ruth Ive in the 1990s.

Mrs Mattuck was very involved in the Women's Society.

My mother [Mrs Mattuck] helped found the Women's Society and was on its committee until my father retired. I joined the committee on my marriage [to Leslie Edgar] and stayed there until my husband retired. Neither of us would accept the offer of chairmanship since we thought it would set an undesirable precedent.

Dorothy Edgar

In this synagogue Mrs Mattuck founded with other women our Women's Society and helped in its development. She accepted the responsibility for making the *sukkah* more beautiful each year and was never overwhelmed by the necessary work to develop the social life of the congregation, which contributed so much to the success of conferences and all kinds of function.

Lily Montagu[208]

By the 1930s the Women's Society was more involved in social work activities, such as arranging annual parties for children from the St George's Jewish Settlement (later the Bernhard Baron Settlement) in the East End of London. More locally, in 1932 the Women's Society set up a play centre for children living close to the synagogue under the chairmanship of Mrs Ricardo. The society also took on responsibility for activities such as arranging the flowers for the synagogue, carrying out inspections of the building to identify necessary improvements and caring for the gardens.

As the decade progressed, the Women's Society organised fewer social events and became more involved in supporting German refugees. It helped to find positions for Jewish girls as companions or governesses and was instrumental in bringing a group of children out of Germany, arranging sponsorship and finding them homes under the aegis of its Hospitality Committee. The Women's Society carried out fundraising on an ambitious scale to support refugees, including organising a major concert just before the outbreak of the Second World War.

Later on, I was very involved in the Women's Society myself. The first time was organising a concert in 1939 to raise money for refugees. I was roped in because Peggy Lewsen, who was the Secretary of the Society, was my cousin and I could type. I had a portable typewriter and I bashed out all the letters on that. On the concert programme you will find all the women who played a prominent part in synagogue life: Mrs Cyril Nathan (Michael's mother); Mrs Kenneth Lazarus (Peter, Norman and Margaret's mother); Mr and Mrs Benedictus (David's parents); Mrs Enoch. They were all friends of my mother. The musicians at the concert were Gerald Moore, a famous accompanist, and Hersha Gluckman, who was German and whom we knew from another source; she had a very nice contralto voice. The concert was in the Sanctuary and we were all in evening dress; my mother made me a new dress for the occasion.

Ruth Ive (Pt. 3)

Once the war started, the Women's Society became heavily involved in wartime activities: arranging comforts for troops, making bandages for the Red Cross, producing garments for the RAF and gathering clothes for evacuated children. In 1940 the Women's Society

---

[208] 'Edna M Mattuck, A memorial tribute', *Liberal Jewish Monthly*, March 1957.

adopted two minesweepers, the crews of which it supplied with items such as warm clothing. A further minesweeper was adopted in 1943. Altogether, 1,200 garments were knitted for the crews.

When the synagogue was damaged in 1940, the twenty-six women involved in the Sewing Guild met twice weekly in the home of Louis Gluckstein in Elm Tree Road, St John's Wood. By that time, it had produced over 1,000 garments for evacuated children, for the Red Cross and it was also making garments for the Armed Forces. Over a two-and-a-half year period, a Knitting Party headed by Doreen Gluckstein knitted up 500 lbs of wool for the Merchant Navy Comforts Service, making 1,500 garments.

Margaret Rigal, who was later to become an active member of the Women's Society, recalls being taken as a child to committee meetings during the war years.

> During the war, while we were at Bognor, she would always try to time our day trips to London to coincide with a day when there was a committee meeting of the Women's Society. On several occasions I went with her to the meetings and was allowed to sit and listen to them all sitting around the table in the old Mattuck Room. I can clearly remember Mrs Mattuck and Dorothy Edgar. The Chairman was Mrs Dorothy Myer, who was always known as Mrs Horace Myer, although I have since learned that her husband was actually called Horatio. The Secretary was Mrs Elsa Espir, who was a rather prim, elderly lady. Everyone was terribly nice to me. My memory is that they were a most charming, well-mannered group of ladies. I was good at keeping quiet, so I don't think that I was a nuisance to them.
>
> Margaret Rigal (Pt. 3)

For the first few years following the war, the Women's Society was very involved in dealing with its aftermath. It raised money for displaced families, orphaned children and those freed from concentration camps. It sent parcels of clothing and other items to charities operating on the continent, such as the Marrainage Scheme, working with orphaned children. The society also helped to support Polish Jewish families arriving in this country without resources.

The society became a major force in restoring the communal life at the LJS. It arranged tea parties to welcome home demobilised members of the synagogue and lunches for ex-soldiers, while continuing to cater for meetings of the ULPS and major festivals.

The Sewing Guild also continued its activities. At this time, between fourteen and seventeen women were engaged in a range of sewing projects each week. It was led by Isobel Coburn who had been one of its initiators in 1912. She continued to be involved until 1959, when she relinquished her leadership at the age of eighty.

Members of the Women's Society began to participate once more in social work activities. It arranged visits to Jewish people in hospitals in and around London. In 1948, a Darby and Joan Club for older people living in the Lisson Grove area was set up under the leadership of Doreen Gluckstein, wife of the LJS President, supported by Dorothy Myer. It was one of the few friendship clubs that existed at that time. Just three members enrolled for the first meeting, which was also attended by the Mayor and Mayoress of St Marylebone. Its membership rapidly escalated to 150 members plus a long waiting list. It continued to operate for over fifty-five years, latterly under the leadership of Rosalie Levinson.

In 1949 the Women's Society set up a group, which each Wednesday morning folded and put into envelopes the LJS weekly newsletter and in 1952 the Women's Society set

30. *Darby and Joan Club helpers. From left: June Goldfaden, Irene Gerchenovitch, Joice Linde, Anita Schwartz, Rosalie Levinson (Club Leader), Nina Schreier, Joan Tobias, Ruby Meerloo, unknown, Elaine Falk. (1992)*

up a Social Services Committee to co-ordinate its welfare activities. By this time, several members of the Women's Society were helping regularly at the Levene Home for the Elderly in Hampstead.

An important post-war development was the affiliation of the LJS's Women's Society to the newly established ULPS Federation of Women's Societies. This was founded in 1946 by Lily Montagu, who had once again identified the need for a national body. The Federation's aims were to promote intellectual, social and religious activities as well as community service, and to foster interfaith work. Its first open meeting was convened at the LJS In January 1947, which was attended by eighty women. Lily Montagu was its first Chairman and remained so for seventeen years. She was succeeded by another member of the LJS, Dora Wolchover, and, at the time it closed in 1987, Margaret Rigal and Tessa Jordan were the joint Chairmen. Fundraising for charitable causes became an important feature of the Federation's work and its May fairs were held at the LJS.

By 1950 membership of the Women's Society had reached 200, and it was again arranging a variety of lectures and other activities, including a Bible Study Group and a study group on Liberal Judaism led by the Rev. Philip Cohen. Regular tea parties had also resumed.

During the 1950s and 1960s, the Women's Society began to change both in its make-up and the way in which it operated. Until that time, its meetings had been very formal affairs.

I joined the Women's Society when Claire went to school forty-five years ago. I remember that some of the ladies wore hats at the committee meetings!

Rosemary Lazarus (Pt. 3)

Until 1961 the members of the Women's Society were referred to by their husband's initials or names, but from then women started to use their own names.

By the late 1950s the Women's Society had had five Chairmen. Lady Sassoon was followed by Alice Model, Dorothy Myer, Peggy Lewsen and Dora Wolchover. Its Committee was mainly made up from the wives of prominent LJS members from well-to-do families, sometimes referred to as the 'Cousinhood' or the 'Jewish Establishment'.[209]

> I didn't cook. I grew up with a staff of five. I've lived my life backwards. I used to have a chauffeur.
>
> Doreen Gluckstein[210]

Before the 1960s there were very few younger women on the Women's Society Committee.

> My mother joined the Women's Society Committee before the war, at a rather younger age than most other women. She always said to me: 'I really don't know why they asked me onto the committee when I was not very active. But it was a great compliment and, so of course, I joined.'
>
> Margaret Rigal (Pt. 3)

Some women had mixed feelings about the way in which the Women's Society operated and were not attracted to participate in its activities.

> As the children grew older, I became involved in the synagogue's Women's Society. I was Honorary Secretary because of my secretarial skills. Doreen Gluckstein was President. The Women's Society did a lot of visiting of the elderly and was quite powerful. I didn't enjoy the Women's Society too much, as I am not a very good listener, and I always steered clear of any activities involving catering!
>
> Elizabeth Lazarus (Pt. 3)

> I remember the members of the Women's Society as formidable, attending their meetings in hats and gloves. As the wife of the student Rabbi, working full-time, nothing was expected of me. But when David returned as Associate Rabbi I felt there was a pressure that I should be involved. But I had two small children, no help, and although I respected what these women did, my feminist instincts rebelled against the idea of being pigeon-holed into 'women's work', i.e. cooking.
>
> Carole Goldberg

The seeds of change were sown when a young mother, Eva Feldman (a refugee from Germany), was invited to join the Committee of the Women's Society as the representative of the Younger Members' Organisation (see below).

> I was one of the first young people to come on the Committee. The Women's Society used to organise a tea on Monday afternoons, and they wanted more young people to come along. I told them: 'You won't get any young people because teatime is the time they collect their children from school.' I also told them that Monday wasn't a good day anyway, because we all did our washing on a Monday. So they changed the meetings to lunchtime on a Tuesday.
>
> Eva Feldman (Pt. 3)

---

[209] This was the name given to the prominent Anglo-Jewish families, the de facto Anglo-Jewish aristocracy. These families included the Mocatta, d'Avigdor, Cohen, Cruse, Goldsmid, Henriques, Kadoorie, Lousada, Marks, Montefiore, Rothschild and Samuel families.

[210] ULPS Oral History Project, interview with Doreen Gluckstein. See Appendix 1.

Eva Feldman eventually became Chairman of the Women's Society and used the role to bring about other changes. She put a proposal to the LJS Council that membership of the Women's Society should be open to all women members of the synagogue, membership fees should be abolished and contributions sought instead. This was agreed and it led to the opening up of the Women's Society which, as a result, started to become involved in new types of activity, particularly those relating to congregational welfare.

In 1967 the Women's Society set up an Advice and Welfare Centre under the guidance of Lillian Hill, a trained social worker. The aim of the centre was to provide help and advice to members of the synagogue, particularly those in need of care. Members of the Women's Society also started to cook monthly hot lunches for people living on their own.

In the early 1970s, under the leadership of Dorothy Edgar and Dora Wolchover, a Women's Society committee looked into the possibility of setting up a small residential home for older members of the LJS community. Nina Nathan and Peggy Lang (the former Organising Secretary of the LJS) were appointed to start the search for suitable premises. A steering committee led by Nina Nathan then oversaw the establishment of the first Jewish Abbeyfield Society home. This entailed a change to the Abbeyfield Society's constitution as it was, until then, a Christian body.[211]

> The committee liked the Abbeyfield philosophy of small residential homes, run on a non-profit making basis. They anticipated employing only a cook-housekeeper and cleaner with the committee stepping in to help if necessary. We could cook for eight people, whereas we would not have been qualified to cook for a larger number.
>
> Jo Kessler

In 1974 a formal committee was set up chaired by Lewis Levy with Edgar Nathan as Treasurer. A suitable property in Willesden was located in 1975.

> Alterations and building work started. We had many problems, including squatters and two burglaries, and during the period when the builders left and before the new Housekeeper moved in, my son, James Kessler, together with a friend, slept in the house.
>
> Jo Kessler

The home was eventually opened in April 1978 by Lord Goodman. It was consecrated by Rabbi Rayner and named after Peggy Lang, who had unfortunately not lived to see the home open.

The home had a number of Admissions' Secretaries during the twenty-seven years of its existence. The first was Nancy Caplin who was much loved by the residents, many of whom were her junior. Peggy Lang House had only two Chairmen.

> I was very fortunate to be involved with the Abbeyfield Camden (Jewish) Society alongside Nina Nathan, Nancy Caplin, Jo Kessler, Maureen Roe, Ann Kirk, Ann and Bernard Hart, Nena and Norman Sofier, Beryl Civval, Susan Goodman, Nicole David, Miles Halford and Bennie Richenberg. The Abbeyfield Society was started by the Nathans, Jo and Nancy, with LJS financial support. The property they bought, Peggy Lang House, was in Walm Lane, Willesden, and Nina was its first Chairman. I took over from Nina – although no one could

---

[211] Later there was to be a Polish, an Afro-Caribbean and an Indian House. The work of the LJS was therefore instrumental in making Abbeyfield an interfaith organisation.

take over from Nina, she was unique. Peggy Lang House continued to flourish for a further twenty-three years with a fantastic committee.

Jocelyne Tobin (Pt. 3)

A dedicated team of voluntary cooks took over occasionally from the Housekeeper, providing meals for special occasions, and members of the Peggy Lang House Committee provided help, care, and entertainment. A Fourth Night *Seder* was run for a number of years by Rabbi Mark Solomon.

Two further Abbeyfield Homes (Lily Montagu House in Edgware – now closed down – sponsored by Harrow and Wembley Progressive Synagogue and The Willows in Stanmore) were subsequently set up modelled on Peggy Lang House with several members of the Peggy Lang House Committee sitting on their boards.[212] Nina Nathan was awarded an MBE for her work with the Abbeyfield Society.

By the mid-1970s there were signs that the Women's Society was in decline. With an increasing number of women going out to work, the society was finding that only older women had time to be involved in its activities. A decade later, women were saying that, not only did they not have the time to be involved, they were also disinclined to be involved in segregated activities and wanted to be part of the mainstream affairs of the LJS. To try and broaden its appeal, an attempt was made to involve men in the activities of the Women's Society, meetings were moved to evenings and discussions convened on topical issues, but to little avail.

31. *Meeting of the Women's Society. At the top table from left: Betty Ungar, Dorothy Edgar, Lady Gluckstein, Ruth Ive, Barbara Brown, Jane Rayner and Nina Nathan. (undated, c. 1986)*

The Federation of Women's Societies (later the Network of Women in the ULPS) was disbanded in 1987, but the LJS Women's Society continued for a further three years. Despite its dwindling membership, in its last few years the Women's Society, with Maureen Roe as its Treasurer, was very successful in raising money for charity.

---

[212] A fourth sister Jewish Abbeyfield Home, Belmont Lodge, was set up in 2002.

And now we think that this is an appropriate time for us to take an honourable retirement. It would be hypocritical for us to say that we accept our demise with equanimity; we do not. Despite all our well-meaning efforts to attract younger women to our ranks, we have failed.

Ruth Ive[213]

As a final gesture, the Women's Society, at this stage chaired by Barbara Brown, presented eight chairs for the *bimah* of the newly built synagogue. These had been embroidered by synagogue members to a design by Jane Finestone, which was intended to complement the surroundings of the Sanctuary, especially the Jerusalem stone, and which represented layers of Jewish civilisation and each of the main festivals in the Jewish year.[214] The project, which was led by Ruth Ive, Rachel Caro and Diana Springall (a well-known professional embroiderer), involved over a hundred people, including some who, until then, had not taken much part in synagogue activities.

32. *Leaders of bimah chairs tapestry project. From left: Ruth Ive, Jane Finestone, Diana Springall, Rachel Caro. Photograph by Carol Gould, Landseer Studios. (undated, c. 1990)*

The project gathered momentum and we had a stitching frenzy. Women, men, teenagers, the elderly, single people, families, couples, our three rabbis, visitors and friends, they all came. Some embroidered entire canvases while others placed a token stitch. On one special LJS open day, the vicar from the church round the corner wielded a needle and stitched his contribution too. We witnessed births, marriages and sadly deaths during the long process, but our achievement went far beyond the objects that we were creating. We discovered connections between people not previously known, feuding family members re-connected and shy lonely widows began to interact and find friendships beyond *Kiddush* on Saturdays.

---

[213] *LJS News*, February 1991.

[214] See special edition of *LJS News*, November 1992, for further information on the *bimah* chairs.

People aired their personal problems and interacted by phone and very often our stitching workshops became little problem-solving sessions, almost a social therapy. The *bimah* chairscape project necessitated that we worked incessantly for two and a half years. Some worked the entire period while others came and went, dipping in only briefly.

Jane Finestone

33. *Bimah chairs embroiderers. From left: Bernard Russell, Jane Finestone and Jean Russell.*
(undated, c. 1990)

The chairs were admired so much and the desire for more tapestry was so strong that a project was set up to replace the chairs in the rear foyer. The new chairs were again designed by Jane Finestone based on an illustration from a medieval Sephardic Bible.[215]

> As the foyer chairs have high backs, I had to elongate and narrow the proportions of the illustration, and with thick wool couldn't possibly embroider the swirling minute lines of ancient script, but the ancient design lent itself perfectly to our chairs and our stocks of surplus wools. It felt right to have evolved a design so deeply connected with our rich history.
>
> Jane Finestone

> One of the first things I got involved in was embroidering a panel for the chairs that are used in the rear foyer. There were a large number of volunteer embroiderers and Michael Adler was the 'wool monitor' preparing a palette for each volunteer with skeins of the wools needed. The chairs were all the same design but two chairs were made in each of three colourways. I was given the large back panel of a brown/orange colourway. By coincidence, Rosemary Lazarus, whom I sat next to in the Members' Choir, was embroidering the identical panel for the other brown/orange chair. When we had both finished, one of the

---

215 The design is from a Bible in Burgos (Spain) dated 1260 (sometimes known as 'Damascus Ketèr), now housed in the Jewish National and University Library in Jerusalem.

brown/orange chairs was made up as a sample by the furniture maker who was putting the chairs together. Unfortunately there was a fire in his workshop which consumed the chair. So Rosemary and I never knew which one of us in fact has their needlework adorning the synagogue and which one of us had our hours of hard work go up in smoke.

Vivien Rose

The chairs were presented to the synagogue in 1995.

Chapter Two: Activities for younger members

YOUNG PEOPLE WERE regarded by the synagogue's early leaders as being an integral part of synagogue life. In 1918 Rabbi Mattuck founded the Alumni Society to provide a forum for the continuing involvement of young people after their Confirmation. The society, which was very innovative at the time, was vital to the rebuilding of the congregation after the First World War had scattered many of its members.

After a rather faltering start, the Alumni Society subsequently went from strength to strength.[216] It was initially largely made up of young people from LJS families, but then grew to include others whose families had no connection with the synagogue, but who nevertheless felt at home there. Rabbi Mattuck chaired it himself for the first twelve months.[217] Ronald Ronalds then took over and its first Secretary was Amy Kirchberger.[218]

During the 1920s the Alumni Society was largely concerned with organising social and educational activities and gave relatively little attention to religious matters.

The Alumni was a very, very active part of one's social life. One was devoted to it when one left Religion School but you have to remember that in my day the people who went to university after leaving school were a minority, there were so many of us who went straight to work after we left school and that [the Alumni Society] was our social life.

Maxwell Stern[219]

In addition to its monthly meetings, at which there were often debates and discussions, the Alumni Society held well-attended *sedarim* and *Chanukkah* dinners and established a popular tennis club. In 1924 a walking group was set up under the leadership of Sam Rich, Head of the Religion School, who organised legendary rambles.

These were well organised and the land had been traversed a week earlier so that there were no arguments and we never got lost. Our tram fares were never to cost more than 1s 6d. The exceptional outings stretched to 2 or 3 shillings. I remember when we walked over Leith Hill, where CGM [Claude Montefiore] and his wife met us to take us to their home to tea. Sam always longed for his pot of tea and one of the star halts was at the Inn at Wootton

---

[216] 'The Years Between 1911–1951', LJS exhibition catalogue.

[217] See list of Chairmen of the Alumni Society in the programme for the Thanksgiving Service to celebrate the 40th Anniversary of the Foundation of the Alumni Society, 26 March 1959, LJS archives. Other notable Chairmen up until 1959 included Leslie Edgar (1929), Sam Rich (1942) and Marjorie Moos (1944).

[218] 'The Years Between 1911–1951', LJS exhibition catalogue.

[219] ULPS Oral History Project, interview with Maxwell Stern. See Appendix 1.

Hatch, Abinger, where he wallowed in cup after cup! Once, when the compartment in the tram on the way home became over-spirited, the chaps were bundled up into the racks to see how many could be accommodated up aloft!

Ruth Hadley[220]

A music group played at Alumni functions, such as at the Alumni annual dinner established in 1925, and also at events held by various Jewish institutions.[221] The group was led by Helen Pyke, who was to become a well-known composer and pianist. Although their prime intent was to socialise, many members of the Alumni Society did become involved in social action, mainly in the East End of London. They had been encouraged to do so by Rabbi Mattuck and by Basil Henriques.

> The Alumni Society wanted to do something for the children at the Settlement. So we decided to give them a *Chanukkah* tea party. I remember that John Cross, Harold Salmon and myself went to the Settlement and collected fifty ten- to twelve-year-old boys and girls. We counted fifty of them when we left Berners Street and when we arrived at Aldgate tube station we thought we had better count them again, and by that stage there were only forty-eight of them! There were cries of 'One's gone 'ome miss, he didn't like it'. Eventually we got them to St John's Wood Station, which was just by Lord's on the roundabout. We counted them again at that point and we found we had fifty-two children. We never found out how the extra ones had tagged along!
>
> Ruth Ive (Pt. 3)

> I must mention Basil and Rose Henriques. When word came round to the Alumni Society that we might go down to help at their club in Betts Street, E1, some of us went along to offer our services. It seemed natural to ask them what duties we were to perform. Nothing was forthcoming in the way of suggestions on their part. We were to fall into things and find our own individual way of joining in. If we were merely 'wall-flowers' – too bad, and their theory was, obviously, that we were unable to overcome the 'them and us' syndrome and we would stay away.
>
> Ruth Hadley[222]

In association with young people from West London Synagogue, the Alumni Society supported a Children's Fund, which contributed to the activities of the boys' and girls' clubs run by Basil Henriques and his wife. This work culminated each year in a variety show at the London Hippodrome.[223]

The Alumni Society also worked with the Social Service Guild and, later, with the Women's Society on charitable activities such as in the running of a play centre, sending parcels to Jewish people in the Ukraine and teaching Austrian children to speak English.[224] It became an established tradition that Alumni members would steward at High Holyday and festival services.

During the 1930s, the Alumni Society played its part in the two main causes taken up by the LJS during the interwar years – supporting refugees from Germany and helping those affected by the high levels of unemployment that followed the Great Depression.

---

[220] Letter from Ruth Hadley to Rabbis Rayner, Goldstein and Goldberg.
[221] LJS Annual Reports.
[222] Letter from Ruth Hadley to Rabbis Rayner, Goldstein and Goldberg.
[223] 'The Years Between 1911–1951', LJS exhibition catalogue.
[224] LJS Annual Reports.

However, the society's social activities continued and by now, river parties, trips to ice skating rinks, mock trials, and short holidays had all become part of the its annual calendar of events.

In 1933 a Younger Members' Organisation (YMO) was established to cater for the post-Alumni age group. The YMO was open to any junior member of the LJS who undertook to do at least one piece of work for the synagogue each year.

The first YMO President was Leslie Edgar, Assistant Minister at the LJS. Leonard Falk was its first Chairman and Ruth Snowman was its first Honorary Secretary. It too organised a range of social activities and was very concerned with social issues of the day. It had regular discussions on topics such as euthanasia and, in 1939, it produced *The Synagogue and Social Issues: A report on an investigation made by members of the YMO*.[225] The YMO, with the help of the Alumni Society, arranged entertainment for young German refugees.

During the war years, the YMO and the Alumni Society merged as there were too few young people left in London to make either group viable on its own.

> The war was a watershed for young people as we were all scattered. We tried to keep in touch, but that was really too difficult. All the boys went into the Forces and got posted around the world and, to a certain extent, so did the girls. So when the war came, the Alumni rather fell apart.
>
> Ruth Ive (Pt. 3)

The young people who did remain in London made contact with young people in other synagogues under the leadership of Rabbi Brasch at North London Progressive Synagogue.[226] Rabbi Brasch organised regular meetings, even during the Blitz, at which young people would listen to an outside speaker and then participate in a discussion.

Soon after its inception, the Alumni Society had set up its own newsletter, the *Alumni Gazette* (later renamed the *Alumni Digest*). This was maintained during the war to ensure that the LJS stayed in touch with young congregants evacuated from London or serving in the Armed Forces. Alumni members in the Armed Forces tried to meet up with Alumnites remaining in London.

> During my officer cadet days I kept in touch with the LJS and associated youth groups, and once joined them on an outing to 'somewhere in Buckinghamshire' led by Rabbi Brasch.
>
> John Rayner [227]

On returning to the synagogue after serving as an Army Chaplain, Leslie Edgar introduced a new programme of activities for young people. The LJS hosted meetings of the London branch of the International Study Group set up under the auspices of the World Union for Progressive Judaism, which looked at the impact of war on the attitude of young Jewish people. Young people became involved in collecting clothing and comforts for relief operations in Holland and at the Belsen concentration camp. Leslie Edgar also

---

[225] Ibid.

[226] Lawrence Rigal and Rosita Rosenberg, *Liberal Judaism: The First Hundred Years*. Rabbi Brasch was a refugee from Nazi Germany who had been recruited by North London Progressive Synagogue before the Second World War (information provided by Jean Russell).

[227] John Rayner, *Before I forget*.

arranged a series of 'In Town Today' meetings at which well-known people met with the YMO and the Alumni Society to discuss subjects such as 'The lessons of Belsen', led by Jane Leverson and the work of the Jewish Fellowship led by Basil Henriques.[228]

In 1946 the YMO and the Alumni Society divided again. Despite restrictions on accommodation because of bomb damage to the synagogue, both groups flourished as young people were keen to form new friendships and to meet up again with old friends.

> I told Bob Kirk the other day when we were honouring him that one of my earliest pictures of being in the Alumni is lying in a punt on the river with Ann lying next to me and Eileen Leapman sitting on the punt drinking out of a bottle. I also remember we had these marvellous hikes in Buckinghamshire. My feet did hurt! Sometimes one tended to get lost. I even managed to get lost with a fellow young female member of the Alumni in the very churchyard where one of the Kray brothers disappeared.
>
> Robert Greenberg

> I joined the Alumni in 1948. I became Secretary and then editor of the *Alumni Digest*. It was at the Alumni that I met John [her future husband]. He was at Cambridge and at that time reading moral science, including psychology, which I found very interesting. He was also very handsome! The Rev. Philip Cohen was very much loved by Alumnites, and I remember reading *Belief and Action* by Viscount Samuel at one of our study sessions with him.
>
> Jane Rayner

Over time, the two groups for young people developed increasingly separate identities – the Alumni was mainly a forum for young people aged from sixteen to thirty, while the YMO became a society for slightly older members, both single and married.

> I was very keen to stay involved with the LJS after my Confirmation, but I was shortly called up to join the Navy. I was in one of the last demob groups coming out in 1948. I then joined the Alumni and was on the committee for some years. John Cross was the Chairman when I first joined. He later became Secretary of the synagogue. The society was very active, with many social events such as rambles and dances. Its object was to keep people together as a social organisation rather than being a religious group.
>
> Michael Nathan (Pt. 3)

> When I was the Chairman of the Younger Members' Organisation ... we held a major fundraising event as part of the synagogue's Golden Jubilee Appeal. We arranged a film show at the Institute Francais in Kensington. We showed the classic silent film *The General* with Buster Keaton, which was accompanied by Arthur Dulay on the pianoforte, and then *The Red Balloon*. Muriel Trent was the Secretary and Kenneth Solomons the Treasurer, but we had help from many others including Hugh Isaacs, my predecessor as Chairman. I believe that we raised enough money to purchase the chandeliers in the new Montefiore Hall.
>
> Anthony Roe (Pt. 3)

By the mid-1950s it had become a long-standing tradition that once a month Friday evening services would be led by the Alumni Society and that annually, during or near *Chanukkah*, the sermon would be given by the Chairman of the Alumni Society.

Under the leadership of Philip Cohen, the Alumni Society grew rapidly, drawing in members not only from London and the Home Counties but from all over the country.

---

[228] LJS Annual Report, 1945.

The society also had a number of associate members in Australia and South Africa who corresponded regularly. It came to be seen as the way in which young people met their future partners.

> Mummy was an active member of the Alumni Society. We have another wonderful photo which shows her and Hilary [her aunt] at a *Chanukkah* dinner held in the Montefiore Hall in the early 1950s. In those days (to quote my dad), the Alumni was 'an excellent social club and marriage agency'. Fellow Alumnite Phillip Leuw brought along his cousin Bob … and that was how my parents met.
>
> Carolyn Simon (Pt. 3)

At the monthly 'Question Time' evenings, Philip Cohen acted as a 'one-person brains trust', answering questions on religious matters, and in 1946, at the behest of Basil Henriques, the members of the Alumni Society became involved once more in the Bernhard Baron Settlement.[229]

> At one point I used to go to the Settlement once a week and sleep there. All the club leaders sat round with cups of cocoa after the clubs finished.
>
> Michael Nathan

34. *Alumni Society three-day ramble, April 1950. Those present included John Aronsohn, Jane Rayner (née Heilbronn), Pat Barder, Jacqueline Pinto (née Blairman), Valerie Leapman, Bill Heilbronn (Jane Rayner's brother), Peter Leapman, Robin Barder, Ian Grant, Ken Schindler, Joel Pinto. (1950)*

35. *Board listing Chairmen of the Alumni Society at 40th celebration of the founding of the society 1958. Rabbi Leslie Edgar presiding. (1958)*

---

229 LJS Annual Report, 1946.

The Alumni Society now often met in an annexe to the synagogue, where the new Lily Montagu Wing was subsequently sited.

> I remember the rebuilding. There was some kind of wooden hut next to the synagogue which was used by the youth groups, and disapproved of by Miss Moos.
>
> Margaret Rigal (Pt. 3)

The Alumni Society started to meet away from the synagogue to assert its independence.

> We used to do all sorts of things and we went to that hotel which has now been rebuilt down in Euston – it used to have dark and panelled rooms – or we went to somebody's house and people were so interested in one another. If you had a drink you'd stand talking for hours on end without doing anything else.
>
> Robert Greenberg

The Alumni Society met up with similar groups that had now been formed in other synagogues but, because it was by far the largest youth group in Progressive synagogues, other youth groups were keen to participate in Alumni Society activities in St John's Wood.

> When we got fed up with our own company we used to go down to Upper Berkeley Street [West London Synagogue], to the over-22s club, and we used to do all sorts of things.
>
> Robert Greenberg

> While I was overseas, my parents moved to Rickmansworth, so our nearest Progressive synagogue was Wembley Liberal. When I came out of the Army, I became a youth leader at the synagogue. The club, 'Two Triangles', was run jointly with Kingsbury United Synagogue for all the Jewish teenagers in that area. We met at the home of a Council member. Sometimes my brother, Lawrence, and I went as visitors to the Alumni Society at the LJS. By comparison to our club, it was a very large and well-run youth club, having all sorts of more advanced and well-organised events.
>
> George Rigal (Pt. 3)

By this time the Alumni Society had broadened its membership still further to include non-Jewish people. However, not everybody thought they had been made to feel welcome by the Alumni Society.

> My earliest memory of the LJS was about 1950 when I had my application for membership of the Alumni Youth group turned down. During my interview, I told the Alumni Chairman I had been brought up in an Orthodox synagogue. He asked me how I felt about attending a Liberal synagogue. I said I didn't think it mattered which synagogue you were from because you were still praying to the same God. This reply was obviously not the one expected. However, through the intervention of friends, including my future husband Joe [Pinto], I was finally allowed to join. Then a couple of months later, I was asked to co-edit the *Alumni Digest*, so presumably I was no longer considered to be an undesirable congregant!
>
> Jacqueline Pinto

Meanwhile, the YMO resumed its pre-war interfaith activities, became involved in visiting sick people in London hospitals and helped with the Darby and Joan Club set up by the Women's Society. Regular talks and lectures were organised and a YMO dance became an annual event.[230]

---

[230] LJS Annual Reports for the 1940s.

36. *Alumni Society Chanukkah dinner in old Montefiore Hall. Those in photograph include: Shirley Banes – later Shirley Leuw (centre front of photo), Bernard Lawton (left of the row of people standing at rear), Rabbi Leslie Edgar and Dorothy Edgar (middle of top table), Joel Pinto, the Rev. Philip Cohen and Mrs Cohen (to right of Dorothy Edgar), Peggy Lang (two places to the left of Mrs Cohen), Jane Heilbronn – later Jane Rayner (seated four places to the left of Bernard Lawton). Photograph owned by Shirley Leuw. (1953)*

Although the Alumni Society and the YMO were both flourishing, Leslie Edgar had a bolder vision. Building on the wartime work of Rabbi Brasch, in 1947 he invited Walter Woyda[231] to work with him in setting up a central ULPS organisation that would bring together congregational youth groups.

> I was extremely close to him [Leslie Edgar] because we were not too far apart in age, and we were involved in the youth movement together. After I had been Chairman of the *Ner Tamid* youth group at South London Synagogue, he asked me to help form the Federation of Liberal and Progressive Jewish Youth Groups (FLPJYG). I became its first Chairman and Leslie Edgar helped me in establishing the group, as did the Rev. Philip Cohen, the third minister at the LJS.
>
> Walter Woyda (Pt. 3)

FLPJYG was a great success. It organised many inter-congregational activities for young people and fostered new congregational groups, including a number of junior groups for those not old enough to join groups like the Alumni Society. The Federation tended to be dominated by the LJS from where a large proportion of its committee came.

---

[231] Then a member of the South London Liberal Synagogue, but for many years now a member of the LJS. See full interview in Part Three.

The youth movement was extremely active. We held annual conferences, which rabbis attended. They gave very good lectures. As the group developed, we started to hold joint conferences with YASGB [Youth Association of Synagogues of Great Britain], which was the Reform youth movement. The culmination of this was the foundation of the Youth Section of the World Union for Progressive Judaism. I was on its first committee, although I was, at that time, establishing my business life.

Walter Woyda (Pt. 3)

When I became editor of the Federation's magazine in the mid-1950s, I travelled up to St John's Wood from South London regularly by public transport to produce it on the LJS's electric stencil duplicator. If we left the slightest trace of ink where it should not have been, we incurred the wrath of John Levinson, which I would not have wished on anyone. Our champion was always Peggy Lang, who encouraged us and always took our side in any dispute.

Rosita Rosenberg

FLPJYG was supported by a number of student rabbis, including John Rayner and David Goldstein, both of whom later became rabbis at the LJS. Because of their interest in young people, Lily Montagu and her sister, Marian, were also very involved.

I remember our General Meetings [of FLPJYG] there with Miss Lily and Miss Marian at the top table. I had not been brought up in Liberal Judaism and regret to say I was more fascinated by their Edwardian clothing and their ability to drop quietly off to sleep during the meetings than with their words of wisdom. If only I had understood their iconic status and spent more time talking to them!

Rosita Rosenberg

In 1956 the YMO set up the *Kadimah* Club for young people aged between thirteen and sixteen involved in the synagogue's Religion School or its correspondence classes. Organised by John and Bobby Cross, its activities included talks, games, gramophone evenings and inter-community quizzes.

By the mid-1960s FLPJYG was becoming less active and in 1968 came to an end. However, the various clubs for young people at the LJS remained well supported, aided by the setting up in 1962 of a Youth Committee, chaired initially by Bertram Jacobs and then by Victor Falk.

The Alumni Society was a very successful youth group in the 1960s of which I served as one-third of the Chairmanship alongside Alan Banes and Nigel Mizrahi. We were referred to as the 'Triumvirate'! We took it in turns to attend meetings of the Youth Committee on which the Chairs of the various groups were represented. The late Bertram Jacobs chaired this particular committee, attending meetings with his restless dog, a red-haired Chow, who spent the meeting running up and down underneath the table between all our legs. Just after his 70th birthday, Bertram decided to retire, stating that he did not think it appropriate for someone of his age to be still chairing a Youth Committee.

Diana Da Costa

We frequently recruited volunteers to help at the Out and About Club at Phase Two and Youth Committee meetings. At that time, the latter were chaired by Victor Falk who impressed us by always wearing his jacket and waistcoat.

Jeffrey Spearman

In 1965 Phase Two came into existence, aiming to fill a gap between the Alumni Society and the YMO.

> My real involvement in the LJS came much later when I was looking for a social life and joined Phase Two. It was a very active group of people, chaired by Esther Rantzen. The members organised an excellent programme of social events and had many speakers from the BBC. There was no need for a Director of Youth or a rabbi organising it as it all seemed to just happen and I met many very good friends to whom I am still close.
>
> Jenny Nathan (Pt. 3)

The setting up of this new society did not detract from the Alumni Society, which in 1969 celebrated its 50th anniversary, although there was some rivalry between the two groups.

By 1968 the *Kadimah* Club was seen as having run its course and was replaced by a new youth group called Square One.

> In the meantime, my group of friends had become involved in the formation of a youth group for thirteen- to sixteen-year-olds. We were supported by the Council and, at the beginning, received some help from Esther Rantzen with finding speakers for events. At the time she was involved in Phase Two and the Out and About Club. We held planning meetings, initially at the home of Sarah Caplin, and I can recall heated discussions about questions like whether to invite someone from the Scientologists to speak to us, whether we could sell alcohol, how much we could charge for entrance fees, or how many adults we needed to supervise in the background ... The most difficult discussion was what to call the group. We went round and round in circles, never quite agreeing and rejecting each idea. 'We seem to be back to square one' said, I think, David Kirk. 'That's it' said several of us ... and that's how the name was born.
>
> Michael Hart (Pt. 3)

Square One was supported by student Rabbi David Goldberg.

> I suppose my fondest memories are of our involvement with the younger members of the LJS. When we came it was an elderly congregation and it seemed important to nurture the next generation. And we found it such fun. When David [Goldberg] was student rabbi we used to have monthly 'coffee evenings' for the mid-teens at our flat. Here they could talk about whatever they wished and they obviously valued the fact that we were not 'old and boring' like their parents. And we still feel a strong bond to so many of those people whom we entertained then, people like George Kessler, David Kirk, Michael Hart, and later with some of the people who were our babysitters when we returned to the LJS. Some of them now have children of the age they were when they babysat: Catherine Loble, Ian Lazarus, Sacha Tobin and Jonathan Adler being among them. But by then we had become 'old and boring' parents ourselves!
>
> Carole Goldberg

However, groups for young married couples fared less well. In 1966, the YMO ceased to exist. It was replaced in 1967 by a new group named 'Focus', but this group operated for only two years.

During the 1970s and 1980s, the LJS gave a great deal of attention to supporting youth groups and societies for young people. In 1976, the New Youth Group was set up by Jo Kessler and Delia Marmor, catering for the 11–14 age range. It ran for several years before being replaced by a succession of groups such as the Aces and the Acorns, which were supported by rabbinic students from Leo Baeck College including Sybil Sheridan and Walter Rothschild.

Increasingly, the membership of both the Alumni Society and Phase Two was made up of young people who were not synagogue members and, as membership of both began to decrease, the two groups were merged before being disbanded in the late 1970s. Over the next decade, a number of short-lived groups were formed (Split Ends, LJSuperkids and Exodus), but by then young people were becoming more involved in the activities of ULPSNYC (the Union of Liberal and Progressive Synagogues Network of Youth Clubs), which had been set up in 1972 to replace FLPJYG, rather than those based at the LJS. Danny Rich and Mark Goldsmith, who were appointed as part-time youth leaders in the 1980s, mainly focused their attention on fostering involvement in inter-congregational activities.

No Strings, a society for unattached people over thirty, was set up in 1978 under the chairmanship of Geoffrey Laventhall.

> Jenny and I met at Rabbi David Goldberg's house – very kosher! He was organising a new group of not-so-young unmarried members. I was elected Chairman of this group and Jenny as Secretary so, in a way, we met over the minutes. David was very pleased with himself that he had got an incorrigible bachelor with many girlfriends married off. Our wedding was held at the time of the Miners' Strike (that was in 1984) and David said that if he could get Michael married off, he felt he would have no trouble in settling the strike.
>
> Michael Nathan (Pt. 3)

It ran successfully for a number of years as did Group Cover, set up in 1982 under the joint leadership of Jacqueline Alpert and Mike Beral to cater for young married couples. By this time, an increasing number of young people were going to university, but they sometimes gathered together at the synagogue during holidays.

More recently, younger Council members, such as Julia Green and then Shelley Salter, have taken responsibility for organising activities for young adults.

> In the mid-1990s I ran the Young Adults' *Chavurah*. It consisted of members and our friends in their thirties. We held them about four or five times a year around the festivals. We averaged around sixty people but at one *Chanukkah* party there were nearly a hundred people. We invited everyone to the Friday service and then had a 'Liberal kosher'-style four-course dinner cooked by Prue Leith-trained chefs. A typical *Chanukkah* menu included smoked salmon blini canapé, salt cod, red cabbage and latke, followed by mini jam doughnuts, apple cream, and freshly brewed coffee with a piece of chocolate. This carried on for about five years. When the novelty wore off and numbers dropped off I decided to call it a day. However, while they were running they were extremely popular, with people even flying down from Scotland to be there.
>
> Shelley Salter

With the advent of new technology, younger members of the LJS now keep in touch with each other by mobile phone and via social networking websites and tend to meet together informally away from the synagogue rather than participating in activities organised by the LJS.

> The girls also attend *Kadimah* – a summer camp – run by Liberal Judaism. The kids constantly keep in touch with each other via BBM/Skype/Text messaging and Facebook.
>
> Caryn Berlingieri (Pt. 3)

Chapter Three: Other groups and societies

A<small>LTHOUGH THE WOMEN'S SOCIETY</small> and the groups for younger people are the ones mentioned most often in interviews and other reminiscences, a number of other groups and societies have existed during the synagogue's hundred-year history. Some of these endured for many years while others were short lived.

In 1922 a Men's Discussion Group was formed with Robert Eichholz as its Honorary Secretary.[232] Subsequently led for twelve years by Ronald Simon, the group met each month to discuss a topic of Jewish or general interest. In 1928 a Synagogue Society was established to promote social, academic, artistic and sporting activities. It had five sub-sections: the Music Group, the Trampers' Group, the Modern Play Readers' group, the Sports Group and the Debating Group.[233] During the 1930s, the society organised a number of major art exhibitions, which attracted a lot of press coverage.[234]

Reconstituted in 1934, the Synagogue Society languished after the Second World War before being re-established in 1960.

> My first 'official' LJS activity was as Treasurer of the Synagogue Society, a social and cultural society open to all synagogue members (chaired at that time by Edith Kahn, a very charismatic lady and Headmistress of Fleet School) as opposed to the Women's Society.
>
> Bob Kirk (Pt. 3)

It operated for just a few years, but was succeeded from time to time by similar groups. In 1968 an Activities Committee was set up under the leadership of the Hon. Hugh Cohen. It organised various events, such as a very successful concert given by Max Jaffa and Jean Grayston (Jean Jaffa) accompanied by Jack Byfield. Its work was taken over by the short-lived Something New Committee in 1970 and then by a Cultural Meetings Committee in 1974. In the 1980s there was a Cultural and Social Affairs Committee chaired by Michael Salmon.

> CASA has gone the way of all flesh but at the time we were rather thrilled that we could have people of such eminence as Lord Denning and Lord Goodman coming to address the synagogue. I was involved in getting these people to come, mainly through my cousin, Louis Gluckstein, who knew both.
>
> Michael Salmon

In 1965 the LJS established a Medical Group, chaired by Dr Sidney Lewsen, which was open to both practising and trainee doctors and also to medical men and women from other ULPS synagogues.

At various times in its history drama groups have flourished at the LJS, During the 1920s, both the Women's Society and the Alumni Society organised and took part in plays. Following the installation of a new stage in the Montefiore Hall in 1930, a drama group, the St John's Wood Players, was set up. It gave its first performance, Noel Coward's

---

[232] 'The Years Between 1911–1951', LJS exhibition catalogue.
[233] LJS Annual Report, 1930.
[234] LJS Annual Reports for the 1930s.

comedy, *I'll Leave It to You*, in May 1931.[235] It continued to put on performances annually for a number of years.

The Alumni Theatre Group, established in 1950, was particularly successful. Its proceeds were used to make charitable donations.

Frederic Raphael (the screenwriter, novelist and journalist) wrote and produced plays, which were staged at the synagogue.

> I was involved in the Alumni amateur dramatic group which put on plays at the Twentieth Century Theatre, including *Hay Fever* and *Dangerous Corners*. Frederic Raphael and his future wife, Betty Glatt, were also members.
>
> Jane Rayner

During the late 1970s, a drama group staged a number of plays including Terence Rattigan's *Harlequinade,* and Alan Ayckbourn's *Confusions.*

37. *Alumni Dramatic Society production of Hayfever. From left: Betty Glatt (married Frederic Raphael), Tessa Jordan (became Tessa Samson), Frederic Raphael and Jackie Weiss. (undated, c. 1951)*

---

[235] LJS Annual Report, 1931.

Chapter Four: Current activities

ALTHOUGH THE LJS continues to organise a number of social activities for synagogue members, more emphasis is now placed on community activities involving caring for members of the congregation.

A number of these were carried forward from the Women's Society. Restaurant Tuesday lunches were introduced in 1969 at the instigation of Margaret Rigal. She suggested that the Women's Society should organise monthly lunches for older members of the synagogue living on their own, which, as well as providing them with a meal, would allow them to socialise. Nina Nathan became the overall co-ordinator of these lunches and Eva Feldman became one of the principal cooks, while Lilian Hill arranged transport. The first lunch attracted six people, but the lunches soon established themselves as a popular activity with a regular attendance of forty to fifty people and began to be run on a twice-monthly basis.

38. *Restaurant Tuesday team. From left: Nina Nathan, Betty Ungar, Rosemary Lazarus, Rose Solomons. (undated, c. late 1970s)*

Forty years later, the Tuesday lunches are still held monthly, now under the leadership of Ann Kirk.

When Ann [Kirk] enters the hall followed by trolleys laden with food, bangs on one of the tins with a ladle and focusses her eyes on us with authority, we all fall silent.

Helga Wolff

While the LJS was based in Loudoun Road, various '1991' initiatives were undertaken to prepare the congregation for making the most of the new building. As the result of discussions at a weekend planning workshop in the Cotswolds, a Keep in Touch (KIT) scheme was launched, co-ordinated by Carolyn Simon.

> I was invited to run a workshop. I'm guessing it was on the subject of change management. One of the needs identified during that gloriously sunny weekend was for something to replace the 'welfare' role formerly undertaken by the Women's Society, which was coming to the end of its natural life. Somehow, I subsequently found myself at a meeting with some key movers and shakers (Trevor Moross, Sir Peter Lazarus and Rabbi David Goldberg, if memory serves) to discuss how to fill this gap. And somehow, I found myself volunteering to set up a new welfare group.
>
> Carolyn Simon

In practice, the group found itself keeping in touch by phone, letter and emails as much as through face-to-face contact. Those involved in the scheme were trained in basic counselling and listening skills, as well as on issues relating to bereavement and illness. Over the years, KIT has run a variety of events and activities, including highly popular tea parties.

> We tried to play to our volunteers' strengths – which meant that I had very little to do with the actual catering, beyond ritually supplying the decorative parsley and cherry tomatoes. Fortunately, we had some star sandwich makers, including Anita Schwartz on egg mayonnaise, Sybil Gottlieb on smoked salmon, and Marie Katz on smoked salmon and cream cheese. Alice Fainberg was famous for her continental-style cheese and pesto sandwiches on dark rye bread. We were blessed with talented bakers too: Jeanne Solomons always baked wonderful home-made biscuits, Rosemary Yablon contributed a fabulous chocolate cake. Barbara Brown would make a gingerbread cake which came from an old Florence Greenberg recipe, and turned out to be so easy that even I was able to replicate it.
>
> Carolyn Simon

KIT is now twenty years old and led by Kate Birk, but several people who were involved with KIT when it was launched are still staunch members: Barbara Brown (who previously co-ordinated welfare visits for the Women's Society), Anita Schwartz and Jeanne Solomons.

Starting in 1997, *Doroteinu* (Our Generations) ran under the leadership of Louise Golding for several years before Bryan Diamond took the helm. Its aim was to foster inter-generational activities and to use the talents of older people. LJS *Doroteinu* projects have included recording reminiscences and staging a pantomime for older people by the Religion School. LJS member Anthony Roe was Chairman of the national level ULPS *Doroteinu* project.

In 2003 Rabbi Kathleen de Magtige-Middleton established a Bereavement Support Group, led initially by Alex Weiss and now by Rabbi Alexandra Wright. The group consists of a number of trained volunteers who support bereaved people in a way that is based on the Jewish concept of the bereavement year.

The Phone a Member (PAM) scheme set up in 2006 provides a means for keeping in touch with older members of the community who live some distance from the synagogue and who are unable to travel. The team of volunteers was initially led by Val Kleanthous, and is now headed up by Mary Rossiter.

39. Keep in Touch (KIT) tea party. (2010)

By 2002 the synagogue was becoming aware that an increasing number of its members were in need of more focussed care, and that more support was needed both for carers and those being cared for. Having sought the views of congregants, a committee involving, amongst others, Jenny Nathan, Anthony Roe, Louise Golding and Margaret Rigal, decided to set up a professional post of Community Care Co-ordinator.

Liz Crossick, who has held the post since it was established, has gradually extended her role. She now offers advice, needs-assessment, assistance and support to older people, people who are sick, those who are housebound and all who need help. She also trains volunteers and liaises with social care workers. Liz Crossick's work and that of the various welfare groups are managed by the Community Care Co-ordination Committee, or the 'Four Cs' as it is known.

Many of the welfare activities that take place at the synagogue have relied on transport being available. A bequest was made to the LJS by Ferry Pilzer enabling the synagogue to purchase a minibus which, as a result, became known as the 'Ferry Bus'. It was used regularly for Restaurant Tuesday and outings organised by Jo Kessler (called 'Jo's

Journeys'). The bus has recently been replaced by Jo and Willie Kessler, but continues to be referred to as the Ferry Bus.

Following a lecture given at the synagogue in 2009 by Baroness Julia Neuberger on her book on age discrimination, the Four Cs set up a discussion group (the Older and Bolder initiative), to develop proposals for responding to the issues raised by Baroness Neuberger, many of which have now been implemented.

> I was truly inspired by Rabbi Baroness Julia Neuberger's lecture on 'Older People and Discrimination' at the LJS. Rabbi Neuberger's arguments clearly resonated with me. In her book, Rabbi Neuberger recommends the setting up of a Grey Power movement. I have always believed in the necessity for such a campaigning self-help group in order to bring about radical improvement to older people's quality of life. Rabbi Neuberger's lecture spurred me on to stand on the fourth plinth in Trafalgar Square and deliver a lecture based on her ten-point manifesto. Unfortunately, as my slot was at 5 a.m. in the morning, I did not have a large audience!
>
> Trixi Blaire

The most recent activity to be launched by the Four Cs is an initiative called Singing for the Brain, which involves the use of singing to stimulate people with memory problems. Sessions are run by volunteers trained by the Alzheimer's Society.

> Thanks to anonymous donors, there is now funding for me to do two full days a week and I have been able to work with the volunteers to develop a number of new projects. The latest one is Singing for the Brain. People with dementia can still remember the words of songs, so the aim is to set up a weekly singing group for them and their carers. After seven years focussed on the older members of the LJS, it feels right that our next project is to set up a Family Support Group, which will look at the needs of the younger grouping.
>
> Liz Crossick

The increased attention given to social welfare has been welcomed by many members.

> On the positive side I welcome the enormous improvements in our Social Care commitments: bereavement counselling, Keep in Touch, Phone a Member, the Out and About Club, Video + Tea, Restaurant Tuesday, help for the disabled, and even a Community Care Co-ordinator – and that doesn't include everything. This certainly makes me proud to be a member of the LJS.
>
> Louise Golding (Pt. 3)

> In recent years, the volunteer efforts of the synagogue seem to have largely focussed on the elderly. There is fantastic provision for this age group, and we should be proud of that.
>
> Ellen Schmidt (Pt. 3)

The synagogue's many and various welfare activities, both past and present, have relied on the huge commitment of time and enthusiasm given by its members.

> Many women did, and continue to have, an enormous amount of involvement in synagogue activities. But several who were exceptional, and would take issue with me for mentioning them individually, still come to mind – some past, and some present. What was so special about them is that they were not sanctimonious 'do gooders' but genuinely good people, the unofficial social workers of the LJS. Names that spring instantly to mind are Nina Nathan, Lilian Hill, Dora Wolchover, Jo Kessler and Jenny Nathan.
>
> Carole Goldberg

Jo Kessler had a special interest in the elderly. She first of all had people to lunch at her home and latterly would arrange for the elderly to go for lunch or tea at interesting venues. She also initiated Tea + Video at the LJS for members and people outside the LJS who lived in the area. John and I really got to know Jo when we were in Cincinnati and she would write us lively letters telling us what was happening at the LJS and about her growing family. Back home, I would occasionally assist her at the *Shabbat* morning nursery where I would flake out after half an hour and she would be unfazed right to the end.

Jane Rayner

I remember when I first started as Community Care Co-ordinator, Rosemary Lazarus arrived in my office. She'd cooked thirty meals for a sick member of the synagogue, in as many days. She was exhausted!

Liz Crossick.

Section Three: A place of learning – the LJS's educational activities

Chapter One: The Religion School

BEFORE THE LJS was set up, the JRU had organised religion classes for children, which were mainly run by its women members.[236] The classes transferred to the Hill Street premises in 1910 before the new synagogue was formally opened and continued in a similar format until Rabbi Mattuck arrived in 1912. The classes were then organised into an embryonic Religion School. Within a year, the number of children enrolled in the Religion School had risen from nine to thirty-seven.[237]

The Religion School was open to the children of both members of the synagogue and non-members. Classes were held every Sunday morning (and therefore initially referred to as the Sunday School). However, the converted chapel in Hill Street was not an ideal setting for educational activities and every conceivable space had to be used for teaching.

> In every corner there was a little class group. The 'tinies', close to the entrance door of the house adjoining the chapel. Another group a little further down the room where there was a skylight, and then came the wooden shutters to divide a raised area, to serve as classroom and the stage for the *Chanukkah* tableaux!
>
> Ruth Hadley[238]

At the outset, Rabbi Mattuck ran the Religion School himself. He was initially assisted by just one volunteer teacher, Rose Solomon, who later became Head Teacher at the Jews' Infant School in Commercial Street. As the Religion School roll increased, she was joined by a number of others, including Sam Rich,[239] a teacher at the Jews' Free School, who in 1923 became Head of the Religion School.

> I can remember when Samuel Rich ('Uncle Sam' or the 'Man in the Moon' to us) asked Eric to close the shutters against disturbance, and when my brother performed this task with all the fervour he could muster: 'You'll be a door-shutter in a nerve hospital when you finish up'! He was a wonderful teacher, and it is to him that I owe my recollection and appreciation of the *Prophetic Scriptures* and the *Apocrypha*.
>
> Ruth Hadley[240]

Gradually from such a tiny start, our teaching staff grew: Mrs Yeatman-Woolf, Mrs Edward Davis, Miss Gladys Joseph (now Mrs Lawrence Woolf), Miss Hayman, Mrs Hayes and Mr Rich came later, and soon a number of confirmees helped us as teachers … Of our older teachers, I shall always remember the names of Mrs [Eileen] Yeatman-Woolf, that writer of

---

236 Lily H Montagu, 'Pioneer Personalities of the JRU', undated manuscript in LJS archives.
237 'The Years Between 1911–1951', LJS exhibition catalogue.
238 Letter from Ruth Hadley to Rabbis Rayner, Goldstein and Goldberg.
239 See photograph 9.
240 Letter from Ruth Hadley to Rabbis Rayner, Goldstein and Goldberg.

children's stories, that delightful teller of children's tales, and Mrs Edward Davis, that scholar, that collector of the excavations of Ur.

Rose Solomon[241]

During the First World War, the numbers attending the Religion School declined, but grew rapidly again after the war ended. To ease the pressure on accommodation at Hill Street, classes were temporarily organised in other venues. In 1919, a class was set up in Gerrards Cross, conducted by Amy Kirchberger, and in 1921 a class was held in the home of Ernest Joseph in Kensington, conducted by Miss Marjorie Moos.[242]

Rabbi Mattuck maintained his leading role in the Religion School, continuing to guide the activities of its increasing complement of teachers. He constantly updated and improved the school's syllabus.

> Those who attended his Teachers' Meetings will not easily forget them. Each teacher's problems were fully discussed; each could rely upon encouragement and all the help that they needed … the discussions on the syllabus were an unforgettable experience.
>
> Marjorie Moos[243]

40. *Religion School class at Hill Street. The teacher is Harry Isaacs, later a prominent pianist. (undated, c. 1925)*

When the Religion School moved into the synagogue in St John's Wood Road in 1925 there was much relief.[244] However, until the building of the new wing in 1963, some classes were still held in rooms used as offices during the week and which therefore had to be cleared every Friday night to provide space for the Religion School.

---

[241] Rose Solomon, 'The Religion School at Hill Street' in *The First Fifty Years*.

[242] LJS Annual Reports for 1919 and 1921. See photographs 6, 41, and 71.

[243] Marjorie H Moos, 'His Greatness As a Teacher', special edition of Liberal Jewish Monthly In Memoriam of Israel I Mattuck, June 1954.

[244] Rose Solomon, 'The Religion School at Hill Street' in *The First Fifty Years*.

41. *Young Miss Marjorie Moos. (undated, c. early 1920s)*

During the 1920s, classes were divided into a Junior and a Senior School, in a similar way to classes in an English school. Separate assemblies were held each Saturday morning, except for a monthly joint assembly intended to maintain the corporate spirit of the Religion School. The school was also grouped into houses (headed by captains), which were awarded points for good work.[245]

In its early days, the Religion School largely concentrated on biblical history and the teachings of the prophets. Very little Hebrew was taught – it was not considered necessary as such a limited amount of Hebrew was used in services. Hebrew classes were introduced in the 1930s as an optional course of study, taught initially by Michael Duparc, Secretary to the synagogue and then by Joe Foreman, Rabbi Mattuck's secretary.

> Hebrew wasn't a subject that was taught, although you could learn it as an extra – you could learn it if you stayed behind after the concluding assembly.
>
> Maxwell Stern[246]

> As a small boy I went with my sister, Josephine, to the Religion School, but then the war came and there was a gap in our religious education. At one time, Joe Foreman, our funeral director, tried to teach me Hebrew, I believe it was before the war when I would have been about seven or eight years old.
>
> Anthony Roe (Pt. 3)

The activities of the Religion School were not confined to lessons. There were special activities such as plays around the time of the main festivals and High Holydays, and also

---

[245] LJS Annual Report, 1928.
[246] ULPS Oral History Project, interview with Maxwell Stern. See Appendix 1.

social events such as sports days, table tennis tournaments and outings to places of interest. The aim of these was to enable the children to make friends and feel an added attachment to the synagogue.[247]

> Every year Mrs Woolf gave a summer party for her own class. Mrs Davis lived in a beautiful period house in St. John's Wood Park close to the 'Admiral's House' and adjoining Gerald du Maurier's on the Heath. We played games in her large walled garden.
>
> Ruth Hadley[248]

> I have a photo of a school picnic in the early 1920s. Dorothy Mattuck and Leslie Edgar were both at the picnic. They were later married.
>
> David Stern

One of Rabbi Mattuck's early educational innovations was the introduction of Confirmation ceremonies. At that time, these did not exist in Anglo-Jewry although they were customary in Reform synagogues in the USA. The Confirmation ceremony marked a young person's graduation from the Religion School at around the age of sixteen. In keeping with one of the LJS's founding principles, Confirmation ceremonies included both girls and boys.

> The girls wore long-sleeved dresses until the war made that impossible because of clothes rationing. The boys, I believe, wore neither skull caps nor *tallitot*. Perhaps the most moving moment was when the rabbi, with his back to the Ark, gathered the confirmees around him for a private talk and prayer and then raised his hands in the priestly benediction. The congregation always found this impressive.
>
> Dorothy Edgar[249]

The Confirmation classes set up by Rabbi Mattuck placed greater emphasis on religious knowledge and principles than on the reading of the scroll. From the outset a high standard of understanding of Judaism and discussion of its significance was required of confirmees.

The first Confirmations were held in April but, thereafter, the ceremonies took place on or close to *Shavu'ot*.[250] Some of the practices introduced by Rabbi Mattuck have been retained through the hundred-year history of the LJS – for example, the Senior Rabbi taking responsibility for the teaching of students and the encouragement given to confirmees to teach in the Religion School.

> After Confirmation, Dr Mattuck used to ask his most promising pupils to teach in the Religion School as they do today, becoming class assistants. So I started teaching in the Religion School, although at the time I was still at school myself, in the sixth form. I was living at that time with the aunts in Hampstead. I continued teaching until I got married. I am told I was called 'Miss Laughypops'.
>
> Ann Kirk (Pt. 3)

With many of the children of the early LJS families away at boarding schools, Rabbi Mattuck also introduced correspondence classes in 1912. They were conducted by Cecile

---

[247] LJS Annual Report, 1936.
[248] Letter from Ruth Hadley to Rabbis Rayner, Goldstein and Goldberg.
[249] ULPS Oral History Project, interview with Dorothy Edgar. See Appendix 1.
[250] Lawrence Rigal and Rosita Rosenberg, *Liberal Judaism: The First Hundred Years*.

Coopman until 1921 when Sam Rich took over their direction. To begin with, fifteen children were enrolled on the correspondence course but within a year this figure had almost doubled.[251]

In 1931 Leslie Edgar became Principal of the Religion School, which had grown by 50 per cent since the opening of the new synagogue in St John's Wood Road.[252] Sam Rich was appointed as Head of the Teaching Staff and Miss Marjorie Moos, who had by then been teaching in the Religion School for over ten years, took on much of the work relating to the correspondence classes as well as continuing to teach in the School.

In the years leading up to the Second World War, the Religion School established a special class for German children refugees, which was taken by Leslie Edgar and Mrs Woolf. As soon as the children had become proficient in the work that they had missed and had perfected their knowledge of English, they were transferred to the ordinary classes.

During the Second World War, the numbers of children at the Religion School decreased significantly as children were evacuated from London and families left the capital, but the numbers taking correspondence classes increased. Sam Rich and Miss Marjorie Moos worked valiantly to maintain these courses assisted by a number of correspondence teachers.

> I was evacuated to Moira House School in Eastbourne but, after a couple of terms there, we were moved to a small, bitterly cold hotel on Lake Windermere. Out of approximately a hundred girls, only three of us were Jewish. Thus, every Sunday, ninety-seven girls marched up the long hill to the church in Sawrey (where, incidentally, Beatrix Potter wrote all her books), while I remained behind to do the Jewish homework sent to me every week from the LJS.
>
> Jean Jaffa (Pt. 3)

> My mother received her religious education by correspondence course. Her teacher was Bessie Hayes who, according to mummy, was a lovely, warm lady who wore tea cosy hats and very long earrings. She wrote her comments in purple ink, and was always very complimentary and encouraging.
>
> Carolyn Simon (Pt. 3)

The weekly correspondence lessons were supplemented by the distribution of orders of service, weekly bulletins and cards on their birthdays. The children also received a magazine on each of the festivals. Sometimes these were put together by those children who remained in the Religion School in London.[253]

Despite his failing health, Rabbi Mattuck maintained his interest in the development of the Religion School for a short while after the war.

> I persevered with the correspondence classes and had the great privilege of being confirmed by Rabbi Dr Israel Mattuck on Sunday 28 April 1946. The ceremony was held in the Montefiore Hall as the main Sanctuary was not in use because of a bomb which fell through the roof of the main building in 1940. My fellow confirmees included Jo Kessler, Ann Kirk, Anthony Levy, Peter Nathan (Michael's brother), Michael Salmon and the Sampson twins,

---

[251] LJS Annual Report, 1913.
[252] LJS Annual Report, 1930.
[253] LJS Annual Report, 1946.

Bettina and Michael; Jo, Ann and Michael Salmon are still active. This was Rabbi Mattuck's last Confirmation class. He had retired the year before and was the Rabbi Emeritus.

Anthony Roe (Pt. 3)

One of the newer teachers in the school in the post-war years was Celia Mintz (later Celia Rapp), who had helped with the correspondence courses during the war. She came to the synagogue in 1942 from Liverpool to take up the post of Rabbi Mattuck's secretary. She became one of the longest-serving teachers in the Religion School, teaching the youngest children towards whom she was very protective and by whom she was adored.

> I started at the LJS Religion School when I was about five years old. Celia Rapp, who taught the first class, was a very special teacher. She was like a tiny bird, scarcely taller than the children she taught, but vivacious and built a wonderful rapport with each one of her pupils.
>
> Alexandra Wright (Pt. 3)

> Endless was the trouble that she took with them. She always came equipped with everything they might need: pencils, paper handkerchiefs, and all sorts of little things that she would buy for them out of her own pocket: Smarties, or apples or oranges to take away with them on special occasions. When they were upset, she would comfort them like a mother ... I don't know *exactly* how successful a teacher she was, but I know that her pupils loved her and she loved them.
>
> John Rayner[254]

In the post-war years, special classes and other activities were established for children undertaking the correspondence classes in their school holidays, which continued over several decades. The tradition of annual outings continued into the 1970s.

> When I was at Religion School in the fifties and sixties there was an annual outing to places such as Whipsnade Zoo, Burnham Beaches and Epping Forest. The trips had a real community feeling; they were very simple, naïve and well-intentioned.
>
> Edward Cross

42. *Religion School picnic. (undated, c. 1970s)*

---

[254] Eulogy by John Rayner at the funeral of Celia Rapp, 'Farewell to Celia Rapp', May 1984. Copy in LJS archives.

עבדו את יהוה בשמחה

43. *60th Anniversary of those confirmed during 1940s. Front row from left: Anthony Roe, Pamela Vos, Ann Kirk (initially known as Hannah Kuhn), Eva Feldman, Peter Rossiter, Rabbi Alexandra Wright. Middle row from left: Norman Lazarus, Jo Kessler (initially known as Inge Rubner), Jean Jaffa, Margaret Rigal. Back row from left: Eustace Maurice (?), Ian Joseph, Michael Cross, Patricia Bronkhurst, Denis Glaser (partly hidden behind Jo Kessler), John Myers (?), Michael Nathan, Alistair Heilbron, Walter Woyda, Peter Nathan, Michael Salmon. (2006)*

Marjorie Moos was Principal of the Religion School for a year in 1958, after which the role was taken over by John Rayner. He carried out a major re-organisation of the Religion School, introducing a new timetable, a more detailed syllabus, new text books and teaching aids, regular homework for pupils and fees for children whose parents were not members of the synagogue. A decision was made by the Council to offer remuneration to teachers. Several teachers declined this offer and, for another decade, the Religion School continued to be run largely on a voluntary basis.

During the early 1960s, there were a succession of Principals and Head Teachers, including the interim rabbis Chaim Stern and Sidney Brichto. The rabbinic students from America who came to the synagogue during the 1960s also taught in the Religion School.

At this time, several of those who had been involved in the Religion School following their Confirmation by Rabbi Mattuck were returning to teach now that they had children of their own who attended the school. The children developed close and long-standing friendships with those attending at the same time.

When my brother Martin and I started attending Hebrew classes, Bob and Ann Kirk, Eva Feldman, John Rich and Michael Alpert were doing a lot of the teaching. I liked the atmosphere in the Religion School. I felt very comfortable there. I made friends and felt part of a community. Andy Kirk, Rachel Goldhill, Ann Myers, Penny Hart, Richard Lissack and Charles Kessler were in my class. My brother Martin felt similarly comfortable. He went to the same school (William Ellis) as David Goldstein's son, Joshua, who was at the LJS Religion School at the same time. They are still firm friends. James Kessler and Ben Rayner were also his contemporaries.

Ellen Schmidt (Pt. 3)

On his return from America in 1965, Rabbi John Rayner once again took a keen interest in the development of the Religion School and, under his leadership, it grew rapidly. Israeli teachers were appointed and classes were gradually moved from Sundays to Saturdays.[255] Celia Rapp was the first teacher to move her class to Saturday mornings and others followed her lead.

During this time we moved the school from its customary Sunday slot to *Shabbat* mornings. One of the major reasons was that, by meeting on *Shabbat*, the children got a sense of being part of a congregation, rather than coming to an apparently unused building.

Bob Kirk (Pt. 3)

Children whose parents belonged to other synagogues started to come to the Religion School because of its growing reputation.

My family had been involved in the founding of the South London Liberal Synagogue where John [Rayner] had his first pulpit, but my late father, who was latterly the Head Teacher of the Religion School at South London, did not believe that it provided a sound enough religious grounding and therefore dragged all four of his children from the depths of Balham in South London to the Religion School at The Liberal Jewish Synagogue, St John's Wood.

Danny Rich[256]

44. *Rabbi John Rayner with Religion School pupils. (undated, c. early 1970s)*

---

255 This move was instigated by the interim Senior Rabbi, Chaim Stern and was, initially, very controversial which is why the shift took several years to achieve. Information provided by Jo Kessler.

256 Rabbi Danny Rich, *Erev Shabbat* sermon in memory of the late Rabbi John Rayner, given at Leo Baeck Education Centre, Haifa, 26 March 2006 to mark the opening of the Hugo Gryn Conference.

Rabbi John Rayner developed and gave increased importance to Confirmation.[257] He updated the course, making the content more traditional and more demanding. In 1967 the scroll was read by a confirmee for the first time and children began to undertake the same role at the school's own services.[258]

During John Rayner's rabbinate, graduation from the Religion School evolved from being referred to as simply Confirmation, to Confirmation/*Kabbalat Torah* (acceptance of the *Torah*) and then to *Kabbalat Torah* (Confirmation) as part of a trend towards the greater use of Hebrew.

> We tend nowadays to refer to it as *Kabbalat Torah*, on the grounds that, as with all Jewish festivals, it must have an international name for Jews all over the world.
>
> John Rayner[259]

> 'Confirmation' sounded too Christian so it was re-titled *Kabbalat Torah*, and John Rayner was very insistent that they shouldn't be called 'confirmees' because you don't confirm someone – its an act of voluntary decision – you are a 'confirmand'. But the terminologies don't change on a logical basis and they are still called 'confirmees'.
>
> Sidney Brichto[260]

The number of Religion School pupils attending Confirmation classes during this period rose dramatically because the 'baby boom' generation was now reaching the age of sixteen. In some years there were around forty Confirmation students, which meant that the class had to be divided into two groups and ceremonies held in both June and September.[261]

The weekends away with the rabbis became one of the highlights of the revised Confirmation syllabus.

> A key event in the LJS calendar was Confirmation. John Rayner and David [Goldberg], took the Confirmation class away for the weekend as part of the course. Most of the confirmees will have fond memories but what I remember are the poems created by John and David which included a verse about each of the young people, catching accurately an amusing incident that had taken place over the weekend. They were often inspired and these weekends built friendships for life. Before my own children were of school age we would join them and I remember those weekends with such affection.
>
> Carole Goldberg

> Our weekend away during the Confirmation year was, I seem to remember in a Convent where games of 'it' up and down several staircases with fellow students, teachers and rabbis were hilarious. My strongest memory of the weekend was John Rayner and David Goldberg singing a fully revised version of *Adon Olam* – one carefully orchestrated verse for each student. Our verse was as follows: 'The Jaffa twins/Are full of grins/Ride horses/While their father Max/Plays Violin!'
>
> Lisa Gershon

---

[257] John Rayner, *Before I forget.*
[258] LJS Annual Report, 1967.
[259] ULPS Oral History Project, interview with John Rayner. See Appendix 1.
[260] ULPS Oral History Project, interview with Sidney Brichto. See Appendix 1.
[261] Record of Confirmation classes kept at LJS.

Also memorable were the parties held after the Confirmation ceremonies.

> And then there were the actual Confirmation weekends. Usually two of them for the large numbers of youngsters. Arrangements had to be made for our children and dogs and together the Rayners and the Goldbergs went to all the parties given for the confirmees. Frequently, this involved journeys across London, from north to south – but no one could be left out. I recall that on one occasion Jane and I went on strike. Somehow we had missed the food everywhere. We arrived too early at some parties and too late at others. At 10.30 p.m. in Hammersmith we demanded that the car was stopped and fish and chips had to be bought for us to eat in the car before we would go on to the next party!
>
> Carole Goldberg

In 1967 male confirmees began to wear a *tallit*.

> The Confirmation service took place in April 1969, and we were one of the larger Confirmation groups, twenty in all, including a couple of late arrivals whom we hadn't met previously – they may have been from the correspondence class. We each had sections of the service to read and I recall being one of those asked to read from the scroll. I read the first part of the Ten Commandments. I wore a *tallit* that had belonged to my great-great-uncle, the *tallit* that I have continued to wear whenever I have been asked to read in a service. At that stage, none of the girls being confirmed wore a *tallit,* but they were expected to cover their heads on the *bimah.*
>
> Michael Hart (Pt. 3)

For some years, girls continued to wear a white dress similar to the Confirmation dresses worn in a church.

During the 1970s, one of the main developments was the setting up of a Parent Teacher Association (PTA), formalising the increasing participation of parents in the life of the Religion School. Initially chaired by Charles Yager and then Hugh Isaacs, the PTA took on responsibility for various Religion School activities, such as providing plants for *Sukkot* processions, organising synagogue sports days and setting up the Marjorie Moos Children's Library. It also initiated Saturday morning sessions for parents to come together to discuss topics of mutual interest.[262]

> The PTA was another area where I became involved for several years. A gang of four of us decided we would organise two events a year as long as it involved no catering. So for *Chanukkah* it was a play and party; only bought junk food [was] provided and much enjoyed by all! But the highlight of the Religion School year was the Religion School picnic. Each family brought their own picnic lunch and tea and we arranged and provided the entertainment and the sports on a field on the Heath! As an event it was a great success, bringing both the kids and their families together for a fun day.
>
> Carole Goldberg

By the late 1970s there was mounting pressure for the introduction of *B'nei Mitzvah* from some congregants who felt that Confirmation at age sixteen was not sufficient. However, Rabbi John Rayner had misgivings about introducing the ceremonies.

> I was on Council for a number of years, first with Sir Louis, then with Lewis Levy and then Maxwell Stern. In the late eighties the big issue was the question of moving or rebuilding.

---

[262] LJS Annual Report, 1974.

Another cause of controversy was the debate over *B'nei Mitzvah.* No one dared say a word against John Rayner, but he was absolutely adamant about not having them, and it caused a lot of trouble. My son David did not mind being confirmed, but Martin, our other younger son, did. He wanted to be *Bar Mitzvah,* and we had to drag him to his Confirmation. A year later everything changed and *B'nei Mitzvah* were introduced. It really caused more argument in our household than anything else, because my husband really wanted *Bar Mitzvah* too. I remember that argument going backwards and forwards.

Ruth Ive (Pt. 3)

[W]e did discuss from time to time whether we should follow the example of most of the ULPS congregations in reintroducing *Bar Mitzvahs / Bat Mitzvahs.* Eventually we did so, but we were almost the last [Liberal] congregation to do so, and many were not happy with the decision. Our main worry was that parents would encourage their sons to have a *Bar Mitzvah* but would not encourage their daughters to anything like the same extent because it is not part of the tradition. We have always attached so much importance to equality of the sexes.

John Rayner[263]

And many others were against the introduction of *B'nei Mitzvah*

I was on Council at the time and remember the debates clearly. There was a huge amount of opposition. Indeed, I think *B'nei Mitzvah* were only introduced because a number of parents threatened to withdraw their membership unless their children could have the ceremony.

In 1981 the synagogue eventually agreed to introduce *B'nei Mitzvah* with caveats about equality and the continued involvement of young people in the Religion School until their Confirmation.

Council tried to insist that there should not be too many *B'nei Mitzvah* ceremonies. This did not work out and I remember remarking that we could not tell parents when to conceive their children so that there should not be too many *B'nei Mitzvah* in any given month! Council also insisted that, if the boy had a sister, he could not be BM unless the girl was also. I don't know if that worked out either. I do recall that I taught fifteen and twenty of the boys and only one or two of the girls.

Michael Alpert

During the 1970s and 1980s, the Religion School grew rapidly, but without the requisite infrastructure to support it. Divergent views about how the Religion School should be run began to emerge amongst parents.

The biggest challenge at the Education Committee was between those parents who wanted the lessons to be quite formal in content, with evidence of lots of learning, and those who were less concerned with the academic side and wanted their children to enjoy themselves and develop a positive association with the synagogue. There was always a lot of debate about how early it was appropriate to start to teach the reading of Hebrew. I was of the view that we should wait till children had been several years in the School, by which time they had the maturity and broader skills to learn to read in a relatively short period of time.

Michael Hart (Pt. 3)

In the early 1970s Geoffrey Ben Nathan, Judith Levy and I were dissatisfied with the Hebrew teaching in the LJS *cheder.* We went to see Rabbi Dr. David Goldstein who was running the School, and made suggestions about putting Hebrew on a firmer basis. David

---

[263] ULPS Oral History Project, interview with John Rayner. See Appendix 1.

was encouraging. It still took a long time and some battles with parents, but I think we changed some attitudes (perhaps even John Rayner's himself!).

Michael Alpert

In 1997 Eric Blaire, assisted by Michael Hart, carried out a thorough review of the operation of the Religion School. They recommended a number of changes, including the appointment of a full-time Director of Education who would take responsibility for the Religion School as well as for educational activities generally in the synagogue. This move reflected the higher expectations of parents and the professionalisation of Jewish education that was occurring across the Anglo-Jewish community.

Jan Roseman was appointed to the role in 1999. One of her first tasks was to place preparation for *B'nei Mitzvah* on a sound footing.

> Jan [Roseman] said, 'If we are going to do them, we are going to do them well' and she began to teach the young people on a one-to-one basis. Tamara [Ellen Schmidt's daughter] was amongst the first group of children to have a *Bat Mitzvah* under Jan's regime and her Hebrew was good enough for her to read from the scroll, translating as she went along, rather than reading from a prepared script.
>
> Ellen Schmidt (Pt. 3)

> My daughter Sarah became a *Bat Mitzvah* at the LJS in March 2010. She studied under Jan Roseman who was the Head of the LJS Religion School for eleven years. Jan came to our house once a week to teach Sarah her *Torah* portion and the prayers for the Friday night and Saturday morning services. Jan was an 'amazing' teacher according to Sarah (the highest accolade a teenager can give!).
>
> Caryn Berlingieri (Pt. 3)

In her eleven years with the LJS, Jan Roseman also introduced a completely new curriculum, professionalised teacher training for Religion School teachers, including teaching assistants, increased the participation of parents in their children's education, and set up family education programmes. In addition, she changed the format of family services and introduced arts activities such as drama, singing and Israeli dancing.

> Within a short time she had made a real difference, not only in improving standards in the Religion School, but in Jewish learning generally. She introduced the adult education programme, now being led by Alex Wright and also family education activities.
>
> Ellen Schmidt (Pt. 3)

The age for *Kabbalat Torah* was lowered from sixteen to fifteen to avoid too much pressure being placed on young people because of studying for it alongside their GCSEs. Although it is made clear to them that they are expected to go on to *Kabbalat Torah* classes, *B'nei Mitzvah* students are no longer required to sign a document agreeing to this. Some congregants are not happy about this but, in recent years, the size of *Kabbalat Torah* classes has been increasing once again.

As part of their course of study, *Kabbalat Torah* (now often referred to as KT) students visit Amsterdam, a tradition introduced by Rabbi Kathleen de Magtige-Middleton, who came from the Netherlands.

> As I am half Dutch, I particularly enjoyed the trip to Amsterdam with the synagogue as part of the KT programme. We attended a service that was led in Hebrew and Dutch, as well as visiting the Holocaust Memorial and Anne Frank's House.
>
> Rachel Brouwer

45. *Kabbalat Torah class 2011. From left: Rabbi David Wilfond, Bertie Mills, Max Loble, Harry Loble, Clayton Sasaki, Chloe Lasher, William Englander, Barney Kass, Rabbi Alexandra Wright, Samuel Rigal. Photograph by Pam Fox. (2011)*

The KT group had two weekends away. The first was in Oxfordshire at a retreat for monks. It was freezing cold, but great fun. The food was horrible, so all we ate were chocolates and crisps. The second weekend away was in Amsterdam. The hostel we stayed in was in the red light district and had a nightclub downstairs. We had the Saturday service in the nightclub. In the centre of the club was a tinted glass box with a pole in the middle and we sat round it for the service. It was surreal. We were allowed to go to the nightclub one night, providing we didn't drink. Needless to say, at least two members of the group were caught with a pint in their hands.

Tamara Schmidt (Pt. 3)

Another innovation in the last ten years has been the painting of *tallitot* by *Kabbalat Torah* classes to wear at their KT service.

It is, of course, always a joy to see the creations of those who are clearly talented artists. It is also a pleasure to witness the sense of achievement in those who started out with low expectations and surprised themselves. I remember one boy, a vision of slouching, hoodied disaffection who turned out to be a wonderful draughtsman, producing a beautiful *tallit*, much to his surprise and genuine delight! There are, too, the awkwardly shuffling boys with huge hands wrapped round small Chinese brushes who, painstakingly and totally absorbed, produce something fine and delicate. Then there was the young artist who would not be swayed from painting a banana, a monkey and a chair, insisting that it was a meaningful existentialist statement! And no, he didn't wear it.

Sally Frankl

Since 2000 the President's Cup (donated by Willie and Jo Kessler) has been awarded to young people who have made an outstanding contribution to youth activities at the synagogue.[264]

> Following KT, I taught for two years at the Religion School. I'm not sure I ever had complete control in the classroom, but I very much hope the Hebrew and Jewish knowledge of the children I taught made some progress. It was fantastic that the Hebrew exercise books had become more focussed on Hebrew as a language and were no longer only about reciting Hebrew from the prayer books. I also worked at the summer school based at the synagogue for those two years. It was during this time I was honoured to receive the first Willie Kessler prize.
>
> Felicity Allen (Pt. 3)

Young people are encouraged to participate in the programmes for young people organised by Liberal Judaism, LJY *Netzer*, which are seen as an important means of complementing the more formal education of the Religion School and as offering valuable leadership training.

An important development in the last decade is the introduction of adult *B'nei Mitzvah* to enable those who, for a variety of reasons, were not able to celebrate this rite of passage at the more traditional age of thirteen.

> During 2006/2007 Michael Simon generously agreed to lead an adult *B'nei Mitzvah* group on Saturday mornings in the 'education slot' before the *Shabbat* morning service. This was the second time he had led such a group, and I remembered having been very moved and impressed by the first adult *B'nei Mitzvah* group who had led a service a few years earlier. I had always wanted to read from the scroll, and thought this would be a great opportunity to learn to do so.
>
> Cathy Lasher

46. *Adult B'nei Mitzvah 29 June 2002. From left: William Carver, Jenny Green, Julie Carlin-Sasaki, Alex Weiss and Paul Newgass.* *(2002)*

---

[264] Names have until recently been suggested by Jan Roseman, Director of Education at the LJS.

The *B'nei Mitzvah* students follow a wide-ranging syllabus and the year of study culminates in the students leading a *Shabbat* service.

> It was a wonderful personal journey for me. Finding my voice as a Jewish woman has always been very hard, and indeed I still find it hard to express just what that year of study, and the day of the *B'nei Mitzvah*, meant to me. That day I read words from an ancient holy scroll for the first time – and I read in my own voice. That was the first time, and I have had the privilege to read from the scroll on a number of occasions since. I have chosen actively to embrace the *Torah*, and the many facets of my Jewish faith and identity, engaging in my own way, just as each of us brings our own uniqueness to all that we do. This enhances my ability – and my joy – in passing the *Torah* and my Jewish heritage on to the next generation, in particular to my daughters, Sarah and Chloe.
>
> Cathy Lasher

> For each participant, the reason for becoming *Bar/Bat Mitzvah* as an adult was a personal one. Some had been brought up as Liberal Jews at a time when the traditional age of thirteen had not been deemed an appropriate age for such an important rite of passage and becoming a 'Child of The Covenant' had not been available; other members had been brought up in an Orthodox tradition where girls had not had become *Bat Mitzvah*; others had come to Judaism at a later time in life. For all of us, having completed our studies, standing before the congregation and reading from the *Torah* was a positive affirmation of our commitment to Liberal Judaism.
>
> Joan Salter

Chapter Two: Lifelong learning at the LJS

Educational and cultural activities

FROM ITS INCEPTION, the LJS has organised educational and cultural activities for all age groups, not just for children and young people. Soon after his arrival, Rabbi Mattuck began to give lectures on a Sunday evening. In 1916 he introduced a programme of lectures by visiting speakers, some of whom were very well known. For example, in 1917 Lucien Wolf spoke on 'The Jewish National Movement'[265] and in 1919 Sidney Webb gave a talk entitled 'Towards Social Democracy'.[266]

When the Alumni Society was established in 1918 its activities included lectures, visiting speakers and discussions. Such educational activities were also a feature of the Women's Society and the Synagogue Society, both of which were established in the 1920s.

In 1927 Rabbi Mattuck and the Rev. Perlzweig introduced study groups on Jewish Religion and Jewish History. The study groups, which continued over the next two decades, were well attended. However, more popular were the Monday Lectures set up by

---

[265] The speech was well publicised because of Wolf's strong anti-Zionist comments, including in *The Jewish Chronicle,* 16 March 1917.

[266] LJS Annual Reports.

Leslie Edgar after the Second World War. They ran from the 1940s through to the establishment of the Evening Institute by the ULPS in the 1960s.

> The Monday evening lectures that we went to were also attended by my brother-in-law, Lawrence Rigal, who later became a rabbi, and quite a few of our friends. When Abram Spiro came to London in 1954 with the idea of starting a rabbinic training college, he took over the Monday classes. He was an outstanding figure in the scholastic world, so anyone he knew who was passing through London and who had any sort of special knowledge came to his classes as guest speakers and gave their own spiel. Afterwards, we would all go back and sit on the floor of Spiro's flat, off the Edgware Road, and have a really good and serious discussion.
>
> Margaret Rigal (Pt. 3)

After the Second World War, the ministers introduced study sessions for each of the main synagogue societies and the Women's Society discussion group flourished under the leadership of Dorothy Isaacs.

1958 marked the 100th anniversary of the birth of Claude Montefiore and in his memory the synagogue instituted annual lectures. The first of these was given on the topic of 'The Hebrew Bible' by Professor D Winton Thomas from Cambridge University.

In 1962 a synagogue Education Committee was set up under the joint leadership of Desmond Feldman and Michael Cross. Its role was to oversee not only the running of the Religion School, but also to advise on all educational matters. From the 1980s, ad hoc adult educational classes began to be organised into more coherent programmes. Wednesdays were earmarked as a recreational study day when a range of talks and short courses took place.

During the 1990s, Rabbi Helen Freeman extended educational activities for young children and their parents, introduced a Sunday Supplement adult education programme and initiated Pre-Service Delights, a weekly programme of talks. In the latter part of the decade, following a Congregation of Learners Review, Peter Spanier ran a very successful annual programme of educational lectures involving some highly-regarded external speakers. To begin with, he ran these informally, but they later became an integral part of the LJS's adult education programme.

Also during the 1990s, Rabbi David Goldberg organised 'Master Classes' held in the Sanctuary. Guests included the renowned cellist Stephen Isserlis, the operatic director and polymath, Dr Jonathan Miller, the actor Janet Suzman, the film director John Schlesinger, and the sculptor Anthony Caro.

> One of the cultural highlights of my membership of the LJS was the wonderful evening 'master class' at which the cellist Stephen Isserlis took Natalie Clein through one of the Bach unaccompanied cello suites. She has recently won the BBC's Young Musician of the Year Award and it was a privilege to be eavesdropping when Isserlis made clear that so far as he was concerned, 'less is more' when playing Bach.
>
> Vivien Rose

In 2006 the Sanctuary was filled to capacity to listen to Rabbi Goldberg interview Vanessa Redgrave who talked not only about her political views, but also about the hazards of sharing a Shakespearean role – and hence costume – with her much shorter colleague Dame Judi Dench.

Throughout the history of the synagogue, lectures have been given and discussions have been led by LJS members either prominent in public life or with interesting experiences to share.

The LJS's adult education programme is now called The Learning Circle and is led by Rabbi Alexandra Wright. In addition to the long-established conversion courses (Exploring Judaism), the programme includes Tuesday evening classes on Jewish History (run with Spiro Ark), Biblical Drama and Hebrew Studies as well as Israeli Dancing. On Monday mornings there is an Art Class and on Tuesday mornings there is a Hebrew class and also a group, led by the rabbis, which reads and discusses different texts (Tuesday Texts).

On *Shabbat* mornings there are classes on a wide range of topics including Hebrew, Talmud and Jewish Knowledge led by experienced members of the congregation, such as Bernie Bulkin, Michael Simon and Gary Lane. Throughout the year, there are various events and lectures and over the last few years there have been a number of *Shabbatons* (whole days of study) and a Language-a-Thon.

The synagogue also continues to organise inter-generational learning activities to enable families to learn about and experience Judaism together. These include festival celebrations and PACE mornings (Parent and Child Education), when parents discover what their children have been learning.

The Nursery School

After a playgroup, run by Monica Huber with Janet Mills and Maria Snider, had operated at the LJS for a number of years, it was suggested that a Nursery School should be set up at the synagogue. In 2004, following lengthy discussions with Westminster City Council about what would be provided, this idea came to fruition.

> I set up the Baby Group. Seventeen years later I am still best friends with the group of women who came to the group and my children are still close friends to their children. I couldn't have wished for more. The LJS helped in the making of the next generation of LJS members. I was so pleased when the Baby Group grew into a Nursery School.
>
> Janet Mills

Caroline Villiers, the Nursery School Head Teacher, was recruited in April of that year and the first class of toddlers aged two-and-a-half years started in September 2004. Since that time, three further classes have been added and the Nursery School has gone from strength to strength. It is open to both LJS members and non-members, and the children attending its classes come from very diverse backgrounds. About 50 per cent of the children are from American families living in the area, who often join the synagogue as a result of their children entering the school.

There are also children whose families belong to other local synagogues, but a significant proportion are non-Jewish, their parents having been attracted by the high quality of education and nurturing provided at the school and its emphasis on interfaith activities. Some of the teachers are non-Jewish and the school celebrates a variety of religious festivals, often with the involvement of parents.

One of the highlights of the Nursery School's week is *Kabbalat Shabbat* held on a Friday morning in the Montefiore Hall. The children sit in a circle to do the blessings with their parents, siblings and other relations around them.

Barbara Fidler

Chapter Three: Fostering Jewish education outside the LJS

A S WELL AS providing opportunities for lifelong learning within the LJS, the synagogue has played a prominent role in promoting educational activities externally and in partnership with other bodies. During the Second World War, the LJS worked with West London Synagogue to run courses for refugees based on its established correspondence courses, the precursor to subsequent co-operation between the Reform and Liberal movements on educational matters.

After the war, young people started to come together on an inter-congregational basis and to voice concerns about how future leaders of the movement would be developed. Meeting in Hertfordshire in 1951, the newly formed Youth Section of the World Union for Progressive Judaism submitted a resolution to its senior body urging it to encourage the Liberal and Reform Movements in Britain to establish a rabbinical training college. The resolution was submitted by the Youth Section Liaison Officer, John Rayner, who was later to become a key figure in implementing the recommendation.

> We decided that the most important need of all in these immediate post-war years was to train a new leadership of rabbis and teachers and youth leaders, and for this purpose we urgently needed to establish a college in which such training could take place. We felt that it was the duty of British Jewry to do this on behalf of the Progressive Jewish World outside the United States of America, which had its own institutions.
>
> John Rayner[267]

The concern was noted by Lily Montagu, who passed it to the rabbinic heads of the two movements – Rabbi Leslie Edgar of the LJS and Rabbi Reinhart of West London Synagogue. However, early attempts to co-operate on setting up a college foundered.

In 1954 an American, Dr Abram Spiro, was appointed as Tutor in Jewish Studies with a brief to lay the foundations for a rabbinic college. He was initially employed by the LJS. A year later, he was appointed as Director of Studies to the ULPS. This appointment was seen as being the first step towards establishing an Institute for Jewish Learning at either Oxford or Cambridge.

Dr Spiro set up a rabbinic library belonging to the ULPS at the LJS. He also set up a bursary fund for prospective rabbis using the Mattuck Memorial Fund established after Rabbi Mattuck's death.

---

[267] ULPS Oral History Project, interview with John Rayner. See Appendix 1.

Then, after the great leader of Liberal Judaism, Dr Israel Mattuck, died there was a scholarship in his memory and I was a beneficiary of this. I came to London, and it took me ages to get a university degree but Lily Montagu was a constant encouragement to me.

Harry Jacobi

Abram Spiro participated in a number of educational activities within the LJS, but failed to develop a rapport with the lay leadership of the synagogue. Although he was officially employed by the ULPS, a high proportion of his salary was paid by the LJS and he remained based in the synagogue. When he was dismissed by Sir Louis Gluckstein, then President of the LJS, it became something of a *cause célèbre*.

> Disagreements developed largely (or even partly, I just do not know) between Abram Spiro and his ideas for the future of the college and the powers that be, which means especially Sir Louis Gluckstein. I think that there was a serious clash of opinions between them, as a result of which Spiro left and returned to America.
>
> John Rayner[268]

For the next seven years, the ULPS continued its established practice for training rabbis: private tuition following a university education. It was therefore left to the Reform Movement to make the next move in establishing a rabbinic college. In 1956 a Jewish Theological College was set up in rooms at the West London Synagogue. Various attempts to engage the Liberal movement in the development of the college failed. When John Rayner took over as Senior Minister at the LJS in 1961, discussions were re-opened, but they were long and protracted and John Rayner had to leave them part way through to complete his rabbinic studies in America.

> Then I was a LJS representative on the Council of the Union of Liberal Synagogues (ULPS) in the 1960s, and I remember Lily Montagu at these meetings. I was present when discussions were taking place about the ULPS joining with the Reform Movement in sponsoring the Leo Baeck College, with Lily Montagu, Edgar Nathan and Leslie Edgar being very vocal.
>
> Ann Kirk (Pt. 3)

When he returned from Cincinnati, John Rayner (now Rabbi Rayner) found the discussions complete and new arrangements in the process of being put in place. He took over the role of Registrar of the College and became deeply involved in re-organising the College. Between 1966 and 1969 he acted as Director of Studies, completely re-planned the syllabus, enlarged the faculty, brought in academics from outside the Liberal and Reform movements, and started a College newsletter.

> Leo Baeck College then worked out of a few rooms at West London Synagogue, but John had begun to get involved in the syllabus and in organising the place … It was due largely to his energy and determination that a ramshackle training college was turned into a serious academic establishment.
>
> David Goldberg[269]

---

[268] Ibid.
[269] Rabbi David Goldberg, 'John Rayner a towering intellect and a man of the highest integrity', *LJ Today,* November/December 2005.

The first Leo Baeck ordination ceremony to take place in a Liberal synagogue was held at the LJS in 1967, using the liturgy from the recently published prayerbook, *Service of the Heart*, edited by John Rayner and Chaim Stern. Since then, ordination services have alternated between the LJS and the West London Synagogue. Between 1968 and 1969, Rabbi Dr Samuel Sandmel of Hebrew Union College, Cincinnati, was Visiting Principal at the College, which greatly increased its profile. Most of the funding to enable this to happen was raised by John Rayner from amongst LJS members.

> The best year of my three there [Leo Baeck College] was when Professor Sam Sandmel came over from Hebrew Union College for a year as Acting Principal. He was a fine man, a very good scholar. He really organised Leo Baeck in a way that was long overdue.
>
> David Goldberg (Pt. 3)

Rabbi John Rayner continued his involvement with Leo Baeck College for the remainder of his life. A number of other members of the LJS also played a prominent role in the college.

> When, in 1965, ULPS joined RSGB (Reform Synagogues of Great Britain) in sponsoring Leo Baeck College, the Evening Institute became part of LBC and I went with it, taken over, you might say, with the furniture. I became Secretary of the College in 1968, again succeeding Greta and, in due course, chaired the College Council from 1978 to 1982. I had the good fortune to be in the chair when we moved the College from West London Synagogue to the Manor House in Finchley – later to become the Sternberg Centre. I am an Honorary Fellow of the College and, like all past Chairmen, an Honorary Life Vice-President.
>
> Bob Kirk (Pt. 3)

> At about that time I joined the Council of Leo Baeck College, on which I served for about twelve years, including three as Chairman. I had an interesting time and found the college fascinating.
>
> Willie Kessler (Pt. 3)

Section Four: A place of righteousness – the values of the LJS and its relationships with wider society

THE ETHICAL STANCE and universalism of Liberal Judaism has shaped both the way in which the LJS has operated internally and how it has related to wider society. In its own affairs, the LJS has demonstrated a continuous commitment to gender equality and to inclusivity and it has always been an outward-looking synagogue. It has consistently been involved in social welfare activities, taken a keen interest in contemporary social issues and been prepared to speak out, even when the views it has voiced have been unpopular, most notably in relation to Zionism and the State of Israel. It has also recognised its responsibility for creating and supporting other Liberal communities and has been proactive in reaching out to other religions to foster mutual understanding.

Chapter One: The values of the LJS

Gender equality

ONE OF THE main aims of the JRU was to enable women to move beyond their traditional religious roles and to work towards the religious emancipation of women. As a result, when plans were being made for the first services at the Wharncliffe Rooms, it was agreed that men and women would sit together and that women would participate in the worship. Accounts of the first service at the Wharncliffe Rooms show how committed the JRU was to encouraging women to participate. Several times in his address, Claude Montefiore referred to 'Jews and Jewesses' and there was a mixed choir.[236]

The importance that the JRU attached to the involvement of women was demonstrated again shortly after the first service when the JRU was approached by the West London Synagogue with a proposal that future services be held there rather than in the hotel. After lengthy discussions, the JRU abandoned the negotiations because the conditions set by the synagogue included what they regarded as an 'archaic requirement' – that men and women should sit separately.[237]

When the LJS was set up, not only did men and women sit and pray together, but a great deal of emphasis was placed on the equal education of boys and girls. The embryonic Religion School was open to both sexes and when Rabbi Mattuck introduced Confirmation classes he insisted that they should be mixed-sex groups. The thinking was that, through equality in education, women would be empowered to take a full part in the life of the community.

---

[236] *The Jewish World*, 24 October 1902.
[237] Lawrence Rigal and Rosita Rosenberg, *Liberal Judaism: The First Hundred Years*.

However, it was some time before women were able to read or preach during services. The suggestion that they might do so was first raised at a JRU meeting in 1905 and also in the following year. On both occasions, a decision was deferred because of concerns raised by Claude Montefiore and others (including Lily Montagu) that such a move might prove detrimental to their cause. The issue was not considered again until 1916 despite the fact that the constitution drawn up for the new synagogue in 1909 had included a clause about the equality of men and women, albeit expressed in a way which women today might find unacceptable.[238]

In its early years, the LJS introduced Saturday morning services designed mainly for children. With the support of Rabbi Mattuck, both Lily Montagu and Rose Solomon, a teacher in the Religion School, preached at the children's services in June 1916. Rabbi Mattuck subsequently sought the Council's agreement to women conducting these morning services, a suggestion that was given unanimous approval.[239]

It was to be two more years before there was any discussion of women leading the main Sabbath services, which were by then held on a Saturday afternoon. Again at the instigation of Rabbi Mattuck, Lily Montagu was asked to preach at the main service on the afternoon of 15 June 1918 and on Rabbi Mattuck's recommendation, in 1920 the LJS Council decided to allow women to act as lay readers. Although these decisions took a long time in coming, they were very radical since it was not until 1928 that women achieved voting equality with men in British parliamentary elections.

> This permission was in logical sequence to the principle of sex equality established since the beginning of our movement, but it is interesting to note, however, that the suggestion was first made to the JRU Committee in 1905, and its acceptance only took place after 13 years' delay, when the existence of the synagogue had already somewhat stabilised the conduct of our services.
>
> Lily Montagu[240]

> It was such an important step in the development of the Liberal Jewish Movement that the sermon was printed. Even those who felt that to allow a woman to preach was going too far, were entirely convinced after hearing her, and they withdrew their objections.
>
> Eric Conrad[241]

Women were also increasingly involved in other aspects of synagogue life. From the very early years, there were women members of the LJS Council, including Lily Montagu. She provided a role model for and encouraged the involvement of women in synagogue activities. Although she apparently had no interest in the Suffragette Movement, she firmly believed that modern Jewish women should be recognised as being articulate and active.[242]

---

[238] Ibid. It said that 'the masculine shall include the feminine'.
[239] LJS Annual Report, 1916.
[240] Lily Montagu, *The Jewish Religious Union and Its Beginnings*.
[241] Eric V Conrad, *Lily H. Montagu: Prophet of Living Judaism*.
[242] Research carried out by Lawrence Rigal revealed that, according to her long-standing secretary Jessie Levy, Lily Montagu took no active interest in the Suffragette Movement although her sister, Netta Franklin, was an active supporter.

When our founders, especially Miss Lily, freed us women from the constraints of orthodoxy, it was not merely to enable us to sit with our menfolk downstairs. Women were expected to share the responsibility with men for the organisation and administration of synagogue affairs, bringing with them a womanly influence (however you might define that) to congregational matters.

Ruth Ive[243]

In 1915 a notable stand was taken by the synagogue in respect of membership of the Board of Deputies. The LJS refused to accept an invitation to be represented on the Board because its constitution did not allow women to vote for delegates to the Board. In fact the LJS did not join the Board until 1922 when the Board changed its constitution.

Notwithstanding the radical innovations and the principled stand taken by the LJS, for many years (as was the case in society as a whole) the main roles undertaken by women congregants tended to be stereotypical ones.

They [the Women's Society] organised all kinds of things, such as hospital visiting, as well as all the catering for the synagogue, which they did on a grand scale. At that time, people did not see any inconsistency between the synagogue's emphasis on equality and the fact that it was the Women's Society who did all the catering.

Ruth Ive (Pt. 3)

While younger men and women did socialise together and have a range of joint involvements, such as in social action, right up to the 1980s the activities of women were mainly confined to their participation in the segregated affairs of the Women's Society.

The Women's Society was a most active part of the social side of the synagogue, but it did not tread on the toes of the male Council members. They were expert in serving tea and producing home-made cakes.

Neil Levitt

For many years the synagogue's committees were dominated by men.

Sir Louis [Gluckstein] then informed me that I would be chairman of the House Committee, and I was immediately drafted on to Council made up exclusively of middle-aged men.

Neil Levitt

And not everybody was in accord with the LJS's commitment to equality of the sexes.

From the very beginning, I was on the Services Committee and it was decided that as far as possible, there should always be one lady participating in the Ark opening, so that we had equality of the sexes. It was very difficult to persuade Louis [Steinman, the *Shammash*] to ask any lady to take part. I constantly had a battle with him and very frequently I would stand with him at the door to ensure that, if possible, we got a lady involved.

George Rigal (Pt. 3)

From the late 1980s, there were signs of change. Two women rabbis were appointed, Rabbi Alexandra Wright in 1986[244] and Rabbi Helen Freeman (previously Horn)[245] in 1990. This helped to raise the profile of women's issues.

---

[243] Address at the special service at the LJS in honour of the Women's Society given by Ruth Ive, 5 January 1991.
[244] See photographs 43, 45, 47, 68, and 85.
[245] See photographs 20, 48, 55, and 59.

Having women rabbis really changed the atmosphere in the synagogue and put women's issues higher on the agenda. I remember Alex Wright's *Yom Kippur* sermon in which she talked about how women were undervalued in the *Torah* reading (Deuteronomy 29). It caused quite a stir amongst the congregation but when Peter Lazarus looked at her sermon afterwards he said that he could see nothing wrong with it and gave her his support.

Prue Baker

47. *Rabbi Alexandra Wright, Associate Rabbi (Senior Rabbi since 2004), saying Kiddush at temporary premises in Loudoun Road. Photograph by Michael S Goldhill. (1988)*

However, the congregation was not always comfortable with the new messages and the new style of leadership.

There was one occasion – *Yom Kippur* – when we were 'in exile'. The synagogue was being rebuilt, and we held the services at Westminster City Hall. I gave a sermon on how the liturgy for the High Holydays didn't necessarily reflect the needs of women and didn't encourage women to assert themselves in a more positive way. Although I quoted from Lily Montagu, it created something of a furore and I was summoned before the Senior Rabbi and Chairman at the time. I gave the Chairman a copy of the sermon. To his very great credit, he sent for me again, apologised and said that what he had *heard* was different from what I had *said*. It was a remarkable moment, but I did learn from that particular episode that it is very easy to bring to what we hear our own preconceptions and assumptions.

Alexandra Wright (Pt. 3)

Rabbi Wright, along with women student rabbis studying at Leo Baeck College, was influential in the decision to use gender-inclusive language in the new ULPS prayerbook, *Siddur Lev Chadash* (introduced in 1995), believing that it would help bring into the community those women who felt distanced by the language of the traditional liturgy. With a major input from Rabbi Freeman, working with Rabbi Marcia Plumb and a number of other women rabbis, a Progressive women's conference, 'The Half Empty Bookcase', was held at the synagogue in 1992. It attracted much interest and publicity.

By the beginning of the 1990s, questions started to be asked about why so few women were involved in LJS committees and subcommittees.

> It seems to me that women are only interested in the 'possibility' of equality, for after nearly eighty years of our LJS existence what do we find? Out of a Council of twenty-two members, there are five women, there is one Woman Chairman of a subcommittee out of five committees; there are no women Trustees.
>
> Ruth Ive [246]

However, the lack of involvement of women in formal leadership did not mean that women had a low profile. In fact some of the major causes pursued by the LJS during the latter part of the twentieth century were led by women, notably Margaret Rigal's outstanding work with the refuseniks and Barbara Brandenburger's work with the Bosnian Support Group.

Today things are very different. Many more women are involved in synagogue committees, two women (Rita Adler[247] and Ellen Schmidt) have chaired the LJS Council, and the Senior Rabbi (Alexandra Wright) is a woman. In 2003 Rabbi Kathleen de Magtige-Middleton[248] chaired the first ever International Women's Rabbinic Network Conference, 'Building Bridges'. The conference, which took place at the LJS, attracted ninety women rabbis from eight different countries and helped to raise the profile of women's issues.

48. *Rita Adler as LJS Chairman. From left: Rabbi Helen Freeman, Rabbi David Goldberg, Rita Adler, Bob Beral and Bob Kirk. (undated, c. 1996)*

---

[246] Ruth Ive, 'Celebration of the Women's Society Achievements', *LJS News*, February 1991.
[247] See photographs 20, 48, 57, and 59.
[248] See photograph 21.

Many LJS members are pleased with the progress that has been made for women.

> What I like is that women have total equality. Everybody sits together, women have equal rights and take part in the service (which is not so in the Orthodox) and there are women rabbis.
>
> Jenny Nathan (Pt. 3)

Others have pointed to inconsistencies in the synagogue's approach to gender equality.

> Just to give an example: the lighting of the *Shabbat* candles used to be one of the few time-bound positive commandments to which women were obligated, as it affirmed their role in the home. Surely in the light of the Liberal principle of equal status for men and women, both men and women should be equally obligated to fulfil the *mitzvot*, and since we no longer define women's role only in the home, lighting candles should not be a typically female prerogative. Nevertheless I have hardly ever seen a man lighting candles in the synagogue. Another remnant from tradition in which men and women are treated differently in our synagogue is the religious obligation of wearing *tallit* when on the *bimah*, which the LJS prescribes as compulsory for males, but optional for females. Surely the principle of equality should demand that men and women are similarly obligated.
>
> Kathleen de Magtige-Middleton[249]

In the last few years, a number of roles that were traditionally undertaken by women are now also carried out by men, such as the arranging of flowers and the serving of coffee before services.

Inclusivity

When Claude Montefiore drew up the 'manifesto' for the JRU, he advocated that no traditional ceremony or institution should be maintained if it were no longer seen as being relevant to modern life. One of his two exceptions to this general rule was the rejection of intermarriage (the other being the retention of circumcision), an issue on which he maintained a hard line for the remainder of his life. He did, however, feel that it was right to admit into Judaism those who were sincere in wishing to convert to Judaism. When the synagogue first opened, decisions on conversions were made by the LJS Council (a major departure from Jewish tradition) and approaches from potential proselytes were not always warmly welcomed.[250]

The approach taken to intermarriage and to conversion became more sympathetic and less dogmatic with the arrival of Rabbi Mattuck, who insisted that decisions on conversion should be made by himself as spiritual leader of the congregation. He altered the rules for accepting converts, fearing that the hard line previously taken by the synagogue ran the risk of being counterproductive and deterring those who were already beginning to drift away from Judaism.

Since that time, the synagogue has taken an increasingly inclusive approach to intermarriage, conversion and the question of Jewish identity.

---

[249] Rabbi Kathleen de Magtige-Middleton, 'Are women really equal in Liberal Judaism', *LJS News,* May 2002.
[250] Lawrence Rigal and Rosita Rosenberg, *Liberal Judaism: The First Hundred Years.*

My parents, Trixi and Eric Blaire, met as students at the University of Bristol in 1965. As my father came from an Orthodox Jewish background, and my mother as a Hungarian refugee had spent time in a Catholic convent on arrival in the UK, it was a challenge for my grandparents to find a synagogue that would accept her Jewish credentials and to which she could feel a sense of belonging. They found that in John Rayner and the LJS.

Felicity Allen (Pt. 3)

Those wishing to convert have been warmly welcomed.

A major reason for my continuing affection and involvement with the LJS was the wonderful support given to Maureen and me. We first met the rabbis Philip Cohen and John Rayner in 1957 and Maureen did her conversion course by these lovely people to enable us to get married in America in 1958. The Organising Secretary, Peggy Lang, who was previously Rabbi Mattuck's secretary, welcomed Maureen and was a great support in her decision to convert to Judaism. When we returned home in 1959, we were totally welcomed and the LJS became our spiritual family.

Anthony Roe (Pt. 3)

Provision has always been made for conversion courses and several generations of proselytes were taught by Marjorie Moos. Following their conversion, proselytes are welcomed to the synagogue with an admission ceremony, usually held on a Friday evening. For many years, Rosa Mintz, sister of the Religion School teacher, Celia Rapp, greeted those coming to the synagogue for an admission ceremony.

Rosa Mintz was a great friend to the proselytes. She was often around the LJS on Tuesday evenings when they had their classes and got to know all of them. Then she saw them on Friday evenings. She took pleasure in their learning and especial pleasure when one of them continued as an active member of the congregation. They all wanted her to be a part of their admission ceremony ... When Rosa died and left a generous legacy to the synagogue, the Council resolved that a copy of *Siddur Lev Chadash* should be presented to each proselyte at their admission ceremony in her memory.

Bernie Bulkin (Pt. 3)

Gradually the LJS came to welcome into its membership those considering or already in a mixed-faith marriage without placing an onus on the non-Jewish person to convert. By the 1980s it had taken this approach a step further by being prepared to provide blessings for mixed-faith marriages.

Rabbi Alexandra Wright performed a blessing on our marriage, the first time she had carried out such a ceremony. It was very well prepared by Alex and was extremely moving for our families and friends. A very positive reflection on the synagogue was the way that it embraced Pam whenever she accompanied me to services and other events, demonstrating very well its commitment to the inclusion of non-Jewish spouses.

Michael Hart (Pt. 3)

Initially mixed-faith marriage blessings were held outside the LJS, but in 2003 it was decided by the rabbis and the Council of the LJS that they could take place in the Sanctuary.[251] However, since the mixed-faith marriage blessings do not constitute marriage ceremonies, the *chuppah*, the distinctive symbol of a Jewish wedding, cannot be used, nor is there a *ketubbah* (Jewish marriage contract).

---

[251] This is in accordance with the general policy of Liberal Judaism.

On the recommendation of Rabbi David Goldberg, in 1994 the LJS introduced the membership category of 'Friends', thereby allowing non-Jewish people to associate themselves more formally with the synagogue. Rabbi Helen Freeman developed a positive response to a ULPS committee's suggestions for welcoming non-Jewish partners and set up a number of groups to do this. In 2003 it was agreed that Friends of the LJS could be buried in the LJS cemetery.[252]

Although some members of the synagogue were concerned that these initiatives would mean that non-Jewish partners might be discouraged from converting to Judaism, the rabbis made it clear that the LJS would still be encouraging those intending to marry a Jew to explore the spiritual richness of Judaism, and ultimately to convert and create a Jewish marriage and Jewish family.

> [W]e decided long ago that all Jews, their partners and their children, should find a place in our [Liberal] synagogues. It is fitting that the LJS, the first congregation in our movement, should take the lead in carrying this principle into a new form of practice, and open the synagogue to acts of prayer and dedication for mixed marriages. Far from diminishing the holiness of our Sanctuary, it will add another dimension of reality to our aspiration, in the spirit of prophetic Judaism, to become 'a House of Prayer for all peoples' (Isaiah 56:7).
>
> Mark Solomon[253]

In the last ten years, the LJS has been at the forefront in welcoming into its membership and supporting blessings for same-sex couples. The first same-sex blessing was carried out by Rabbi Mark Solomon in 2006.

> Civil Partnerships for same-sex couples became legal late in 2005. Susan and I decided to enter into this commitment in June 2006, and we were keen to have a spiritual dimension to recognise and celebrate this step. By this time, Lily was an enthusiastic four-year-old in *Gan* class at the LJS Religion School. Rabbi Mark Solomon, who had been one of a few rabbis who had worked hard to secure Liberal Judaism's celebration of same-sex commitment ceremonies, and who had collaborated on Liberal Judaism's 'Covenant of Love' service of commitment for same-sex couples, officiated at our commitment ceremony on 18 June 2006, the first to be held at the LJS. This made the occasion very special for us.
>
> Karen Newman (Pt. 3)

Most members have supported, or are at least accepting of, the LJS's ever-increasing inclusivity, which has brought into its membership many people who might not otherwise have belonged to a synagogue or who might have left Judaism. However, some people are concerned about the potential dilution of the basic tenets of Liberal Judaism.

> The practice of the Liberal Jewish religion is different now because many Orthodox people have joined Liberal synagogues for the sole purpose of marrying someone outside their religion. This is a crisis for the movement, and I do not accept how it has been handled. I think it should have been made explicit right from the start that they should adhere to the Liberal philosophy.
>
> Walter Woyda (Pt. 3)

---

[252] *LJS News*, May 2005.
[253] Rabbi Mark Solomon, 'Council Sanctions Mixed Blessings in the Sanctuary', *LJS News*, May 2005.

Chapter Two: Social welfare and social action

EVEN BEFORE THE LJS was established, its founders were heavily involved in various forms of social welfare and social action. Lily Montagu had already established her West End Girls' Club and was active in organisations aimed at improving the working conditions of women industrial workers. She later served as a Justice of the Peace in the juvenile courts because of her interest in youth work and she played a major role in founding the National Association of Girls' Clubs and the Maude Nathan Home for Little Children. Claude Montefiore was involved in various educational activities, generously supported many charities and was also an active worker in several welfare organisations such as the Jewish Association for the Protection of Girls and Women. These involvements provided a model for the early members of the LJS.

A Social Service Guild was set up in 1912 with the remit of making social work an integral part of the life of the synagogue. Under the leadership of Mr S Lazarus, it started to organise lectures on relevant topics and to provide workers for a range of charities, such as the Invalid Children's Aid Association and the Jewish Board of Guardians. During the First World War, the Guild discontinued most of its activities, but it did support a home for Belgian refugees. Members of the Guild found longer-term accommodation for the refugees, visited them in their new homes and helped them to become self-supporting. This work was led by Francesca Gluckstein, mother of Sir Louis Gluckstein, who in 1918 was awarded an MBE for her work and the Order of Queen Elizabeth of Belgium.[254]

Basil Henriques (later Sir Basil), a member of the synagogue, regularly spoke about his work in the East End of London at gatherings of the congregation. In 1914 he formed a Jewish Boys' Club, the Oxford and St George's Jewish Lads' Club, at 125 Cannon Street Road, which was dedicated to improving the lives of young Jews in the East End. This proved successful, so Henriques subsequently founded a similar girls' club led by Rose Loewe whom he married in 1917. The Social Service Guild appealed to the Council to give money to support these initiatives.

> Basil [Henriques] had a commanding presence. He was very tall and had a voice that could silence even the most raucous and loudest youngster when the club evenings came to an end with an assembly and a final prayer. Many other LJS members also became involved in helping in both the boys' and girls' clubs, and a number of marriages arose from this.
>
> Michael Nathan[255]

The clubs continued while Henriques served in the First World War, but on his return he made plans for a Progressive Jewish settlement similar to the Christian settlements he had seen in the East End. With financial help and other support from both the LJS and the West London Synagogue, the St George's Jewish Settlement was set up Betts Street in 1919 and became one of the main causes supported by the LJS during the 1920s and 1930s. Many members of the synagogue went to work on a voluntary basis at the Settlement.

---

254 Mentioned in LJS Annual Report, 1958 on the death of Francesca Gluckstein.
255 Amongst those who met their future spouses while working at the Settlement were Geoffrey Kahn, Max Caplin and Susan Goodman.

Now in the congregation there were two ladies, the Misses Millie and Sophie Levy, who had been LJS members since Hill Street days. They were unmarried sisters, voluntary social workers in the East End of London with an office at the Bernhard Baron Settlement.

Ann Kirk (Pt. 3)

Dr Mattuck encouraged us to go down to the Jewish Settlement in the East End in Berners Street. It was financed by a member of the LJS, Bernhard Baron, and it was named after him – it was the Bernhard Baron St. George's Settlement. It helped the thousands of poor Jews who lived in the East End. They would come off the immigrant ships and many of them were living in great poverty and deprivation in the East End. The Settlement was run by Sir Basil and Lady Henriques. It was absolutely their baby and it was a wonderful organisation. Basil was known as 'the Gaffer' and she was known as 'the Missus'. I had ties with the Settlement inasmuch as there was a family connection to Lady Henriques. So I used to help down there as did many of my contemporaries such as Jenny Nathan's uncle, Alan Rubenstein, (Justin's father), who was a 'poor man's lawyer', and Bill Frank helped out with the accounts.

Ruth Ive

49. *Sir Basil and Rose Henriques (the 'Gaffer' and the 'Missus'). Photograph owned by the Civval family. (1930)*

Their involvement in the activities of the Bernhard Baron Settlement opened the eyes of some LJS congregants to conditions prevailing in the East End at the time.

I remember running round Berners Street with a chicken casserole. I saw poverty such as I had never dreamed of – down in basements, in tenements, old women and men dying of consumption and I thought: 'How terrible it is; what an unequal society it is'. It turned me into a good socialist as I began to realise that there was something very wrong with a society that could tolerate such appalling poverty ... Added to that, there was the fear of the Blackshirts. They were a very real threat to Jewish people in the East End. I returned from my East End visits to a middle-class home where my dinner was waiting for me, served by the parlour maid. The contrasts were absolutely extraordinary. When people say there was a wonderful spirit in the East End, of course there was, because they were all in it together.

But the hardship and the illness and the poverty were not to be admired. I don't like it when people present a rosy view of what it was like – they were not easy times because there was so much unemployment.

Ruth Ive

When they were established, the Alumni Society and the Women's Society both had objectives that included supporting social action. In 1918, the Alumni Society worked with the Social Service Guild to set up and run a play centre (the Marylebone Play Centre) at an LCC school in Whitfield Street for the Jewish Children of East St, Marylebone. Within a year, the play centre was attracting nearly 200 children between the ages of eleven and fourteen.[256]

Members of the Alumni subsequently became involved in various other schemes.

Dr Mattuck saw that his lessons inspired us to social work. To mention a few of the things we did, there was the Little Brothers and Sisters scheme, when every boy or girl was attached to a poor child in the East End and had to look after them. My particular job on Fridays was to choose a chicken which was suitably cooked for the Sabbath weekend. The next thing we did was teas and we used to have a service on Saturday afternoons and afterwards, we bought some lovely checked tablecloths and provided teas for all those people who wanted it before they went home.

Marjorie Moos[257]

The Marylebone Play Centre closed after two years, but the Alumni Society opened another at the synagogue in 1920.

One of the most interesting experiments was a play centre for the children of the neighbourhood, both Christian and Jewish, which met at the synagogue twice a week.

Michael Duparc[258]

The involvement of the Women's Society in social action included making garments for children in need, arranging activities for disadvantaged children and visiting sick people. Even children were involved in social action. A children's club, which met at the synagogue on a Saturday afternoon, was involved in making dolls' houses which were given to disadvantaged children.[259]

As the influence of the LJS grew, invitations to be involved in inter-communal social action began to flow. In 1929 the synagogue was invited to join the Visitation Committee of the United Synagogue, which supplied visitors to Jewish people in institutions, such as hospitals and prisons, and which nominated Jewish Chaplains to the Armed Forces.[260]

By the 1930s, members of the LJS were involved in a wide variety of Jewish and non-Jewish charitable organisations and had started to undertake formal social work training. Phyllis Gerson, a lifelong member of the LJS, was a pioneer professional social worker in the East End of London. As a young woman in the 1920s, she started as a volunteer in the Stepney Jewish Girls' (*B'nai Brith*) Club and Play Centre and in a small girls' club run

---

[256] LJS Annual Report, 1918.
[257] Talk by Marjorie Moos to LJS Women's Society.
[258] J M Duparc, 'Our Congregations', *Liberal Jewish Monthly*, December 1950.
[259] LJS Annual Report, 1935.
[260] LJS Annual Report, 1929.

by Anna Schwab (grandmother of Baroness Julia Neuberger). Having obtained a social worker's qualification at the LSE in the 1930s, she became the Warden of the Stepney Jewish Settlement, a role from which she reluctantly retired in the late 1970s.

> Phyllis was Chair of the local Juvenile Magistrate Court as well as being involved in any committee, local or national, which was in any way concerned with welfare. Her networking was astonishing and, without so much as referring to an address book, she could magic out of thin air the name of an individual or organisation guaranteed to come up with the necessary support – financial or otherwise – for any given task or individual in need.
>
> Joan Salter

The two biggest causes to which the synagogue lent its support during the 1930s were helping unemployed men and supporting refugees from Nazi Germany. Rabbi Mattuck was very concerned about the impact of the Great Depression and ensured that the congregation were fully aware of the plight of the unemployed.

Now Assistant Minister at the LJS, Leslie Edgar encouraged the setting up of a club for unemployed men at the synagogue with finance raised from amongst LJS members. The club had a membership of over 400 and became self-governing. The Women's Society ran a canteen for the club in the Montefiore Hall under the leadership of Mrs Starrels, wife of the Assistant Minister, and the Younger Members' Organisation ran various classes for the men and singing lessons were given by the Choirmaster, Ivor Warren.[261] The LJS also arranged for the men to have access to the cricket nets across the road at Lord's Cricket Ground.

> A delightful incident occurred towards the end of the Club's existence. One of the men, a butcher by trade, got a job as a window cleaner. At the end of the first week of work he went to Smithfield market and bought a large joint – an enormous joint of beef. It was cooked in the canteen kitchen and all the men were invited to lunch. It was a very fine gesture and I have rarely been more proud to be, as I was then, the guest of honour.
>
> Leslie Edgar[262]

> The men worked mending each other's and children's shoes or chairs and all kinds of things and this went so well that the local mayor came and approved and he gave the men an empty house and the wherewithal so that they might manage it for themselves and have their club. And when the men left, they all clubbed together and they gave a pipe to Mr Nathan who was our Housekeeper to thank him for what he had done for them.
>
> Marjorie Moos[263]

Rabbi Mattuck worked zealously to raise funds to enable German refugees to come to England. To avoid their reliance on public funding, the Government required refugees to have sponsorship. The money that Rabbi Mattuck raised was sufficient to enable 156 refugees to escape from Nazi persecution.[264] It was administered by a Refugee Committee led by Leslie Edgar.

---

[261] Cited in Lawrence Rigal and Rosita Rosenberg, *Liberal Judaism: The First Hundred Years*.
[262] Rabbi Dr Leslie I Edgar, *Some Memories of My Ministry*.
[263] Talk by Marjorie Moos to LJS Women's Society.
[264] Following the depression of the 1920s and the years of high unemployment it created, Britain passed laws to limit the entry of refugees. The Government insisted that refugees had a guarantee of £250 and later £500 so that they would not be a burden on the state.

It proved difficult for the synagogue to obtain visas for refugees and, even when this was achieved, it was often hard for the refugees to find work because of the general hostility towards them. Members of the synagogue sometimes used their social and family connections to help.

> The ever-pressing subject was Germany. My cousin, Bernard Davidson, who was on the LJS Council, got to know the Home Office officer in charge of visas. He spent his life on the telephone to Major Morrison trying to get visas, and I must say that he had some success; we did get people out.
>
> Ruth Ive (Pt. 3)

When the War Office decided to call upon young refugees for military services and the Pioneer Corps was formed, a prominent LJS member, Bernard Davidson, was invited to assist in their recruitment and given the rank of Major.[265]

The Women's Society was very involved in supporting those affected by the rise of Nazism. In 1934 the society's Social Service Committee 'adopted' eight children placed in emergency open-air nurseries in distressed areas. The Hospitality Committee for German Refugees chaired by Lily Montagu's sister, Henrietta (Netta) Franklin, helped to find domestic posts for married couples who had no other means for leaving Germany, to educate and find holiday hospitality for children (twenty-three children were supported in this way) and, in conjunction with the synagogue's Refugee Committee, to find hospitality for refugees awaiting permanent homes.

The Women's Society tried to ensure that the children they helped had a Jewish education, especially if they lived with non-Jewish families. Many of them were taken into the homes of members of the synagogue.

> We looked after a boy called Henry Worth. His name had been Wortheimer. He came from Austria. His father had been a master printer. He had seen his mother killed ... My father got his father over here. My father paid to get him here.
>
> Doreen Gluckstein[266]

> It just so happened, at a party there, they met my mother's best friend, Edith, who had recently emigrated from Berlin. They got into conversation and Edith explained that her friend, Hertha Kuhn, was desperately trying to get her little girl, Hannah, out of Germany. Well, they thought about it and, bearing in mind what Dr Mattuck had said, agreed to take me. They were actually even prepared to come over to Germany to collect me, but that wasn't allowed, so my parents enrolled me on the *Kindertransport*.
>
> Ann Kirk (Pt. 3)

The synagogue hosted a club for German refugees, which sometimes organised dances attended by as many as 200 young people.[267] A room was set aside in the synagogue to enable older German refugees to meet together under the leadership of Mr and Mrs Schlesinger, who organised lectures and music recitals.[268] Supported by the LJS, the German refugees ran language lessons and, supported by Lily Montagu, started to hold

---

[265] LJS Annual Report, 1960.
[266] ULPS Oral History Project, interview with Doreen Gluckstein. See Appendix 1.
[267] LJS Annual Report, 1936.
[268] LJS Annual Reports, 1935 and 1936.

their own services as they wanted forms of worship that were more traditional than those of the LJS. They eventually formed their own congregation in Belsize Square.

After the war, the LJS continued its involvement in social action, mainly under the auspices of the Women's Society. In the immediate aftermath of the war, the Women's Society sent clothes to displaced Jewish people in Europe, especially those living in temporary camps, collected toys for orphaned children in France, Germany and Austria (the Marrainage Scheme), and raised money for the British Fund for Jewish Relief and Rehabilitation. After the foundation of the State of Israel in 1948, the Women's Society started to raise money for Jewish immigrants in camps and reception centres in Israel.

In the post-war period, many individual members of the synagogue continued to be involved in social welfare activities in the East End.

> While I was a student I was invited by Lillian Hill and Phyllis Gerson to the East End to see the social work they were carrying out there. They were part of a generation of Anglo-Jewish families who had been influenced to become involved by Lily Montagu and Basil Henriques and had a very strong sense of social responsibility. The work they did was amazing. They worked with some very tough young people and took it all in their stride.
>
> David Goldberg (Pt. 3)

> It was about this time that I began going to Stepney one evening each week to help in the Boys' Club at the Bernhard Baron Settlement, usually staying the night there, which gave me much insight into youth work and communal social work. On at least one occasion, I went with the club to camp for a week at High Down near Worthing. This was my first active involvement with a Jewish charity. Soon after this I became the Treasurer of the Association for Jewish Youth and of the Stepney Jewish Club and Settlement, of which I was later President for seventeen years. I was also the Treasurer for twelve years of what was then the Jewish Board of Guardians, later Jewish Welfare Board and now Jewish Care.
>
> Michael Nathan (Pt. 3)

In 1949 the Younger Members' Organisation visited the Bernhard Baron Settlement where they gave a *Chanukkah* tea party for over 400 children and 100 adults, described by Basil Henriques as 'the biggest in my memory of the Settlement'.[269]

By now, the congregation included an increasing number of prominent dedicated social workers, such as the remarkable Leverson sisters.[270] Nancy, who married Dr Max Caplin, was confirmed at the LJS in 1929. She was first involved in social work working in children's clubs in London's East End in the 1930s and was still actively engaged there sixty years later. Her commitments included volunteering in two homes for older people that she originally helped to establish and where she continued to be involved even when she was considerably older than many of the residents.

> She organised the annual camp for the Berhard Baron Settlement, where she met her husband Max, a junior doctor at the time, who had been sent to help – and very firmly told him that the latrine he had been digging 'was not nearly deep enough'.
>
> Jo Kessler

---

[269] ULPS *Union News*, March 1949.
[270] For further information on the Leverson sisters see, Pam Fox, 'The Remarkable Leverson Sisters', *LJS News*, May 2011.

During the Second World War, Nancy Caplin worked as a military social worker in an Army hospital. In 1945 she worked in the Gorbals, helping ex-service men return to normal life. She then took a job as one of the first children's welfare officers in Tottenham where she was a pioneer in highlighting child abuse. She worked for over twenty years for Willesden Citizens Advice Bureau, and after an accident which affected her mobility, she continued to give advice by telephone.

Katherine Leverson, who became Katherine Rantzen (mother of Esther Rantzen), also worked in the East End, with Phyllis Gerson, among others, at the Stepney Jewish Settlement. Jane Leverson was one of the first Jewish welfare workers with the Friends Relief Service to enter the Belsen concentration camp.[271] Nancy's fourth sister, Marion (later Green), worked with Lilian Hill, who was responsible for the Welfare of the Aged Department at the Jewish Welfare Board.[272]

> Another person who was very involved with the LJS was Lilian Hill. She had been a senior social worker at the Jewish Welfare Board with special responsibility for the elderly. She had a cottage in Suffolk where John [Rayner] and I stayed from time to time and occasionally took our children. Lilian had parties for the elderly and even for the not-so-elderly from the LJS to visit her there.
>
> Jane Rayner

Many LJS members continued to undertake voluntary work in organisations such as the Citizen's Advice Bureau and other charitable bodies.

> I was a compulsive volunteer. I worked for about eight years for the Citizens Advice Bureau and then became a Magistrate, eventually sitting on the Inner London Family Panel and Youth Courts. I was Vice Chair of the Family Panel for a while. I also worked as a volunteer for the Spinal Injuries Association and was a Governor of a Church School, Christ Church Bentinck, for about eight years, finally chairing the Governors.
>
> Barbara Godfrey (Pt. 3)

Some of the synagogue's social welfare activities took place at the LJS, including the Darby and Joan Club founded in 1948 by Lady Gluckstein with the help of Dorothy Myer. It was a non-denominational friendship club open to all older people living in the Lisson Grove area which had been badly devastated during the war. It earned a national reputation, which led to it being inspected by social workers considering setting up similar clubs.

> As I have already mentioned, my parents were among the earliest members of the LJS. They were also among the most active. For quite a long time, my mother was Chairman of the Women's Society, and she also started the Darby and Joan Club. I remember the latter meeting every Wednesday. It proved very popular with the thirty or so attendees, none of whom were members of the LJS. They chatted, played cards and bingo, and frequently some form of entertainment was provided (I sang for them regularly). Members of the LJS helped, and always organised an excellent tea for everybody.
>
> Jean Jaffa (Pt. 3)

---

[271] She gave talks about her experience at the synagogue.
[272] The Chairman of the department was George Maitland, another LJS member.

50. *Darby and Joan Club outing. Photograph by Mark Gerson. (1949)*

In addition to the regular meetings at the synagogue, there were outings and members of the Club who were sick were visited in their homes. Lady Gluckstein ran the Darby and Joan Club for twenty-seven years with the assistance of a number of faithful helpers. It was subsequently led by Rosalie Levinson, who ran the club for a further twenty-five years before it was finally disbanded in 2003.

> I started helping at the Darby and Joan Club in 1984. The club served the local area, and most of the people who came weren't Jewish. It was held on Wednesday afternoons, from 2.00 until 4.00 pm. We'd put out magazines and cards ready for when people arrived. Then, at 3.00 p.m., we'd serve tea and cake, followed by bingo. Sometimes Fred (the caretaker) was the caller for us; we took it in turns. The prize was a bar of chocolate! We also had an annual bring and buy sale, to raise funds for the club. I stopped in 2000. By then there wasn't really the need for it, there were other clubs around, such as the Out and Abouts, that had more going on, although, when it started, I think it was one of the first of its kind.
>
> Anita Schwartz

The Out and About Club, founded in the 1964 by Esther Rantzen and Diana Da Costa (née Mohr), was a non-denominational club for disabled people living in St John's Wood and the surrounding area. Many young people from the LJS's various societies and groups assisted with the running of the club.

It has often been stated that the founding of the Out and About Club had been my idea. This was not the case. The Committee of the Alumni Society wanted to undertake a charitable project and so I volunteered to visit the London Council of Social Services to get some ideas. One of the LCSS's suggestions was to run a club for disabled people under the auspices of the Greater London Association for the Disabled [GLAD]. The Alumni Society Committee liked this suggestion, the GLAD were delighted, the LJS Council readily agreed and the Club was born. The Alumni soon realised that this project was too big to undertake by ourselves and so Phase Two, then under the Chairmanship of Esther Rantzen, were invited to join us which they readily accepted. Jane Green, Esther Rantzen and I were the first of many Chairs. The rest is history.

Diana Da Costa

In the late 1960s and early 1970s the Out and Abouts grew at quite a rate with Westminster Council eventually providing four buses for club members and with a fleet of volunteers bringing members from further afield. I did a stint as Co-Chair with Malcolm Brown which was always amusing as our styles were so different. (We were followed by Sue Barnard [now Wolf] who is, I believe, still a member of the Elstree Community.) The monthly planning meetings were great fun with up to twenty-eight volunteers descending on someone's home in North London. I also vividly remember one occasion when two shy but very bubbly seventeen-year-olds came to the Out and Abouts. Both were called Michael (Hart and Beral!).

Jeffrey Spearman

51. *Out and About Club. From left: Jenny Nathan, Mary Carter and Esther Rantzen. (1991)*

52. *Out and About Annual Dinner. (undated, c. mid-1980s)*

Under the Chairmanship of Jenny Nathan, who received an MBE in 2006 for her work with the Out and About Club (and other activities for disabled people), the club continues to meet once a fortnight at the LJS where various activities are arranged, including talks and musical entertainment. The club is supported by a number of local churches and only a handful of its forty members are Jewish. For many years, the President of the Out and About Club was Dr Max Caplin. His role has now been taken over by Rabbi Emeritus David Goldberg, who plays a very active role in its affairs.

> It has always been a very active, social thing to be involved with; people who were helpers remained friends for years afterwards. Geoffrey Laventhal and Joany Weinberg, who is still a member of the LJS, were two of the original helpers and so was Fleur Hoffman. All sorts of people were Chairman, among them Jeffrey Spearman, Nick Feldman and Stephen Lazarus. Stephen and I ran it together for a while; but when Nick married and moved to Suffolk and there was a vacancy for a Chairman, I took it on and have been doing it ever since. I enjoy it. We had a reunion last year and seventy people who had been helpers came. It was amazing!
>
> Jenny Nathan (Pt. 3)

Young people were also prominent in establishing a number of other post-war social welfare activities at the LJS. Towards the end of 1968, a number of young people met with Rabbi and Mrs Jane Rayner to discuss the possibility of undertaking voluntary work with children. The outcome of the meeting was the formation of a junior Gateway Club set up to provide social activities for young people with special needs to complement the work of special needs schools and training centres.[273] The club met at the synagogue for a number of years on a Sunday afternoon with support from the Jewish Youth Voluntary Service. The club expanded and, by the early 1970s, the young LJS members involved

---

[273] LJS Annual Report, 1969.

were also visiting and organising outings for young people from Brent Council's Halfway Home in Winchester Avenue.[274]

At the initiative of Rabbi Helen Freeman, in 1992 the LJS set up a Social Action Group to co-ordinate its various social welfare and social action activities. During the 1990s, it concerned itself with helping asylum seekers who were in need of charitable support, sending food to a refugee centre in Vauxhall and supporting Jubilee 2000, an international movement dedicated to eradicating debts owed by developing countries. Its first two Chairmen were Bryan Diamond and Joshua Dubin. The group was re-designated as the Social Action Committee and refreshed in 2001 when Michael Hart became its Chairman.

> The Committee was a little unsure what its role should be and, after several meetings, I was asked to take over as Chairman. We formed a small, new Committee, which focussed on a limited number of objectives, organising some special events such as a *Shabbaton* about refugees, a soapbox session like the ones at Hyde Park Corner, and activities to increase the involvement of members with disabilities.
>
> Michael Hart (Pt. 3)

One of the first activities that the revived committee promoted was the twinning of the LJS with a Progressive congregation in Eastern Europe. The impetus for this came from a talk at a Friday evening *Chavurah* given by Linda Kann on behalf of Exodus 2000, a Progressive Jewish organisation set up to promote congregational support for communities in the former Soviet Union.

> The next phase seemed the simplest but took a little longer than anticipated … who would be our twin? Linda works closely with Rabbi Alexander Dukhovny, Chief Rabbi of Kiev (or Kyiv according to the correct spelling) to find suitable twins. The first suggestion was a relatively large and established congregation which already had a twinning arrangement with another congregation. There were many attractions to this suggestion but, after some consideration, the Social Action Committee decided to ask for an alternative in the hope of finding a twin which was at the early stages of development and was not as yet linked with any other congregation. The second proposal from Rabbi Dukhovny was Vinnitsa, which we quickly agreed would be an excellent twin for the LJS.
>
> Michael Hart[275]

The twinning arrangement was confirmed and a visit to the community was organised.

> With Michael Hart, David de Magtige and Rabbi Mark Solomon, I visited our new partner community in Vinnitsa in the Ukraine, which was a fascinating experience. One of the most memorable and moving moments was when we went to a forest clearing where many Jews had been murdered. We were accompanied by a lady whose parents were among the victims and Mark chanted the *El Maleh Rachamim* memorial prayer.
>
> Tim Simon (Pt. 3)

A return visit was made by a delegation from the community the following year and since then the synagogue has continued to support the Vinnitsa community financially.

The Social Action Committee also initiated support for the Bayswater Family Centre for asylum seekers, refugees and homeless families located close to Westbourne Grove.

---

[274] LJS Annual Report, 1972.
[275] 'The LJS Twinned with Ukrainian Jewish Congregation', *LJS News*, October 2002.

For a number of years now, the synagogue has collected tins of food and pharmaceutical goods for the centre and members of the congregation volunteer there.

> Margaret and I have also been involved in the Social Action Group on and off since its beginning. It has always supported the Bayswater Family Centre. We got involved because our doctor, Richard Stone, was active in various social activities and he put us in touch with the Bayswater Centre. His practice was about 100 yards from it. Living locally, we were able to assist in a variety of ways. The LJS supplied the funding for a computer room for children at the centre who had nowhere to study in the evenings.
>
> George Rigal (Pt. 3)

In recent years, the Social Action Committee has been chaired by Sue Bolsom, who has taken the lead in organising a range of events and activities, including one which has now become an annual event. As part of national *Mitzvah* Day, the Social Action Committee and other volunteers spend a day outside Sainsbury's at the O2 Centre on Finchley Road where shoppers are encouraged to add items to their shopping trolleys and then hand them over to the collectors after they have been purchased. The food and other goods are then distributed to relevant charities.

53. *LJS volunteers at Sainsbury's, the O2 Centre Finchley Road, Mitzvah Day 2009. George Rigal in centre of photograph. (2009)*

In April 2006 the Social Action Committee, in partnership with World Jewish Relief, organised a collection of items to be transported to Belarus, one of the poorest and most disadvantaged states in the former Soviet Union. The project was linked with the counting of the *Omer* in the seven weeks between *Pesach* and *Shavu'ot*. The congregation donated different items in each of the weeks of the *Omer*. This resulted in ten large bags and boxes of items being sent to Belarus.

Charitable giving

Charitable giving is central to the Jewish ethic and throughout its history the LJS has been involved in raising money for both Jewish and non-Jewish causes. When it was established in 1912, the main focus of the Social Service Guild was to encourage fundraising for major charities of the day such as collections for the Jewish Board of Guardians and the Hospital Sunday Fund.

All of the synagogue's main societies and groups were heavily involved in fundraising for charities, especially the Women's Society and Alumni Society and, later, the Younger Members' Organisation. For example, during 1919, the Alumni Society raised money so that it could take disadvantaged children on a picnic. Concerts and dramatic performances were frequently held at the synagogue as a means of fundraising.

From its early days, the Religion School collected money each week for causes such as famine relief, a tradition which continued for over fifty years. Albeit less frequently, Religion School collections are still made today.

In 1925 the LJS set up a committee to look at methods for collecting funds for charities, which led eventually to the establishment in 1929 of the synagogue's United Charities Fund (UCF) as a separate registered charity. The aim of the UCF was to simplify the collection of charitable giving and increase support for Jewish charities. The costs of setting up the UCF were paid for by Leon Rees, who subsequently became its Chairman for twenty-five years, followed by Michael Nathan.

> I remained Chairman for the next forty-five years, so that in the first seventy years of its existence the Fund only had two Chairmen. The object of the Fund was to assist LJS members in making their charitable donations through knowledge of the more deserving causes and allocating funds to the Jewish charities which seemed to be most in need, sometimes a rather difficult task. Occasionally, the Fund would receive a substantial legacy from congregants and, on occasion, from completely unknown people. As Chairman, I was responsible, together with the rabbis, for choosing the recipient charities for the synagogue's Day of Atonement appeal.
>
> Michael Nathan (Pt. 3)

During the 1930s and throughout the Second World War, the congregation was involved in major fundraising activities to support Jewish refugees from Europe. Later the synagogue launched urgent appeals for Israel and for causes such as the Soviet refuseniks. In 1985 the LJS's Junior Council held a disco and a food fair to raise money for Soviet Jewry. During the 1980s, the synagogue also raised money for the refugees from Laos, Cambodia and Vietnam.

Over time, it became a tradition at the LJS that monies raised as the result of a charitable appeal at *Yom Kippur* were divided between an Anglo-Jewish Charity, an Israeli charity and a non-Jewish charity. Members of the LJS have always pursued innovative ways of raising money.

> Arguably, Michael's most creative contribution was as the instigator of 'Red *Kippah* Day' in March 1996, inspired by and coinciding with Comic Relief's 'Red Nose Day'. 152 red silk *kippot* were sold in advance, raising over a £1,000 for the synagogue. That *Shabbat*, the Sanctuary was a sea of red *kippot*. David Rigal sportingly raised extra money by dyeing his beard bright red. A couple of splendid photos appeared in the newsletter.
>
> Carolyn Simon (Pt. 3)

Chapter Three: Involvement in social issues

IN 1916 RABBI MATTUCK established a programme of lectures, talks and discussions by high-profile speakers. His Sunday morning services introduced in 1925 became a forum for debating contemporary social issues.

> To a remarkable degree, Dr Mattuck had already achieved this, [that is, making an impact on the social problems of the time] by his great eloquence and penetrating analyses of social problems from the religious point of view. Over and above his writings on the application of Judaism to contemporary social problems, the Sunday Services which he initiated at the St John's Wood Liberal Jewish Synagogue had a particularly great influence.
>
> Leslie Edgar[276]

Rabbi Mattuck was an ardent believer in social justice and became known as someone who was always on the side of the working man. During the Great Depression, he was outspoken on the plight of workers, describing the miners' strike as a 'lock-out', which was too controversial even for the socially conscious lay leadership of the LJS.[277] He was asked by Claude Montefiore to temper his sermons, but he remained resolute and even offered to tender his resignation. Montefiore demurred and the principle of 'freedom of the pulpit' was established at the synagogue.[278]

During the 1920s, the Alumni Society invited to its meetings speakers who talked about topical issues. The society founded a League of Nations Group under the leadership of the Rev. Perlzweig, which attended the League of Nations Union demonstration at Westminster Hall on Armistice Night in 1926 that was protesting at Germany's admission to the League.

When he was appointed as Assistant Minister in 1931, Leslie Edgar set himself three main tasks one of which was to bring the synagogue's influence to bear on the main social issues of the time.[279] As a vehicle for achieving this, he set up a synagogue Social Issues Committee made up of men and women widely experienced in public affairs. The Committee discussed and drew up reports on contemporary social issues, analysing problems from a religious perspective and making recommendations.

> [T]he reports were of considerable value in making the synagogue members generally conscious of the need to apply Jewish teachings to contemporary social problems and in helping them to form their own instructed judgements.
>
> Leslie Edgar[280]

An example of the committee's work was the report that it produced on the topic of Artificial Insemination, submitted to a Home and Scottish Office Committee set up by

---

[276] Rabbi Dr Leslie I Edgar, *Some Memories of My Ministry*.
[277] Pamela Fletcher Jones, 'Mr Duparc remembers'.
[278] Ibid.
[279] Rabbi Dr Leslie I Edgar, *Some Memories of My Ministry*.
[280] Ibid.

the Government. When the Committee's findings were published, they were largely in agreement with the views expressed by the LJS Social Issues Committee.[281]

The LJS's involvement in social issues continued after the Second World War. The synagogue maintained its involvement in the St Marylebone branch of the United Nations Association and, in 1965, a branch of Amnesty International, the '28 Group', was set up under the leadership of Rabbi Dr David Goldstein. The branch was successful in securing the release of two political prisoners, one in Rhodesia and one in Spain.

During the 1970s and 1980s, most Jewish organisations gave their support to Jewish people in the Soviet Union. The LJS was particularly supportive of those referred to as the 'refuseniks'. These were Jewish people living in the USSR who applied for and who were refused visas to emigrate, especially in the period following the 1967 Six Day War and who were subsequently persecuted or discriminated against for having done so.

An LJS Soviet Jewry Committee was set up in 1977 under the leadership of Doreen Isaacs. Over a twenty-year period, the Committee co-ordinated action by the synagogue. Members supported demonstrations and marches, they visited refusenik families in Moscow, Leningrad (St Petersburg), Kiev and Odessa. They adopted refuseniks and sent them messages of support, *Rosh Hashanah* cards, *Chanukkah* greetings and *seder* services for *Pesach*. The congregation 'adopted' Misha and Galina Kremen from Moscow throughout the fourteen years they were refused exit and supported them when they finally arrived in Israel. The Committee produced 100,000 Russian/Hebrew *seder* services, which were sent into the Soviet Union.

The Committee was particularly supported by Margaret and George Rigal who felt passionately about the issue.

> From the 1970s onwards, Margaret and I were very active in the Soviet Jewry movement and did our best to involve the congregation in its activities. We had met the father of an ex-Soviet prisoner early on and he introduced me to the movement. We wrote letters of appeal, signed by members of the synagogue, whenever various refuseniks were in trouble and we would deliver them to the Soviet Embassy ... Later on, the LJS Soviet Jewry Group attracted a significant number of people who were not otherwise active in the synagogue. A number of the people involved could be described as 'politicals' and not ones who normally attended services.
>
> George Rigal (Pt. 3)

The Soviet Jewry Committee attracted to the synagogue people who were not normally involved in its activities and interest in the Soviet Jewry permeated the synagogue, including the Religion School.

> There were also quizzes involving the whole school, special activities to stimulate the interest of the older classes and one event that stood out because of the enthusiasm it generated, a Soviet Jewry morning. We transformed The LJS into 'Soviet Russia' and organised activities in which the children experienced the frustrations for Jews of living under the Soviet regime. It was a large-scale 'game' in which lots of learning took place. Several former pupils mentioned the impact of this activity several years later.
>
> Michael Hart (Pt. 3)

---

[281] Ibid.

54. *George and Margaret Rigal (second and third from left in front row) with 'adopted' refusenik family, the Kremens (Mrs Kremen to George Rigal's right and their sons and Mr Kremen to Margaret Rigal's left). Friends and family of the Kremens to rear of the photograph. (undated)*

During the 1990s, the Soviet Jewry Committee took on the new role of helping and advising ex-Soviet Jews coming to settle in London, a number of whom were encouraged to become active members of the synagogue.

> My daughters have gone through the LJS Religion School; they also had their *Bat Mitzvahs* and *Kabbalat Torah* here. My wife and I did security and I sat on Council, but it was a little bit too early for me. My spoken English was not yet good enough. When we first joined the LJS, Rabbi David Goldberg helped me a lot, and Margaret and George Rigal became personal friends.
>
> Tim Sandler (Pt. 3)

Despite protests by some of those involved, the committee was disbanded in 1998.

George and Margaret Rigal were very active in raising awareness about the Soviet Jews outside the synagogue and beyond the Jewish community.

> I can remember going down the cricket queue in Lord's collecting signatures for petitions.
>
> George Rigal (Pt. 3)

Margaret Rigal gained a particularly high profile as a leading member of the intra-community pressure group, the Women's Campaign for Soviet Jewry, which is known as

55. *Soviet Jewry Group, April 1991. Yom ha-Atzma'ut celebration with Ukrainian dancers. LJS dancers include Bob and Ann Kirk (far left), Rabbi Helen Freeman (to rear of Bob Kirk), Yakov and Sue Paul (to left of Ann Kirk) and Michael Adler (far right). (1991)*

'The 35s'[282] This group organised protests and other activities designed to attract media attention. Political lobbying had proved effective, but Margaret Rigal and her colleagues felt that more was required to secure the safety and future of Russian refuseniks. The group went on to organise demonstrations, protests, education activities and publicity campaigns.

> Our overriding aim was that no Jew should be ignorant of the plight of Soviet Jewry. We hailed it as the Second Exodus. I feel blessed to have seen this happen in my lifetime.
>
> Margaret Rigal[283]

The work of The 35s group continues today. It now supports a Jewish Aid Committee, which gives financial assistance to new immigrants to Israel and also promotes cross-community children's organisations bringing Israeli Jewish, Muslim, Christian and Bedouin and Druze together in many parts of Israel. A second charity, the One to One

---

[282] See previous mention in Part One. The other leader was Rita Eker. The group was called 'The 35s' because this was the approximate age of the women involved. They were dubbed thus by the press in an article when they demonstrated on behalf of a Jewish dissident who was arrested and incarcerated in Odessa in 1971. The group operated from an office in Golders Green.

[283] Interview with Margaret Rigal, *LJ Today,* July/August 2008.

Children's Fund, supports children in need in South Africa, Kosovo, and southern India.[284] Margaret Rigal remains involved with these activities.

Under the leadership of Barbara Brandenburger, the multi-faith Bosnian Support Group was set up in 1991 to respond to the 'ethnic cleansing' taking place in Bosnia.

> Muslims, Orthodox and Catholic Christians and Jews lived harmoniously together until roused by nationalist politicians such as Milosevic and Tudjman to hate and fear each other. When we launched the Bosnian Support Fund in 1992, fired by a wish to do something, we chose to reflect that past and to spell out the strength that can spring from diversity.
>
> Barbara Brandenburger[285]

56. *Barbara Brandenburger, founder of the Bosnian Support Group. (undated, c. 1995)*

Initial membership of the Bosnian Support Group (BSG) included Rabbi John Rayner and his wife Jane, the novelist Lynn Reid Banks, and Fred Tuckman, President of the Anglo-Jewish Association (AJA), as well as a number of LJS members including Vivien Rose, Patricia Hartwig, and Prue and Stanley Baker.

To begin with, the BSG concentrated its attention on sending clothing and blankets to Ljubljana in Slovenia before 'adopting' an under-resourced Bosnian refugee community in Hrastnik hosted by the Slovenian Social Services. A Family Link Scheme was set up to match refugees to families in the UK, including many from the LJS, so they could send gifts and letters. A LJS work group met fortnightly to make blankets to be sent to the refugee community.[286]

> I got involved in the Bosnian Support Group through a notice in the *LJS News* asking people to make up packages containing little treats to send to refugees in the Hrastnik refugee camp. I eventually became the Group's secretary and liaised with the Charity Commission to broaden the objects of the charity to cover the longer-term needs of the refugees once the fighting had subsided. The organisers, Barbara Brandenburger and her friend Claude Murray, were an inspiration to me. Though they appeared at first sight to be

---

[284] Ibid.

[285] Barbara Brandenburger, 'Symbols Matter: Interfaith work improving the lives of those most in need', *LJS News*, December 2002/January 2003.

[286] *LJS News*, March 1993.

rather diffident and even slightly disorganised, in fact they were indefatigable in their determination to help the refugees. Through persistent and imaginative fundraising they provided a huge amount of practical and financial help to refugees in the camp, particularly through the courageous field-worker Bernard McMahon.

Vivien Rose

57. *Thursday Workshop knitting blankets for Bosnia. At head of table to left are Rita and Michael Adler. To Michael Adler's right are Daphne Isaacs and Betty Ungar, and the second person to Rita Adler's left is Joice Linde. Others unknown. (undated, c. 1996)*

The BSG successfully raised large amounts of funding to help the Hrastnik community, including from the LJS which, in 1995, donated £14,500 from the synagogue's *Yom Kippur* Appeal. The Bosnian Support Group later became the Bosnian Support Fund and continued to support the adopted camp for many years and help refugees to return to their homes when this was possible. The LJS helped to fund some of the activities, which included paying for medical care, purchasing livestock, paying for repairs to refugees' homes and providing educational grants.

A major event in 1998 was our Bosnian Lunch and Art Sale held in the Montefiore Hall, attended by the Bosnian Ambassador. The food cooked by refugees in this country was delicious – an amazing feat since most of them had been struck down by flu in the week before, but had struggled out of bed to help us.

Barbara Brandenburger[287]

The BSF's work in Bosnia continues today.

LJS members were also active in the Jews against Apartheid campaign and were vocal in criticising controversial legislation on asylum seekers which passed through Parliament in the 1990s. Rabbi David Goldberg led a deputation to meet the Home Secretary to express concern.

---

[287] Undated email from Barbara Brandenburger to David Rigal, kept by Barbara Brandenburger.

Chapter Four: Zionism and the State of Israel

A T THE TIME that the JRU was founded in 1902 there was very little interest in Zionism. For quite different reasons, both Orthodox and non-Orthodox Jewish people were opposed to the notion of a national homeland. Some Orthodox Jews were antipathetic because they believed that a homeland should not be established until the Messiah came. Progressive Jews feared that the existence of a Jewish state might place at risk the equal rights for which Jewish people in Britain and other countries had fought so hard. The idea of a Jewish homeland also seemed inconsistent with the JRU stance that being Jewish was a matter of belief rather than of nationality. Since the JRU had been set up to bring back to or retain people in their Jewish religion, Zionism, by offering a secular alternative to Jewish identity, ran counter to the Union's aims.

The three main leaders of the LJS – Rabbi Mattuck, Claude Montefiore and Lily Montagu – were all fervent anti-Zionists. They all wrote to the government opposing the Balfour Declaration of 1917, which pledged British support for the founding of a national entity in Palestine after the ending of the First World War.

> Rabbi Israel Mattuck was a formidable and intellectual opponent of Zionism, that is to say, he was in fundamental disagreement with it, but he understood it, and respected it, and kept himself extremely well informed about its affairs.
>
> John Rayner[288]

However, not all of the early leaders of the LJS were anti-Zionists. Harry S Lewis, one of the founder members, and the synagogue's second minister, the Rev. Maurice Perlzweig, were both outspoken Zionists. Rabbi Mattuck strove to work amicably with those holding Zionist views for the good of the Liberal movement, but his desire to do so was sometimes put to the test. For example, during the founding conference of the World Union for Progressive Judaism held at the LJS in 1926, Dr Stephen Wise challenged delegates to make positive statements about Zionism. Chairing the conference, Rabbi Mattuck ruled that the conference should remain neutral in its attitude towards Zionism.[289]

In 1929 the Board of Deputies invited the LJS to join the Jewish Agency which aimed to show the support of Anglo-Jewry for the British mandate for Palestine. The synagogue turned down the invitation on the grounds of its policy of neutrality towards Zionism.[290]

Although Rabbi Mattuck and the Rev. Perlzweig agreed to differ on the issue of a Jewish homeland, the situation proved unsustainable and Maurice Perlzweig eventually left the LJS in 1938 to serve at the North Western Reform Synagogue in Alyth Gardens.[291]

One of the LJS representatives on the Board of Deputies during the Second World War was Louis Gluckstein who, in 1942, became President of the synagogue. Although

---

[288] *Progressive Judaism Zionism and the State of Israel*, four talks given by Rabbi John Rayner at The Liberal Jewish Synagogue, in January and February 1983, Liberal Jewish Synagogue (1983).

[289] Ibid.

[290] LJS Annual Report, 1930.

[291] The Rev. Perlzweig left Alyth Gardens Synagogue in 1942 to emigrate to America where he sat on the Executive of the Jewish Agency and worked for the Zionist cause.

he claimed to be neutral on the issue of Zionism, he was actually seen as being an anti-Zionist. He had a major difference of opinion with the Board of Deputies, which by then was dominated by Zionists, and which passed a resolution urging the Government to make Palestine a Jewish state. Louis Gluckstein resented being instructed to follow this line in his utterances as a Conservative MP.[292]

As the movement for establishing a Jewish homeland gained momentum, Rabbi Mattuck became more vocal in his opposition to it.

> I very distinctly remember that when people were discussing the birth of the State of Israel as a national home, he was firmly against it. He went to America and had a very strenuous programme of visiting congregations there to dissuade them from supporting the idea of a national homeland in Israel. He gave a very, very strong sermon about it at the synagogue. He wanted the Jews to be scattered throughout the world so that they would share their message worldwide. He was terrified that once there was a homeland there would be troubles and anti-Israel feeling and that the Jews in the Diaspora would become second-class Jews.
>
> Margaret Rigal (Pt. 3)

The synagogue supported the Jewish Fellowship, which was established to promote the concept of Jews being a religious people united by their beliefs, history and traditions rather than being a national group with a homeland in Palestine.[293]

> During the 1940s, there was quite a lot of anti-Zionism, encouraged by Dr Mattuck and Basil Henriques and formally expressed through an organisation called the Jewish Fellowship. These anti-Zionist views were entirely based on religious beliefs. It was considered that a theocratic State would, through its policies, debase the fundamental religious tenets of Judaism, which is a view taken today by some ultra-Orthodox Jews who refuse to recognise the State of Israel. I was for a time actively involved as Vice Chairman of the Jewish Fellowship, as were Jane and Nancy Leverson, later Jane Levy and Nancy Caplin.
>
> Michael Nathan (Pt. 3)

The Fellowship was short-lived (it disbanded in 1948), although it continued to define the attitude of many Liberal Jewish people. By the time that the State of Israel came into being in 1948, the LJS was beginning to change its stance on matters, mainly because of concern for the fate of displaced European Jews. Rabbi Leslie Edgar, who succeeded Rabbi Mattuck as Senior Minister, discernibly shifted his views.

> The rise of Hitler and the Nazi movement put for me, at any rate, a complete end to this noble illusion and disappointed idealism. It was indeed a noble and worthy vision and I still greatly admire it and am glad that I shared it.
>
> Leslie Edgar[294]

Because of this shift, Leslie Edgar refused invitations from within the UK and from America to lead an anti-Zionist movement. He maintained a philosophy that Israel and

---

[292] Lawrence Rigal and Rosita Rosenberg, *Liberal Judaism: The First Hundred Years.*

[293] The Jewish Fellowship published a newsletter, *The Jewish Outlook,* which appears to have had an editorial input from the LJS. News relating to the synagogue dominates its pages.

[294] Rabbi Dr Leslie I Edgar, *Some Memories of My Ministry.*

the Diaspora were complementary to each other.[295] However, his more supportive attitude towards Israel did not prevent him from condemning those Israeli actions he saw as being unacceptable. In 1953, he described the slaughter of fifty people in the Jordanian village of Qibya as a 'shocking departure from Jewish moral standards'.[296]

Other LJS leaders remained wedded to their anti-Zionist views, including Louis Gluckstein (now Sir Louis), who came into conflict with Rabbi Herbert Richer, Minister of North London Progressive Synagogue because of Richer's unquestioning support for Israel at the time of the Suez Crisis. Rabbi Richer's speaking engagements at the LJS that year, arranged to cover Rabbi Edgar's absence on a sabbatical, were cancelled by the lay leadership of the synagogue because of the dispute.[297]

> Lily Montagu was equally vehement in her anti-Zionism. I believe that she refused to shake hands with Herbert Richer, who was a Zionist, when he gave a sermon at the LJS in favour of Israel. Lily Montagu was very upset by it.
>
> Margaret Rigal (Pt. 3)

As Israel began to establish its identity and to make progress in developing its economy, an increasing number of LJS members started to express support for Israel. The Women's Society raised money for Jewish immigrants in camps and reception centres in Israel. It was a sign of the times when, in 1953, the LJS established a Group of Friends of the Hebrew University of Jerusalem of which the President was synagogue member, Sir Keith Joseph.[298] When the new prayerbook, *Service of the Heart*, edited by Rabbi John Rayner and Rabbi Chaim Stern, was published in 1967, it contained several prayers for Israel, including a prayer for Israel Independence Day.

In 1966 Rabbi John Rayner co-produced with Rabbi Richer a statement recognising that the neutral stance of the Liberal movement was no longer appropriate. They recognised that, since both the World Union and other Progressive institutions had by now been established in Israel, there was an obligation on Liberal Jews to support them. Lily Montagu had already been doing so prior to her death in 1963.

> So, yes, we had our misgivings and our disappointments, but in the main our attitude to the State of Israel was in those twenty years a very positive one.
>
> John Rayner[299]

Those who knew him well suggested that, had he lived, even Rabbi Mattuck might have changed his stance.

> Mattuck was a pragmatist – given time, he would have seen the need and changed his mind [on the issue of Israel].
>
> Joe Foreman[300]

---

[295] Ibid.
[296] Rabbi Dr Leslie I Edgar, *Progressive Judaism Zionism and the State of Israel*.
[297] Lawrence Rigal and Rosita Rosenberg, *Liberal Judaism: The First Hundred Years*.
[298] Rabbi Dr Leslie I Edgar, *Progressive Judaism Zionism and the State of Israel*.
[299] Ibid.
[300] Rabbi David Goldberg, 'Mattuck the Boss', *LJS News*, December 1991.

The Six Day War in 1967 and the *Yom Kippur* War in 1973 accelerated the growing support and sympathy for Israel amongst LJS members. In 1967 the LJS raised £67,000 for the Israel Emergency Appeal.

> [R]emember it was the Six Day War in 1967 and suddenly everybody became a Zionist – even Sir Louis Gluckstein! At The Liberal Jewish Synagogue on the Friday after June 6 the service was packed. Everybody was coming to the synagogue to thank God for the miracle of the Jewish salvation because everybody thought that the Jews would be wiped out at the end of May because the United Nations had pulled out their troops and how could poor Israel defend itself?
>
> Sidney Brichto[301]

> By 1967 we were about as Israel-orientated as any other synagogal body in Anglo-Jewry, and the Six Day War both demonstrated the trend and advanced it still further. Like all other Jews, we identified ourselves with Israel as never before, both in her hour of peril and in her moment of triumph, and made common cause with all British Jewry in an emergency fundraising campaign of unprecedented magnitude.
>
> John Rayner[302]

While the two wars acted as a bonding experience for Anglo-Jewry, they also planted the seeds of disagreement on whether the victories should be used as an opportunity to make peace with the Arabs or as a chance to achieve the ideal of a 'Greater Israel' cherished by many. The leadership of the LJS was decidedly in the former camp. As time went on, and Israelis continued to occupy the West Bank, many people in the congregation began to feel concerned about the situation.

> I became a representative on the Board of Deputies of British Jews. I decided to do that because both Danya and I felt quite strongly that what was happening in Israel was wrong. We were in Israel just after the 1967 war. Two Israeli cousins of Danya did a tour of the West Bank, which is now called 'the Occupied Territories', including Jericho and everywhere. Everybody was really very kind. We broke down and got a puncture and someone mended the puncture for us. Kindness all round even though they knew this was an Israeli car with Israelis going down there. That sort of set us off on another line of how we felt about what was happening there and this continued and ended up by feeling that something needs to be done very actively to get the Jewish community in England to have a more supportive role of the left-wing in Israel in saying that the occupation is wrong. That is when we joined various groups, such as 'Peace Now'.
>
> Denis Glaser

> We had similar, very meaningful discussions when the Six Day War broke out in Israel in 1967. It really shocked and excited our class, the congregation and the whole of Anglo-Jewry. At that stage, we were pleased that Israel had managed to defend itself when attacked from all sides. Later, differing views began to emerge about whether Israel was right to hold on to the territories it had occupied and the impact this had on a lasting peace.
>
> Michael Hart (Pt. 3)

In 1970 the LJS launched an Israel Committee under the chairmanship of Joe Pinto which, the following year, invited the Israeli Ambassador to address one of its meetings. Over the

---

[301] ULPS Oral History Project interview with, Sidney Brichto. See Appendix 1.
[302] Rabbi Dr Leslie I Edgar, *Progressive Judaism, Zionism and the State of Israel.*

next two decades it was reconstituted on a number of occasions, including between 1974 and 1975 when it operated as the Joint Israel Appeal Committee (JIA) under the chairmanship of Malcolm Slowe. This marked the synagogue's increasing interest in supporting new immigrants to Israel. The JIA concentrated its attention on raising funds for *Magen David Adom* (the Israeli emergency ambulance service). The Israel Committee that followed it became involved in a wide range of activities, including arranging tours of Israel for young people and a trip to the first Progressive Kibbutz, *Yahel.* In 1978, the LJS was twinned with *Kedem* Synagogue, Tel Aviv, a Progressive congregation of 150 families.

By the late 1970s, the rabbis at the LJS were starting to voice their concerns publicly. In January 1981 Rabbi David Goldberg published an article entitled, 'Rather the bite of a friend than the kiss of an enemy', in the *ULPS News*. In this article he attacked the Begin Government's policy in the Occupied Territories. He saw these concerns as being a moral rather than a political issue and criticised the Liberal movement for not being similarly concerned. The article caused a furore in the movement and very divergent opinions were expressed.

Rabbis David Goldberg and John Rayner reiterated their criticisms of the Israeli Government in their 1981 High Holy Day message to the LJS. This was quoted extensively in the *Jewish Chronicle,* leading to calls for the ULPS to dissociate itself from the opinions voiced by the LJS rabbis. Major tensions developed between the LJS rabbis and Rabbi Sidney Brichto, Executive Director of the ULPS. With the backing of the lay leadership of the synagogue, Rabbis Rayner and Goldberg continued to condemn the occupation of the West Bank and, subsequently, the war in Lebanon.

> I also had many disagreements with Sidney about Israel. Sidney did some fairly 'political' things to try and discredit the views expressed by John and me on Israel and the Middle East, since they were very controversial at the time. We spoke out in our sermons and I wrote articles in *The Times* (such as my 1979 piece called 'Passover for the Palestinians too'), and in other newspapers, which questioned the occupation of the West Bank and Gaza and, subsequently, the war in Lebanon. This caused a big furore. At that time, Jewish people would criticise Israel privately, but not in public. John and I were disowned by the ULPS as well as the Board of Deputies, but fortunately we were backed by Council and the LJS tradition of 'freedom of the pulpit'. We stuck it out because we were very conscious of our duty as Liberal Jews to carry forward the tradition of speaking out on controversial issues of the day which had been established by the founders of the LJS.
>
> David Goldberg (Pt. 3)

They were at pains to point out that the criticism they made of Israeli policy did not mean that they were anti-Israel. They felt that, by being prepared to speak out on the things they saw as being wrong, they were in fact better friends than those who were prepared to support Israel whatever its actions.

Disagreements in the Liberal movement continued to rage for many years with Rabbi Rayner expressing repeated concerns about those whom he felt were supporting the expansionists rather than the peacemakers (the 'hawks' and the 'doves'). Despite these tensions, the LJS and other Liberal synagogues developed more effective support for Progressive Jewish communities in Israel and supported peace initiatives.

In 1985 Rabbi David Goldberg accepted an invitation to address a pro-Arab lobby group, which had been widely condemned by the Anglo-Jewish establishment. When asked to comment on this by the *Jewish Chronicle*, the then Chairman, Maxwell Stern, said that it could never be wrong to talk about peace.[303]

Today, the LJS does not stand alone in its questioning of Israeli policy, but differences of opinion still abound within the Liberal movement.

> The ULPS gradually became more nuanced in its approach – not exactly challenging but pointing out the need for a greater emphasis on peace – and John and I were eventually proved to be vindicated in our stance, although we had been 'prophets without honour.'
>
> David Goldberg (Pt. 3)

In general, younger members of the congregation are now more pro-Israel (although not unquestioning of some of Israel's policies), especially those who have been involved in the ULPS/Liberal Judaism pro-Israel youth groups and those who have been on organised tours of Israel. However, some longer-standing members remain very concerned about the existence of the State of Israel and current Israeli policies.

> The so-called remedy was a pseudo-messianic one which made a mess of Arab Jewry, resulting in a country which did not have frontiers. The international community set the State up. It should have insisted that it had frontiers, it never did.
>
> Walter Wolfgang

> Going to Israel for the first time was a very special experience, and I am deeply saddened by the current situation there and some of the policies adopted by the Government in response to the Palestinians. This is not the place to attempt a lengthy discussion on the issues, the background and possible solutions, but suffice it to say – as of course others have in other places with greater eloquence and knowledge, and less simplistically – that any course of action needs to be morally justified and to respect the strong ethical imperative of the Jewish faith.
>
> Deborah Lazarus

In recent years the congregation has largely concentrated its attention on supporting Progressive communities, fostering Arab/Israeli activities designed to promote friendship and mutual understanding, and exposing inequalities, especially the treatment of the Women of the Wall group praying at the Western Wall.

Under the chairmanship of Carol Roberts, the now long-standing Israel Group continues to organise events designed to promote understanding of political, religious, social, cultural and other issues connected with the State of Israel and the Middle East. It aims to offer LJS members and other interested people wide-ranging, high quality, balanced information, analysis and opinion, together with forums at which members are able to express their views.

> At a time when opinion is polarised and many throw up their hands in despair at the ever-decreasing prospects for peace amid calls for a one-state solution we continue to offer moral and financial support to our friends and colleagues in Israel. Whether it is co-existence among Arab and Jewish youth in Acre, or the success and growth of the Israel Movement for Progressive Judaism (IMPJ) and the Israel Religious Action Centre (IRAC), together with the Leo Baeck Education Centre-Haifa, LJS members help to provide hope that a new generation, imbued with a Liberal Jewish ethos, can and do have an impact in the areas of Human Rights and Social Action.
>
> Carol Roberts

---

[303] Eulogy at the funeral of Maxwell Stern, Golders Green, 13 January 1997, given by Rabbi John Rayner.

Chapter Five: The relationship between the LJS and the Liberal Jewish movement

IN 1909 THE Jewish Religious Union (JRU) changed its name to the Jewish Religious Union for the Advancement of Liberal Judaism as a signal of its intent to establish a new movement in Anglo-Jewry. To begin with, little progress was made in expanding the movement since the leaders of the JRU were preoccupied with establishing the new Liberal Jewish Synagogue.

For the first few years of the LJS's existence, the movement and the synagogue were almost synonymous. The JRU was based in the synagogue, its affairs were discussed by the synagogue Council rather than at separate meetings, and the leadership of the JRU and of LJS were the same.

> My memories as a child of Hill Street (which strictly speaking is the LJS rather than the JRU, but in those days, the two were not easy to differentiate from each other since exactly the same people were involved in both), Miss Montagu and my father, Rabbi Mattuck, ran both of them with Claude Montefiore.
>
> Dorothy Edgar[304]

However, the JRU and the LJS did have separate membership lists. It was possible to be a member of the JRU without being a member of the LJS, but not vice versa.

The arrival of Rabbi Mattuck from America in 1912 allowed more attention to be given to establishing a separate identity for the JRU and to setting up new Liberal congregations. In 1913 a subcommittee, chaired by Michael Green, was established to consider how the JRU should evolve.[305] Its members proposed that the JRU should have its own constitution and should consist of autonomous local sections, which would set their own subscription rates but pay a contribution to the central JRU body. It was also agreed that the JRU should produce a monthly magazine and should hold an annual religious conference.

These decisions determined the shape of the Liberal Jewish movement for many years to come. Michael Duparc, Secretary of the LJS, became Secretary of the newly constituted JRU and, early in 1914, the first *Bulletin of the Jewish Religious Union* appeared.

For the next twenty-five years Rabbi Mattuck, Lily Montagu and Claude Montefiore worked tirelessly to form new congregations. By 1920 the North London Synagogue in Stamford Hill and the West Central Synagogue in Bloomsbury had been set up. When the new congregations were established, Rabbi Mattuck, and later other ministers from the LJS, helped to run the services since there was a shortage of Liberal rabbis. In 1921 the Rev. Maurice Perlzweig was appointed as Assistant Minister at the LJS, but for the next few years he worked part-time at the North London Synagogue while he finished his studies at Cambridge. Similarly, when Rabbi Solomon Starrels was appointed by the LJS in 1928 he spent most of his time at the West Central Synagogue. Until that time, Lily Montagu had conducted most of the services with help from visiting ministers and lay readers.

---

[304] ULPS Oral History Project, interview with Dorothy Edgar. See Appendix 1.
[305] Lawrence Rigal and Rosita Rosenberg, *Liberal Judaism: The First Hundred Years*.

When Leslie Edgar became Assistant Minister at the LJS in 1931, he took on the role of preaching at new and emerging Liberal synagogues.

> My father [Rabbi Mattuck] and later on my husband [Leslie Edgar] preached one after the other at all these outlying congregations, some of which had ministers and some of whom didn't. I remember them, of course, going to West Central frequently, to South London and to North London as well as over to Dublin when that congregation was founded and to Liverpool, very many times. When they went to Dublin, of course, they had to stay overnight. I think it was many years before Dublin had a rabbi of its own. There was of course an enormous shortage of rabbis. They had to do all the JRU work as well as the LJS work.
>
> Dorothy Edgar [306]

The new synagogues largely modelled themselves on the LJS, but the congregations did sometimes adopt different approaches. The North London Synagogue decided to use its own prayerbook rather than the ones produced by Rabbi Mattuck, and the congregation of the West Central Synagogue wanted more traditional services.[307] However, for many years, differences in the operation of the new synagogues and the LJS were quite slight.

By the time of the 25th anniversary of the founding of the JRU, it had become recognised as a separate movement, but the LJS was still the dominant force within the movement. The LJS had a large congregation when the other Liberal synagogues were still struggling to establish themselves and it was far wealthier. As a result, well into the 1930s the LJS Council was still considering matters concerned with JRU policy, such as the relationship between the Liberal and the Reform movements and the content and production of prayerbooks. The JRU Committee largely confined itself to spreading Liberal Judaism and noting the progress being made by its constituent sections.

The central JRU body had limited funding and could not always afford to support the new congregations Lily Montagu was starting to develop outside London. Most newly formed congregations had the salaries of their ministers paid for either by the JRU or the LJS. The LJS was the main source of the Spread Liberal Judaism Fund, but it was by then finding it hard to raise the sums required.

During the 1930s, the JRU started to bring the different communities together for conferences and other activities. After the end of the war, the Union prepared itself for a programme of expansion by appointing its first Organising Secretary, Henry Solomons, a member of the West Central Synagogue. He was assisted by Peggy Lang who was appointed as Organising Secretary of the LJS in 1945. From this point onwards, there were increasing signs of a changed relationship between the LJS and the ULPS (as it had been renamed in 1944).

Following a disagreement between the Board of Deputies and LJS over the matter of marriage secretaries in 1949, the ULPS issued an instruction that Liberal synagogues should not nominate representatives to the Board until the matter was resolved. A decade previously it would have been the LJS Practices and Rites Committee which would have issued such policy guidance rather than the Liberal movement.

---

[306] ULPS Oral History Project, interview with Dorothy Edgar. See Appendix 1.
[307] Lawrence Rigal and Rosita Rosenberg, *Liberal Judaism: The First Hundred Years*.

Towards the end of the 1940s, the ULPS set up a committee that evolved into a Ministers' Meeting (later the Ministers' Conference and subsequently the Rabbinic Conference), to bring together the ministers, rabbis and lay minsters[308] of Liberal synagogues. These meetings started to discuss religious practices which had previously been decided by the LJS.

When in 1961 Rabbi Leslie Edgar resigned from his post as Senior Minister at the LJS for health reasons, he was succeeded by John Rayner, who decided that the time had come for a more democratic approach to be taken to the leadership of the ULPS. Rabbi Mattuck and Leslie Edgar had, until then, automatically been accepted as the leading ministers within the movement.

> In those days, the Senior Rabbi of the LJS was de facto religious head of the movement, and my impression was that Leslie [Edgar] rather fancied himself as presiding over a synod of gaitered bishops at the Athenaeum.
>
> David Goldberg[309]

John Rayner proposed that there should be an election for the chairmanship.

> When Rabbi Edgar retired as Chairman of the Ministers' Conference in 1963, he thought that I should take over. I was persuaded by my American colleagues that we should become more democratic and that the Chairman of the Ministers' Conference should be democratically elected from time to time. I therefore insisted to Rabbi Edgar (much to his dismay), that I would not take over as Chairman unless I was elected.
>
> John Rayner[310]

When the election took place at the Ministers' Conference in 1962, equal votes were cast for John Rayner and for Rabbi Bernard Hooker. Since John Rayner was shortly to depart for America to complete his rabbinic studies at the Hebrew Union College, it was agreed that he should hold the chairmanship for that year and that Bernard Hooker should then take over. Since that time there have been regular elections for the role.

The ULPS adopted a new constitution in 1962, increasing the size of its Executive. Although the aim was to make the movement more inclusive, the LJS's primacy was maintained by a clause stating that at least three members of the Executive should be from the LJS.

However, the real watershed in the evolving relationship between the LJS and the ULPS occurred in 1964 when Rabbi Sidney Brichto,[311] who had been appointed as interim Assistant Rabbi at the LJS, was offered the appointment as the first Executive Director and Vice-President of the ULPS. This new role had been established following the publication of a report on the Union's future organisation and structure produced by Rabbi Bernard Hooker.

---

[308] As there were no systematic arrangements for training Liberal and Progressive rabbis at this point, there were insufficient ministers to serve the new congregations being established. It was therefore decided to establish 'lay ministers', who could preach and lead services at the new synagogues.

[309] David Goldberg, 'Rabbi Leslie Edgar', *LJS News*, July 2011.

[310] ULPS Oral History Project, interview with John Rayner. See Appendix 1.

[311] See photograph 23.

Rabbi Brichto was intent on creating a separate identity for ULPS and set about doing so by acting on another recommendation contained in Rabbi Hooker's report. This was that the ULPS should move to its own premises. Since the LJS's inception in 1911, the JRU (later the ULPS) had been based at the synagogue. For many years ULPS affairs were administered by the same people who supported the work of the synagogue and the Union did not have its own telephone number until 1958.[312]

> The LJS was seen as the Liberal Jewish movement. And it was my first role as Director to make the ULPS independent of St John's Wood, to the extent that other congregations would not feel that the Union was the LJS of St John's Wood. Everyone used to say, 'Well St John's Wood says this, St John's Wood says that' because its President was the Senior Minister of the LJS. Lily Montagu, the founder, of course, of the Liberal Movement, would attend the LJS Council meetings, and at the end she would be asked to talk about the other groups. It always felt, at the time, that really all the Liberal synagogues were sort of groups, to some extent, of the LJS. So it was my objective to give it independence, which eventually we did, first of all by making it financially independent, by every congregation giving the same amount (in proportion to their members), and the LJS not giving more than any other congregation; secondly, eventually by moving to Whitfield Street.
>
> Sidney Brichto[313]

The new ULPS headquarters in Whitfield Street, adapted from the West Central Liberal Synagogue, were opened in 1971 and the building named the Montagu Centre.[314]

The other development reinforcing the distinction between the LJS and the ULPS was the opening of the Edgwarebury Cemetery in Edgware in 1975. Since it was acquired by the LJS in 1913, the Pound Lane Cemetery in Willesden had provided burial space for other Liberal congregations in London. However, by the 1960s the LJS was becoming concerned that it would run out of space at the cemetery if this arrangement were to continue. It asked the ULPS to start looking for other facilities.

After protracted investigations, a site was located in Edgwarebury Lane and a consortium established between the ULPS, the West London Synagogue and the Spanish and Portuguese Synagogue. This meant that no financial and administrative arrangements were now needed between the LJS and other London Liberal synagogues and therefore placed the LJS on the same footing as other ULPS congregations. Although it remained the oldest and largest Liberal congregation, it no longer dominated the movement.[315]

The leadership of the LJS was not opposed to the independence of the Liberal movement, but tensions now developed between the synagogue and the leadership of the ULPS. Over the years, the LJS had become accustomed to speaking for the movement, and it was some time before a new equilibrium in the balance of power between the LJS and ULPS was established.

> The synagogue's relationship with Liberal Judaism and the Rabbinic Conference has had its ups and downs. There used to be some tensions between John Rayner and Sidney Brichto.

---

[312] Lawrence Rigal and Rosita Rosenberg, *Liberal Judaism: The First Hundred Years*.

[313] ULPS Oral History Project, interview with Sidney Brichto. See Appendix 1.

[314] The site was redeveloped in 1993 and the entrance to the Montagu Centre was relocated around the corner in Maple Street.

[315] Lawrence Rigal and Rosita Rosenberg, *Liberal Judaism: The First Hundred Years*.

The ULPS had offices in the old LJS building, and they were very keen to move out from under the influence of the LJS and have their own building. John and Sidney disagreed about who should speak for Liberal Judaism. John felt it should be the Senior Rabbi of the LJS, as it were by historic right, whereas Sidney felt it should be the Executive Director of the ULPS. My view was always: 'let a hundred flowers bloom'. Everybody should speak for Liberal Judaism; the more people who get in the papers, get on the radio, write articles, the better for the movement.

David Goldberg (Pt. 3)

There were also tensions during the late 1960s and early 1970s relating to the setting up of new Liberal and Progressive communities. The LJS was concerned about the loss of its members to the new communities, which it saw as weakening the position of the LJS, while the Liberal movement maintained that having a nucleus of knowledgeable and committed Liberal Jews was essential to establishing viable congregations.

Notwithstanding these tensions, in 1983, after a gap of nearly ten years since the death of the previous President of the ULPS (Eva, Marchioness of Reading), Malcolm Slowe, a prominent member of the LJS and ULPS Chairman from 1965 to 1970, was appointed as ULPS President. He established a good rapport with both the professional and lay leadership of the movement. On his death in 1987, he was succeeded by Lord Goodman, also a loyal member of the LJS and an admirer of John Rayner.[316] The current Chairman of Liberal Judaism is an LJS member (Lucian Hudson) and Rabbi Danny Rich, Chief Executive of Liberal Judaism is the son of John Rich who taught for a long time in the LJS Religion School.

Over the last twenty years or so there has been a further shift in the relationship between the LJS and the ULPS which was renamed Liberal Judaism in 2002 on the occasion of its 100th anniversary. Although the synagogue continues to exert significant influence on the movement because of its size and its age, it no longer holds sway in the movement, nor occupies the role of 'first among equals'. There is now a two-way relationship, with the LJS influencing ULPS thinking and vice versa. However, some commentators think that the pendulum has swung too far and the LJS is too detached from the Liberal movement.

Chapter Six: Interfaith dialogue

RABBI MATTUCK'S SUNDAY services instigated during the 1920s became a focus for interfaith dialogue. They were attended by many non-Jewish people and provided a forum where they and Jewish people could meet and gather information about Judaism at a time when anti-Semitism was being fomented in Germany and spread by British Fascists such as Oswald Mosley.

---

[316] Arnold Goodman, *Tell Them I'm On My Way*, cited in ibid.

The synagogue's involvement in interfaith dialogue was placed on a more formal footing during the latter part of the 1920s. In 1924 leading members of the synagogue involved in its Social Service Committee, which was chaired by Mrs McArthur, consulted a number of other religious bodies, set up an organising committee and convened an interfaith conference. The aim of the conference was to provide 'an opportunity for Jews and Christians to confer together on the basis of their common ideals and with mutual respect for differences in belief'.[317] The conference had as its theme 'Religion as an Educational Force'.

Despite the criticism levelled at the synagogue by Orthodox communities because of this involvement, a further conference was held the following year on the topic of 'Religion and the Race Problem'. This led in 1927 to the founding of the London Society of Jews and Christians, the oldest interfaith organisation of its kind and out of which subsequently grew the Council of Christians and Jews.

Rabbi Mattuck delivered many addresses on Jewish religion and theological language at meetings of the London Society of Jews and Christians, some of which were later published in a book, *In Spirit and in Truth*.[318] He preached at a number of churches and was a member of the Religious Bodies Consultative Committee chaired by the Dean of Chichester.

> [A]s a rabbi he [Rabbi Mattuck] threw himself into the work of promoting understanding between Jews and Christians, and through his work and by his public pronouncements on religious issues, he exerted great religious influence, far beyond the Jewish community itself, and became one of the leaders of religious thought in our generation.
>
> Lily Montagu[319]

Rabbi Mattuck's role in the London Society of Jews and Christians was taken over by the Rev. Leslie Edgar in 1951. He then held the position of Joint Chairman with Dr Edward Carpenter, Archdeacon and later Dean of Westminster until 1978.

> In the field of Jewish-Christian relationships, I was already taking a considerable part even in this early part of my Ministry before 1939. I was associated with the Council of Christians and Jews from its inception in 1942 and frequently lectured for it. I took part in trio Teams – a joint platform of an Anglican, a Roman Catholic and a Jew – who expounded some aspect of their various religions – their agreements and their differences – or who spoke of their various religious attitudes to some contemporary problems.
>
> Leslie Edgar[320]

Involvement in interfaith activities was not confined to LJS rabbis. All of the LJS's main societies set up in its early years invited non-Jewish people to talk at their meetings about their different practices and perspectives. When it was formed in 1933, the Younger Members' Organisation (YMO) established contact with a Quaker organisation and organised informal meetings with other young Christians.

---

[317] LJS Annual Report, 1924.
[318] Rev. George Alfred Yates (Editor), *In Spirit and in Truth, Aspects of Judaism and Christianity*, Society of Jews and Christians (1934). This was first Jewish/Christian symposium ever published in England.
[319] Lily Montagu, 'Rabbi Dr Israel Mattuck, Memorial Tribute', In Memoriam issue of *Liberal Jewish Monthly*, June 1956.
[320] Rabbi Dr Leslie I Edgar, *Some Memories of My Ministry*.

During 1936 the YMO met on a monthly basis with students from the Theological College of London. Regular meetings were also held with young Catholics and with Wesleyans. The meetings were sometimes held at the synagogue, but the YMO was also invited to meet with other religious groupings at their respective meeting places.[321] These meetings helped to generate an understanding of the plight of Jewish people in Europe and, after the German pogroms of 1938, large numbers of Christians attended services at the synagogue to show their sympathy.[322]

In 1949 Leslie Edgar organised the first act of joint worship at the LJS. Representatives from local churches were invited to participate in a Friday night service at which Canon Collins of St Paul's Cathedral gave the address.[323] This service became the first of many occasions when Christians were invited to the LJS to take part in services.

Rabbi Leslie Edgar was also involved in a number of other interfaith organisations and was often asked to give lectures on interfaith issues, such as his lecture on 'Co-operation Between World Religions', given to the General Assembly of the Unitarian and Free Christian Churches in 1952. In 1961 he invited The World Congress of Faiths to hold its annual service at the synagogue.

When Rabbi Leslie Edgar retired, Rabbi John Rayner was equally involved in interfaith activities and in 2002, he received a CBE for his contribution to interfaith dialogue, especially for his work with the Council of Christians and Jews.

58. *Rabbi John Rayner with Archbishop Gregorios of Thyateira and Great Britain at the Council of Christians and Jews interfaith award ceremony at the LJS. (1996)*

---

[321] LJS Annual Report, 1936.
[322] LJS Annual Report, 1939.
[323] Ibid.

59. *Bishop of London preaching at the LJS. From left: Rita Adler, Willie Kessler, Rabbi Helen Freeman, Dr David Hope (Bishop of London), Rabbi David Goldberg, and the Israeli Ambassador and his wife, Moshe and Hannah Raviv. (1994)*

During the 1970s, Rabbi David Goldberg extended the synagogue's interfaith work by promoting dialogue with the rapidly increasing Muslim community in London. He initiated meetings involving a tripartite dialogue between the LJS, St John's Church and the recently built London Central Mosque in Regent's Park.

> In respect of interfaith work, I was something of a pioneer. As Associate Rabbi, I organised the first 'trialogue meetings', as we called them. They were with John Slater, the vicar of St John's Church (the church at the roundabout), who was a lovely, lovely man and, alas, died too young, and with Zaki Badawi, who sadly is also dead. He was the first Director at the mosque in Regent's Park. There was a lot of Christian-Jewish dialogue going on at the time, but no meetings with the increasing Muslim population. So, when they built the mosque in the late 1970s, we decided at Council to send a gift to the mosque as a gesture of friendship and welcome. Zaki (later Sir Zaki) was a great Director and a good public face for Islam. He was very outward-looking, and had to overcome a lot of suspicion amongst his own flock, many of whom really did not want this connection with either the synagogue or the church. But he prevailed and the early meetings drew very large audiences.
>
> David Goldberg (Pt. 3)

> I was on the Services Committee many years ago. I enjoyed interfaith events, including the tripartite ones before 1988 with the Muslims from the London Central Mosque and members of the St John's Wood Church on the roundabout.
>
> Jocelyne Tobin (Pt. 3)

The meetings continued for a number of years, even after the Lebanon War in 1982. A decision was eventually made to discontinue the meetings when they started to become a focal point for political discord.

60. *Rabbi David Goldberg presenting an inscribed copy of Siddur Lev Chadash to the Pope John Paul II, at a small audience with Liberal and Reform rabbis in January 1999 at the Vatican. Photograph owned by Rabbi David Goldberg. (1999)*

> There were very strongly opinionated Muslims as well as strongly opinionated Jews and it was turning unpleasant and bitter.
>
> David Goldberg (Pt. 3)

However, interfaith dialogue continued in other forms. History was made in February 1994 when the Bishop of London, the Right Reverend David Hope, became the first non-Jew to give a sermon at the LJS, becoming one of only a handful of Christian clergy to preach at a British synagogue. The newly appointed Israeli Ambassador, Moshe Raviv, and his wife, Hannah, were present at the service. During the following year, Rabbi Helen Freeman organised a series of 'dialogue meetings' with St Mary's in Primrose Hill in which many congregants participated.

> [I enjoyed] the meetings in the 1990s at our local church, St Mary's in Elsworthy Road. These were very fruitful – we discussed our comparative approaches to life events.
>
> Jocelyne Tobin (Pt. 3)

In 1999 David Goldberg was awarded the Gold Medal of the International Council of Christians and Jews for his 'outstanding contribution to interfaith harmony'. He was also awarded an OBE for his interfaith work in 2004.

> Interfaith work has always given me great pleasure because it is such a civilised discourse. I have said, and people like Zaki and my Christian friends have always agreed with me, that we have more in common with a liberal person, with a small 'l', of another faith than with fundamentalists of our own. Liberal people can always find common cause; it's the fundamentalists who cause problems.
>
> David Goldberg (Pt. 3)

In recent years, the synagogue has continued to host a variety of interfaith events such as the Multi Faith Service of Reconciliation (sometimes also referred to as the Service of Remembrance), held on 21 July 2005 to remember the victims of the London bombings of 7 July. In December 2007 Rabbi Mark Solomon officiated at the Westminster Abbey celebration of Advent and *Chanukkah,* the first such event to be held in London.

> I attended the Multi-Faith Service of Remembrance and Hope at the LJS on 21 July and found it uplifting. In spite of travel problems on that day, it was heartening to see the packed synagogue ... When Sheikh Dr Zaki Badawi opened his address pointing out that 'We are all children of Abraham', it gladdened my heart.
>
> Alice Lovell[324]

A group of committed Jews, Christians and Muslims from the St John's Wood area continue to meet on a monthly basis to study each other's sacred texts. Meetings of the Tuesday Texts group rotate between the LJS, St John's Wood Church and the London Central Mosque.

In January 2006, the Social Action Committee organised a visit by a group of LJS Members to the London Central Mosque in Regent's Park. In 2007 a similar visit was made to the Hindu temple in Neasden. Rabbi Wright continues the LJS's long involvement in the London Society of Jews and Christians and is a founder member of a local Jewish, Christian and Muslim clergy group called Pathways: Faiths in Conversation, which has not only facilitated good relations with mosques and churches in North West London, but also improved intra-faith working relationships with local Masorti and Orthodox synagogues.

> The Pathways Roadshow takes clergy from each faith into schools to meet staff and pupils, and answer their questions. It's not just a chance for children to learn about different faiths, it's a powerful demonstration of interfaith co-operation and harmony.
>
> Steven Derby

In 2010, as the result of its long history of interfaith work, the LJS was awarded a grant by the Community Development Foundation's Faiths in Action Programme. Further funding followed from Awards for All, which enabled the synagogue to appoint an Interfaith Consultant, Steven Derby, to continue and develop the LJS's interfaith work. On 6 December 2010 a *Chanukkah* open house party was attended by representatives of many different faiths including the Church of England, the Catholic Church, the Greek Orthodox Church, the London Central Mosque, the Hindu Forum of Britain and the Sikh community, which attracted wide publicity. Since then there has been a successful interfaith *Tu bi Sh'vat* celebration and Communal *Seder.*

> I was proud of our community, and everyone there, and that it [the *Tu bi Sh'vat* celebration] was a beautiful little reminder of what is possible between people.
>
> Harriett Goldenberg

---

[324] *LJS News*, November 2005, letter to the Editor.

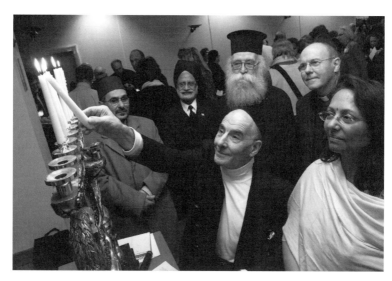

61. *Open House Chanukkah Service December 2010 showing back row from left: Sheikh Seddiki Sidi Fawzi (London Central Mosque and Islamic Cultural Centre), Rajinder Singh Bhasin (Central Gurdwara, Khalsa Jatha, London), Rev. Deacon Meliton Oakes (Chapel of the Annunciation Thyateira House), Fr. Richard Sloan (Hospital and Hospice of St John and St Elizabeth), front row from left: Bob Kirk (President, The Liberal Jewish Synagogue), Bharti Tailor (Hindu Forum of Britain). Photograph by Polly Hancock. (2010)*

62. *Pathways interfaith dialogue group visit to St Clement Danes School 29 November 2010 to celebrate Interfaith Week. LJS Rabbi, David Wilfond, with children from the school. (2010)*

Section Five: The people and the place

Chapter One: LJS rabbis

S INCE THE SYNAGOGUE was established in 1911, there have been five Senior Rabbis at the LJS: Israel Mattuck (from 1912 until 1948 and Rabbi Emeritus until his death in 1954), Leslie Edgar (Assistant Minister from 1931 and Senior Minister from 1948 until 1961 and Rabbi Emeritus until his death in 1984), John Rayner (Assistant Minister from 1957 until 1961, Senior Rabbi from 1961 to 1989 and Rabbi Emeritus until his death in 2005), David Goldberg (Associate Rabbi from 1975, Senior Rabbi from 1989 to 2004 and now Rabbi Emeritus), Alexandra Wright (Associate Rabbi between 1986 and 1989 and Senior Rabbi since 2004). Each of the Senior Rabbis has made or continues to make a distinctive contribution to the LJS and its congregation.

Personal recollections for the first three Senior Rabbis are given below followed by brief formal biographies. As they are both still very involved in the LJS as Senior Rabbi and Rabbi Emeritus respectively, there are fewer memories relating to Rabbi Wright[325] and Rabbi Goldberg.[326] Readers are referred to Rabbi Wright's foreword to this book and to her memories in Part Three, and to Rabbi Goldberg's memories (also in Part Three).

This chapter also covers other rabbis who have served at the LJS over the last hundred years who are remembered well by congregants.

Rabbi Israel Mattuck

Despite the early challenges he faced as the first Liberal minister in Britain, Rabbi Mattuck's contribution was immense.[327]

He is remembered foremost as an exceptionally powerful and compelling preacher. He was sometimes referred to as 'Dr Dramatic'.

> I was very impressed with him because, at that time of my life, I was very interested in the English language and he had a wonderful flow and way with words. I could sit almost enthralled, listening to how he would form a sentence and develop a theme. I was interested in the fact that I could understand what he was trying to put over – when you are young you think you don't have to listen but I was very interested ... I envied his command of the English language and tried to emulate him.
>
> Hannah Feldman

> When I was a child we used to come down to London from Glasgow where we lived and stay with my grandparents and they took us to synagogue on a Saturday. I still remember the dramatic sermons Dr Mattuck would give, one would sit there and no one would move.

---

325 See photographs 43, 45, 47, 68, and 85.
326 See photographs 20, 48, 59, 60, and 68.
327 See photographs 5, 14, 18, and 63.

63. *Rabbi Mattuck preaching. From left: Rabbi Leslie Edgar, the Rev. Philip Cohen,*
Rabbi Mattuck, Lily Montagu. Photograph by Krongold. (1951)

He was more like an actor really; everyone was mesmerised. Even today I can visualise him in my mind's eye giving his sermons.

Aileen Davis

He varied his style to maintain the interest of his audiences and his oratory was accompanied by theatrical arm and hand movements.

I also remember Dr Mattuck as a very charismatic character, throwing his arms around.

Violet Levy[328]

At the end of each service Rabbi Mattuck would put his hands in the air and bless us all; he looked as if he was going to fly up in the air.

Martin Slowe

He captured the imagination of young people with his theatricality.

I remember seeing Dr Mattuck preach when I was just nine years old. Although his sermons were too learned for me at that age, he still captured my imagination. When he gave the priestly benediction, he stood up on his tippy toes to give it emphasis. I thought he was going to levitate to heaven and was very disappointed when he didn't! I had recently been to a performance of *Faust* and become confused between Marguerite, who I had seen hoisted up above the stage, and Mephistopheles because Dr Mattuck, like Mephistopheles, was smallish and saturnine. After this first encounter with Dr Mattuck, whenever I saw him I recalled my disappointment. Many years later I told this story to his daughter, Dorothy Edgar, who thought it was hilarious.

Jean Russell

---

[328] 'Anniversaries: Milestones in Liberal Judaism'.

Under Rabbi Mattuck's leadership the LJS developed rapidly.

> But in 1912 they [the leaders of the JRU] had only laid the foundations. It fell to Rabbi
> Mattuck, far more than any single individual, to build on them, to create the superstructure,
> to transform the tentative experiment into an abiding reality and he did it with a superb
> combination of qualities – of learning and wisdom, of oratorical and literary power, and
> administrative skill – and with unremitting dedication.
>
> John Rayner[329]

Rabbi Mattuck was a prolific liturgist and the contents of his prayerbooks for the
synagogue endure and are still admired today.

> The Liberal Jewish Prayerbook which he edited in three volumes, and which was used
> throughout our movement for some forty years, was strikingly innovative, if somewhat
> idiosyncratic, and ranks amongst the most interesting creations of its genre.
>
> John Rayner[330]

He was able to communicate with all manner of people, but especially young people with
whom he was able to strike up a strong rapport.

> As a youngster, I found him in fact extremely approachable … We had these 'Brains Trusts'
> where you could ask him questions ... I well remember on one occasion when afterwards I
> was talking to Mrs Mattuck and was saying, cheeky young fellow that I was, 'The trouble
> with your husband is that he never answers the question you ask him but he tells you so
> much that you feel that you've got to be satisfied.' The old boy came by, 'Eh, eh what are
> you saying?' I said he hadn't heard, but he had heard. He said, 'The trouble with Greenberg
> is that he always gets the right answer but he doesn't like the answer.'
>
> Robert Greenberg

People felt able to turn to him for advice and support.

> [H]e cared for the problems of every individual. We could all come to him with our
> difficulties and these were straightened out by his clear intellect and practical sympathy.
>
> Lily Montagu[331]

He was a gifted teacher of both young people and adults.

> He had that characteristic of a good teacher in that he never told you anything – you told
> him – and if you were in the Confirmation class that Mattuck took, it was quite unforgettable
> … although I can't remember everything that Mattuck said. I just remember the feeling of
> being there and taking in the wonderful ideas that one had never thought of before.
>
> Maxwell Stern[332]

> Whether he was teaching children in a class or sitting in his study with a group of young
> people around him or taking an adult study group, he roused such interest in his hearers
> that he made each one feel the need and the desire to learn more.
>
> Marjorie Moos[333]

---

[329] 'The Spirit of Israel Mattuck', sermon by Rabbi John Rayner at the LJS, 25 January 1992.
[330] John Rayner '80th Anniversary of Rabbi Mattuck's induction', *LJS News*, January 1992.
[331] 'Address given at the memorial service on Tuesday April 8 1954', special edition of *Liberal Jewish Monthly*, *In Memoriam of Israel I Mattuck*.
[332] ULPS Oral History Project, interview with Maxwell Stern. See Appendix 1.
[333] Marjorie H Moos, 'His Greatness As a Teacher', special edition of *Liberal Jewish Monthly In Memoriam of Israel I Mattuck*.

Rabbi Mattuck was particularly good at interpreting Judaism for non-Jews.

> I was once told by Dr James Parkes, the leading Christian historian of Jewish-Christian relations, that when he had a query about Judaism, he would go to Dr Mattuck in preference to Orthodox Jewish Scholars because he would be sure that from him he would get an objective answer to his queries.
>
> John Rayner[334]

He often spoke and wrote on social issues, never hesitating to challenge what he regarded as reactionary views. However, his forthright opinions sometimes aroused controversy in the wider Jewish community, such as his reference to *kashrut* as 'an ancient Jewish prejudice', and his willingness to marry divorced women who had not obtained a *Get* (a Jewish divorce certificate), the institution of which, he declared, violated the principle of equality for men and women.[335]

> Conferences were organised in London and the provinces. These provoked lively reactions from Orthodox Jewish opponents, but usually his eloquence, personal charm, and formidable Jewish knowledge carried the day.
>
> David Goldberg[336]

He was a democrat and was always very supportive of working people. He was vehemently opposed to Zionism, a stance that he brought with him from America.

Although Rabbi Mattuck had a keen sense of humour, he was quite austere in his tastes.

> He was very much against dressy wedding parties and one of his objections to *Bar Mitzvahs* was the ostentatious parties associated with them.
>
> Ann Kirk

Rabbi Mattuck was not always the easiest person with whom to work. He was clearly fair in his dealings with LJS staff, but he was also quite demanding. Being capable himself of working long hours under pressure, he expected the same of others.

> He expects grand opera on tuppence halfpenny.
>
> Ivor Warren[337]

Rabbi Mattuck played an outstanding role in the development of other Liberal Jewish congregations and a key role in the development of the World Union for Progressive Judaism.

> To Dr Mattuck we owe, more than to anybody else, the building of the other Liberal congregations throughout this country. He felt the urgency of every call that came to us. No group should starve because of the delay in satisfying their spiritual hunger.
>
> Lily Montagu[338]

He was well known for his press articles and his broadcasts, but wrote comparatively few books.

> Dr Mattuck's time for literary work was limited, for he was a man of action.
>
> Lily Montagu[339]

---

[334] ULPS Oral History Project, interview with John Rayner. See Appendix 1.
[335] *The Jewish Chronicle*, 9 April 1954.
[336] Rabbi David Goldberg, entry in *Oxford Dictionary of National Biography*.
[337] Quoted in 'The Spirit of Israel Mattuck', sermon by Rabbi John Rayner at the LJS, 25 January 1992.
[338] 'Address given at the memorial service on Tuesday April 8 1954', special edition of *Liberal Jewish Monthly*, *In Memoriam of Israel I Mattuck*.
[339] Ibid.

On a personal level, Rabbi Mattuck enjoyed tennis, walking, mountain climbing and a good cigar. He also enjoyed visits to theatres and galleries and was a very amusing storyteller.[340] He was a keen gardener and relished spending time with his family in their country home in Long Crendon, Buckinghamshire.

> He was a great lover of the country, of flowers, and of beauty. He was a great gardener.
>
> Leslie Edgar[341]

He received a great deal of support from his wife, Edna, who was very involved in the Women's Society and synagogue affairs generally.

> Mrs Mattuck was particularly charming to me. She was small, roundish and had very sharp, bright black eyes. She always appeared to be having a wonderful time and she made everybody around her, as far as I was concerned, have a wonderful time too. She was very efficient and fully involved in the synagogue.
>
> Margaret Rigal (Pt. 3)

Rabbi Mattuck's contribution to the synagogue (and generations of Liberal Jews beyond the LJS) was, above all, a spiritual one. Many were inspired by him to become rabbis or take on leadership roles in the Progressive movement. In March 1987, at the end of the celebration of the LJS's 75th year, Rabbi John Rayner summed up Rabbi Mattuck's contribution as follows:

> What Rabbi Mattuck did then – with power and fervour that still communicates over the decades – was to insist on honesty in thought and practice, to demand that Judaism be a living faith that unifies the love of God and love of man in practical everyday behaviour, and to reaffirm boldly that Tradition, no matter how hallowed, must always remain subservient to the still greater priority of the Truth.
>
> John Rayner[342]

Rabbi Leslie Edgar

64. *Rabbi Leslie Edgar, Assistant Minister 1938–48, Senior Minister 1948–61 (became Rabbi 1951), Rabbi Emeritus 1961–84. Photograph by Elliott and Fry Ltd. (undated, c. 1980)*

---

[340] 'Dr Mattuck's seventieth birthday', *Liberal Jewish Monthly,* February 1954.
[341] Rabbi Leslie I Edgar, 'A personal appreciation', special edition of *Liberal Jewish Monthly, In Memoriam of Israel I Mattuck.*
[342] 'The Spirit of Israel Mattuck', sermon by Rabbi John Rayner at the LJS, 25 January 1992.

Rabbi Leslie Edgar[343] was identified at an early age as a potential future rabbi and was prepared by Rabbi Mattuck for the role.[344]

> Well, Leslie Edgar was in Religion School at the same time as I was but he was senior to me and even then I can remember that when they were short of a teacher, he took a class. I think he always seemed to know where he was going.
>
> Maxwell Stern[345]

> Dr Mattuck gave me lessons in more advanced Hebrew. It was clear that he hoped I would train for the Liberal Jewish Ministry.
>
> Leslie Edgar[346]

He became Rabbi Mattuck's son-in-law when he married Dorothy Mattuck in 1934. However, he apparently struggled to establish himself as rabbi at the synagogue.

> Rabbi Edgar took on an enormous burden in succeeding his father-in-law, Dr Mattuck. He obtained a double first at Cambridge, and he was like his father-in-law a very fine chairman of meetings, a great organiser, and above all a great perfectionist. When he had to write something he wrote it several times until he was satisfied with it. To be a perfectionist is of course a handicap as it can be very time-consuming. In this way Rabbi Edgar suffered where Dr Mattuck did not.
>
> John Rayner[347]

In striving to make his mark, Rabbi Edgar was not helped by the fact that, despite being highly intelligent, he had a poor memory, particularly for recalling people's names.

> There was a story about Leslie that I never quite dared ask him to confirm. Coming into the old no. 28 building one morning, he saw an elderly congregant whose name he actually remembered. 'Good morning, Mrs Cohen, and how are you?' he enquired. 'I'm very well, thank you' replied the congregant. Foolishly emboldened by his success, Leslie continued: 'And how is your brother?' The flustered lady replied: 'But Dr Edgar, I don't have a brother!' To which Leslie's response was: 'Oh, are you sure?'
>
> David Goldberg[348]

When he became Senior Minister in 1948, Leslie Edgar found himself in conflict with the lay leadership of the synagogue.

> My father used to say that it was a tradition that the Senior Rabbi argues with the Council and he would have said that while they were all arguing with Dr Mattuck. Leslie Edgar was lovely and easy, although after Dr Mattuck had retired and Leslie Edgar became the Senior Rabbi, he wasn't quite as easy. Louis Gluckstein (or Luigi as he was known) was a very difficult Chairman and President; he and Leslie Edgar disagreed on many matters.
>
> Margaret Rigal (Pt. 3)

As well as having to contend with the powerful legacy of Rabbi Mattuck and a problematic relationship with Sir Louis Gluckstein, Rabbi Edgar also suffered several episodes of illness and eventually retired on ill health grounds.

---

343 See photographs 15, 18, 35, 63, and 64.
344 Rabbi Dr Leslie I Edgar, *Some Memories of My Ministry*.
345 ULPS Oral History Project, interview with Maxwell Stern. See Appendix 1.
346 Rabbi Dr Leslie I Edgar, *Some Memories of My Ministry*.
347 ULPS Oral History Project, interview with John Rayner. See Appendix 1.
348 David Goldberg, 'Rabbi Leslie Edgar'.

He was ill very early in his life. He preached at Friends' House just after he had come out of the Army where he had served as a Chaplain. That was a very memorable sermon, but gradually, as he got more ill, he really started taking more of a back seat, and that was when John came to the LJS from the South London Liberal congregation.

Ann Kirk (Pt. 3)

He was a fairly reserved man.

For the first ten years of our acquaintanceship he called me 'Goldberg' and I called him 'Sir'. Then he intimated that we could be less formal with each other and used my first name, but I could never bring myself to take the same liberty. He was 'Sir' until the end.

David Goldberg[349]

Nevertheless, Rabbi Edgar is remembered fondly as a very sincere man and as someone to whom people felt able to turn for comfort and guidance.

Leslie Edgar was willing to stick his neck out further than anyone else I had ever known. In later days, after his illness, he became a much more nervous individual and I don't think many people remember how outspoken and clear-thinking he was. He was absolutely splendid, a man to whom I would have gone with any kind of problem. I remember while I was a student being upset by seeing some of the malformed babies that were being kept alive for many years. I took this concern to him and he had no hesitation at all in saying that he felt babies who had no appreciation of anything and were obviously uncomfortable or unhappy, should not be kept alive year after year, unless there was a purpose in their continued existence. I don't think many people would have said that. He was a great comfort to me.

Margaret Rigal (Pt. 3)

He was a fluent, albeit slow, speaker.

He would speak quite freely from his notes, rather than read his notes. He had been Chairman of the Debating Society at Christ's College Cambridge and was an experienced speaker.

John Rayner[350]

I have very early memories of the LJS, going back to the days of Rabbi Dr Leslie Edgar in the early 1960s. I must have been about four years old, as my parents allowed me to stand on the brown leather seats of the old synagogue in order to see the scroll being taken out of the Ark, and I recall Rabbi Edgar's deep and resonant voice and the way in which he would elongate his vowels in a distinctive and memorable way.

Alexandra Wright (Pt. 3)

Retrospectively, Rabbi Edgar's role came to be seen as that of a bridge between generations.

He was brought up in, and was a firm adherent and exponent of, the principles of the founders but at the same time, being of a younger generation and a Chaplain during the war he naturally realised the changing climate and what was required for the rebuilding of the movement after the war when the members of the congregations were so scattered.

Dorothy Edgar[351]

---

[349] Ibid.
[350] ULPS Oral History Project, interview with John Rayner. See Appendix 1.
[351] ULPS Oral History Project, interview with Dorothy Edgar. See Appendix 1.

Rabbi John Rayner

65. *Rabbi John Rayner, Assistant Minister 1957–61, Senior Minister 1961–89 (became Rabbi 1965), Rabbi Emeritus 1989–2005. (undated)*

Rabbi John Rayner[352] became involved in the LJS as the result of the respect for Rabbi Mattuck he developed as a young man. He had a long association with the synagogue and its congregants before he became Assistant Minister in 1957. Within just a few years of his arrival, he was promoted to the role of Senior Minister (subsequently Senior Rabbi). This appears to have come as surprise to him, but not to others who quickly recognised his stature.

> There was no doubt, then, but that this young man, whose intellect and integrity shone through, was destined to be a great leader, scholar and teacher of Liberal Judaism.
>
> Rosita Rosenberg[353]

He was able to develop a rapport with long-standing members of the LJS, and also with newer members, particularly those who had arrived in the country as refugees and had similar backgrounds to his own.

> John was my guru. I admired him. What helped was that John also came on a *Kindertransport*, so we had the same background. We also discovered many years later that his parents and my mother were actually taken on the same transport, so that was something else we had in common.
>
> Ann Kirk (Pt. 3)

> I remember John well, because, like me, he was a refugee. He was highly intelligent and, later on, he studied at the Hebrew Union College in America, and became an inspiration to his congregation.
>
> Walter Woyda (Pt. 3)

---

[352] See photographs 20, 23, 44, 58, 65, and 68.
[353] Quoted in Rabbi David Goldberg, 'John Rayner a towering intellect and a man of the highest integrity'.

Rabbi Rayner is remembered as quite a reserved man.

> I was very fond of John Rayner. He came across as being a bit aloof because he was quite shy. He was a little intimidating because he was so intelligent. He had some quite traditional views on certain issues, such as abortion, which I recall being angry about when I was a teenager.
>
> > Ellen Schmidt (Pt. 3)

> We complemented each other well. He was quite a shy man, enormously imposing with a great deal of dignity. He was the most delightful, amusing companion, but he could appear rather formal and a lot of people found that a little forbidding.
>
> > David Goldberg (Pt. 3)

His shyness masked his warmth and keen sense of humour.

> His sense of humour was in some ways legendary. He would look at you with a very slight twinkle in his eye and, just when you thought that he was about to talk to you about Maimonides' concept of revelation, he would tell you a joke.
>
> > Alexandra Wright[354]

> I once told him [John] that he had no sense of humour. He responded by making a very witty address to my wife and myself – in verse.
>
> > Robert Greenberg[355]

Some were taken by surprise in finding him fun-loving with a zest for life.

> I recall going out for a *Shabbat* afternoon walk and being amazed to see John Rayner do a gate-vault over a country gate, not the sort of thing that fitted with our previous image of him.
>
> > Michael Hart (Pt. 3)

Notwithstanding his light-heartedness, John Rayner had very firm views on certain issues, such as events in Israel and he was not afraid to voice them.

> [A]s a prophetic preacher [he] confronted his community with sometimes brutal honesty. When, in October 2003, his *Yom Kippur* sermon on the topic of 'Ashamnu', 'We have sinned', expressed his belief that the Israeli government had strayed a long way from the prophetic teachings of justice and compassion, some of his closest friends and members attacked him fiercely. Rayner did not retreat an inch.
>
> > Albert Friedlander[356]

He was very persuasive when putting over an argument and was not afraid of standing up to people if he felt that it was necessary.

> John had stood up to Luigi on a number of occasions about the new prayerbook and other things. This took enormous courage on John's part. I remember the AGM at which Luigi criticised the new High Holyday prayerbook that eventually came out in 1973. This was *Gate of Repentance*, which John had edited with Chaim Stern, and for which David

---

[354] Rabbi Alexandra Wright's contribution to prayers held at the LJS on 25 September 2005 following the death of John Rayner.

[355] Email from Robert Greenberg to Jane Rayner following the death of John Rayner, document kept by Jane Rayner.

[356] Rabbi Albert Friedlander, Obituary for Rabbi John Rayner, *Independent*, Thursday 22 September 2005.

Goldstein had done a lot of the excellent translation. John responded and the atmosphere became quite electric because people did not easily refute or disagree with Luigi and, in those days, an AGM went on for no longer than twenty minutes. This one went on much longer because it became a big debate about the new prayerbook.

David Goldberg (Pt. 3)

Although he had occasional differences of opinion with people, he succeeded in retaining their friendship and respect.

After I left, I thought, in spite of the deep differences between us on certain issues, which at times had led to angry exchanges, how close I felt to him. For my part, it was because he had been such a good friend when I needed him, but also because I respected him.

Sidney Brichto[357]

He had clear views on issues and could, on occasion, be quite firm.

I remember a leading Council member and future Chairman grumbling about there being too much Hebrew in services. John remarked something like: 'There are no good reasons why you should not, and some good reasons why you should, make an effort to learn a little Hebrew'. Not even that particular gentleman would have dared to answer back to John Rayner.

Michael Alpert

However, he was not dogmatic.

There was an occasion when the best man forgot to bring the head covering for the men under the *chuppah*. A small disaster was speedily averted when John Rayner, who was conducting the wedding, said, 'Not to worry. So the men won't have their heads covered'. And removing his *kippur*, he continued the wedding ceremony.

Raymon Benedyk

He is frequently remembered for the quality of his sermons.

It feels a great privilege to have belonged to the LJS for at least some of the years when John Rayner was preaching there. His sermons were consistently brilliant, both in their structure and content. The message was always profoundly humane. The line that stays with me to this day is: 'As God loves all His creatures, so should we.' His voice would have been a pleasure to listen to even if he had been reading telephone directories.

Carolyn Simon (Pt. 3)

When John gave a sermon, it was a real sermon. His sermons were like well-crafted symphonies: there was a beginning, a development section and an articulate and succinct conclusion. And it was all relevant. I always came away feeling uplifted.

Yakov Paul

And also for his teaching of both adults and young people.

In about 1974 John Rayner invited anybody who was interested to [come] his house in Armitage Road, Golders Green to be taught Classical Hebrew. Besides John's son Ben, my daughter Jacqueline and I went there every Sunday for about eighteen months. We took and passed the GCE O Level in Classical Hebrew. This made an enormous difference to our understanding of *Torah* and the *Siddur*. Jane Rayner smilingly welcomed us with coffee or

---

[357] Sidney Brichto, 'In memoriam of John D Rayner', *European Judaism*, Vol. 39, No. 1, Spring 2006.

orange juice every Sunday morning when we arrived. I remember that time with great affection. I have had three or four teachers to whom I owe a great deal, and John is one of them. Now that he is gone, I feel bereft if I need to ask a question on a matter of Judaism.

Michael Alpert

He is generally regarded as having been a very kind, sincere man.

We got to know John Rayner on a sad occasion when our daughter Claire died at the age of thirty-two. He was absolutely brilliant – a very warm and wonderful man. We always enjoyed his services. He was a tremendous scholar, thoughtful and kind.

Barbara Godfrey (Pt. 3)

John Rayner meant every word of the blessing. He was absolutely sincere when he said, 'May the Lord bless you and keep you.'

Jane Kessler

But he permitted no errors by others or by himself.

[H]e could be impatiently critical of faulty theological reasoning, mispronounced Hebrew, incorrectly attributed Talmudic sources or homiletic inadequacies.

David Goldberg[358]

He always wrote me lovely letters thanking me but there was always a sting in the tail! He would tell me where I had gone wrong, but he was always right and his criticisms were constructive.

Yakov Paul

He was particularly precise about his use of the English language and of Hebrew.

Any texts submitted to him were subjected to an exacting grammatical examination alongside the demands for intellectual clarity.

Albert Friedlander[359]

After one service, John Rayner approached me and complimented me on my Hebrew, then pointed out the three mistakes I had made during the service. Later, I approached him during the afternoon break one *Yom Kippur*, when I saw him sitting alone, and asked him if he could help me with one aspect of Hebrew pronunciation. Before I told him what it was, he said, 'No doubt you want to learn about the *kamatz katan*', which, of course, I had been doing all wrong. I still have the sheet he gave me explaining the rules. John had a wonderful gentle way as a firm but caring teacher, and I learned much from him in various conversations, particularly about rabbis and sermons, as well as correct Hebrew pronunciation.

Bernie Bulkin (Pt. 3)

He was a sociable man and a personal friend of many LJS members.

I have many happy memories of our discussing Liberal Judaism and the wider issues of the world. We often used to go places in his car. On those occasions, I recall taking a bucket of water with me as he never refilled his car radiator and, after some miles, steam would come out of the engine.

Walter Woyda (Pt. 3)

---

[358] Rabbi David Goldberg, 'John Rayner, a towering intellect and a man of the highest integrity'.
[359] Rabbi Albert Friedlander, Obituary for Rabbi John Rayner.

Rabbi John Rayner was my friend as well as my minister for over forty-five years. He married my two sons. He also blessed my daughter as a baby, married her and when she suddenly lost her husband at the age of thirty, comforted her.

Robert Greenberg[360]

He was revered by his students at Leo Baeck College, where he lectured for over thirty years. He loved children and was a devoted family man.[361] He was steadfastly supported by his wife Jane.

[H]e said that he was lucky to have married Jane. No human being has given her husband as much love, devotion and support than Jane gave John through the good times and the bad times, as have his children Jeremy, Ben and Susan and his grandchildren Lev and Max of whom he was so proud.

Sidney Brichto[362]

John Rayner bore his periods of ill health with fortitude. Despite his increasing disability in his latter years and the trauma of his early years, he retained his optimistic outlook on life and remained committed to the LJS and to its congregation.

I said that it [his greatest achievement] was his courage in facing whatever life brings and seeking to overcome the bad – as illustrated by the way he faced his illness and disability for the last two years; how he greeted everybody with a smiling face and looked on the bright side, taking the view that he was fortunate to be alive and things could have been worse.

Sidney Brichto[363]

Yes, I remember being asked to visit Rabbi John Rayner in the Royal Free Hospital, just before his major heart surgery. I entered the ward to hear an exasperated nurse calling: 'Mr Rayner, Mr Rayner, will you *please* get back into bed!' Apparently he had just heard that one of his congregants had been admitted to a nearby ward and he was sneaking out to comfort him. He could only be got back into bed when I said, 'Why don't you let me hold the overflow service on your behalf, John. Give me your message and I'll take it to him!'

Louise Golding (Pt. 3)

When he died in 2005, John Rayner was celebrated as one of the foremost Progressive rabbis in the country and as a worthy successor to Rabbi Mattuck, by whom he had been inspired.

He deeply admired Rabbi Mattuck of whom he had once written: 'his ideas had influenced me as much as those of Claude Montefiore: especially his uncompromising rationality, which was not a negation but an expression of his spirituality, and his combination of profound Jewish scholarship, as well as a sense of mystique of the Jewish people's role in history, with unreserved universalism.' He could have been writing about himself.

Alexandra Wright[364]

---

[360] Email from Robert Greenberg to Jane Rayner following the death of John Rayner.
[361] This is fully apparent in his memoirs, John Rayner, *Before I forget*, in which he talks about all of the time he gave to family activities as well as to the LJS.
[362] Sidney Brichto, 'In memoriam of John D Rayner'.
[363] Ibid.
[364] Rabbi Alexandra Wright's address at the prayers held at the LJS on 25 September 2005 following the death of John Rayner.

As we [his family] got to know Rabbi Rayner, like so many others, we fell under his spell, or rather his aura. He exuded compassion, humility, learning and quiet authority. He listened and he communicated gently and softly on the big and small questions. He was an inspirational figure who wore his learning and his great intellectual powers with such modesty. We owe him a great deal. We think of him often.

Michael Grade

Biographies for LJS Senior Rabbis

Rabbi Dr Israel Mattuck: Israel Isidor Mattuck was born on 28 December 1883 in Shirvint (now Sirvintos) near Vilnius in Lithuania. His parents, Benjamin and Ida, adopted the name Mattuck when they arrived in the USA in around 1890. He was one of eight children. The family settled for a number of years in Worcester, Massachusetts, but later moved to New York.

Israel Mattuck attended the Classical High School in Worcester, and in 1901 he entered Harvard University where he specialised in Semitics, graduating with the highest honours. His teachers included C H Toy, the eminent biblical scholar, and George Foot Moore, the outstanding authority on rabbinic Judaism. In Mattuck's leaving testimonial of 1905 Toy described him as 'an exceptionally promising man, both in scholarship and character'.

From an early age, Mattuck studied the Talmud with his father but he diverged radically from his traditional background when he enrolled at the Hebrew Union College, Cincinnati, the foremost American seminary for training Reform rabbis. Part of his studentship was spent serving a congregation in Lincoln, Nebraska, where he met Edna Mayer whom he married in 1910. They had their first child, Robert, in 1911, and subsequently also had two daughters, Dorothy and Naomi.

After his ordination in 1910, Rabbi Mattuck became the rabbi of a fledgling congregation in Far Rockaway, New York. He was there for only a few months when he was approached by The Liberal Jewish Synagogue (LJS) to become its first rabbi.

In 1927 he co-founded with W R Matthews, Dean of St Paul's, the London Society of Jews and Christians, the first interfaith group in the country. He considered it his task to spread Liberal Judaism beyond the LJS and was prominent in establishing several new Liberal congregations in London and elsewhere.

During the years of the Nazi oppression he laboured devotedly for the emigration and welfare of refugees from Germany, especially children.

Mattuck wrote a number of pamphlets, monographs, and essays, and broadcast regularly. His significant publications include: *What are the Jews?* (1937), a religious interpretation of Jewish history and mission, *The Essentials of Liberal Judaism* (1947), a concise summation of its principles and beliefs, and which was the seminal work for Liberal Jewish people for many decades, and the three volumes of the Liberal Jewish Prayerbook.

The war years took a heavy toll on his health. In 1948 he retired as Senior Minister of the LJS, and became Minister Emeritus. Despite continuing ill health, he managed to write two books, *The Thought of the Prophets* (1953) and *Jewish Ethics* (1953) before he died on 3 April 1954 at his home at Wildwood in Hampstead. His death was reported on the BBC national news, received obituary notices in the major newspapers, and occasioned widespread tributes in Anglo-Jewry and beyond.

Rabbi Dr Leslie Edgar: Leslie Edgar had a distinguished career at Cambridge where he obtained a Double First in History and Oriental Languages. He was a Scholar and Prizeman of Christ's College and Bishop Gell Prizeman for Biblical Hebrew. After rabbinic study under Rabbi Dr A Marmorstein at King's College, London, he entered the Liberal Jewish ministry in 1931. He was Assistant Minister to Rabbi Mattuck from then until 1948 when he took over as Senior Minister

During the Second World War he served for five years as Chaplain to the Forces, and for a time as Acting Senior Jewish Chaplin.

In 1951 the Hebrew Union College in Cincinnati conferred on him the title of Rabbi and, in 1958, the honorary degree of Doctor of Divinity.

In addition to his role within the LJS, Leslie Edgar was for many years Deputy President of ULPS (now Liberal Judaism) and subsequently President and Honorary Life President. He was Co-Chairman of the World Union for Progressive Judaism and from 1972 Honorary Life Vice-President. He was involved in a variety of interfaith organisations including his membership of the Executive Committee of the Council of Christians and Jews which he Co-Chaired from 1951–1978.

He was the author of numerous articles, pamphlets, papers and booklets including *A Jewish View of Jesus* (1940), *Some Theological Problems of Jewish-Christian Dialogue* (1968), *Co-operation Between World Religions* (1952), *The Jewish Conception of God* (1954). His memoirs, *Some Memories of My Ministry*, were published posthumously in 1985.

He married his wife Dorothy, the daughter of Rabbi Mattuck, in 1934 and had two children, Gillian and Robert.

✡

Rabbi Dr John Rayner: John Rayner was born as Hans Sigismund Rahmer in Berlin in 1924. He came to England on one of the last *Kindertransport* in 1939. He was sent to Durham School and lodged in the school holidays with a Christian clergyman, William (later Bishop) Stannard, by whom he was encouraged in his religious vocation and to go on from school to Emmanuel College, Cambridge. His parents meanwhile were killed in the death camps.

Rabbi Rayner studied for six years at Cambridge. He started by reading French and German, then Philosophy and finally Hebrew and Aramaic. He changed his German name when he joined the Durham Light Infantry in 1943 where he attained the rank of Captain.

He met and was heavily influenced by Rabbi Mattuck of the LJS while he was still in the Army and decided to become a rabbi. He was ordained by Rabbi Mattuck at the LJS in 1953. His first congregation was at South London Liberal Synagogue where he served for four years before being invited to join the ministerial team at the LJS, initially as Assistant Minister and then, from 1961, as Senior Minister (later Senior Rabbi) until his retirement in 1989 when he became Rabbi Emeritus, a position he held until his death.

Between 1963 and 1965, Rabbi Rayner completed his rabbinic studies at the Hebrew Union College in Cincinnati (HUC), taking two years' leave from the LJS to do so. He was awarded an honorary Doctorate of Divinity by the HUC in 1980. He was Director of Studies, Lecturer and then Vice-President of Leo Baeck College where his special areas of instruction were liturgy and rabbinic codes. He shaped its curriculum and influenced several generations of student rabbis taught at the College.

Rabbi Rayner chaired the ULPS Rabbinic Conference and was also a Chairman of the Council of Reform and Liberal Rabbis. He became Life President of the Union of Liberal and Progressive Synagogues (ULPS) in 1994. In his interfaith work he was Co-Chair of the London Society of Jews and Christians and also played a significant role in the Council of Christians and Jews for which he was awarded a CBE in 2002.

Rabbi Rayner's many publications include: *The Practices of Liberal Judaism* (1958), *An Understanding of Judaism* (1997), *Jewish Religious Law: a Progressive Perspective* (1998), *A Jewish Understanding of the World* (1998), *Principles of Jewish Ethics* (1998), *Aspects of Liberal Jewish Thought* (1999), A *Guide to Jewish Marriage (1975)*, *Judaism for Today (1978)* (co-authored with Rabbi Bernard Hooker), and *The Jewish People: Their History and Their Religion (1987)* (with Rabbi Goldberg).

✡

Rabbi Dr David Goldberg: David Goldberg is Rabbi Emeritus at the LJS. He was educated at Manchester Grammar School, Oxford University, and Trinity College, Dublin. He is the son of Reform rabbi, Selvin Goldberg, and received his Rabbinic Ordination from the Leo Baeck College in 1971, having been a student rabbi at the LJS for two years during his training.

He served the Wembley Liberal Synagogue (now Harrow and Wembley Progressive Synagogue) for three and a half years years before his appointment as Associate Rabbi at the LJS in 1975. He was appointed Senior Rabbi in 1989, and Rabbi Emeritus on his retirement in 2004.

He is widely known in Jewish and wider circles for his trenchant criticisms of Israeli policy in the Occupied Territories. He has been a regular contributor on religious and political topics to BBC programmes and leading newspapers such as *The Times*, the *Sunday Times*, the *Guardian* and the *Independent*.

He is a former Chairman of the Rabbinic Conference of the Union of Liberal and Progressive Synagogues, and Co-Chairman of the London Society of Jews and Christians. In 1999, he was awarded the Gold Medal of the International Council of Christians and Jews for his 'outstanding contribution to interfaith harmony' and, in 2004, he was awarded an OBE in 2004 for services to interfaith work.

He is the author or editor of several books including *The Jewish People* (1989) with Rabbi John Rayner. The translation of his book, *To the Promised Land: A History of Zionist Thought* (1996) was awarded the 1999 Premio Iglesias for its Italian edition. His most recent book, *The Divided Self: the Jewish Psyche Today*, was published in April 2006.

✡

Rabbi Alexandra Wright: Alexandra Wright, current Senior Rabbi at the LJS, grew up at the LJS. Her grandmother was an early member of the synagogue when it was based at its first premises in Hill Street.

She was educated at London's Francis Holland School and Exeter University where she studied English, specialising in Mediaeval Arts. She graduated in 1978 and trained as a teacher before entering Leo Baeck College in 1981 from where she was ordained in

1986. She served as Associate Rabbi at the LJS working alongside Rabbi David Goldberg and Rabbi John Rayner between 1986 and 1989.

From 1990 until 2003 she was the rabbi at Radlett and Bushey Reform Synagogue in Hertfordshire where she founded and established The Learning Circle, the only Jewish adult learning centre in the area sponsored by four Liberal, Reform and Masorti synagogues in conjunction with Spiro Ark.

During her time at Radlett and Bushey Synagogue, she taught classical Hebrew at Leo Baeck College, was an elective in the Maharal of Prague and for a number of years co-ordinated the tutorial system for students. She was also involved with the Council of Christians and Jews and served for five years as the North London Hospice's Jewish Chaplain. She returned to the LJS as Senior Rabbi in March 2004 since when she has developed a special interest in interfaith and pastoral work.

Rabbi Wright continues the LJS's long involvement in the London Society of Jews and Christians and is a founder member of the group called Pathways: Faiths in Conversation, which has not only facilitated good relations with mosques and churches in North West London but also intra-faith working relationships with local Masorti and Orthodox synagogues. She is part of the Spiritual Care Team at St John's Hospice, part of the St John's and St Elizabeth's Hospital.

She has contributed to *Hear our Voice* (1998) and *Taking up the Timbrel* (2000), anthologies of essays and liturgies by women Rabbis and edited by Rabbis Sybil Sheridan and Sylvia Rothschild. She has also edited a *Pesach Haggadah* together with Reform and Liberal colleagues.

Other LJS rabbis

During the synagogue's hundred-year history, many other rabbis have worked at the LJS, each of whom has left a legacy. Brief biographies for rabbis who served the congregation in the last two decades for more than a five-year period (Rabbi Helen Freeman,[365] Rabbi Kathleen de Magtige-Middleton,[366] and Rabbi Mark Solomon) are given below and a full list of LJS rabbis is provided at Appendix 3. Personal recollections for two rabbis – Philip Cohen and Dr David Goldstein – who are frequently remembered for their particular contribution are given below.

Biographies for other LJS rabbis

Rabbi Helen Freeman: Helen Freeman was born in Croydon, Surrey and was involved in Bromley Reform Synagogue from an early age, where her mother was a choir leader and her father senior warden. She qualified first as a speech therapist in Leeds and taught at Sinai Synagogue where she also served on the Council.

---

[365] See photographs 20, 48, 55, and 59.
[366] See photograph 21.

Following her ordination in 1990, Rabbi Freeman worked for nine years as a rabbi at the LJS. During this time she contributed to two books of essays by the women rabbis of the United Kingdom, *Hear Our Voice* (1998) and *Taking up the Timbrel* (2000).

More recently, Rabbi Freeman has contributed to two books edited by Rabbi Jonathan Romain, the first a response to Richard Dawkins and the second entitled *Really Useful Prayers*. She contributed a chapter on Rabbi Hugo Gryn for a book to celebrate 200 years of Reform Judaism and also a chapter on 'Judaism and Serious Illness' to *Festschrift* for Rabbi Tony Bayfield's retirement.

During her years as a congregational rabbi, she has also qualified as a Jungian analyst. She serves as a trustee of the Guild of Pastoral Psychology and on the Central London Council of Christians and Jews. She has served West London Synagogue since 1999 where she has become involved in Jewish-Muslim dialogue groups.

Rabbi Freeman is continuing her training in psychotherapeutic skills and is a tutor and teacher for *Shiurs* at the Leo Baeck College. She is married to David, a Jungian analyst and rabbi.

✡

Rabbi Kathleen de Magtige-Middleton: Kathleen de Magtige-Middleton worked as a rabbi at the LJS from September 2000 until June 2007.

She was born in Utrecht, Holland and read Semitic Languages and Culture at the University of Amsterdam where she obtained an MA in 1994. She commenced her rabbinic training at Leo Baeck College in 1995. Whilst at the college, she worked as a student rabbi at Finchley Reform Synagogue, Manchester Reform Synagogue and Woodford Progressive Synagogue.

Rabbi de Magtige-Middleton was Assistant Librarian of the Hebrew and Judaica Department of the University Library of Amsterdam (1992–95). She also lectures at Leo Baeck College and is an active member of the UK Christian-Jewish Women's Dialogue Group: Kent House Group and was an occasional lecturer on Judaism at the Muslim College.

She contributed to *Women's Voices, New Perspectives for the Christian-Jewish Dialogue* edited by Helen Fry and Rachel Montagu (2005).

Whilst at The LJS she was instrumental in setting up the Bereavement Support Group and a Community Care Coordination Team. In 2003 she co-chaired the first ever International Women's Rabbinic Network Conference, which was held at the LJS, and co-chaired several Liberal Judaism Biennial Conferences. In June 2008 she took up the post of Rabbi at Middlesex New Synagogue in Harrow.

She is married to David de Magtige and has two children.

✡

Rabbi Mark Solomon: Mark Solomon was born and educated in Sydney, Australia, where as a boy he sang in the choir of the Great Synagogue. He later served there for a year as *Torah* Reader and Assistant Cantor. He studied at the *Lubavitcher Yeshivah* in Melbourne and in Israel, then read for a BA (Hons) in English Literature at the

University of Sydney. He came to Britain to study at Jews' College, where he was ordained in 1991. Shortly afterwards, he left Orthodox Judaism and became Lecturer in *Talmud* at Leo Baeck College, where he also completed an MA in Jewish philosophy.

After eight years as Rabbi of West Central Liberal Synagogue, he was appointed Rabbi at the LJS in 2000 and made a significant contribution to the life of the synagogue with his lectures and cantorial singing. He introduced the cantillation of the *Torah* as an option for rabbis and *B'nei Mitzvah*, and was instrumental in the move to allow mixed-marriage blessings and same-sex commitment ceremonies at the synagogue.

In August 2009, he left the LJS to take up the post of Interfaith Consultant with Liberal Judaism. He is part-time Rabbi to both Manchester and Edinburgh Liberal congregations and Associate Chair of the *Beit Din* of Liberal Judaism.

Rabbi Solomon has a special interest in the field of interfaith dialogue, is Co-Chair of the London Society of Jews and Christians and the Interfaith Alliance UK, a Governor of the Ammerdown Centre, Radstock, Somerset, Co-Convenor of Westminster Scriptural Reasoning and trustee of LEAT (London Ecumenical AIDS Trust). He is an honorary rabbi of the Jewish Gay and Lesbian Group and editor of the liturgy *Covenant of Love: Service of Commitment for Same-Sex Couples*, published by Liberal Judaism in 2005.

The Rev. Philip Cohen[367] was Assistant Minister at the LJS between 1946 and 1958. He was born in Manchester and had an Orthodox background. He studied at the Jews' College in London, but he never had the title of 'rabbi' conferred on him.[368]

> But he was more rabbinical than most of us who bear the name ... He was our teacher in the rabbinic tradition, and one of the best.
>
> John Rayner[369]

In 1939 he took up his first post at the Central Synagogue in Great Portland Street but soon after the war started he volunteered for the Army as a Chaplain. During the war he became disillusioned with Orthodox Judaism and therefore accepted the rabbinic post at the LJS following his demobilisation.

> Philip Cohen was very interesting because he had journeyed from Orthodoxy to Liberalism and had a rather non-committal approach. When we spoke to him privately he was able to give guidance and decisions which he would have been reluctant to express in front of a full congregation. He was much more outspoken in private than he was in public.
>
> George Rigal (Pt. 3)

His main role at the synagogue was to work with young people with whom he had a great affinity.

> The minister principally connected with the Alumni Society was the Rev. Philip Cohen, a very sincere, very warm and caring person.
>
> Denis Glaser

---

[367] See photographs 18, 36, and 63.
[368] At that time, rabbis were ordained as 'ministers'.
[369] Thanksgiving for the life of the Rev. Philip Cohen, eulogy given by Rabbi John Rayner at the funeral of the Rev. Philip Cohen, 19 January 1986, document in LJS archives.

Actually, when my wife and I got married, we were the first Jewish people to get married, to have our reception at the Trocadero and no Orthodox minister would come to that, so Philip Cohen came and said the blessing and grace and the rest of it. When I met him years later, he always reminded me that I still hadn't paid him his fee.

Robert Greenberg

He had a very wide knowledge of Judaism and could be relied on to come up with the correct quotes.

> He could have become a considerable Jewish scholar, as the little-known fact is that he was one of the contributors to the Soncino Translation of the *Talmud* indicates, except that for him life was to be primarily with people rather than with books.
>
> John Rayner[370]

He gave short, pithy sermons, which were particularly brief during the cricket season to enable him to take his seat at Lord's across the road from the synagogue.[371] His sermons were rarely written down and often started with phrases such as, 'Reading *The Times* on the bus as I came here today I saw an article on ...'.[372]

> My fondest memory of Philip is of him giving a sermon on the theme of 'Don't ignore the old. You never know what you can learn from them'.
>
> Rita Adler (Pt. 3)

He had a keen wit and was always cracking a joke. He is remembered fondly for his joviality and his relaxed attitude.

> Philip Cohen was the kindest, most laid-back minister you could imagine. He even forgot to bring the marriage certificate to the ceremony [for her wedding]!
>
> Rita Adler (Pt. 3)

Rabbi Dr David Goldstein was the Rabbi at South London Liberal Synagogue for five years before joining the LJS as Assistant Minister in 1964, where he served for the next eleven years. He was an outstanding Jewish scholar and left the LJS to become a curator at the British Library's Department of Hebrew manuscripts and printed books, eventually becoming curator. He was not, however, an aloof intellectual and is remembered for his warmth.

> David Goldstein was very intellectual and 'dreamy', but very friendly and accessible.
>
> Ellen Schmidt (Pt. 3)

> David Goldstein's directness was a quality I experienced when I sought his advice on a difficult problem. His warmth and concern drew one towards him.
>
> Ruth Hadley[373]

He had a particular affinity with young people.

---

[370] Ibid.
[371] Ibid.
[372] Article on website for Alyth Gardens Synagogue, 'Rabbis of Alyth Gardens Synagogue who came from the LJS', undated.
[373] Tributes to Rabbi Dr David Goldstein', pamphlet to accompany the service held at the LJS to commemorate his death in 1987.

66. *Rabbi David Goldstein, Associate Rabbi 1964–75. (undated)*

David Goldstein was the best rabbi I have ever experienced. He – and his wife Berry – had a unique ability to relate to teenagers and to take an interest in them without being patronising. He held a teenagers' open house once a month for coffee, discussions and chit chat. We were made to feel very welcome.

Edward Cross

He delivered highly regarded sermons and was a gifted teacher.

His sermons were 'out of this world' and we missed him terribly when he left the synagogue to go to the British Library as Keeper of Hebrew Manuscripts.

Ann Kirk (Pt. 3)

He had an ability to appear to learn from all. In group discussions he had an uncanny ability to obtain contributions from most present, to build on them and to draw out new angles – a great teacher.

Jenny Stephany[374]

Despite his acknowledged ability as a rabbi, he was not an ambitious man.

When I came back from America, the late Dr David Goldstein had also been appointed to join the ministry here. He was a tremendous asset and we worked together very closely. He said to me right at the beginning: 'I'm very happy to do the routine work', and anything in the way of new ideas and activities he left largely to me.

John Rayner[375]

Rabbi Goldstein had many involvements outside the LJS, including lecturing at Leo Baeck College, serving as Principal of the ULPS Evening Institute, and taking services at a number of ULPS congregations, most notably at Hertsmere Progressive Synagogue (now The Liberal Synagogue, Elstree). Many LJS congregants followed his lead and became involved in these activities.

It was a sermon that he gave at the LJS on *Shabbat Shuvah* 1980 that encouraged me to start attending the ULPS Evening Institute.

Gordon Higgott[376]

---

[374] Ibid.
[375] ULPS Oral History Project, interview with John Rayner. See Appendix 1.
[376] Tributes to Rabbi Doctor David Goldstein.

Many years ago I attended the *Tikkun Leyl Shavu'ot* and on arrival found that I was almost the only person who was not a Leo Baeck student. However, within a few minutes Rabbi Goldstein made me feel one of the group on the same level as the students. We spent an absorbing and fascinating night studying commentaries on the *Shem*a.

Jenny Nathan[377]

He was a consummate writer and published many revered works including *The Jewish poets of Spain, Jewish folklore and legends, The Ashkenazi Haggadah,* and *Hebrew manuscript painting*. He was particularly renowned for his Hebrew translations, including his *magnum opus* translation of Tisby's *The Wisdom of the Zohar*.

When he died aged just 54 in 1987, David Goldstein was remembered with great fondness.

David exists in my mental reference gallery of the truly righteous by whose lives I measure my conduct as a Jew.

Robert Greenberg[378]

He really was the most polite man. I worked as his secretary for ten years and it spoilt me for working for anyone else!

Jean Russell

American rabbis at the LJS

Throughout its history, the LJS has been served by student rabbis and ordained rabbis from America. To begin with, this was due to the fact that, until Leo Baeck College was established, there was no organised system for training Progressive rabbis in the UK, which meant that the synagogue had difficulty in obtaining the assistance it needed from the limited pool of British-trained ministers of a liberal persuasion.

Most of the American rabbis came via the Hebrew Union College in Cincinnati, where both Rabbi Mattuck and Rabbi John Rayner trained. However, some came to the synagogue via other routes.

A fully trained rabbi from America who served us for a substantial amount of time was Rabbi Jack Spiro. He was Chaplain to the American Forces in this country, but he had enough time to give a good deal of service to us for three years.

John Rayner[379]

Many of the early American rabbis, such as Rabbi Solomon Starrels and Rabbi Raphael Levine, stayed at the LJS for significant periods of time and became well integrated into the congregation. Attracted by his experience when he had been a delegate at the World Union for Progressive Judaism conference held at the LJS in 1926, Rabbi Starrels was appointed as Assistant Minister in 1928, but he also worked part-time at the West Central Synagogue founded by Lily Montagu.

---

[377] Ibid.
[378] Ibid.
[379] ULPS Oral History Project, interview with John Rayner. See Appendix 1.

One Friday night, Rabbi Levine was the guest of Mrs Goldstein who lived in Cholmley Gardens, West Hampstead. Because of an air raid warning, she persuaded him to stay overnight. The synagogue was bombed that night so this saved him from being killed.

Denise Franklin

It was the American rabbis who served at the LJS after the end of the Second World War who made the most impact on the congregation and who were most integrated into the LJS community. Rabbi Chaim Stern left a particularly strong legacy because of his work with Rabbi John Rayner in editing the new prayerbooks introduced during the 1960s and 1970s. His cousin, Sidney Brichto,[380] is also remembered because of his subsequent role with ULPS.

However, the American rabbis did not always find favour with the lay leadership of the LJS.

Chaim Stern and Sidney Brichto both came over from America to work at the LJS as young rabbis. After a few years Sidney moved on to the ULPS. We thought Chaim was outstanding, a wonderful character, thinker and intellectual. We were very upset when he and Louis Gluckstein failed to get on and Chaim returned to America. We were pleased that he and John Rayner continued to work together on writing the ULPS prayerbooks. Chaim made a great contribution during the drafting process.

Margaret Rigal (Pt. 3)

67. *Sir Louis Gluckstein, President of the LJS, presenting Rabbi Chaim Stern with a presentation copy of Service of the Heart. (1967)*

As well as being generally appreciated by the congregation, the rabbis themselves appear to have enjoyed their time at the synagogue.

I was Assistant Rabbi at The Liberal Jewish Synagogue during the period that John Rayner had two years' leave of absence to study. And at that time, sure enough, my cousin Chaim Stern was appointed to be the acting Senior Minister at The Liberal Jewish Synagogue. And so he and I became the joint ministers at the LJS and had wonderful times together, sharing preaching engagements, etc., and doing the Communal *Seders*. It was a very nice period.

Sidney Brichto[381]

---

[380] See photograph 23.
[381] ULPS oral history project, interview with Sidney Brichto. See Appendix 1.

Most of the rabbis who served at the LJS eventually returned to the United States, but some remained in contact with LJS members.

> I recall the many friendships Maureen and I made in the 1960s with the young rabbis who came to the LJS for a short time, particularly Chaim Stern and his wife Susan. Many years later when we were visiting the States with Adam, we made a surprise visit to them. Seeing a sign on the Throughway to the small town of Chappaqua where they lived, we made a detour and asked at a delicatessen if they knew of Chaim Stern. We were directed to the wooden synagogue in the woods, where they were rehearsing for a play, and someone gave us directions to the Stern's home. We were given a great welcome and very soon Chaim and I were back in the deli buying some supper!
>
> Anthony Roe (Pt. 3)

As the result of an arrangement set up between the ULPS and Rabbi Sam Sandmel of the Hebrew Union College in 1959,[382] a number of American student rabbis also served at the LJS for twelve months during the 1960s. The arrangement proved vital at a time when the LJS was finding it difficult to appoint full-time rabbis to assist with its rapidly growing congregation.[383] The student rabbis included Richard Zionts, Jonathan Brown, Howard Smigel, Michael Abrahams and Michael Barenbaum. Now a retired rabbi in America, Jonathan Brown continues to visit the LJS when he is in the UK and others retain warm memories of their time at the LJS.

> On the evening of November 22, 1963, Rabbi Sidney Brichto and his wife invited me to join them for *Shabbat* dinner after the Friday *Shabbat* Eve services at the LJS. When we arrived at their flat, Mrs Brichto opened the door and said, 'President Kennedy has just been shot in Dallas, Texas and is in the hospital there. It's all on the BBC.' We were shocked and horrified at the news and had a very sad *Shabbat* dinner that night. Later, I walked from the Brichto flat to the American Embassy at Grosvenor Square where US Marines were posted all around the building. News reports were being taped to the front doors detailing what had happened on that terrible day in Dallas. The next morning we held special prayers relating to the assassination of the President. The LJS was packed with members – it resembled *Rosh Hashanah* or *Yom Kippur* in attendance. Rabbi Chaim Stern gave a very comforting and meaningful sermon that day that touched everyone's hearts. I will always remember that event and even more, the kindness and sympathies extended by the people of the LJS and throughout all of London at that trying time. I felt as though we were all part of one great family.
>
> Richard Zionts

Two American rabbis have been appointed in more recent years. For twelve months Rabbi Michael Feinberg bridged the gap between the departure of Rabbi Alexandra Wright in 1989 and the arrival of Rabbi Helen Horn (later Freeman) in 1990 and in 2010, the LJS appointed Rabbi David Wilfond[384] who returned to his substantive post in Israel in 2011.

---

[382] Lawrence Rigal and Rosita Rosenberg, *Liberal Judaism: The First Hundred Years*.
[383] LJS Annual Report, 1960.
[384] See photographs 45 and 62.

Chapter 2: The lay leadership of the LJS

The changing nature of the lay leadership of the synagogue

To begin with, the lay leadership of the synagogue was synonymous with the leadership of the Jewish Religious Union (JRU). As President of the JRU, Claude Montefiore became the first President of the synagogue and the first LJS Council was formed by the members of the JRU Committee.

> Those were the days of the spiritual giants of the movement led by Claude Montefiore, Lily Montagu (whom he affectionately called his 'gadfly'), Israel Abrahams and Israel Mattuck. The Council of those days was formidable and I fear occasionally a rather contentious body of men and women, proudly and courageously proclaiming the principles of Liberal Judaism by their words and by their lives.
>
> Louis Gluckstein[385]

However, the complexities involved in managing a growing congregation and a building meant that a range of specialised committees needed to be set up. After the LJS opened, there was therefore a rapid expansion in the type and nature of lay leadership roles and the numbers of those involved.

Claude Montefiore and his successor, Sir Louis Gluckstein, also acted as the Chairman of the LJS Council as well as President until the two roles were separated in 1963.

Before 1926 the LJS had one Treasurer. The arrangement of having two Co-Treasurers was then introduced. The first LJS Treasurer was Harry R Lewis, a solicitor interested in Jewish education and youth work.[386] In 1913 he was succeeded by Sidney Mendelssohn who had previously been Co-Treasurer of the JRU and who discovered the Hill Street premises which served as the synagogue building for fifteen years.[387]

From the outset, the synagogue also had an Honorary Solicitor (now Ellen Schmidt), but the number and nature of other honorary roles have varied. Some roles, such as that of Honorary Architect, which Ernest Joseph held for many years, are now carried out on a professional basis. In its centenary year, the honorary roles at the synagogue, apart from those of the Chairman (Rita Adler and then Michael Hart) and the Treasurers (Barbara Fidler and Eric Blaire), are those of Honorary Archivist (Bryan Diamond) and Honorary Librarian (Barbara Godfrey).

> My main job at the synagogue has been as Archivist, using experience I gained at Northwood and Pinner Liberal Synagogue. I volunteered to do this in 1993 when the archive boxes came out of store after the rebuilding of the synagogue. I arranged a move of much older material to the Record Office, now the London Metropolitan Archive, and I continue to receive and supervise the accession of new material. My help in supplying photocopies has been acknowledged in a book entitled *Lost Synagogues of London* by Renton, which was

---

[385] Sir Louis Gluckstein, 'The Work of Our Hands'.
[386] Obituary in *The Jewish Chronicle*, 2 March 1934.
[387] Lily Montagu, *The Jewish Religious Union and Its Beginnings*.

published in 2000. I have written several articles for the LJS newsletter. I have taken photos at many events, which I have deposited in the archive.

Bryan Diamond (Pt. 3)

After Claire [her daughter] died I became more involved with the synagogue and became the Honorary Librarian, as I always loved books and knew a little about libraries following my year at Hopkins. I have always been a 'bookworm'.

Barbara Godfrey (Pt. 3)

For many years, lay leadership roles were mainly filled from amongst those families sometimes referred to as the 'Cousinhood' or the 'Jewish Establishment', who were prominent amongst the membership of the LJS in its early years. It was not until the late 1960s that the lay leadership of the synagogue began to be drawn from a much wider pool of congregants. When Council membership was broadened, it included a significant number of those who had come to the country as refugees and had gradually taken on higher profile roles in synagogue life, such as Bob Kirk and Willie Kessler.

When the LJS was first established, members of its Council and other synagogue committees were invited to join them rather than being elected. It was not until the 1960s that there were contested elections for the Council.

It was Sir Louis Gluckstein, then President, who invited me to join the Council. When I was YMO Chairman he said: 'Willie, you are going to be important here, why you don't come on the Council'. He was always very kind to me.

Willie Kessler (Pt. 3)

When the generation of Joe Pinto, Desmond Feldman, Bob Kirk and my father, Michael Cross, started to get involved with the Council it was (to them) like the cabin boys taking over the ship. Until then it felt like no one under the age of forty or who wasn't a gentleman was invited on the Council and a contested election was unheard of.

Edward Cross

Another change in the lay leadership of the LJS is that Honorary Officers and other lay leaders previously tended to serve for much longer than they do now.

[My father, Kenneth] was a very active Chairman of the House Committee for many years and a member of the Council for as long as I can remember. In those days there was no question of anyone resigning after three or six years.

Margaret Rigal (Pt. 3)

My grandfather, Julian Simon, was one of the first Treasurers of the synagogue, and he was followed by my father, Ronald. I do not know exactly when my father retired as Treasurer, but it must have been in the 1960s, and so between them they covered the first fifty years or so. I was also Treasurer, but not immediately after my father, so there was an interregnum!

Tim Simon (Pt. 3)

Initially the LJS Council met in the homes of its members and it was some time before meetings were placed on a more formal footing and were convened at the synagogue.

In those spacious and gracious days we met at his [Claude Montefiore's] home in Portman Square, and Council meetings were partly social functions with Miss Montagu presiding over the cups of coffee before we started the business of the evening.

Louis Gluckstein[388]

Those who joined the Council and other committees when their membership began to diversify found meetings very formal.

Council meetings were courteous and proper and people went to them well prepared. They were conducted with a great deal of formality and were over in a couple of hours, which is how it should be. I am sure there were occasional disagreements, but no voting because the understanding was that you would always reach a consensus. If there was a vote, it was an exceptional happening and I can't recall in my time there ever being a vote at Council.

David Goldberg (Pt. 3)

They also tended to be dominated by the Chairman.

I was asked to stand for Council in 1974. At the time I was twenty-seven and although I had already had active roles in both the Alumni Society and the Out and About Club as Co-Chairman, I was surprised to be asked as the average age of most Council members was a lot older! One of my main memories was that of the late Sir Louis Gluckstein, who as President attended every Council meeting, always sitting below his portrait. Sir Louis said little, but when he spoke there was no muttering or whispering and you could hear a pin drop. Sir Louis' memory was phenomenal. On one occasion, there had been a lengthy discussion (I cannot remember now what it was about) when Sir Louis stated that this very point had already been discussed and agreed by Council in 1926 on… specifying the exact date. Someone was then asked to find the Minute Book to look this up. Sure enough, Council had decided this issue in 1926, over fifty years earlier, and this concluded the discussion with no suggestion that the original decision could be reviewed.

Diana Da Costa

I attended Council during the rebuilding project. When I first went I didn't realise that employees weren't encouraged to speak. After one meeting when I had given an opinion, Sir Peter took me aside and suggested that if I wanted to raise something in future I should pass him a note. From then, Peter acted on all the many 'notes' that passed between us with discretion and firmness, so they appeared to be his intervention! Council was at times autocratic. I remember seeing Rabbi Helen Freeman being asked to leave a Council meeting when they wanted to discuss something privately.

Prue Baker

As a new generation of people became involved in the Council and other committees, they became less formal.

Much of what I did when I was on the Council is recorded in the Council minutes, but there were other things I got involved in too. I was Chairman of a number of the committees that were established at that time, such as the Services Committee and the Education Committee. I was also Treasurer of the synagogue for seven years. I enjoyed working with the people who were on the various committees. I considered myself one of the leaders of

---

[388] Sir Louis Gluckstein, 'The Work of Our Hands'.

the 'Young Turks' who wanted to bring the Council and the Synagogue into the post-war era. With my reputation and my family connections, I was able gradually to influence people in various ways.

Desmond Feldman (Pt. 3)

However, the Council and other synagogue committees still tended to be male-dominated, despite the role model provide by Lily Montagu. It was not until the late 1980s that women started to play a significant part in the lay leadership of the LJS.

> Committees used to be very male-dominated affairs conducted in smoked-filled rooms and women rarely went to them. Women are now properly involved in every aspect of synagogue life.

David Goldberg (Pt. 3)

68. *Council meeting. From left: Simon Davis, Neil Levitt, Leslie Kanaber, Patricia Hartwig, Ronald Berg, Brenda Nathanson, Ian Lipton, David Gluckstein, Bob Beral, Rosemary Lazarus, Rabbi David Goldberg, Peter Rossiter, Elizabeth Riberio Dos Santos, Willie Kessler, Rabbi Alexandra Wright, Sir Peter Lazarus, Rabbi John Rayner, Julian Tobin, Raymon Benedyk. (1987)*

Today, synagogue committees are much more democratic, participative and inclusive, but leadership roles remain quite demanding.

> By then, I was back on the Council. During the last two years of my six-year term, I served as a Treasurer. This was a difficult role as the synagogue was going through some financial problems. Expenditure had risen significantly, and was exceeding income. I tried to ensure everyone involved took responsibility for making realistic predictions of likely expenditure and income. We had many lively debates on other matters, and took some important decisions, such as the one to agree that same-sex ceremonies could take place in the synagogue.

Michael Hart (Pt. 3)

Prominent lay leaders of the LJS

Over the years, the LJS has had many prominent lay leaders, all of whom have contributed significantly to the development of the synagogue. The following paragraphs provide information on the most prominent lay leaders and those who are most frequently mentioned in reminiscences and memoirs. The contributions of the two more recent Presidents, Willie Kessler[389] and Bob Kirk,[390] are not included as their memories are included in full in Part Three.

69. *Willie Kessler, LJS President 1999–2006. Photograph by Foto Schmelz, Klosters, Switzerland. (undated, c. 1999)*

Lily Montagu

Lily Montagu[391] was a spiritual as well as a lay leader. However, she has been included in this chapter on lay leadership because it is predominantly in her role as a lay leader that people of the LJS have memories of her.

Although she was a member of the LJS Council from its inception until the end of her life, Lily Montagu held no formal leadership role at the synagogue. She was, nevertheless, one of its outstanding leaders. She is often described as a 'good organiser', but her contribution was far greater than that. She was the source of inspiration to many and universally revered by those who encountered her.

> For one thing, one always worked 'with' her and never 'for her', however humble one's part in the activity might be. She always spoke of something achieved by us, never, never, by 'me'. It goes without saying that she was incapable of distinguishing between a voluntary and a salaried worker.
>
> Phyllis Jacobs[392]

---

[389] See photographs 20, 59, 68, 69, and 77.
[390] See photographs 20, 26, 48, 55, 61, and 85.
[391] See photographs 3, 14, 17, 18, and 70.
[392] Phyllis Jacobs, 'A Debt Not Yet Repaid', *Community*, Vol. No 5, January 1968.

My mother adored both Miss Lily Montagu and Miss Marian Montagu; she adored the two of them. She regarded them as something quite holy when they came.

Hannah Feldman

She was a lifelong influence on many of those who met her.

In July 1949 I came over as a youth delegate from Holland to the World Union Conference and Lily Montagu, who was then World Union Secretary, received every delegate kindly … After the conference, I went to see her again and she changed the course of my life because I came to London with the intention of *aliyah*, a poor student, and no family at all, having lost all my family in the Holocaust and Lily Montagu said, 'Why don't you start teaching Hebrew at my club?' She persuaded me to stay in London and I went to teach in her club.

Harry Jacobi[393]

I want to pay tribute to the two women who most influenced my life: Rose Layman who adopted me, and her mentor The Hon. Lily Montagu, 'Miss Lily', as she was known, who was always ahead of her time.

Barbara Shortt

In the interwar years Lily Montagu devoted herself to supporting refugees from Nazi persecution. Eric Conrad,[394] who came to the LJS as a refugee from Vienna in 1938 and married Lily Montagu's niece, Sheila Myers, recalls:

He [a noted Hebrew scholar in Vienna] gave me a written introduction to an English lady. He said that she was a quite exceptional woman, a member of the Anglo-Jewish aristocracy. She had spent her life devoted to social and religious work. He had met her in Vienna several years earlier when she was on one of her many missionary travels, and had worked closely with her on developing a progressive type of Judaism in Austria. He described her as the sort of lady who would help me. As you may have guessed by now, that lady was Lily Montagu. I went to see her very soon after I arrived in London. I immediately fell under her spell and, very luckily for me, she also seemed to have taken to me.

Eric Conrad (Pt. 3)

She regularly welcomed members of the congregation into her own home, although the fare and the surroundings were quite spartan.

Both women [Lily and her sister Marian] spent very little money on themselves. My wife and I were often invited to dinner at Red Lodge and we would find that the meal was certainly not substantial!

John Rayner[395]

My parents were very fond of them and used to go there [Red Lodge] for an occasional Friday night. My father gave us very graphic accounts. The usual fare was two fishcakes. I don't know what went with it. They had a very large dining room, which in the wintertime was very cold … there was a single, small, electric fire with one bar.

Margaret Rigal (Pt. 3)

---

[393] Transcript of talk given by Rabbi Harry Jacobi, 'Memories of Lily Montagu' at West Central Synagogue in 2009.

[394] Eric Conrad was the son of Emil Conrad, Editor of the Vienna *Neue Frie Presse* at the time of the Dreyfus Affair. Eric was a member of the Austrian Bar. He enlisted in the Pioneer Corps at the outbreak of war, was transferred to the intelligence Corps in 1944 and attached to the American Army. In 1949, he married Sheila Grenville, a daughter of one of Lily Montagu's sisters, Elsie.

[395] ULPS Oral History Project, interview with John Rayner. See Appendix 1.

Lily Montagu preached regularly at the LJS and was very devout.

> I would describe her as a saintly figure. She always sat in the front row wearing a heavy coat with her sister, Marian, who fell asleep in later life. When she preached it was very spiritual and special.
>
> Michael Nathan (Pt. 3)

She had simple tastes bordering on austerity.

> Miss Montagu impressed us as children with the fact that she walked, since she would not ride on the Sabbath, with Miss Marian and Miss Connie Lewis to the LJS on a Saturday from her home. They brought their sandwiches and went on to the West Central for the afternoon service.
>
> Dorothy Edgar[396]

She was aware of the incongruity of her wealthy background and her frugal lifestyle.

> Because I worked very hard, dressed badly, went out very little, was always shy and awkward at social functions, I was held up as a warning by my mother's acquaintances … They kept their daughters away from my bad influence.
>
> Lily Montagu[397]

Despite her remarkable organising skills, she was not the most orderly or practical of people.

> I was privileged to work with Lily Montagu when John and I were in South London, on the committee of the Maude Nathan Home which she and her sister Marian had founded. She was very idealistic about it but totally impractical.
>
> Jane Rayner

> Miss Lily was really spiritual, but also very absent-minded. I remember, at one dinner laid on by the Women's Society in the Montefiore Hall, the dessert was blancmange or something similar. Miss Lily would never eat anything – she never had time. My mother said to her at this dinner, 'You really must have something to eat, dear,' and Miss Lily said, 'No, dear Mrs Magnus, not now, but I'll take it home and have it for supper,' and with that she simply poured it into her bag – not on the plate, but just into the bag – and my mother had to take the whole thing into the kitchen to sort out.
>
> Ruth Ive (Pt. 3)

She is remembered for her determination and optimism.

> When we discussed some insoluble problem she would always say, 'Well, we must peg away.'
>
> John Rayner[398]

But she is also remembered for being formidable at times and for the strictness of some of her views.

---

[396] ULPS Oral History Project, interview with Dorothy Edgar. See Appendix 1.
[397] Lily H Montagu, *My Club and I: The Story of The West Central Jewish Club*, Herbert Joseph, (1941).
[398] ULPS Oral History Project, interview with John Rayner. See Appendix 1.

I went to the Alumni and did quite a lot of activities with them, and then there was a Young Members' Organisation where I met many leading people. Rabbi Mattuck and Lily Montagu were totally opposed to anything to do with gambling such as a raffle and did not approve of a tombola. On one occasion I had organised a dinner party at which everyone wore formal dress. We wanted to run a tombola and I went to see Lily Montagu but she said, 'No, no my dear, we cannot have that'.

Ruth Ive

In one respect only she seems to be sometimes too exacting in her demands on others. Though she is a great believer in co-operation between Christians and is one of the founders of the London Society of Jews and Christians – she is a member of the Executive Committee – she is uncompromising in her objection to mixed marriages, however secure and happy they may be.

Eric Conrad[399]

However, Lily Montagu also had some passions. Both she and her sisters, Marian and Netta, were keen cricket fans and enjoyed the cinema and the theatre. Lily Montagu loved books, embroidery and flowers.

Her life was not all prayer and incense. She loved good music, literature and biography. She loved flowers and when she once made a confession to that effect in the course of a speech, the floral department of Harrods was emptied and deposited on her door-step. In common with Marian and Netta, she was a keen sportswoman, loved cricket and tennis, and all three would often be seen in the members' enclosure of Lord's and Wimbledon in large hats and parasols, among other ladies similarly attired, a sight so imposing, so formidable that it was difficult to watch them and believe that the Empire was no more.

Chaim Bermant[400]

The walls of her study are covered from floor to ceiling with a very fine collection of books, and she greatly enjoys novels and biographies.

Eric Conrad[401]

70. *The three sisters. From left: Mrs (Netta) Franklin, Lily Montagu and Marian Montagu. Copyright Daily Mail. Man on left unknown. (undated)*

[399] Eric V Conrad, *Lily H. Montagu: Prophet of Living Judaism.*
[400] Chaim Bermant, *The Cousinhood, The Anglo-Jewish Gentry,* Eyre and Spottiswoode (1971).
[401] Eric V Conrad, *Lily H. Montagu: Prophet of Living Judaism.*

Biography for Lily Montagu

The Hon. Lilian Helen Montagu (1873–1963) was the first Jewish woman in Britain to become directly involved with the ideology of religion. She was one of the ten children of Sir Samuel Montagu who was a wealthy banker and Liberal Member of Parliament for Whitechapel. He later became Baron Swaythling and President of the Federation of Synagogues. Her mother was Ellen, née Cohen.

Lily Montagu was educated at Doreck College, London until she was fifteen and then privately by tutors.

The Montagu home was a very traditional one in which Orthodox traditions were closely observed. The family belonged to the New West End Synagogue. It was here that Lily Montagu received her early religious education from the Rev. Simeon Singer, who subsequently became her guide and mentor.

By the age of fifteen, Lily Montagu was already questioning the rituals associated with Orthodox Judaism, which she felt constrained the religious development of Jewish women. Her concerns and the indecision she faced in choosing between a traditional Jewish marriage and community service are evident in the two novels she wrote as a young woman. Aged seventeen, she set up services for children in English at the New West End Synagogue.

In June 1898 she attended a conference on Jewish Elementary Education. As a result, she developed a concern that the traditional Jewish educational methods were not meeting the needs of the young people of that time and that the demands of traditional rituals were too difficult for working people, who found them hard to combine with their everyday lives. Within four months of the conference she had written the paper which inspired Liberal Judaism, 'Spiritual Possibilities of Judaism To-day', which appeared in the *Jewish Quarterly Review* in 1899.

With the help of Dr Claude Montefiore, Lily Montagu went on to bring together a group of people who were interested in modernising Judaism – what became known as the Jewish Religious Union (JRU), the initial aim of which was to win back to Judaism those who were drifting away from the faith.

Although Dr Claude Montefiore became the President and greatest scholar of the JRU and Rabbi Israel Mattuck its religious interpreter and mouthpiece, it was Lily Montagu who provided the visionary leadership which led to the setting up not only of The Liberal Jewish Synagogue but also many other congregations. She founded the World Union for Progressive Judaism in 1926 and became its President in 1954 and Honorary Life President in 1959.

With her sister Marian, who was to become her inseparable companion throughout her life, Lily Montagu while still in her teens became involved in youth activities and social work. She was nineteen when she founded and became Secretary of the West Central Jewish Girls' Club for young women living in the Soho area and was one of the principal founders of the National Association of Girls' Clubs. She was an active in a number of campaigning societies such as the Anti-Sweating League and the Women's Industrial Council, the aims of which were to improve the working conditions of women industrial workers.

She was one of the first women to be appointed as a JP and served for many years on the Bench of the London Borough of St Pancras. Later she became a member of various juvenile courts and during the Second World War she was appointed as Chairman of the Westminster Court.

In 1942, Lily Montagu and Marian founded the Maude Nathan Home for Little Children.

Although Lily Montagu is remembered principally for being an organiser and a woman of action, she was also an experienced spiritual leader. From the inception of the JRU, she participated in the Saturday afternoon and Sunday services. She also gave special talks for children and arranged children's services in the Soho area. Lily Montagu was the first Jewish woman to serve as a lay minister. She preached regularly at The Liberal Jewish Synagogue from 1918 and had her own congregation, the West Central Liberal Jewish Congregation, where she officiated regularly

In 1930 Lily Montagu received from the Hebrew Union College in Cincinnati an honorary degree of Doctor of Hebrew Law. In 1937 she was awarded an OBE and in 1955, a CBE in recognition of her services.

Marjorie Moos

Marjorie Moos[402] was a long-standing teacher in the LJS Religion School and was involved in variety of other educational activities at the synagogue. Described by Rabbi Leslie Edgar as 'one of the most conscientious and imaginative teachers',[403] Marjorie Moos came to the LJS as a teacher as a result of her involvement in Lily Montagu's West Central Jewish Girls' Club.

> Clever woman that she [Lily Montagu] was, she spotted me and invited me to go to the West Central Club and when I got there, she was taking a Bible class and she said, 'I wonder if you could do this for the younger ones'. And that's exactly how it all happened, just as easily as that.
>
> Marjorie Moos[404]

She became something of a legend at the synagogue and is sometimes referred to as the 'Fourth M' alongside Rabbi Mattuck, Lily Montagu and Claude Montefiore.

She started teaching in the Religion School in 1922 and was also involved in producing materials for the LJS's correspondence courses. She became well known amongst children attending boarding schools and those who were evacuated from London during the Second World War.

> My earliest memories of the LJS were of the redoubtable Miss Marjorie Moos who took Religion School classes and was quite keen on tracing the origins of the Jewish people. We were instructed to make little Israelite and Palestinian villages, which I proceeded to do, made out of little red blobs of clay in the shape of huts. I made them into a little village. Miss Moos was very curious about that and asked, 'but why have you made the huts in the shape of a swastika pattern?' I couldn't answer. That was just before the war.
>
> Denis Glaser

---

[402] See photographs 6, 41, and 71.
[403] Rabbi Dr Leslie I Edgar, *Some Memories of My Ministry*.
[404] ULPS Oral History Project, interview with Marjorie Moos. See Appendix 1.

In the war years, she also took over the running of the activities of the combined Younger Members' Organisation and Alumni Society and travelled tirelessly to keep in touch with young people.

Marjorie Moos, taught many children of LJS families in their own homes.

> As regards my religious education, Miss Moos (she was an old friend of my mother) would come to our house once a week and give me an hour's 'teaching'. This was essentially based on biblical stories and involved getting me to make drawings of, for example, David's fight against Goliath, or Moses with the Israelites in the wilderness. As I remember it, Miss Moos had a huge India rubber to rub out my mistakes and was, as others can testify, a great character with a remarkably strong voice even on her 100th birthday.
>
> Michael Nathan (Pt. 3)

> I began my religious studies at home, where I was taught by the redoubtable Miss Marjorie Moos, the ever-in-demand first teacher for North and West London's Jewish children.
>
> Jean Jaffa (Pt. 3)

71. *Marjorie Moos, long-standing Religion School and correspondence course teacher. Photograph by Sidney Harris. (1987)*

She was generally seen as being very stern until her students came to know her better.

> One of my teachers was Marjorie Moos, who wrote comments in bright red ink on such work as I sent back. Once she wrote 'can I have the pleasure of hearing from you again?'. For me, as a young boy, she was a most terrifying lady. Later, of course, we came to love and respect her as a very fine person and teacher. I was delighted when her former pupils were asked to send a short biography and a photograph for a compendium that was to be presented to her on her 80th birthday.
>
> Anthony Roe (Pt. 3)

On Sam Rich's retirement in 1946, Marjorie Moos became Director of the Correspondence Class and was Principal of the Religion School between 1958 and 1959. She took on this role when she retired from South Hampstead High School (her own old school) where, in a professional capacity, she had taught Jewish Scripture for over twenty years. She continued her involvement in the Religion School until 1965 when she was asked to retire by the LJS President, Sir Louis Gluckstein.[405]

> For twenty-two years I taught in the Religion School and got to know Miss Moos very well. She was formidable and it was only after I had known her about twenty years did she invite me to call her 'Marjorie' rather than Miss Moos. Actually, she virtually ordered rather than merely allowed me to call her 'Marjorie'. She was a very good teacher but you didn't argue with her!
>
> Michael Alpert

Marjorie Moos did not confine herself to teaching in the Religion School. She also arranged a number of extra-curricular activities for the children, including picnics and other outings. She produced several publications for use by young people, including a series of Bible stories for the very youngest children.

Marjorie Moos was a member of the LJS Council for over thirty years and taught several generations of proselytes, many of whom became firm friends. This work continued long after her formal retirement from the Religion School.

> Then, thankfully and miraculously, Marjorie Moos came on the scene. She became Sharon's friend and mentor, guided her, encouraged her and brought her through the journey, which was both a journey into Judaism, but also an amazing introduction to the LJS, its history and heritage.
>
> Trevor Moross (Pt. 3)

She continued her involvement with the synagogue until well into her nineties, but regretted that she no longer had any regular pupils. Reviewing her eighty-year career as she was approaching her 100th birthday in April 1994, Marjorie Moos described it as a 'vocation' and said it had been 'utterly joyous'.[406] She died later that year.

LJS Presidents

Claude Montefiore (President 1911–38)

Dr Claude Montefiore[407] was the first LJS President (and Chairman of the Council). He was a philosopher and theologian whose teachings inspired the thinking of the Liberal Jewish movement in its early years. He is described as:

> a very tall imposing man with piercing eyes who appeared to look right through me … He always walked with his hands behind his back.
>
> Dorothy Edgar[408]

> Tall, with somewhat Semitic features, close cropped hair and a beard, his eyes were arresting, even to a stranger. When a few years ago his portrait was painted by a leading artist of the

---

[405] Letter in LJS archives.
[406] *LJS News*, December 1994.
[407] See photographs 2, 6, and 14.
[408] ULPS Oral History Project, interview with Dorothy Edgar. See Appendix 1.

day, the picture was criticised because the eyes had not been accurately portrayed. 'You cannot expect me to paint stars' replied the artist.

Basil Henriques[409]

Another personal recollection of Montefiore is that he was a prodigious letter writer, who seldom used the telephone.

> Four or five letters at least would arrive daily at our house from him, never dated – or very rarely. They would simply say *Monday* or whatever, no superscription. They were short, to the point and commented either on the previous day's sermon or a topical subject or whatever view he had (usually very firm views), very well phrased, sometimes hilariously funny.

Dorothy Edgar[410]

He is remembered best by members of the LJS for his addresses at synagogue services. He was on the *bimah* every Saturday, entering the synagogue with the ministers. He preached occasionally, but always on the afternoon of *Yom Kippur*.

> I think for at least two, possibly three times, I was given the honour and responsibility of reading passages from Isaiah and Jeremiah parallel with Dr Montefiore.[411] One year, as I was set to start the passages, not a word of sense could I make of it and suddenly realised that *he* was making an impromptu speech about Isaiah. I quickly decided to go ahead with reading the passages and then had to keep the timing right by making an impromptu talk myself on the sermon. Never had I had such a dreadful thing to do … I wrote to Dr Montefiore and wailed a little and he wrote: 'Gee whiz, did I do that to you? How awful!' The next year I wrote to him and asked if he was making a speech on Isaiah that time and if so, how long. 'Two minutes,' I was told. So I prepared my speech from Isaiah and all went well.

Marjorie Moos[412]

> His reading of Jonah on the Day of Atonement was a notable annual event. He always preached on the afternoon of the Day of Atonement on a subject relating to death leading up to the Memorial Service.

Dorothy Edgar[413]

Although his sermons were memorable, they tended to be rather erudite and somewhat lofty for some members of the congregation.

> Yes, we have wonderful memories of Claude Montefiore. He was beyond my intellectual sphere (if you know what I mean). As you know, he was not only an intellectual but a wonderful preacher and I used to sit enthralled at how any one individual could express himself (it didn't mean a great deal to you religiously) so well. I was much more interested in his wording and general information, rather than from the religious point of view … I was very fond of him. He was marvellous.

Hannah Feldman

---

409 Taken from the diary of Sir Basil Henriques, quoted in introduction to Henriques Music Archive produced by Sally Civval, 2011.

410 ULPS Oral History Project, interview with Dorothy Edgar. See Appendix 1.

411 Given the large attendances on High Holydays, the LJS has traditionally organised parallel services in the synagogue and in the Montefiore Hall with the choir and the music serving both services. To ensure that the choir and the music was correctly cued, the speakers at the two services had to ensure that their precisely co-ordinated. See section on the spiritual life of the synagogue, chapter on festivals and High Holydays.

412 Talk by Marjorie Moos to the LJS Women's Society.

413 ULPS Oral History Project, interview with Dorothy Edgar. See Appendix 1.

I should be inclined to say that the sermons I heard my father deliver were preached rather over the head of his audience. They were I suspect caviar to the general … He never preached extempore and used to express unbounded admiration for a preacher who could go on or stop short at will.

Leonard Montefiore[414]

Although Claude Montefiore supplied the philosophy that underpinned Liberal Judaism, he was in fact quite a conservative man.

[H]e had sentimental piety for certain traditions and a horror of doing anything that might offend the susceptibilities of his more Orthodox relations. And, in weightier matters, his attitude was conservative. How often do I remember people coming to discuss the question of marriage. There he would make no concessions … The synagogue cannot and will not give the blessing to the marriage of those of different faiths.

Leonard Montefiore[415]

Like Lily Montagu, he lived a very simple life.

Montefiore had some endearing idiosyncrasies. Although he was a wealthy man, he spent little on himself, always travelled third class, patronised the cheapest shops, and would hesitate to ring a bell for fear of troubling the servants.[416]

However, he was not without warmth of character.

He was so full of whimsical fun, and endowed with such a sense of humour, that either when presiding at a public meeting, or at a Committee, or when talking privately to an individual, he was able to fill his audience with a joy of life, which was delightfully exhilarating, even in the most serious, the dullest of saddest of moments.

Basil Henriques[417]

Biography for Claude Montefiore

Dr Claude Goldsmid Montefiore (1858–1938), the son of Nathaniel and Emma Montefiore, was descended from two famous Anglo-Jewish families. He was the great nephew of Sir Moses Montefiore, the philanthropist and champion of Jewish rights, who was honoured for his services to the Jewish community and a prominent member of the Board of Deputies. He was also the nephew of Horatio Montefiore, one of the founders of the West London Synagogue. His maternal grandfather was Sir Isaac Goldsmid, another founding member of West London Synagogue and of University College, London.

Montefiore received his early education privately because of his delicate health but went on to study Classics at Balliol College, Oxford, where he formed a close friendship with the Master, the classicist and theologian, Benjamin Jowett, who was to be a lasting

---

[414] Leonard G. Montefiore, OBE, 'Memories of My Father' in *The First Fifty Years.*
[415] Ibid.
[416] Anonymous article, 'The Life and Work of C G Montefiore', *Liberal Jewish Monthly*, Claude Montefiore Centenary Number, June 1958.
[417] Taken from the diary of Sir Basil Henriques.

influence on him. Intending to enter the Jewish ministry, he subsequently spent some time studying theology in Berlin.

On his return from Germany, Montefiore quickly became involved in various educational activities such as the London School Board, the Froebel Institute and later the University College of Southampton (now Southampton University). He also worked on behalf of the Jewish Education Board and sat on the Council of the Jews' College. Given these many involvements, Claude Montefiore abandoned his original plans to become a rabbi.

Montefiore soon established his reputation as a scholar and spiritual authority as the result of the lectures he gave (notably the Hibbert lectures on *The Origins of Religion as Illustrated by the Ancient Hebrews*) and his publications through which he aimed to dissipate tensions between Jews and Christians and to modernise Jewish beliefs.

His early publications included his *Bible for Home Reading* (1907) which made a permanent contribution to the science of theology. In 1898 he founded, with the outstanding Rabbinic scholar, Israel Abrahams, the *Jewish Quarterly Review* which they subsequently jointly edited.

Montefiore ranked as one of the leading philanthropists in the Anglo-Jewish community and held office in various important bodies. He was elected as President of the Anglo-Jewish Association in 1895, was a prominent member of the Council of the Jewish Colonization Association and was President of the Society for the Protection of Women and Children.

At the urging of Lily Montagu he became President of the Jewish Religious Union when it was established in 1902 and the first President of the LJS, a role which he held until shortly before his death in 1938. During his time as President he gave regular addresses at the synagogue, which were very popular and attracted large congregations. Montefiore's publications were highly influential, especially his 1903 book *Liberal Judaism – An Essay* and his *Outlines of Liberal Judaism,* which was for many years the standard text on Liberal Judaism. In 1926, when the World Union for Progressive Judaism was founded, he became its President.

At the age of twenty-eight, Montefiore married Therese Schorstein, the granddaughter of a Polish rabbi. She died three years later having given birth to a son, Leonard Montefiore, who became a well-known communal worker and leader of Anglo-Jewry. Montefiore remarried in 1902. His second wife, Florence Ward, was a convert to Judaism and Vice Mistress of Girton College, Cambridge.

Sir Louis Gluckstein (President 1942–79)

The second President of the synagogue was Sir Louis Halle Gluckstein[418] who had, since 1933, been its Vice-President.

> When Claude Montefiore, our first President, died in 1938, my father was asked to succeed him, but he felt he could not follow immediately in the footsteps of such a great man, and it took two years before he agreed. My father then remained President for some forty years,

---

[418] See photographs 18, 67, and 72.

a period which covered the Second World War and the disastrous bombing of the synagogue on 1 November 1940.

Jean Jaffa (Pt. 3)

Sir Louis Gluckstein, sometimes referred to affectionately as 'Luigi', was very prominent in public life.

He had been an MP, and it was the great regret of his life that he did not make it to Cabinet rank, for which he undoubtedly had the calibre. The war came and he was not in the right place at the right time.

David Goldberg (Pt. 3)

He devoted an inordinate amount of time to LJS affairs and had many skills and extensive experience, which benefitted the synagogue.

He was President for many years. He talked to somebody at the synagogue every day to see how things were going.

Doreen Gluckstein[419]

During his presidency, he mounted many campaigns on behalf of the synagogue and Liberal Judaism. He had a number of differences of opinion with the Board of Deputies, such as over his right as an MP to express his misgivings on the establishment of the State of Israel.

He was a very religious man, wedded to Liberal Judaism in the form that it was shaped by the founders of the synagogue.

Of the past presidents, Louis Gluckstein was an imposing figure, very establishment. He was opposed to change. I didn't have any changes to advocate, but I got the impression that whatever changes were advocated, he was against them.

Denis Glaser

Many people found Sir Louis to be a kind man.

I got on quite well with Sir Louis Gluckstein, the President of the synagogue, until his death in the 1970s. He sort of mentored me, saying, 'If you have any problems and I can help, come to me and I will do what I can.' A real gentleman of the old school!

Raymon Benedyk (Pt. 3)

However, he was a very forceful character.

When I came to the LJS, Sir Louis Gluckstein was President. Known as 'Luigi', he had the style of a patrician and could be fearsome by all accounts.

David Goldberg (Pt. 3)

As Chairman, Luigi ran the whole show. I had known him all my life – he was 'Uncle Luigi' – but I never did anything of which he disapproved.

Margaret Rigal (Pt. 3)

But not everybody was daunted by him.

Aged six, and recently into gymnastics, I was a bridesmaid to my mother's brother. Standing behind the bride and probably bored, I started to practise my exercises. The best man, my

---

[419] ULPS Oral History Project, interview with Doreen Gluckstein. See Appendix 1.

father (who don't forget was more than six-and-a-half feet tall), turned round, waved a long finger at me and whispered loudly: 'Stop it!' Apparently I waved my finger back at him, and continued to amuse the congregation.

Jean Jaffa (Pt. 3)

72. *Sir Louis Gluckstein, LJS President 1944–79. Photograph by Geremy Butler Photography. (undated, c. 1975)*

Biography for Sir Louis Gluckstein

Sir Louis Halle Gluckstein (1899–1979) was born in Hampstead, the son of Joseph Gluckstein who was one of the founders of the J. Lyons and Co. coffee house and catering empire in London. His mother, Francesca Halle, was an American opera singer, and his elder sister, Hannah, was the noted portrait painter, Gluck.

He was educated at St Paul's School and Lincoln College, Oxford, where he gained an Honours Degree in Jurisprudence.

Louis Gluckstein was commissioned into the Suffolk Regiment during the First World War and also saw action as a Colonel in the Second World War, being Mentioned in Dispatches in the early part of the war. He remained in the Territorial Army until his retirement in 1948, and was awarded the Territorial Decoration in 1947.

He was called to the Bar by Lincoln's Inn in 1922 and became King's Counsel in 1945, Bencher in 1952, Officer of the Inn in 1966, and Treasurer in 1970.

Louis Gluckstein was elected as a Conservative MP for Nottingham East at the 1931 general election, a seat which he held until 1945. He was a very tall man and at over 6 foot 7 inches, is believed to have been the tallest MP until the election of Daniel Kawczynski in 2005.

He was Deputy Lieutenant of the County of London in 1952 and a member of the LCC from 1955 until 1964. He then became a Conservative councillor on the Greater London Council (GLC) for the Cities of London and Westminster from 1964 to 1967. He became an Alderman and Chairman of the Finance Committee in 1967 and in 1968 he was appointed Chairman of the Greater London Council. He was President of the St Marylebone Conservative Association.

His other involvements included: Chairman of the Bernhard Baron St George's Jewish Settlement, Commandant of the Jewish Lads' Brigade, Vice-President (1961) and then President (1965) of the Royal Albert Hall, President of the St John's Wood Protection Society, Board Member of British Transport Hotels and Life Vice-President of the Services Kinema Corporation.

He was knighted in the Coronation Honours of 1953, was made a Commander of the Order of the British Empire (CBE) in the 1964 New Year Honours, and was promoted to Knight Grand Cross (GBE) in the 1969 Queen's Birthday Honours.

He married Doreen Klean in 1925 with whom he had three children, Jean[420] (who became a famous contralto singing under the name of Jean Grayston), Roy and David.

Maxwell Stern (President 1987–92)

After a gap of eight years, Maxwell Stern[421] followed Sir Louis Gluckstein as President, having been Chairman of the LJS Council since 1981. He was President for five years.

> It has always been felt that the presidency of the LJS should be an honour that is kept for outstanding people, not just automatically conferred. So there was a gap after Luigi died. Maxwell Stern then became President. We had quite a formal relationship. I found he could be a bit difficult and rather tough financially.
>
> David Goldberg (Pt. 3)

Biography for Maxwell Stern

Maxwell Stern (1910–1997) was the son of a Czech farmer's son who emigrated to London in 1906 to work with his two uncles who had already established a timber firm in the Victoria Docks.

Maxwell Stern won scholarships to St Paul's School and then the Ecole de Commerce in Lausanne. He subsequently joined the Royal Marines and served in Alexandria, Colombo and, after D-Day, in France. He had reached the rank of Captain by the time that he was demobilised.

He rejoined the family hardwood business which had virtually ceased to exist during the war and, with his brother Geoffrey, built it up to a successful public company. He served on the Committee of the Timber Trades Federation and became Chairman of the Hardwood Section.

---

[420] See her memories in Part Three of the book.
[421] See photograph 75.

In 1945 he and his wife, Anne, were married at the LJS. They had two daughters, Felicity and Jenny.

He was involved in a wide range of charitable and voluntary activities. He and Anne were among the founders of Sunridge Court care home and Maxwell Stern served on its committee for many years. He was also Justice of the Peace in the Tottenham Bench.

Maxwell Stern had a wide range of interests which included music, art, literature, bridge, photography, trains and cricket.

He was one of the first members of the LJS. He was educated in the Religion School in its Hill Street days and was one of those who laid a brick in 1924 when the new synagogue was being constructed in St John's Wood Road.

For a number of years he was the synagogue's Senior Treasurer and then Chairman. It was during his Chairmanship that the 'Climate of Change' had to be faced when the building was found to have major structural problems. He prepared the way for the rebuilding of the synagogue under the leadership of Sir Peter Lazarus. He was elected as the third President of the LJS in 1987.

Sir Peter Lazarus (President 1995–96)

73. *Sir Peter Lazarus, LJS President 1994–95. (undated)*

Sir Peter Lazarus was President for just a year, but he had previously served twice as Chairman of the Council, first between 1972 and 1975 and then between 1987 and 1992.

His grandparents were amongst the founding members of the synagogue and his father, Kenneth Lazarus, was a member of the LJS Council for more than twenty years, many of them as Chairman of the House Committee. Sir Peter's family remain involved today as the fourth and fifth generations of Lazaruses in membership of the synagogue.

In his early days as a member of the Council, which he joined on his father's death in 1961, Sir Peter sought to bring about changes in the LJS and in doing so came into conflict with Sir Louis Gluckstein, then synagogue President.

> Sir Peter Lazarus was a very nice guy ... I am not very much into politics so I don't really know what happened. I think what he wanted to do, he didn't always achieve. My impression was that he was under-voiced.
>
> Denis Glaser

He was a very ambitious man, both in his professional career and regarding his role in the synagogue.

> I knew Peter when we were both young men and I remember going for a walk with him. They had a house in Bognor Regis and invited us down for weekends every so often and I went for these hikes with him and we must have both been in our late twenties then and I said to him, 'Peter what is your objective?' He said, 'I want to get to the top.' And he did. I said, 'I want to build up a business.' We both succeeded in what we aimed at.
>
> Willie Kessler (Pt. 3)

He had a reputation for correctness.

> He was a stickler for doing and saying the right thing. When we had Council meetings, I would prepare the minutes for him or get my secretary to type up a draft and we would ensure that he received a copy of that draft almost within twenty-four or forty-eight hours of the meeting. I would get it back with his amendments and there were always plenty of them. I might put something down in one sentence and he would make two or three paragraphs of it, which was perhaps right.
>
> Raymon Benedyk (Pt. 3)

> The best Chairman or President I had in my thirty years here was Peter Lazarus. I loved Peter. He was an outstandingly capable person. He was very, very tough in his judgements and if he thought you were not pulling your weight or if he didn't respect you intellectually, you were out. However, if you measured up to his exacting standards, which John and I obviously did, he was wonderful – he would fight for you financially, work with you very closely. For a long time after he died, I would think about him almost daily and ask myself, 'What would Peter have done?' or 'How would Peter have dealt with this?'
>
> David Goldberg (Pt. 3)

Some people found him stern and somewhat autocratic.

> I knew Peter before he got autocratic and a little pompous, some people thought. It never struck me that he was. This happens with old friends, doesn't it? You remember them as they were when you are both youngish and you forgive them any oddities as they get older.
>
> Willie Kessler (Pt. 3)

He was, however, less stern in private settings.

> Sir Peter Lazarus could seem intimidating, but when I was co-ordinating the rebuilding of the synagogue I got to know him quite well and saw another side to him. Although when he chaired Council he was quite stern and very correct, in private he was very supportive and also open about his feelings. While I was working out of Tim Simon's offices in the City, Peter would drop by for a coffee and to smoke his pipe and share his anxieties about

the project. His commitment was total and when we were nearing re-opening he set himself the task of visiting the synagogue every day in case there were problems for the new administrator.

Prue Baker

He was much admired, especially for the leadership he displayed during the rebuilding of the synagogue.

> Peter Lazarus stayed on as Chairman to see us into the new building and he was very, very good at it.
>
> Michael Salmon

> David respected him enormously and loved working with him, and the rebuilding of the new synagogue was very much a shared passion supported by an immensely able and enthusiastic team of professionals and congregants.
>
> Carole Goldberg

He had many friends amongst the congregation.

> My parents had a huge respect and love for Peter Lazarus. The fact that the LJS is still there is due in no small measure to his commitment and his leadership.
>
> Edward Cross

> Peter Lazarus and his wife, Elizabeth, gave a memorable dinner in the City on their Ruby wedding. His sons and his brother, Norman, did a hilarious 'turn' mentioning 'Sir Peter, as he is informally known at home', which raised a great laugh. He was very kind to my daughter, Annabel.
>
> Jocelyne Tobin (Pt. 3)

He is remembered as having made an enormous contribution, both to the synagogue and to the wider community.

> Peter Lazarus was 'old school', the essence of integrity and decency. He came from a background where it was believed that those who were fortunate in life had an obligation to 'give something back'. He was a man of huge intellect and achievement in the outside world but was proud of his family and loyal to his Jewish roots.
>
> Carole Goldberg

Biography for Sir Peter Lazarus

Sir Peter Esmond Lazarus was born in 1926. He attended Westminster School during the war years. On leaving school he joined the Army, was commissioned in the Royal Artillery and was still under training when the war ended.

He was demobilised in 1948 and went to Wadham College, Oxford, to read Greats, but after a year decided to enter the Civil Service. Having passed the entrance exam he joined the Ministry of Transport as an Assistant Principal where he remained for twenty-one years.

He was rapidly promoted and became Principal by 1953, Assistant Secretary in 1962 and Under Secretary in 1968. In 1971 he was seconded to the Treasury for two years before moving to the Department of the Environment as Deputy Secretary. He was made Companion of Order of Bath in 1975. He became a Permanent Secretary in 1982 and was knighted in January 1985. He retired a year later.

Following his retirement he was very involved in the Jewish Lads' and Girls' Brigade as a Commandant. He was also Chairman of the Jews' Temporary Shelter and a member of the Allocations Board of Jewish Continuity.

Sir Peter was Chairman of the LJS between 1972 and 1975 and again during the time that the synagogue was rebuilt and was President of the synagogue between 1994 and 1995.

He met his future wife, Elizabeth Atwell, at her 19th birthday party and they married in 1950. They had three sons, Richard, Stephen and James and ten grandchildren. He died in 1995.

Chapter Three: Volunteering and the LJS's professional staff

Volunteering

FROM ITS EARLY days in Hill Street, many of the activities involved in managing the synagogue have been carried out on a voluntary basis. Early memories of voluntary contributions include the maintenance of the synagogue linens.

> My mother was the custodian of the scroll covers and other fabrics, because Mrs Mattuck had said to her, 'Mary, dear, will you look after the scroll covers?' She would go in and iron anything that had become creased, and saw to it that the rabbis' gowns were cleaned when necessary. She looked after the *tallitot* too, but there weren't very many then. I don't think anybody wore a *tallit* other than the rabbis. My mother continued as custodian until she was a very old lady, when I took over.
>
> Margaret Rigal (Pt. 3)

The activities that have been carried out on an unpaid basis are numerous.[422]

> Following my retirement from Council, I took over as Chief Steward from Martin Slowe for three years before retiring in 2007. Martin had acted as Chief Steward for many, many years and had done so with wonderful efficiency, endearing himself to our members, especially the elderly. He was indeed a hard act to follow. The High Holydays require over a hundred volunteers, and it is something of a logistical nightmare to ensure that every slot is filled.
>
> Tim Simon (Pt. 3)

> One of my other preoccupations is the care of our scrolls (not the mantles, which are looked after lovingly and generously by Christine Stevenson). I have a particular interest in our Czech scroll, which we hold on permanent loan from the Czech Memorial Scrolls Trust. Until recently we had a second one, which has now been transferred to a newly formed Liberal community whose need is greater than ours.
>
> Bob Kirk (Pt. 3)

---

[422] The LJS Annual report for 2010 listed 200 volunteers.

Lottie Nash was a member of the synagogue who was a registered blind person. She came every Saturday to services, and one day was telling me how frustrating it was for her not to be able to read the synagogue newsletter. Now, I knew Lottie was getting the *Jewish Chronicle* and the local newspaper on tape, so I thought, why don't I put the newsletter on tape for her too? This was in the days when Ann and Bob Kirk were the editors. I spoke to them and they said, 'Fine'. So every month I read the newsletter aloud and recorded it on to a tape for Lottie. After she had listened to it, she would ring me up and we would discuss it. She really cared about the synagogue and was interested to know what was going on. I carried on taping the newsletter until Lottie died. Then Ann and Bob told me there was another lady who would appreciate the recordings, so I carried on. This lady was a Hungarian refugee and she was so grateful that when she sent back the tape for me to re-use, she also enclosed another tape with a thank you message. When she died, she left me her antique china candlesticks.

Anita Schwartz

The other main piece of work that I have done is on the synagogue's burial records, which I have corrected and computerised. In order to do this, I spent probably two years recording stones in the cemetery and then computerising the records. I have also subsequently computerised the marriage records.

George Rigal (Pt. 3)

Some members of the congregation have developed specialisms.

I have now been on the Library Committee for about five or six years and Chairman for about a year. Our committee is quite small and there is a very good team of volunteers. They supervise the library on a Saturday morning. Once a year we have a joint meeting when we update them on what has happened during the year and hold a party to say, 'Thank you'.

Barbara Godfrey (Pt. 3)

In the beginning I hardly ever came to the LJS, leaving Alex to go on her own. However, after a few years, Trevor Moross, the then Chairman, announced that he would be hosting a new members and volunteer evening. Alex and I went along and I heard someone say that the LJS was looking for a security co-ordinator. I had not a clue what that meant but it sounded inviting and curiosity got the better of me and I said I'd give it a go, still hardly knowing how to spell security ... The rest is history except to say that I obviously discovered my niche. Not being a 'Services' person I prefer to make my own 'Service' being outside in all weathers trying my best to ensure the safety and security of all who enter the LJS.

Tony Weiss

Others have taken on multiple roles.

Apart from her teaching, Celia Rapp attended every service and meeting in the synagogue, served on various committees, started and ran the Brownies pack, acted as Secretary of the United Charities Fund, helped with the Out and About Club, and the Darby and Joan Club, and the Communal *Seder*, and just about everything else that took place at the LJS. She did it voluntarily, conscientiously lovingly and enthusiastically.

John Rayner[423]

My parents were on so many rotas at one stage that my mother had to keep a written record to make sure none of them were overlooked.

Michael Hart (Pt. 3)

---

[423] Eulogy by John Rayner at the funeral of Celia Rapp, 'Farewell to Celia Rapp', May 1984. Copy in LJS archives.

One of the more demanding roles undertaken in a voluntary capacity is that of editing the synagogue's newsletter, the format and content of which has evolved in a variety of directions over the years.

> Editing the newsletter was a difficult, but interesting and enjoyable job. I used the old methods, with everything on hard copy, paste-ups, etc. We used a jobbing printer (no computers for us at that time), but I had to do the layout for him, although he produced the camera-ready copy. Also we didn't have the advantage of emails, so it was quite time-consuming chasing people for their articles. We used to have an editorial meeting once a month, when David Goldberg and we would decide what should be the lead article and what we should commission. Obviously, people were also encouraged to submit contributions. At that time, we produced eleven issues per year with July/August a joint edition. It was quite hard to find a stand-in so that we could take a holiday.
>
> Ann Kirk (Pt. 3)

In 2003 a seminar for Community Magazines was organised by the Board of Deputies in conjunction with the *Jewish Chronicle*. The *LJS News* was awarded first prize in the category of Best Synagogue Newsletter for 2003, from among more than ninety entries. Bernie Bulkin attended the seminar and collected the certificate and engraved plate which is on display in the synagogue.

Some members of the LJS have been able to contribute using their professional skills.

> In 1958 I was approached by Sir Louis Gluckstein, the then President of The Liberal Jewish Synagogue, who asked me if I would join the House Committee with my experience of furnishing and furniture. At that time the chairman of the committee was Bernard Lawton and we were responsible fully for all the buildings at the cemetery, the cleaning staff and the caretaker as well as the main building at no 28 St John's Wood Road.
>
> Neil Levitt

> One of the more interesting and sad problems on which I was called upon to advise as Honorary Solicitor, was whether the marriage performed at the LJS of a former Bond girl was valid. She was not originally Jewish, but went through the full conversion process at the LJS. She had appeared in *For Your Eyes Only*, was strikingly beautiful, but it turned out was a transsexual. Although she was legally married according to European law, that was not the case in England, so the marriage was deemed to be void. British law regards gender reassignment as merely a cosmetic procedure, and the changes in legal status that are allowed are similarly only cosmetic. She could be called female on her passport, and that was about it. To all intents and purposes, in the eyes of the law, she was male because it said so on her birth certificate. As a male, she obviously was not allowed to marry another man. They were apparently forced by her husband's family to come back from their honeymoon and they separated.
>
> Tim Simon (Pt. 3)

> Within the LJS there are so many families and family friends who contribute much to the synagogue. My own input has been relatively limited by comparison – although I did have a 'professional' look at the old building with Maxwell Stern all those years ago when the decision to repair or rebuild was under consideration.
>
> Deborah Lazarus

> Andrew [Hart], year after year, has taken on the role of doctor available (along with Stephen Kahn) for any medical emergencies that occur occasionally during the High Holydays, rarely moving from his assigned seat throughout the whole of the *Yom Kippur* service.
>
> Michael Hart (Pt. 3)

Others have developed skills as a result their voluntary roles, which have sometimes helped them in their professional careers or made contacts which have led on to other involvements.

> I have learned many things from all the rabbis at the LJS, not just about Judaism, but also about how to teach through observing their different styles.
>
> Bernie Bulkin (Pt. 3)

> I was on the Education Committee when Anthony Roe chaired it. I met interesting people, including Edith Kahn, who was the Headmistress of Fleet School. She said to me, 'I've got just the job for you when you retire.' She said I should become a steward at the Festival Hall. And I remembered that, and wrote in, and was indeed a steward there for many years.
>
> Sybil Gottlieb

Some volunteering roles are very visible; others are less so.

> I consider it a privilege to be able to be part of the volunteer group of the LJS, whether it is in big things like being Treasurer or *LJS News* co-editor, or in the smaller and less noticed things like greeting people on Friday evening, visiting Rosa Mintz and Harold Young in hospital, or teaching a small group of members on Saturday.
>
> Bernie Bulkin (Pt. 3)

While some activities formerly carried out on a voluntary basis are now carried out by professional staff, the reverse is the case for other activities.

> When Louis Steinman retired as the Beadle in 1993 after about thirty years of service, we decided that his duties should become a congregational responsibility. Martin Slowe, George Rigal and I became the first *shammashim* and I still lead the team, which is now sixteen-strong, with a great deal of support from the synagogue office. For several years I organised member participation in services.
>
> Bob Kirk (Pt. 3)

Building on the early example of Lily Montagu, volunteering has included assisting the rabbis in the spiritual leadership of the synagogue.

> I know he [Michael Simon] gained much satisfaction from his pseudo-rabbinic activities, which have included designing and running two adult *B'nei Mitzvah* programmes, a *Talmud* class and an alternative *Kol Nidre* service, as well as leading and participating in services.
>
> Carolyn Simon (Pt. 3)

Professional staff

Soon after it was established, the LJS found it necessary to employ professional staff to assist with the management of its affairs. The first professional post to be established was that of Secretary to the synagogue. The person appointed to this position (a Miss Wilson), stayed only a short time.[424] The second person appointed was Michael Duparc,[425] who

---

[424] First LJS Annual Report, 1913.
[425] His full name was Isaac Michael Duparc, but was also known as 'Jack'. He signed himself under the initials of JMD. See photographs 10 and 74.

had previously been a journalist with the *Jewish Chronicle*. He held this position from 1913 until he partially retired in 1961, except when he was temporarily replaced by Bethal Halford during the First World War.

> The appointment of Mr Duparc in 1913 helped further to consolidate the work of the congregation at Hill Street. Besides being Secretary of The Liberal Jewish Synagogue, he became Hon. Secretary of the JRU, and his capacity and devotion assisted our work in every possible way.
>
> Lily Montagu

> He was a great character with a great sense of humour. He was always very proud that Dr Mattuck had once said to him, 'Both you and I are men of the world'.
>
> John Rayner[426]

74. 'Jack' Isaac Michael Duparc 1881–1980, Synagogue Secretary 1913–61 and thereafter 'loyal servant to the congregation' until his death. (undated)

When work began on the new purpose-built synagogue in St John's Wood Road, much of the work connected with the building plans fell to Michael Duparc. When the synagogue was opened in 1925, it became the centre of Michael Duparc's life. He was therefore devastated when he received the call on 2 November 1940, telling him that the synagogue had been bombed.[427]

Michael Duparc taught for many years in the Religion School and his many responsibilities included acting as Marriage Secretary for the LJS, a post he held from 1934 until this role was taken on by Raymon Benedyk in 1973 (see below). After his partial retirement, Michael Duparc became Financial Secretary, regularly travelling thirty miles from his home in Little Chalfont, Buckinghamshire to the LJS until his 96th birthday in 1977.[428] He died in his hundredth year in 1980.

---

[426] ULPS Oral History project, interview with John Rayner. See Appendix 1.
[427] Pamela Fletcher Jones, 'Mr Duparc remembers'.
[428] Ibid.

Of course, the Secretary for many years was the same man, Mr Duparc, who was devoted and went on long after he ceased to be Secretary. He came and did odd things because his heart was in the synagogue.

Maxwell Stern[429]

As the Liberal movement grew and membership of the LJS expanded, the roles of managing the synagogue and supporting the JRU (later the ULPS) were split and the number of staff increased. While Michael Duparc remained responsible for supporting the LJS, various committees and subcommittees dealing with governance issues were set up and the post of Organising Secretary was established to deal with matters relating to synagogue members.

Charles Berwitz, previously Secretary to the JRU, was appointed as first Organising Secretary to the LJS before the Second World War. In 1945 he was replaced by Peggy Lang,[430] who in 1965 became the Editor of ULPS Publications. Peggy Lang remained very involved in LJS affairs, especially those relating to community care. Her knowledge of the LJS was encyclopaedic.

She [Peggy Lang], more than anyone else, gave up her life for the LJS, and the ULPS ... She was often here at the synagogue for a great many hours. She was extremely able and dedicated all round, as well as knowledgeable. In a sense she has never been replaced. The LJS Publication Fund was named after her.

John Rayner[431]

John Levinson, a member of the synagogue, took over the role of Secretary to the synagogue on Michael Duparc's retirement in 1961. His health deteriorated quite rapidly and John Cross was appointed as Joint Secretary, leaving John Levinson to concentrate mainly on the production of the then fortnightly newsletter.

There was the infamous stencil duplicator but, by then, the LJS had also acquired an early version photocopier, which was kept in John Cross's office. The ULPS was not allowed to use it, but if John was in a good mood, you could give him the paper you wanted copied and he would do it for you. Mr Duparc would wander along the corridors and occasionally talk to us, but I doubt whether he ever used the duplicator or the photocopier.

Rosita Rosenberg

John Cross had been a prominent member of the Alumni Society and, with his wife Bobbie, went on to support youth activities at the LJS and in the wider Liberal movement. Following John Levinson's death in 1967, John Cross continued in the role of Secretary until his own death a few years later

A huge gap was left in the smooth running of the secretariat with the deaths of John Levinson and then John Cross within five years of each other. At that time there were no computers and other records were limited. Lionel Symonds, who had joined the staff shortly before, took over as acting secretary when John died. The staff rallied round, particularly Marianne Ghosh who was John Rayner's secretary. Previously she had worked closely with Peggy Lang. She had an amazing memory for procedure such as High Holyday arrangements,

---

[429] ULPS Oral History Project, interview with Maxwell Stern. See Appendix 1.
[430] See photographs 23 and 36.
[431] ULPS Oral History Project, interview with John Rayner. See Appendix 1.

the Communal *Seder*, etc. Remember at that time there was an overflow service for the High Holydays held in Porchester Hall, Paddington.

Pam Herson

John Cross and John Levinson were succeeded by Raymon Benedyk in 1973.

At first, I found it quite difficult. There was no guidance available because both my immediate predecessors had very recently died, leaving part-timer, Lionel Symonds, holding the fort as best he could. Whatever I learned, I picked up for myself, such as taking minutes and dealing with members' enquiries.

Raymon Benedyk (Pt. 3)

In the office each rabbi had his own secretary and the Secretary of the synagogue ran all aspects of the rest, taking on new members who were interviewed on Sunday mornings by a rabbi and then a member of Council. My impression was that most things ran extremely efficiently.

Neil Levitt

Raymon Benedyk[432] in his memories (see Part Three) provides interesting insights into the organisation of the synagogue and the relationships between staff, lay and spiritual leaders during the 1970s and 1980s.

The original Synagogue Secretary was Mr Michael Duparc, who had been in office from 1912 until 1961. He was still around when I first started, and was a mine of interesting information about 'the old days'. He warned me that if ever there was a disagreement between the secretariat and the rabbis, the Honorary Officers would always side with the rabbis and it was therefore better not to have any disagreements with the rabbis. As it happens, I had no arguments with the rabbis. In fact, think I got on quite well with them all.

Raymon Benedyk (Pt. 3)

His job provided him with a wealth of anecdotes.

I did have one or two funny experiences as Synagogue Secretary. When I first started, the standard annual membership rate was £32.00 per year (we mustn't compare that with today's amount). When I found someone paying only £10.00 per year, although living at a smart address in Maida Vale, I asked him to increase his contribution to the standard rate. His response was, 'I can't afford to increase my subscription as I have to go to the Bahamas every winter for my health.' He was quite serious!

Raymon Benedyk (Pt. 3)

One of the characters of the synagogue's Hill Street days was the first Beadle and Sexton, Isaac Nathan, who was appointed in 1913.

One of the duties that Mr Nathan carried out, possibly self-appointed, was to walk in front of each bridal procession up the aisle to the LJS *bimah*. When Michael [Duparc] and Ursula [Bamberger, daughter of one of the founding families of the synagogue] were to be married, she confided to Dr Mattuck that the sight of that familiar, formal figure walking just ahead of her might reduce her to giggles, so Dr Mattuck decided that the time had come to

---

[432] See photographs 20, 68, and 76

change the wedding procedure and he tactfully suggested to Mr Nathan that he felt the bridegroom needed his support more than the bride, on these occasions, and said that, from then on, he should accompany the bridegroom to the *chuppah* and await the bride with him!

Michael Duparc[433]

After Isaac Nathan's retirement in 1945, he was succeeded by Joe Foreman who had, for many years, taught Hebrew in the Religion School as well as being secretary to Rabbi Mattuck. He was designated as Clerk to the synagogue with responsibility also for cemetery matters.

> Mr Foreman had his own room where he looked after all the burials and the cemetery. One could hardly get into his office as his files were strewn all over the floor and tables, but he seemed to know exactly what he was doing.
>
> Neil Levitt

> The contribution Joe Foreman made as the Funeral Secretary is frequently not recognised. In fact he enlarged on the job he inherited and built up quite a reputation for his sympathy and efficiency when dealing with the bereaved both among the congregation and with non-members. As a result he attracted outsiders to the Liberal movement some of whom became members. He worked from a gloomy office in the bowels of no. 28 surrounded by urns containing unclaimed ashes which he took to Pound Lane every so often. His desk was always covered with papers because he had to do his own secretarial work although a couple of us used to assist him in a voluntary capacity from time to time.
>
> Pam Herson

75. LJS President, Maxwell Stern, making a presentation to Joe Foreman, LJS Sexton, in honour of his fifty years of service at the synagogue. (1982)

---

433 Pamela Fletcher Jones, 'Mr Duparc remembers'.

He remained with the synagogue in the role of Sexton for many years but was followed as Beadle by Louis Steinman[434] in 1961.

> Louis Steinman was full of good stories, particularly one about Leslie Edgar who, on hearing that Louis had been in the Guards as a bugler, got him to demonstrate his bugle and bring his busby along so he could see it.
>
> George Rigal (Pt. 3)

76. *Raymon Benedyk (left), Synagogue Secretary and Lionel Symonds (right), Assistant Synagogue Secretary. (undated, c. 1974)*

The synagogue has had a number of dedicated caretakers, who are remembered with warmth.

> The caretakers at that time were Mr and Mrs Temple and their dog called Paul which seemed to be constantly walking up and down the main stairs to the caretaker's flat. Either the son, or was it Mr Temple himself, was also called Paul, which was very confusing.
>
> Michael Hart (Pt. 3)

> They [the Temples] retired in the early 1970s, to be followed by Don and Mrs Eaton. He was a very charming man and a hard worker. In particular, he was most concerned about the cleanliness of the building. He washed down walls that had not been cleaned for years. He also scrubbed the floor of the Sanctuary where, over the years, dirt and grime had accumulated around the feet of the benches. The improvement was obvious for all to see. When he died, Mrs Eaton's son-in-law, Fred Shelley, took over and, once again, we were in good hands.
>
> Raymon Benedyk (Pt. 3)

---

[434] See photograph 22.

Fred Shelley served for thirty-two years in the Royal Navy, retiring as a Chief Petty Officer – the highest non-commissioned rank. His wife, Marcia, worked in the LJS office for many years.

> With his imposing frame and Navy background, he did appear daunting at times – but it did not take long for me to realise that underneath is a kind and warm-hearted person, who would do anything to help in a genuine situation.
>
> Tim Farrell

> Their greatest hour was the move to the church in Loudoun Road in 1987 when the old building was pulled down and the new one was being built. Marcia readily moved her files and the flow of activities was never interrupted. Fred worked all hours ensuring that everything was in place for the continuation of services, and no task was too much for him. His adaptability was no doubt due to his experiences in the Navy. On returning to the new building in 1991 Fred had much to learn about the state-of-the-art air conditioning and sound system, and all the intricacies of modern architecture. Meanwhile Marcia learned and became an expert in computer skills. Despite the increased activities in the building one could always be sure that Fred would welcome one at the security door with a little story and help as to where the meeting they might be attending was.
>
> Neil Levitt

77. *Farewell to Fred Shelley (caretaker) and his wife, Marcia. On left Willie Kessler. (2006)*

In recent years, further professional posts have been established, including that of Community Care Co-ordinator to take on some of the congregational welfare work previously carried out on a voluntary basis. Since its establishment in 2003, this post has been occupied by Liz Crossick.[435] In 1999 the post of Director of Education was set up, which was held by Jan Roseman until August 2010. She was succeeded by Dov Softi as Head of the Religion School.

---

[435] See section on the community life of the congregation.

The LJS professional staff and volunteers have a symbiotic relationship; they work side by side in the running of the synagogue. Sometimes the volunteers provide support for paid workers but in some instances the roles are reversed as in the case of the work of the Community Care Co-ordinator.

> When I first started, the job was only 11¼ hours a week. It was clear to me that my role needed to be to co-ordinate and support the synagogue volunteers rather than to do a lot of visiting myself. My approach is to work with a volunteer group leader to get a project going, provide training and then support the volunteers. That's my ethos: the volunteers do the work, and I support them.
>
> Liz Crossick

Chapter Four: The congregation of the LJS

Journeys to the LJS

SOME OF THOSE who joined the newly established LJS were attracted there because they had attended the early JRU services.

> My first knowledge of Liberal Judaism came from attending a service in the Wharncliffe Rooms in the Central Hotel at Euston, before there was a synagogue. Then I came to the services at that little synagogue in [Hill Street].
>
> Marjorie Moos[436]

Others were probably attracted by the rationality and simplicity of what was being offered by the LJS, but also because of the distinct 'Englishness' of its approach. Many early members were from families who were assimilated into the life of the country and, although they did not want to abandon their Jewish faith, they wanted a religious institution that could be compared to an English church, where hymns were sung and where sermons were of a high quality.

> Some members were primarily drawn to it [the LJS] by the Liberal Jewish presentation of Jewish thought and belief. They wanted services and teaching which expressed ideas in harmony with modern thought and life ... For one thing, they could understand the prayers so that the services meant something to them; they were not just a formal repetition of incomprehensible words. And the services had an outstanding beauty derived both from the prayers and from the music.
>
> Israel Mattuck[437]

> I think that my mother liked to be 'more "English" than the English' and she would have liked the services to be in English rather than Hebrew, therefore I think she was casting around for a different synagogue to join. She lit upon The Liberal Jewish Synagogue in St John's Wood Road.
>
> Denis Glaser

---

[436] Talk by Marjorie Moos to LJS Women's Society.
[437] Rabbi Dr I Mattuck, 'Liberal Judaism in Great Britain' in *The First Fifty Years*.

In particular, the early members wanted an institution noted for its decorum, and which could be differentiated from the 'oriental murmurings'[438] generally associated with Orthodox synagogues. However, some members of the congregation had, on occasion, to be reminded of the differences between The Liberal Jewish Synagogue and the more Orthodox ones to which they had previously belonged.

> The decorum was excellent. I well remember on a Holy Day at no. 28, my father telling the women of the congregation what he thought of them for wearing furs and jewellery to a service. It took many years to expunge some of the less desirable Orthodox behaviour, such as tipping the rabbi after a wedding or funeral.
>
> Dorothy Edgar[439]

Some early members of the synagogue were drawn there because of their connections with its leadership, either because they were related to them or they were involved in activities promoted by LJS leaders. This was particularly the case with Lily Montagu because of her prominent role in the World Union for Progressive Judaism and the girls' club she ran in Bloomsbury. A significant number of the initial congregants came from the West London Synagogue where Claude Montefiore was and remained a member throughout his life.

Once the synagogue had been in operation for some time, people began to join the LJS for other reasons. Some followed friends and family who had formed the initial congregation, others because they wanted to take advantage of the flourishing Religion School classes.

> Thanks to the enthusiasm and work of a band of voluntary teachers, the classes grew steadily and children of members and non-members led their parents into the congregation.
>
> Israel Mattuck[440]

> We were first made aware of the existence of the LJS through the Schlesingers, Frances and Erica's parents, who were friends of my parents. So it was considered a good idea that we should be sent off to Hill Street Sunday morning Religion School. I am not certain of the date, but it must have been about sixty-one years ago, when I was about six years old, and my brother, Eric, thirteen months older than I.
>
> Ruth Hadley[441]

A number of the early members of the synagogue were or became leading social workers of the day, such as Alice Model, Lilian Hill and Phyllis Gerson. They would have been attracted by the synagogue's ethical stance and the emphasis that was being placed on social service by the synagogue's leadership.

For others, the attraction was being in the vanguard of a new movement.

> Not all of the people may have come from conviction; the novelty itself aroused the interest of many.
>
> Eric Conrad[442]

---

[438] Interview with Rabbi Alexandra Wright 18 June 2010.
[439] ULPS Oral History Project, interview with Dorothy Edgar. See Appendix 1.
[440] Rabbi Dr I Mattuck, 'Liberal Judaism in Great Britain' in *The First Fifty Years*.
[441] Letter from Ruth Hadley to Rabbis Rayner, Goldstein and Goldberg.
[442] Eric V Conrad, *Lily H. Montagu: Prophet of Living Judaism*.

It is not easy to sketch a picture of the very early atmosphere. [It was about the] enthusiasm of pioneering, the pleasure in making do with such inadequate premises, resources and personnel.

Dorothy Edgar[443]

Another attraction would have been its accessibility. The LJS organised its activities to fit with people's lives, holding services on a Sunday as well as a Saturday afternoon to attract those who worked for five-and-a-half or six days a week.

The idea of the Sunday services was, I suppose, for business people. A man in the garment trade or a man who had a shop would be working on Saturdays and so it was an idea I remember to have Sunday services.

Maxwell Stern[444]

However, one of the biggest attractions was Rabbi Mattuck – people appreciated his powerful preaching and his willingness to address controversial and contemporary social issues. Some of those who attended his popular Sunday services subsequently became synagogue members. The Sunday services received a great deal of press coverage and raised the profile of the synagogue and so attracted more members.

[I]t was the force of Mattuck's personality, the sway of his preaching, and the quality of his religious instruction that turned curious newcomers into ardent disciples.

David Goldberg[445]

Rabbi Mattuck and his family lived originally in Buckland Crescent, NW3, and we lived round the corner in Belsize Square. My parents were Orthodox but they had a great respect and admiration for Rabbi Mattuck and Mrs Mattuck too. I was allowed to go to Hill Street one Saturday morning and I can still remember the surprise and joy that I felt – so different from all of the others I had attended before.

Elaine Falk[446]

Because of its high profile, the LJS attracted members whose Judaism had lapsed or who were not previously members of a synagogue.

Others joined The Liberal Jewish Synagogue who had not previously belonged to any synagogue, because they found in it an appeal which the others lacked.

Israel Mattuck[447]

The setting up of the Women's Society in 1923 brought new congregants to the LJS as many of its members were socially well connected. However, more significant growth occurred after 1925 when the grand new synagogue was opened in St John's Wood Road. This appears to have been pivotal in convincing people that this was a synagogue that was now well established and worth joining. For some people, the new building represented the beginning of the LJS.

---

[443] ULPS Oral History Project, interview with Dorothy Edgar. See Appendix 1.
[444] ULPS Oral History Project, interview with Maxwell Stern. See Appendix 1.
[445] Rabbi David Goldberg, entry in the *Oxford Dictionary of National Biography*.
[446] 'Anniversaries: Milestones in Liberal Judaism'. Elaine Falk was the grandmother of Rabbi Alexandra Wright.
[447] Rabbi Dr I Mattuck, 'Liberal Judaism in Great Britain' in *The First Fifty Years*.

One frequently hears the expression, 'I was one of the first members of The Liberal Jewish Synagogue', when what the speaker means is that he or she was in the front rank of those who joined when the present building [the first building at 28 St John's Wood Road] was opened in September 1925, The Liberal Jewish Synagogue is, of course, very much older than that.

Michael Duparc[448]

In the decade that preceded the Second World War, the LJS continued to capture the imagination and support of many of those in Anglo-Jewry who were looking for something new in respect of religious observance.

I was first introduced to Liberal Judaism in the early days of Hill Street when I was a young officer on leave in 1917. I had been brought up in the Orthodox tradition, but after the First World War I found myself in spiritual doubt and unhappiness within its narrow and unacceptable approach to Judaism. It was, therefore, an immense relief to me to find in Liberal Judaism what I had unsuccessfully been seeking as the religious guide and purpose of my life.

Louis Gluckstein[449]

My father had served for five years during World War One and he grew away from Orthodox Judaism. He liked the fact that men and women were able to sit together and that the LJS held services on Sunday mornings. Men didn't have to wear hats, and that appealed to him also.

Denise Franklin

During the interwar years, the synagogue was involved in a range of social welfare activities, which enhanced its reputation further. Although during the years of the Great Depression a number of members left as they could no longer afford the subscription, people continued to join the synagogue. The new members included refugees from Germany and elsewhere, including many who came to the country via *Kindertransport*.

My younger brother and I travelled on a *Kindertransport* to Belgium, where my uncle and aunt lived. We waited there until, through the enormous efforts of Miss Montagu and Rabbi Mattuck, my father was released from the camp at Sachsenhausen, where he was sent after *Kristallnacht* in 1938. He and my mother picked us up in Belgium to come to England. We found a flat in Kilburn, but Miss Montagu decided that we needed some rest and we moved to a cottage on a large estate in a village called Hasfield, Gloucestershire. My brother and I were schooled first of all in a local village school where the first priority was for us to learn English as neither of us could speak the language.

Walter Woyda (Pt. 3)

Some of these new members came because they had belonged to Progressive synagogues in Europe and, as Secretary of the World Union for Progressive Judaism, Lily Montagu was their first point of contact in Britain. However, a few came by accident not having a full understanding of the nature of the Liberal movement in Britain.

---

[448] J M Duparc, 'Our Congregations', *Liberal Jewish Monthly*.
[449] Sir Louis Gluckstein, 'The Work of Our Hands'.

> My parents belonged to the Liberal Synagogue in Germany, corresponding to the Reform synagogue here. One of the first things they did when they arrived in this country was to join the Liberal Synagogue. In fact they joined it by mistake because they thought it was Reform, as in Germany.
>
> Eva Feldman (Pt. 3)

By this time, many of the younger members of the synagogue were starting to marry and they brought into the congregation their new partners, who sometimes also brought with them their own families. Gradually there was established a pattern of intermarriage between the LJS and the Hampstead and West London Synagogues, which has persisted until today. However, not all families have been comfortable when their relations moved to the LJS.

> My father's parents, Michael and Sarah Abrahams, belonged to Hampstead (Orthodox) Synagogue in Dennington Park Road, where my grandfather was a warden. When my parents were engaged and then planned to be married at the LJS, the idea of their getting married in a Liberal synagogue was something of a shock to the Abrahams family!
>
> Jenny Nathan (Pt. 3)

> Because of my Benzimra grandparents' involvement with West London, my parents had to handle the move very carefully. My grandfather was disappointed about it, mainly because the family would no longer be involved in the same congregation.
>
> Michael Hart (Pt. 3)

In some cases, to avoid family rifts, families held dual membership of the LJS and the synagogue to which their families had traditionally belonged.

> My three children all went through the Religion School. Michael, the middle child, was very keen on doing that. He was the most religious of all three. When he came to age thirteen Danya insisted that the eldest, Daniel, should have a *Bar Mitzvah*. At that time the LJS did not allow *Bar Mitzvah*s, so we decamped to Alyth Gardens Synagogue (Reform). He had his *Bar Mitzvah* and Michael in his turn. Then Elaine also sang her portion for *Bat Mitzvah* there. We continued our membership at the LJS, so we were paying burial fees for both, which could have caused problems. We realised that we could not be buried in both places so we decided to make the LJS our main synagogue.
>
> Denis Glaser

Rabbi Mattuck worked valiantly to maintain contact with the scattered congregation during the Second World War and was rewarded by the return of many families to the synagogue in the post-war years. Some of those who might otherwise have left the synagogue felt a pressing need to remain involved because of the Holocaust.

As well as existing members returning, many new members joined as the result of a general renewal of interest in religion following the war and because some people had, as a result of the upheavals of 1939–45, broken their ties with their former synagogues. Many of the services conducted for members of the Armed Forces during the war had been progressive in character, with prayers often being said in English. This encouraged some to look for similar types of service when they were demobbed.[450]

---

[450] Lawrence Rigal and Rosita Rosenberg, *Liberal Judaism: The First Hundred Years*.

This [the rebuilding of the synagogue after it was bombed] was a great joy to me as was the reinforcement of numbers of young, keen members of the Anglo-Jewish community, who during their war services had reflected deeply about Judaism and had come to believe that the answer to their spiritual problems was to be found within the Liberal movement.

Louis Gluckstein[451]

However, the rapid growth of the synagogue's congregation during the post-war years was, in large part, due to an influx of young people. Many of them were attracted to the synagogue by the reputation of the Alumni Society, which was seen as being the foremost youth group in London and a means for people to meet their future partners.

Now, the most important aspect of things, when I came here, was the strength of the Alumni Society … in those days, I mean, we had a very active youth movement.

Robert Greenberg

I came into contact with Progressive Judaism when my younger sister, Adele, joined the Alumni Society for the sixteen to thirty age group in the late 1940s, and I tagged along.

Willie Kessler (Pt. 3)

Despite the death of Rabbi Mattuck in 1954, the LJS continued to have a high profile and to be seen as a significant force in Anglo-Jewry. Its activities were, by then, regularly covered in the national press and on the radio. The eminence of both its lay and its religious leaders not only attracted new members, but helped to retain existing members.

[My link with the LJS] wouldn't have lasted if I hadn't been one of many privileged congregants to be influenced and inspired by John Rayner, a man for whom I have undying, everlasting gratitude.

Michael Grade[452]

I was aware by this stage that the synagogue was a good place to be. Its rabbis were people of substance, and had lots of influence on the wider Jewish world. It was regarded as being the 'cathedral' of Liberal Judaism.

Ellen Schmidt (Pt. 3)

People continued to be attracted by the nature of Liberal Judaism and forms of worship at the LJS.

I became associated with the LJS when Brian [her son] got married here. Brian got married in 1960 or 1961, I think. We became members in 1962. We visited a couple of times before he got married. We both liked it. Before then we used to belong to an Orthodox synagogue because that was all we knew but we very rarely went because we couldn't understand what they were saying and couldn't follow what they were saying in the books so we hardly went but coming here was a real eye-opener. It was beautiful. It was quiet. You could understand every word and follow the Hebrew. It was wonderful.

Diana Gould

Some people joined the LJS having had bad experiences in an Orthodox synagogue.

My second experience of Orthodox inflexibility was closer to home. My mother's father, Dick Levy, entered the Licensed Trade in the 1890s. Together with his son Teddie and his

---

[451] Sir Louis Gluckstein, 'The Work of Our Hands'.
[452] Quoted in 'Grade's tears for late rabbi', *The Jewish Chronicle*, 3 March, 2006.

son-in-law Arthur Franks, they founded the firm Levy and Franks which traded under the name, Chef and Brewer. The firm prospered and became a public company. Shortly afterwards Teddie died. He and the firm had many non-Jewish connections and friends who wished to pay their respects, so naturally the family wanted to hold a memorial service at their home synagogue in Great Portland Street. They were told that the Chief Rabbi had expressly forbidden the holding of such services and the family would have to look elsewhere … My sister Frances and her husband Derek Merton had been long-standing members of the LJS and I had witnessed the Confirmations of their three children, Roger, Linda and Bryan with pleasure and admiration so it was natural that to there we should first turn for help. Rabbi Rayner was, as one would expect, both sympathetic and welcoming and Josephine and I speedily became members.

Richard Langton

The Religion School, which had gone from strength to strength after the move to the new synagogue in St John's Wood Road, was a major factor in the expansion and cementing of the LJS congregation.

My ongoing involvement started when our elder son, David, joined the Religion School in 1960 and I was asked to help run the school. I became the Administrator – a post I held for twelve years. It must have been hard for David and his younger brother Andrew – with both parents active in the school (Ann was still teaching) there was never a chance to duck out.

Bob Kirk (Pt. 3)

During the post-war years people continued to join the synagogue though marriage and social connections.

My father knew Joe Foreman (Dr Mattuck's secretary) from helping in the boys' clubs in the East End. He said, 'Why not join the Liberal Synagogue as I am sure you will be happy there?' So we joined the LJS in 1945.

Rita Adler (Pt. 3)

In 1967, I married Penny, then Levinson, and her family were all members of the LJS at St Johns Wood so that was my first introduction. Under the 'Choopa', my late and beloved Grandmother Olga Winogradsky, unaccustomed to any 'shuul' that permitted men and women to mix (!) uttered in a stage whisper audible throughout the congregation: 'It's like a church!' Nevertheless, that introduction served my family and I so well. We all rediscovered our faith and found a spiritual home, my father, others in the family, and myself.

Michael Grade

By this time, however, an increasing number of people were beginning to join the synagogue as a result of its inclusive approach, especially its openness to conversion and the importance it attached to gender equality.

When Nicholas, our eldest child, was ready to start Religion School, I said to Desmond: 'You can have Nicholas educated in the United Synagogue, but no daughter of mine is going to be a member of the United Synagogue'. So Desmond joined the LJS in around 1958. It was as simple as that. We both went to a class run by John Rayner that led to Desmond becoming very enthusiastic about Liberal Judaism. Within three years he was on the LJS Council.

Eva Feldman (Pt. 3)

After a sharp decline during the previous decade, in the 1990s the size of the congregation began to stabilise. This was partly due to the synagogue's willingness to adapt to the needs of its changing congregation (see below), but also because of the attraction of the warm and beautifully designed new building.

> The new building brought in a wave of 'bright young things'. After it was opened quite a few well-known people joined.
>
> Prue Baker

Some of the families who had moved to the suburbs and had become involved in another synagogue when their children were young, returned to the LJS when their children were grown-up.

> When our children had left home, we moved to Hampstead in 1990. Our eldest daughter, Lynette, lives near us and is a member of the LJS. The middle one, Naomi, has two young sons and is a member of Leicester Progressive Jewish Congregation. We rejoined the LJS when it was 'in exile' in Loudoun Road and attended services regularly. At first, we still went back to Northwood for some services and Judith for some classes, but over time this was less frequent.
>
> Bryan Diamond (Pt. 3)

In more recent years, many people have joined the synagogue because of its ever-increasing inclusivity, its establishment of the category of Friends of the synagogue, and its openness to same-sex commitment ceremonies.

> In the last ten years, since becoming members we have become part of the community. We are regular worshippers almost every *Shabbat*, we participate in regular duties and enjoy the friendship and spirit that is so much part of the synagogue. We have made some very good friends. We entered into our Civil Partnership in February 2006.
>
> Alex Rosen and Armand Azoulay (Pt. 3)

The synagogue's changing congregation

A significant proportion of the synagogue's initial membership was drawn from the members of what is referred to as the 'Jewish Aristocracy'. They were often either related to each other or closely connected socially.

> We pride ourselves at the LJS on being democratic. Nevertheless we have an aristocracy ... They belonged to our synagogue in the Hill Street days. They were pioneers: adventurers.[453]

Although the LJS never became established as the 'synagogue of choice' for the 'Cousinhood',[454] it did include a significant number of families who came from that *milieu*. These families included the Nathans, the Samuels, the Levys, the Salmons, the Glucksteins, the Lazaruses, the Franklins, the Myers and so on, who often lived close to each other.

> My mother and her family had been members of the LJS since the 1920s, being connected to the Salmons, Glucksteins and Josephs, who were founding members.
>
> Martin Slowe

---

[453] Foreword by unnamed author, 'The Years Between 1911–1951', LJS exhibition catalogue.
[454] Chaim Bermant, *The Cousinhood, The Anglo-Jewish Gentry*.

Before the war, we lived in Lansdowne Crescent, Holland Park, where I was born, as was my younger brother Peter. It was then quite a popular area for Jewish families with the Walford, Henriques, Karminski and Franklin families, amongst others, all living nearby. I began going to LJS services before the war. It was quite a long walk to St John's Wood Road for a six or seven-year-old, and the best part of it was always along the canal seeing the barges.

Michael Nathan (Pt. 3)

She [Molly Salmon] was my best friend always. We were brought up together, we lived five doors apart, our parents were friendly; our nannies were friendly.

Doreen Gluckstein[455]

People from these families chaired many of the main committees and societies in the synagogue. Some became Chairmen of the Council and took on other lay leadership roles.

The particular person who, of course, I had most connection with was my cousin, Louis Gluckstein, who was Chairman and later President. I was a great admirer of his. I had a certain amount to do with him.

Michael Salmon

Children of these families socialised with each other and often married.

During this time I met George and we got married. In those days all our parents gave parties for the young generation and we all met the children of our parents' friends as well as our own friends. It was a very pleasant way for men and women to meet. George is a distant cousin of Elizabeth [Lazarus], the wife of my brother, Peter Lazarus. George and I met in many, many houses; we couldn't get away from each other really.

Margaret Rigal (Pt. 3)

The families were very close to the LJS rabbis, particularly Rabbi Mattuck.

I remember Dr Mattuck very well as he was a personal friend of my family. He and his wife would come to dinner at Pembridge Place.

Margaret Rigal (Pt. 3)

Before the war we would often lunch after services on a Saturday at what was then the Tavern Restaurant at Lord's. We always hoped that Dr Mattuck would join us at our table since he was such good company and a close family friend.

Michael Nathan (Pt. 3)

However, the composition of the congregation was never completely homogenous and always included some who came from other walks of life and a range of Jewish backgrounds. While the families who made up the Cousinhood were mainly Sephardic in origin, a number of LJS members were from Orthodox and Ashkenazi backgrounds. Their families had come to this country in the late nineteenth century and early twentieth century as a result of the pogroms in Eastern Europe.

Both my parents were teenage immigrants, arriving separately in 1912 from Poland. They were observant Jews from very traditional backgrounds. My mother's father was a Chassid – a sweet, tolerant man. He and his wife – they were called Israel and Rosa Mintz – had seven surviving children, practically all of whom, including their descendants, have remained within the United Synagogue.

Jocelyne Tobin (Pt. 3)

[455] ULPS Oral History Project, interview with Doreen Gluckstein. See Appendix 1.

> There were pogroms and really terrible things going on, but the people in the village thought a great deal of my father and used to warn him when the police were coming with the soldiers and they used to hide the boys but then eventually I was born so mother was able to come to London and she came by train with my brother who was two-and-a-half at the time and my other brother who was about eight, I should think. I had a sister, Bertha and she came over too.
>
> Diana Gould

During the 1930s, the congregation began to be even less homogenous when its numbers were increased by refugees from Germany and other European countries. Although some of these newer members eventually formed their own congregation (the Belsize Square Synagogue), a number remained as members of the LJS. However, it was some time before the impact of this diversification became evident because the more recent members initially felt unable to discuss their experiences.

> At that time, it felt as though there were strong social distinctions in the synagogue, especially between the paid staff and the congregation, but also between those established Anglo-Jewish families and others. Those with continental origins had a very low profile and didn't talk about their past. It took me some time to realise that John Rayner came from a similar background. I was just aware that he was very warm towards me, and I felt a sense of affinity with him. I had also noticed that when he came to *Onegei Shabbat* he sang songs to different tunes, which I had previously only heard my mother sing. It wasn't until much later that he and others started to talk about their past.
>
> Ellen Schmidt (Pt. 3)

Significant changes in the make-up of the congregation started to become more evident after the end of the Second World War when, as with society as a whole, the imposition of new taxes and increasing educational opportunities led to a decline in the numbers of those with unearned incomes and a rise in those involved in middle-class occupations such as teaching, law, medicine and accountancy.

Another change in the post-war years was the diminished involvement of some of the families who had been founder members of the synagogue since a number of them had moved out of London during the war and remained outside the capital after the war. This led to the partial breaking down of the pronounced family atmosphere that had existed in the pre-war years. This breaking down was also the result of the movement of some established LJS families to the suburbs. Whereas in the past most members had lived close to the synagogue in areas such as Hampstead, Bayswater, St John's Wood, a rapidly increasing number now lived in areas such as Wembley, Northwood and Pinner. It therefore became more difficult for the leadership of the LJS to maintain the cohesiveness of the geographically dispersed congregation.

In 1953 groups of members from the outskirts of London and the Home Counties were invited to meet together at the synagogue. These meetings were repeated for other areas and were sometimes held in members' homes. A few years later, Rabbi John Rayner placed these arrangements on a more formal footing. He divided the congregation among fifty areas and, over a period of years, encouraged congregants to meet with each other in their respective Areas Groups. A committee led by Edith Kahn with a great deal of support from Peggy Lang, Organising Secretary for the synagogue, administered the scheme. The Area Groups sometimes set up their own study groups and activities such as *Onegei Shabbat*, which eventually led to the establishment of new congregations.

John Rayner also organised receptions for new members and changed the format of the LJS newsletter to provide more information on what was being planned and to encourage people to exchange views, news and ideas.[456]

During the 1960s, an increasing number of young people went on to university after they left school, which meant that, for several years, the life of the synagogue tended to be dominated by an ageing congregation and remained quite conservative.

> In the 1960s the synagogue seemed still very formal. There was no chatting before services; there was nowhere to chat. It resembled a superior learned club.
>
> Edward Cross

> Services, mainly in English, were brief, cold and formal. No men in the congregation wore head covering or *tallit*. It was a Liberal Judaism pickled in aspic and unlikely to have survived into the present.
>
> David Goldberg[457]

From the mid-1970s, many of those who had grown up in the LJS were now marrying, starting families and becoming involved in new Liberal and Progressive communities closer to their homes in the suburbs.[458] This not only reduced the size of the congregation but also further increased its age profile.

> When I was on Council there was a possibility that a Progressive synagogue might open in Finchley. There was uproar as we did not wish our members to leave and join another closer to where they lived. The establishment since of a dozen Liberal congregations in the north-west suburbs of London in the last forty years has reduced the LJS membership from over 3,000 to 1,800.
>
> Martin Slowe

Although services and forms of worship had evolved since the setting up of the synagogue and more traditional approaches had been reintroduced, particularly after the arrival of John Rayner, a proportion of the long-standing members of the congregation held out against the re-introduction of some traditions. A number of those who had joined the synagogue from Orthodox backgrounds because of its more welcoming approach to intermarriage and also some younger members were now looking for services which were less 'austere' or devoid of ritual. Some families decided to leave the synagogue when change was slow to occur.

Assimilation into wider society, as for Anglo-Jewry generally, was also a reason for the declining membership of the synagogue and, perhaps inevitably, the LJS lost some members when it was based in temporary premises in Loudoun Road while the synagogue was being rebuilt.

During the 1980s and 1990s, it was noticeable that a number of people with a high profile in public life were joining the synagogue.

---

[456] John Rayner, 'Bigger and Better', *Community*, (the LJS newsletter), Vol. 1, No. 1, September 1967.

[457] David Goldberg, 'Rabbi Leslie Edgar', *LJS News*.

[458] The reduction was also partly explained by the fact that a number of people were taken off the membership list following a review of records which showed that the list was very out of date and a number of people were no longer in membership of the synagogue.

It was an enormously prestigious congregation then, with a fair sprinkling of the 'great and the good', including several High Court Judges. However, there was still a strong representation from several extended, interlinking families, with some of their numerous children, grandchildren and great grandchildren still with us. Even now I can be surprised to discover unknown family connections. But I learned one thing very quickly: that I should never gossip because I didn't know who was connected to whom. This did not mean I couldn't listen to the latest exciting news!

Carole Goldberg

There was, however, continuity in the membership of the synagogue.

Another [early LJS member] who later became Treasurer, was Julian Simon. I mention this because it so happens that today is the 125th anniversary of his birth, and because we have with us one of his sons and two of his grandsons: a reassuring sign of continuity.

John Rayner[459]

In more recent years, the size of the congregation has not only stabilised, but the average age has been reducing. This has resulted from the fact that an increasing number of young families are joining the LJS, largely because of its burgeoning Religion School. Amongst those who have joined the LJS in the last decade are a number of American families who have come to live in London for a few years and who settle in St John's Wood because of the nearby American School.

While there are probably a smaller proportion of academics, scholars and intellectuals in the congregation today than there were when the LJS was first established, the LJS's membership is much more representative of the population of London and includes people from all walks of life.

The synagogue used to be very much dominated by the 'Cousinhood', generations of families who had grown up together. This did not start to break down until the 1970s and 1980s when different people began to join the synagogue because it was seen to be an exciting, relevant and diverse place as a result of the causes in which it was involved, such as the refuseniks, the Bosnian Support Group and our stance over Israel. The LJS has now become much more cosmopolitan and less hierarchical. Class differences, as in society as a whole, are now much less obvious.

David Goldberg (Pt. 3)

The make-up of the congregation has evolved over the years. Someone once described the Church of England as 'the Conservative Party at prayer'; in the same vein the LJS was the Anglo-Jewish establishment at prayer. That has changed a lot, of course. We now represent a much broader cross-section of the Jewish population of London.

Willie Kessler

Despite the fact that the congregation of the synagogue has changed immensely it is still a very cohesive community and many people are involved in all aspects of synagogue life.

The synagogue is much more egalitarian generally than it used to be. There is much less separation between the congregation and the rabbis, perhaps because many members are at least as well educated secularly as the rabbis, and are at the top of their own professions. The changing make-up of the membership of the synagogue reflects changes in society at large.

Ellen Schmidt (Pt. 3)

---

[459] 'The Spirit of Israel Mattuck', sermon by Rabbi John Rayner at the LJS, 25 January 1992.

Although some young people may prefer to meet up away from the synagogue, many are very committed to the community.

> On Saturday mornings I see my little sister, my younger brother, my mother and I, all involved with our separate groups of friends. The synagogue is the one place in which we can all separately be absorbed, knowing that the others are nearby and we can find them whenever we need them. A lot of religious establishments have kids of my age who are anxious to get out of the place and distance themselves from it. However, there is something about the LJS which makes many kids happy to remain engaged at my age and stick around, so it must be doing something right.
>
> Reuben Ruiz-Daum [age 16]

Chapter Five: The synagogue building

THE CURRENT BUILDING is the third in which the synagogue has been housed (or the fourth if the temporary premises in Loudoun Road are included). As described in the Part One, the synagogue was initially located in a small disused chapel in Hill Street[460] near Baker Street Station.[461] Although some of the first congregants became quite attached to this first building, it is mainly recalled as being rather dilapidated and uncomfortable.

78. *Hill Street interior. Rabbi Mattuck's office and classrooms to the left, organ far right with choir invisible behind the organ. (undated, c. 1925)*

---

[460] See photographs 4, 7, 8, and 78.
[461] This is where the block of flats called Rossmore Court is now located.

The rapidly expanding congregation soon outgrew the Hill Street premises and a new, much larger synagogue was built in St John's Wood Road during 1924.[462] The site on which it was built was purchased from a firm of motor engineers, L K Bennett Ltd, who had purchased and cleared the site in 1919.

> They demolished what had been a coachman's cottage and stables fronting the Lodge Road boundary of the property, where they made a garage, and converted no. 28 into a car showroom with offices above. When our Building Committee, having visited a number of sites including the Regent's Park villa now next to the mosque, first viewed premises at no. 28 in 1922, the relative absence of planning restrictions must have been a major consideration. Despite occasional criticism from West Enders anxious about the distance of St. John's Wood Road from their homes, no. 28 emerged as the popular choice, and what soon became known as 'the New Liberal' opened its doors in September 1925.
>
> Malcolm Brown[463]

The new building was designed by Ernest Joseph, Honorary Architect to the synagogue, who had been connected with the Liberal Jewish movement since its inception in 1902. When it was decided to establish The Liberal Jewish Synagogue in 1909, Ernest Joseph and his wife became founder members and he had overseen the adaptation of the Hill Street building.

His design for the new building in St John's Wood Road was regarded at the time as being 'one of simple dignity and beauty'.[464] The building was rendered with Portland stone and had a Greek Ionic portico presented to the LJS by Bernhard Baron, a cigarette manufacturer and philanthropist, who was another early member of the LJS.

Inside, the main synagogue was a 'basilica' (a perfect double cube) and the side aisles were built in tiers. The seats were wooden with leather cushions. The *bimah* (referred to as the *almemar*) was made of walnut. The *ner tamid* was adapted from an old Spanish oil lamp purchased in Madrid and presented to the synagogue by Michael Green, one of the original members of the synagogue. Above the Ark was a choir gallery, screened from view by a bronze balustrade. On each of the short sides of the synagogue there were circular-headed doors.[465]

To one side of the vestibule was a small room that was used for worship when there were small gatherings. It was the gift of Nathaniel Joseph, Ernest Joseph's father. Behind the synagogue was a *sukkah* with a sliding roof that was sometimes used for receptions and meetings. Also behind the synagogue was Montefiore Hall which was used for social gatherings and overflow services. Above the synagogue were three galleries, two over the aisles and one over the entrance vestibule, classrooms for the Religion School and offices for the rabbis and professional staff.

---

[462] See photographs 11, 12, 13, 79, and 80.

[463] Malcolm Brown, ' Our Domestic Prehistory', *LJS News,* February 2004.

[464] Charles Magnus, *E.M.J: The Man and His Work*, published for private circulation, (1962).

[465] This description of the building is taken from Ernest Joseph, 'The Liberal Jewish Synagogue, London Built 1924; Rebuilt after war damage 1940–1951, An Account by the Architect, Ernest M Joseph'. Copy of undated article in the LJS archives.

79. *Interior of first synagogue sited at 28 St John's Wood Road. Shows the seating arrangement. Photograph by E H Emanuel. (undated)*

80. *Interior of first synagogue building sited at 28 St John's Wood Road showing the bimah and the Ark. Photograph by E H Emanuel. (undated)*

The move to St John's Wood Road was overseen by Michael Duparc, Synagogue Secretary. The deadline of the synagogue opening for High Holydays was met, but only one office was habitable. Until the office accommodation above the synagogue was completed in 1928, Michael Duparc and other staff remained at Hill Street, which meant frequent walks between the two buildings.[466]

Once the new building in St John's Wood Road was opened, Ernest Joseph gave a great deal of attention to its maintenance and adaptation as the activities of the synagogue developed.[467] In November 1940 the building sustained serious bomb damage.

> It was a tragic morning, that morning of November 1940. I was travelling from my home in Hampstead to my war job in Esher, after a noisy night, when I found the warning word 'Diversion' at the end of St John's Wood Road. The disaster which had happened was soon apparent: tumbled masonry, twisted steel, great blocks of brickwork, unbroken by the blast, were lying across a gaping crater, the whole interior of the synagogue from its western approach exposed to view, yet – unbelievably – the great saucer dome of the roof, though much out of level and cracked here and there, was intact, the northern and eastern galleries, with all their seats, and even their glass windows, appeared unharmed, as also was the Ark.
>
> Ernest Joseph[468]

81. *The bomb-damaged synagogue. (1940)*

While Ernest Joseph was considering the extent of the damage, a demolition squad had arrived on the morning after the bomb fell on the synagogue. They had to be persuaded not to pull down the building.[469]

Restoration works overseen by Ernest Joseph, were carried out between the years 1948 and 1951.

---

[466] Pamela Fletcher Jones, 'Mr Duparc remembers'.
[467] Charles Magnus, *E.M.J: The Man and His Work*.
[468] Ernest Joseph, 'The Liberal Jewish Synagogue, London Built 1924; Rebuilt after war damage 1940–1951'.
[469] Ibid.

He [Ernest Joseph] again rendered service comparable to that given by him when the synagogue was originally created and, under his direction, it was restored to its former beauty – this time with additional facilities … Frequently, he was at the synagogue in the early morning supervising the work and evolving new plans.

Charles Magnus[470]

Although the effect of the bomb was staggering, it failed to stop the continuity of the synagogue's activities. Montefiore Hall was quickly restored and was used for many synagogue activities while the restoration works progressed. However, bigger events had to be held away from the synagogue.

I do remember going to Communal *Seders*, which were conducted by Dr Mattuck at Lord's (not in the members' section, but in the Tavern upstairs) after the bombing of the synagogue. They were popular, with at least a hundred people attending despite the problems of wartime. The High Holyday services, some of which I helped to steward, were held at the Friends' Meeting House in Euston Road.

Michael Nathan (Pt. 3)

The synagogue was gradually restored.

My very first memory of going to the LJS is when I was about five years old. There was a special service after the war, the last held in the synagogue before it closed for restoration. I can remember it clearly. I was sitting downstairs and my main occupation during the service was looking upstairs to the part which had been bomb-damaged and watching the pigeons flying in and out through the empty space.

Jenny Nathan (Pt. 3)

As well as being Honorary Architect to the synagogue, Ernest Joseph was also a long-standing Council member.[471] Shortly before he died in 1960, he donated a panelled screen for the choir gallery. When it was complete, the small synagogue (the Lily Montagu Wing) that was added in 1963 was largely furnished by bequests from Ernest Joseph and his family.

82. *Ernest Joseph, LJS Honorary Architect, with Lily Montagu. (1950)*

---

[470] Charles Magnus, *E.M.J: The Man and His Work*.

[471] Ernest Joseph was elected to the Council in 1927 and remained a member for twenty-nine years. He was Honorary Treasurer and Vice-President from 1953 to 1956. On his retirement from Council, he joined the Synagogue Advisory Committee.

83. The new Montagu Wing, dedicated on 7 March 1963. (1963)

The discovery of serious structural defects made it necessary for the LJS to decide either to carry out major repairs or to rebuild the synagogue. After long deliberations lasting over three years, the decision was eventually taken to redevelop the site.

> I joined the LJS House Committee and we were charged with the general maintenance of the building, which had been repaired after the bomb damage. I don't think the problems were any different from now until the LJS very sensibly took the decision that either they carried on repairing an even more expensive building or they built a new one. This was a very brave and wonderful decision.
>
> Michael Salmon

A long lease on part of the land was sold to Abbey National Homes to help finance the rebuilding project, which commenced in 1988. The farewell service was held on 30 April 1988, after which the congregation moved to temporary premises in a deconsecrated church in Loudoun Road.

> While we were at the church in Loudoun Road, the Council used to meet in a very dark and dingy room behind the body of the old church. I suppose it must have been a sort of vestry room. In the church itself, we covered up all the obvious Christian symbols for the purposes of our own services. It was rather chilly. During that period only one marriage took place in the church and that was of my daughter, Mary. The church was totally unsuited for any form of Jewish marriage. There was nowhere for the bride to prepare herself before going into the ceremony, so we had to rig up some curtains. It caused a great deal of hilarity in my own family because we had always told our children that they should not think that we would come to their wedding if they got married in a church.
>
> George Rigal (Pt. 3)

The design for the new building was put out to competition. The Fitzroy Robinson Partnership, in association with Preston Rubin, was chosen to design the shell (and the adjoining block of flats). A firm of Israeli architects, Kantor Schwartz, working closely with their London associates, Koski Solomon, was commissioned to design what was to become known as the Sanctuary.[472]

> Les Koski was an excellent community architect. He really listened to what people had to say and acted as a sensitive intermediary between Kantor Schwartz and the LJS. He was terrific; he really cared. Not many architects would be such a patient and skilled communicator.
>
> Prue Baker

A Steering Committee chaired by Sir Peter Lazarus oversaw the whole project, while a Design and Use Committee, chaired by Neil Levitt, focussed on the use of all areas of the new building, furnishings, fittings and equipment.

> When I look back on my involvement at the LJS, the people I enjoyed working with most were those involved in the rebuilding. It was an incredibly harmonious and constructive time because there was such respect for everyone else's point of view. I also remember that it was also very scary. I can well remember the sleepless nights. On the second floor of our home outside our bedroom we had a balcony which overlooked Peter Lazarus's garden, far away but you could see into his garden. I can remember several times standing on that balcony in a cold sweat after a particularly worrying night wondering whether Peter too was in the same state of anxiety.
>
> Trevor Moross (Pt. 3)

Every attempt was made to involve the congregation in all aspects of the design of the new building, including the setting up of a range of specialist subcommittees of the Design and Use Committee representing interests such as classrooms, kitchen/catering, nursery, library, garden and the choir.

> I worked (with others) on the structure for the *bimah* chairs with the furniture designer Bob Pulley. The chair's finely curved and rather graceful sprung back is a special feature. The pairs of chairs are designed to sit equally well in twos as singly. Each chair has only one outside arm – so that two people can be close together, or separate and turned away private in meditation. The wide supportive arm can hold an open prayer book and the grooved splayed edges of the wooden arms even suggest the open pages of a book.
>
> Jane Finestone

For some, the dismantling of the synagogue was an emotional experience

> Another moving recollection was seeing the portico pillars being driven away for storage on the back of a huge lorry. It felt almost like the end of an era; the old synagogue had been very much associated with my childhood and teenage years, and with the early years of my rabbinate.
>
> Alexandra Wright (Pt. 3)

Some members were keen to retain certain aspects of the old building, but their views sometimes proved difficult to accommodate.

---

[472] The designation 'the Sanctuary' to denote the part of the building to be used for worship was a new development – it had not previously been used in the old building. It is a designation that is commonly used in America.

A number of meetings were held with members under the then Chairman Sir Peter Lazarus and promises were made that we would insist that the Compton organ would be kept and that the fine mahogany-lined *almemar* would be reinstated. Circumstances were such that there was no room for all the organ pipes and the interior architect had other ideas for the *almemar*.

Neil Levitt

A strong professional team guided the building project on a day-to-day basis. The full-time Project Co-ordinator, Prue Baker, was based at the law firm of LJS Honorary Solicitor, Tim Simon. The Project Manager was Chris Hill, a professional quantity surveyor.

The intention was that as Project Co-ordinator I should be the single contact point for both professionals and LJS membership, to make sure the architect and project manager were not bombarded with too many queries. For their part, the professionals were in constant touch by phone, wanting decisions, or reporting progress – sometimes as many as half a dozen times in a day. We had at least two meetings every week and I recorded everything on a typewriter – no computers at this stage!

Prue Baker

However, the project did not proceed without its difficulties and, at one point, the LJS became locked in a major legal battle with the builders, John Mowlem plc, about responsibility for miscalculations on the siting of the portico.

Working with Sir Peter, Trevor and Neil Levitt on the rebuilding of our fine new synagogue was a wonderful, if taxing, experience. A particularly fraught problem lay in our having to sue the builders, Mowlem. I well remember a meeting we had with Mowlem at the offices of Singer & Friedlander, of which Anthony Solomons was the Chairman at the time. I think Mowlem came to the meeting assuming that, as a religious body, we were a soft touch and not to be feared. Anthony Solomons soon put them right, and they realised they had a serious fight on their hands, which, in due course, we won.

Tim Simon (Pt. 3)

In 1990, while the building was still just a shell, the World Union had its biennial conference in London and one part of its programme was to come and visit the new building. A WUPJ Service of Dedication was held on the site on 5 May 1990.

There was a great deal of nervousness as the opening of the new building approached.

I can also remember our anxieties about the first service. Would the sound and air conditioning systems work? Would there be enough seats for people? Would they be comfortable? That first *Rosh Hashanah* and *Yom Kippur* it was very warm but the air conditioning wasn't working. The only way we could get it to work was manually. Neil Levitt, Fred Shelley (the caretaker) and I ran up and down the stairs to and from the basement to move a lever which would open and close the valves to regulate the temperature. People complained it was too cold. I can well remember the words of Ludwig Spiro, an engineer and a very nice man, who said, 'You've got the design wrong, but don't worry. Everybody will forget about it after a time'.

Trevor Moross (Pt. 3)

The building that eventually emerged from all the detailed planning and discussion was very different from the old synagogue.

But I used to find the old LJS a rather forbidding building. It was dark and it was cold and there was brown everywhere. It was very impressive on the High Holydays when it was full and the choir was above the Ark singing down. There would be a wonderful atmosphere. On an average *Shabbat* morning there would be maybe 100 or 150 people in a 1,200-seat building; they rattled around like peas in a pod. The acoustics were bad and it was impossible to instil any atmosphere with people sitting so far from the *bimah*. The foyer was cavernous and unwelcoming. This meant that, when we rebuilt, I was determined that we should have a warmer, friendlier building ... We certainly achieved that. The first comment people make when they come to the synagogue is, 'what a welcoming building', which gives me great pleasure.

David Goldberg (Pt. 3)

I think that when we were in Loudoun Road we shared the difficulties – it was good for us. But of course we were delighted when we moved to 28 St John's Wood Road. To us it seemed absolutely the last thing in modernity.

Maxwell Stern[473]

84. *The Sanctuary in the new synagogue in St John's Wood Road. (2011)*

---

[473] ULPS Oral History project, interview with Maxwell Stern. See Appendix 1.

PART THREE

Memories

The memories of individuals

Rita Adler
Felicity Allen
Raymon Benedyk
Caryn Becker Berlingieri
Bernie Bulkin
Eric Conrad
Bryan Diamond
Barbara Godfrey
Rabbi David Goldberg
Louise Golding
Michael Hart
Ruth Ive
Jean Jaffa

William Kessler
Lady Lazarus
Jacob Lovick
Trevor Moross
Anthony Roe
Tim Sandler
Ellen Schmidt
Tamara Schmidt
Carolyn Simon
Tim Simon
Jocelyne Tobin
Walter Woyda
Rabbi Alexandra Wright

Joint memories

Eva and Desmond Feldman
Ann and Bob Kirk
Rosemary and Norman Lazarus
Jenny and Michael Nathan

Karen Newman with Susan Crane
Margaret and George Rigal
Alex Rosen and Armand Azoulay

Readers please note: The memories that follow were recorded or written at different times so some information contained within them is now out of date.

Rita Adler

Rita Adler's family, the Raymans, joined the LJS in 1946 where she met and married Michael Adler. Her first major involvement was with the Women's Society. She was then elected to the Council in 1974 and became an Honorary Treasurer in 1988. She was Chairman of Council from 1992 until 1998 and from 2007 until 2011.

I was born on 1 May 1940. My parents, Jack and Zelda Rayman, were second- and third-generation British Jews respectively. My father was born in London, in Church Street, Kensington, where his father had a silver shop. My father also became an antique silver dealer. He died in 1983. My mother, who was born in Cardiff, did not work. They are both buried in Pound Lane Cemetery. Each of my parents had a sister, but neither of my aunts had children. My parents are now both dead, as is my unmarried brother.

My parents were married in 1938 at Hampstead Synagogue, Dennington Park Road, by the Rev. Philip Cohen. They then moved to West London Synagogue as they wished to sit together in services. That was not a great success. My father knew Joe Foreman (Dr Mattuck's secretary) from helping in the boys' clubs in the East End. He said, 'Why not join the Liberal Synagogue as I am sure you will be happy there?' So we joined the LJS in 1945.

I have consulted my mother's diary and see that my first visit to the LJS Sunday School was on 15 September 1946. I attended the Religion School, where I was taught by Celia Rapp and Marjorie Moos. I was confirmed in 1956 and then became a teaching assistant. Marjorie Moos prepared the lessons and told me, 'One must make a bridge between what goes on today and what was in the past, as this will interest the class.' This lasted for about eighteen months until my patience wore out.

As regards my memories of the synagogue in those days, I remember a grave Miss Lily Montagu. I also recall Rabbi Edgar rarely remembering anyone's name. I recall going to services in Friends' House in Euston Road because the synagogue had been severely damaged by the bombing in 1940, and waiting for Dr Mattuck, hands raised high, to pronounce the final blessing.

I did not go to university, but became a draughtsman apprentice and eventually a graduate of the Institute of Heating and Ventilating. I worked as an engineer before I met and married Michael Adler, who was also an LJS member. We married at the LJS in 1962. Michael ran a family couture business until he decided to close it in 1970. We then both had second careers jointly running a mail order business and shop for elderly and disabled people. Very sadly, Michael died suddenly in 1997. He had a strong commitment to the community side of the synagogue. He was a dedicated and, I gather, much-loved member of the Keep in Touch team, and revelled in being 'Keeper of the Embroidery Threads' for the tapestry project.

Michael's parents, Max and Renée Adler, belonged to the LJS too. They used to sit on one side of the old Sanctuary and my family sat facing on the opposite side. Although we were friendly with Rabbis Rayner and Edgar, when Michael and I decided to get married we requested Philip Cohen (who had been Associate Minister from 1946 until 1958) to marry us, because he had married my parents at Hampstead Synagogue. Philip Cohen was the kindest, most laid-back minister you could imagine. He even forgot to bring the marriage certificate to the ceremony! My fondest memory of Philip is of him giving a sermon on the theme of 'Don't ignore the old. You never know what you can learn from them'. He also had a wonderful way with young people.

I was not very involved with Liberal Judaism until 1968 when my mother died. I was twenty-eight at the time. Rosemary Lazarus, who was Chairman of the Women's Society, said, 'Why don't you come along to a meeting and see what help you can give?' In those days, the Women's Society did visiting, cooking and catering. It catered for the Communal *Seder* and I remember a recipe starting with, 'Take 12 lbs of apples...'.

I joined the Council in 1974. My children were growing up and I was only working part-time. The Women's Society thought it would be good to have another woman on Council. Sir Louis Gluckstein was President at the time, and I was briefed that one did not speak during one's early years on Council, and certainly not at one's first meeting. However, as I found it difficult not to say anything, I put up my hand and Sir Louis asked, 'Do you want to say something, Rita?' Unfortunately I cannot recall my question. Sir Louis, known to those who knew him well as 'Luigi', ruled the synagogue with a rod of iron.

Sir Louis was succeeded by Sidney Levine and he, in turn, by Rosemary Lazarus's father, Lewis Levy. He was a much more relaxed figure. He brought in his own secretary one day a week to do all the clerking. He was a benign, charming man who looked after the staff. We were all a great big family. Lewis played bridge most of the time, so if you wanted to put forward an idea to him, you had to ring at 10.30 a.m. on a Sunday morning!

As I became more involved with the synagogue, I found I enjoyed helping people and meeting others socially. Getting to know and benefitting from the knowledge of a wide variety of rabbis was also stimulating. After a number of years I became an Honorary Treasurer (1988–92). Julian Tobin had been the Treasurer since 1984 and it was decided that I should be his assistant. He was a neighbour of ours so I knew him very well, although we were quite different in our outlook. At the time of the rebuilding of the synagogue in the late 1980s, when we were in the church in Loudoun Road, I took over from Julian as Senior Treasurer, and Bob Beral came in as Junior Treasurer. I was never good at figures, but I bought a book and my husband also helped.

Peter Lazarus was the Chairman at this time and we got on extremely well together. He had great faith in me. Things were very different in those days: Honorary Officers used to meet for supper in an Italian restaurant in St John's Wood High Street, and we would split the bill between us. During the synagogue redevelopment, the project managers would occasionally be invited to join us there.

On completion of the new building, Peter decided it was time for him to retire and he said: 'Why don't you become Chairman?' and I said, 'I don't think so.' There was another member of Council who wished to take up the position and I said, 'Let him be Chairman,' but Peter said, 'No, let the Council vote.' This was most unusual. There was a vote on Council, but before the votes were counted the opposing candidate withdrew his nomination. I was Chairman from 1992 until 1998.

I greatly admired Peter and he taught me much. He was a very experienced senior civil servant. When finances were particularly tight he did his own Council minutes. On more than one occasion, he had written the minutes before the meeting took place, and I would diffidently suggest there might be a need for minor alterations before their circulation! Had it not been for Peter's grasp of the enormity of the rebuilding project and his care for the LJS congregation, we would not be where we are today. Now after a break of some years, I am once again Chairman.

I have many memories of the rabbis. David Goldstein was a lovely, gentle person. He had a wonderful way with young people. He went on to be Keeper of Hebrew manuscripts at the British Library. Sadly he developed cancer and died. John Rayner had a wonderful sense of humour and always had a funny story. He loved his food. David Goldberg was a good leader with whom the Honorary Officers had little to query and he led from the front. He ran a very organised office with a good team of staff. Life was simpler in those days – there were fewer rules and regulations and contracts were much more elastic.

My two children were both confirmed at the LJS, and are both now married, but not to members of the LJS. Jonathan Adler (born 1965) lives in Wellington, New Zealand, with his wife and three children. Jozelda Sparks (born 1969) lives in Barnet with her husband and three children.

Currently, we are involved in celebrating the Centenary of The Liberal Jewish Synagogue. It is important that we do not look back all the time, but look forward to how the synagogue might be in the future. We are very lucky to have Michael Hart and Pam Fox overseeing the events for the centenary year – it's in very capable hands.

When one looks back on the past one can see that the social, caring and catering sides of the synagogue are much more active than ever before, despite the fact there is now no Women's Society. We still have Tuesday lunches and we serve coffee and biscuits before the service on Saturday, as well as *Kiddush* afterwards. We have members welcoming visitors at services and a professional Community Care Co-ordinator. Previously, this work used to be done by the rabbis in their pastoral role with help from the Women's Society.

All this needs many volunteers. With all the charity and government regulations that one has to keep up with, together with Ofsted, Health and Safety and many other requirements, precious time is taken to ensure that all is recorded and returned to the department concerned. Sometimes this delays the staff and Council from looking after our membership, and hinders us from moving forward as a community.

There is now much more Hebrew during services, and although I can read Hebrew, I am not proficient enough to read it at speed let alone understand it. I must say, I preferred the past when more of the service was in English. However, many new members seem to like the form of the service now, and so one must embrace change and follow the swing of the pendulum. Sincerity of belief and action are more important than outward form.

I have learned much from being Chairman of Council. First and foremost, you have to work in partnership with the rabbis. You must be proactive and you have to try to anticipate what might come up. You also have to get people to agree. You have to have patience, as it often takes a long time for a new idea to become accepted. Everyone likes to be thanked and the Chairman has to be available to thank people on behalf of the congregation. You have to be able to identify the right people for the right tasks and be able to work to people's strengths. You have to learn how to stop people from talking too much in meetings and I've also had to learn to curb my tongue.

The role of Chairman has a few frustrations. For example, sometimes you have to clear up other people's messes and you have to be able to cope with more criticism and behind-the-scenes politics than in the past. However, the role can also provide tremendous pleasure when you see a project through, such as Singing for the Brain, a new initiative led by Jenny Nathan, which provides singing sessions for anyone with Alzheimer's in the local community. My philosophy of life has always been to 'get on with it', but I certainly could not have found the time to be Chairman on top of a full-time job.

One great delight has been to see LJS publicity established on a professional basis. You get a sense of pride when a service goes well or when you hear from a new member what a warm welcome they have received.

See photographs 20, 48, 57, and 59.

✡

Felicity Allen

Felicity Allen is a third-generation member of the LJS. She attended the Religion School where she subsequently worked as an assistant teacher and was the first recipient of the Willie Kessler Award. Last October her daughter, Rebekah, had her naming blessing there.

My name is Felicity Allen, née Blaire, and I was born in 1979. My maternal grandparents, George and Vera Baracs, joined the LJS in 1969 having come here as refugees after the Hungarian uprising in 1957. They had survived both the Holocaust (my grandpa in forced labour camps in the Ukraine, and my grandma in hiding) and the Russian occupation in Hungary. My grandpa had been a lawyer in Budapest and re-qualified as a solicitor here, which was no mean feat for a man in his forties with a wife and two children. My grandpa eventually became a partner in the law firm Mischcon de Reya, and the LJS was recommended to him by his colleagues there.

My parents, Trixi and Eric Blaire, met as students at the University of Bristol in 1965. As my father came from an Orthodox Jewish background, and my mother as a Hungarian refugee had spent time in a Catholic convent on arrival in the UK, it was a challenge for my grandparents to find a synagogue that would accept her Jewish credentials and to which she could feel a sense of belonging. They found that in John Rayner and the LJS.

The whole family became very involved in the synagogue in various ways. Grandpa was an avid bridge player and, on retirement, wrote a bridge column for the LJS newsletter for some time, while my father's brother, Stuart Blaire, who is a professional chef, ran some Sunday cookery lessons at the synagogue in the 1980s.

My older sister, Camie, and I both began our LJS Jewish studies from the age of four. However, for Camie, they began through the correspondence course as we were living in Staffordshire until she was seven. I have very clear memories of Religion School from my first days in *Alef* all the way to *Kabbalat Torah* [KT]. My first teachers were (at times confusingly) Caroline and Carolyn whose strengths complemented each other very well. Caroline provided less serious singing and Jewish stories and Carolyn gave us our first taste of Hebrew. We subsequently had John Hagard whom I adored. It would never have felt out of place to have hugged him and we were delighted he found love and happiness in Caroline and, of course, devastated to have cancer take him away from us so prematurely.

My closest friend at Religion School in those years was Rebecca Marsden. Her sister, Katy, was in the same LJS class as Camie and was also lovely. She always had a very cool denim jacket covered in badges. Rebecca and I had a fantastic year the year we were taught in Abercorn Place by Seth and Esther who I suppose were only seventeen at the time but of course seemed very grown-up to us aged eleven or so. We looked at the Holocaust from the perspective of Raoul Wallenberg, an absolute hero of mine, who forged Swedish passports for many Jews, saving their lives and who at the end of the war was arrested by the Soviets never to be seen again. I can't remember ever not knowing about the Holocaust or the horrors of Soviet Communism as my mother's family, living in Hungary until 1956, were survivors of both and you don't live through something like that without scars that pass down the generations. So I found it an extremely helpful, albeit emotional, opportunity to learn about the war in a more structured and less personal setting.

I later on became close to Jenny Afia. We did our *Kabbalat Torah* together and also went on tour to Israel together aged sixteen where we met Naomi Spencer, an LJS member who is now a student Rabbi. Jenny and I spent a lot of time at synagogue laughing. And we weren't alone – if Fred, the caretaker, or Sharon Moross were not joining in our laughter it was Ann and Bob Kirk. We used to sit in the upstairs of the synagogue during the service eating sweets when no one was looking and made the most of the games room in the basement. We talked a lot about boys. We had a hilarious weekend away in preparation for our KT where, at Jenny's instigation, we dyed our hair purple (her) and red (me). On me, you could barely notice any colour, but on her it was quite obvious and if you couldn't spot it on her you knew something had happened, given the red and purple handprints on the bathroom walls!

Following KT, I taught for two years at the Religion School. I'm not sure I ever had complete control in the classroom, but I very much hope the Hebrew and Jewish knowledge of the children I taught made some progress. It was fantastic that the Hebrew exercise books had become more focussed on Hebrew as a language and were no longer only about reciting Hebrew from the prayerbooks. I also worked at the summer school based at the synagogue for those two years. It was during this time I was honoured to receive the first Willie Kessler Prize.

The rabbis of my formative years were Alex, David and Helen. David and Helen took us through KT. This was again a very complementary combination of teachers. Like all rabbis, Helen was extremely hard-working but was also especially committed to connecting with her students. I personally don't think you can ask for more inspirational leaders than David Goldberg and Alex Wright. In my opinion you can't beat some of David's sermons for their pertinence, truth, quality and moral rightness. And as a working mother, I couldn't ask for a more personally special rabbi than Alex who knew me as a little girl, and who has now blessed my little girl. She also provided a huge comfort to my mother when my Gran died just over a year ago.

It was always my father who took us to synagogue, but over the years my mother has become increasingly involved in LJS life. She even now has a few formal responsibilities (no longer having an Orthodox mother-in-law to react against!) and my father seems to be on every committee going. The LJS is very much his second home.

Outside of synagogue I attended the local comprehensive girls' school, where I was extremely happy. It was an extremely inclusive school. The head was an active member of Radlett Reform Synagogue and a classmate of mine was Charley Baginsky, who has gone on to be the Rabbi at Kingston Liberal Synagogue. I went on to study German and Politics at the University of Bristol, which gave me the opportunity to spend a year teaching English in Germany. A very memorable moment I had there was discovering that the grandfather of my closest friend – a fellow teacher, Katja – had been killed in the war when her father was very young with obvious consequences for the financial and emotional well-being of her father's family. It felt significant to me that it was her grandfather who had died and not mine – there are no clear winners in war. But it was also uplifting that it had only taken two generations for the 'oppressor' and the 'victim' to become friends again.

On the Politics side of my degree, for my final year dissertation I wrote about the 1956 Hungarian revolution which was the event that gave my mother's family the opportunity to escape. Like the Wallenberg experience at *cheder*, this enabled me to objectify and study an event in history that I had previously only connected with emotionally and personally.

During the summer break between my first and second year at university I went travelling in Africa and met my future husband, a New Zealander, on his way to the UK. I was both the first Jewish person and the first vegetarian he had ever met! Whilst he and his family are of course accepting of the former, they have still not come to terms with the latter! We now have a beautiful sixteen-month-old daughter. My husband was allowed to choose her name within the confines that it had to be from the Old Testament. We certainly hope that she has as enriching an experience of the LJS as I have had. The Tiny Tots services are already a very promising start.

I am extremely proud to be a member of the LJS. I am proud of the heterogeneity of its rabbis, its pioneering liberalism, its interfaith work, its perspective on Zionism and its commitment to gender equality. From the age of four to eighteen I went to the LJS weekly and have gone regularly albeit less frequently since. I therefore feel a constant ease there even as the number of people who recognise me ebbs and flows. One particular aspect I have always enjoyed about going to synagogue is how it is the only place where different generations mix meaningfully. Observing oneself moving up the generations is almost like a rite of passage in itself – an apt experience for one's place of worship.

✡

Raymon Benedyk

Raymon Benedyk was Synagogue Secretary from 1973 to 1991. He was also a Marriage Secretary, a role which he continued for seven years after his retirement.

My name is Raymon Benedyk. Of my parents, I think my father may have even been described as an atheist. He was a very intelligent person, self-educated, and very well read. He wasn't a member of any synagogue. I think my mother was probably brought up in a religious home and, for the first few years of her married life, kept her home as she had been taught as a child. However, one Friday night when I was about four years old, the window curtains over the lit candles caught fire and my mother bravely pulled the curtains down and extinguished the flames. So, if we had Friday night candles after that, they were not lit.

As to my own Jewish education, from 1932 to 1937 I went to the Jewish Orphanage in West Norwood, South London, not because I was an orphan, but because it was a London County Council school which all local children, Jewish and non-Jewish, attended. I learned some Hebrew, but regret to say I did not retain the knowledge.

At the beginning of the war I joined the Air Training Corps, the cadet force for young men, hoping to join the Royal Air Force when conscription arrived. In 1944, I duly volunteered, but the Recruiting Officer turned me down, saying: 'We don't want any more air crew. If you want to volunteer for anything, join the Army!' I declined, thinking to myself that, because of my ATC training, when my conscription notice came I would surely still end up in the Air Force.

However, I was to be disappointed, because I found I had been conscripted to work in the coal mines. I became a 'Bevin Boy', called such because it was Mr Ernest Bevin who, as Minister of Labour and National Service, had called up coal miners for the armed services, but later realised that, with dwindling stocks, men were urgently needed to help get coal to the surface. It was he who devised the scheme whereby men with a specific number on their call-up papers were automatically directed to this work without any choice. Those who refused were sent to prison. Of the 48,000 men conscripted in this way, some 3,000 were killed or seriously injured. It was not the easy option that people even today still think it was, and we were most certainly not conscientious objectors.

I was invalided out after some eighteen months with a damaged back, an injury from which I have suffered ever since. We Bevin Boys got no medal, not even a demob suit. When I applied for a disability pension, I was refused because 'the injury was not sustained in combating the enemy'. I appealed, pointing out that my injury was sustained in combating the enemy in the manner the government of the day directed, but the refusal was upheld.

Back in 'Civvy Street', I rejoined the family business, which was in waste reclamation. I married in 1951 and my two sons were born in 1953 and 1955. However, by 1962 it became obvious that the business could no longer support the four families who lived from it. One by one we left, eventually leaving my father to continue on his own. For the next four years, I job-hopped trying to maintain a familiar standard of living. Between 1962 and 1966, I worked at Liberty's in Regent Street selling jewellery. I then sold refrigeration maintenance for a few months, and also the *Encyclopaedia Britannica* and did not do too badly. In 1966 I became a casino cashier in one of London's most prestigious gaming houses, a job I did for the next seven years, eventually becoming Chief Cashier. However, I found that the night work involved was not conducive to married life.

In 1973 I decided I ought to seek a daytime job and answered an advert in the *Jewish Chronicle* inviting applications for the position of Synagogue Secretary. I had no idea what a Synagogue Secretary did, but I applied and, one Sunday morning, I was successfully interviewed by Peter Lazarus and Lewis Levy. I took up the post in October 1973.

At first I found it quite difficult. There was no guidance available because both my immediate predecessors had very recently died, leaving part-timer, Lionel Symonds, holding the fort as best he could. I picked up a lot for myself, such as taking minutes and dealing with members' enquiries.

From the beginning, I tried to run the place as I would a business in order to try and show a profit (sorry, wrong word, I mean surplus of income over expenditure!) and tried to impose various economies. I supervised the staff and originally had my own secretary, as did each of the Rabbis who, at the time, were Rabbi David Goldstein, Rabbi Alan Mann and Rabbi John Rayner. There was a Bookings Secretary, a Records Secretary, a Book Keeper and another person who prepared the wages each week. They were nearly all part-timers doing two or three days per week. When one left, I tried not to replace them, distributing their tasks among the remaining staff. I dealt with subscriptions and accounts and the payment of bills. I also ensured that the needs of the House Committee were dealt with and obtained estimates for any necessary maintenance work.

There was a succession of caretakers during my time. The first were Mr and Mrs Temple. Mrs Temple was quite temperamental. They retired in the early 1970s, to be followed by Don and Mrs Eaton. He was a very charming man and a hard worker. In particular, he was most concerned about the cleanliness of the building. He washed down walls that had not been cleaned for years. He also scrubbed the floor of the Sanctuary where, over the years, dirt and grime had accumulated around the feet of the benches. The improvement was obvious for all to see. When he died, Mrs Eaton's son-in-law, Fred Shelley, took over and, once again, we were in good hands.

When I came on the scene, Peter Lazarus was the Council Chairman. He was a stickler for saying and doing the right thing. At Council meetings, I would take the minutes and prepare a draft for him, usually within twenty-four hours of a meeting. However, frequently items I had covered in a sentence or two, he would expand into three or four paragraphs, providing much more detail of the matters discussed. After him came Lewis Levy, from 1975 until 1980. He was followed by Maxwell Stern, who, although being rather stern by nature as well by name, was in fact a kind person. However, he was also a stickler for doing things the right way.

I got on quite well with Sir Louis Gluckstein, the President of the synagogue until his death in the 1970s. He sort of mentored me, saying: 'If you have any problems and I can help, come to me and I will do what I can.' A real gentleman of the old school!

The original Synagogue Secretary was Mr Michael Duparc, who had been in office from 1912 until 1961. He was still around when I first started, and was a mine of interesting information about 'the old days'. He warned me that if ever there was a disagreement between the secretariat and the rabbis, the Honorary Officers would always side with the rabbis and it was therefore better not to have any disagreements with the rabbis. As it happens, I had no arguments with the rabbis. In fact, think I got on quite well with them all.

I knew the Rev. Philip Cohen slightly and, as the LJS's Marriage Secretary, I did several weddings with him. Rabbi Alan Mann was the third minister at the LJS when I came, but he left soon after I arrived. As it happened, I had known Rabbi Rayner from when I was living in South London. As Minister at the local Liberal Synagogue, he tried to persuade my wife and me, then newly married, to join his synagogue. In those days I was a bit 'bolshy' about Judaism and tried to belittle some of the Jewish beliefs. He countered my arguments brilliantly, which made me an admirer of his ever after.

I soon found I rather liked this liberal kind of Judaism and that I much preferred it to the Judaism of the Orthodox. I liked the fact that men and women could sit together, and that the decorum during the service was much better than in an Orthodox synagogue, with the rabbi having to pound on his desk to stop people talking during the service. This was something I could understand and enjoy.

I was never a regular synagogue-goer, preferring to attend only when I felt the need to do so, such as for the *Yahrzeit* of my late wife and, of course, on the anniversary of the death of my older son who died in 1998 at the age of forty-four. I received a lot of comfort from attending and found Rabbi David Goldberg particularly sympathetic. He always has just the right words at the right time.

When it was announced that I was about to retire, the Honorary Officers set up a Testimonial Fund for me. I was most gratified to be the recipient of so many people's contributions as a mark of appreciation of my work.

I did have a few funny experiences as Synagogue Secretary. When I first started, the standard annual membership rate was £32.00 per year (we mustn't compare that with today's amount). When I found someone paying only £10.00 per year, although living at a smart address in Maida Vale, I asked him to increase his contribution to the standard rate. His response was, 'I can't afford to increase my subscription as I have to go to the Bahamas every winter for my health.' He was quite serious!

Because of the hours I kept, I was always available when members phoned to speak to me or came to see me. I also often visited people at home if they were unable to get to the synagogue. I was able to give advice and guidance on all manner of matters relating to weddings and funerals, grave maintenance and upkeep, problems with finding homes for sick parents, etc. Rabbinic or religious matters, however, were always referred to the rabbis.

My departure was somewhat precipitated when, at the end of 1990, about six months before my 65th birthday, I happened to mention to an officer that, if they were considering replacing me at sixty-five, they might like to plan ahead. I went off on a two-week holiday and, when I returned, there was a total stranger at my desk who said that she was to be my successor. From then on I was very much less involved in the running of things. I don't recall her name, but she lasted just thirteen months. Her replacement lasted eight weeks. Over the following years there were several more changes, some, I understand, more successful than others. I lasted almost twenty years, so I must have been doing something right.

When the new synagogue was consecrated I had the great honour of carrying in one of the scrolls – I have a splendid photograph of the event. After my official retirement I continued to do various jobs on a part-time basis, particularly as Marriage Secretary. Of course, there was pressure on office space, and I operated in a very small room off the Assembly Hall. As Marriage Secretary I did not always use LJS rabbis, and sometimes used the services of outside ministers. The Rev. Philip Cohen was one of these. That is how I knew him.

The last wedding at which I officiated was the rather famous one of Simon and Santa Sebag-Montefiore. Prince Charles was one of the witnesses to the wedding documents. When he was about to use his pen I said to him, 'I would be obliged if you would use the official pen,' to which he replied, 'Why do you want me to use your pen?' I said, 'Because mine has ink in it which won't fade.' He said, 'But mine has ink in it which won't fade,' to which I responded, 'Nevertheless I would prefer you to use my pen!' So he put away his pen and used mine. I dined out on that incident for months, but maybe it cost me a knighthood!

During the time the synagogue was being rebuilt, we continued to operate as a community in a deconsecrated church in Loudoun Road, Swiss Cottage, with the authority of the Bishop of London. All very legitimate! However, there was some hostility shown by one or two members of the local community, who objected to 'their' church being used by what they referred to as 'Christ killers' and 'heathens'. On one occasion, the verbal abuse got so bad that our receptionist at the time, Fred Shelley's wife Marcia, became quite upset prompting me to intervene. I very gently and quietly pointed out to the woman that the Bishop of London had authorised our use of the premises, but this did not pacify her. When I also told her that Jesus was a Jew, and that all the original disciples were Jews, she promptly slapped me round the face. Fred quickly escorted the lady off the premises and we never saw her again. Yes, one of the dangers of being a Synagogue Secretary!

See photographs 20, 68, and 76.

Caryn Becker Berlingieri

Caryn Berlingieri was born in New York. After being brought up in a Reform synagogue there, and then participating in the Jewish youth movement, she moved to London in 1994. Her family joined the LJS in 2001 when her children were of Religion School age. She and her husband Chris are very involved in supporting the Religion School and the wider LJS community.

My name is Caryn Berlingieri and I was born in Brooklyn, New York. I was named for my great-grandmother, Clara who was originally from Vienna, Austria. This is the story of how I arrived in London from America and became a member of the LJS.

My Hebrew name is Chaya Simcha – which I translate to mean joyous life. I was born on April 18th 1963 to Howard and Sheila Becker. My given name was Caryn Sue Becker. My parents owned a house in Brooklyn where I spent my early years. We lived on the upper level of the house and my parents rented the lower level of the house to a Puerto Rican couple. One of my earliest memories from Brooklyn was listening to 'Georgy Girl' by The Seekers on the radio. Even though we were in the heart of the city, we had a backyard and two pets – a duck and a chicken!

My brother Eric was born in 1965. We lived in that house in Brooklyn until I was four years old and then we moved to a suburb of New York called Hewlett, Long Island. My parents still live there today.

I attended the local primary school – Hewlett Elementary – which was across the street from my house. I started school already knowing how to read. My father taught me while we were still in Brooklyn. One day when I was in the second grade (I was seven years old), I was taken out of class and given a number of puzzles and tests to complete and I was timed against a stop-watch. I think I passed the tests, because my parents were told that the school wanted to move me into the third grade. Going into the third grade would make me a year younger than my peers, but I told my parents I wanted to skip a grade. Even at that time, I thought that being the youngest in the class would give me an extra year in life to play with.

My family joined Temple Emanu-El of Lynbrook in the early 1970s. Although my mother was brought up in the Orthodox tradition and we kept kosher at home, Temple Emanuel-El was a Reform synagogue. My parents chose that synagogue because the members were friendly, the men and women could sit together and most importantly, the rabbi at that time was the distinguished Harold I Saperstein.

My earliest memories of Temple Emanu-El are of going to Hebrew School. While the boys and girls were taught together in the same classroom, the boys were able to study towards a *Bar Mitzvah* ceremony, but the girls were not offered a *Bat Mitzvah*.

The Reform movement at that time wanted to move away from holding *Bar/Bat Mitzvah* celebrations altogether, preferring instead to hold a Jewish Confirmation ceremony for teenagers reaching the age of fifteen. The Board decided that too much emphasis was put on lavish *Bar Mitzvah* parties, and the significance of the *Bar/Bat Mitzvah* (becoming a son or daughter of the commandments) was being lost.

However, a *Bar Mitzvah* ceremony was such a traditional event that some members of Temple Emanu-El did not want to give it up. So the girls were sidelined in favour of keeping up the *Bar Mitzvah* tradition for boys only.

Somehow this didn't seem right. I was well aware of the Women's Liberation Movement of the 1970s and I was inspired to bring some equality to this situation. I enlisted the help of my good friend Abby Plotkin, and together we organised a petition to allow girls to have *Bat Mitzvah* ceremonies at Temple Emanu-El. We received signatures from girls, boys and their parents supporting our cause. We then asked the Temple office for a meeting with Rabbi Saperstein.

On the day of the meeting, Abby and I nervously went into the rabbi's office. Rabbi Saperstein was a man we respected and perhaps even feared. With shaking hands we presented the signatures and then our petition verbally. I thought lightning would strike. Instead, Rabbi Saperstein looked at us thoughtfully, accepted our petition, and said he would bring it up with the Board.

And so it came to pass that in the autumn of 1975, *Bat Mitzvah* ceremonies were introduced to Temple Emanu-el of Lynbrook. We were delighted! Abby had her *Bat*

Mitzvah on 29 November. As I was younger, my *Bat Mitzvah* ceremony took place on 8 May 1976 – just after my 13th birthday.

Abby and I continued our Jewish studies in a Confirmation class that was taught by Rabbi Saperstein and other dedicated members of the synagogue. I remember enjoying my Confirmation classes even more than studying for my *Bat Mitzvah*. As teenagers we wanted to discuss more difficult and challenging topics. One of the teachers taught us Transcendental Meditation. A required reading was *Night* by Elie Wiesel, the famous author and Holocaust survivor.

When I was fifteen years old, my parents agreed to send me on a summer 'teen-tour' to Israel. There were many types of teen tours around. They allowed American teenagers to travel around America or to Europe in groups over the long summer holidays. The one I joined was organised by the American Zionist Youth Federation (AZYF). It was called 'Israel Summer Happening' and had an itinerary that would take us around the State of Israel for two months. This was at a time when bombs were going off in the market places, but we were not afraid.

During the summer, we toured Jerusalem, Tel Aviv, Haifa, Tiberias and Eilat with our leaders. We travelled thirteen hours on a rickety school bus, with no air conditioning, into the stifling heat of the Sinai desert to Sharm el Sheikh which, at that time, was also part of Israel. On the way, we stopped to ride camels across sand dunes, drink black coffee with the Bedouin and eat bread baked by the sun on a rock.

When we arrived in Sharm el Sheikh, we stayed at a disused army barracks where the only source of water was from a trough that looked like it was meant for horses. We woke up at 3 a.m. to climb Mount Sinai. We participated in a three-day-long programme about the Holocaust. We were immersed in what life was like for Jews before, during and after the war. After that, we were exhausted, physically and emotionally, but our support for Judaism and Zionism was strong.

A few years later I attended the State University of New York at Albany, which is where I met my husband Chris. We liked the same music, and talked about different bands. We worked at the college radio station and the university concert board. Chris played guitar in a band in his spare time. We moved to Manhattan after leaving Albany. Chris and I dated for seven years, and with our parents' blessing, we decided to get married. I was disappointed that at that time, the rabbi in Temple Emanu-El of Lynbrook wouldn't marry us.

We then heard about Cantor Robert Abelson in New York. Not only did Cantor Abelson perform wedding ceremonies, he sometimes performed on Broadway. We met him at a deli in the Soho section of Manhattan. Over pastrami sandwiches, Cantor Abelson told us that he believed in love. He wanted to know if we decided to have children, how we would raise them. Chris said we are planning to raise them Jewish. Once he heard that, he agreed to perform our wedding ceremony, which took place in Glen Cove, Long Island on 1 September 1991. We had 200 guests – dancing both the hora and the tarantella. It was the happiest day of my life.

In July 1994 we decided to visit London together (we had both been to London separately before). During our holiday, Chris (now a qualified Doctor of Chiropractic), met with a few people about joining practices in London. We knew it might be a long shot, Chris would need a work permit to work in the UK, but he had a few good meetings and by the time we left, he had two offers to join practices.

Back in New York, a work permit for Chris arrived from Sayer Clinics. He was to start work in September at the Chelsea Harbour Club, where Princess Diana was a member. I was working for Merrill Lynch at the time and I asked my boss if he would consider transferring me to London. He agreed. So Chris went off with two suitcases in hand to London in September, and after tying up some loose ends at my job in New York, and packing up the rest of our apartment, I joined him in December of 1994.

By 2001 Chris was an established Chiropractor working at two offices in London and we had two beautiful little girls, aged four-and-a-half and three. At that point, I started looking at synagogues to find one that we would be comfortable joining and that would have a good religion school for our girls. I cannot remember who recommended The Liberal Jewish Synagogue to us, but I was due to have a meeting with Rabbi Kathleen de Magtige-Middleton after work on 11 September 2001 to discuss becoming a member.

At 2.30 p.m. on that infamous day, I was in my office when someone came running in to say that the Twin Towers were on fire. I went into the conference room where the large television screen was showing the burning buildings. I watched with disbelief – this could not be my city. The intensity of what was happening slowly sank in. My boss asked me if I wanted to go home, but I stayed glued to my office. I remembered my appointment at the synagogue and quickly cancelled it. There were a lot of phone calls I was going to have to make to New York that evening – if I could get through.

That Friday night Chris and I went to the service at The Liberal Jewish Synagogue. The Sanctuary was overflowing with people. Chris and I sat in the balcony. Rabbi Goldberg gave the sermon. I then met Rabbi Middleton whom I had been due to meet earlier that week. I couldn't speak – tears just streamed down my face. Kathleen looked at me with kind sympathy. There was nothing to say. I was working at the World Financial Center in New York in 1993 – the first time terrorists tried to blow up the Twin Towers and failed. Now they succeeded. Seeing the strong and supportive community at the LJS, we decided to join.

We enrolled our daughters in the Religion School held on Saturday mornings. Sarah went into class *Gan* taught by Caroline Hagard. Our younger daughter, Rachel, wanted to be with her sister and so spent two years in class *Gan* with Caroline.

Caroline still teaches class *Gan*, complete with her stories about the *Shabbat* Ghost who miraculously sets the *Shabbat* table while Caroline leaves the room. (The children actually set the table – and Caroline acts surprised!) She also allows the children to light the *Shabbat* candles. ('I always use safety matches,' she says to the parents.)

The children still remember the first Jewish holiday songs they were taught by Caroline. There were easy rhyming songs about Passover (like the 'on *pesach* we eat matzoh, lots and lots of matzoh' song), or about *Chanukka*h (The eight-candles burning song) as well as the *Tzedaka* song ('give to the poor, give to the sick, give to those who have no home'), complete with the actions. Caroline has a wonderful gift for engaging the youngest ones in our synagogue. We will always remember her guitar – it has a sticker on it that one of my girls gave her: a Hebrew letter in the shape of a cat. Caroline also loves cats.

Our son Michael was born when Sarah was seven and Rachel was six. We held his baby naming ceremony at the LJS on 11 September 2004. It was a very symbolic day for us.

When he was four years old, Michael attended Caroline's class too. He now recites the *Shabbat* prayers at our Friday night dinners.

My daughter Sarah became *Bat Mitzvah* at the LJS in March 2010. She studied under Jan Roseman who was the Head of the LJS Religion School for eleven years. Jan came to our house once a week to teach Sarah her *Torah* portion and the prayers for the Friday night and Saturday morning services. Jan was an 'amazing' teacher according to Sarah (the highest accolade a teenager can give!).

At her *Bat Mitzvah* service, Rabbi Alexandra Wright gave a beautiful sermon, in which she spoke about the work of Rabbi Harold Saperstein. Interestingly enough, one of Harold Saperstein's sons, Professor Rabbi Marc Saperstein, is currently the Principal at the Leo Baeck College in London. He has been a guest speaker at the LJS several times.

Rachel is currently studying for her *Bat Mitzvah*, which will take place at the LJS in November of its centenary year. Through the LJS she has made close friendships with her *cheder* classmates, even though they attend different secular schools. The girls also attend *Kadimah* – a summer camp – run by Liberal Judaism. The children keep in touch with each other throughout the year via BBM/Skype/Text messaging and Facebook.

Dov Softi has taken over the post of Head of the Religion School. Dov is introducing Hebrew at an earlier stage. Michael, who is now in class *Bet* learns a new Hebrew letter each week.

As a family, we are very supportive of the synagogue. We attend most Saturday mornings and have run events for the Religion School children and their parents, as well as an 'Auction of Promises' that raised some additional funds for the Religion School. Sarah is now part of the *Kabbalat Torah* class held on Sundays.

For the centenary year, we organised a gala event called A Midsummer Night's Celebration. Chris (who still plays guitar), along with his band, Sound of the Suburb, entertained LJS members with music from different decades of the past hundred years.

We look forward to watching our children continue to grow with Liberal Judaism being a part of their lives. Each end-of-year family service makes us realise how much they have matured and how much they have learned. The LJS community is helping to prepare them socially, morally and spiritually for a very complex world.

We know that the synagogue will continue to be a positive force for all of us as it embarks on its next hundred years.

Bernie Bulkin

Bernie Bulkin regards himself as being new to the LJS, having joined twenty years ago. He is a past Council member and a former Honorary Treasurer. He has been very involved in Friday night services and was *shammash* for five years. He was also joint newsletter editor with his wife, Vivien Rose, and has led various educational activities.

I was born in a New Jersey farmhouse. My father was a chicken farmer, producing eggs for the New York market. There were a large number of Jewish farmers in the 1930s in central New Jersey, men like my father who had accumulated enough money to buy a small farm and escape the Depression, or at least be more in charge of their own livelihoods. My parents were Zionists, but the War and small children kept them from emigrating to Palestine. They eventually moved to Israel in 1970 when my father retired.

When I was just four years old, my parents sold their farm and moved to New York City, where we lived in an apartment in the East New York section of Brooklyn. From the age of five I attended an Orthodox Hebrew School from 3.30 to 5 p.m. Mondays to Thursdays after my day school, services on Saturday morning and, when I was a little older, Sunday morning classes as well. The education was mostly rote-learning of prayers from our *Siddur*, plus a lot of Jewish history and culture. Through the special Saturday morning services run by older boys, we learned how to conduct a service, how to *davven* and how to behave in services.

When I was ten years old, my parents moved to a middle-class suburb in Queens, and joined a Conservative synagogue. Here my Hebrew education was reduced to four-and-a-half hours per week, but there was much more history and explanation. I also became part of the large Conservative youth movement, United Synagogue Youth or USY, and several times attended a USY week at Camp Ramah in Connecticut. There we were introduced to some of the great teachers from the Jewish Theological Seminary and, of course, it was also a major social gathering for teenagers. Later, as a student, I was active with *Hillel* and often led services, including on High Holydays, along with others.

In New York, as an adult, I lived in Roosevelt Island, a 'new town' in the City and, with friends, founded a congregation there which still continues. Again, with various part-time rabbis, I participated in leading services, especially on High Holydays. It is a great feeling to start a congregation from the beginning, make all the decisions about liturgy and practices, and see it thrive.

I came to the United Kingdom in October 1988, supposedly for a two-year secondment, and bought a house in the village of Hinchley Wood, Surrey. Not long after my arrival, I saw a card in the local library giving information about Kingston Liberal Synagogue, which had just hired Danny Rich as its rabbi. I went along there one Friday evening and was overwhelmed by the friendliness of the congregants. Before long, Monty Alfred, who was Chairman, asked if I could possibly help as Treasurer, and I became an officer of KLS, joining Monty, Pam Fletcher Jones and others. My son, David, had his *Bar Mitzvah* at Kingston.

In 1992, when it became clear that my stay would be longer and that I would be working at BP headquarters in the City, I decided to move to somewhere more central and found a house in Belsize Park. When I told my friends at Kingston that I was moving, they said that I would, of course, want to join the LJS. Through other friends I already knew a few LJS members, and so I came along one Friday evening. I was given a warm welcome and a small inquisition by Rosa Mintz, with whom I later became close friends. Soon I met John Rayner, David Goldberg, and Helen Freeman and became a member of the congregation.

Rosa Mintz was the *shammash* on Friday evenings for a long time. She decided who lit the candles and who opened the Ark for the *Shema*. She had no hesitation in walking up to someone whom she did not recognise with the greeting: 'Hello, I'm Rosa, are you Jewish?' When Rosa became ill, the first of many illnesses, she asked me to substitute for her. Eventually I took over this role, and was *shammash* every Friday evening for about five years until I helped create a rota to do this.

Few congregants attend Friday evening services, which have changed format over the years, but they remain a wonderful, meditative way to end the week. The Sanctuary can be lit so that it is dim at the back, and those gathering at the front feel part of an intimate congregation. Visitors from all over the world come on Fridays, and I have had the pleasure of greeting and getting to know some of them, sometimes seeing them at intervals of two or three years.

In the early 1990s, the custom was for a cup of tea to be available before the service and tea and biscuits at *Kiddush*. Once *Kiddush* had been made, the rabbi and those congregants who wished to stay would gather around the table for a short *Oneg* discussion. When I first came to the LJS these were random topics. Later, David Goldberg had the idea of going through great Jews of all time alphabetically. We did this for a year. As I led Friday evening services from time to time, I recall doing the *Oneg* on Bialik and, later in the year, on Miriam. Alexandra Wright later changed this *Oneg* element to a short discussion or presentation on the week's *Torah* portion during the service instead.

On the first Friday of the month we have a *Chavurah* supper. Everyone brings a non-meat dish to share and there is a short programme of some sort. When I first arrived, these arrangements had been suspended by Rabbi Goldberg because the suppers had begun to attract a large number of people who ate a lot and contributed little or no food. One woman regularly turned up with two small pots of yoghurt and, if they were not eaten, she took them back home with her. For a time, while the service was in progress, Fred Shelley, our caretaker, would look at what food had been contributed and decide how many pizzas to order.

Through the efforts of several people the suppers were revived. Joyce Whitman, a congregant who later worked for a time as Organising Secretary of the LJS, was a terrific cook and started to bring a carful of food for the suppers. This meant that we all had enough to eat, at least when she was cooking, but it gradually reduced the incentive for others to contribute. More recently, congregants have been much better at bringing food and we can feed those who are unable (or unwilling) to contribute.

Friday evening is also a time when many of those converting to Judaism come to services, and I have participated in many admission ceremonies. Most of those converting are doing so in preparation for marriage, but not all. Many have stayed on and become active LJS members. Rosa Mintz was a great friend to the proselytes. She was often around the LJS on Tuesday evenings when they had their classes and got to know all of them. Then she saw them on Friday evenings. She took pleasure in their learning and especial pleasure when one of them continued as an active member of the congregation. They all wanted her to be a part of their admission ceremony,

I find admission ceremonies most moving. The new member of our congregation says the *Shema*, holds the *Torah* scroll for the first time, takes a Hebrew name, and we say to them, 'You are our brother' or 'You are our sister'. When Rosa died and left a generous legacy to the synagogue, the Council resolved that a copy of *Siddur Lev Chadash* should be presented to each proselyte at their admission ceremony in her memory.

Through my Friday evening activities, I gradually became more active at the LJS. Because I had a more traditional Orthodox and Conservative Jewish education in the United States, my Hebrew reading is reasonably fluent. However, I was brought up with Ashkenazi Hebrew pronunciation and the transition to the Sephardi pronunciation used in the Liberal movement took some time. At Kingston, when I occasionally read in services, this was received with gentle humour, my Hebrew being referred to as 'Ashkephardic'. But at the LJS, standards are high. After one service, John Rayner complimented me on my Hebrew, then pointed out the three mistakes I had made during the service. Later, I approached him during the afternoon break one *Yom Kippur*, when I saw him sitting alone, and asked him if he could help me with one aspect of Hebrew pronunciation. Before I told him what it was, he said: 'No doubt you want to learn about the *kamatz katan* which, of course, I had been doing all wrong. I still have the sheet he gave me explaining the rules. John had a wonderful gentle way as a firm but caring teacher, and I learned much from him in various conversations, particularly about rabbis and sermons, as well as correct Hebrew pronunciation.

Towards the end of Rita Adler's first period as Chairman, she approached me about joining Council, which I agreed to do. After about a year, Rita was succeeded by Trevor Moross, and Trevor asked if Tim Simon and I would become Treasurers. The LJS has two Treasurers, one for money coming in (subscriptions), and one for money going out – I took over the subscriptions role. But Trevor, Tim, and I, as the three officers of the congregation, would gather regularly, usually over dinner, and discuss all the issues.

Before my term as Treasurer, there had been several attempts at computerising the subscription process for the LJS, none successful, and when I took on the role, the preparation of the annual invoices was still being done manually. It was a complex job because, over time, some members had, due to financial circumstances, paid reduced subscriptions, some paid nothing at all, and a number of generous members paid more than the official subscription.

Another new member of Council when I joined was Vivien Rose. Trevor asked her if she would help me with the subscriptions. Gradually we sorted through the mass of paper, made lists of members in various categories and began to systematise the process. What we needed was a database and a way to manipulate it. Trevor hired his office assistant to type the names and addresses of all the LJS members onto an Excel spreadsheet over one weekend. We then added columns to indicate the correct amount people paid and gradually learned about all sorts of quirks, such as members paying for their grown children, children paying for their parents, etc. All of this information was recorded on the spreadsheet.

Finally, Vivien and I learned how to do a mail merge, creating hundreds of invoices and letters in Word by automatically inserting the correct information from the database. It sounds pretty trivial now, and it is, but assembling and checking the information for many hundreds of congregants took us a very long time. The first year we did the invoicing, we finished it over the Easter weekend. By the second year, we had it done by mid-February, and. by the third year, everyone got an invoice by the first week in January. I think by that time Vivien and I had realised that if we could achieve this, we could actually have a life together and we were married at the LJS in 2002.

When Rabbi Helen Freeman left to go to West London Synagogue, Trevor asked me to chair the Rabbinic Appointments Committee to recruit a new Assistant Rabbi. We formed a committee made up of Council members and others, with someone from every age decade from twenties to eighties. To maintain confidentiality, particularly for those rabbis we were interviewing, most of the meetings took place in my house in Belsize Park.

As a first step, I discussed the position with John Rayner and David Goldberg. As it turned out, David had an idea who we would finally appoint before we even started, but both gave a lot of helpful ideas. Although the position was advertised, we spent a lot of time talking to potential candidates to encourage them to apply. At that time, several rabbis realised that David Goldberg would be retiring in a few years as senior rabbi and that there had been cases in the past of the Associate Rabbi succeeding the LJS Senior Rabbi, as David himself did. Several rabbis were interested in the post only if that was part of the deal, but in the end the Committee decided that the succession would be a separate process and should not be pre-empted by this search.

Rabbi Mark Solomon, who taught at Leo Baeck College but was also a rabbi at West Central Synagogue on a part-time basis, had been at the LJS for extended periods of time and was well known to the congregation. We were also very much impressed by a final year student at Leo Baeck College, Kathleen Middleton, from the Netherlands. In the end, the Committee recommended to Council that we appoint Mark Solomon part-time and Kathleen Middleton full-time, so that we would have two-and-a-half rabbis instead of two. This was agreed and they both started in 1999.

I also chaired the Rabbinic Appointments Committee when David Goldberg's retirement was approaching. Of course, the appointment of a Senior Rabbi is a much more challenging task. The LJS had only had four Senior Rabbis in its history, all of whom were distinguished intellectually. We once again formed a committee. Drawing on the experience of our previous search, and that of other congregations, we decided that we would only consider rabbis of whom we had personal knowledge, that is, either they had served United Kingdom congregations now or in the past, or someone on the Committee knew them. We contacted every graduate of Leo Baeck College and advertised widely. However, we received relatively few applications. We also drew up a list of those rabbis we knew who we would like to invite to apply and I contacted all of them personally. I spent quite a long time discussing the post with David Goldberg, and with John Rayner. With John, I reviewed every rabbi on our list and he was very frank in his assessment of their strengths and weaknesses.

Several of our favoured candidates did not apply, but we still had a strong slate of applicants. The Committee worked very hard and, in the end, we had a long discussion about four final candidates. There was unanimity in the choice of Rabbi Alexandra Wright.

The LJS has been a big part of my life for the last two decades. Until I came to the LJS, I always thought I would prefer a smaller congregation to a large one, but I was wrong. I have made many close friends and, most importantly, met my wife through the synagogue. I have learned many things from all the rabbis at the LJS, not just about Judaism, but also about how to teach through observing their different styles. I consider it a privilege to be able to be part of the volunteer group of the LJS, whether it is in big things like being Treasurer or *LJS News* co-editor, or in the smaller and less noticed things like greeting people on Friday evening, visiting Rosa Mintz and Harold Young in hospital, or teaching a small group of members on Saturday morning.

✡

Eric Conrad

This interview is based on a lunchtime talk that Eric Conrad gave after a Tuesday Lunch at the LJS in 1998. A refugee from Vienna, he became the nephew-in-law, biographer and literary executor of Lily Montagu.

I left Vienna for England in early May 1938, aged twenty-seven, just seven weeks after Hitler's Nazi army invaded Austria. We lived dangerously and had to keep our departure absolutely secret. Nevertheless, I did visit two old and trusted friends of mine to say goodbye before I left. One of them was a noted Hebrew scholar who, fourteen years earlier, had prepared me for my *Bar Mitzvah*.

He gave me a written introduction to an English lady. He said that she was a quite exceptional woman, a member of the Anglo-Jewish aristocracy. She had spent her life devoted to social and religious work. He had met her in Vienna several years earlier, when she was on one of her many missionary travels, and had worked closely with her on developing a progressive type of Judaism in Austria. He described her as the sort of lady who would help me. As you may have guessed by now, that lady was Lily Montagu. I went to see her very soon after I arrived in London. I immediately fell under her spell and, very luckily for me, she also seemed to have taken to me.

She introduced me very soon afterwards to Dr Mattuck and I was deeply impressed with my first Sabbath morning service at the LJS. From then on, I never missed a morning service on Saturdays and, very soon, was drawn into the service. I was asked to read from time to time and, almost every Saturday, I was called up to help open and close the Ark and with undressing and dressing the scroll. In the meantime, Lily Montagu also introduced me to her social circle and asked me to her house. She had a big family and introduced me to the Franklins, the Samuels and the Montefiores.

When war broke out, she kept in touch with me while I was interned and, later, for nearly six years when I was in the Army. In the meantime, something had happened, the significance of which I did not realise at the time. I got an invitation – a very formal one – which said Miss Myer and Monica Myer would be 'at home' from 3 to 6 p.m. for tea and entertainment on a certain date and at a given address, RSVP. I had no idea who the Myers were or how they had got hold of my name and address, but I accepted anyway. When I went to their home, I discovered that the two Myer sisters had decided to have one of their afternoon teas for about twenty or thirty refugees, as many as they could accommodate, in order to give them a good time for a few hours. They were both members of the LJS, and had consulted a list of refugees kept by the synagogue. I happened to be one of those they had drawn from the list.

Monica Myer, the younger sister, was a plump, bouncy, cheerful and happy girl, who tried her hardest to entertain us. The older sister, Miss Myer (for I knew her by no other name), was a complete contrast. For one thing, she was more attractive, but she also had a fascination for me, which I found, at the time, difficult to explain. She was very shy and quiet, and had a serious expression on her fine face, which was lit up by an enchanting smile. She had the most gentle and beautiful voice. However, Miss Myer faded out of my life. I would have loved to have met her again, but I couldn't even afford to send her a bunch of flowers, which would have been *de rigeur* for a young man who had been asked to a party.

When the war was over and I was demobbed in July 1946, I immediately resumed my contact with Lily Montagu and the synagogue. She drew me more and more into her activities, especially the World Union for Progressive Judaism, the West Central Girls' Club, which she had founded when she was nineteen, and the West Central Synagogue, where she was a minister. She also continued to ask me to her home.

She lived with her older sister, Marian, in a very fine Victorian house called the Red Lodge at Palace Court in Bayswater. There the two sisters celebrated the Sabbath eve every Friday night with a family party, which consisted of twelve to fifteen guests, most of them from their very large family. The parties followed the same pattern: prayers for twenty minutes led by Lily Montagu, then dinner when the candles were lit, after which we ate. Later, we went back to the sitting room, where we had animated conversation for an hour or two.

On one Friday night in spring 1949, I was asked again to one of the family parties. Just before we sat down for prayers, the telephone rang and Lily answered the phone. She said to her sister, Marian, in a loud voice, as Marian was very deaf, 'Sheila says she is unfortunately delayed, but she will be in time for dinner'. After prayers, we went to the huge dining room. When I had found my seat, I noticed that the one next to me was empty. While soup was being served, the door opened and a lady, obviously 'Sheila', came in. She was very apologetic and embarrassed, and was shown to the seat next to me. To my joy, I immediately recognised that Sheila was the Miss Myer whom I had met many years earlier. She had no idea who I was of course, but I reminded her of the party eleven years ago. It was only then that I discovered that she was a niece of the Montagu sisters. In fact, as it turned out later, she was their favourite niece.

We decided to meet again soon, and we did so. We met frequently and, after a short time, dated. On 9 July 1949 we officially celebrated our engagement, again at the Red Lodge on a Friday night. Aunt Lily (as she soon became known to me), spoke a few lovely words and wished us happiness. She married us at the LJS on 6 October 1949, and later came to our house at Fitzjohns Avenue, where she blessed us. When we had our two lovely daughters, Jane at the end of February 1951, and Barbara in September 1952, we took them to synagogue and Aunt Lily blessed them. Lily Montagu remained the biggest influence in my life.

Sheila died two years ago, in November 1996. During our forty-seven years of marriage, our mutual love and understanding grew from year to year until I can really say that we became a single mind. There was never, ever heard a single harsh or cross word between us. It is said that some marriages are 'made in heaven'. I have a certainty that ours was made in heaven, because it resulted directly from a seemingly, quite trifling incident: the visit to my old Hebrew teacher. If it had not been for that, I would never have met Miss Montagu, would not have been involved with The Liberal Jewish Synagogue and would not have met Sheila.

Aunt Lily, before she died, made me her literary executor. When the National Federation of Temple Sisterhoods in America commissioned a biography of Lily Montagu for her 80th birthday, she reluctantly consented and asked me to write it.

Editorial note: Eric Conrad's closeness to Lily Montagu and her high regard for him is evident from a message on the rear of a photograph taken at a WUPJ conference in which is held in the LJS archives. It reads: '*Eric Conrad, With greetings from his friend Lily Montagu who has great confidence that he will achieve much that is good for he belongs to the opposition party who as Dr Baeck said at the conference belong. August 1946*'

✡

Bryan Diamond

Bryan Diamond is the LJS Honorary Archivist. He was very involved in the synagogue as a young man, particularly in the Alumni Society, and returned to the synagogue in 1990 once his family had grown up. He was a member of the LJS Council between 1994 and 2000 and, in the late 1990s, he led the synagogue's *Doroteinu* project. Since 1994 he has been a member of the Services Committee and, since 1995, also a member of the Building and Facilities Committee. For a number of years he chaired the synagogue's Social Action Group and, more recently, joined the Library Group.

I was born in 1936 in Leamington Spa, the second of three boys. I had little Jewish upbringing until my parents, Claude and Anne, joined the Birmingham Liberal Synagogue when I was fourteen. Previously, they had been members of the Orthodox Singers Hill congregation. I had lessons with Rabbi Bernard Hooker for my Confirmation, which took place at the synagogue when I was sixteen. I also became involved in the Knesset Youth Group. When I went to Birmingham University, I joined the Jewish Society, which was dominated by Orthodox Jews, and continued to attend the Birmingham Liberal Synagogue.

My involvement with The Liberal Jewish Synagogue began in 1957 when I came to London. I recall Peggy Lang introducing me to a shy John Rayner, as he then was. I also have a dim memory of seeing Lily Montagu with her sister, Marian, at the front of the Sanctuary. I attended a meeting at their home in Palace Court.

I was a keen member of the Alumni Society, which became the centre of my social life. The society was very active, having a wide age range from about seventeen to thirty-five. We had much support from the convivial and popular Assistant Minister, the Rev. Philip Cohen. We held our own services, study groups, debates and discussions, cultural events, including theatre visits and drama productions, social activities, rambles at the weekend and tennis in the summer. In 1960, I was the Secretary and organised the first Alumni Weekend Conference in June at Quaremead. On a few occasions, I went ice-skating with the Alumni at the rink in Bayswater. The *Chanukkah* dinner and dance in 1958 had an attendance of 110. I was elected Vice Chairman in 1961 and drafted a revision of the constitution, but I resigned soon afterwards on becoming engaged to Judith Letchner. She was from Edgware Reform Synagogue. In 1985 I suggested and helped to organise a reunion dinner for past members. About eighty people attended.

The Federation of Liberal and Progressive Jewish Youth Groups (FLPJYG) organised monthly discussions, for example on Israel and intermarriage. I attended these meetings in different synagogues, thus becoming familiar with other clubs. There was also an annual drama competition held in the Montefiore Hall at the LJS. I attended the annual conference in April at Dorking and appear in photographs, such as one that was used for the centenary history of the Liberal movement. At the request of Rabbi David Goldstein, in 1958 I became the Treasurer of the World Union for Progressive Judaism Youth Section conference held in Italy.

In 1967 Judith and I settled in Pinner, but we remained members of the LJS until 1970 when our eldest daughter was due to attend *cheder*. We joined the Northwood and Pinner Liberal Synagogue where Judith, our three daughters and I took an active part in that lively congregation. My parents, Claude and Anne, had joined the LJS when they moved to London in about 1968 and remained members till their deaths in 1985 and 1988. My mother was on a committee which arranged an annual exhibition of members' art.

When our children had left home, we moved to Hampstead in 1990. Our eldest daughter, Lynette, lives near us and is a member of the LJS. The middle one, Naomi, has two young sons and is a member of Leicester Progressive Jewish Congregation. We rejoined the LJS when it was 'in exile' in Loudoun Road and attended services regularly. At first, we still went back to Northwood for some services and Judith for some classes, but over time this was less frequent. The nature of the congregation and the services at the LJS were very different and took some time to get used to, but I have now adjusted to the changes in the *Siddur* and in the services.

Rabbi Helen Freeman was friendly to me, and John Rayner, the Rabbi Emeritus, was always courteous. I also got to know the new Rabbis Solomon, Middleton and Wright. After first being advised that it was not usual to stand for the Council soon after joining the LJS, despite my experience at Northwood and Pinner Liberal Synagogue, I was unsuccessful in a contested election when Sir Peter Lazarus was Chairman. I then joined the Council in 1994 under the chairmanship first of Rita Adler and then of Trevor Moross. I stayed on the Council for the maximum six-year term. Judith has also been on the Council for six years and has been very active in the synagogue.

I had previously represented Northwood and Pinner Liberal Synagogue on the Council of the Union of Liberal and Progressive Synagogues (ULPS). After we joined the LJS, I continued to serve on the ULPS Council, representing the LJS. In this role I went to several meetings around the country, including in Bristol, Liverpool, Birmingham, the Beth Shalom Holocaust Centre and, in 2010, Brighton.

In 1994 I joined the LJS Services Committee and find the discussions very interesting, with the opportunity to hear the views of the rabbis. Sometimes there have been strong differences of opinion between members of the committee, such as about the frequency of *B'nei Mitzvah*, the amount of the sermon directed to the child, the proportion of English and Hebrew in services, the chanting of the *Torah* portion, selection of passages from Leviticus, non-Jews being on the *bimah*, who can have an *aufruf*, and the continuance of 'Tent' services.

Since 1995 I have also been a member of the Buildings and Facilities Committee. Apart from attending meetings, this has involved noting defects in the building and making suggestions for improvement. In 2009 I revised extensively and re-published the booklet, *A Guide to the Building*, which included many of my own photos.

I ran a National Theatre Visits group, which was much appreciated by our older members. In 1995 I became the chair of the Social Action Group, which had been struggling for a while, and I arranged some pre-service talks, including four on mental health. I continued on the group until it was reorganised in 2000. I also started a group, as part of the Union of Liberal and Progressive Synagogues' *Doroteinu* programme, to support the many older members of the congregation and, in 1999, I chaired a well-attended talk given at the LJS by Rabbi Julia Neuberger on the problems of health in an ageing population. She talked again on this subject in 2008. I joined the Library Group, taking part in the Saturday rota.

However, my main job at the synagogue has been as Archivist, using experience I gained at Northwood and Pinner Liberal Synagogue. I volunteered to do this in 1993 when the archive boxes came out of store after the rebuilding of the synagogue. I arranged a move of much older material to the Record Office, now the London Metropolitan Archive, and I continue to receive and supervise the accession of new material. My help in supplying photocopies has been acknowledged in a book entitled *Lost Synagogues of London* by Renton, which was published in 2000. I have written several articles for the LJS newsletter. I have taken photos at many events, which I have deposited in the archive.

Until recently, there was little regular help with the archives, but I now have some assistance from Carol Roberts and Albert Herskovits. In 2008 I commenced a series of interviews of staff and older members, which have been transcribed, and which were the starting point for this book. In 1994 I taped interviews with several people, including Mrs Dorothy Edgar (Rabbi Edgar's widow), Rabbis John Rayner and Bernard Hooker, and Maxwell Stern (former LJS President) for the ULPS Oral History project.

I have also continued to be involved with our movement, the ULPS, now Liberal Judaism. I was a member of the committee, chaired by Walter Goldsmith, which organised the celebration of the 50th anniversary of our youth movement in 1997, held at the LJS. In 1999 I became the first Archivist to the ULPS and have had a major job in organising their papers into a logical arrangement as they had been in great disorder. I have had some help from Malcolm Brown, Ken Solomons and my daughter, Lynette. Rosita Rosenberg has assisted with identifying photos. I also came across various papers relating to my own history. I began listing the earliest documents and, in 2000, wrote a first archive entry for the yearbook. In the early months of 2002 I listed all the prayer books I could find at the Union of Liberal and Progressive Synagogues and at the LJS. This bibliography was published with a paper by John Rayner. I have continued to attend the Liberal Judaism Council as their Archivist.

In conclusion, I appreciate the dignity of the services at the LJS, the music, and the thoughtful sermons. I enjoy playing my part in the various groups, relating to other volunteers, and especially the expertise I have acquired as Archivist and the help I can thus offer.

✡

Barbara Godfrey

Barbara Godfrey joined the synagogue twenty-seven years ago. She is the synagogue's Honorary Librarian and Chairman of the Library Committee.

I was born in Edgware in 1934. My parents were founder members of the Reform Synagogue there but they both came from Orthodox families.

My mother was born in Manchester and went to the local Jews' School. She won a scholarship to Manchester High School, which was unusual for a girl at that time. If you were a scholar, you had to sit in the front and were asked to do chores because as a scholar you were looked down upon. My mother was very bright and had a very good education. She was also an excellent pianist. She didn't go to university as her parents were very Victorian in their outlook. Instead they sent her to secretarial college, after which she obtained a very good job.

My father was born in Szrensk in Poland. He used to say that on Monday, Tuesday and Wednesday it was in Poland and on Thursday, Friday and Saturday it was part of Russia. I don't know much about his life. He died in 1962 when he was sixty-five. I think that he came over here when he was quite young, and that he returned to Poland in his early twenties to bring his siblings over to the UK when his parents died. He worked his way up from nothing and was a successful businessman.

During the war I was moved from pillar to post. We went to live in Wales, where I learned a bit of Welsh. I went to boarding school at the age of five and moved schools several times, which was not good for my education. Because of the war I didn't receive much religious education. At boarding school in Yorkshire I remember being accused of killing Christ. I was only seven at the time and didn't know how to deal with it. I am sure the Headmistress of that school didn't like me. On one occasion, in school prayers, I was asked the number of the hymn by one of the girls and, when I replied, the Headmistress ticked me off and told me that, because I had talked in prayers, I must go to church. This made me feel as if I had committed a crime. I remember sitting in church, feeling very uncomfortable and thinking that I should not be there. I was probably well into adulthood before I got over this incident.

After the war, we went to live in Chessington Avenue at Henly's Corner in Finchley. It was a very nice area, but everyone knew everyone else's business, which I didn't like. We joined the North-Western Reform Synagogue in Alyth Gardens and I attended Hebrew classes there. I found them incredibly boring as we just learned Hebrew, which I could already read. I must have had some lessons at home. When I was sixteen I was due to be confirmed. I asked the rabbi, Dr Van der Zyl, how one could reconcile the Big Bang with religion and God. Dr Van der Zyl was a marvellous man, whom I really liked and respected, but he looked at me and didn't reply, so I decided not to be confirmed.

I went to North London Collegiate School in Edgware and stayed there until I was sixteen, after which I studied Speech and Drama at the Royal Academy of Music (RAM). They had a Drama Department at that time, and I absolutely loved the course. I received an LRAM (Licentiate of the Royal Academy of Music) in Speech and Drama and a RAM teaching diploma at the end of it. When I left the Academy, I taught voice and speech at the London Academy of Music and Dramatic Art (LAMDA) for about ten years.

I have a brother, Michael, who is seven years older than I am. I had another brother, David, who was three years older. He had heart trouble and died following an operation when he was thirty years old. Two days after his death my father, who'd had a stroke, also died. We had a double funeral, which was very traumatic. I was in my late twenties at the time with two small children.

I had met my husband, Malcolm, who was a qualified doctor, in quite a conventional way. There was a synagogue dance at the Savoy, which my parents wanted my brother, Michael, and me to attend. I didn't particularly want to go, but I met Malcolm there. We hadn't known each other very long before we decided to get married. We met in November and married the following September. He was twenty-nine and I was twenty. I had to obtain permission from my parents, which was required in those days as I was under twenty-one!

When we had been married for about a year, Malcolm obtained a Research Fellowship at the Johns Hopkins Hospital in America, and I took a job in the library at the same university, which I found most interesting. As we didn't have a family then, we travelled around the States a great deal.

On our return to the UK, Malcolm went to work at the headquarters of the Medical Research Council. Eventually he changed jobs and became Dean of the Royal Postgraduate Medical School at Hammersmith Hospital, where he stayed for nine years. He then returned to the Medical Research Council as their Second Secretary. He received the CBE, which he wouldn't want me to mention as he is very modest. Malcolm is also the most religious member of the family; he really believes in God, for which I admire him. He very much likes the decorum and the feeling that services are a sincere form of prayer, rather than mere ritual.

I continued teaching at various drama schools, and also became an examiner in Speech and Drama for the Associated Board of the Royal Schools of Music. This took me all over the UK, visiting schools and examining children of all ages. I also held drama classes at our house in Wimbledon and taught the sixth form at King's College School. I studied with the Open University in the late 1980s and obtained a BA Hons., a truly mind-expanding experience. I had learned the piano as a child and, when I was in my thirties, I took up the clarinet. I now also play the tenor and alto saxophone. I play in two different groups.

Over the years I have been a compulsive volunteer. I worked for about eight years for the Citizens Advice Bureau and became a magistrate, eventually sitting on the Inner London Family Panel and Youth Courts. I was Vice-Chair of the Family Panel for a while. I also worked as a volunteer for the Spinal Injuries Association. For about eight years I was a governor, and later the Chair of Governors, of Christ Church Bentinck School.

During our first years of marriage, we lived in Wimbledon and belonged to the local Reform Synagogue. Malcolm wanted to join a Liberal synagogue because he had read a number of the writings of the 'founders' and had been very impressed by their approach to Judaism. So when the Kingston Liberal Synagogue was established, we became members. However, our three children were blessed at the Wimbledon Reform Synagogue. Our son, Richard, had his *Bar Mitzvah* at Kingston. We had to persuade the synagogue to hold a *Bar Mitzvah* as, at that time, they only wanted the children to be confirmed. Jenny, our eldest daughter, was also confirmed at Kingston.

After about twenty-four years, we moved to the centre of London and, for a while, joined the West London Synagogue, where our youngest daughter, Claire, was confirmed and joined the youth club. We then moved to St John's Wood and joined the LJS. Malcolm was keen to join the Liberal Synagogue and now that I am familiar with the service, I feel very much at home there. I love the singing of the choir and all the music, which I think is led brilliantly by Cathy Heller Jones. We have now been members for twenty-seven years.

We got to know John Rayner on a sad occasion, when our daughter Claire died at the age of thirty-two. He was absolutely brilliant, a very warm and wonderful man. We always enjoyed his services and found him to be a tremendous scholar, thoughtful and kind. We also admire David Goldberg for his way with words. His sermons have always been stimulating and have raised issues that we could talk about afterwards. We are very fond of Alexandra Wright, who is a warm and compassionate person. I feel that, if I ever were to have a problem, I would be able to talk to her with complete confidence. Her sermons are fantastic, so I feel lucky to have had this contact with the rabbis.

After Claire died, I became more involved with the synagogue and became the Honorary Librarian. I have always loved books and knew a little about libraries following my year at Johns Hopkins. I have always been a 'bookworm'. Rabbi Kathleen Middleton was on the Library Committee, so we got to know her quite well. She was very helpful, so I was very sad when she left the LJS. Mark Solomon came onto the Committee, but he was quite busy and was not able to attend many meetings. I have now been on the Library Committee for about five or six years and Chairman for about a year. Our committee is quite small and there is a very good team of volunteers. They supervise the library on a Saturday morning. Once a year we have a joint meeting when we update them on what has happened during the year and hold a party to say 'Thank you'.

I feel that the LJS has become less progressive. There is much more Hebrew than in the past and the *B'nei Mitzvah* often chant their portion. I preferred it as it was, and I associate the chanting with Orthodoxy.

I enjoy my family and am fortunate in having four English grandchildren and three American ones. The latter belong to a modern Orthodox congregation!

✡

Rabbi David Goldberg

Rabbi Goldberg was a student rabbi at the LJS during the late 1960s. He returned as Associate Rabbi in 1975 and became Senior Rabbi in 1989. He is now Rabbi Emeritus. He is well known for his outspoken views on Israeli policy and developments in the Middle East and for his interfaith work.

I was born in 1939, just before the start of the war, in the East End of London, but moved to Manchester as a young boy when my father was appointed as the rabbi of the Manchester Reform Synagogue. At that time, it was housed in temporary premises as the synagogue had been destroyed by an enemy bomb. I therefore had a sense of *déjà vu* when, as rabbi of the LJS some forty years later, I was involved in the rebuilding of the synagogue.

My father came from a conventional United Synagogue background. His family were originally from Russia, but settled in Sunderland, where they joined the Orthodox Synagogue. My father trained at Jews' College, but I think he always had doubts about the way the United Synagogue treated women, and about what he was taught at Jews' College, so when the opportunity came to go to Manchester to the largest and oldest Reform congregation outside London, he took it.

My mother (née Yudt or Judt), also came from a very Orthodox background. Her family were rabbis and scholars from Poland. I haven't traced the line in detail, but I do know that a member of my family was one of the seventy-two delegates whom Napoleon convened in the Sanhedrin in 1804 to deal with the 'Jewish problem' in French territories. My mother's family were greatly upset when my father became a Reform rabbi. Family mythology has it that they felt he was 'deserting the ship' for 'those reformers'.

My own religious education was a Reform one. I was *Bar Mitzvah* at my father's synagogue, but I did not have a Confirmation, it was not on offer. When I was older, I taught a little in the religion school and also helped out when I went to university.

We were closer to my mother's family than to my father's. I was particularly close to my maternal grandfather, whom I admired and liked enormously. He had been quite a scholar back home in Poland and, along with my father, he was one of the main influences on my becoming a rabbi, although I fought against it for a while because I wanted to write.

My boyhood was not a particularly happy one. My father was quite stern and held strong views on how my younger brother and sister and I should behave as the children of a rabbi. We were often reprimanded for our behaviour in synagogue. I had a bit of a wild streak, which was not totally repressed by my father's strictness. I sometimes got into scrapes with the children of Orthodox families living close to us, which caused tensions between our respective parents. Relations between the Orthodox and Reform communities were somewhat acrimonious at the time, which was another reason why my childhood in Manchester was not easy. I couldn't wait to get away!

I was, however, very happy at Manchester Grammar School, then under the High Mastership of Eric James (later Lord James of Rusholme), especially as a sixth-former. I was a prefect and played lots of football and cricket. I gained a scholarship to Lincoln College, Oxford, to read English, but deferred taking up the place for two years.

Emerging from the restrictions and austerities of the war, my generation were full of 'derring-do'. At the age of sixteen I went on a camping holiday with school friends to the Loire Valley in France. This would now be seen as quite tame, but it was very adventurous at the time. I regretted the ending of National Service the year before I left school. I thought that I would have enjoyed the strenuous lifestyle that the Army would have provided. So I went travelling instead. I was so keen to go, I even left school early and missed out on a season's cricket!

Just before I left, I walked into the offices of the *Manchester Evening News,* and persuaded them to commission me to write monthly articles on my travels as a means of supplementing my income. In the eighteen months I was away, I had more than enough adventures to submit these regular articles: the time I slept in a police cell in a small Swedish town; my eventful trip with a Swiss driver who gave me a lift across Germany, Holland and Belgium to reach Paris; the various gruelling jobs I took to earn money, such as cleaning boats in a dockyard and scrubbing floors in a restaurant; my artistic tour of Italy.

After about six months, my family came to meet me in Italy. They brought with them the good news that my *bubba* had offered to pay half of my fare to Israel, so I quickly got labouring work to earn the other half of the ticket. I set off without much thought of what I was going to find there. I fell in love with the country at my first sight of Mount Carmel as the boat reached Haifa. It was very liberating to see Jewish people in all walks of life rather than being a minority as they had been in Manchester.

I stayed a year in Israel, abandoning my plans to see India. It was then a young and quite dangerous country, and I had some wonderful experiences. I worked on two *kibbutzim*. The first was a very left-wing one. I loved the communal experience, but left to travel round the country for six weeks. After that, I needed to earn more money so I applied to join a *kibbutz* in the Negev Desert. I liked the idea of working with horses as I had been a proficient rider from an early age, but also because of the resonance of the environment with the cowboy movies I had come to love as a child. Soon after I arrived at *Kibbutz S'de Boker*, I heard Ben Gurion speak. He had recently resigned as Prime Minister and was living on the *kibbutz* to encourage young people to become pioneers. I found his speech inspiring and met him on a number of other occasions. He became a formative influence; his wife adopted me as a sort of grandson.

I loved the spartan existence in the desert, and also the contact with the super-fit soldiers, even though I felt that I was an inferior 'Diaspora Jew'. It was one of the most fantastic times of my life. I was beginning to think about giving up my place at Oxford and going instead to study agriculture at the Hebrew University. However, the dream was brought to an end when I had an accident which hospitalised me for two months. After that, I was not able to work properly and began to be a bit bored and homesick so, when my parents wrote to me suggesting that I should go home to prepare for Oxford, I did.

I found it very difficult to adjust to life at Oxford which, in comparison to the casualness and bustle of Israel, I found stuffy and steeped in restrictive traditions. But, after a two-month trip back to Israel at the end of my first year, I found my dreams had waned a little and I was therefore more settled when I returned. During my second year, I became involved in the college drama society and helped to produce the first college production to play at the Oxford Playhouse. In my third year I wrote a novel based on my experiences in Israel, which I thought was going to be published. When it wasn't, I realised that I needed to get a job, so I went into teaching.

Comprehensive schools had just been introduced, and I taught in one of those in South East London. As I was something of a socialist *manqué*, I thoroughly enjoyed teaching English to a group of young people who had been written off as not having the ability to take 'A' levels. Although I was proud to get some of them to university, I soon found teaching to be very repetitive. It was at this point that I had a telephone call from Rabbi Reinhart at West London Synagogue, who had left an impression on me as an adolescent when he'd visited Manchester to preach. He was a very powerful speaker, preaching in the style of the era – in a very declamatory way with lots of arm movements. Israel Mattuck would have preached in the same vein. It's not how we preach nowadays, but it impressed me mightily as a thirteen-/fourteen-year-old. I remember his phone call well. The essence of it was: 'The apple never falls far from the tree. Why don't you consider it, David?'

The seed was planted. I decided I would ease my way into the rabbinate by studying Semitics first to get a competent background. I studied for two years at Trinity College, Dublin, where there was a very well-known professor of Semitics, Professor Jacob Winegreen. There was also a small Liberal congregation looking for somebody to take services. I was therefore able to combine postgraduate work at Trinity with taking services and see if I liked it. There were very bitter relations between the Progressive and Orthodox communities in Dublin, and the fact that many people were emigrating because the Irish economy was so bad, was rather depressing. There was also much factionalism and politicking within the Liberal community. This all proved to be a good grounding for synagogal politics later on!

At the end of my two years in Dublin I thought: 'Yes, I do actually quite like this'. So I came back to England to study at Leo Baeck College for three years. I found myself very sought after as a student rabbi. The first approach came from Rabbi Reinhart, now at Westminster Synagogue. His admirers had bought Kent House in Knightsbridge, and he was quite keen that I go there as his assistant. Another offer came from Middlesex New Synagogue. Rabbi Michael Goulston was joining Hugo Gryn at West London, so they were looking for a successor to him. The third, and financially least attractive offer, was from the LJS as a student rabbi to John Rayner and David Goldstein.

I had met John in Dublin when he'd come over with Sidney Brichto and some ULPS lay leaders to celebrate the community's 21st anniversary. I was bowled over by John – his approach, his scholarship, his way of looking at Judaism, all of which accorded with my own developing views. I'd previously met Rabbi Albert Friedlander from Wembley Liberal Synagogue when he had come to Dublin to conduct a wedding. I was impressed by his kindliness towards me and his thoughtfulness. I found a refreshing honesty and integrity about both his and John's Liberal approach which, to my young mind, contrasted favourably with what I saw as the hypocrisy (I use that word thoughtfully) of the Reform movement on issues like mixed marriage, or saying that it is a *halachic* movement, when quite obviously no non-Orthodox movement can claim to be *halachic*.

I had also met David Goldstein, a great scholar with a pleasant similarity of viewpoints. He, John and I were all Oxbridge people, which gave rise to a collegiality. David loved cricket, as I do. So without any hesitation I chose the LJS. I came as a student rabbi in 1968. In those days Leo Baeck College liked to move their students around, but I was quite adamant that I wanted to be here and so I managed to stay for three years. Carole and I met and married while I was a student rabbi.

I enjoyed my rabbinic training very much. Leo Baeck College at that time worked out of a few rooms at West London Synagogue, but John had begun to get involved in restructuring the syllabus. The best year of the three I spent there was when Professor Sandmel came over from Hebrew Union College for a year as Acting Principal. He was a fine man, a very good scholar. He really organised the College in a way that was long overdue.

While I was a student, I was invited by Lilian Hill and Phyllis Gerson to the East End to see the social work they were carrying out there. They were part of a generation of Anglo-Jewish families who had been influenced to become involved in social work by Lily Montagu and Basil Henriques. They had a very strong sense of social responsibility and the work they did was amazing. They worked with some very tough young people and took it all in their stride.

As I was about to finish my studies at Leo Baeck College and to be ordained, I decided to speak about my future to the Chairman of the LJS Council, Teddy Joseph, and the Honorary Officers since there was the possibility of my going to Wembley Liberal Synagogue because Albert Friedlander was leaving to go to the College as the full-time Dean. Teddy suggested that it might be better for me to wait to become Associate or Senior Rabbi rather than taking on the role of third rabbi. So I went to Wembley. By a piece of good fortune for me, David Goldstein left to go to the British Library as Keeper of Mediaeval and Hebrew manuscripts. Thus I returned to the LJS in 1975 having spent three-and-a-half years at Wembley, which, in those days, was a thriving congregation. I had a very enjoyable time there, but John Rayner asked me if I would be interested in becoming Associate Rabbi at the LJS.

The vacancy was properly advertised, but there were no trial sermons as part of the interview process in those days. I was given a brief letter of appointment, which mentioned my salary. We shook hands on it. I think the understanding was that if a rabbi and the congregation get on, then you don't really need to draw up a lengthy contract. If they don't get on, then all the contracts in the world won't make it better.

Duties were divided very amicably between John and me. He explained what we would do together, like going to Council meetings, and what we would do separately. Things were divided straight down the middle rather than it being based on status, which is how I arranged things when I became Senior Rabbi myself. I took on the Religion School and responsibility for working with young people. Carole and I used to have monthly coffee meetings at our flat, at which adolescents talked openly about the things in which they were interested.

John and I became great friends. We used to go on long walks together to get into the right frame of mind for *Yom Kippur*. Our wives and our children were also very friendly, so it was a family relationship as well as being a work relationship. We complemented each other well. He was quite a shy man, enormously imposing with a great deal of dignity. He was the most delightful, amusing companion, but he could appear rather formal and a lot of people found that a little forbidding, whereas I have always been, I think, a bit easier to approach. People used to say that if they needed spiritual advice they would go to John, if they needed human advice they would go to David.

John and I preached for each other. We were both very, very critical of slipshod scholarship and badly turned phrases, so we would spend far too long crafting every word of our sermons and making the perfect sentence rather than getting on with it; it's part of the fastidiousness that John and I always shared.

When I came to the LJS, Sir Louis Gluckstein was President. Known as 'Luigi', he had the style of a patrician and could be fearsome by all accounts. We got on because we had been at the same Oxford College. He had been an MP, and it was the great regret of his life that he did not make it to Cabinet rank, for which he undoubtedly had the calibre. The war came and he was not in the right place at the right time. When he died, he left me a gift (which I still have) of cufflinks in his will, which is more, John said, than he had left him.

John had stood up to Luigi on a number of occasions about the new prayerbook and other things. This took enormous courage on John's part. I remember the AGM at which Luigi criticised the new High Holyday prayerbook that eventually came out in 1973. This was *Gate of Repentance*, which John had edited with Chaim Stern, and for which David Goldstein had done a lot of the excellent translation. John responded and the atmosphere became quite electric because people did not easily refute or disagree with Luigi and, in those days, an AGM went on for no longer than twenty minutes. This one went on much longer because it became a big debate about the new prayerbook.

It has always been felt that the presidency of the LJS should be an honour that is kept for outstanding people, not just automatically conferred. So there was a gap after Luigi died. Maxwell Stern then became President. We had quite a formal relationship. I found he could be a bit difficult and rather tough financially. Maxwell had followed Lewis Levy, his cousin, as Chairman.

The best Chairman or President I had in my thirty years here was Peter Lazarus. I loved Peter. He was an outstandingly capable person. He was very, very tough in his judgements and if he thought you were not pulling your weight, or if he didn't respect you intellectually, you were out. However, if you measured up to his exacting standards – which John and I obviously did – he was wonderful. He would fight for you financially and work with you very closely. For a long time after he died, I would think about him almost daily and ask myself, 'What would Peter have done?', or, 'How would Peter have dealt with this?'

Council meetings were courteous and proper and people went to them well prepared. They were conducted with a great deal of formality and were over in a couple of hours, which is how it should be. I am sure there were occasional disagreements, but no voting because the understanding was that you would always reach a consensus. If there was a vote, it was an exceptional event, and I can't recall in my time there ever being a vote at Council.

In the mid-1980s, when Maxwell Stern was still Chairman, we got the report from our surveyors saying that there was serious structural damage to the synagogue. It had been repaired after the enemy bomb in 1940, but they said there were still serious problems, which would cost £500,000 immediately and then an equivalent amount would have to be spent over subsequent years. So, in 1987, Council took the decision to rebuild the synagogue. At this point John was easing towards retirement and doing more at Leo Baeck College. I had taken over a lot of the Senior Rabbi's responsibilities in 1986, although John did not formally retire until 1989.

The decision to rebuild was a major one – the redevelopment was estimated at over £14 million. We gathered together an outstanding group of people, and the next few years were the best and the most rewarding years of my rabbinic career. Trevor Moross was responsible for the building and development side. He was a great fund of original ideas. Neil Levitt was a marvellous House Committee Chairman. He oversaw our move to Loudoun Road. I should also mention Prue Baker, who was a really efficient Project

Co-ordinator. There were contributions from many more people, but it was essentially a quartet of Peter, Trevor, Neil and myself who looked after the congregation in the 'wilderness years', as we called them, in Loudoun Road. I was fit and healthy and full of energy in those days!

We raised the money we needed and overcame a small financial crisis thanks to the enormous generosity of several people. It was a very, very exciting time with everybody pulling together There weren't any arguments, just some most productive discussions about what to do, which way to go and the architecture. It was very creative stuff and turned out to be a wonderfully successful achievement.

Orthodox rabbis tell a lot of jokes about how demanding congregants are and how badly they might be treated by them. A nice thing about the LJS in my day is the great courtesy and respect which was accorded to the rabbis. But I used to find the old LJS a rather forbidding building. It was dark and it was cold and there was brown everywhere. It was very impressive on the High Holydays when it was full and the choir was above the Ark singing down. There would be a wonderful atmosphere. However, on an average *Shabbat* morning when there would be maybe 100 or 150 people in a 1,200-seat building, they rattled around like peas in a pod. The acoustics were bad and it was impossible to instil any atmosphere with people sitting so far from the *bimah*. The foyer was cavernous and unwelcoming. I was therefore determined that, when we rebuilt, we should have a warmer, friendlier building.

We certainly achieved that. The first comment people make when they come to the synagogue is: 'what a welcoming building', which gives me great pleasure. But I think we have lost out slightly in that, before a High Holyday or Saturday morning service, people tend to chat because it is such a friendly building. It upsets me that they don't listen to our outstanding organist, Tim Farrell, when he is playing music beforehand and don't get into a reflective mood for the service. I think there is perhaps a bit too much informality now. On the other hand, it is a building which does buzz, especially when there are kids around. I like that.

I think my greatest lasting contribution to the LJS is being one of those responsible, along with Vikki Slowe and a few others, for the Anish Kapoor Holocaust Memorial. We must have looked at over 150 submissions to come up with a shortlist of two. One was Anish Kapoor; the other was Antony Gormley. What an amazing shortlist! We went for Anish Kapoor because his concept best combined those elements of spirituality, awe and eternal mystery that we wished to convey in a non-representational manner. It was only afterwards that we discovered that, on his mother's side, he is a sixteenth-generation Iraqi Jew. The last thing in our mind was: 'Is the guy Jewish or not?' Our main criterion was artistic excellence.

In respect of interfaith work, I was something of a pioneer. As Associate Rabbi, I organised the first 'trialogue meetings', as we called them. They were with John Slater, the vicar of St John's Church (the church at the roundabout), who was a lovely, lovely man and, alas, died too young, and with Zaki Badawi, who sadly is also dead. He was the first Director at the mosque in Regent's Park. There was a lot of Christian-Jewish dialogue going on at the time, but no meetings with the increasing Muslim population. So, when they built the mosque in the late 1970s, we decided at Council to send a gift to the mosque as a gesture of friendship and welcome. Zaki (later Sir Zaki) was a great Director and a good public face for Islam. He was very outward-looking, and had to overcome a lot of suspicion amongst his own flock, many of whom really did not want this connection with either the synagogue or the church. But he prevailed and the early meetings drew very large audiences.

Several hundred people attended the first meeting in the mosque, and the American Ambassador, whose residence was nearby in the Park, intended to come to the first meeting in the church. He couldn't make it in the end, but he sent several representatives from the Embassy. We kept the meetings going for quite a few years, even for a while after the Lebanon war in 1982, which was terribly divisive. We then took a joint decision that the meetings were becoming a battleground for political discord. There were very strongly opinioned Muslims as well as strongly opinioned Jews, and the atmosphere of the meetings was turning unpleasant and bitter.

Zaki left the mosque, but I always had a warm relationship with him. I taught a course in Judaism for his Muslim College. After Zaki left, they put in a Saudi Arabian Director. He was a delightful man, but the various groups we had set up, like groups for doctors, social workers and teachers, to talk about common problems, stopped. This was partly down to the new Director, but I must take some of the blame myself as I was so involved in the rebuilding of the LJS, and it took up all my energies keeping things going at Loudoun Road. The last time I was at the mosque was for Zaki's funeral when he died a few years ago. John Slater left St. John's Church and went to St George's, Handel's Church in Hanover Square, but our friendship continued.

However, there was still plenty of interfaith work going on. I was Co-Chair of the London Society of Jews and Christians for many years; I am now Co-President. Interfaith work has always given me great pleasure because it is such a civilised discourse. I have said, and people like Zaki and my Christian friends have always agreed with me, that we have more in common with a liberal person, with a small 'l', of another faith than with fundamentalists of our own. Liberal people can always find common cause; it's the fundamentalists who cause problems.

There have been many changes during my time at the LJS. When I first arrived people were invited to join rather than elected to Council. Things are now much more democratic. There is also more equality for women. Back in my early days at the LJS, women from the families who ran the LJS rarely had a full-time job. They got involved in the Women's Society, but also had time for major causes such as Margaret Rigal's amazing 35s Committee for Soviet Jews. I supported the closure of the Women's Society and the taking on of wider roles by women in the synagogue. Committees used to be very male-dominated affairs conducted in smoked-filled rooms and women rarely went to them. Women are now properly involved in every aspect of synagogue life.

The synagogue's relationship with Liberal Judaism and the Rabbinic Conference has had its ups and downs. There used to be some tensions between John Rayner and Sidney Brichto. The ULPS had offices in the old LJS building, and they were very keen to move out from under the influence of the LJS and have their own building. John and Sidney disagreed about who should speak for Liberal Judaism. John felt it should be the Senior

Rabbi of the LJS, as it were by historic right, whereas Sidney felt it should be the Executive Director of the ULPS. My view was always: 'let a hundred flowers bloom'. Everybody should speak for Liberal Judaism; the more people who get in the papers, get on the radio, write articles, the better for the movement.

I also had many disagreements with Sidney about Israel. Sidney did some fairly 'political' things to try and discredit the views expressed by John and me on Israel and the Middle East, since they were very controversial at the time. We spoke out in our sermons and I wrote articles in *The Times* (such as my 1979 piece called 'Passover for the Palestinians too'), and in other newspapers, which questioned the occupation of the West Bank and Gaza and, subsequently, the war in Lebanon. This caused a big furore. At that time, Jewish people would criticise Israel privately, but not in public. John and I were disowned by the ULPS as well as the Board of Deputies, but fortunately we were backed by Council and the LJS tradition of 'freedom of the pulpit'. We stuck it out because we were very conscious of our duty as Liberal Jews to carry forward the tradition of speaking out on controversial issues of the day which had been established by the founders of the LJS.

I subsequently became involved in unofficial tripartite meetings between PLO and Israeli representatives and Anglo-Jewish intermediaries. After the Oslo Accords, I met Arafat when he came to England in 1992. Afif Safieh, the PLO representative here in London, came to our *seder* one year. The ULPS gradually became more nuanced in its approach, not exactly challenging, but pointing out the need for a greater emphasis on peace. John and I were eventually vindicated in our stance, although we had been 'prophets without honour'.

The liturgy and music of the LJS have changed enormously. Liturgy has never been a major interest of mine – that was John's speciality; he was a great liturgist. My concern has always been a rather fastidious grammarian's concern that translations are accurate and that the English flows well. Again this meant that John and I worked well together. John had a very good style, but I had a slightly lighter one in terms of idiom and so forth. So, often when he would do a translation or write a prayer, he would show it to me and I might suggest some amendments or alterations. David Goldstein was a splendid translator from Hebrew, and Chaim Stern was a very poetic innovator in prayer. However, it is interesting that when I look at old prayerbooks, or even our modern ones, it is invariably John's prayers that have stood the test of time.

As for the music, I think that our high standards have been maintained because of the work of Cathy Heller Jones and Yakov Paul before her, whom I brought with me from Wembley. They have been eclectic in their musical choices and would rather go for a John Rutter setting of 'The Lord bless you and keep you' than some mediocre Jewish setting that you can strum on a guitar.

As far as I know, I did the first mixed-faith wedding blessing in this country. I also instituted the category of 'Friends of the Congregation'. The idea is commonplace now, but I remember it was quite daring then and made front page headlines in the JC. People have their own good reasons for not wishing to convert, but if they are sympathetic to our aims and wish to support them, they should feel part of the community. In addition, I initiated the participation of non-Jewish parents in *Bar* and *Bat Mitzvah* services. They had previously not been allowed on the *bimah*.

The synagogue used to be very much dominated by the 'Cousinhood', generations of families who had grown up together. This did not start to break down until the 1970s and 1980s when different people began to join the synagogue because it was seen to be an exciting, relevant and diverse place as a result of the causes in which it was involved, such as the refuseniks, the Bosnian Support Group and our stance over Israel. The LJS has now become much more cosmopolitan and less hierarchical. Class differences, as in society as a whole, are now much less obvious.

Writing books is very difficult to combine with running a congregation, but I did write while still working as a full-time rabbi. I was approached by Viking/Penguin to do their standard work on Judaism, which is still in print. I asked John to join me in this because it was an enormous undertaking. My 'bent' has always been towards history, while John was a great authority on law and lore, so we wrote the book together. One of us would go off on a mini-sabbatical for three months or so and get on with his part, and then the other would have time off and get on with his. I then did a second Penguin book, *To the Promised Land*, which has been reissued by Faber Finds. It wasn't popular, because it was really quite critical of Zionism, but I think it is well written. It is mentioned in complimentary fashion in academic circles. I then wrote *The Divided Self* for I.B. Tauris. I have also edited several books such as *Liberal Judaism – The First Hundred Years* by Lawrence Rigal and Rosita Rosenberg.

I hope there might still be another book in me and indeed I have recently been commissioned by Faber & Faber to write a book whose title is, 'This Is Not the Way: Jews, Judaism and Israel' and is due out in February 2012.

See photographs 20, 48, 59, 60, and 68.

Louise Golding

Louise Golding joined the LJS in 1952. She served on the House Committee and the Council. She has been very supportive of the synagogue's congregational welfare activities – she is a committee member of both the Keep in Touch and the Video + Tea groups.

My name is Louise Golding (née Davies). My background was originally Orthodox, my forebears being Ashkenazi Jews who settled in the City of London way back in the 1760s, possibly even earlier. In 1806 my maternal great-great-grandfather was a subscriber to one of the first English translations of a Hebrew *Haggadah*. We still possess the family copy. It was the discovery of notices of family deaths, handwritten in the fly-leaf of this *Haggadah*, which helped me to trace my maternal ancestors.

My maternal grandmother was a pupil teacher, then Head Teacher, at a small Jewish infants' school in London. She and her husband were among the first members of Brondesbury Synagogue in Chevening Road, where my parents were married.

On my father's side of the family, I have traced a great-grandfather, somewhat impoverished, who lived in Birmingham with his large family. He merited a glowing obituary in the *Jewish Chronicle*, extolling his family's hospitality and his lifetime of religious, political, committee and charitable work 'for the well-being of the working class'.

My father had a half-sister, who trained as a nurse, together with three half-brothers who all served abroad with the British Forces throughout World War One, and who amazingly all survived. Dad was finally invalided out after fighting in the Dardanelles at the end of the war, married my mother, and decided to open a shop, a 'Gentlemen's Outfitters', in a property owned by his father in Brighton. So although I was born in Adelaide Road in Swiss Cottage, I was in fact brought up at the seaside.

My parents gave me a happy, easy-going Jewish upbringing. We observed Friday nights and the High Holydays, but apart from my mother's attendance at the *Kol Nidre* service, which she so loved, my parents didn't attend synagogue. My sister and I were taught the rudiments of Hebrew by a kindly elderly gentleman who had coached my father for his *Bar Mitzvah*. Most Sabbaths I (though not my rebellious elder sister!) accompanied my grandmother to the Orthodox Synagogue in Middle Street, Brighton.

I was a pupil at the Brighton and Hove High School. The Jewish girls sat in an adjoining room during morning prayers, filing in for assembly. But when I became Deputy Head Girl, one of my occasional duties was to read the lesson during school prayers. The Headmistress made sure that my readings were always from the Old Testament.

Because of the wartime bombings, another High School from London was evacuated to join us. Space was somewhat cramped. When we had lessons in the classrooms, they had to have theirs in the cloakrooms, and vice versa. If an air raid warning sounded, I was allowed to run down the road from school to take up my position as a fire watcher. My father joined the Sussex Home Guard. It was a genuine and courageous 'Dad's Army', determined at all costs to defend the coast from the expected German invasion. Before they were issued with rifles, the men had to train with wooden poles. As a defensive precaution, the pier was blown up in the middle and the beaches were mined.

The war greatly affected the trajectory of my education and future career. In order to take up a scholarship from the USA (which had been offered to a pupil from war-torn England), I switched from the study of English literature to the more appropriate and relatively new subject of Dietetics. But there were still U-boats in the Atlantic and the scholarship had to go to an English girl already in America.

So there I was, still in England and all set to study Dietetics. Fortunately, I managed to win a scholarship to study Household and Social Science at King's College, University of London. But even then the war altered the course of events. An enemy aircraft landed on the college roof, which meant that I spent my London University years evacuated to Leicester, sharing premises and laboratories with Leicester University College. Incidentally, it was here that the Christian Principal of the college, Dr Attenborough (the father of Richard and David), brought up two young Jewish refugees with his own family. I didn't actually know this at the time and only heard about it years later.

There were just two Jewish students on my course, and we happily socialised with the local Jewish youth groups, as well as with the Leicester College lads. Our student war work included trimming (with nail scissors) the surplus rubber from newly manufactured gas masks. We began our final exams with the roar of aeroplanes flying overhead to Normandy. D-Day had begun!

My family had no relatives still living abroad (they had all emigrated by the 1890s), and I feel almost guilty when I say that I lost no one in the Holocaust. But I still mourn the death of my favourite cousin Robert, who was killed, aged only eighteen, fighting in the Battle of Britain.

It was in the Brighton Middle Street Synagogue that I married another cousin's brother-in-law, Leonard Golding, and immediately came up to London where, in 1952, I joined his synagogue, the LJS.

Leonard and I had two daughters, but tragically they were only thirteen and seven years old when my husband suddenly died. Later, the girls were confirmed at the LJS and Paula came back to St John's Wood Road after twenty-five years for a group reunion. Both my daughters married non-Jews, but one of the highlights of my year is when the whole family gathers round the *seder* table to read in turn from the *Haggadah*, with the three grandchildren asking the Four Questions together. So I am truly content that the traditions of my ancestors have been passed down 'from generation to generation'.

Paula now lives in St Albans and has recently joined Radlett and Bushey Reform Synagogue. Before that she was Treasurer and Member of Council at Southgate Progressive Synagogue. Her twins, Rory and Jessica, celebrated their *B'nei Mitzvah* at SPS and then, in 2009, their *Kabbalat Torah*. Jessica is one of the youth leaders and dancers in their Israeli Dance Group (for girls aged eight to eighteen). They have entertained us at our LJS Keep in Touch tea party, and have been invited to return. Rory gives spirited performances at the Southgate Progressive Youth Club annual show. My younger daughter, Ruth, has been teaching at Religion School, first at Nottingham, and then at Leicester Progressive Synagogue. Now that her daughter, Emma, has celebrated her *Bat Mitzvah*, she too has begun to teach at the Leicester Adult and *Bar Mitzvah* classes.

Looking back to the time before I had children and was embarking on my career, it was towards the end of the war when I took on my first job at the London Headquarters of the Ministry of Food. It was the ideal combination of literature and science, editing a monthly magazine for Domestic Science teachers and dietitians. At the age of twenty-one, I was meeting and interviewing some of the leading scientists of the day, avoiding the night-time blitz by commuting to Brighton. I published all the current food and rationing news and also undertook the linking of this subject with the whole school curriculum: food and geography, history, mathematics, art, current affairs, and, of course, cookery.

Following the end of rationing, I was asked by the BBC in 1954 to present a shopping programme to advise listeners on consumer choice, and on the quality, nutritional value and cooking of the new foods appearing in the shops. It was scheduled to run for twelve weeks, but it continued as *Shopping List* in the morning *Today* programme twice a week for the next twelve years.

My darling husband's sudden death at the age of forty-four found me, as already mentioned, with two young children, and the need for a full-time career. I needed work that would permit me to regulate my own hours. I needed to be at home in the early morning when the children left for school and to be back home again by the time they returned.

I returned to my old college and, with the support of Professor John Yudkin and others, raised funds for a small team. This was an independent research unit to investigate nutritional and other needs of the older generation. Later we investigated the periods just before and just after retirement from work. The aim was to bridge the gap between research and its practical applications for the rapidly increasing numbers of older men and women, and their carers. This work entailed organising surveys, writing scientific papers, producing posters and leaflets, publishing books (including paperback cookery books), and giving lectures on the prevention of malnutrition, with audiences ranging from old people's homes to international conferences.

There was one memorable trip when I was the only Jew in a small group of medical experts invited to Israel from Britain to advise on the reception and treatment of the vast numbers of elderly, and often desperately ill, refugees expected soon to arrive in large numbers from Russia. We were shown some of the amenities already put in place, and the warm welcome that was being planned.

These days, I still don't really consider myself retired. I became a Consultant in Gerontology Nutrition, and now I'm using my early *Haggadah* as a stepping stone to look at the influence of heredity in my own family. I find that I come from a long line of elderly widows, none of whom remarried. Several managed both children and a career, even in the ninteenth century. What is more, I can tell from early photos that all we women look alike. And certainly I've inherited my parents', and probably their parents', food habits and lifestyle.

It was through my husband, Leonard, that I became involved with the LJS. Leonard had earlier joined the LJS with his mother and brother because of the sympathy and kindness shown to them on the death of his father. I still remember the culture shock I experienced when I joined Leonard in 1952, hearing for the first time an organ in a synagogue and female voices in the choir! But I was thoroughly impressed by the unfamiliar decorum, and the wonderful experience of a service conducted almost entirely in English. At last I could follow, understand and participate in all those beautiful prayers.

Leonard had been a member of the Education Committee. Much later, I served on the House Committee and became a member of Council. Now I go to the stimulating discussions that take place at Tuesday Texts, and I'm a committee member of both Keep in Touch and Video + Tea. I also helped to stitch the synagogue's tapestry chairs!

Particular memories of the LJS include being asked to visit Rabbi John Rayner in the Royal Free Hospital just before his major heart surgery. I entered the ward to hear an exasperated nurse calling, 'Mr Rayner, Mr Rayner, will you *please* get back into bed!' Apparently, he had just heard that one of his congregants had been admitted to a nearby ward and he was sneaking out to comfort him. He could only be persuaded back into bed when I said, 'Why don't you let me hold the overflow service on your behalf, John. Give me your message and I'll take it to him!'

I've mentioned my joy at coming to The Liberal Jewish Synagogue and finding a service read in English by the whole congregation. So if I have any regrets, they are that nowadays not just a few, but more and more of our synagogue prayers are being recited in Hebrew. I would like those of us who are not Hebrew scholars to be spared a thought! Increasingly I'm finding myself unable to participate fully in the service. So I just sit, or stand, and silently read the translations, feeling somewhat isolated and on my own.

However, on the positive side I welcome the enormous improvements in our Social Care commitments: bereavement counselling, Keep in Touch, Phone a Member, the Out and About Club, Video + Tea, Restaurant Tuesday, help for the disabled, and even a Community Care Co-ordinator – and that doesn't include everything. This certainly makes me proud to be a member of the LJS.

✡

Michael Hart

Michael Hart has been involved in the synagogue since he was ten years old when he started attending the Religion School. He was a founding member of the Square One youth group. Later on he held a variety of positions in the synagogue, including Head Teacher of the Religion School, Chair of the Education Committee, Chair of the Social Action Committee, Honorary Treasurer and, more recently, Co-Chair of the Centenary Committee. Since June 2011 he has been Chairman of the Synagogue Council.

Born in 1953, I am the eldest of three children in a close-knit family that consisted of my parents, Ann and Bernard, my sister, Penny, and my brother, Andrew. My family were very involved with the synagogue over many years. My parents were on so many rotas at one stage that my mother had to keep a written record to make sure none of them were overlooked. Penny, with her husband Mike, has been very involved with Liberal Judaism and with The Liberal Synagogue, Elstree, where they are members and where they have each served as Chairman. Andrew, year after year, has taken on the role of doctor available (along with Stephen Kahn) for any medical emergencies that occur occasionally during the High Holydays, rarely moving from his assigned seat throughout the whole of the *Yom Kippur* service.

My grandparents were key influences in our lives. They lived fairly close to our home in Willesden, and a normal weekend would include visiting both sets of grandparents for a meal. Sometimes we saw them at other times during the week as well. My mother's parents, Harold and Bertha Benzimra, were very involved at West London Synagogue. Harold was a warden and Bertha at one stage chaired the Women's Guild. My grandfather's family came from Gibraltar and my grandmother's from Poland. My father's parents, Albert and Esta Hart, were also members of West London Synagogue, but had very little contact with it.

My first memory of the LJS was the *Chanukkah* service in 1963, which my family attended to see whether we liked the synagogue. I had not been happy at the Religion School at West London Synagogue and my parents were exploring alternatives. The West London classes at that time were held in an office block in Charlotte Street, which felt very cut off from the synagogue, and I didn't get on with one of the teachers.

We enjoyed the service and so my parents decided to move to the LJS, where there were many families whom they knew socially, such as Rosemary and Norman Lazarus, Jacqui and Joe Pinto (relations of my father), Jo and Willie Kessler, Bob and Marion Beral, and Elizabeth and Peter Lazarus. Peter and Norman's father, Kenneth, was an old friend of my grandfather. Because of my Benzimra grandparents' involvement with West London, my parents had to handle the move very carefully. My grandfather was disappointed about it, mainly because the family would no longer be involved in the same congregation.

I went to the Religion School for the first time at the start of January 1964. At that time there were Religion School classes both on Saturdays and Sundays, but this was in the process of changing to classes only on Saturdays. I understood later that the decision to make the change had been taken by Rabbi John Rayner in the hope that this would encourage Religion School parents to attend services while the classes for the children were taking place. At that time there was no coffee before services to act as an incentive for parents to remain in the building after dropping off the children.

That first day we went into the synagogue we were greeted by Bob Kirk, who was in charge of running the Religion School. I was placed in a class taught by Michael Cross for Jewish Knowledge and by an Israeli teacher, Gideon Giladi, for Hebrew. In the class there were already two young people whom I knew: Michael Beral, with whom I had gone to school at the age of five, and George Kessler. The Harts and the Kesslers had been friends for a long time. Other members of the class soon became friends including David Kirk, Paul Carton, Sarah Caplin and later Deborah Feldman and Judith King. I developed some long-standing friendships from the Religion School. We were a very demanding class and I heard it said that the only teacher who could control us was Michael Cross.

Over the years we had a number of teachers who were very involved in the synagogue such as Desmond Feldman and Hugh Isaacs. At that time, the teachers of the younger classes were Celia Rapp, Ann Kirk and Eva Feldman. The classes were referred to as 'grades'. It was only much later, I think in the 1990s, that the classes became known by Hebrew letters, probably a reflection of more Hebrew also being used in the synagogue generally. Apart from several Israeli teachers, there were others who took a major role in the Religion School, including Michael Alpert and, later, John Rich.

The format of the Religion School was that we had one lesson lasting forty minutes, after which we went down to the Montefiore Hall and lined up for a Children's *Kiddush*, when we said the blessings over the wine and the bread. We were allowed to let off steam, running round the Hall before lining up again in our classes to go into the first part of the main synagogue service. Bob Kirk and the other teachers sat behind us to keep us in order, to check we were following the service and, sometimes, to tell us to be quiet. I have a strong memory of Celia Rapp reading aloud very slowly to help the younger children. She always seemed to finish several seconds after the rabbis, which made it sound like an echo! We came out of the service when the scroll was returned to the Ark at about 11.40. Services must have been shorter because that usually happens at about 12 noon now. This was probably because the liturgy was not so long, there was no special theme and the introduction to the scroll reading was brief.

I was fascinated by the *ner tamid* and for a long time could not understand how it remained alight. I remember staring up at the long chain from which it was suspended, and only much later realised that there was a long thin electric cable wound around the chain. The synagogue was full of other surprises. The rabbis emerged from a door built into the back wall behind the *bimah* and it took me some time to work out how you reached the choir loft, somewhere high above the Ark. After we left the service we returned to our classrooms for the second lesson, either Hebrew or Jewish Knowledge.

Once or twice a term the pattern changed and we had a short children's service instead of joining the main service, where one of the rabbis, often Rabbi David Goldstein, gave a short talk. I still remember one of these in which David likened all of those present to links in a chain, passing on Judaism from generation to generation and stressing what would happen if the links broke. The teachers taught us the importance of speaking slowly and projecting our voices when reading at the children's service. I also remember being shown by Bob Kirk how to undress and dress the scroll, and how to lift it correctly from the reading desk.

These children's services took place in what was known as the New Synagogue. Just before my family joined the LJS, a new wing had been added on the synagogue site, the Lily Montagu Wing. This housed a new smaller synagogue and classrooms designed as such rather than as offices. Two innovations in the new synagogue were the sliding Ark doors and the choir seating at the rear of the hall, not hidden away in an ethereal space above the congregation.

I had enormous admiration and affection for Rabbi David Goldstein, so I was delighted when he suggested that I should read from the scroll in a children's service. I think I may have been one of the first young people at the LJS to do so before their Confirmation class. I read the first part of *Lech L'cha*. On reflection, it was probably about the time that I would have been *Bar Mitzvah*, but that was never discussed as this was a long time before the LJS introduced *B'nei Mitzvah* ceremonies.

Each *Chanukkah* we used to take part in a specially written play. I was usually a soldier who had one line before dying on stage. In the summer we had Religion School outings to Whipsnade Zoo. One of my main memories was a discussion with our teacher, Edith Kahn, the day after the Aberfan disaster, which filled our television screens. The syllabus was set aside that day to discuss the human issues arising from the catastrophe. We had similar, very meaningful discussions when the Six Day War broke out in Israel in 1967. It really shocked and excited our class, the congregation and the whole of Anglo-Jewry. At that stage, we were pleased that Israel had managed to defend itself when attacked from all sides. Later, differing views began to emerge about whether Israel was right to hold on to the territories it had occupied and the impact this had on a lasting peace.

When my family first joined the LJS we attended High Holyday services at the Porchester Hall. These were the 'overflow services', as there wasn't room for the entire congregation to fit into the synagogue in St John's Wood, so newer members had to go to Porchester Hall. Later on we graduated to the main synagogue and, in time, the need for services in a separate building reduced as the overall membership declined from its peak, which I believe occurred in the early 1970s.

Amongst the readers at the Porchester Hall was Walter Wolfgang. Imagine my surprise when, about forty years later on my honeymoon, I found a picture of the same Walter Wolfgang in his eighties, hitting the headlines after being ejected from the Labour Party conference.

There was no need for overflow services for the afternoon of *Yom Kippur*, so we started attending these services at St John's Wood Road. Often Rabbi Leslie Edgar, the Rabbi

Emeritus, led one of these services. His diction was very measured and precise. For us, as children, it seemed very slow and it felt as if the service would never end, especially the Memorial and Concluding Services. One of the enjoyable memories of the High Holydays was that on *Rosh Hashanah* afternoon, the rabbis and their wives (John and Jane Rayner and David and Berry Goldstein), invited all members of the congregation to tea at their homes. Lots of members went and their houses were always packed.

In 1967 the new prayerbook, *Service of the Heart,* was introduced. Rabbis John Rayner and Chaim Stern had written it, communicating across the Atlantic. It was more modern and accessible than the previous ones by Rabbi Mattuck, which had included lots of different services and hymns that were sung in English. The new prayerbook also contained several very meaningful readings and poems in the 'special themes' section. Above all, it was comfortable to hold and a much friendlier book to use than anything before or after it. I always remember, for example, that we had to turn to page 364 for the *Aleynu,* which I associated with being one number less than the days in the year. *Service of the Heart* was a definite step forward.

The following year, we moved on to the Confirmation class. We had our lessons in Rabbi Rayner's office and were taught each week by one of the rabbis. During that year, a student from Leo Baeck College, David Goldberg, arrived at the LJS. John and the two Davids led our Confirmation weekend which took place in Cambridge. At that time it was definitely called 'Confirmation'; it was not till the 1980s that the term *Kabbalat Torah* was introduced. The weekend in Cambridge was a memorable time for learning, praying and socialising. I recall going out for a *Shabbat* afternoon walk and being amazed to see John Rayner do a vault over a country gate – not the sort of thing that fitted with our previous image of him!

The Confirmation service took place in April 1969, and we were one of the larger Confirmation groups, twenty in all, including a couple of late arrivals whom we hadn't met previously – they may have been from the correspondence class. We each had sections of the service to read and I recall being one of those asked to read from the scroll. I read the first part of the Ten Commandments. I wore a *tallit* that had belonged to my great-great-uncle, the *tallit* that I have continued to wear whenever I have been asked to read in a service. At that stage, none of the girls being confirmed wore a *tallit,* but they were expected to cover their heads on the *bimah.* I think it was the advent of women rabbis that led to some women congregants deciding to wear a *tallit.* After the Confirmation service, which included a sermon in which Rabbi Rayner made links between the space programme and our launch into our role in the community, we celebrated in a very crowded Montefiore Hall.

As a result of the Confirmation class, we got to know the rabbis quite well. They were each different in personality. Rabbi John Rayner came across as being rather serious, but he could also display a more light-hearted side, for example, with his enthusiastic leading of communal singing of Jewish tunes after Friday night services. A particular favourite was the round based on the one word 'Hallelujah'. None of us could claim not to know the words! Rabbi David Goldstein combined an academic approach with the great ability to communicate ideas in simple fashion. Young people felt able to talk to him on all sorts of controversial topics of the time such as euthanasia, Northern Ireland, the Six Day War, apartheid in South Africa. I recall his strong support for Amnesty International in its early days. Many of the Confirmation class also identified closely with David Goldberg. As a student rabbi, he brought his wit and fresh insights from his studies, as well as being closer in age to us than the other rabbis.

In the meantime, my group of friends had become involved in the formation of a youth group for thirteen- to sixteen-year-olds. We were supported by the Council and, at the beginning, received some help from Esther Rantzen with finding speakers for events. At the time she was involved in Phase Two and the Out and About Club. We held planning meetings, initially at the home of Sarah Caplin, and I can recall heated discussions about questions like whether to invite someone from the Scientologists to speak to us, whether we could sell alcohol, how much we could charge for entrance fees, or how many adults we needed to supervise in the background.

The most difficult discussion was what to call the group. We went round and round in circles, never quite agreeing and rejecting each idea. 'We seem to be back to square one,' said, I think, David Kirk. 'That's it,' said several of us... and that's how the name was born. We had a busy programme with meetings every fortnight, ranging from music and discos to guest speakers and games evenings. Some seem dated now, but at the time we enjoyed the social interaction. I was the first Treasurer. We started the group with a big social event, which attracted lots of our friends from within and outside the synagogue. I had to collect the membership money and entrance fees. I remember at the end of the first event adding all the cash up and proudly telling the rest of the committee that we had made a surplus, after allowing for costs, of thirty-two shillings and sixpence. Imagine my feelings when I discovered the next day that I had miscalculated by ten shillings. We had not made such a big profit after all. What should I do? I feared that no one would trust me as Treasurer if I now said we had ten shillings less, so I made up the difference from my pocket-money savings!

With Square One meetings, and for other synagogue events, it was important to have the support of the caretakers. At that time they were Mr and Mrs Temple, which seemed an appropriate name for synagogue employees. It was always important to keep the Temples on side and I recall that my mother frequently baked cakes to take for Mrs Temple. They had a dog called Paul which seemed to be constantly following the Temples up and down the main stairs, past the classrooms, the Ministers' Robing Room and the New Synagogue to and from the caretaker's flat. I seem to recall that the Temples' son was also called Paul, which was very confusing.

During the years after the Confirmation service I was occasionally asked to open the Ark or read in a service, steward at the High Holydays and at the following year's Confirmation service. I took part in services for young people on *Yom Kippur* afternoon, which were held in the New Synagogue and, later on, incorporated into the main service.

In 1971 I went to Exeter University for three years, and I recall Rabbi Rayner coming to lead a service for the Jewish Society at the university. Members of the small local community were also invited and a few turned up to the service. I remember being rather surprised when I overheard a conversation that the leader of the Exeter synagogue was having with Rabbi Rayner after the service. He asked John, 'I know we believe in one

God, but is there anything else we believe in?' I'm sure John gave, as always, a very polite and straightforward answer.

Another memory during this period was at *Yom Kippur* in 1973 when Rabbi Rayner was handed a note during the service and shortly afterwards made an announcement that war had broken out in Israel, the start of the *Yom Kippur* War. This left the congregation very shocked and keen to leave quickly afterwards to hear the news.

Back in London and working as a teacher in the mid-1970s, I continued to be involved at the LJS, helping to organise some Friday evening services, especially those for young people. I was also a supervisor for four years at *Kadimah*, the Union of Liberal and Progressive Synagogues' summer school, run by Rabbi Andrew Goldstein and his wife Sharon. I learned a lot from Andrew and the other supervisors about how to make the teaching of Judaism exciting for children and young people. I acquired skills from all of these activities, which were to be useful in my career in future years.

I also read from the new High Holyday prayerbook, *Gate of Repentance*, several times on the afternoon of *Yom Kippur*. *Gate of Repentance*, published in 1973, brought the High Holyday liturgy into line with the style of *Service of the Heart* with a number of modern prayers and a more creative Additional Service, involving a narrator with musical accompaniment and a range of readers. In 1980, just after my grandfather Benzimra had died, Rabbi Rayner rang on the morning of *Yom Kippur*. He explained that one of the rabbis was not well enough to take part in the service and he would be grateful if I would read a section of the service that afternoon. That led to lots of quick preparation, but it all went well. I recall trying to put a special effort into my reading in memory of my grandfather.

In the 1970s there were some moves to make the services a little more traditional. More of the reading and most of the singing was now in Hebrew. Rabbi Rayner was encouraging people to wear *kippot*. There was occasional experimentation with processing the scrolls around the synagogue, but this stopped after a while, because the congregation didn't like it. John wrote or preached about these changes, setting out the pros and cons and why he recommended a particular view. During this period he also introduced some new practices, such as the *Tikkun Leyl Shavu'ot*, modelled on the concept of the *Seder* Service, which was followed by an all-night study session.

In the late 1970s, while I was living and teaching near Camberley, I was very involved in the setting up of the Thames Valley Progressive Jewish Community, now known as Reading Liberal Jewish Community. This was founded by the ULPS with the support of those of us living in the area and who were members of the LJS or of other ULPS congregations. Links with the LJS continued and services in the early days were taken by visiting rabbis including Rabbi David Goldstein, Rabbi Rayner, Rabbi Harry Jacobi and, later, by student Rabbi Alexandra Wright.

In the early 1980s, I had been working for several years as a teacher and I was asked by Rabbi David Goldberg, the Principal of the Religion School, to teach in the school and, a little later, to take on the role of Head Teacher. I agreed to this and continued in the role for about five years. There was a well-established and reliable team of teachers including Celia Rapp, Lynn Levy, Michael Alpert, John Rich, Nena and Norman Sofier, Morris Fishman, Caroline Hagard and Carolyn Leuw (now Carolyn Simon), with Marie Alpert as the Administrator.

Gradually I introduced some new ideas into the Religion School, building on my experience at *Kadimah,* and developing a programme of services and alternative activities during the middle period of the morning. Highlights of this period were the mornings when we suspended normal lessons and replaced them with a 'circus' of special activities on a theme, with the children rotating between different rooms and teachers. There were also quizzes involving the whole school and special activities to stimulate the interest of the older classes. One event that stood out because of the enthusiasm it generated, was a Soviet Jewry morning. We transformed the LJS into 'Soviet Russia' and organised activities in which the children experienced the frustrations for Jews of living under the Soviet regime. It was a large-scale 'game' in which lots of learning took place. Several former pupils mentioned the impact of this activity years later.

This was a very busy time as I was working full-time and acting as Head Teacher in my spare time. There were many happy events, but also some sad ones during that period. The most significant was the sudden death of Celia Rapp. She had taught generations of younger children at the LJS and at other synagogues. Rabbi Goldberg rang me soon after Celia died to discuss what we should do that Saturday morning. We decided I would tell the school the news at the assembly, which took place at the start of the morning. It was a very sad occasion, but one which all the teachers handled very well with their classes. Later there were discussions about a collection in memory of Celia and the dedication of a classroom in her memory.

During this period, I was aware of other changes taking place in the synagogue. Rabbis Rayner and Goldberg responded to Israel's attacks on the Lebanon with some outspoken criticism of Israel at a time when this was considered unacceptable by other parts of Anglo-Jewry. I respected their views and their decision to take a stand in the face of a lot of opposition. At the same time, there were gradual changes in the membership of the synagogue, with more families moving out to Progressive Jewish congregations in the suburbs. There also appeared to be a greater proportion of LJS families who did not consist of the traditional make-up of both parents coming from a Jewish background. New members, some of whom became quite involved with the synagogue, such as some American families living in London for a few years, came from a variety of backgrounds, which meant that there was less reliance on the influence of the previous core group of LJS families.

Much the biggest issue in the 1980s was whether to rebuild the synagogue. After the Council had made the decision to do so, I contributed to the planning of the new building by being a member of the Design and Use Committee, which later became the Facilities and Use Committee. My role was to try to gauge what facilities would be needed for the Religion School: the number of rooms, their size and the equipment. It involved a lot of guesswork about future trends, and was affected by changes about how much space would be available for the Religion School. I found many of the meetings held at the temporary premises in Loudoun Road very frustrating, but somehow the key decisions were made. There were also some good discussions about the future of the synagogue, including a residential weekend at Bloxham and it was very exciting when the foundation stone for the new building was laid and when the first services were held.

I gave up being Head Teacher when I could no longer accommodate it alongside an increasingly demanding teaching job during the week. Sharon Moross (now Lewison) took over, and I continued my involvement by remaining on the Education Committee, then chaired by Brenda Nathanson. Later I took over as Chairman of the Committee. Sharon brought lots of new ideas and coped very well with arranging classes in temporary facilities in Abercorn Place.

The biggest challenge for the Education Committee at that time was handling the differences between those parents who wanted the lessons to be quite formal in content and those who were less concerned with the academic side and wanted their children to enjoy themselves and develop a positive association with the synagogue. There was always a lot of debate about the age at which it was appropriate to start to teach the reading of Hebrew. I was of the view that we should wait till children had been several years in the school, by which time they had the maturity and broader skills to learn to read in a relatively short period of time. The other ongoing debate was about *Bar* and *Bat Mitzvah* ceremonies. Although these were now an established part of the synagogue's practices, there was still controversy about how we ensured that the young people would continue their education until *Kabbalat Torah*, something which we did not always achieve.

About that time I was elected to the Council for three years. Sir Peter Lazarus was the Chairman and he was trying to include some younger members on it – I was in my late thirties! I remember finding the Council rather formal compared with other meetings I had attended. There were lots of prepared speeches and, although discussion was encouraged, it sometimes felt as if the important decisions had already been taken by the Honorary Officers.

In 1999, although I had not been the Chair of the Education Committee for several years, I was involved in appointing a new Director of Education, to take responsibility for all education matters in the synagogue, not just the Religion School. We appointed Jan Roseman and she soon made a real impact, bringing rigour to the curriculum and supporting teachers in lesson planning. There also seemed to be more emphasis on *Bar* and *Bat Mitzvah* ceremonies, including longer introductions before the *Parashah* read by the young person. This is one development that I have not particularly liked. The introductions have become overly long and are too polished. A related change is that the *Torah* reading is now rarely translated after every few verses, a practice which used to occur more frequently, and which I preferred.

Other developments over the years seem much more positive, such as the inclusion of baby blessings in the *Shabbat* service rather than as a separate event afterwards, the availability of the *Torah* and *Haftarah* readings within the service sheets rather than needing to take a Bible or *Chumash* into services, and the now generally accepted gender-inclusive language of our current prayerbooks, *Siddur Lev Chadash* and *Machzor Ruach Chadashah*. I remember that John Rayner became convinced about the use of gender-inclusive language after encouragement from Rabbi Wright, who was a student rabbi at the LJS at the time when the prayerbook was being compiled.

In 2001 I joined the Social Action Committee as I was keen to become involved in a different area of synagogue life. The Committee was a little unsure what its role should be and, after several meetings, I was asked to take over as Chairman. We formed a small, new Committee, which focussed on a limited number of objectives, organising some special events such as a *Shabbaton* about refugees, a soapbox session like the ones at Hyde Park Corner, and activities to increase the involvement of members with disabilities. It was during this time that Rabbi Mark Solomon suggested we should investigate a twinning arrangement with a Jewish community in the former Soviet Union. After much communication with the co-ordinator of these twinning arrangements, we reached an agreement for the LJS to be twinned with Vinnitsa in the Ukraine.

The twinning started in 2004, and resulted in lots of emailing to the leader of the small Vinnitsa progressive Jewish community, Igor Kulyavtsev, to find out how we could help. I wrote articles for the LJS newsletter and we raised money for the community. In 2004, we organised a visit to Vinnitsa by Rabbi Solomon, Tim Simon, David de Magtige and myself to meet the community and see the local religious sites. We agreed to provide financial support to develop the community's use of the Internet and to pay for their religious leader and some of their education activities. In 2005 I organised a return visit by some of the Vinnitsa community, and we had special *Shabbat* services to welcome them. It was an enriching experience for all those involved, and I was very impressed by the response of synagogue members in supporting the visit. Accommodation was offered, interpreters appeared, gifts were given, members provided whatever we needed. We organised activities around London for our visitors, who travelled to and from the Ukraine by coach, taking two days each way.

By then, I was back on the Council. During the last two years of my six-year term, I served as a Treasurer. This was a difficult role as the synagogue was going through some financial problems. Expenditure had risen significantly, and was exceeding income. I tried to ensure everyone involved took responsibility for making realistic predictions of likely expenditure and income. We had many lively debates on other matters, and took some important decisions, such as the one to agree that same-sex ceremonies could take place in the synagogue.

At the end of July 2003 my mother, after a relatively short period of illness, died unexpectedly. The community was wonderful in its support for my family during this period. It made us appreciate what a key role the synagogue plays at such difficult times. During the year after my mother's death all of the key events were particularly poignant, but it helped having the support of friends and acquaintances at the synagogue.

Early in 2005, to everyone's surprise, I became engaged to Pam and subsequently we were married on 18 September. Rabbi Alexandra Wright performed a blessing on our marriage, the first time she had carried out such a ceremony. It was very well prepared by Alex and was extremely moving for our families and friends. A very positive reflection on the synagogue was the way that the congregation embraced Pam whenever she accompanied me to services and other events, demonstrating very well its commitment to the inclusion of non-Jewish spouses. In the year after we were married, I gradually realised that I was not finding enough time to carry out my duties as a Council member, Treasurer and Honorary Officer as well as I wanted, so when my six-year term on Council ended in 2006, I stepped down to take more of a back seat.

This only lasted for a couple of years. In spring 2009 I was approached by Bob and Ann Kirk about becoming involved in the preparations for the LJS's centenary celebrations in 2011. Subsequently we agreed that Pam and I would take over the role of co-ordinating the centenary planning, building on the groundwork already put in place by Bob and Ann and their previous committee. Just as Pam and I began to realise the scale of that task, I was also asked by Rita Adler, Chairman of the Council, to lead the recruitment process for a new rabbi after Rabbi Mark Solomon left. I gave this much thought before agreeing as it was a great honour. After considering very carefully the key requirements for a new rabbi, the Rabbinic Appointment Panel carried out a recruitment process, which resulted in the appointment of Rabbi David Wilfond for a year. The panel worked very effectively together and we were all delighted with the experience, knowledge and personal qualities that Rabbi Wilfond brought to the LJS. After his decision to return to Israel with his family in October 2011, the search for a successor to David Wilfond continued. Meanwhile, planning for the centenary led to the creation of a programme of events to celebrate the anniversary, whilst looking back at our history and considering the future direction of the congregation.

In January 2011 I was co-opted back onto the Council, taking on the role of Vice Chairman, followed in June 2011 by election to the role of Chairman. The LJS has been a key influence in shaping my life. It has enabled me to learn a lot about my religious heritage, to make many long-standing friends, to be stronger after key life-cycle events and to benefit from skills that I have learned at the synagogue. More importantly, the synagogue has given me a strong ethical framework and I hope to contribute to the congregation's development as it continues to influence the shape of Liberal Judaism in this country.

Ruth Ive

Ruth Ive's family joined the LJS in 1936. She became very involved in the Alumni Society and later the Women's Society of which she was Chairman in its latter years. She played a leading role in the *bimah* chairs Tapestry Group.

I was born in June 1918. My father's name was Cyril Steinman Magnus and he came from a respectable, very old Anglo-Jewish family. Branches of the family came to England in about 1770. They came originally from Hamburg, but settled for a while in Holland where they were successful in marrying bankers. There is a very old synagogue in Chatham, the Magnus Memorial Synagogue.

My mother's name was Rose, née Davidson. Her family was quite different. They had come originally from Romania and Jaffa and became cotton traders in Manchester. They had suffered appalling conditions in Romania with terrible anti-Semitism. What made them decide to leave was that when their new baby was being pushed in the pram by the nursemaid, she threw the baby into the lake.

My mother's family were very far-sighted. They decided they would go into the postcard business years ahead of their time. They printed the original funny postcards, of which my son has quite a good collection. When my grandfather died and we went into the attic, my mother looked at these cartoons of postcards and couldn't think what we would do with them, and so tore them all up. I remember sitting there helping her. Now I am buying back as much as I can, because Davidson Brothers postcards really are collectables. The family was also very musical, and quite a few of them were politically-minded. They were great patrons of the arts in the thirties and forties and they were amongst the founders of the Israeli Symphony Orchestra.

My parents were very socially aware. My mother taught dressmaking at the Brady Street Girls' Club and played piano for their concert parties. There were many of these clubs, and mother met my father at one of them. The clubs were organised by Jews who had attained a little comfort in life and wanted to help their poorer brethren. They didn't look on it as charity and it was not received as such. They felt it was their Jewish duty to help – if they didn't, who would?

I lived in London for the first three years of my life and then my family moved to Westcliffe. I went to an independent girls' school there. Of the 250 girls in the school, I was the only Jewish one. In those days they made no concession for religion and as the school was strictly Protestant, I went to every church in Essex and got a very good grounding in *Hymns Ancient and Modern*.

However, I was always aware that I was Jewish. Once we attended the Orthodox Synagogue in Southend; it was such a ghastly experience that we never went near it again. My parents did not belong to a Jewish community in Westcliffe but, at one point, my father had a fit of conscience and thought he had better teach us something and arranged for the local *shochet* to give me Hebrew lessons. I was absolutely appalled and said, 'Look, there's blood underneath his finger nails! I won't have him!' He was awful. He didn't teach me Hebrew; what he taught me was Yiddish writing.

After I left school, I auditioned at the Guildhall School of Music and joined the drama course because I wanted to go on the stage. Both my father, who worked in London, and I found it rather a bore commuting as it was such a long journey. So we moved back to London in about 1936. My parents had attended the LJS before the move to the south coast, so they knew the LJS from Hill Street days. As I had no friends and no siblings, when we moved back to London, the Davidsons took me in hand and suggested that I go to the Alumni Society at the LJS.

The Alumni was the young people's society and was very well established. This was where you met your dates and future husbands. I was really rather overwhelmed by it. All the people there seemed to be so much older, so much part of a Jewish community, for which I had absolutely no feeling at all. At that time, I didn't know the prayers or any Hebrew. However, I made a lot of very good friends and, within two years, I had become the Secretary of the Society because I was a pushover when it came to volunteering for jobs.

We had a committee of about a dozen and we arranged all sorts of activities. There were various kinds of social events, with everybody really enjoying themselves. I remember we organised treasure hunts, but as very few of us had cars then, it meant *schlepping* around on public transport. As we didn't know any better, it didn't really matter. We also arranged many competitions, where you not only had to follow clues of one sort or another over London, but you had to pick up objects from various unlikely places. I remember very vividly rushing through the kitchens of the Dorchester Hotel trying to get a dustbin lid. Once we rented a rather large beach hut on the coast. About fifty of us ended up there at about two o'clock in the morning.

We also had dances in the Montefiore Hall with a three-piece band when we could afford it. Anybody that you talk to today who was a member of the Alumni Society remembers it with great affection. Sadly a lot of my contemporaries have died.

The war was a watershed for young people as we were all scattered. We tried to keep in touch, but that was really too difficult. All the boys went into the Forces and got posted around the world and, to a certain extent, so did the girls. So when the war came, the Alumni rather fell apart. However, after the war, John Cross and Geoffrey Kahn became joint chairmen and revived the Alumni, which flourished until the early seventies.

In the 1920s and 1930s Dr Israel Mattuck and Rev. Maurice Perlzweig were the rabbis at the LJS. Dr Mattuck held services and meetings on a Sunday morning. Some people said, 'Ah, now the Orthodox will say that they have just moved the Sabbath to Sunday.' But that wasn't it. The services were for the many people who could not get to the Saturday morning services, and to give people a chance to expand their knowledge of Judaism and of contemporary and religious subjects, but there was no reading from the scroll. The Sunday morning talks were advertised, so they were really a public forum, and the meetings were packed. Dr Mattuck always spoke on very controversial subjects. We used to have question-and-answer sessions; people would write questions on slips and runners – myself included – would take these to Dr Mattuck.

We discussed absolutely everything, every aspect of human life and moral attitude, even sex. That wasn't discussed in those days, but Dr Mattuck most certainly did. It was the first time that anyone had mentioned the word 'sex' in public. He spoke very sensibly about human relationships. It certainly got an audience. This was in the days of the outspoken Dr Alex Comfort, and Dr Mattuck carried on in the same vein. He emphasised that Liberal values of gender equality had to be carried through into sexual relationships. That I do remember very vividly. The audience consisted mainly of young people. Some may have been unhappy about it, but I don't think we cared.

Dr Mattuck certainly influenced me. I was at an impressionable age and I was a voracious reader – and still am – and his ideas very much appealed to me. Dr Mattuck opened a door to intellectual thinking that I had never found before then. He was a wonderful orator and really reached out to all types of Jew. He was very much lampooned by the Orthodox for his rather flamboyant style of speaking. But he was an American and he didn't have the same reserve as the English rabbis. In those days, most of the rabbis in England came from Poland or Lithuania and they had that indefinable sort of Yiddish feel to them. Anglo-Jewry wanted something different, something with which they could empathise.

London in the 1930s was just recovering from a really dreadful recession. Times were very hard and there was great unemployment, great hardship and great misery. The synagogue was very aware of this; it was not an inward-looking congregation. It was the teaching of Miss Lily and Dr Mattuck that we must look outwards into the community and play our part as British Jews in it. And we did.

The famous Lily Montagu soup kitchen was before my time, but it hadn't been forgotten. Dr Mattuck, Miss Lily and Marjorie Moos had opened a soup kitchen in the

Montefiore Hall. I think it was held once or twice a week. A hot lunch was served to the unemployed; anybody that wanted to come, could. I remember not so long ago when we had another recession, somebody suggested that we again open a soup kitchen; there was a horrified gasp: 'You never know who you would let in' and I thought: 'That wouldn't have been Dr Mattuck's reaction at all'. Nowadays they are so security-mad.

Dr Mattuck encouraged us to go down to the Jewish Settlement in the East End in Berners Street. It was financed by a member of the LJS, Bernhard Baron, and it was named after him – it was the Bernhard Baron St George's Settlement. It helped the thousands of poor Jews who lived in the East End. They would come off the immigrant ships and many of them were living in great poverty and deprivation in the East End. The Settlement was run by Sir Basil and Lady Henriques. It was absolutely their baby and it was a wonderful organisation. Basil was known as 'The Gaffer' and she was known as 'The Missus'. I had ties with the Settlement inasmuch as there was a family connection to Lady Henriques. So I used to help down there as did many of my contemporaries such as Jenny Nathan's uncle, Alan Rubenstein (Justin's father), who was a 'poor man's lawyer', and Bill Frank helped out with the accounts.

I started off, believe it or not, taking a ballet class at the Settlement! But then 'The Missus' (or Cousin Rose as I called her in private), took me out of the ballet class and said I was to be her personal runner. She wanted me to check how certain families were getting on. I remember running round Berners Street with a chicken casserole. I saw poverty such as I had never dreamed of – down in basements, in tenements, old women and men dying of consumption and I thought: 'How terrible it is; what an unequal society it is.' It turned me into a good socialist as I began to realise that there was something very wrong with a society that could tolerate such appalling poverty.

Added to that, there was the fear of the Blackshirts. They were a very real threat to Jewish people in the East End. I returned from my East End visits to a middle-class home where my dinner was waiting for me, served by the parlour maid. The contrasts were absolutely extraordinary. When people say there was a wonderful spirit in the East End, of course there was, because they were all in it together. But the hardship and the illness and the poverty were not to be admired. I don't like it when people present a rosy view of what it was like – they were not easy times because there was so much unemployment.

The Alumni Society wanted to do something for the children at the Settlement. So we decided to give them a *Chanukkah* tea party. I remember that John Cross, Harold Salmon and myself went to the Settlement and collected fifty ten- to twelve–year-old boys and girls. We counted fifty of them when we left Berners Street and when we arrived at Aldgate tube station we thought we had better count them again, and by that stage there were only forty-nine of them! There were cries of 'One's gone 'ome miss, he didn't like it'. Eventually we got them to St John's Wood Station, which was just by Lord's on the roundabout. We counted them again at that point and we found we had fifty-two children. We never found out how the extra ones had tagged along!

We took them into to the Montefiore Hall and, of course, they absolutely fell on the tea. I remember we had sardine and egg sandwiches and chocolate cupcakes from Lyons, because the Lyons family were all members of the LJS. It was cleared in about ten minutes. There were no picky children in those days and they were hungry. Afterwards we said,

'Would you like to give us a concert?' We nearly got mown down in the stampede because these East End kids were terrific. They knew all the latest hit songs. I will always remember one little tot – she was about eleven or twelve years old – belting out 'Oooh Johnny! Oooh Johnny! How you can love! Oooh Johnny, Oooh Johnny Heavens above!' She definitely had a career in show business ahead of her! There were comedians and storytellers, one of whom told stories in Yiddish, which we couldn't understand. That party was something that has probably not been done since.

Life at that time was terribly difficult and we were all beset with awful ethical questions. We knew war was looming. Dr Mattuck encouraged us to think about things and wanted us to explore different religions and different political thinking; we became very politically aware. For instance, one of the Cross boys, Edward, joined the International Brigade during the Spanish Civil War and was killed.

We had an open debate one evening on 'Can there be a just war?' I remember the case for war was made by a barrister called Desmond Marks who was later killed in action. The case against was led by the chairman of the Alumni, Bill Frank, who was a conscientious objector, and who later served with great distinction as a stretcher bearer during the war. Bill belonged to the Peace Pledge Union and there were other sympathisers amongst the audience. There were two girls who were members of the Communist Party because the Alumni encouraged young people to join in from the wider community, not just members of the LJS.

The ever-pressing subject was Germany. My cousin, Bernard Davidson, who was on the LJS Council, got to know the Home Office officer in charge of visas. He spent his life on the telephone to Major Morrison trying to get visas, and I must say that he had some success; we did get people out.

The most extraordinary thing happened then. My parents and I moved into a really large flat with five bedrooms and three reception rooms. Because it was so large, Bernard asked if we could take some of the younger refugees off the trains and give them temporary accommodation until they got themselves sorted out. My family and I provided accommodation for several people and we had a terrible time with some of them. After my father died, we were asked if we would carry on doing this great service and my mother said of course she would. Bernard said he had a young woman coming over from Vienna – she was a violinist and he thought he could get her a visa to America. I remember meeting this girl, Heidi, in mid-December. The train came in the middle of the night and I went with Ma down to Victoria Station and the girl came off the train from the Continent. She took off her gloves and she had huge diamond rings on nearly every finger. My poor mother nearly died!

This girl was very difficult as she had to wear gloves all the time to protect her hands for playing the violin. But she had all this jewellery – not just a chip, a real diamond! Before Christmas she asked could she have her fiancé over. Eventually the fiancé turned up – a very small and not very prepossessing little man. My mother and I went off for Christmas dinner and left them alone. The next morning on Boxing Day, Heidi came to Ma and asked if her fiancé could stay here because he was a deserter from the German army! He was in the *Wehrmacht* and he wanted to go to America. As he wasn't Jewish, it would have been criminal for us to harbour him. So we phoned Bernard and asked,

'What are we going to do now?' Bernard came over by taxi and he literally picked the fiancé up by the scruff of his neck – he was a very large man – threw him into the taxi, took him down to Victoria and put him onto the next boat train back to Germany. That was not a very pleasant incident. Heidi then left.

One night in 1940, Ma and I were sitting under the dining room table in the Blitz and Ma said to me, 'I had a postcard today from California.' She read it out to me, 'Dear Mrs Magnus you will be glad to know that I am sitting under an orange tree in the baking sun in California.' It was from Heidi – she was the only one we ever heard from after they left us.

In March 1939 Bernard said he had a very nice young man to send us. His name was George, who was Polish but not a refugee – he was in England on a work permit. His father had died and left him a big factory and he was over here to undertake a technical course leaving his family back in Poland. He got more and more worried, poor chap, about his family and in August 1939 he said that he felt he really ought to go back. I remember Ma sitting on the couch trying to talk him out of it and saying he could stay with us rent free. He said he couldn't, he had a mother and two sisters. So he went back to his town, Kattovice, which was among the first to be strafed by the Germans. So that was a very sad ending.

By this time, because my father had died and left us rather badly off, I had to go out and earn my own living. I went to commercial school and learned shorthand, but not very willingly because I had wanted to go on the stage; that was why I was at the Guildhall School. I left the commercial school with verbatim speed. I do the 'Gregg' Method, the American System. I got two shillings a week extra for using my shorthand.

I knew Lily and Marian Montagu. Ma and I loved them and they were very nice to us. There were always the three old girls sitting in the front row of the synagogue – Miss Lily, Miss Marian and the Hon. Mrs Horace Myer. Miss Marian was a great doer. She was very fond of and played a lot of cricket, never mind having a wooden leg! Miss Lily was really spiritual, but also very absentminded. I remember, at one dinner laid on by the Women's Society in the Montefiore Hall, the dessert was blancmange or something similar. Miss Lily would never eat anything – she never had time. My mother said to her at this dinner, 'You really must have something to eat, dear,' and Miss Lily said, 'No, dear Mrs Magnus, not now, but I'll take it home and have it for supper' and with that she simply poured it into her bag – not on the plate, but just into the bag – and my mother had to take the whole thing into the kitchen to sort out! Miss Lily lived in a house that was always in a state of chaotic disorder, but she was a dear soul. She espoused the cause of equality in religion and she fought our battles for many years. I don't think she ever bought any new clothes, or even sent the ones she had to the cleaners.

After the bombing in 1940, the synagogue couldn't be used. The congregation trooped down to Friends' House in Euston Road for the High Holydays; I was working then and I couldn't go. The Montefiore Hall was made useable – they put the pews in there and there was only a small aisle at the side. So when it came to my wedding, we ended up getting married in the New West End Synagogue in St Petersburg Place. The wedding was conducted by the rabbi there. He was a card, he really was, I'm sure he married us and then rushed off to the races. It was a great shame that they wouldn't let Dr Mattuck in because he was a progressive rabbi. But he did come to the reception where he acted as my father.

I married Ronald Ive. Ronald had an Orthodox upbringing. He had been to a public school (Polack's House, Clifton College), which wasn't strictly Orthodox although they didn't play games on Saturdays. His family's surname was really Zussman. My father-in-law had a chain of pharmacies around London under the Zussman name. In the First World War, bricks were thrown through the shop windows because people thought the business was German, so he changed the name to Ive.

Ronald was quite a lot older than I. When I came up to London with my family, we stayed in a Jewish boarding house in Canfield Gardens and I met Ronald there. His father had just died and he had wanted to move and had nowhere to move to. He was not involved in the Alumni. He was very hard-working. He had had a very tragic life. His mother had died when he was eight years old. That was why he was sent to boarding school. He had an older sister who married, had a baby, developed leukaemia and died. Ronald was in the OTC (Officers Training Corps) and he was called up in 1939.

I was on Council for a number of years, first with Sir Louis, then with Lewis Levy and then Maxwell Stern. In the late eighties the big issue was the question of moving or rebuilding. Another cause of controversy was the debate over *B'nei Mitzvah.* No one dared say a word against John Rayner, but he was absolutely adamant about not having them, and it caused a lot of trouble. My son David did not mind being confirmed, but Martin, our other younger son, did. He wanted to be *Bar Mitzvah,* and we had to drag him to his Confirmation. A year later everything changed and *B'nei Mitzvah* were introduced. It really caused more argument in our household than anything else, because my husband really wanted *Bar Mitzvah* too. I remember that argument going backwards and forwards.

My mother served for twenty-five years on the committee of the Women's Society, which was a really innovative body of women before the war. They were very active in looking after the German children that came to London. They organised all kinds of things, such as hospital visiting, as well as all the catering for the synagogue, which they did on a grand scale. At that time, people did not see any inconsistency between the synagogue's emphasis on equality and the fact that it was the Women's Society who did all the catering.

For the *seder,* the entire congregation were asked to bring pieces of fried fish. They all turned up in the morning, bringing to Mrs Mattuck and my mother all different sizes of fish, from large pieces of cod to small sardines. It was a disaster, and they decided they could never go through that again. My mother said it gave her backache. However, there was a wonderful feeling of togetherness which I rather miss now. The Women's Society also cooked the *matzah* balls with a huge batch of fish stock, which one of the cooks had made. That was on the boil and people were asked to bring along their *matzah* balls. Apparently Ma stood and lobbed them all in, the *matzah* balls varying from the size of pin heads to almost the size of cannon balls. They also varied in texture.

Later on, I was very involved in the Women's Society myself. The first time was organising a concert in 1939 to raise money for refugees. I was roped in because Peggy Lewsen, who was the Secretary of the Society, was my cousin and I could type. I had a portable typewriter and I bashed out all the letters on that. On the concert programme you will find all the women who played a prominent part in synagogue life: Mrs Cyril

Nathan (Michael's mother); Mrs Kenneth Lazarus (Peter, Norman and Margaret's mother); Mr and Mrs Benedictus (David's parents); Mrs Enoch. They were all friends of my mother. The musicians at the concert were Gerald Moore, a famous accompanist, and Hersha Gluckman, who was German and whom we knew from another source; she had a very nice contralto voice. The concert was in the Sanctuary and we were all in evening dress; my mother made me a new dress for the occasion.

The Women's Society supported a number of charities by fundraising through bazaars, raffles etc. We raised a lot of money to give to causes such as Wireless for the Blind. Maureen Roe was the very efficient Treasurer. Then we started the Abbeyfield Project with Nina Nathan, Nancy Caplin, Vi Levy and Jo Kessler – it involved hours and hours of work. I have little patience with the argument that 'now people work and haven't the time to get involved'. We all worked, and shopping and housekeeping was much harder then. We gave a gala lunch once a year and I remember I got David Batty from the Antiques Roadshow to come one year and that was a terrific success.

I was involved in the Women's Society right up until it ended in 1991. We took the decision to close down because we simply couldn't encourage younger people to join the committee. The argument was that the 'new men' were coming along who would do the catering. Well, I've yet to see that happen! I remember when I was Chairman of the Women's Society I arranged a meeting at the synagogue on euthanasia because Rabbi David Goldstein was very interested in it and we got a full house. I also invited Leslie Abdela to come and talk about International Human Rights. I think there is still a place for social issues like that to be discussed in the synagogue.

See photograph 31 and 32.

✡

Jean Jaffa

Jean Jaffa is the daughter of Sir Louis Gluckstein, long-serving President of the LJS, and Doreen Gluckstein who established a long-running Darby and Joan Club at the synagogue. She had a distinguished career as a contralto singer and was married to the well-known violinist, Max Jaffa.

I was born on 3 May 1926 on the first day of the General Strike. I was the eldest of three, my brothers Roy and David being respectively two and four years younger. We were all born and grew up in the same large family home in Elm Tree Road, St John's Wood, where my parents lived happily for over half a century. Luckily they were able to afford the staff necessary to run our home. During our childhood, the extended family of many Glucksteins, Salmons and other relations enjoyed a busy social life.

My parents, Louis and Doreen Gluckstein, were among the earliest members of the LJS. They were married in the Central Synagogue in Hallam Street in 1925, because the new building in St John's Wood Road was not yet completed. Being very progressive, my parents joined the LJS because they liked its ethical values and regularly attended the services, which were important to them.

First, a little about the family tree. My father's great-grandfather was Lehmann Meyer Gluckstein, a professor of languages, who had come to England from Rheinberg in the late nineteenth century. He married Helena Nathan Horn, and they had six sons and one daughter. Samuel, one of their sons, was born in Rheinberg in 1821, was my great-grandfather. He married Hannah Colman Joseph (born in 1819 in Amsterdam) in 1845. They had twelve children (two died in infancy) and one of their surviving sons was my grandfather, Joseph Gluckstein. Joseph had two marriages: first to Kate, who died young, and then to Francesca Halle, born in St Louis, USA.

Francesca was a stunning, nineteen-year-old redhead with a lovely voice. She came to London from Berlin, where she was studying singing, to visit some of her relatives. She was many years younger than Joseph, but I have a clear memory of their very happy marriage. They lived in Avenue Road, St John's Wood, and had two children: Hannah, who was always known as 'Gluck' when she grew up, and became an extremely distinguished artist (her paintings are still much sought after), and her brother Louis, my father.

While Louis was growing up, his family's firm, Salmon and Gluckstein, became the biggest chain of cigar and tobacco merchants in the UK. Given the rapid growth of both the family and its business, Montague Gluckstein, one of the cousins and a driving force, realised that they would have to look to other opportunities. While at a trade fair in Newcastle demonstrating his tobacco products, he realised that, although there were plenty of alcoholic beverages available, what he really wanted most was a cup of tea. He had this same problem at every exhibition he visited throughout the country: no teashops anywhere to be found! Clearly he'd discovered a gap in the market and this germ of an idea led to the founding of the J. Lyons and Co. catering empire. Why the name J. Lyons? Well, Montague Gluckstein didn't want any confusion with the existing and well-known tobacco business, so he turned to Joe Lyons, a very good family friend, who permitted his name to be used for the new business.

My mother's maiden name was Doreen Klean. Her parents, Alexander and Esther, lived in Frognal, Hampstead, and were originally members of the Hampstead Synagogue in Dennington Park Road, although my grandmother later joined the LJS. My grandfather was highly respected in the jewellery trade and he founded H A Byworth and Co., who were specialist diamond setters who made beautiful jewellery and supplied shops such as Aspreys. My grandmother, affectionately known to my children as 'Gran Gran', was an accomplished and inveterate bridge player, who loved entertaining, and who lived to the great age of ninety-eight. I seem to come from a long-lived matriarchal line as her daughter, my mother Doreen (another outstanding bridge player, who was also brilliant at tennis), made it to ninety-seven.

I began my religious studies at home, where I was taught by the redoubtable Miss Marjorie Moos, the ever-in-demand first teacher for North and West London's Jewish children. At about the age of eleven, I joined the Religion School at the LJS, and had just started to learn Hebrew when war broke out. I was evacuated to Moira House School in Eastbourne but, after a couple of terms there, we were moved to a small, bitterly cold hotel on Lake Windermere. Out of approximately hundred girls, only three of us were Jewish. Thus, every Sunday, ninety-seven girls marched up the long hill to the church in Sawrey (where, incidentally, Beatrix Potter wrote all her books), while I remained behind to do the Jewish homework sent to me every week from the LJS. I'm ashamed to say that I never returned to learning Hebrew.

I matriculated and left school at sixteen and, even though the war was still raging, came back to London and was confirmed in the old LJS building by the never-to-be-forgotten Rabbi Israel Mattuck. He was a great orator who, with his passion, wonderful voice and American accent, mesmerised the congregation. The thing I remember best about my Confirmation was reading Shelley's *Ode to the West Wind*.

Because of the war and the heavy bombing of London, my family had taken a house at Shiplake, near Henley. It was right on the River Thames and even had a boathouse underneath the drawing room! My father Louis, who had been an oarsman at Oxford, and was always interested in rowing, insisted that my two brothers and I learned how to do it properly. We also had a punt, which proved much trickier to handle.

Throughout the period of the family's Shiplake sojourn, my father continued to be based in London, where he was working in the Judge Advocate General's department (he shared an office with David Niven, no less!). My father was a towering man both physically (at six foot seven-and-a-half inches), and professionally. A QC, he was elected the Member of Parliament for Nottingham North East in 1931 and retained his seat there until 1945. He was also a full Colonel with the 51st Highland Division and extraordinarily lucky to escape from France ten days after the main army evacuation from Dunkirk. Although his entire Division had been captured and remained prisoners for the rest of the war, my father had been ordered as an MP to return immediately to the War Office. Thank goodness he managed to, given that he was on Hitler's 'most wanted' list of 500 names.

While my father was working in London during the war, living in the family house in Elm Tree Road where the garden had been turned over to vegetables and chickens, I was also 'commuting' daily between Shiplake and London. I attended Mrs Hoster's Secretarial College and then, once my course was completed, got my first job as a secretary in the Religious Broadcasting Department of the BBC.

Elsa Swartz was a particularly good friend during those years and as a Wren, she was stationed in Chelsea, where we often met up for dinner. She was a lovely pianist and had a beautiful voice. I had always sung at school, but was painfully shy about doing so in public – I would only perform from behind a curtain. On one occasion, we met up in the Officers' Mess, where there was a piano, and my friend persuaded me to sing and promptly insisted that I should go to her singing teacher, Mrs Davis Reynolds, at the Wigmore Hall Studios. I did as I was told and began my studies and, after a year or so, realised how much I wanted to become a professional singer.

From the outset, I worried that my surname would be too quickly connected with J. Lyons and Co. and I really wanted to succeed on my own merit. (I also wasn't convinced that 'Gluckstein' went too well with singing oratorios such as Handel's *Messiah* and the Verdi *Requiem*.) So I became Jean Grayston, contralto, when I auditioned along with some 400 others in 1951 to join Glyndebourne Opera. There were five places in a chorus of just twenty-four – I got one of them, and the next four years proved some of the happiest of my singing life. Embarking on a career as a soloist is never easy, but luckily engagements soon began to come my way. I passed the BBC audition which, unbelievably, led to fifty years of broadcasting a rich variety of music, mainly on the Third Programme (now Radio 3) and the Light Programme (now Radio 2).

In December 1955 I was engaged to sing at a concert in Portsmouth. On the same bill was the Max Jaffa Trio: violinist Max Jaffa, pianist Jack Byfield and cellist Reginald Kilbey. They were immensely popular, never off the wireless (as they called it) and the television. Before the concert, Max came to my dressing room to introduce himself and say hello… and that was that. It was an amazing moment – truly love at first sight!

It took nearly four years before I could become Jean Jaffa (although separated, Max had to get properly divorced). Even though my father was LJS President, and I had never been married, Rabbi Leslie Edgar refused to marry us in the synagogue. This upset us all very much. Consequently, we had a non-religious marriage ceremony in the Registry Office of the Marylebone Town Hall on 24 June 1959.

We then embarked on thirty-two wonderfully compatible years of exceptionally 'close harmony', living and working together until Max's death in 1991. He was my soulmate and I miss him every day. We were blessed with three daughters (beautiful, of course, as far as I'm concerned!): Naomi (born 1961) and twins Jenny and Lisa (born 1965). Sadly, Max never lived to meet his four lovely grandchildren: Nathan, Louis, Lena and Noah.

Lisa, her husband Steve, and their sons, Louis and Noah Gershon, live nearby and are committed members of the LJS, where the boys currently sing in the Junior Choir. I think we're so lucky to have the inspirational Cathy Heller Jones and Tim Farrell in charge of our music. Lisa is a gifted and much-sought-after tennis coach, and her boys already demonstrate great ability on the court. Clearly they've all inherited my mother's fabulous tennis genes!

Nathan and Lena aren't so close to home, living as they do in Los Angeles with Jenny – who is now Marketing and Communications Vice-President at Starlight/Starbright Foundation – and her husband, Barry Isaacson. Happily Nathan seems to have inherited some of the Gluckstein/Grayston/Jaffa musical genes and is showing promise and dedication to his piano studies. Lena, on the other hand, loves playing soccer.

Naomi lives in Suffolk, where she is Director of The Poetry Trust, which runs the annual, internationally acclaimed Aldeburgh Poetry Festival. She is a published poet, a dedicated dressage rider, and a leading member and sometime soloist in the Britten-Pears Chamber Choir.

Following our marriage, Max and I continued to work together until about thirty years later when he retired in 1986. We gave concerts up and down the country and made countless recordings and television shows, as well as appearing as guest performers on many QE2 world cruises. But it was Yorkshire, of all places, that became our much-loved second musical and family home.

Before meeting Max, I had been singing in Scarborough at the Spa Grand Hall, and had done a couple of musicals (*King's Rhapsody* by Ivor Novello and *Carousel* by Rogers and Hammerstein) at the Open Air Theatre, which was on a large island in Peasholm Park. Across the water from this island stage sat an audience of 8,000! It had nothing to do with me when, in 1960, Max was offered the job of directing the summer season of music at the Spa Grand Hall in Scarborough. This involved auditioning and engaging an orchestra to play for five mornings and seven nights a week from May to September, and a different guest singer each week.

He wasn't keen, but I told him that the beautiful Victorian concert hall, seating about 2,000, had marvellous acoustics, and that the surrounding countryside was magnificent. He was persuaded and agreed to a year's contract, but 'only' to play evenings. Twenty-seven years, and a mind-boggling 3,213 performances later, he retired. (Actually he missed just one concert, to attend the funeral of his beloved pianist, Jack Byfield.) Once it became clear that Scarborough was to be an annual commitment, we bought a second home in the nearby village of Scalby, and the girls were able to indulge their passion for all things pony in every school holiday.

For his services to music in the town, Max was delighted to be given the Freedom of the Borough of Scarborough in 1987 (together with playwright and theatre director Alan Ayckbourn). He was almost as thrilled as when he received an OBE from Her Majesty the Queen in 1982.

But back to the LJS. When Claude Montefiore, our first President, died in 1938, my father was asked to succeed him, but he felt he could not follow immediately in the footsteps of such a great man, and it took two years before he agreed. My father then remained President for some forty years, a period which covered the Second World War and the disastrous bombing of the synagogue on 1 November 1940. (With the power station just round the corner in Lodge Road, it became a prime target for the German bombers.) Amongst the many memories of my father in synagogue is his reading of the Book of Jonah on *Yom Kippur*, which was always very special.

In my lifetime, the LJS has gone through two major incarnations, calling for us to worship elsewhere. The first was after the war when I remember attending High Holydays at the Friends' Meeting House in Euston Road. I also remember that, before the badly bombed synagogue was rebuilt, it became infested with pigeons. My father, being eminently practical, gave an air gun to my brother Roy (a good shot), and told him to dispatch the pigeons that were flying about the building. Although he managed to hit quite a few, Roy told me that they were so tough he doubted any of them had actually been killed!

The second rebuild, which created our current, wonderfully modern synagogue, entailed a temporary relocation to a lovely church in Loudoun Road (where Max and I once gave a concert). In fact, we worshipped there for three years, during which time I became increasingly aware of the work of John Rayner and David Goldberg and what charismatic and outstanding rabbis they both were. It was while the new LJS was under construction that John officiated at the marriage of our daughter, Jenny, to Barry Isaacson, permission having been given to use the West London Synagogue in Upper Berkeley Street. Eleven years later on 7 September 1997, John and David joined together (which was rare) to conduct the marriage ceremony of Lisa (Jenny's twin) to Stephen Gershon back in St John's Wood Road in our new 'home'.

Mentioning the marriages of Jenny and Lisa reminds me of an amusing incident at the LJS. Aged six, and recently into gymnastics, I was a bridesmaid to my mother's brother. Standing behind the bride and probably bored, I started to practise my exercises. The best man, my father (who don't forget was more than six-and-a-half feet tall), turned round, waved a long finger at me and whispered loudly: 'Stop it!' Apparently I waved my finger back at him, and continued to amuse the congregation.

As another aside, having just mentioned my father's height, it actually saved his life in the First World War. He was riding a motor bike in France, when he was hit on the top button of his tunic by a piece of shrapnel. A man of average height would have been killed. He hung on to that piece of shrapnel and had it mounted. I have it still, a permanent reminder of his escape from death.

These days, I spend as much time as possible with my grandchildren – the London ones are obviously easier to see more often than their Los Angeles cousins! I am also involved with The Westminster Society for People with Learning Difficulties and, in recent years, have organised two very successful fundraising 'evenings' with Sandi Toksvig and with Ronnie Corbett. We arrange all sorts of events, which recently included a Jazz Brunch in Regent's Park and a wonderful concert with the outstanding Cellist Natalie Clein at the Amadeus Centre in Maida Vale.

As I have already mentioned, my parents were among the earliest members of the LJS. They were also among the most active. For quite a long time, my mother was Chairman of the Women's Society, and she also started the Darby and Joan Club. I remember the latter meeting every Wednesday. It proved very popular with the thirty or so attendees, none of whom were members of the LJS. They chatted, played cards and bingo, and frequently some form of entertainment was provided (I sang for them regularly). Members of the LJS helped, and always organised an excellent tea for everybody. My mother made another valuable contribution when she came up with the idea of the Penny Jar. This still sits on the reception desk and, over the years, has raised thousands of pounds, helping to buy items the synagogue wouldn't otherwise have been able to afford. The piano in the Montefiore Hall is one of them.

My father dedicated his life to public service. In 1953, the Queen's Coronation Year, he was given a knighthood. He was Treasurer of Lincoln's Inn and Treasurer, and then Chairman of the Greater London Council. He was particularly overjoyed to receive the GBE (Knight Grand Cross of the Order of the British Empire), because it is a personal honour solely in the gift of the Queen. He was also President of the Royal Albert Hall for twenty years, which, of course, reminds me of our daughter Naomi presenting the bouquet to the Queen as part of the Hall's centenary celebrations.

Both of our parents cared deeply about the synagogue, and Roy, David and I have, in our different ways, always wanted to continue the family's involvement. In the end though, family was the most important thing in their lives, and continues to be so in mine.

See photographs 18, 67, and 72 (Sir Louis Gluckstein)
and photograph 31 (Lady Gluckstein).

✡

William Kessler

Willie Kessler has been involved with the synagogue since the late 1940s when he joined the Alumni Society. He has held many prominent roles, including being a Council member, Vice Chairman and, between 1999 and 2006, President of the synagogue.

My name is William Kessler, known as 'Willie'. I was born on 6 April 1927 in Vienna. My father's name was Leopold, and my mother's name was Cecily (neé Feldsberg). Neither was particularly religious, but my mother was more so than my father. They belonged to the local United Synagogue in London. My father died in 1963 and my mother in 1975. They are both buried in Pound Lane. When they retired to Brighton, they joined the Liberal Synagogue there, but they had previously been connected with the LJS.

I came to London in 1938 when I was eleven. My father had actually had a business in London since the mid-1920s, so it was easy for us to escape from Austria. I went to Enfield Grammar School. My grandfather, who came to London from Vienna in 1939, wanted me to have a *Bar Mitzvah* and found an ageing and very nice rabbi in Enfield to teach me. I'd attended Religion School in Vienna but, although I was generally an excellent scholar, religious education was one subject which did not appeal to me. Whatever I was taught bounced off like water off a duck's back. I did have a *Bar Mitzvah*, but it didn't mean very much, and I did not perform particularly well. It took place at Egerton Road United Synagogue in Stamford Hill, to which my grandfather belonged.

I came into contact with Progressive Judaism when my younger sister, Adele, joined the Alumni Society for the sixteen to thirty age group in the late 1940s, and I tagged along.

I had met Jo in 1947 at the London School of Economics (LSE), where we were both evening class students. Jo studied Economics and Sociology, and I studied Commerce. Jo also had a connection with the LJS because she was sponsored by members of the synagogue on a *Kindertransport,* and she had been in Dr Mattuck's last Confirmation class. We occasionally attended Alumni Society meetings, Jo more frequently than I. We were married at the LJS in 1952 by Rabbi Leslie Edgar.

I began to attend services more regularly when the children, George (born 1953), Charles (1956), James (1959) and Edward (1963), started to attend the Religion School. All our children were confirmed, they did not have a *Bar Mitzvah* – that was not offered at the LJS at that time. Jo was a great supporter of the Religion School, and was instrumental in starting a new post-Confirmation group, Square One.

I got involved with the Younger Members' Organisation (YMO), and eventually became its Chairman. The YMO was an extremely useful organisation as it brought young people together, both married and unmarried. It is sad that it too has ceased to exist, but perhaps this type of group is no longer appropriate.

In due course, I joined the Synagogue Council – in the late sixties – and after a few years became a Treasurer. There are always two Treasurers, and my first partner was Julian Tobin, followed by Tony Margo. We didn't worry too much about LJS office back-up, as we had our own office facilities to support us. We saw what needed doing and got on with it. There are always headaches associated with any financial job, but none with which we felt we couldn't cope.

When Rita Adler became Chairman of the Council for the first time, I was her Vice Chairman. At about that time, I joined the Council of Leo Baeck College, on which I served for about twelve years, including three as Chairman. I had an interesting time and found the College fascinating. I had left the LJS Council because I couldn't do both roles, but I always kept in touch. Someone would phone up if there was a problem that needed sorting out informally. Eventually I was invited to become President.

I think that a Synagogue President's role is an extremely flexible one – you can do as much or as little as you want to. I personally took a very active role during my Presidency, and got involved with as many people as I possibly could. I used my role to firm up links with the College. I also tried to firm up links with West London Synagogue and I used my role as President very broadly, both internally and externally. I retired in 2006 at the end of my six-year term of office. I then had my back operation and so would not have been able to do very much more.

I am now involved very informally. I firmly believe that if someone takes over from me, I don't want to sit in their pocket and interfere.

I didn't know Rabbi Mattuck. I heard him preach when we came to services here and at Porchester Hall, where the LJS held its High Holyday overflow services. I knew Leslie Edgar better because he married us. He was a highly dedicated man, and a very nice person. John Rayner became a close personal friend, as did David Goldberg. We liked David Goldstein very much, it was a great loss when he left us. We also knew the Americans who came over, Rabbi Chaim Stern, Rabbi Sidney Brichto and all the students. We were really friendly with all the Rabbis and their wives.

It was Sir Louis Gluckstein, then President, who invited me to join the Council. When I was YMO Chairman he said, 'Willie, you are going to be important here, why don't you come on the Council.' He was always very kind to me. He was followed as President by Maxwell Stern, whom I knew slightly. He was a nice man.

Sir Peter Lazarus was a personal friend; I was on the Council with him. The family had a house in Bognor Regis, and he invited us down for weekends every so often – I went for walks with him there. At that time, we must both have been in our late twenties. I said to him, 'Peter, what is your objective?' He said, 'I want to get to the top.' And he did. I said, 'I want to build up a business.' And I did, so we both succeeded in what we aimed to achieve. I knew Peter before he got autocratic and, in the view of some people, a little pompous. It never struck me that he was. This tends to happen with old friends. You remember them as they were when you are both youngish and you forgive them any oddities as they get older.

Over the years, services at the LJS have become more 'High Church', as one might call it which, on the whole, the younger people like. The trend towards more traditionalism may not be so popular with older members who remember the 'Mattuck' line. Otherwise, to me, the LJS has been a marvellous place. It has given us our personal, social, and religious roots more than any other institution. Obviously, one has many other friends outside as well, but in terms of our rootedness, I think the LJS plays a major part.

The make-up of the congregation has evolved over the years. Someone once described the Church of England as 'the Conservative Party at prayer'; in the same vein the LJS was the Anglo-Jewish establishment at prayer. That has changed a lot, of course. We now represent a much broader cross-section of the Jewish population of London.

Ours is a family business started by my grandfather, Bernhard, in Vienna. My father, Leopold, managed a London branch from 1926. He ran the business on a small scale, which is what he wanted. I first got involved as a 'Saturday boy' at the age of eleven and, when I took it over, I enjoyed making the business grow; and it has indeed grown. Two of our sons, George and Charles, joined the firm in the mid-seventies. Of our other two sons, James is a QC, and Edward is the Executive Director of the Wolff Institute for Abrahamic Faiths in Cambridge.

As the business expanded, we moved several times and our state-of-the-art factory and headquarters are now in Stratford, East London. We are involved in three fields: designing and making shop display and marketing equipment, distribution and property. We changed our name to Kessler International Ltd to reflect our increasing export market and in 2008 to 2009, we won eleven European POPAI and Display Industry awards. We were also chosen as the Best Employer of Apprentices in Greater London in recognition of our excellent apprentice and training schemes.

There are other Kesslers, but we are not related to any of them. I knew David Kessler of the *Jewish Chronicle*, but we decided that any connection was unlikely as his family came from Silesia in Eastern Germany (now Poland) and mine from Austria.

The LJS has certainly been a source of joy and activity for me and it has also been the same for Jo, who had a tremendous input as Secretary of the Women's Society. That doesn't exist any longer, but there are many activities such as the 4Cs, Keep in Touch, the Out and About Club and Tea + Video, in which she is deeply involved. So the LJS continues to be a major part of both our lives.

See photographs 20, 59, 68, 69, and 77.

✡

Lady Lazarus

Elizabeth Lazarus has been a member of the LJS since the 1930s. Shortly after the Second World War, she married Peter Lazarus (later Sir Peter), who became Chairman and President of the synagogue. She was involved in the Alumni, the Younger Members' Organisation, and the Women's Society.

I was born Elizabeth Atwell on 18 June 1927. My mother's maiden name was Nina Levy and my father was Leslie Atwell. His name was originally Apfel, but it was anglicised to Atwell, probably during the First World War. My father was sent to Shrewsbury public school, which was unusual for a Jewish boy in those days. My paternal grandmother was Hannah Gluckstein. Her family founded the Lyons tea houses.

My father owned a chocolate factory called Lesme in Blackpool, and a biscuit factory called BB Biscuits. During the Munich crisis in 1938 we all went to stay in Blackpool in case London was invaded.

I have two sisters, Susan and Jennifer, and a brother, David. We grew up in Hampstead, North London, but also had a home in Henley-on-Thames. I attended the Frognal School, a day-school in Hampstead. As children, we had a nanny and, later on, a governess. My mother would come to see us every day after tea. I was a little bit difficult as a child as I wanted my mother to spend more time with us.

When the Second World War broke out, there was a real fear of bombings, so we moved out of London. I was sent to Courtfield School in Bognor Regis. In 1940, after just one year at the school, we had to leave the coast in case of a German invasion. They were only forty miles away on the other side of the Channel!

My mother was originally a member at Hampstead Synagogue, but as there was too much Hebrew in the services there, we moved to the LJS as a family during the 1930s. I was let off Religion School because of the war, and was spared having Miss Moos as a teacher! However, my sisters were taught by Miss Moos. She was a good teacher and managed the Religion School correspondence course as we were all so scattered during the war.

After leaving Bognor Regis, I became a boarder at Wycombe Abbey, a public school in High Wycombe. I was happy at this school as one was treated like a 'semi-adult'. I was fourteen at the time.

However, the Americans requisitioned Wycombe Abbey, and we all had to leave without even being able to say goodbye. We were evacuated to Ancaster House, a school which had been a stately home. It was near Buscot Park in Berkshire and belonged to Lord Faringdon. My classroom was in the stables. It was damp and horrible! The school was very strict. I once said to Matron, 'This is not what life is about.' I stayed at this school until I was seventeen.

My father was very sensible and wanted me to do something practical after school, so I was sent to Shropshire College of Domestic Science for a year to learn to cook. After school, the college was absolute bliss! We were allowed out until 5.30 p.m. when the troops used to come into town. I was next sent for a year to St James' Secretarial College in London to learn shorthand and typing. I hated it! It was very boring.

After the war I was a member of the Alumni Society at the LJS and later, a member of the YMO (Younger Members' Organisation). We used to hold dances at Camden Town Hall.

I met my husband-to-be, Peter Lazarus, at a party my parents gave for me at the end of the war, when I was nineteen. Peter's family were also LJS members. Peter wasn't my first boyfriend; I had one or two before him. I liked Peter. He was a year older than I and was very clever. He had read Greats – Latin and Greek – at Wadham College, Oxford.

After secretarial college, I got a job at Carreras, the Craven 'A' cigarette factory in Camden Town. I worked as a secretary in the employment department, where I met everybody. I had a good sense of humour and liked people. I always found members of the working class much more tolerant than the upper class. I didn't tell anyone at work that I lived in a posh flat in St John's Wood. I used to take the 74 bus to work. The fare was 1½ d. I used to get off the bus early to save the bus fare as I was saving to get married. My generation was much thriftier than people nowadays.

I worked at Carreras for eighteen months until I got married. In those days, it wasn't done for a woman to have a job after marriage. While I was working, I also volunteered one day a week at Brady Girls' Club in Whitechapel, where I ran the library. I gave this up too when I got married.

We were married at the LJS by Rabbi Leslie Edgar in April 1950. I became a Lazarus and called myself 'Liz-Laz'.

Our wedding had to take place in the Montefiore Hall, as the synagogue had suffered serious bomb damage. The MCC was very good to the LJS – they let us use rooms there while the synagogue was being repaired. We used to have High Holyday services in Friends' House in Euston, so that we could all be together.

Peter was in the Army when we were married. He entered the Civil Service as an Assistant Principal, and eventually became Permanent Secretary at the Department of Transport. He got a good pension when he retired, but there weren't many perks on the way up!

We had three boys: Richard, Steven and James. As we were in Henley-on-Thames at weekends, all three children followed Miss Moos's correspondence course and were, in due course, confirmed at the synagogue. There were no *Bar Mitzvahs* at the LJS in those days, but we would not have wanted them for the boys in any case. Peter and I were much more anglicised and wanted the children to be confirmed. The Confirmation weekend away is very important. My children have made lifelong friends through their Confirmation classes.

When Peter retired he received a knighthood. Going to Buckingham Palace for the ceremony was rather fun. I wore a blue dress, hat and gloves. My father lent us his chauffeur-driven car, so we arrived in style. Subsequently, we were invited to many Palace garden parties. They went on too long and there was nowhere to sit down!

Peter's father was deeply involved in the organisation of the LJS, and Peter was elected to Council in the 1950s. He was an extremely able planner. He was Chairman from 1987 until 1992. I always tried to support Peter in his work at the LJS – that is essential, otherwise one starts living separate lives.

As the children grew older, I became involved in the synagogue's Women's Society. I was Honorary Secretary because of my secretarial skills. Doreen Gluckstein was President. The Women's Society did a lot of visiting of the elderly and was quite powerful. I didn't enjoy the Women's Society too much, as I am not a very good listener, and I always steered clear of any activities involving catering!

My sons are all married now. My youngest son, James, has become a devout Christian. I am not very happy about it, but as my middle son says, 'It's all right – there is only one God after all.' I have three wonderful daughters-in-law and ten wonderful grandchildren, five boys and five girls. Some of them are already in their twenties.

In terms of LJS Rabbis, Rabbi Mattuck was American and rather alien to me. Leslie Edgar was much liked. Philip Cohen was his Assistant Minister. Later, we had Sidney Brichto. He was American and very good with people. Rabbi Rayner served South London, before coming to the LJS. He was very much loved. He was a very warm, well-educated man. I think Rabbi David Goldberg has done a good job. He is always available and he is very good at funerals. He is very anglicised. Rabbi Alexandra Wright is rather serious.

The LJS is part of my life. I am deeply religious. My favourite festival is New Year as it's rather joyous. However, I find the Day of Atonement rather difficult, and I've never fasted.

Although I was quite involved in the Women's Society, when you get to eighty plus, you begin to do a bit less. I still go to the Tuesday Lunches once a month and to the Keep in Touch tea parties. I enjoy them as I know half the people there such as Margaret Rigal, my sister-in-law; she is a very good person. Ann Kirk and Jo Kessler are refugees. They are so sane, in spite of everything they have been through. They are all wonderful, delightful people.

See photographs 68 and 73 (Sir Peter Lazarus).

✡

Jacob Lovick

Jacob Lovick has been coming to the synagogue since he was very young. Following his *Kabbalat Torah* **he became an assistant teacher and then a teacher in the LJS Religion School. He is now its Head Librarian.**

The Liberal Jewish Synagogue certainly forms a basis for much of my youth. It means so much more than the name of a building – it is a community that I feel part of, and have felt included by. My time at the LJS has been something that I will always treasure and, hopefully, continue to treasure, but has, by no means, been a thoroughly Edenic ride. There have been ups and downs. There will be people whose company I will never regret, and others that I could maybe say less of. But the positives of the community, congregation, friendship and learning will always be the ones that stay with me.

Coming from what is loosely termed as a 'mixed' background, that of one Jewish parent, my mother, and one Christian parent, my father, being a member of the congregation here has been less what one might term 'a journey of faith', but rather 'a journey of discovery'. My mother takes a very active role in the community, as I'm sure she would be pleased for me to mention, whilst my father takes a much more hands off, passive role to religion. So whilst I prefer to refer to myself as 'half-Jewish, half-Christian', and reap the benefits of both, it has to be said that I do nurture the Jewish side to me a little more than the Christian side.

I have been told that, before my birth, my parents came to some sort of agreement with regards to my faith in my youth. They took me to synagogue from an early age, something that I was more passive than active in instigating, but I really do not remember much of these early years. Vague flashes of brightly coloured Hebrew-lettering-covered books seem to occupy that area of my memory, but as a comprehensive review of *Naftali's Journey to Jerusalem* and *Naftali Meets A Camel* is unlikely to interest you, I will move swiftly on. That is not to say that I discredit the fine late-eighties writings of young Naftali on the subject of the Diaspora and its relationship to the Jewish homeland, indeed it is what I mostly read now in my role as Head Librarian for the Religion School.

Growing up, I was ferried by my caring mother from the western suburbs of Acton along the much-loved Western Avenue into St John's Wood every Saturday, not quite sure what that morning's lesson would bring. Reflecting on this now, I seem to remember a certain sense of trepidation stepping into the foyer, perhaps brought on by the prospect that there might be another 'surprise visit' to the service, or the fact that in those years I had an irrational terror of my teacher, despite her soft, dulcet, soothing Israeli tones and caring demeanour. This perhaps explains my current *laissez-faire* attitude to the staff room in the Religion School.

A big landmark for me, as for any Jewish child with a passion for being the centre of attention, large parties, glorious present-giving, and performing in front of much of the congregation, was my *Bar Mitzvah*. I distinctly remember standing in the Montefiore Hall beforehand, with my father, who was bemoaning my choice to get a frankly ludicrous haircut only days before the biggest day of my Jewish life which, retrospectively, was certainly a mistake. I was also struck then, as I still am now, by a certain sense of irony that the portion that I was reading, Exodus 29, verses 1–14, depicted in meticulous detail the fantastically over-the-top garments that Moses's brother Aaron was to wear during the ceremony of making him High Priest, whilst I, at the time, was still reluctant to put on a shirt and tie. The ceremony all went to plan, my mother burst into tears, my grandmother told me how handsome I looked, relatives that I had never met came up to me and confided how well I read, and that was that. I was a man.

Or not quite. There was still the small question of the *Kabbalat Torah* course and service to complete. This, for me, now feels to be the true stepping stone from the apathetic Jewish youth to the more proactive member of the community, one who takes a sincerely interested attitude to the events in the building around him, and feels a closer bond and friendship with the community. Fittingly, the theme for our KT service was 'Friendship and Community'. For me, religion, Jewish or otherwise, is almost a synonym for 'friendship and community'. Whilst the growing numbers of the non-religious of our country state that religion is a waste of time, and that it is a fruitless endeavour to believe in something that one has absolutely no proof of whatsoever, I merely respond that religion is all about a sense of belonging, a feeling of being part of a supportive and close-knit community. The KT year, and its service theme, only served to amplify these sentiments within me. As Mark Twain put it, 'the universal brotherhood of man is our most precious possession.'

After leaving the Religion School as a pupil, I took the natural next step, and I became an assistant to a teacher. The education of young minds, not all quite eager or willing to learn, is certainly a skill that one acquires over time, and mostly gets picked up by osmosis. Teaching can be gruelling, satisfying, exasperating, humorous, enjoyable, hateful, pointless, cheering, draining or pleasing, and, occasionally, all ten. I found that I learned a lot whilst teaching, namely a greater grasp of the grisly production of *kosher* food, and the names of all of the seas in Israel. I learned how one can simply drop the name of a Head Teacher, and all will fall deathly quiet, and, later, how a trip to the Religion School Library is seen as a form of punishment, rather than stimulation, for the children. Moving from position to position, assistant to teacher, teacher to Head Librarian, stuffy, blinding classroom to boiling, windowless classroom, I built a relationship with other teachers, younger and older, and, needless to say, with the children as well. As a teacher, I found that I had more interaction with the children's parents and grandparents, a not always rewarding opportunity, but one that nonetheless increased and developed my interaction and engagement with the LJS community, and helped me to further integrate and make myself known to many people.

The experiences that I have enjoyed, and friendships that have gone from strength to strength, will never leave me, nor will my truly sincere sense of belonging that I can enjoy being a member of the congregation of the LJS. The buildings might not be the prettiest in the world, and the classrooms might not be the best climate-controlled, but these are all simply part of the charm of this hundred-year-old community. When Lily Montagu, Claude Montefiore and Israel Mattuck, the 'Three Ms' as we tell the students, chatted about the idea of forming a less Orthodox, more welcoming, more inclusive and more egalitarian synagogue, I'm not sure whether they would have predicted what a thriving community it would eventually become. It is something I am proud to belong to, something that I, indeed most of us, have grown up into, and is as much a part of my life as is my school or where I live. In our modern, hectic, stressful lives, it is easy to consign ideas of community and religion to the over-filled recycling bin of the past, but I argue that the LJS can be as much an integral, supportive, caring and, above all, enjoyable part of our lives as it was to the first members of the LJS in 1911.

Editorial note: In 2011 Jacob Lovick was awarded the President's Cup (donated by Willie and Jo Kessler), which is awarded to young people who have made an outstanding contribution to youth activities at the synagogue.

Trevor Moross

Originally from South Africa, Trevor Morass served continuously on the LJS Council from 1987 before becoming Chairman in 1998. He played a leading role in the rebuilding of the synagogue between 1988 and 1991.

My name is Trevor Moross. I was born in Johannesburg in 1948. There was a strong Jewish community in Johannesburg, and a significant Reform/Liberal congregation, founded just before the war. The founder was a very charismatic and inspiring American rabbi, Moses Cyrus Weiler. The congregation attracted a large German-Jewish community that had been building up in South Africa as a result of the Holocaust, and also from those disaffected, largely Lithuanian, Jews who were looking for a more meaningful form of Judaism.

My paternal grandmother died very young. My paternal grandfather had come from a strongly religious family. I believe that his father or uncle was a rabbi in Lithuania. I did not know my grandfather as he died when I was two years old, but I believe he was a synagogue-goer and was an esteemed member of the large United Synagogue congregation in Johannesburg. As South Africa was part of the Commonwealth, the same structure existed as in the UK with a Chief Rabbi drawn from the largest, Orthodox community.

My maternal grandparents were very much part of my life. My grandfather went to an Orthodox synagogue for all the festivals and, as a child, I sometimes went with him to his synagogue. My grandmother was very observant, but not in a fundamentalist way. I don't remember her going to synagogue very often as she was a little agoraphobic, but she acted out some of the practices of her childhood by rote. She could not read Hebrew, which was a great sadness to her. She read her prayerbook almost every day.

My father was never interested in organised religion. He never goes to a synagogue. He claims that it had been rammed down his throat as a child and he wanted nothing to do with it. My mother was the opposite. She was keen to instil a Jewish upbringing into the family and made sure that my two sisters, my brother and I attended the synagogue very regularly. It was my mother who joined the Temple Israel Synagogue and encouraged our connections with it.

Temple Israel was the mother synagogue of Reform Judaism in South Africa. Rabbi Weiler built a huge congregation and, in the sixties, it grew two additional congregations in Johannesburg alone. The services there were very similar to those at the LJS today. There was an organ and a very good professional choir and the system was very similar with Religion School on Saturday mornings. However, we also had to go on Tuesday afternoons. I have a 1957 copy of the prayerbook at home. It was a reprint, slightly adapted, of an American prayerbook printed in South Africa in 1951.

I was very taken by Rabbi Weiler and enjoyed the services very much. From an early age, I sang in the choir and soon got involved in youth activities, both at the synagogue and in the national movement. I was a regular camper and in my late teens, a leader of all kinds of camps. The movement in South Africa had two permanent campsites with excellent facilities, one at the coast and one near Johannesburg so there were lots of opportunities for going on organised camps.

It is probably fair to say that, until I went to university, my social life mainly revolved around the synagogue, so much so that there was some concern voiced by my parents about whether I might want to become a rabbi, which I think worried them a bit. During those years, the rabbis changed several times. Rabbi Weiler emigrated to Israel around the time of my *Bar Mitzvah* and was succeeded by Michael Elton, a British rabbi whom I didn't like a lot. He in turn was followed by a very charismatic and quite liberal American, Aaron Opher, who introduced confirmations and *Kabbalat Torah*, in which we all took part.

When I went to university, the University of Witwatersrand in Johannesburg, my involvement with the synagogue became less intense as I became immersed in student politics. However, it was about that time that a wonderful man, Rabbi Arthur Super, became the Senior Rabbi. Rabbi Super was an amazing, amazing man. A polio victim in a wheelchair, he was highly articulate, had been editor of the *Jewish Chronicle* in South Africa, and took a strong anti-apartheid political stance. That was very inspiring for me. He was often seen leading marches in his wheelchair, and he was a very outspoken anti-government critic, which was hugely important to me at the time. I was very proud of being a Progressive Jew with a leader who was so brave and outspoken.

Although I was not too involved with the synagogue whilst at university, I did get embroiled in some of the community politics of the time. The American rabbi with his liberal ways had split the community, as those who felt that he was too liberal formed a splinter congregation. I can't remember the detail, but I do recall that I was involved in quite a lot of the issues that this created for the Jewish youth movement in South Africa.

I worked for three years in South Africa before going to university in the UK and became involved in national politics. I was an election agent and ran the campaign for a Progressive Party candidate. This was the party of Helen Suzman.

When I came to England I left all that behind me. I first spent three years at Reading University, where I was completely uninterested in anything to do with Judaism. I was in my early twenties and excited about making a life for myself here and sorting out my career. There was a Jewish Society at Reading, but as it was Orthodox, I had nothing to do with it.

During my first year at Reading I met Sharon (now Sharon Lewison). She was born a Catholic and came from a large, practising Catholic family. That was very troubling to me and particularly troubling for my parents. There was no question of my marrying somebody who was not Jewish. I couldn't cope with it and my parents certainly couldn't. Fortunately, Sharon was very willing to think about conversion. She had rejected her rigid Catholic upbringing and was interested in exploring Judaism.

When we paid our first visit to South Africa together, my parents arranged for us to meet someone who could arrange a quickie conversion in Israel. In the ghetto-like community of the time, the fact that Reform conversions were not recognised was a problem for my parents. This meeting was a catastrophe as the requirements were very onerous and also required Sharon to obtain consent from her parents. Most importantly, there was absolutely no integrity to the process. At the same time I went to see Rabbi Super who knew me very well. He said, 'If you're going to do this, there is only one person in England you should go and see and his name is John Rayner.'

So we returned to London, and made an appointment to see John. I can't remember whether we went together or whether I went on my own. He was typically John, rather aloof and clinical, and I confess that it wasn't love at first sight. We were encouraged to join the LJS and started attending services. We did that for the High Holydays whilst we were living in Reading and, having resolved to get married when we came to London, Sharon started the conversion process.

Her initial experiences with David Goldstein were not brilliant. After he left to work in the British Library, things began to lapse. Then, thankfully and miraculously, Marjorie Moos came on the scene. She became Sharon's friend and mentor, guided her, encouraged her and brought her through the journey, which was both a journey into Judaism, but also an amazing introduction to the LJS, its history and heritage.

We had a civil wedding before Sharon's conversion and, soon afterwards, a synagogue wedding in South Africa. By this time, we had become quite familiar with the LJS and enjoyed going there, which was easy because we lived in St John's Wood. Richard was born in 1977. His *brit* was arranged through the LJS and John officiated.

Not long after that we moved to Muswell Hill and Daniel was born in 1981. As young parents, our attendance was much less regular. We moved about the time when Richard needed to go to Religion School, and hesitated about continuing our membership because of the distance. In fact, I wrote a letter to Raymon Benedyk, who was the Organising Secretary at the time, saying as much. A letter came bounding back from David Goldberg saying, 'Don't leave, this is where you belong.' So we stayed.

David wisely realised that he needed to capture my interest and persuaded me to join the House Committee and, if I remember correctly, the Cemetery Committee for a while. That was the first time I met Neil Levitt and Bob Beral. I think Bob was the chairman of the Cemetery Committee. Bob had a shop in Muswell Hill and I could pigeon-hole him, which helped to make me feel at home.

Kate was born in 1986. With three children and a busy job, the committee work became too much for me and I became less involved for a period until the question of the rebuilding arose. Despite this, during the period that our children were in the Religion School, we were both very regular attendees at the LJS and at services. We were very integrated into LJS communal life. Sharon became very involved in education matters and, for a time, ran part of the Religion School. She was engaged in a great deal of Jewish education work and initiated quite a number of projects both at the LJS and for ULPS.

I can't remember when it was exactly but, during this period, David Goldberg called me and said, 'We have got an issue with the building. We don't know how we're going to go about it. Would you be interested in getting involved?' I already respected and enjoyed working with Neil Levitt. I also knew Tony Margo quite well because we had professional dealings, and I had a great deal of respect for him. I thought he was a fabulous chap.

I started attending meetings and was invited by Maxwell Stern, the Chairman from 1981 to 1987, to join the Council. I got more and more sucked in, probably because I was very concerned about the direction in which the project was going. At the first general meeting at which the project was discussed, I was horrified to see how much opposition there was to what seemed to me to be a no-brainer. I was also concerned about the number of special interest groups who were trying to muscle in for their own personal gain.

When I saw the first drawings that emerged from the initial discussions between Tony and the architects, I was even more determined to get involved. I felt strongly that we had the opportunity to make something special of the project, and I was keen to see an architectural competition. The first design was an awful slab of a building rather like *Lord's View*, with a hole punched through, giving access to a synagogue at the back.

Very soon afterwards Peter Lazarus (later Sir Peter Lazarus), became Chairman. Peter was an amazing and able person. He had remarkable people skills, was an excellent leader and had huge experience from his big government job. From the moment I met him, I liked him. We got on well and worked well together.

We formed a good team under Peter's leadership: Neil Levitt, Tony Margo and me. Tim Simon gave us careful, quiet counsel. David Goldberg was at his best. John provided wonderful gentle guidance. We each had different roles and got on with them. The rebuilding of the LJS, together with the relationships I formed in the process, was unquestionably one of the most enjoyable and rewarding things I've ever done. It was an incredibly harmonious and constructive time because there was such respect for everyone else's point of view. It was also very scary. I can well remember the sleepless nights. On the second floor of our home, outside our bedroom, we had a balcony which overlooked Peter Lazarus's garden from a distance. I can remember several times standing on that balcony in a cold sweat after a particularly worrying night, wondering whether Peter was in the same state of anxiety.

Peter used to pop round to the house quite often in the evenings for a chat. He was allowed one pipe a day and he used to walk round the block and, as he passed, he used to knock on my door. I used to walk the other half of the block with him and we finished the walk together, chewing over the problems and challenges of the week.

There were moments of huge anxiety about money and also a terrible dispute with Mowlem, the main contractor, about the portico. It was in the wrong place because the architects had not measured its location correctly and the building, as designed, and for which we had planning permission, did not fit on the site! We thought we were in big trouble and we knew it wasn't our fault, but we didn't know how we were going to get it sorted out. We decided to invoke the help of Tony Solomons, who was one of the 'big hitters' in the congregation. He was and still is a tough cookie. He took on Mowlem, and tried to persuade them to pay the cost without the need for litigation. We had a plan that, if all else failed, we would go to Arnold Goodman. In those days he was the person people were most frightened of. In the end we didn't need to involve Arnold Goodman because we got very good legal advice that said we could win a case. We did win, which was a huge relief to everybody.

I can also remember our anxieties about the first service. Would the sound and air conditioning systems work? Would there be enough seats for people? Would they be comfortable? That first *Rosh Hashanah* and *Yom Kippur* it was very warm but the air conditioning wasn't working. The only way we could get it to work was manually. Neil Levitt, Fred Shelley (the caretaker) and I ran up and down the stairs to and from the basement to move a lever which would open and close the valves to regulate the temperature. People complained it was too cold. I can well remember the words of Ludwig Spiro, an engineer and a very nice man, who said, 'You've got the design wrong, but don't worry. Everybody will forget about it after a time.'

We never got the sound right. There were things we put into the building that were completely crazy and were never used. We always felt we needed a remote control system for the sound so that we could control the PA system from the balcony. However, this never worked. Then there was the choir loft. We only used it once or twice, because the logic of separating the organ and the choir (necessary because we could not fit the organ into the choir loft!) and the acoustics of the choir from the top of the building just did not work. It was very good that we had to move the choir into the body of the congregation; this changed the LJS for ever.

It took probably five or six years for us to 'wear' everything in. The rebuilding of the LJS was tremendously rewarding. It is probably the most rewarding thing I have done in my life other than father my children.

I served on the Council continuously from 1987 until I resigned as Chairman in 2002. During that period I served on almost every committee there was and chaired the Membership, Finance, Services Committees and, I think, for a time also the Cemetery Committee.

I became Chairman following Rita Adler in 1998. I felt strongly that there was the need for some change and quite a lot of things required determined action. My relative youth and energy were directed into trying to achieve that. I thought that there was the need for a fresh approach. I chose two new Treasurers: Tim Simon (1998–2002) and Bernie Bulkin (1998–2001).

During my Chairmanship Rabbi Helen Freeman left, we changed the management, we reformed the cemetery arrangements, we appointed two new rabbis, and we invested in the Religion School, appointing Jan Roseman as Director of Education. We also made a CD of the choir, revamped the newsletter and introduced more technology into the office. We tackled the problem of the virtual non-existence of David Goldberg's pension and tried to change the culture of relying on legacies to fund our deficit. I found it all exhausting, but very rewarding.

I resigned from the Chairmanship before the end of my second three years of office. I had really had enough by then. The main problems in my final few months were staffing decisions, which I found did not have the full support of some pillars of the congregation. I began to feel that David Goldberg was right when he said that the Chairman should never stay for more than three years because 'whilst they will argue for the first three they will hate you for the next three'. I quoted this at a speech I made recently when I finished my term as Chairman of the Academy of St Martin in the Fields.

The moment of decision came when I had the opportunity to join the board of the orchestra (the Academy of St Martin in the Fields), of which I later became Chairman. I knew that the Chairman at work would not approve of me doing both that and the LJS, so I gave up the role at the LJS, having persuaded Tim Simon to take over. Tim is another member whom I greatly respected and admired for his commitment, discretion and ability. I then took a really big step back. I was exhausted by the role of Chairman and did not feel our achievements during my period in the role were sufficiently appreciated.

By this time, my children had all grown up, Kate had completed her *Bat Mitzvah*, I was divorced and I had met Patricia. I owe my current happy circumstance and life with Patricia to the LJS as well. Our children are similar ages and had got to know each other at *Kadimah*. When Patricia left Cambridge after her divorce and came to London she joined the LJS. It was the year before the *Bar Mitzvah* of Alexander, Patricia's youngest son. Patricia attended services regularly and our relationship started and grew in the back rows of the synagogue!

I have had very little to do with the LJS in the past nine years. Patricia and I are often away on weekends, and we have lots of commitments when we are in London. I must also confess that something has gone out of the place for me since John's death and David's retirement. I have continued to be involved with the Finance Committee and, more recently, have run the Centenary Appeal. The LJS is very important to me and I always feel that I have an obligation to give as much as I can to it.

I am less worried than others about the changes in the services as my upbringing was slightly more Reform than the LJS. I would have left the LJS if there had been no *B'nei Mitzvah,* and was very put off by the 'no head-covering' policy in place at the LJS for many years.

I think that we have done a lot to become more inclusive. What is really important about the LJS is that it is a place where all kinds of non-affiliated Jews can come. We have to recognise that the bulk of non-affiliated Jews have a United Synagogue heritage and therefore they are generally more comfortable if the LJS is slightly more traditional. We have to offer both tradition and radicalism, including moments of extreme liberality. We should be more responsive, less rigid, more adventurous and more open-minded about some things that we are not open-minded about. We also need to be warmer, more spiritual. That can come from being slightly more traditional than the 'old' LJS.

See photograph 20.

✡

Anthony Roe

The LJS has been Anthony Roe's spiritual home for over seventy-five years. During that time he has served on the House Committee, chaired the Education Committee and been a Council member. His wife Maureen was very active in the Women's Society and was for several years its Treasurer.

According to my birth certificate, I arrived in this world at number 8 Lydford Road, Cricklewood on Friday 13 December 1929, and I have been fortunate ever since.

My father, Percy Alex Roe, was born in London on 25 April 1886. He was the son of Felix and Josephine Rosenstiel. He had a brother, Edgar, a sister, Nita, and a half-brother, Hugo. The story of Felix and Josephine is really quite romantic but also rather sad. Josephine was born on 27 February 1857 in Jassy (now known as Iasi), Romania. She was the daughter of Alter Rosenthal and his wife Berthe (née Kohn). She married a man called Loewenthal who, according to Auntie Nita, was a beastly man. Shortly after Hugo was born, Loewenthal died and Josephine went with her baby to live with her parents and sister, Babette, who had moved to Berlin. An eligible young man called Felix Rosenstiel (born in Glogau, Silesia, on 9 December 1844) was invited to visit as a suitable husband for Babette. However, Felix used to watch Josephine pushing the pram in the garden. He fell in love with her, wanted to marry her and offered to adopt Hugo. The families agreed and they were married in Berlin on 8 September 1880. Very shortly afterwards they moved to London, where Felix started a business in London as a fine art publisher.

The business must have flourished, but Felix died on 4 April 1895 and was buried in the Pound Lane Cemetery in Willesden. Josephine, who by all accounts was a remarkable woman, ran the business until my father was old enough to join her. Father was at the City of London School and wanted to be an engineer. However, at the age of fifteen, he had to join his mother in the business when it was rather distinctively renamed Felix Rosenstiel's, Widow and Son. The business continues under this name, and today is run by David Roe (a great-grandson of Felix) and his son, Nick. I often wonder what Felix and Josephine would think if they could know that their descendants had been honoured at Buckingham Palace as recipients of two Queen's Awards for Export!

Percy Rosenstiel married Flora Sara Kisch in 1913 at the Abbey Road Synagogue. The family name was changed to Roe during the First World War. They had four children: Peter Felix, Jervis Royalton (known as Jerry), Josephine Angela and Anthony Maitland Roe (me).

My mother's parents were Augustus and Sara Kate Kisch (née Davis). I only knew my maternal grandmother, who was called 'Gargar' by all her grandchildren. The Kisch family were pretty distinguished in many fields. It is documented back to Hirsch Kisch (1651–1698) a pharmacist, who lived in Prague. Sir Cecil Kisch (1884–1961), a diplomat, was a member of the LJS Council for some years – there are many references to him in the newsletters. My mother's eldest brother, Ernest Royalton Kisch MC, was an early supporter of the JRU, a founding member of the LJS and a great supporter of Rabbi Mattuck. He was instrumental in getting my family and my Uncle Maitland, who was my godfather, to join the LJS.

Why was I born in Lydford Road? My parents had just sold their home at 228 Walm Lane, and were not able to move into no. 2 Frognal Lane until early in 1930. We lived in Frognal Lane until 1940 when the bombing forced us to leave London.

I have been involved with The Liberal Jewish Synagogue all my life. I cannot remember being taken to any other synagogue. My two older brothers, born in 1914 and 1918, were *Bar Mitzvah*, but I am not sure where the ceremonies took place. It might have been the synagogue in Walm Lane, Willesden, when the family lived there (quite close to Peggy Lang House, the Abbeyfield Home run by members of the LJS). I was told that my eldest brother, Peter, placed a brick in the new LJS building in 1925 when he was eleven years old.

As a small boy I went with my sister, Josephine, to the Religion School, but then the war came and there was a gap in our religious education. At one time, Joe Foreman, our funeral director, tried to teach me Hebrew. I believe this was before the war when I would have been about seven or eight years old.

I took the correspondence classes. One of my teachers was Marjorie Moos, who wrote comments in bright red ink on such work as I sent back. Once she wrote: 'Can I have the pleasure of hearing from you again?' For me, as a young boy, she was a most terrifying lady. Later, of course, we came to love and respect her as a very fine person and teacher. I was delighted when her former pupils were asked to send a short biography and a photograph for a compendium that was to be presented to her on her 80th birthday. I was especially pleased because it was just after I appeared in Who's Who? and I included a copy of my entry.

I persevered with the correspondence classes and had the great privilege of being confirmed by Rabbi Dr Israel Mattuck on Sunday 28 April 1946. The ceremony was held in the Montefiore Hall as the main Sanctuary was not in use because of a bomb which fell through the roof of the main building in 1940. My fellow confirmees included Jo Kessler, Ann Kirk, Anthony Levy, Peter Nathan (Michael's brother), Michael Salmon and the Sampson twins, Bettina and Michael; Jo, Ann and Michael are still active in the synagogue. This was Rabbi Mattuck's last Confirmation class. He had retired the year before and was the Rabbi Emeritus.

My sister Josephine was confirmed in 1943, together with Jean Jaffa (née Gluckstein), Pamela Vos (née Heilbuth) and Walter Woyda. Later, my Aunt Nita taught in the Religion School for many years until she moved to Brighton, where she continued teaching in the Brighton and Hove Progressive Synagogue.

I was at Harrow School. The School song is 'Forty Years On', so I thought it would be appropriate for the 1946 Confirmation class to have a reunion in 1986. On Saturday 26 April, John Rayner, with my assistance, arranged a lovely service. Several of us read and John gave a sermon entitled 'The Fourth Freedom' – this was during *Pesach*. That evening, Maureen and I hosted a supper at home: seven fellow confirmees, including Elizabeth Lewsen, came, together with John and Jane Rayner, Dorothy Edgar, Ruth Ive, Maxwell Stern and Michael Cross.

The question arose about what should happen sixty years on. With Rabbi Alexandra Wright's help, we were planning a further reunion for the 1946 confirmees but, quite rightly, she suggested that we should expand the group to include all those confirmed in the 1940s. Everyone that could be contacted was invited, and a service was held on 29 April 2006. Fifteen former confirmees took part, Rabbi Alexandra preached and a special *Kiddush* took place afterwards.

There is a happy example of family continuity. My eldest son Adam, who was born in 1963, was confirmed in 1979. Six of the confirmees that year were children of my Confirmation Class: Edward Kessler, Charles Levy, Andrew Salmon, Adam Roe, and Bettina Samson's twins, Deborah and Simon Pantel. My second son, Michael Felix Edward, was confirmed in 1981, and Miriam Lucy, in 1984.

In 1950 there was a youth conference at the LJS entitled, 'The Future of Liberal Judaism', with Walter Woyda as Chairman. There were three speakers: John Rayner from Emmanuel College, Cambridge, Herbert Richer from University College, London (both of whom became rabbis) and myself from Oriel College, Oxford. Rabbi Mattuck summed up and I recall that Lily Montagu was sitting at the high table.

In those days, it was thought by some that I might become a rabbi, and I may have disappointed one or two people. However, perhaps I was partly responsible for one rabbi. At Oxford, I met Michael Leigh, who was a member of the Oxford Union where we used play chess and discuss Judaism. Michael came from an Orthodox background, but we started to write letters to the ULPS Newsletter about Liberal religions. At this time I became friendly with John Rayner, who wrote scholarly replies to our letters. I believe that writing these letters prompted Michael to start thinking about the rabbinate; he and Lionel Blue were the first students to graduate from Leo Baeck College. Michael went on to become an influential Reform rabbi.

Leslie Edgar encouraged me to form a Liberal Jewish group at Oxford, which I did with like-minded people such as Denis Glaser, Ian Grant and Michael Rich. I insisted that this group should be part of, and not separate from, the University Jewish Society. We held meetings on a wide variety of subjects and a Liberal rabbi sometimes came to speak to us. In July 1951, there was a World Union for Progressive Judaism Congress at West London Synagogue where Rabbi Dr Leo Baeck was one of the speakers. I was one of the stewards and I remember shaking his hand! Another important speaker was Martin Buber.

During my long membership of the LJS, I was Chairman of the Younger Members' Organisation in 1962. In that year we held a major fundraising event as part of the synagogue's Golden Jubilee Appeal. We arranged a film show at the Institut Français in Kensington. We showed the classic silent film *The General* with Buster Keaton, accompanied by Arthur Dulay on the pianoforte and then *The Red Balloon*. Muriel Trent was the Secretary and Kenneth Solomons the Treasurer, but we had help from many others including Hugh Isaacs, my predecessor as Chairman. I believe that we raised enough money to purchase the chandeliers in the new Montefiore Hall. In those days the YMO was a flourishing and vital organisation with a paid-up membership and regular events throughout the year, which included an annual *Chanukkah* service and dinner which, as I recall, regularly attracted well over fifty young people.

At about that time, Bernard Lawton was Chairman of the House Committee and he invited me to join the Committee. Later Bob Kirk asked me to succeed him as Chairman of the Education Committee, which I chaired from 1974 to 1986. That was in the days before we had a Director of Education and I had a most enjoyable and productive time. David Goldstein was closely involved and one of the issues that came up whilst I was Chairman was that several children were leaving the Religion School because their families wished them to have a *Bar Mitzvah*. We drew up some pretty strict rules, which we presented to Council, if it was decided to introduce *B'nei Mitzvah*. I recall saying to Council that these rules should be adhered to. However, since those days they have been very much relaxed.

I always tried to sit next to Peter Rossiter at Council meetings because he wrote very amusing notes and limericks during the meetings. On one occasion, the Council was considering the syllabus used in the Religion School, but it was clear that many were not very interested in the subject. John Rayner and Rabbi Bernard Hooker had recently written a book published by Penguin Books, and Peter suggested to the Council that the children should 'p-p-pick up a Penguin'! (At that time there was a television advertisement for chocolate biscuits, which used the phrase 'p-p-pick up a Penguin'.) I was invited by Peter Lazarus, then Chairman of the Council, to help interview two rabbis for the position of Associate Rabbi, following the departure of Rabbi Goldstein. They were very informal interviews – just Peter Lazarus, Maxwell Stern (the Treasurer) and myself. David Goldberg was selected; clearly it was a *fait accompli* and the interviews were hardly necessary.

Since those days, I have been involved with various committees, including the Area Groups, the Keep in Touch Group, and the Library. I have also been quite active outside of the LJS with the ULPS, as it used to be called. Having been on the ULPS Development Committee, Maureen and I were involved in starting the Beds/Herts congregation (now the Bedfordshire Progressive). The driving force was Sidney Brichto, together with Rosita Rosenberg. I wrote a letter to the JC announcing there would be a meeting in St Albans Town Hall for those interested (this was about forty years ago) and the congregation was formed with Cedric Rigal as its first Chairman. We held services in members' homes, and the Religion School was held at Francis Bacon Grammar School in St Albans. Maureen was a teacher in the school's early days. Among those she taught was Rachel Benjamin, who became a rabbi, and Jennie Isaacs, now married to Bob and Ann Kirk's son, David. One of my other interests was chairing the *Doroteinu* Group, an ULPS inter-generational project.

A major reason for my continuing affection and involvement with the LJS was the wonderful support given to Maureen and me. We first met Rabbis Philip Cohen and John Rayner in 1957, and Maureen was fast-tracked in her conversion course by these lovely people to enable us to get married in America in 1958. The Organising Secretary, Peggy Lang, who was previously Rabbi Mattuck's secretary, welcomed Maureen and was a great support in her decision to convert to Judaism. When we returned home in 1959, we were totally welcomed and the LJS became our spiritual family.

Maureen was involved in the Women's Society as Treasurer when Doreen Gluckstein, Dora Wolchover and Ruth Ive were in the Chair. With Rosemary Lazarus, she cooked for the monthly lunches under the strict supervision of Annie Loeffy, and she helped design the kitchen during the rebuilding. She did some of the needlework on the *bimah* chairs and acted as Treasurer for the project. Later she was asked to join the United Charities Fund and, for many years, was the House Treasurer of Peggy Lang House. Maureen derived enormous pleasure from singing in the Members' Choir and made many friends. Outside the LJS, Maureen served for twenty-three years as an adviser in the Citizens Advice Bureau and she edited the local Talking Newspaper for the Blind.

We produced three children, who all went to the LJS Religion School. Adam, our eldest, was blessed as a baby by Rabbi Chaim Stern, when John Rayner was on sabbatical. Michael was involved in the correspondence classes and received nothing but As and A pluses from Margaret Rigal, who was his teacher. He won a competition for designing a New Year card. Later, Adam's involvement with the LJS included helping to design the first synagogue website. He served on the Council, the Education Committee and the security team. His daughter, Anna, was *Bat Mitzvah* four years ago, prior to her *Kabbalat Torah,* and was the first *Bat Mitzvah* ever in our family. All our children and Anna regularly went to the *Kadimah* Summer Schools. In 2010 Anna was a supervisor at Spring Camp and Lucy's daughters, Poppy and Daisy, went to Spring Camp and *Kadimah.*

In the fifty years of our marriage, there were really only two major crises, both in 1999. That year, our second granddaughter, Poppy, was born very prematurely, and Michael, working for the medical aid NGO Merlin in Liberia, was kidnapped along with five others. Thankfully, these events are now past history.

I recall the many friendships Maureen and I made in the 1960s with the young rabbis who came to the LJS for a short time, particularly Chaim Stern and his wife Susan. Many years later when we were visiting the States with Adam, we made a surprise visit to them. Seeing a sign on the Throughway to the small town of Chappaqua where they lived, we made a detour and asked at a delicatessen if they knew of Chaim Stern. We were directed to the wooden synagogue in the woods, where they were rehearsing for a play, and someone gave us directions to the Stern's home. We were given a great welcome and very soon Chaim and I were back in the deli buying some supper!

The services at the LJS have now become more traditional. Initially I was not overly sympathetic to all these changes. My cousin, Alma Royalton-Kisch, was one of many who castigated our rabbis for introducing more traditional services and rituals, but I found that I could adjust to the new trends, and as I get older I do not mind the more traditional services so much. I really enjoy the fine music we have. I never cover my head unless I am on the *bimah*, but as I look round now many more men are covering theirs. I thought I was going to have problems with the new prayerbooks, but I was so impressed with the High Holyday *Machzor* that, the first year it was used, I wrote to Rabbis Andrew Goldstein and Charles Middleburgh to express my satisfaction and congratulate them on producing such a meaningful and stimulating prayerbook. It was an advance on the prayerbooks written by Rabbi Mattuck on which I had been brought up. We are very fortunate to have such dedicated and gifted liturgists as John Rayner and his successors.

As regards my career: after school, I took up the Byng Scholarship at Oriel College, Oxford, and studied Chemistry with supplementary pharmacology. It was a four-year course and, in spite of spending much time coxing the College and other boats, I satisfied the examiners, obtaining a First Class degree. This led to three years of research for a D. Phil in organic chemistry under Sir Robert Robinson OM, Nobel Laureate. Having had a very sheltered upbringing, I elected to do National Service at the age of twenty-five.

I was, in fact, head-hunted by an intelligence group based at Nuneham Park, just a few miles down the river. To join them, I had to get a commission: I did my officer's training at Eaton Hall with eighteen-year-old infantry men – but I survived! The attraction of Nuneham Park was its proximity to Oxford, which allowed me to continue tutoring some medical undergraduates.

However, another attraction soon arose: Maureen Curtayne was a Wren officer working in Naval Intelligence at Nuneham. The first time I saw her was when I was shown round the site. In the miniature range three ladies in dark blue were lying flat on the ground shooting the tops off bottles – Maureen was one of them! I was pleased to be promoted to Captain for the last few months of my service. I had to be given regular Captain's pay because there were no National Service Captains in the Intelligence Corps, but I did not complain.

Maureen and I had a wonderful summer in 1957 and then I went to the University of Rochester NY to take up a one-year research Fellowship. This was when Maureen decided to change her religion with the intention that we should marry on my return. However, the position that I thought I had back in the UK was not available. Rochester asked me to stay another year and so, with the families' agreement, Maureen sailed to New York where she was, I know, very relieved to see me on the quay. We were very honoured to have been married by Rabbi Philip Bernstein, a very distinguished and much-loved rabbi.

On our return in 1959, I started work in a newly opened Research Institute set up by the American pharmaceutical company, SmithKline and French (SK&F), in Welwyn Garden City. In 1963 I became Head of Chemistry. The great excitement was our work from 1964 to 1977 in discovering and developing the anti-ulcer blockbuster medicine, cimetidine (Tagamet). It is an understatement to say that I was very privileged to have worked with Jim Black who was Head of Pharmacology; Jim, who became Sir James Black OM, Nobel Laureate, came to us from ICI, where he had been responsible for the discovery of beta-blockers.

I ended my career with the company as Director of Chemistry and, along with most of my senior colleagues. I left the company in 1986. One memorable experience was as a participant in a three-week mission from the Department of Health and the UK pharmaceutical industry, which visited the People's Republic of China in 1975 when it was still in the throes of the Cultural Revolution. I gave lectures on the cimetidine story in Peking, as it then was, Shanghai, and Canton and met many interesting scientists. Looking back, the whole trip was somewhat surreal.

Before leaving SK&F, I was fortunate to have been offered a part-time position as Executive Secretary of the Council of Science and Technology Institutes (now the Science Council). Maureen called this my retirement hobby! Although it was a totally different area of work, I had held various positions in the Royal Society of Chemistry and had worked with analysts, biologists, physicians, physicists, chemical engineers, pharmacists and statisticians, which was probably why I got the job. I found it an enjoyable challenge and it brought me to contact with many influential organisations and people in Parliament, universities, research councils, the Civil Service and the European Commission, etc.

Following my 'first retirement' I was a volunteer in our local hospice for fifteen years and, after several years on the Management Committee of Welwyn Hatfield Citizens Advice Bureau, I became Chairman of the Trustees.

Maureen and I were able to take some great holidays all across this wonderful world we inhabit. Our last major holiday was to Fiji and New Zealand. Shortly after our return in February 2007, Maureen was diagnosed with a fatal illness. We told the oncologists that we had to make our Golden Wedding in November 2008. And we did! I have been very fortunate to have shared fifty happy and fulfilling years with such a wonderful friend, wife, mother and grandmother.

See photograph 26.

✡

Tim Sandler

Tim Sandler has been a member of the LJS since 1988. Born in the Soviet Union, he is a former refusenik. He has been a member of the security team and of the LJS Council.

I was born in 1946 in Ufa, capital of Bashkiria, in the Soviet Union. Bashkiria was then, and still is, a republic in the Russian Federation. By the time I was born, the Soviet authorities had managed to suppress religious affiliations for the majority of the Soviet people, but my family was considered Ethnic Jewish by the Soviet regime. My parents were in their forties when I arrived. They already had one son, who was fourteen years older.

My father was orphaned when he was ten years old. He was a teenager when the communists came to power, and he joined the communist movement. After a career in the Red Army, he was sent by the movement to Moscow University to study banking. However, in time, Moscow University was seen to be disloyal to the communist regime, so the whole university – staff and students – were sent to Tashkent, to 'restructure'. This is where my parents met.

Once qualified, my father held several responsible positions in Soviet banks until 1937, the height of the repressions. While he was manager of the Bank of Siberia in Omsk, he was suddenly arrested and imprisoned. The official local paper said he was guilty of financing counter-revolution and was 'an enemy of the people'. My mother and brother were forced out of their home, and had to go to live with my mother's family thousands of miles away. My father was released three years later without ever having had a trial. I still have the document stating that his release did not mean that he wasn't guilty! My parents' fate was common. People were constantly being moved around, so that they would not be able to put down roots anywhere.

At the outbreak of the Second World War, my father was not mobilised due to ill health, but was given employment as a low-level bank clerk. In 1947, when I was a year old, we moved to Vladimir, near Moscow. I don't think my father was allowed to move to Moscow itself. So, I grew up as a son of 'an enemy of the people'. At the same time, there was a lot of anti-Semitism. You had to state your ethnic origin on your documents, even in a kindergarten. I therefore knew I was Jewish, but I didn't know what it meant. I thought it meant some sort of deficiency. I dreamed of being of Russian ethnic origin.

After Stalin's death and the twentieth Communist Party Congress in 1956, my father was rehabilitated. Later still, after Khrushchev and then Brezhnev, the regime got softer, and some Jews were allowed to emigrate to Israel. My father died when I was a nineteen-year-old student, in 1966. My mother died three years later.

My first real encounter with Judaism was while I was a science postgraduate student in Leningrad. I was working in the same laboratory as Grigori Wasserman's brother (at that time Grigori Wasserman was a quite well-known 'refusenik'; he now lives in Israel). Grigori's brother gave me a book translated into Russian and printed in Israel, but originally written for American secular Jews to help them understand the meaning of Judaism. The book was printed on very thin paper, and had been smuggled into the Soviet Union.

The book was Herman Wouk's *This Is My God*. It changed my life by helping me to understand that being Jewish is not a deficiency, but rather, the other way round! I stopped being loyal to the Soviet Union and in 1979 I applied to emigrate to Israel. However, just at this point the Soviet Union invaded Afghanistan, and there was such anti-Soviet feeling in the West that, in retaliation, the Soviets stopped *aliyah*. And that's how I became a 'refusenik'.

I started meeting young Jewish people from the West and met Grigori Wasserman. We used to meet in Grigori's studio apartment, which was searched several times by the KGB, probably to frighten him.

When my application to emigrate was refused, I had no Plan B. I had already given up my job and had no money, even for food. As the Soviet government was allowing elderly Jews with relatives abroad to leave, I started earning some money by helping these people with the bureaucracy involved in leaving the Soviet Union. When this was stopped, I had to learn something else. I learned how to repair cars damaged in accidents, panel beating and spraying. I had to earn my living somehow.

In the meantime, I had started learning English at evening class. One evening, when I went to sit down at my usual desk at the front of the class, I found a girl sitting next to me. She was young and pretty, but as all my thoughts revolved around leaving the Soviet Union, I didn't notice her, and we did not speak to each other for a long time. I think I was a challenge for Maria Glouzman. Eventually we did fall in love, started living together, and had two daughters, Masha and Paulina. Maria was Jewish, but to start with, she was scared that if she married me, her family could lose their jobs.

In January 1987 I received a white postcard from AVIR (Department of Visas and Registrations), a Soviet government department which handled the applications to leave. I'd made my 26th application and the answer was positive. It arrived completely out of the blue. It was a very cold winter – minus 40 degree centigrade – and, like many refuseniks, I had long hair and a beard, which froze!

I made arrangements to leave very quickly. I flew to Vienna on 12 April 1987. My wife and children would join me a year later. I spent one month in Vienna. There, you had choices! If you did not want to go on to Israel, you could apply to emigrate to the United States, Canada or Australia. I applied to go to the US. All those not going on to Israel had to travel to Rome.

I had been on the third plane for Vienna after a gap of several years. Probably the Jewish agencies helping emigrants in Vienna were not completely ready yet. I think the people on the plane before us were attacked by Arab terrorists somewhere in Vienna. For this reason, when we travelled to Rome by night train, we were in the last two carriages with members of *Mossad*, carrying machine-guns. The train stopped before we reached Rome, and our group transferred to coaches in case terrorists had anticipated our arrival.

I was in Rome for about six weeks. We were looked after by HIAS (the Hebrew Immigrant Aid Society), and the American Jewish Joint Distribution Committee. We received some training about life skills in the West, including how to be entrepreneurial! I was granted a Green Card for the US by June and was due to arrive in the US by September 1987. However, I had a cousin in London, and I wanted, if possible, to see him before leaving Europe. HIAS arranged a week's visit to my cousin, even obtaining Italian travel documents for me.

In London, my cousin and his wife were keen for me to stay. They contacted the CBF (the Central British Fund for World Jewish Relief), where Margaret Rigal was Co-Chairman, and explained my situation. A letter was written to the Home Office; the reply was positive. I later learned that I was one of only three people entering the UK from the Soviet Union that year! My family joined me in June 1988. By then, Masha was nearly five, and Paulina two.

I decided that I had to join a synagogue, and my cousin Alex, who lived in Hampstead, recommended that I go to the library to ask for information about synagogues. The librarian said he had no idea, but suggested I look in Yellow Pages. About twenty synagogues were listed. I chose the LJS because it was near to my cousin and because I liked the fact that it was called Liberal. On the phone I was told to come to the LJS before the service one Saturday morning. I still had my beard and my long hair and it was raining. I was stopped by Leslie Kanaber, on security duty, at a distance of about 100 metres! Since then, Leslie and I have become good friends.

My daughters have gone through the LJS Religion School, and they each graduated through *Bat Mitzvah* and *Kabbalat Torah*. My wife and I did security and I sat on Council, but it was a little bit too early for me. My spoken English was not yet good enough. When we first joined the LJS, Rabbi David Goldberg helped me a lot, and Margaret and George Rigal became personal friends. I also feel quite close to Rita Adler.

I always come to the LJS with pleasure. We have a very balanced rabbinical team. Our Senior Rabbi, Alexandra Wright, is excellent, and I like the American approach of Rabbi David Wilfond. Both Rabbis Alex and David are Liberal: they bring Judaism to modern life and develop our approach to God. This approach needs to be alive and always needs to find new ways.

✡

Ellen Schmidt

Ellen Schmidt's parents were refugees from Nazi Germany. As a young person she was involved in the Square One youth group, and later in educational activities. She was Chairman of the Education Committee between 1998 and 2003, Treasurer between 2002 and 2004 and Chairman of the Council between 2002 and 2005. She sings in the Members' Choir.

I was born in St John's Wood and have lived there, or close to it, all my life. My parents, Thilde and Ernst Fraenkel, were both refugees from Nazi Germany. My mother came to England in 1936 when she was thirteen to be educated in a school in Kent founded by a German educationalist, Anna Essinger, who was a relative by marriage. My mother had previously attended a Jewish boarding school near Ulm in Germany. My father came to England in April 1939 on one of the *Kindertransporte*. He discovered only quite recently he was on the same boat from Hamburg as Ann Kirk.[474]

My parents actually knew each other in Germany. They went to the same school for a while, but they had very different backgrounds. My mother's parents, Isidore and Elsa Weil, owned a clothing shop, which my grandmother, a trained milliner and quite a businesswoman, seems to have run because my grandfather was frequently ill as a result of having served in the First World War. My maternal grandparents and my mother's sister all died in concentration camps – my grandmother and my mother's younger sister, Edith, in Auschwitz and my grandfather in Theresienstadt. Fortunately my mother's older brother had come to England as a refugee before the war.

My father's background is more complicated. His father, Ernst Fraenkel, was from a well-off family. He served as a cavalry officer during the First World War for which he was awarded the Iron Cross. After the war, he became involved in left-wing politics, organising Jewish ex-servicemen. He was outspoken against Nazism, and should probably have made arrangements for the safety of his family. However, like many well-assimilated German Jews, perhaps he just did not appreciate the risk, despite having been imprisoned by the Nazis very early on. My father's mother, Margarete, who was not Jewish, was an educated woman. She had a degree, which must have been unusual for a woman at that time. My grandmother ran a school for training nursery school teachers.

My father was one of five children. Three of the four sons came here on *Kindertransporte* (on different boats), but the eldest one went to Argentina. Their sister, Anne Marie, came to England on a visa as a maid. She later worked with Anna Freud, and married an English conscientious objector. The Fraenkel children had quite a liberal upbringing by German upper-middle-class standards, but they did not have a Jewish upbringing. However, with the coming of Hitler they were made only too aware of their origins.

My paternal grandmother was trapped in Germany, but somehow survived the war. My father joined the American Army after the war, in order to be able to go back to Germany and find her before she died in 1947. My grandfather was able to obtain a visa

---

[474] Ann Kirk's memories are recorded later in this part of the book.

and came to live in Belsize Park during the war. He went back to Germany afterwards, married an English woman and became a Professor at Frankfurt University – he was part of the 'New Germany', due to his first wife's pre-war connections.

My parents had what might be called a 'good emigration'. They became a couple when they were quite young, having met again in England through a mutual school friend from Germany. They had many friends in this country in the same situation as themselves – refugees without their families. They were – and are – a strong couple, and supported each other. They were able to deal openly with what had happened to their families, and my younger brother Martin and I always knew of our family's history. We also knew and visited our paternal grandfather in Germany until his death aged eighty.

My parents were not members of a synagogue, but I think that my mother decided that my brother and I should have some Jewish education. My mother, who was a physiotherapist, was recommended to join the LJS by a doctor she knew – Dr Lewsen, whose wife Peggy Lewsen was very involved in the Women's Society and lots of other activities at the synagogue. My mother is more religious than my father, who is definitely an atheist. However, he is very aware of being Jewish and, particularly since his retirement, he has been very involved in Holocaust education through the Wiener Library. He also has strong connections with the University of Haifa. He didn't go to the synagogue much at all until I was confirmed, but he now comes occasionally because of the grandchildren. He always accompanies my mother to synagogue on *Kol Nidre*.

When my brother Martin and I started attending Hebrew classes, Bob and Ann Kirk, Eva Feldman, John Rich and Michael Alpert were doing a lot of the teaching. I liked the atmosphere in the Religion School. I felt very comfortable there. I made friends and felt part of a community. Andy Kirk, Rachel Goldhill, Ann Myers, Penny Hart, Richard Lissack and Charles Kessler were in my class. My brother Martin felt similarly comfortable. He went to the same school (William Ellis) as David Goldstein's son, Joshua, who was at the LJS Religion School at the same time. They are still firm friends. James Kessler and Ben Rayner were also his contemporaries. I learned a lot from Rabbi David Goldstein, who was Principal of the Religion School when I started.

As well as attending Religion School, we went to the *Onegei Shabbat,* which used to be organised by the Women's Society on Friday nights. There were lots of people at them and they had a lovely feeling. I enjoyed being able to go into the kitchen and getting involved in the preparations. It felt very special to be able to do that. My mother came to help, having been encouraged to become involved by Jo Kessler and other parents with children in the Religion School. However, she wasn't part of the crowd that was very active in the synagogue at that time.

I belonged to the Square One youth group, which was purely a social group – just discos and meetings, but no religion! We sometimes met in people's houses. I was aware by this stage that the synagogue was a good place to be. Its rabbis were people of substance, and had lots of influence on the wider Jewish world. It was regarded as being the 'cathedral' of Liberal Judaism.

At that time, it felt as though there were strong social distinctions in the synagogue, especially between the paid staff and the congregation, but also between those established Anglo-Jewish families and others. Those with continental origins had a very low profile and didn't talk about their past. It took me some time to realise that John Rayner came from a similar background. I was just aware that he was very warm towards me, and I felt a sense of affinity with him. I had also noticed that when he came to *Onegei Shabbat* he sang songs to different tunes which I had previously only heard my mother sing. It wasn't until much later that he and others started to talk about their past. Because of their common background, Rabbi Rayner became friendly with my parents.

When I first started going into services at the synagogue, English was used a lot more and many men still wore formal hats rather than *kippot*. There was a ticketing system for High Holyday services. Only long-standing members of the LJS were able to get a seat downstairs in the main synagogue. Others had to go to the overspill services held at Porchester Hall. We felt like second-class citizens and it took some time to graduate even to sitting upstairs in the gallery at the synagogue, let alone downstairs.

I went to Camden School for Girls, and then went on to Bristol University where I studied Law. I was less involved in the synagogue as a young adult, only coming back for High Holydays. For a while, I stayed in touch with Penny Hart, with whom I had become close in the Religion School. I did see Mike Beral (whom I also knew from Religion School), as he was at Bristol University. He later married Penny.

I met Richard at university and eventually we got married. Our wedding took place in a registry office, partly because neither of our fathers would have wanted us to have a religious ceremony! Actually, nor would either of us at that stage. My mother would have liked us to have a blessing, and she did get this in a funny sort of way. She happened to meet David Goldberg in St John's Wood High Street one day and mentioned it. He said a blessing for us there and then in the street!

Richard's background is not dissimilar to mine. His mother Sylvia was not Jewish (she came from a non-conformist background), but his father, Hans, was and took him to an Orthodox synagogue on the High Holydays. Hans came from Germany in 1939 on a visa sponsored by Marks and Spencer. During the war, he was sent by the War Agricultural Committee to work in Cumbria, where he met Sylvia, who was a teacher there. They later married and moved to Watford, where Richard was brought up. He positively opted into Judaism once we had children and is a member of the LJS.

After leaving university, I became articled to Tim Simon, and trained at his firm, Birkbeck Montagu's, in Ludgate Circus where I stayed for several years after I qualified as a solicitor, eventually becoming a partner. I got to that firm because of synagogue connections. My mother happened to sit next to Tim's mother at a meeting of the London Society of Christians and Jews and mentioned to her that I was looking for a summer job while I was at university. Margot Simon arranged for me to meet Tim. I worked for him for two summers, and was subsequently invited back for my Articles.

I became involved with the synagogue again when my own children went to the Religion School, which they started at the age of eight. I found the Religion School very different from when I had attended it. There were many more classes, and everything was a lot more informal. Some parents were not particularly committed to ensuring their children had a good Jewish education. They just saw the LJS as a safe place for their children to be when they were busy on a Saturday morning. There was, by now, a paid Head Teacher and the rabbis weren't so involved.

Because of concerns expressed by some parents, Stanley Baker, then Chairman of the Education Committee, called an open meeting to seek our feedback. I was quite vocal, and so Stanley said I should join the Education Committee! I did, and within a year I became Chairman because Stanley wanted to step down. In this role I worked closely with Helen Freeman, who had by this time become Principal of the Religion School. We decided to establish the post of Director of Education and Michael Hart, Sue Head and I appointed Jan Roseman. Within a short time she had made a real difference not only in improving standards in the Religion School, but in Jewish learning generally. She introduced the adult education programme, now being led by Alexandra Wright, and also family education activities.

Jan took the *Bar/Bat Mitzvah* classes in hand and put them on a proper footing. They had been introduced because of demand from the congregation, many of whom felt that Confirmation/*Kabbalat Torah* at age sixteen was not sufficient. Some people were leaving the synagogue because there were no *B'nei Mitzvah,* and others were not joining. Some people came to the LJS because they had married non-Jewish partners, but they wanted to retain some of the Orthodox practices they were used to. Jan felt that if we were going to do *B'nei Mitzvah*, then we were going to do them well, and she began to teach the young people on a one-to-one basis. My elder daughter, Tamara, was amongst the first group of children to have a *Bat Mitzvah* under Jan's regime, and her Hebrew was good enough for her to read from the scroll translating as she went along, rather than reading from a prepared script. David Goldberg gave people space to develop and Jan flourished in that environment and, consequently, the Religion School did too.

As a result of my involvement in the Education Committee, I was encouraged by Bob Kirk to stand for Council, which I did. Trevor Moross and then Tim Simon were the successive Chairmen of Council when I first joined. I served as Treasurer for a year with Tony Yablon before Michael Hart took over this role and I became Chairman.

During the time that I have been involved with the synagogue, I have got to know several of the rabbis. David Goldstein was very intellectual and 'dreamy', but very friendly and accessible. I was very fond of John Rayner. He came across as being a bit aloof because he was quite shy. He was a little intimidating because he was so intelligent. He had some quite traditional views on certain issues, such as abortion, which I recall being angry about when I was a teenager. I remember David Goldberg from my teenage years. He and Carole had a flat in Belsize Park and they used to invite groups of young people to go there to talk about topical issues. It was fun, but I don't recall ever saying a word!

I have seen the role of women in the synagogue change through the years. They were always involved in volunteering and 'good works', and there have been some very powerful women who have had very influential roles, such as Margaret Rigal's involvement with the refuseniks. Some women, like Jo Kessler, Ann Kirk, Ann Hart and others, were very active in the community and some of them still are. The committees used to be quite male-dominated, but now women are very involved in decision-making, and take on more roles beyond those relating to education and welfare. Ironically, it is now quite hard to recruit men to take an active role in synagogue committees and on the Council.

The synagogue is much more egalitarian generally than it used to be. There is much less separation between the congregation and the rabbis, perhaps because many members are at least as well-educated secularly as the rabbis, and are at the top of their own professions. The changing make-up of the membership of the synagogue reflects changes in society at large. In particular, many of the families joining over recent years have one Jewish and one non-Jewish parent.

I am aware of how services are changing. There was a shift to using more Hebrew when John Rayner was Senior Rabbi, and that trend has continued under Alexandra Wright. Music has become more important, and is of a very high standard. Cathy Heller Jones has really put it on a professional footing. There are some very fine soloists, and it is a great pleasure to listen to the professional choir.

The synagogue is now a much busier place than it was. If you went into the building during the week it used to be very quiet, but now there is always something happening. The Nursery School in particular has brought it alive during the day. However, we are not doing enough to attract and keep young adults, which is concerning for the future. The Religion School is much bigger and there is a large cohort of parents who are involved in synagogue life through the PTA and security rota, but unfortunately we don't seem to be able to hold on to many of these families once the children have completed their schooling.

In recent years, the volunteer efforts of the synagogue seem to have largely focussed on the elderly. There is fantastic provision for this age group, and we should be proud of that. But looking forward, I would like to see this same energy applied lower down the age scale too, so that the membership and community can continue to flourish in the future.

Tamara Schmidt

Tamara Schmidt is a third-generation member of the LJS. She attended the Religion School, where she subsequently worked as an Assistant Teacher. She has been involved in LJY Netzer (the Liberal Jewish youth movement) as both a participant and a leader, most recently leading Kayitz.

I was born on 6 March 1988. My involvement with the LJS goes back to my maternal grandmother, Thilde Fraenkel, who is now in her late eighties. When I come to the synagogue with my grandmother, it's like coming with the Queen, as she knows everyone. My grandmother is very different from my mum in that my grandmother has never been on any committees, but she has always been active in the community.

My mother, Ellen Schmidt, went through Religion School and had her Confirmation at the LJS. She is still friends with many of her classmates. My mum taught at the Religion School until she went to Bristol University to study Law. She met my dad, Richard Schmidt, at Bristol – he was a fellow Law student.

My dad's father was a Jewish refugee from Germany. He married my grandma, who was born in Wales, and became an English teacher. My paternal grandfather did not keep up his involvement with Judaism and didn't bring my dad up as Jewish. When my mum met my father, she naturally assumed a student by the name of Schmidt must be a nice Jewish boy!

I have two younger siblings: Matthew, who is now twenty, and Isabel, who is sixteen. We started being involved in LJS children's activities from when we were quite little. Dad used to bring us most of the time, although he didn't attend services. He eventually ended up on the LJS security rota – I think he loves it.

When I started Religion School at the age of eight, I was put in a class of six- to seven-year-olds, as I couldn't read Hebrew. Every Saturday we coloured in a different letter of the Hebrew alphabet. My mum spent the whole year trying to convince Gill Fisher, the Head Teacher of the Religion School at the time, to move me up a class. In the end, I just started going into the eight-year-olds' class. My mum complained so much that she was told that she might as well join the Education Committee. Then she was told she might as well chair it! Eventually, she came to chair the whole LJS Council.

Religion School was much more relaxed at this time, and many people preferred it that way, but it was quite shambolic and 'do-it-yourself'. Then Jan Roseman was appointed Head Teacher. That definitely shook things up!

I learned a lot at Religion School, where there were a number of very good teachers. I was in a really good group, and ten to fifteen of us worked towards our *B'nei Mitzvah* together. My *Bat Mitzvah* was one of my two acts of teenage rebellion in that I asked to have one! My mum was opposed to a *Bat Mitzvah*, as it went against the LJS ethos, but all the Jewish girls in my year-group at school were having them, so I wanted one as well. I had lessons with Jan Roseman for six months – it was brilliant! Jan and I wrote our own translation, and because it was my own, I remembered it really well. My portion was extremely boring; it was about the clothes the High Priest wears. So, my commentary was about shopping! There was a great sermon from Rabbi Goldberg, all about what fun my grandparents are.

I was the subject of lots of changes and experiments at Religion School when I was about fourteen. I was in quite a large class and we trialled a new timetable. Everyone studied Hebrew, but then you could choose between two to three options, such as Israeli Dancing. We had a great time, but we just ran riot.

My class at Religion School was the last one to have *Kabbalat Torah* at sixteen. Now, it is held when you are fifteen, so that it doesn't clash with GCSEs. This change meant that my class celebrated their KT in April, and the year below followed in June of the same year. Therefore, we formed an enormous KT group. Many of us are still in touch with each other. Two of my closest friends, Gabi Frankl and Gabby Wright, were in my KT class – Gabi and I had been in the same class since we were about eight, and Gabby joined us when Alexandra became Senior Rabbi.

The KT group had two weekends away. The first was in Oxfordshire at a retreat for monks. It was freezing cold, but great fun. The food was horrible, so all we ate were chocolates and crisps. The second weekend away was in Amsterdam. The hostel we stayed in was in the red light district and had a nightclub downstairs. We had the Saturday service in the nightclub. In the centre of the club was a tinted glass box with a pole in the middle and we sat round it for the service. It was surreal. We were allowed to go to the nightclub one night, providing we didn't drink. Needless to say, at least two members of the group were caught with a pint in their hands.

The KT service was an amazing experience. It was so interesting to listen to each other's speeches. For me the speech that stands out the most was Vic Feinstein's, which was really honest, insightful and funny. Five of us from the KT group signed up to go on the Israel tour with LJY [Liberal Jewish Youth] at the end of that year, which was a great way to end the process.

My other act of teenage rebellion was leaving South Hampstead High School at the age of sixteen. I had been there for eleven years and had ceased to enjoy it. I made fantastic friends, but felt I had outgrown it. My gran had gone to boarding school, and I had always wanted to go too. So we visited quite a few boarding schools, but in the end I decided against it. I was lucky as, instead, I got a scholarship to Highgate School – it was the year the school had gone co-educational. I loved it there and went on to do really well.

I taught in the Religion School for over two years until I finished school. I considered my work at the LJS was finished, but I have been back twice during summer holidays – when I had no money – to help out in the office.

After a gap year, I went to Birmingham University to study English. There is a really big JSoc at Birmingham, but I wasn't involved. I felt that I didn't want to be defined as Jewish, as that's not how I define myself. However, I was 'outed' to my flatmates within two days of arriving by a Jewish boy with whom my flatmates and I had made friends. Thereafter, my defining characteristic was being Jewish, in the same way that another flatmate was 'the blonde one'. While at Birmingham, I was asked by Rabbi Margaret Jacobi if I'd like to teach in Birmingham Progressive Synagogue's Religion School, and I went on to teach there during my second and third years.

In my last year at Birmingham, LJY rang me and asked if I would act as a leader for them, so I did. I had an absolute whale of a time. This is ironic since, as a child, I had resisted all my mum's attempts to send me to *Kadimah*! I led for LJY the next summer too and also during the year. This summer, I led on their Europe tour. It was brilliant.

I am very fond of the LJS. I have a lot of memories, and I have made so many friends through the synagogue. However, I am trying not to be too involved. I don't think my mum or I want there to be a Schmidt female dynasty! But I was in the synagogue for three weeks in the summer helping to archive building plans in the basement. There are a few of us who are currently seen, for better or worse, as the 'voice of youth'. However, I find myself agreeing to do things when I'm asked and I also enjoy the odd bit of reading in services. I imagine I'll stay involved with the LJS, and I hope that it'll continue evolving as I've seen it evolve over the past years.

Carolyn Simon

Carolyn Simon taught in the Religion School in the 1980s and co-ordinated the Keep in Touch Group from 1991 until 2006. Here she shares not only her own reminiscences of the LJS, but also memories handed down by her parents and grandparents.

My name is Carolyn Simon, née Leuw, and I was born in 1960. I am fourth-generation LJS. My maternal great-grandparents joined in the early days. My grandparents were married there in 1932 and my parents in 1958.

When Michael Simon proposed to me in 1993, I said yes, provided we could have our wedding at the LJS! However, Michael was interested in us also having an Orthodox *ketubbah*. This necessitated a trip to the headquarters of the United Synagogue (then at Woburn House) to prove that I was halachically Jewish. Rabbi Julian Shindler rummaged through the record books, culminating in the 'eureka' moment when he found the entry for my maternal great-grandparents, Alfred and Rose Edgar, who, we learned, had married in the Western Synagogue (now Marble Arch Synagogue), in 1904.

Soon after the LJS was founded, my great-grandparents became members and that was where my grandma and her siblings went to Sunday School. I remember my grandmother telling me that John Slater (known to me as Sergeant Stone in the television programme *Z Cars*) and Maxwell Stern had been in the same class, and that she had laid a brick in the wall of the then new synagogue building. The other thing she told me was that they had a teacher who always wore dresses with buttons from collar to hem. My grandma would pass the time counting the buttons.

Alfred Edgar (originally Etgart) had been something of an adventurer before he married. My mother still has a couple of books he brought back from South Africa, full of photos of semi-dressed African women. Soft porn posing as anthropology! However, he settled down with his family in the Kensal Green area, where he had a draper's shop. Alfred and Rose had five children. The youngest, Phyllis, died in 1926 when she was only fourteen or fifteen. The others were Leslie, Dudley, Irene and Jessie (my grandma), who was known as Jackie.

We have a wonderful photo of a grand LJS dinner at the Savoy in 1930, celebrating the 5th anniversary of the laying of the cornerstone of the new building. The four young Edgars are in the foreground. Leslie, of course, went on to become Rabbi Leslie Edgar. For some reason, Auntie Irene found this difficult. When I was growing up she gave that as the explanation as to why she no longer belonged to the LJS. However, she was a regular helper at the Darby and Joan Club and Restaurant Tuesday Lunches. As she and her Russian-French-Jewish husband, Benia Gerchenovitch, lived round the corner from the synagogue, in Maida Vale, she would invite us to lunch every *Yom Kippur* after the morning service, on the basis that my brother and I were too young to fast. She, on the other hand, didn't attend the service, but would just serve us the meal without eating herself.

I remember going to High Holyday services as a child, and looking down from the balcony at the congregation below. Given the family precedents, I wondered whether my future husband was sitting down there somewhere. At the end of the service Uncle Leslie, in black robes and biretta, would, with fatherly presence, stretch out his arms to bless the congregation.

Like Margaret Rigal,[475] I have a vague memory of visiting the *sukkah* when I was little, and being given a piece of fruit. Apart from the High Holydays, the only other time I remember coming to the LJS in the 1960s was to board a coach to the London Palladium. My parents had read in the newsletter that free tickets for the pantomime dress rehearsal were being offered to LJS members, courtesy of Sir Lew Grade. We saw a wonderful production of *Aladdin*, starring Cilla Black, Leslie Crowther and Alfred Marks.

---

[475] See Margaret Rigal's memories later in this part of the book.

The first Jewish book I ever read was a children's version of the *Shema*, by Uncle Leslie, with illustrations in black and red. It was a significant influence on my nascent Jewish soul. But oddly it was a gift from the other side of the family, from my paternal grandfather, Cyril Leuw.

Our branch of the Leuw family came from Holland in 1860. We have a copy of an official document dating back to 1811, recording our ancestor Abraham Levie's change of name to Abraham Leuw. The family were meat traders, and although originally it was the cattle trade that caused Abraham's son Marcus to settle here, throughout much of the twentieth century the Leuw business at Smithfield sold pork! Cyril, however, eschewed the family firm, leaving his younger brother Maurice to take it over. In the 1920s he entered the brave new world of the motor car and went on to become the owner of the Mayfair Carriage Company, with showrooms and petrol stations in Colindale and Canons Corner, Edgware. In time, his sons Bob and David would also follow him into the motor trade.

Cyril was a tall, good-looking young man. Apparently a tailoring company gave him suits for free, by way of advertising. In 1927 he eloped with a lovely Irish Catholic woman called Florence Prangnell and they had a registry office wedding. Because he knew and liked the rabbi, Maurice Perlzweig, Cyril subsequently brought Florence to The Liberal Jewish Synagogue to discuss the possibility of a conversion. Mr Duparc asked Florence why she wanted to convert to Judaism. She replied, 'I'm doing it for my husband.' This wasn't considered a satisfactory response, and Florence was sent away.

Cyril and Florence agreed between themselves that, if their first child was a boy, all their children would be brought up Jewish. If the first child was a girl, all the children would be brought up Catholic. In 1930 my father, Robert Leuw (known as Bob), was born. As a child he attended Dennington Park Synagogue with his grandfather, Sidney Leuw, but he didn't have a *Bar Mitzvah*.

In 1932 Jackie Edgar married Bernard Banes. Bernard was the third of seven children. His father, Jacob Baneshik, had come from Krakow when a teenager. Jacob married his cousin, a Manchester Jewess called Esther Weisgard, and changed his name to Jack Banes. Soon after my grandfather was born, the family moved south, initially to Ilford and then to Muswell Hill. Apparently the air quality was one reason they chose this high part of London, as my grandfather had had rheumatic fever. When their first house was demolished to make way for the Muswell Hill Odeon, they moved to 255 Creighton Avenue.

Jack Banes was a furrier. Although Bernard wanted to be a doctor or a lawyer, family finances had meant higher education was out of the question, and he was required to go into the family business. After a few years, he extricated himself from this, and for most of his working life he was a confectionery trade representative. This may not have been his ideal vocation, but in the 1960s it pleased his grandchildren, as there were always chocolate brazils and hazelnut clusters in his dining room cupboard.

The Banes family attended Muswell Hill synagogue. My grandfather learned to read Hebrew fluently, though not to understand it. As a young man, he grew to detest certain Orthodox practices (such as paying money for *aliyot*), so he joined the LJS. His parents, along with all their other children – Ruth, Lionel, Wilfred, Stella, Stanley and Laura – followed him there. Leafing through the diaries of Alumni rambles in the 1930s, I found Wilfred Banes frequently Mentioned in Dispatches.

After their marriage, Bernard Banes and Jackie Edgar lived in East End Road, Finchley, for the rest of their lives. They had two daughters, Shirley (my mother) and Hilary, who went to the convent school up the road on the site now occupied by the Sternberg Centre. There's a quite different school there now – Akiva – and my son is one of its pupils. My mother received her religious education by correspondence course. Her teacher was Bessie Hayes who, according to mummy, was a lovely, warm lady who wore tea cosy hats and very long earrings. She wrote her comments in purple ink, and was always very complimentary and encouraging. Bessie's son was another person who had been at religion school with my grandma!

Mummy was an active member of the Alumni Society. We have another wonderful photo which shows her and Hilary at a *Chanukkah* dinner held in the Montefiore Hall in the early 1950s. In those days (to quote my dad), the Alumni was 'an excellent social club and marriage agency'. Fellow Alumnite Phillip Leuw brought along his cousin Bob … and that was how my parents met.

Because daddy's mother wasn't Jewish, and he had not had a *Bar Mitzvah*, my parents were advised to have a civil marriage as well as a Liberal Jewish one, to make sure they were legally married. My father was also required to have a series of one-to-one lessons with the Rev. Philip Cohen. Of necessity, this was something of a crash course, as the wedding date had already been set for 26 August 1958 and it was only on 21 July that the synagogue told my parents that there were problems with my father's Jewish status.

I grew up in Stanmore, in the house where my parents still live. Until I was about ten, we belonged, fairly nominally, to the LJS. Then in around 1970 my parents' friend, Hugh Isaacs, was instrumental in setting up a local 'satellite', the Stanmore Liberal Jewish Congregation. My parents joined, and my brother Marc and I were sent to the Religion School. One of my teachers was Celia Rapp; another was the congregation's first rabbi, Alan Mann, who was also briefly an Associate Minister at the LJS. I remember thinking that if people like these believed in Liberal Judaism, it must be a good thing.

My Confirmation service took place in a local community hall, on the same day as Marc's *Bar Mitzvah* (how economical!). In time, the congregation acquired a building (with my dad helping with the DIY) and a new name: Hertsmere Progressive Congregation. It's now the Liberal Synagogue, Elstree, which gives more of a clue as to its location. I went on the 'Senior Kadimah' holiday that Alan Mann led in the Peak District. This was a seminal moment, as it introduced me to ULPSNYC, the Liberal Jewish youth movement, and to a bunch of teenagers who were to become lifelong friends. I became 'Jewish Awareness Officer' on the ULPSNYC executive and, on the advice of the ULPS *sh'licha*, *Nurit Be'er*, spent half of my gap year at the Hebrew University of Jerusalem. Here I met my great friend Vivien Rose. Thereafter, Vivien and I were at Cambridge together, and helped run 'Prog Soc', the university's Progressive Jewish group.

I was a youth leader on several ULPSNYC weekends while a student but, when I returned to London, I felt I should graduate to a more mature kind of role. Rabbi Julia Neuberger, who had been an inspirational overseer while I was in ULPSNYC, invited me to teach at the South London Liberal Synagogue Religion School, which I did quite happily for a while, and learned a very useful route from Marylebone (where I lived) to the hitherto uncharted territory of Streatham. But when I bought a flat in East Finchley, the journey was no longer feasible.

At Michael Hart's suggestion, I switched to teaching at the LJS. Rather confusingly, John Rich – who was the Head Teacher at South London on Sunday mornings – turned out to teach at the LJS on Saturdays as well. My students included Emily and Rupert Goldberg, Robyn Paiba, Richard Moross, Ben Wiseman, Jonathan Grade, Bertie Albert (who is now married to Jonathan) and Rachael Young. One morning, Jonathan, Bertie and Rachael's class were so badly behaved that I walked out, and took myself along the corridor (upstairs in the old building) to an empty classroom. Fortunately Rachael and a friend had the guts to come and seek me out and apologise!

I liked the LJS so much that, after a gap of some twelve years or so, I rejoined, now as an adult member in my own right. When I changed careers from publishing to management consultancy, I found I needed my weekends to recuperate and gave up teaching in the Religion School. By this time, I had done a foundation course for religion school teachers at Leo Baeck College. I remember Hannah Jacobs coming along to the LJS to present me with my certificate (which I still have, dated 1986). Who'd have guessed that years later I would be a faculty member of Leo Baeck College myself? Since 2002 I have taught the personal and professional development module on the College's Advanced Diploma programme.

It feels a great privilege to have belonged to the LJS for at least some of the years when John Rayner was preaching there. His sermons were consistently brilliant, both in their structure and content. The message was always profoundly humane. The line that stays with me to this day is: 'As God loves all His creatures, so should we'. His voice would have been a pleasure to listen to even if he had been reading telephone directories.

Although Michael and I were married at the LJS, we brought along our own rabbis – my close friends Michael Shire and Marcia Plumb – to conduct the ceremony. So the only time, happily, that (so far) I have needed LJS rabbinic support in a quite personal way was when my grandfather died. Rabbi Helen Freeman was marvellous. By this time I had set up the Keep in Touch Group (KIT) and attended some bereavement support training. But it was moving to be on the receiving end of Helen's pastoral expertise, and to experience what it felt like to be given space to talk about the details of organising the funeral and to be listened to attentively and compassionately.

Apart from running KIT from 1991 to 2006 and introducing Vivien to the synagogue, my other significant contribution has been to bring my husband Michael into the LJS's orbit. He has a religious background that spans membership of Federation, Reform and United synagogues, and insists that he is not really a Liberal with a capital L. Nevertheless, for thirteen long years he devoted great chunks of his time to helping the synagogue administer its finances. Michael is a chartered accountant by profession, so this role represented something of a busman's holiday. I know he gained far more satisfaction from his pseudo-rabbinic activities, which have included designing and running two adult *B'nei Mitzvah* programmes, a *Talmud* class and an alternative *Kol Nidre* service, as well as leading and participating in services.

Arguably, Michael's most creative contribution was as the instigator of 'Red *Kippah* Day' in March 1996, inspired by and coinciding with Comic Relief's 'Red Nose Day'. 152 red silk *kippot* were sold in advance, raising over £1,000 for the synagogue. That

Shabbat, the Sanctuary was a sea of red *kippot*. David Rigal sportingly raised extra money by dying his beard bright red. A couple of splendid photos appeared in the newsletter.

When our son Reuben was born, it really felt as though we were reaping the benefit of our involvement with the LJS. The congregation was clearly delighted on our behalf, and we were overwhelmed by the number of cards we received from LJS members. Margaret Rigal (who had already given me helpful advice to do with breastfeeding, involving surgical spirit) popped round almost immediately, and Rosemary Lazarus knitted a beautiful cream wool blanket. Reuben's baby blessing was held at the LJS in December 2002, conducted with grace, warmth and charm by Rabbi Kathleen Middleton.

While Reuben was little, the 4Cs (Community Care Co-ordination Committee) meetings were held in my dining room. If Reuben was grizzling, Jo Kessler would rummage in her handbag and keep him entertained with her car keys. Once Alexandra Wright became Senior Rabbi, she came to our meetings too. Although she has a reputation for being quite earnest, glimpses of her sense of humour would be discernible. I was actually already acquainted with this side of Alex, as our paths had crossed socially about twenty-five years earlier. In fact I remember being at a dinner party hosted by David Kirk at the end of the seventies when Alex, who was working as a teacher, confided in me that what she'd really like to do was to become a rabbi. In our 4Cs meetings, Alex, like Liz Crossick, our Community Care Co-ordinator, laid great stress on confidentiality. Alex was also very emphatic about the Jewish concept of *l'shon ha-ra* (not speaking ill of anyone). I like to think that I have become a slightly better person as a result.

Indeed, the ways I have benefited from my involvement with the LJS are numerous: not just spiritually and socially, but from coming alongside some great role models. I served on two Rabbinic Appointments Committees under Bernie Bulkin, and, albeit briefly, on the Olga Field Committee under Trevor Moross. Both Bernie and Trevor were quite brilliant at chairing meetings, combining charisma, gravitas and a clear sense of direction. When I'm in a meeting nowadays and hear myself saying: 'May I make a suggestion?' I know I owe a debt to Trevor. I am also a big fan of Rita Adler; I admire her directness, courage and energy to get things done. People like Ann and Bob Kirk, Jo Kessler and Margaret Rigal are wonderful human beings and it is a privilege to know them.

See photograph 36 (Shirley Banes, later Leuw).

✡

Tim Simon

Tim Simon is a lifelong member of the LJS. Like his father and grandfather before him, he was an Honorary Treasurer of the synagogue. He has also been Chairman of the LJS Council, Honorary Solicitor and Chief Steward. He is now a Trustee and Chairman of the United Charities Fund.

Both my paternal and maternal grandparents, Julian and Florence Simon and Stanley and Dorothy Cohen, were founder members of the LJS. My father's grandfather, Julius, had come to England from Celle in the Kingdom of Hanover in 1850. The family of his mother, Florence, had been here since the eighteenth century. In addition to the passport issued to Julius by the Kingdom of Hanover, I have his Certificate of Naturalisation dated 21 November 1870, together with his Oath of Allegiance to Her Majesty Queen Victoria, her Heirs and Successors. At that time, the family lived in Bayswater.

I also have a bound copy of *Werther* by Goethe, translated by Julius into French. It was written in Paris as he passed through on his way to London where he settled. It is in longhand in a beautiful script, and is dedicated to 'Madame E Oulemann née Cohen'. I have no idea who she was, but she certainly was not Eliza Leon, whom he subsequently married!

Florence's father was Hyman Montagu, who founded the firm of solicitors of which my father was in due course a partner, and which I joined in the early 1960s. Hyman Montagu was a great scholar, linguist, entomologist and, above all, a numismatist. He gave a large part of his collection to the British Museum and, when he died, his collection of coins and medals was sold over three days at Sothebys. About ten years ago, I had cause to take a medal of his to the British Museum and, when they heard that I was a descendant of Hyman Montagu, they got most excited and reached immediately for the catalogue of the sale.

My mother's family came here even earlier. Her mother Dorothy Lazarus's side originally arrived in England when Cromwell allowed the Jews to return in the seventeenth century. They came from Toledo in Spain via Holland. Her father Stanley Cohen's ancestors had arrived from Australia, and had started a penny bazaar, which was Lewis's of Liverpool – nothing to do with John Lewis. It acquired Selfridges and was ultimately sold to Charles Clore's Sears Holdings. My mother was brought up in Liverpool, but the family came to London just about the time when the LJS was founded.

My grandfather, Julian Simon, was one of the first Treasurers of the synagogue, and he was followed by my father, Ronald. I do not know exactly when my father retired as Treasurer, but it must have been in the 1960s, and so between them they covered the first fifty years or so. I was also Treasurer, but not immediately after my father, so there was an interregnum!

I know that my grandmother, Florence, was involved in the Women's Society at the synagogue because, a short time ago, I helped Rita Adler in finding a cleaner for an embroidered tablecloth. The names of all the women involved were embroidered on the back, and one of them was Florence Simon. I do not think that my mother, Margot, was similarly involved, but she was very active in the Brook Clinics, which were one of the first places in the UK where young girls could get contraceptive and sexual health advice. I recall that it caused quite a scandal when it was founded by her great friend, Helen Brook.

In addition to being Treasurer, my father was Honorary Solicitor from the early 1920s until I took over from him in the early 1960s. I carried on until Ellen Schmidt relieved me about four years ago, so between us, my father and I must have held this post for about eighty years! During my period of office, I drafted two synagogue constitutions, which is not a job I would want again. Rather like Parkinson's Law of Triviality concerning the bicycle shed, everyone has an opinion, so progress was always slow and tortuous.

The first of these constitutions was drafted by me whilst Sir Louis Gluckstein was President and also Chairman of Council. Fortunately for me, he always acted in a most autocratic manner and would never brook any opposition. Indeed, he considered, I think, that Council was superfluous and unnecessary. I am not at all sure that he wasn't right! There were no long debates or extended Council meetings when he was in the Chair.

One truly great pleasure relating to drafting that first constitution was getting to know John Rayner better. He was Senior Rabbi at the time, and he helped me draft the objects, which are really the most important part of any constitution. He was delightful, insightful and diffident; he had a way of simplifying problems and getting to the very essence. He had a fine analytical brain and, because English had not been his mother tongue, like many in that position, he always chose his words with particular care.

John married Doreen and me in 1969. When I was Chairman, towards the end of John's life, I used to have lunch with him now and again and learned much from his wisdom. I recall him telling me what a disappointment it was to him that the Liberal and Reform movements could not find a *modus vivendi*, principally he said because they felt it necessary to have a common policy on patrilineality, which they could not reach.

Doreen and I have had three children, all of whom have become more observant than we are and are, therefore, not members of the LJS. Between them they have (so far…) produced for us twelve wonderful grandchildren, who consume a great deal of our time. Suzi, our middle child, now lives with her five children in Israel, where we go to visit them quite frequently. The other two, Matthew and Devorah, live in North London.

One of the more interesting and sad problems on which I was called upon to advise as Honorary Solicitor, was whether the marriage performed at the LJS of a former Bond girl was valid. She was not originally Jewish, but went through the full conversion process at the LJS. She had appeared in *For Your Eyes Only*, was strikingly beautiful, but, it turned out, was a transsexual. Although she was legally married according to European law, that was not the case in England, so the marriage was deemed to be void. British law regards gender reassignment as merely a cosmetic procedure, and the changes in legal status that are allowed are similarly only cosmetic. She could be called female on her passport, and that was about it. To all intents and purposes, in the eyes of the law, she was male because it said so on her birth certificate. As a male, she obviously was not allowed to marry another man. They were apparently forced by her husband's family to come back from their honeymoon and they separated.

From some time in the 1960s and, for what seemed to me most of the subsequent forty and more years, I was on Council. Why I agreed to subject myself to this I cannot now imagine. I cannot stand committees and much prefer Sir Louis' way of managing our affairs. I served under Sir Louis, Lewis Levy, Maxwell Stern, Sir Peter Lazarus – who stood out as a very fine Chairman – Rita Adler and Trevor Moross. I myself was Chairman after Trevor, but I think the only mark that I made was to ensure that Council meetings were shorter than previously.

Working with Sir Peter, Trevor and Neil Levitt on the rebuilding of our fine new synagogue was a wonderful, if taxing, experience. A particularly fraught problem lay in our having to sue the builders, Mowlem. I well remember a meeting we had with Mowlem at the offices of Singer & Friedlander, of which Anthony Solomons was the Chairman at the time. I think Mowlem came to the meeting assuming that, as a religious body, we were a soft touch and not to be feared. Tony Solomons soon put them right, and they realised they had a serious fight on their hands, which in due course we won.

I believe I was instrumental through clients of mine, Michael Gillingham and Donald Findlay, in finding our temporary lodgings in the deconsecrated church in Loudoun Road near Swiss Cottage.

I recall when I was a child listening to Israel Mattuck and Lily Montagu. Although I was too young to appreciate Mattuck, I was brought up on his book *The Essentials of Liberal Judaism,* which was required reading pre-Confirmation. (There was no *Bar* or *Bat Mitzvah* in those days.) If I recall correctly, the weekly correspondence assignment for confirmees, who were at boarding school like me, was a chapter of this book. Lily Montagu lived until I was in my early twenties, and I well remember being inspired by her. From that era another name to conjure with was Marjorie Moos, who I believe taught my father (that is probably apocryphal), me, and my son Matthew. Since the 'Three Ms', I have slept through the sermons of, enjoyed and/or been inspired by those who have followed – Leslie Edgar, David Goldstein, John Rayner, David Goldberg, with whom I have spent many delightful hours walking over hill and dale and, more recently, Helen Freeman, Kathleen de Magtige-Middleton, Mark Solomon and, of course, Alex Wright.

No account of my doings at the LJS would be complete without mentioning my father's brother, Arthur and his wife Sybil. Although I do not believe they ever held any office, they were throughout their lives extraordinarily generous supporters, contributing hugely to the rebuilding fund of the synagogue and on many other occasions. They had no children and, both before and especially after the death of my father in 1971, they took a great interest and pride in the involvement of my family in synagogue affairs.

In my time, I have also been involved in a number of other aspects of the LJS. With Michael Hart, David de Magtige and Rabbi Mark Solomon, I visited our new partner community in Vinnitsa in the Ukraine, which was a fascinating experience. One of the most memorable and moving moments was when we went to a forest clearing where many Jews had been murdered. We were accompanied by a lady whose parents were among the victims and Mark chanted the *El Maleh Rachamim* memorial prayer.

Following my retirement from Council, I took over as Chief Steward from Martin Slowe for three years before retiring in 2007. Martin had acted as Chief Steward for many, many years and had done so with wonderful efficiency, endearing himself to our members, especially the elderly. He was indeed a hard act to follow. The High Holydays require over one hundred volunteers, and it is something of a logistical nightmare to ensure that every slot is filled.

I have now been put out to pasture as a Trustee, a position that carries honour without much responsibility. I continue, for the moment, to chair the United Charities Fund, taking over from my cousin, Michael Nathan, who had been in that position for more than forty years. I have no intention of emulating his example. Indeed at my age it will (fortunately) be impossible to do so!

As I think back over the years that I have been involved with the LJS, I reflect on the changes that have taken place. The move from almost no Hebrew in our services to its inclusion today; the central part played by the State of Israel and the permissible criticism of its policies; the physical change from the austere wood-lined *bimah* to the bright modern Jerusalem stone. But the greatest change is, I think, the part which youth today plays at the LJS, for which much credit must go to Jan Roseman, Caroline Villiers and, of course, our rabbis. It is there that our great and continuing success can be seen and it is there that the hope for our next one hundred years rests.

See photographs 6 (Julian Simon) and 20.

✡

Jocelyne Tobin

Jocelyne Tobin joined the LJS in the 1960s. She was Chairman of Peggy Lang House, a home for older people in Willesden set up by the LJS. She was also on the synagogue's Services Committee, involved in interfaith activities and sang in the Members' Choir. She is now a member of the Library Committee. Her husband, Julian Tobin, was an Honorary Treasurer.

I was born in Golders Green on 3 December 1929, the youngest of four children, to Bertha and Bernard Prevezer. Both my parents were teenage immigrants, arriving separately in 1912 from Poland. They were observant Jews from very traditional backgrounds. My mother's father was a Chasid – a sweet, tolerant man. He and his wife – they were called Israel and Rosa Mintz – had seven surviving children, practically all of whom, including their descendants, have remained within the United Synagogue. My parents married in 1918 and eventually settled in Dunstan Road, Golders Green, in 1925 with three children. I was born four years later. I went to a little preparatory school called 'St Dunstans', which was on the corner of Finchley and Hodford Roads run by Miss Forder and Miss Arthur, two lovely ex-missionary ladies.

The Golders Green United Synagogue is also in Dunstan Road, and we were very much part of the congregation, with many people popping in for *Kiddush* on their way home from the Saturday service. We all attended on most Saturdays, and I went to Religion School until I was thirteen. A very flourishing youth club was started during the war, and there was also a Guide company. I was Patrol Leader of the Blue Tits!

In 1941 I went to South Hampstead High School where I met Ann Kirk. Although she was two forms above me, I got to know her because we met at Jewish prayers, which were held at least twice a week in the school library. On other days, we joined the remainder of the school for assembly and prayers. Any verses mentioning Jesus were dropped from the hymns! Marjorie Moos was our 'Scripture' teacher; she was also Head of the LJS *cheder*.

A very important activity in my social life during the war was *Habonim*, which met at 57 Eton Avenue (now a private preparatory school). Many of the members were refugees, some of whom had arrived on the *Kindertransport*. They were an extremely interesting group. We had many social and intellectual events, including some stimulating lectures. I went to a summer school in 1945, which was held at the David Eder Farm in Harrietsham in Kent. We were camping, and I remember having a great time. While we were camping the war with Japan ended and we celebrated by dancing round the camp fire. Quite a few members of *Habonim* made *aliyah* to Israel.

I left school after the Upper V, attended the London College of Secretaries, and then worked for a short time at the City Literary Institute, and for the concert impresarios Lynford Joel Promotions Ltd. I next applied to the BBC, which I joined in 1948. Eventually, I became a production secretary in the Sound Radio Drama Department, where I stayed for seven years before I became a Studio Manager at Bush House, retiring in 1963.

In 1959 I married Julian Tobin. His family lived in Cambridge, and were members of the independent Orthodox Thompson's Lane Synagogue. We were married in London's Bayswater Synagogue with Rabbi Louis Jacobs officiating. I had never been truly at home in the United Synagogue – although I cannot say the same for Julian – but eventually, after much discussion, we decided that we would both be happy at the LJS, which we joined in the early 1960s. And so it proved to be. As Julian was already a Hampstead Borough Councillor and as, in those days, a councillor had to be domiciled in the Borough they represented, we had to find a house in Hampstead. So we bought 18 Eton Villas, where I still live fifty years later.

After retiring from the BBC, I worked part-time on Tribunals, first with the Central London Valuation Tribunal (a lay tribunal dealing with rate appeals), and then with the London Rent Assessment Panel, where I sat as a lay member alongside lawyers and valuers dealing with appeals against Fair Rents. I also became Chairman of the Hampstead Branch of the *Save the Children* charity.

Julian became a Council member of the LJS and was also Co-Treasurer from 1984 until 1989 with Willie Kessler.

I always had great respect for our rabbis and presidents. I very much enjoyed talking to Rabbi David Goldstein and admired his sermons. He eased my mind about not going to *Shabbat* morning services when we went to our country cottage. I attended David Goldberg's Hebrew classes before he became a Rabbi. Rabbi John Rayner had a great sense of humour, but we didn't know him that well.

I remember our then President, Sir Louis Gluckstein, taking part in the first High Holyday overflow service at Porchester Hall. His daughter, Jean Jaffa, an opera singer, gave some amazing concerts.

Peter Lazarus and his wife, Elizabeth, gave a memorable dinner in the City on their Ruby wedding. His sons and his brother, Norman, did a hilarious 'turn' mentioning 'Sir Peter, as he is informally known at home', which raised a great laugh. He was very kind to my daughter, Annabel.

I was very fortunate to be involved with the Abbeyfield Camden (Jewish) Society alongside Nina Nathan, Nancy Caplin, Jo Kessler, Maureen Roe, Marian Steafel, Ann Kirk, Ann and Bernard Hart, Nena and Norman Sofier, Beryl Civval, Susan Goodman, Nicole David, Miles Halford and Bennie Richenberg. The Abbeyfield Society was started by the Nathans, Jo and Nancy with LJS financial support. The property they bought, Peggy Lang House, was in Walm Lane, Willesden, and Nina was its first Chairman. I took over from Nina – although no one could take over from Nina, she was unique. Peggy Lang House continued to flourish for a further twenty-three years with a fantastic committee.

A second Jewish Abbeyfield home, Lily Montagu House, was started by Hugh Isaacs in Edgware; then a third, Belmont Lodge in Bushey, by a consortium of local Progressive synagogues. Belmont Lodge is still flourishing, but Peggy Lang House closed about six years ago because our residents were too elderly for the care we were able to provide. Two of them are still with us, well into their nineties and living at Sunridge Court.

I was on the LJS Services Committee many years ago. I enjoyed interfaith events, including the tripartite ones with Muslims from the Regent's Park Mosque and members of the St John's Wood Church at the roundabout, and also the meetings in the 1990s at our local church, St Mary's in Elsworthy Road. These were very fruitful – we discussed our comparative approaches to life events.

For quite a few years, I was a member of the Members' Choir as an alto. I cannot sight-read, so I don't think I was a very effective member, but I did my best! When I first joined, Edward Cross was the conductor and, when he moved to Radlett, Norman Lazarus took over.

I have finally retired from my past activities, but I am an enthusiastic member of the London U3A (University of the Third Age) in Belsize Park, catching up on my education. I go to a lecture on European History, and I also attend classes on the History of Philosophy, on Mahler, a Poetry class and one on the Contemporary Novel. I enjoy my connection with the LJS library under the Librarian, Barbara Godfrey (who also goes to the Poetry Class at the University of the Third Age). We repair and clean books regularly and we find that very satisfying.

Julian died in November 1999 and I am very fortunate to have my children – Rupert born in 1963, Sasha in 1965 and Annabel in 1968 – and three grandchildren. The children were confirmed but did not marry at the LJS, although Sasha is a member.

See photograph 68 (Julian Tobin).

Walter Woyda

Walter Woyda is the son of Bruno Woyda, who was prominent in establishing the World Union for Progressive Judaism. Having come to Britain on a *Kindertransport*, Walter helped to form, and was the first Chairman of, the Federation of Liberal and Progressive Youth Groups. He served on the LJS Services Committee and chaired the Concert Committee for the celebration of a hundred years of Liberal Judaism.

I am the fourth-generation Liberal Jew in my family. I was born in Berlin on 20 June 1926. We belonged to the *Reformgemeinde* in Berlin, an ultra-Liberal congregation founded in 1845, from which many congregations in England and America took their lead. The Liberal movement was outstandingly important to me as my father was the General Secretary of the congregation. He and the three ministers made me realise that the spirituality, liturgy, music and philosophy were the right interpretations of Judaism for the modern world.

My younger brother and I travelled on a *Kindertransport* to Belgium, where my uncle and aunt lived. We waited there until, through the enormous efforts of Miss Montagu and Rabbi Mattuck, my father was released from the camp at Sachsenhausen, where he was sent after *Kristallnacht* in 1938. He and my mother picked us up in Belgium to come to England. We found a flat in Kilburn, but Miss Montagu decided that we needed some rest and we moved to a cottage on a large estate in a village called Hasfield, Gloucestershire. My brother and I were schooled first of all in a local village school where the first priority was for us to learn English as neither of us could speak the language.

Once my father's health improved, we moved back to London to a flat in Streatham. We were sent to St Joseph's College, which was a Roman Catholic Brothers school. We were the only Jewish children in the school, but we were accepted because they wanted to help as we were refugees. It was an immensely impressive school and my brother learned enough to become a teacher eventually. I was evacuated with the school to Haywards Heath, where I took lessons from the LJS Religion School by correspondence course. I still remember the comments I had from Rabbi Mattuck and Miss Moos. They gave me a very good education.

My father was the German delegate at the first conference of the World Union for Progressive Judaism when it was founded in London in 1926. The second conference was held in Berlin when my father helped with the arrangements. Once we were living in England, my father helped Lily Montagu, first as Financial Secretary of the World Union, and then as General Secretary of the Union. Both the UK Liberal and Reform movements became important constituents of the Union.

I was confirmed in 1942 at the LJS and many of the participants in the ceremony are still friends of mine. The service made a big impression on me – it was totally different from the present day *Kabbalat Torah*. When I was confirmed at sixteen, I knew much about religion thanks to the teachers at Religion School and the correspondence course that I took, together with what I had learned in Germany in my younger days. After my Confirmation I recall my father saying to me, 'You are now a man, and there are two things that matter: keep Liberal Judaism in your family and do good and help people.'

As I grew up, I was proud to have Rabbi Israel Mattuck as our minister at the LJS. He was highly intelligent, and a most charismatic Liberal Jew. His sermons were meticulously wise in their philosophy, and his books and booklets were all of great importance. I still re-read them constantly. He kept Liberal Judaism to the forefront in Anglo-Jewry. His assistant was Leslie Edgar, who later became an Army Chaplain. I was extremely close to him because we were not too far apart in age, and we were involved in the youth movement together. After I had been Chairman of the *Ner Tamid* youth group at South London Synagogue, he asked me to help form the Federation of Liberal and Progressive Youth Groups. I became its first Chairman and Leslie Edgar helped me in establishing the group, as did the Rev. Philip Cohen, the third minister at the LJS.

The youth movement was extremely active. We held annual conferences, which rabbis attended. They gave some very good lectures. As the group developed, we started to hold joint conferences with YASGB (Youth Association of Synagogues of Great Britain), which was the Reform youth movement. The culmination of this was the foundation of the Youth Section of the World Union for Progressive Judaism. I was on its first committee, although I was, at that time, establishing my business life. I was also active in South London where I was Financial Secretary and then General Secretary.

Rabbi John Rayner was a close friend of mine and I was delighted when he became the first minister to come to South London before he came to the LJS. It is interesting that, at that time, South London was considered the training ground for some of the rabbis that we had in the movement. David Goldstein and Baroness Neuberger were both there.

I remember John well, because, like me, he was a refugee. He was highly intelligent and, later on, he studied at the Hebrew Union College in America, and became an inspiration to his congregation. I have many happy memories of our discussing Liberal Judaism and the wider issues of the world. We often used to visit places in his car. On those occasions, I recall taking a bucket of water with me as he never refilled his car radiator and, after some miles, steam would come out of the engine.

As the family were growing up I rejoined the LJS and served on the Services Committee and the Library Committee, I was also Chairman of the ULPS Concert Committee, which was held at the LJS marking a hundred years of the Liberal Movement. I also participated in a number of ULPS conferences. I wrote two articles on liturgy and gave a talk on 'Why I am a Liberal Jew' as part of a series of lectures at the synagogue. I also spoke at a conference about the world-wide Liberal movement.

My wife and I were married at the LJS on 16 March 1952. It was the second marriage there after the synagogue was repaired following bomb damage, and we were lucky enough to have Leslie Edgar conduct the ceremony. Miss Montagu also participated. We encouraged our children to remain Jews and to take an interest in the Liberal movement. Both my son and daughter were very active in the youth movement before they were married. When he married, my son joined Alyth Gardens, and my daughter, having been in Israel for two years, became very Orthodox. She and her family now belong to the Federation of Synagogues. This was all a surprise to me, but I respect both of them because whatever their interpretation of Judaism is, it helps to keep the whole of Judaism alive.

Beyond the Liberal movement, I became a representative on the Association of Jewish Refugees and helped as a volunteer at Nightingale House, because my in-laws were resident there. I always tried to work on the basis that one should not only live a Jewish life as a Jew, but one should also give a portion of one's income to help other people – that is one of the ways in which Judaism has a part to play. I have considered it important to support Israeli, Jewish and non-Jewish charities, and that it is incumbent on us to help people who are much poorer than we are living in other parts of the world.

I am now eighty-four years old, and still happy to be a member of the LJS, but I hope that Liberal Judaism will regain the commitment it had in its early days, and that it will continue for centuries to come because it has been an important influence during my life. The practice of the Liberal Jewish religion is different now because many Orthodox people have joined Liberal synagogues for the sole purpose of marrying someone outside their religion. This is a crisis for the movement, and I do not accept how it has been handled. I think it should have been made explicit right from the start that they should adhere to the Liberal philosophy. I feel we have moved away from the liturgy of the

Liberal movement, and the services are not as they used to be – I am not happy with the amount of Hebrew. However, I know I should not complain and I have come to accept it. I am happy that the sermons are still built on the ethics of the movement.

See photograph 43.

✡

Rabbi Alexandra Wright

Rabbi Alexandra Wright grew up at the LJS. Her grandmother, Elaine Falk, was an early member of the LJS and her parents have been very involved in many aspects of synagogue life. Taught in the Religion School, Rabbi Wright became Associate Rabbi at the LJS from 1986 until 1989 and has been Senior Rabbi since 2004.

I was born Alexandra Levitt. My great-grandfather on my father's side came from a small town in Lithuania, called Plungyan. He was one of several brothers and cousins who left, perhaps to avoid conscription, perhaps because of the terrible poverty and economic deprivation there, or because of anti-Semitism. Some made their way to South Africa and settled there. Joe Levitt, my great-grandfather, travelled to Ireland and arrived in Dublin in the 1890s with next to nothing.

I am not sure how he met his wife Tilly Leventon. She was a highly cultured and musical woman, who had won many singing prizes in Ireland, and who could have had a successful musical career. It may have been that her father, Israel Leventon, the Polish-born rabbi of the Adelaide Road Synagogue, and the community's *shochet, mohel* and *sofer,* had taken pity on the impoverished pedlar and felt bound to offer him hospitality. Israel's portrait used to hang in the Jewish Museum in Dublin, while the *Sefer Torah,* which he took ten years to complete, is now in the Orthodox synagogue in Terenure in Dublin. When a group of Israel Leventon's descendants visited Dublin some years ago, we were shown his *Sefer Torah* with its fine and even calligraphy. It is still in use for *Shabbat* services today.

My maternal grandparents, Elaine and Cecil Falk, lived in Hampstead and, later on, in St John's Wood. It was my grandmother who first moved from her Orthodox roots to the LJS. I think she had gone with a friend to hear Rabbi Mattuck speak. He was a powerful and charismatic orator and many were drawn to listen to his sermons and lectures.

During the Second World War, Elaine was evacuated with her four children to Cheltenham, and when they returned to London she joined the synagogue. The youngest, William, who now conducts the Members' Choir, was confirmed at the LJS in 1959. My grandmother was particularly active in the synagogue: she was a member of the Women's Society, and helped for many years with the Darby and Joan Club, founded after the war by Lady Gluckstein. She was still helping well into her eighties, giving lifts to the members, some of whom were several years younger than she was.

My parents, Susan and Neil Levitt, were married at the New West End Synagogue (the synagogue to which Lily Montagu's family belonged), but they joined the LJS soon afterwards and became involved in the Younger Members' Organisation (YMO). In the 1960s, my father joined the House Committee, was on the Council and appointed Vice

Chairman and, during the rebuilding of no. 28, he chaired the Design and Use Committee, which oversaw the design of the new Sanctuary. Both my parents have strong social networks in the congregation, but my mother's main involvement has been with the Members' Choir. My father regularly attends services, sitting in his favourite seat in the Sanctuary.

I have very early memories of the LJS, going back to the days of Rabbi Dr Leslie Edgar in the early 1960s. I must have been about four years old, as my parents allowed me to stand on the brown leather seats of the old synagogue in order to see the scroll being taken out of the Ark, and I recall Rabbi Edgar's deep and resonant voice and the way in which he would elongate his vowels in a distinctive and memorable way.

I started at the LJS Religion School when I was about five years old. Celia Rapp, who taught the first class, was a very special teacher. She was like a tiny bird, scarcely taller than the children she taught, but vivacious and built a wonderful rapport with each one of her pupils. Harry Rapp, her husband, was quiet, but always supportive as was her sister, Rosa Mintz. Another Religion School teacher was Eva Feldman. One of my most vivid memories of Religion School is a lesson with Eva in the 'new' classrooms that were built in the 1960s on the floor above the small synagogue. Eva got us to act out the story of Rahab and the two spies sent by Joshua into Jericho.

By the age of twelve, I was ready to rebel and decided that I no longer wanted to go to Religion School. To their great credit, my parents didn't insist on my return, but a year later, I suddenly realised the loss of friendships and the Hebrew as well. I had some lessons with Mrs Rapp to catch up, and returned to the classes with John Rich, Michael Cross and Professor Michael Alpert. Much later on, Michael Alpert tutored me in Hebrew before I went to Leo Baeck College. I never imagined for one moment that I would end up teaching classical Hebrew at the College many years later!

Kabbalat Torah classes (or Confirmation as they were called then) were with Rabbis John Rayner and Dr David Goldstein. I don't suppose we fully appreciated the intellectual calibre and greatness of both these rabbis, although we respected them hugely and liked them. David Goldstein was a marvellous rabbi, and I think many remember the warmth of his Family Services. He had a fund of stories drawn from folklore and *midrash*, which he would relate from the pulpit. Later he published a volume of these stories, which we loved as children. His last, monumental *oeuvre* was a translation from Hebrew of Isaiah Tishby's *Wisdom of the Zohar*. It is an absolutely indispensable work for the student of the *Zohar*, the great mediaeval work of Jewish mysticism by Moses de Leon.

The very first time I read from the *Torah* was October 1972, the date of my Confirmation. John Rayner was an exacting and precise teacher, and I remember, to my very great surprise, volunteering to read the second half of the Ten Commandments. About four or five years later, I was invited to read part of the service on *Kol Nidre*. That was an enormous honour, but it still never occurred to me that perhaps my vocation lay in the rabbinate.

My closest friends at Religion School were Jenny Stephany, Ruth Steinman, daughter of the synagogue Beadle, Louis Steinman, who blew the *shofar* so memorably and wonderfully, and Griselda (later Ruth) Cross. I have a feeling we weren't terribly well behaved, and Edward Cross, Michael's son, who conducted the Children's Choir at the time, has never forgotten (or forgiven) me for crawling under his seat while he was playing the organ and untying his shoelaces. He wasn't very amused.

It was while I was at university that I began to think about becoming a rabbi. I met Julia Neuberger at the LJS in the mid-seventies. She was a rabbinic student at Leo Baeck College and I remember thinking: 'So women *can* be rabbis!' At the same time, I was taking a lead in the tiny Jewish Society at my university, and every Monday used to attend a *Shiur* given by Rabbi Dr Bernard Susser, who was doing a law degree at the same university. By a curious coincidence, many years later after he had died, I met up with his daughter Hanna Jaffe who lives in Jerusalem, and who is a professional storyteller. She was in London with a group of children visiting the LJS from the St John's Wood Adventure Playground.

My interview for Leo Baeck College took place in the Council Room on the first floor at West London Synagogue, where the College was housed until it moved to the Sternberg Centre in Finchley in 1982. Prospective and hopeful candidates sat in the corridor, awaiting their turn, and when I was called the Principal pointed to a lone chair in front of an interminably long table, behind which, I can only imagine, the great and good of the College were seated. I cannot remember any of their faces, which were screened by swirls of cigarette smoke!

I joined the LJS as Associate to Senior Rabbi David Goldberg in 1986. At my interview with the Chairman, Maxwell Stern, I rather presumptuously asked about a day off. He looked a bit shocked and said, 'Why do you need a day off? Rabbis have Fridays off!' I said no more, but I still find Fridays the most onerous and difficult day of the week, writing a sermon for *Shabbat*, often adding to that a *D'var Torah* for *Erev Shabbat* services, preparing a lesson for the Religion School, and trying to put together a meal for Friday evening.

I was very involved in the Religion School, and enjoyed the pastoral aspect of visiting people at home or in hospital. I do remember spending hours on the telephone trying to get practical welfare help for congregants. I had no idea how to navigate the complexities of Social Services, and often felt as though I was getting nowhere. It is only now, with Liz Crossick as our Community Care Co-ordinator, that I really appreciate having someone with a strong social work background to take care of the practical and pastoral needs of our more frail congregants.

Did my arrival at the LJS help to raise the profile of women's issues? I'm not sure. I hope so. I don't think I was necessarily challenging, because I was from a generation of women rabbis who knew we had to behave as 'honorary men' if we wanted to get anywhere. We dressed in black (I still do) and I think we probably felt we had to work much harder to get anywhere near as far as our male colleagues.

There was one occasion – *Yom Kippur* – when we were 'in exile'. The synagogue was being rebuilt, and we held the services at Westminster Central Hall. I gave a sermon on how the liturgy for the High Holydays didn't necessarily reflect the needs of women and didn't encourage women to assert themselves in a more positive way. Although I quoted from Lily Montagu, it created something of a furore and I was summoned before the Senior Rabbi and Chairman at the time. I gave the Chairman a copy of the sermon. To his very great credit, he sent for me again, apologised and said that what he had *heard* was different from what I had *said*. It was a remarkable moment, but I did learn from that particular episode that it is very easy to bring to what we hear our own preconceptions and assumptions.

One of the highlights of being at the LJS during that period was serving on the Editorial Committee for the new prayerbook, *Siddur Lev Chadash*. John Rayner's scholarship was formidable and we immersed ourselves in the history, variety and development of the liturgy. We all contributed to the prayerbook, but John was very firm about what he wanted. I remember submitting a draft of a special theme and he almost completely rewrote it, but generously attributed parts of it to me.

When it came to gender-inclusive language in the *Siddur*, the real influences came from Rabbis Sheila Shulman and Elli Tikvah Sarah, who were rabbinic students at the time. Over a period, they convinced John that the new prayerbook should be gender-inclusive, and I think we all worked tremendously hard to produce a *Siddur* that had integrity, but was also poetic and read well.

My daughter, Gabby, was born in 1988. We were about to go into 'exile' for thirty-three months and she had her baby blessing in the church hall of St John's Church at the roundabout because the Loudoun Road premises weren't quite ready for us to occupy. By the time she was eighteen months, the building works at no. 28 were under way and she was invited to lay one of the bricks for the foundation of the new building. Another moving recollection was seeing the portico pillars being driven away for storage on the back of a huge lorry. It felt almost like the end of an era, the old synagogue had been very much associated with my childhood and teenage years, and with the early years of my rabbinate.

Ben was born on a Friday evening, the night before I was supposed to say farewell to the congregation for pastures new. Perhaps it was significant that I never got to say goodbye!

I was at Radlett and Bushey Reform Synagogue for nearly fourteen years – they were very happy, hard-working years. New families moving out into Hertfordshire were joining all the time, and as the only full-time member of staff, but with active volunteers and a wonderful Head Teacher, Ora Warren, whom I adored and worked with very closely, I was kept very busy.

Coming back to the LJS in March 2004 was very different from my first experience as a junior rabbi. I knew many of the older members who hadn't changed one bit, but there were many younger families who had joined the LJS in the years I had been at Radlett.

I know that for many members who had been used to a male, more hierarchical model and very charismatic form of leadership, having a Senior Rabbi who was a woman, was a challenge. It's difficult to be objective about oneself in this role. I want to be more consultative, to offer something a little quieter and more reflective.

I hope I have tried to integrate the Religion School more fully into whatever is going on in the Sanctuary on *Shabbat* mornings and during festivals, and to create an active adult education programme where people feel committed to learning about Judaism. I have tried to allow for more spontaneity and warmth in the services. Certainly, there is scarcely a *Shabbat* without a celebration or commemoration, whether communal, family or individual. Above all, I hope that I am creating a place at the LJS where people can engage meaningfully with each other and with their Judaism. How we are with each other and with those who are different from ourselves, beyond the walls of the synagogue, seems to be the necessary response in such changing and uncertain times.

Since I became Senior Rabbi, there have been some remarkable occasions. Two weeks after the London bombings on 7 July 2005, the LJS held a service of reflection and reconciliation, together with St John's Wood Church and the London Central Mosque. Coming together so soon after this tragedy, and on the day when there was another, this time attempted bombing, was very moving and powerful. From that service emerged Pathways, the local clergy group which has become a place of great friendships and influence in the local community.

A service to mark the 70th anniversary of *Kristallnacht* was another highlight, with the cellist Andrea Hess playing extracts from Ernest Bloch, and readers re-enacting the terrible events of the pogrom that swept through Germany on the night of 9 November 1938.

Why do people join the LJS? Why do they continue in their membership? There is enormous loyalty to the LJS – among young and senior congregants. But I think it's because the LJS is, above all, a diverse and inclusive community that seems to be able to find a place for people from many different kinds of backgrounds – the third- or fourth-generation Liberal Jew who has grown up in the congregation; newcomers passing through London temporarily – Americans, Israelis, South Africans; Jews from all over the world who have made London their home; Jews who enjoy the cultural and festive aspects of our faith; the intellectual who wants to question Jewish tradition and faith, but still wants to belong to a community; the individual who has Jewish ancestry and passionately wishes to find their way back to Judaism; those in mixed-faith relationships and those who sometimes feel on the margins of the 'establishment'.

What is important to me in my Judaism? I love studying and want to impart my love of texts to the congregation. *Talmud Torah* (the study of *Torah*), in its widest sense, is a way of opening up a dialogue, a conversation among ourselves. but also something of a metaphysical nature. If, as has been said, prayer consists of our words and thoughts addressed to God, then study is God's words to us.

My vision for the LJS is to provide a place where the individual can engage with their Judaism in order to find a sense of renewal and purpose; a place where life-cycle events, *Shabbatot*, festivals, the critical moments and journeys in individuals' lives can be acknowledged sensitively and gently. When we are more anchored and more secure in our own identities, then we are more willing to go out and engage in the world beyond the four walls of our own homes and community. If the LJS encourages us to contribute to the growing goodness and peace of the world then, although our task is far from over, our congregation will have begun to fulfil its purpose in the world.

**See photographs 43, 45, 47, 68, and 85 plus 20 and 68 (Neil Levitt),
26 (Susan Levitt), and 30 (Elaine Falk).**

✡

Eva and Desmond Feldman

Eva and Desmond Feldman were both involved in the Younger Members' Organisation. Desmond, whose family had been long-established in England, went on to join the Council, becoming an Honorary Treasurer and Vice Chairman. Eva, who was from Germany, became Chairman of the Women's Society. She was a founder member of Restaurant Tuesday, which is still operating today. Eva and Desmond were both involved in educational activities and in running a marriage guidance service.

Desmond: My father was born in England in 1888 or thereabouts. He became a medical student, qualified as a doctor and joined the Army in 1914. He was affiliated with the United Synagogue, which effectively was Anglo-Jewry at that time – indeed he became Warden of the Great Synagogue.

My mother was Belgian and before the Second World War lived with her family in Antwerp. She came over to England and worked for the Red Cross. It was the usual story: my father was wounded, she nursed him and then they married. They were married in Antwerp and then set up home living in Hampstead. My parents were Orthodox throughout their lifetime.

I was born in 1923. My religious education was pretty slim. I was prepared for my *Bar Mitzvah*, which I learned by rote, and I had no understanding of what it all meant.

Eva: My maiden name was Coleman. I was born in 1924 in Germany and came to England when I was eight years old with my parents, grandmother and my sister. My father had a brother who had been in England running a business since before World War I, so my father was able to settle here and had a job to go to.

My parents belonged to the Liberal Synagogue in Germany, corresponding to the Reform synagogue here. One of the first things they did when they arrived in this country was to join the Liberal Synagogue. In fact they joined it by mistake because they thought it was Reform, as in Germany. But once they had joined, they stayed. I was very smitten with Judaism after the War. I'd had a bad experience with a rabbi at a religion school in Germany and I swore then that when I left the LJS Religion School and was confirmed, I would never enter a synagogue again. But I changed my mind.

I think it must have been in early 1934 that I started at the Religion School at the LJS. I couldn't have started any earlier than that because I didn't have any English. I remember my first teachers there very well – they were Joe Foreman and Marjorie Moos. Sam Rich also taught me later on. In those days, learning Hebrew was optional. I quite enjoyed Hebrew because I liked languages, but when I moved up to the next class I opted out of this. Any Hebrew I have learned since then is what I have taught myself.

I went on to Confirmation during the Second World War. My family lived in Barton-on-Sea on the south coast. It was some way from London, and although we had the odd bomb, it wasn't too bad. I took the correspondence course organised by Miss Moos and came up to London for my Confirmation on 8 April 1942. My uncle who was living here took us out for lunch. The Confirmation service took place in the Montefiore Hall and was a low key affair. When I arrived, Alfred and Lilly Loebl, asked me, 'Have you got the prayer that you were going to read?' I said, 'I don't know anything about a prayer.' They then asked, 'Which passage were you going to read?' I said I hadn't been told about this.

I was handed something and told, 'This is it,' so I went up onto the *bimah* and read it. I have not kept in touch with any of the other confirmands. Of the names on the flier that I have kept from the service, the only one I recognise is Peter Lazarus.

My family moved back to London in 1945 and I immediately got involved with the Younger Members' Organisation. This was amalgamated with the Alumni during and for a while after the War. Then when things settled down again and more members joined, the two organisations separated again. I ended up as the Secretary of the Alumni Committee. There was little religious content to the activities organised by these societies, apart from the Alumni Friday evening services, which members ran themselves with the Chairman giving the sermon, and debates on ethical subjects. But, on the whole, the social side predominated.

Desmond: Eva and I met in 1948 at Joe Pinto's house. Joe was an old school friend of mine. Eva and I got married in the Great Synagogue in 1949, but because the synagogue building had been bombed, the ceremony actually took place in a hut. For a while I continued to go to the Orthodox synagogue and Eva to the Liberal. My journey to the Liberal movement started with my children because Eva felt very strongly that she did not want them to be brought up as Orthodox.

Eva: When Nicholas, our eldest child, was ready to start religion school, I said to Desmond, 'You can have Nicholas educated in the United Synagogue, but no daughter of mine is going to be a member of the United Synagogue.' So Desmond joined the LJS in around 1958. It was as simple as that. We both went to a class run by John Rayner and that led to Desmond becoming very enthusiastic about Liberal Judaism. Within three years he was on the LJS Council.

Desmond: Much of what I did when I was on the Council is recorded in the Council minutes, but there were other things I got involved in too. I was Chairman of a number of the committees that were established at that time, such as the Services Committee and the Education Committee. I was also Treasurer of the synagogue for seven years. I enjoyed working with the people who were on the various committees. I considered myself one of the leaders of the 'Young Turks' who wanted to bring the Council and the Synagogue into the post-war era. With my reputation and my family connections, I was able gradually to influence people in various ways. The synagogue became less formal during our lifetime and the congregation grew. On a *Shabbat* morning when I first joined you might get only twenty or thirty people.

Eva: When I was on the YMO Committee, Michael Cross rang me one day and asked if I would like to represent the YMO on the Women's Society. He later told me that his phone call was made the day after he had heard that our young daughter, our second child, was going to nursery school, so he thought that I would have some more free time. I wasn't thinking quickly enough, so I agreed, and I did it for a year.

I was one of the first young people to come on the Committee. The Women's Society used to organise a tea on Monday afternoons, and they wanted more young people to come along. I told them, 'You won't get any young people because teatime is the time they collect their children from school.' I also told them that Monday wasn't a good day anyway, because we all did our washing on a Monday. So they changed the meetings to lunchtime on a Tuesday.

When my year was up I was asked if I would like to serve on the Women's Society permanently. Peggy Lewsen was Chairman when I first joined. When she became ill, Dora Wolchover became Chairman and Nina Nathan was the Secretary. Then when Dora retired, I was asked to take over from her, and I was Chairman for five years.

Initially you had to pay to be a member of the Women's Society – there was a membership fee of ten shillings a year. However, anybody could go to any of our activities whether they had paid or not. I felt this should be changed as it was unfair that those that had not paid could take advantage of these activities. I wrote to the Council to ask for £200 a year for our expenses, which they agreed to pay. We wrote to all the members of the society to tell them what was happening and also to the rest of the congregation who weren't members.

During my Chairmanship I also started a Saturday morning nursery. It ran from ten o'clock when the parents brought their older children to the school and dropped their younger children off. It took me about a month to organise this with the help of Peggy Lang who gave me the names and phone numbers of people to ask to help me. There was no suitable room for the nursery and there were no educational materials. However, someone donated some scissors from the Women's Society and I drew a lot of the pictures myself, tracing them from books for the children to colour in. I tried to teach the older children a few Bible stories. Desmond and some of our friends got involved with teaching as well. This meant that we didn't often get to go into the Saturday morning services.

I also started weekly Hebrew classes for the women. This went on for quite a long time, but everything packs up eventually, doesn't it? We had a teacher whom the rabbis had organised, but I was the person who set it up. Over time, there weren't enough people to keep it going. A number of women wanted to go on to further study, so they themselves paid a small fee for the teacher. Eventually the synagogue started to hold its own Hebrew classes.

Two other activities that started under my Chairmanship of the Women's Society are still going. The first is the Judaica shop in the foyer and the second is Restaurant Tuesday, which started in 1967. We started Restaurant Tuesday because there was a complaint that not enough was being done for older members, particularly for those who lived on their own and did not want to cook for themselves. It is still going strong and I have kept up my involvement; I am still cooking.

Desmond: Eva and I were involved in the ULPS Marriage Guidance for engaged couples. John Rayner encouraged us to set it up at the synagogue. We received training, of course, from the Marriage Guidance Council. It is obviously all confidential so we can't talk about particular cases. So many things came up and we thought: 'My goodness! They should have discussed this before they got married!' Sometimes things would have caused someone to walk out; whether it was finances, attitudes to parents and in-laws. Also the physical side, we had a lot of questions on that. I think it was terribly useful and I think it may have stopped the odd divorce. It got people talking to each other. It was interesting work.

Eva: I was very taken with Leslie Edgar. During the war, he came to visit us once or twice in our evacuation home. He was Chaplain to the Forces.

As to the services, I think it has gone a little bit too far towards the Orthodox at the moment. The Liberals went the wrong way to start with. They threw out the baby with the bath water. I am dead against young people having *B'nei Mitzvah*, and there is too much Hebrew in the service. We don't agree with celebrating *Purim* because we are real 'Old Liberals'. A lot of members have come in recently from the Orthodox synagogues and they have their own preferences. I realise that you have to go with what your congregation wants, to an extent. But sometimes I feel that there is a little too much accommodation of their views.

Desmond: Rabbi John Rayner was a great influence in our lives. We were friendly with most of the American rabbis who came over. We remember David Goldstein and admired him greatly. He was also a great influence. The LJS has really been a home-from-home for us.

Editorial note: Desmond Feldman sadly died in February 2010.
See photograph 43.

✡

Ann Kirk

Ann Kirk came to England on a *Kindertransport* in April 1939 sponsored by two sisters who were long-standing members of the LJS. They introduced her to the synagogue and, since then, she has been enthusiastically involved in all aspects of LJS life.

My name is Hannah Kirk. I was born in Berlin on 15 August 1928 as Hannah Kuhn. When I was naturalised, I decided that I didn't want to keep the surname of Kuhn, so anglicised my father's forename of Franz to Francis. So I became Hannah Francis, asking my friends to call me Ann and that's the name by which I became known in the synagogue.

My early upbringing was in a moderate Orthodox environment in Germany. I was sent to a Jewish kindergarten where we were taught Hebrew and, so from the age of four, I had a Jewish education. When I left the kindergarten, I entered a state school and joined the Religion School of the local synagogue in Cottbus.

My mother was quite religious. One of her ancestors had been a rabbi. My father really only went to synagogue to get married as he was an atheist. However, he did support my mum – we had Friday nights at home and kept the festivals. I went with mum to an Orthodox synagogue, sitting upstairs in the women's gallery.

I discovered very many years later that amongst the possessions that I had brought with me from Germany, there was a prayerbook that had belonged to my father's mother, the grandmother whom I never knew because she died before I was born. Rabbi John Rayner told me that this was one of the early Liberal prayerbooks produced in Germany, which rather pleased me.

The conditions in Germany from 1933 gradually worsened for the Jewish population, from petty restrictions to Jews losing all their civic rights, culminating in *Kristallnacht* on 9 November 1938. After *Kristallnacht*, the British government agreed to allow 10,000 unaccompanied Jewish children into this country provided the Jewish community made itself responsible for their upkeep. Dr Mattuck, who was the Senior Rabbi at the LJS, preached a sermon in which he asked the congregation to really think seriously about providing a home for a child from the *Kindertransport*.

In the congregation there were two ladies, the Misses Millie and Sophie Levy, who had been LJS members since the synagogue's Hill Street days. They were unmarried sisters, voluntary social workers in the East End of London with an office at the Bernhard Baron Settlement. It just so happened, at a party there, they met my mother's best friend, Edith, who had recently emigrated from Berlin. They got into conversation and Edith explained that her friend, Hertha Kuhn, was desperately trying to get her little girl, Hannah, out of Germany. Well, they thought about it and, bearing in mind what Dr Mattuck had said, agreed to take me. They were actually even prepared to come over to Germany to collect me, but that wasn't allowed, so my parents enrolled me on the *Kindertransport*.

After all the emigration procedures were completed, I finally arrived in England on 21 April 1939, and the very first Saturday that I was in this country, the 'aunts' – that is what I was told to call the Misses Levy – took me to the LJS. Well, my first impression really was that I was going to a church. Men and women were sitting together, the men wore no *kippot*, no *tallit*, and there was very, very little Hebrew. As far as I remember, it was only the *Shema* and the *Kaddish*, which is Aramaic (although I didn't know that at the time). I do remember Leslie Edgar, who was then the Associate Minister, coming down from the *bimah* when it was time for the sermon and, taking me by the hand, leading me out for the children's talk. I wrote to my parents for reassurance: Were these ladies Jewish? Was I taken to a Jewish synagogue? They replied that, yes, the Misses Levy were indeed Jewish, and this was a modern form of Judaism. They were sure that I would soon learn to love it. How right they were!

The aunts had been advised to send me to a boarding school to learn English. So I was only with them for a fortnight before being sent off to a boarding school in Kent. I was kitted out in school uniform, which was unheard of in Germany – so that was yet another culture shock. I was the only Jewish child at that school and that was a real problem. The girls thought that, since I came from Germany, I had to be a Nazi. They bullied me and I was really very miserable and lonely. While there, I received the LJS correspondence school lessons, sent out by Marjorie Moos, who was a brilliant peripatetic teacher. She used to visit many boarding schools, teaching Jewish children, but she was also a teacher in the Religion School at the LJS.

When war broke out in September, it so happened that the aunts missed the evacuation train of that boarding school and, in the first place, I was evacuated with the school of one of the aunt's friends. It was an elementary school, which went to Berkhamsted. Well, also evacuated to Berkhamsted was South Hampstead High School [SHHS] and, in fact, it had been the Headmistress of that school who had recommended that the aunts should send me to a boarding school in the first place. The Headmaster of the elementary school went up to see the Headmistress at South Hampstead and said, 'I have got this little girl in my school. She has only been in this country for a few months, but she honestly doesn't belong in an elementary school, she is already well ahead of her peers. Would you just see her?' The Headmistress agreed. She asked me a few questions, which involved a spelling test and some reading and sums, and I was accepted. I stayed at SHHS from the age of eleven to eighteen and I was very happy there.

There were many Jewish girls at SHHS and we used to have separate Jewish Prayers at Assembly twice a week taken by a prefect. Marjorie Moos, the Scripture teacher, came from London to teach Jewish Knowledge and History. She usually also came to take the High Holyday services – she used Dr Mattuck's *Liberal Jewish Prayerbook*. Marjorie used to stay with us, as the aunts, thinking that I'd had enough trauma in my short life to be billeted, had given up their London flat and rented one in Berkhamsted.

When the school returned to London, I continued to attend Marjorie Moos's Scripture lessons, so at that point I didn't go to the LJS Religion School, but I did join the Confirmation class and I was confirmed by Dr Mattuck in 1946. That was Dr Mattuck's last Confirmation class. Interestingly, in that class were Jo Kessler, Anthony Roe, Michael Salmon and Peter Nathan. Jo, Michael, Anthony and I are still very active. After Confirmation, Dr Mattuck used to ask his most promising pupils to teach in the Religion School as they do today, becoming class assistants. So I started teaching in the Religion School, although at the time I was still at school myself, in the sixth form. I was living at that time with the aunts in Hampstead. I continued teaching until I got married. I am told I was called 'Miss Laughypops'.

I wanted to go to University, having obtained the required grades, but the aunts would not agree to this. They felt that I had to be in a position to support my parents if, by some miracle, they had survived the camps. So they sent me to St Godric's Secretarial College, from where I obtained a secretarial post with the University of London Press. I soon enrolled in a two-year evening Production and Editorial course at the London School of Printing. I graduated with a first class pass, the only woman in a class of fifty men, and my firm promoted me to Editorial Assistant.

I joined the Alumni Society, which was the youth club at that time, where I was quite active. I made a lot of friends, some of whom are still our close friends now. I also went to a club for young refugees, which a friend of mine had recommended, and I met Bob there in 1949. I brought him to an Alumni Friday night service at which the Alumni Chairman, Bernard Lawton, gave the address. Bob was very impressed.

Bob and I were married at the LJS on *Erev Shavu'ot,* 21 May 1950 by the Rev. Philip Cohen, who was then the Associate Minister. At that time, services were still taking place in the Montefiore Hall because the synagogue had been bombed during the war and was out of action. The Women's Society decorated the Hall with flowers earlier than they normally would have done for the *Shavu'ot* services, so we had beautiful flowers for our wedding.

After our wedding, we joined the LJS as adult members, although, of course, I had been a junior member. I remember we were interviewed by a Council member, Major Davidson, a very friendly avuncular gentleman.

I left the Alumni Society and we joined the Younger Members' Organisation. I remember the Rededication service in 1951 when the synagogue was repaired. We were stewards in the gallery, as we were not yet allowed to be stewards downstairs. Later, I became the YMO representative on the Women's Society.

I left the University of London Press when I became pregnant, but continued to freelance for various publishers. When our elder son, David, was enrolled in the Religion School in 1960, I started to teach in the school again, and I taught for about twelve years until after both David and our younger son, Andrew, were confirmed.

Then I was an LJS representative on the Council of the Union of Liberal Synagogues (ULPS) in the 1960s, and I remember Lily Montagu at these meetings. I was present when discussions were taking place about the ULPS joining with the Reform movement in sponsoring the Leo Baeck College, with Lily Montagu, Edgar Nathan and Leslie Edgar being very vocal. I was on the ULPS Council for approximately ten years, and then Bob took over. We've always tried not to sit on committees together.

Bob and I joined the newly formed Members' Choir in 1974 and I sang soprano for thirty years. It was formed by Pamela Cross and our first conductor was Israel Hoffman, the LJS Director of Music. However, he soon gave up and Edward Cross took over. We continued under him for some years until he moved to Radlett, and then Norman Lazarus became our conductor for very many years. He handed the baton to William Falk a few years ago, although he still sings with the choir occasionally.

The next thing, as far as the LJS is concerned, is that the Council asked Bob and me to become joint editors of *LJS News* and we did so from 1992 to 1998. By that time I was the Senior Medical Editor of Heinemann Medical Books and I had already occasionally deputised for Peggy Lang when she was on holiday. Peggy was the Technical Editor of *Service of the Heart* and also used to edit the *ULPS News*.

Editing the newsletter was a difficult, but interesting and enjoyable job. I used the old methods, with everything on hard copy, paste-ups, etc. We used a jobbing printer (no computers for us at that time), but I had to do the layout for him, although he produced the camera-ready copy. Also we didn't have the advantage of emails, so it was quite time-consuming chasing people for their articles. We used to have an editorial meeting once a month, when David Goldberg and we would decide what should be the lead article and what we should commission. Obviously, people were also encouraged to submit contributions. At that time, we produced eleven issues per year with July/August a joint edition. It was quite hard to find a stand-in so that we could take a holiday.

Then, as a sideline, I was Admission's Secretary at Peggy Lang House, which was an Abbeyfield Home, sponsored by and originally funded by LJS members, who also provided the majority of the committee.

I joined the Restaurant Tuesday team of cooks in 1988, as at that time my firm had relocated to Oxford and I became freelance once again, so I was off the 9-to-5 treadmill, and had a bit more time during the day. Eva Feldman, who was then the Co-ordinator of Restaurant Tuesday, asked me to come and help, because Nina Nathan had recently died. Then, when Desmond became unwell, Eva asked me to become Co-ordinator, and I have done that since 2001. At each lunch, we decide what the menu should be for the following month, who is going to cook what and who is going to do the shopping. Bob is the chauffeur for the Northwood crew, as Sue Paul and Eva also live in Northwood, and he drives us all down with the food. He is also the RT Treasurer. We leave at 8.30 a.m. and do not actually get back home until around 4 p.m., so physically it is quite tiring, but it is very worthwhile and our clients enjoy it. It is one of the successful LJS events. In fact, Restaurant Tuesday celebrated its Ruby anniversary in October 2009.

In 1994 John Rayner and Chaim Stern asked me to become Technical Editor of *Siddur Lev Chadash* and I worked very closely with him until the *Siddur* was published in 1995. Then Andrew Goldstein and Charles Middleburgh invited me to repeat my role for the

Machzor, which was published in 2003. I consider that working with the Rabbis on our prayerbooks has really been among my most fulfilling and enjoyable LJS activities.

Apart from that, I was on the coffee rota for many years. I am a member of the Library, KIT and 4Cs committees and I am a greeter on the *Shabbat* morning rota.

A highlight for us was when we had our Golden Wedding anniversary at the LJS in 2000. We had a Thanksgiving Service under the *chuppah* with the family around us. John gave a short address and David Goldberg also officiated. We were trying, at the time, to encourage others to take up the idea and have a little religious ceremony for their Golden Wedding under the *chuppah*. But I don't think it has caught on. In 2010 we celebrated our Diamond Wedding with the Kirk family participating in the *Shabbat* service and Bob reading from the Scroll.

You wouldn't recognise the LJS now compared to how it was at my first service in 1939 when I thought I was going to church. Now, many men wear *kippot*, not all wear *tallit*, but quite a large number do. We have a woman as our Senior Rabbi. There are still a number of Dr Mattuck's prayers in our liturgy. Interestingly, they were incorporated into *Service of the Heart* and from there into the *Siddur*. There is much, much more Hebrew; also more ritual. Some of us don't like all the rituals. Thank goodness we still don't process the scrolls, although some Liberal synagogues do. Our new Sanctuary provides a far warmer atmosphere; previously it was somewhat cold, although, in a way, the old building was beautiful with all its wood.

We noticed a change in the language of the services from 90 per cent English to more Hebrew under John Rayner's leadership. It occurred very gradually but, once *Service of the Heart* was introduced, it was very evident. It is left to the leader of the congregation to choose what will be read in Hebrew or English. They take a measure of the congregation and decide how to proceed. If there are a lot of non-Jewish visitors, they might do more English.

The acoustics in the old synagogue were not very good. The choir would sing from the gallery – 'angels from above'. Now the choir sings downstairs, which is much better. This practice was actually started by the Members' Choir in the New Synagogue in our old building. They wanted to be part of the congregation, and not be hidden away. When we entered our new building in 1991, there was a choir loft and the Professional Choir was meant to sing from there, but they found the acoustics difficult and they moved downstairs.

I always remember Lily Montagu sitting in the front row of the old synagogue wearing a long brown coat, brown hat, with her head down. You thought she was asleep, but occasionally her head would come up and she would nod her head vigorously, and then down would go her head again. She was usually there with her sister, Marian. She was very impressive.

Dr Mattuck was a wonderful, charismatic orator. His sermons were always thought-provoking, and one listened spellbound. I well remember his blessing the congregation with arms held aloft, a ritual also followed by his successor, Dr Edgar, who was a very dear man, but with a rather poor memory. It was quite common for him to meet you with a 'good morning', and a short while later he would greet you again. He was a very sincere, genuine man. He was ill very early in his life. He preached at Friends' House just after he had come out of the Army where he had served as a Chaplain. That was a very memorable sermon, but gradually, as he got more ill, he really started taking more of a back seat, and that was when John came to the LJS from the South London Liberal congregation.

John was my guru. I admired him. What helped was that John also came on a *Kindertransport*, so we had the same background. We also discovered many years later that his parents and my mother were actually taken on the same transport, so that was something else we had in common. John had no small talk, he was a very private man, but when you got him talking at a party, he was very funny. He would write limericks about everybody, quite spontaneously.

Philip Cohen, who married us, was wonderful with young people, and a good pastoral rabbi. He was followed by David Goldstein, who used to hold coffee evenings for the Confirmation class and the youth groups and was very popular. His sermons were 'out of this world' and we missed him terribly when he left the synagogue to go to the British Library as Keeper of Hebrew Manuscripts.

Of the presidents, I remember Louis Gluckstein very well. He was very tall, even taller when he had his top hat on. He was very kind to Bob and me. Bob has more stories about him than I do, because of the Council meetings. Then came Maxwell Stern, who was succeeded by Peter Lazarus, a personal friend whom we admired very much indeed. Willie Kessler is also amongst our close friends. As I mentioned earlier, his wife Jo and I were confirmed together. Our sons grew up together and we had joint Confirmation parties. We have also sat happily alongside each other on many committees.

The LJS has been my home since 1939 and Bob's since 1950. Although we now live in Northwood, we just cannot leave the LJS. All our friends are here. Spiritually, this is where we belong, even though it does mean coming every Saturday from Northwood. We have very little family, so the synagogue is our extended 'family'.

Our son David is a member of Northwood. He was a Treasurer there, and is still very much involved in various committees. Andy does not really believe in organised religion. He will come to special services; for instance, he came to the final service in the old synagogue and to the first service in the new Sanctuary. He occasionally comes on *Erev Rosh Hashanah*.

Our grandchildren, Devora, Ben and Joshua all had their *B'nei Mitzvah* at Northwood as well as their *Kabbalat Torah,* and they have all been very active in *Kadimah* – so, hopefully, the family commitment to Liberal Judaism continues.

See photographs 26, 43, and 55.

✡

Bob Kirk

Bob Kirk came to Britain in 1939 as a child refugee on a Kindertransport. He joined the LJS on meeting his future wife, Ann. Over the years he has been involved in most aspects of synagogue life, a commitment recognised by his election as President in 2007.

I am Robert Samuel Kirk, (usually called Bob), born in Hanover, Germany on 19 May, 1925, as Rudolf Kirchheimer. My parents, Josef Kirchheimer and Hedwig Heller, met in Frankfurt-am-Main. After their marriage in 1912, they settled in Hanover, where my mother's family lived and where my father established a textile business.

My father came from Berwangen, a small village in Baden, where his family had been cattle dealers since at least 1701. Some members of the family emigrated to America in the mid-1800s, but he and his brothers were among the first to leave to pursue other livelihoods in Germany.

My maternal grandfather, a soap and candle maker, came from Crailsheim in Wuerttemberg, where he had settled after leaving Postelberg, in Bohemia, in 1893. I never found out why he moved on from Crailsheim to Hanover.

I was the youngest of three children; a fourth sibling had died at the age of seven before I was born. My father had served in the 1914–18 war, had been wounded several times and was awarded a number of decorations including the Iron Cross.

We were members of an Orthodox community – in 1925, it was the ninth largest in Germany, with about 5,000 members – where my parents were regular worshippers. There was a large circle of friends and a lively youth scene.

I celebrated my *Bar Mitzvah* in the beautiful synagogue in the old city (built by Edwin Oppler in 1870, in the same year as, and very reminiscent of, West London Synagogue) in May 1938, one of the last *B'nei Mitzvah* to take place there before the building was destroyed during *Kristallnacht*, 9 to 10 November 1938.

Kristallnacht was the catalyst for the *Kindertransport*, under whose auspices I arrived in the UK on 4 May 1939. My elder sister Helga had emigrated to South Africa in 1936, then aged twenty-three and, in 1948, had moved to Brazil where her husband had been sent by his employers. My brother Frank had come to Britain a few months before me on a trainee work permit although, at the age of fifteen, he would have qualified for inclusion in a *Kindertransport*. He has lived in Lancashire since 1948. My parents were transported to the concentration camp in Riga in December 1941. After the war, in 1949, I went back to Germany to seek information, but at that time all that was known that 'they had not returned from the East'. Now they are commemorated by name, together with the other 2,500 murdered Jews of Hanover, on a memorial in front of the Opera House in the city centre.

When the *Kindertransport* organisation was first set up, there was a requirement for a £50 deposit in respect of each child to be brought into the country, intended as a guarantee that the child would not become a charge on public funds and to cover re-emigration – we were not really meant to stay here. However, I had no knowledge of that at the time, nor for years afterwards. That requirement was later waived, but when I arrived, the arrangement was still in place and for the first eight days after my arrival I stayed with my guarantor. But as he had sponsored a number of children, it was soon time to move on to make room for the next one. I was lucky to be sent to a young family, with whom I stayed for about eight weeks until the boy they had sponsored arrived. They sent me to school, and we have always remained in touch, although the family moved to Canada.

After a spell at a hostel in Westgate, I returned to London, just in time to join a school and be evacuated at the outbreak of war. Evacuation proved to be a great leveller – we refugees were no longer the only ones away from home and family.

After two years at what had become the village school, I was directed to a factory for war work, and in 1944 volunteered for Army service. At that time I also changed my name. Kirchheimer was not considered safe for active service. The name 'Kirk' seemed appropriate as I was stationed in Scotland. After training in the Royal Artillery, I eventually became an interpreter, dealing with German prisoners of war.

On demobilisation in 1948, I returned to London, where I found work with my one-time youth club leader from Hanover. I also joined a club for young Jewish refugees. One day the chairman brought along a prospective new member, Ann Francis. And that is where my involvement with the LJS started.

Ann had been at the LJS since her arrival on a *Kindertransport* in April 1939. She was an active member of the Alumni Society (a club for sixteen- to thirty-year-olds, established by Rabbi Dr Mattuck in 1918) and taught in the Religion School. She introduced me to the LJS at an *Erev Shabbat* service run by the Alumni. It was a real eye-opener to find laymen thoroughly involved, including delivering the sermon – on that occasion by the Society's Chairman, Bernard Lawton, later a long-serving Chairman of the House Committee and Chief Steward.

At that time, the Sanctuary had not yet been repaired following extensive war damage, and so we were married in the Montefiore Hall of the old building on 21 May 1950. The Hall was temporarily furnished with the pews from the Sanctuary, where they were later reinstated. As a result, the gangways were extremely narrow and the bride had to sidle up the aisle. This was *Erev Shavu'ot,* and thanks to the kindness of the Women's Society in decorating in the morning rather than, as usual, in the afternoon, the stage (used as the *bimah)* was ablaze with flowers. We could never have afforded that. We were married by the Rev. Philip Cohen, then our Associate Minister. Our Senior Rabbi was Leslie Edgar. Dr Israel Mattuck was Rabbi Emeritus, having retired in 1947.

I was not much involved in synagogue life for the first few years of membership. Having missed a great deal of education, I spent ten years in correspondence studies alongside full-time work, finally qualifying as a Chartered Company Secretary in 1960. After a few false starts I became Company Secretary and Finance Director of a company dealing with textiles for the automotive and marine industry. That was a little ironic since, in the normal course of events, I might well have taken over my father's textile business.

My first 'official' LJS activity was as Treasurer of the Synagogue Society, a social and cultural society open to all synagogue members (chaired at that time by Edith Kahn, a very charismatic lady and Headmistress of Fleet School), as opposed to the Women's Society. My ongoing involvement started when our elder son, David, joined the Religion School in 1960 and I was asked to help run the school. I became the Administrator – a post I held for twelve years. It must have been hard for David and his younger brother

Andrew – with both parents active in the school (Ann was still teaching) there was never a chance to duck out.

At that time, our teaching staff consisted entirely of dedicated volunteer members, including the much-loved Celia Mintz (later Rapp), Eva Feldman and Ann among many others. The school had a succession of Principals, including a number of American rabbinic students, and the rabbis Chaim Stern and Sidney Brichto whilst they were at the LJS during John Rayner's studies at HUC in Cincinnati and, from 1964 to 1975, our Associate Rabbi, Dr David Goldstein. David, a brilliant scholar and poet, eventually left to become Keeper of Hebrew Manuscripts at the British Library. He died far too young, and there is a photograph and plaque in his memory in our library, which he cherished and cared for. David and his wife, Berry, used to hold very popular open evenings for our young people, with discussions over coffee and music played by David on his guitar.

During this time we moved the school from its customary Sunday slot to *Shabbat* mornings. One of the major reasons was that, by meeting on *Shabbat*, the children got a sense of being part of a congregation, rather than coming to an apparently unused building. The school was organised in four houses (Carmel, Hermon, Lebanon and Tabor), which made for a certain amount of rivalry. That system was abandoned after much pressure from Edith Kahn, who objected to the competition element. The idea was resurrected in 1995, with the houses being named Montefiore, Montagu, Mattuck and Moos, but that too has been discontinued, and the classes are designated by the letter of the Hebrew alphabet.

One of the duties of the school administrator was to act as supply teacher and so, in order to improve my Jewish knowledge, I joined the Evening Institute then being run by the ULPS (Union of Liberal and Progressive Synagogues – now known as Liberal Judaism, or LJ). At that time, Greta Hyman, the Organising Secretary of ULPS, was Registrar of the Institute. Pretty soon, she persuaded me to take over from her.

When, in 1965, ULPS joined RSGB (Reform Synagogues of Great Britain) in sponsoring Leo Baeck College, the Evening Institute became part of LBC and I went with it, taken over, you might say, with the furniture. I became Secretary of the College in 1968, again succeeding Greta and, in due course, chaired the College Council from 1978 to 1982. I had the good fortune to be in the chair when we moved the College from West London Synagogue to the Manor House in Finchley – later to become the Sternberg Centre. I am an Honorary Fellow of the College and, like all past Chairmen, an Honorary Life Vice-President.

I joined the LJS Council in 1966 under the chairmanship of Sidney Levine. At that time Sir Louis Gluckstein was President, having combined that office with the chairmanship until 1964. Sir Louis was very tall – six feet seven inches – which made having a conversation with him from my five-foot level problematic. He solved the difficulty by having me stand on the third step of the stairs leading up from the foyer of the old building. That just about brought me to eye-level with him!

I succeeded Michael Cross as Chairman of the Education Committee in 1968. In 1973 we decided to revive the Services Committee (there had been one in the 1950s under the chairmanship of Desmond Feldman). I was its Chairman for a number of years and still serve as a member.

Having left the Council in 1981, I was re-elected in 1985 in time to become involved in the plans for the rebuilding of the synagogue. I served on the Design and Use Committee headed by Neil Levitt, and chaired the *Shoah* Memorial Committee. That was probably the most difficult assignment I have ever had to deal with. At our first meeting in April 1989, we established our criteria: Beauty, Simplicity, Dignity and Permanence, together with the need for low maintenance. First we ran a competition, which produced several interesting proposals, none of which, however, really met our criteria. Over the next six years, we considered and discarded many suggestions, and the committee understandably became very frustrated. We were very fortunate that a number of members, Vikki Slowe, Jeremy Lewison and Edward Mendelsohn, together with Rabbi David Goldberg, were willing and able to devote much time to the search which finally led us to Anish Kapoor. Once we had seen his work, we knew we had found our man.

The dedication of the memorial, on 10 November 1996, was one of the most emotional events I have ever attended. There was a sermon by Rabbi David Goldberg, a reading from Primo Levi's *The Truce* by Janet Suzman, a short but very moving address by Anish, *El Maleh Rachamim* sung by Rabbi Mark Solomon, culminating in the dedication prayer by Rabbi John Rayner, the text of which hangs next to the memorial. Since the installation of the memorial we have held a service around it every year to commemorate *Kristallnacht,* when many German and Austrian synagogues and communal buildings, as well as homes and shops, were destroyed and the persecution of Jews started in earnest.

For the last fifteen years or so, both Ann and I have often spoken to schools and other groups about our life as children in Nazi Germany and as refugees in England. We are on the speakers' circuit for the Jewish Museum, and participate in the Holocaust Memorial Day programme at Northwood & Pinner Liberal Synagogue, where we are Friends, and at Finchley Reform Synagogue.

Two other dedications remain in my mind: the return to our Sanctuary in 1951, dramatically led by Rabbis Mattuck and Edgar, after the war damage had finally been repaired (Ann and I, as very junior members, were allowed to steward in the gallery), and the entry, forty years later, into the new Sanctuary, at the conclusion of the rebuilding project between 1988 and 1991, with the *ner tamid* being lit by Marjorie Moos and a Religion School pupil.

Ann and I helped to found the Members' Choir and we sang in it for nearly thirty years. I am Treasurer for Restaurant Tuesday (which Ann leads) and for the Library, where we are both on the executive committee.

From 1992 to 1998, we were joint editors of *LJS News.* In 1986, I had the pleasure of masterminding the celebrations for the 75th Anniversary of the synagogue, with a great deal of hard work by Dorothy Moncrieff, who mounted an extremely interesting exhibition, and Prue Baker. Prue was also one of the driving forces behind the *Sho'ah* Memorial, and the extremely efficient co-ordinator of the synagogue's rebuilding project.

In 1973 Raymon Benedyk succeeded Michael Duparc as Marriage Secretary. When in 1992 he felt it advisable to ask for assistance – we had considerably more marriages then than we do now – I was asked to become an additional Marriage Secretary. I continued in that role when Joan Shopper took over.

When Louis Steinman retired as the Beadle in 1993 after about thirty years of service, we decided that his duties should become a congregational responsibility. Martin Slowe, George Rigal and I became the first *shammashim* and I still lead the team, which is now sixteen-strong, with a great deal of support from the synagogue office. For several years I also organised member participation in services. One of my other preoccupations is the care of our scrolls (not the mantles, which are looked after lovingly and generously by Christine Stevenson). I have a particular interest in our Czech scroll, which we hold on permanent loan from the Czech Memorial Scrolls Trust. Until recently we had a second one, which has now been transferred to a newly formed Liberal community whose need is greater than ours.

I became a Trustee in 1982 and from 1992 was Joint Treasurer with Bob Beral, until I left Council in 1998. And finally, the most amazing event of all was to be elected President in 2007, the sixth in line after Claude Montefiore, Sir Louis Gluckstein, Maxwell Stern, Sir Peter Lazarus and Willie Kessler. What does a President do? Opinions vary. I have always thought it important not to interfere in the management of the synagogue – that's the job of the Honorary Officers. I attend Council meetings by standing invitation, which helps me to understand members' thinking if asked to give advice. Of course – as I said in my acceptance speech – I do sometimes give advice even if not asked! The really important thing, to me, is to be around and to be accessible to all members, and smooth ruffled feathers when necessary – I'm glad to say that's very rare. I also represent the synagogue when invited to do so.

For many years I was an LJS representative on the Council of ULPS. I was also a member of the Education Committee and of the Advisory Committee, which addressed problem topics before they were presented to Council. Two of the most important subjects for discussion I remember were the proposal to move the Union headquarters from Whitfield Street (now Maple Street) to the Sternberg Centre (it was eventually decided that it was necessary to retain a presence in Central London), and the proposition to merge the two Progressive Movements – Liberal and Reform. Although strongly supported by, among others, John Rayner, David Goldberg and West London's Senior Rabbi Hugo Gryn, eventually the opposition won out. In my view this was a great pity.

Ann and I have attended many of the ULPS Biennial Conferences, starting from 1952. There are always interesting discussions about Liberal Judaism and its place in the world, but the really important aspect is meeting and talking to members of other Liberal congregations. It is a great pleasure every time to meet up with friends from all over the country.

When I joined the LJS, the atmosphere at services was very formal. No one wore a *kippah*. If one wanted to cover one's head one wore a hat – and *tallitot* were worn only on the *bimah*. For the High Holyday services, many men wore top hats or bowlers. Over the years, that has changed. We used to be accused of being rather 'cold' – possibly 'reserved' would have been a better description – a feeling perhaps not helped by the beautiful but nevertheless somewhat austere appearance of the Sanctuary, with its subdued colour scheme and impressive carved mahogany Ark screen.

The new building has dispelled any feeling of coldness. Quite apart from the beauty of the 'new' Sanctuary – it's already twenty years old! – much of the change in atmosphere has come from the way in which we greet members and visitors. The institution of *shammashim* and greeters manages to counteract the need for a strong security presence, which a lot of people find rather disturbing even if necessary. Visitors are often surprised to be met by the offer of a cup of coffee before the service – an innovation introduced shortly before our 'exile' at the church in Loudoun Road while no. 28 was being rebuilt. It's a great way for members to meet and helps to set an informal tone for the morning.

At the time I arrived at the LJS, we were using the 1937 edition of the *Liberal Jewish Prayerbook*, written largely by Rabbi Dr Israel Mattuck. That was quite a culture shock. Hebrew usage was at a minimum and, coming from an Orthodox background, I was greatly struck by the very different format of the liturgy.

All that changed with the introduction of *Service of the Heart* in 1967 and *Gate of Repentance* in 1973, the work of Rabbis John Rayner and Chaim Stern. The language was modernised (no more 'thees' and 'thous'), there was rather more Hebrew and the liturgy took much more account of the traditional format. This didn't please everybody because it was a major change from the 'Mattuck tradition'.

The next generation of prayerbooks, *Siddur Lev Chadash* (1995) and *Machzor Ruach Chadashah* (2003), took the modernisation of the liturgy a step further with their de-gendered language. I am quite proud of the fact that I was invited to be a member of the lay consultancy panel for both the *Siddur* and the *Machzor*. I had frequently attended study sessions with the rabbis, particularly with John Rayner, but this was quite different. John's meticulous preparation, with many pages of background on the history and text of prayers, with reasons why he favoured a particular formulation, was an educational experience like no other. These prayerbooks, together with more accessible music and greater use of lay readers, have done much to improve participation in services.

The day I met Ann was, without a doubt, the luckiest day of my life. Not only did it lead to the happiest of marriages and a family, but it also introduced me to the community of the LJS which, for both of us, became our extended family and a lifelong focus of involvement.

See photographs 20, 26, 48, 55, 61, and 85.

✡

Rosemary and Norman Lazarus

Norman Lazarus is a lifelong member who still attends synagogue most Saturdays. He was a member of the Alumni Society and the Younger Members' Organisation and ran the LJS Religion School football team. For twenty-five years he conducted the Members' Choir. Rosemary joined the LJS in the 1960s. She became Chair of the Women's Society and was involved in many other congregational activities including Restaurant Tuesdays, flower arranging and the Tapestry Group which completed the *bimah* chairs. She was also a member of the Keep in Touch Group and was, in effect, the *LJS News* Social Secretary.

Rosemary: My name is Rosemary Lazarus (née Levy) and I was born on 10 September 1935.

My father, Lewis Levy, was born in Hampstead in 1910 and died in 1984. He worked for the 600 Group, a scrap metal and engineering business that still exists, and which was so-called because it was located at 600 Commercial Road. My mother, Violet, was born in Manchester, as was her mother, Nettie Heyman. Violet's father, Max, originally came from Alsace-Lorraine. Dad's family were Orthodox, and my parents were married at Dennington Park Road Synagogue. Although we continued to belong to the Orthodox synagogue, I did not have any religious education there. I was taken to *cheder* once, but the behaviour of the other children was so disgraceful that my mother said, 'She's not going again!' My parents knew Marjorie Moos, and they arranged for her to come about once a fortnight to teach me and my brother Bryan. We didn't learn Hebrew, just Religious Knowledge. At home, we kept Friday nights, so I did pick up a little Hebrew that way.

My mother's family were Liberal. My grandfather was a founder member of Hill Street, and my mother was Treasurer of the Alumni Society when Leslie Edgar was Chairman in the early days. Granny Heyman was very infirm. She had terrible arthritis, so when I was about thirteen I used to come to the LJS on High Holydays on her ticket, which was allowed in those days, with my great-uncle John. I much preferred the service to the Orthodox synagogue. It was less noisy and more peaceful.

Norman: My name is Norman Lazarus, and I was born on 7 September 1928. My mother's name was Mary Halsted and my father was Kenneth Lazarus. My parents were married at the Bayswater United Synagogue, where the Halsteds were members. My parents were members of the LJS and I used to go to services with them from time to time. My father was on the Council and chaired the House Committee for many years. My mother started and ran the nursery on High Holydays.

During the war we lived in Bognor Regis, and only came up to the synagogue for the High Holydays. I did not go to Religion School as a child. My brother Peter, sister Margaret and I were taught by the formidable Miss Moos before we were confirmed. I remember her being particularly strict, she was quite authoritarian. We certainly learned a lot, but no Hebrew. I have made up for it since. I travelled to London for my Confirmation classes and I was duly confirmed in 1945. The Senior Rabbi, Dr Israel Mattuck, conducted the service, which I well remember to this day. Most of my fellow confirmands are no longer with us, but Roy Gluckstein, with whom I was very friendly, is still going strong.

I remember Dr Mattuck very well. He had a commanding presence. He and Rabbi Leslie Edgar, the Assistant Minister, conducted the services and delivered some wonderful sermons. They were great friends of my family. There was a professional choir, who sang beautifully from the choir loft, which made them rather remote.

Not long after my Confirmation I had the pleasure of joining His Majesty's Army, and didn't really come back to the LJS until I was about twenty-one. I was a member of the Alumni Society and, later, of the Younger Members' Organisation. We had many enjoyable outings. For a time, I was Treasurer of the Alumni. It was all very 'English', in the sense that there was not much religious content, though we did have a *Chanukkah* service.

I met Rosemary at the engagement party of my sister Margaret and George Rigal.

Rosemary: Norman and I became engaged before my 21st birthday. We had no engagement party, as my 21st party had already been organised at my home in Northwood. We were married at the LJS on 10 April 1957, and our reception was at the Trocadero Hotel.

Norman: Dr Mattuck had died, so it was Leslie Edgar who married us. It was a very large, wonderful wedding. Our first home was in Sidmouth Road, Willesden Green.

Rosemary: By then, my mother had crept back to the LJS. My father followed some time later, but he also kept up his membership of Dennington Park Road until his mother died in 1972. In 1975 he became Chairman of the LJS Council for six years.

When we first got married, Norman and I attended Hebrew classes at the LJS. I was in a class above Norman! We had four children, Roger, Claire, Ian and Janet, who were all confirmed at the LJS. While they were young, we were tied to the home, and I didn't start attending the synagogue regularly until they went into the Religion School.

We thought one shouldn't send children to classes without going oneself, so I used to alternate with Norman in attending *Shabbat* services. That was when we really got involved. I remember Janet, the youngest, getting a little fidgety during services, so I used to take her out into the corridor where we would often meet Tony Solomons with his daughter Jennifer.

Janet is the only one of our children who is still actively involved in the synagogue. She helped to set up the Mothers and Toddlers Group, and was on the selection committee when we were seeking a new rabbi. She is Janet Mills now, and her children, Freddie, Bertie and Matilda, are fifth-generation LJS.

Norman: I conducted the Members' Choir for many years. Pamela Cross actually started this amateur choir with Israel Hoffman as its conductor. He handed the baton on to Pamela's son, Edward, who was a very fine musician. Under his leadership, the choir grew in strength and proficiency. When Edward moved to Radlett, I took over and ran the choir for the next twenty-five years. Choir rehearsals were held once a week and we sang on the first *Shabbat* of the month, as well as at the High Holyday and Festival services. Our standard improved considerably, and we also sang at weddings and old people's homes. I recall that we went all the way to Nightingale House in Clapham as well as singing at Sunridge Court, a Blind Club and to the Out and About Club.

The Members' Choir was my great love. I have loved music since I was a boy, and I played the piano, which I still do. I really wanted to take music up professionally, but, in fact, I became a chartered accountant and was the Finance Director of several companies including Sutcliffe's, the catering firm.

Rosemary: I joined the Women's Society when Claire went to school forty-five years ago. I remember that some of the ladies wore hats at the committee meetings! All women members of the LJS were automatically members of the society of which I became Chairman when I was only forty years old. We had bazaars, coffee mornings, and two lunches a month – one with a speaker. The Speaker's Lunch was eventually discontinued, but Restaurant Tuesday, of which I am one of the team, is still thriving today. We also visited the elderly, both in their homes and in hospital, which KIT does today.

I also compile the People's Page for the Newsletter which keeps me quite busy. I like working with people, both young and old, and I am on the Management Team of Sunridge Residential Home, where there are many LJS members.

Professionally, I taught in various schools for many years. My final teaching job was working mornings at Glendower Preparatory School from 1977 to 1995.

Norman: About thirty-five to forty years ago, I used to be in charge of the football team for Religion School children who, after matches, regularly came back to tea in our kitchen. We held training sessions, and we also went to 'away' events against other youth groups. It was a great way for the children to form friendships. Later, Charles Kessler became involved.

Rosemary: I also remember looking through the members' index cards with Celia Rapp – a brilliant teacher who took the 'baby' class of five- to six-year-olds in the Religion School. In those days the LJS had no computers! We wanted to identify those children who were the right age for starting in the school in order to send letters to the parents with all the details. At one point there were about 3,000 LJS members. We also organised groups by postcode – everyone living in St John's Wood, etc. Celia knew a huge group of children and their parents, so between us we covered a large percentage of the congregation.

Norman: Rabbi John Rayner was the leading light of the LJS. His three children are the same ages as our oldest three and they used to come to tea with us. John's best effort was when he went round the garden standing on his hands. John had hidden talents, which not many people saw. He could be very light-hearted. He loved children and he liked to amuse them.

Rosemary: Maxwell Stern, my father's cousin, was an excellent Chairman. I joined the Council the day my father retired from Council. Unfortunately, he died three weeks after that, and since he had never spoken about what went on at Council meetings, I never really learned anything from him which was a great shame.

Norman: Liberal Judaism is in our blood, and I am so pleased that Rosemary and I were able to contribute to the life of the LJS. I used to help Neil Drapkin and then Ergun Arican with the synagogue accounts. Looking back, I did quite a bit in that accounts office – but, of course, nowadays it is run far more professionally.

Rosemary: We have thoroughly enjoyed being LJS members – we feel really 'married' to the synagogue.

Editorial Note: Rosemary died suddenly on 30 September 2009. The above memories do not come close to reflecting the manifold nature of her involvement in LJS activities. As Ann Kirk recalls, Rosemary was also 'an enthusiastic embroiderer in the Tapestry Group working on the beautiful *bimah* chairs, a committed Restaurant Tuesday cook, a repairer of library books, and a *Shammash* and Greeter. She was a founder member of the Members' Choir. I treasure sitting next to her for over thirty years, chatting away in between singing at rehearsals, sometimes to Norman's displeasure! Rosemary loved a good-natured gossip'. (*LJS News*, November 2009)

See Photographs 1, 26, 27, 38, 43 and 68.

✡

Jenny Nathan

Jenny Nathan has memories of the LJS that date back to just after the Second World War. Having attended the Religion School, she was a prominent member of Phase Two prior to her involvement in the Out and About Club, in which she has now played a leading role for over thirty years. Jenny is also involved in a range of community care activities and has chaired the Community Care Co-ordination Committee since its inception in 2003.

My name is Jenny Nathan and I was born in London on 16 April 1943. My parents, Joan and Eric Abrahams, were married at the synagogue on 4 August 1940, three months before the bomb damage occurred. Daddy was in the Army at the time and had just forty-eight hours' leave to get married, have a reception at the Grosvenor Rooms in Willesden and take a honeymoon.

My maternal grandfather, Samuel Rubenstein, came from Plungyan in Lithuania with his father when he was thirteen years old. He arrived in Swansea in 1895. Shiploads of wood for pit props were exported at that time and many Jews managed to escape the pogroms in this way. He married Phoebe Greenstone from Wolverhampton and they lived in Swansea where my mother, Joan, and her brothers, Alan and Norman, were born before the family came to London in the 1920s. When they were looking around for a new community to join, they were excited when they heard about the opening of a new synagogue in St John's Wood. They apparently came to the opening service at the LJS in 1925 and were very proud of being long-standing members of the synagogue.

My father's parents, Michael and Sarah Abrahams, belonged to Hampstead (Orthodox) Synagogue in Dennington Park Road, where my grandfather was a warden. When my parents were engaged and then planned to be married at the LJS, the idea of their getting married in a Liberal synagogue was something of a shock to the Abrahams family! However, all was well and you can see from the wedding photographs that they all looked very smart, wearing silk top hats and stylish outfits. It was very difficult to get things in 1940 and I was told that the wedding cake was only partly a real cake – two layers were cardboard as you could not get enough sugar for the icing. The only sadness was that my mother's brother, Norman, was at the time missing, having been taken prisoner of war and this was obviously an enormous worry to all the family. He survived the war, having spent five years as a prisoner and later wrote a book called *The Invisibly Wounded*, a copy of which is in the LJS library.

My father was stationed at Lord's Cricket Ground with an anti-aircraft unit, which apparently deflected a bomb from damaging the ground. My father was rewarded the next day by Sir Pelham Warner, Chairman of the MCC, who gave him a hundred cigarettes for preventing a bomb from falling on the hallowed turf.

My grandfather, Sam Rubenstein, died in 1946, before my brother Peter was born. This was sad because it meant that I was the only grandchild he knew. He was buried in the LJS cemetery in Pound Lane and we used to go every month with my grandmother to take flowers and look at the names of the people buried there. I mention this because people sometimes feel that cemeteries are sad places, but this has colour because of the rose bushes and other flowers. I think it is important for young people to be taken and shown the cemetery; it is an extension of the LJS and part of their history.

My brother Peter, who was also married at the LJS to Eva Kilgast, was Chairman of the Cemetery Committee and did a huge amount of work there. My husband Michael's parents, Cyril and Violet Nathan, whom sadly I never met, have rose bushes around their grave and they are just across the path from where my grandparents are buried, which is an extraordinary coincidence.

My very first memory of going to the LJS is when I was about five years old. There was a special service after the war, the last held in the synagogue before it closed for restoration. I can remember it clearly. I was sitting downstairs and my main occupation during the service was looking upstairs to the part which had been bomb-damaged and watching the pigeons flying in and out through the empty space.

The services were then moved to the Montefiore Hall and I can distinctly remember the *sukkah,* which used to be in the Mattuck Room where Council meetings were held. There was lattice work on the walls and glass in the ceiling, which opened up so that you could convert it into a lovely *sukkah.* I always remember the wonderful smell of the greenery at *Sukkot.*

I also remember the rededication service that was held in 1951 when the synagogue was re-opened. It was an important service and part of it was broadcast on the radio. There were only enough tickets for adults to go and I can remember sitting at home by the radio trying to get the right spot to hear the little bit from our synagogue – that was very exciting.

I started going to the LJS Sunday School, as it was then. Miss Moos, the Head Teacher, was rather frightening and awe-inspiring, but Miss Mintz (who became Celia Rapp) was completely the opposite. She was small and petite and an excellent teacher.

However, I did not continue my studies at the Religion School because, at that time, there was no *Bar* or *Bat Mitzvah* at the LJS and my parents were very keen that my brother should have one, so we went to the Hampstead Synagogue. I liked the services there because the Rev. Harry Levy was the most liberal and open-minded of all Orthodox rabbis. We had a mixed choir which proves the point, I think. I did enjoy the *chazan* singing. But I also liked going to the LJS and being able to read the prayers in English, join in the hymns and have the whole family sitting together. I feel I had a very balanced upbringing, having experience of both Orthodox and Liberal services.

My real involvement in the LJS came much later when I was looking for a social life and joined Phase Two. It was a very active group of people, chaired by Esther Rantzen. The members organised an excellent programme of social events and had many speakers from the BBC. There was no need for a Director of Youth or a rabbi organising it as it all seemed to just happen and I met many very good friends to whom I am still close.

I worked as a Medical Secretary at the Middlesex Hospital, then the Royal London Hospital for many years until I met Michael and married, a bit later than most of our friends. I was involved with the Jewish Historical Society in the East End which researched Jewish medical personnel who had practised in the area. I also wrote a paper about Mrs Alice Model, who was a pioneer in Nursery Education and after whom the Alice Model Nursery School was named. I was a Governor of the school for fifteen years. I am hoping that someone will write some papers on pioneering women of the East End of London.

The Out and About Club, which has been my main interest at the LJS, was founded by Esther Rantzen and Diana Da Costa (née Mohr) in 1964. It was set up as a non-denominational club for disabled people living in the area and this is how it has remained. It has always been a very active, social thing to be involved with; people who were helpers remained friends for years afterwards. Geoffrey Laventhal and Joany Weinberg, who is still a member of the LJS, were two of the original helpers and so was Fleur Hoffman. All sorts of people were Chairman, among them Jeffrey Spearman, Nick Feldman and Stephen Lazarus. Stephen and I ran it together for a while, but when Nick married and moved to Suffolk and there was a vacancy for a Chairman, I took it on and have been doing it ever since. I enjoy it. We had a reunion last year and seventy people who had been helpers came. It was amazing!

The Out and About Club continues to meet once a fortnight at the LJS where we arrange musical entertainments and a have variety of talks ranging from 'Travels with Pam Fox and Michael Hart' to what it was like to work at Bletchley Park. At present we have four Jewish members out of a total of forty, which is nice as we have a lot of local churches involved in this way, especially St Paul's, Rossmore Road and the Catholic Church of Our Lady in Lisson Grove. Usually people introduce one another to the Club. Dr Max Caplin was our President until recently, but due to ill health he has retired and has been succeeded by Rabbi David Goldberg who is a very active President and takes an interest in everything that is going on.

We have an annual outing and an annual dinner, which is a major event. We had 125 people at the dinner last December. Every member is invited to bring a friend, some perhaps bring two, and then we invite people who have helped us during the year or have entertained us, together with some members of Council. Although the annual dinner is a big event, we still manage to organise the catering between us with a little outside help. We appeal to LJS members once a year, which keeps us going. In return, the Out and About members themselves often put all their pennies in the Penny Jar which goes to the LJS.

I also chair the Community Care Co-ordination Committee (known as the 4Cs), which deals with all aspects of Community Care at the LJS. We are lucky enough to have a professional Social Worker, Liz Crossick, leading the work together with the KIT (Keep in Touch) Group, Bereavement Support Group, Family Care Group, Restaurant Tuesday, Tea + Video and the Out and Abouts. This is an essential part of synagogue life as we now have a large number of congregants over the age of eighty-five and many families have four generations needing help.

The other thing that I was asked to do, which I was told would not take up too much time, was to form a Personnel Committee. That is a bigger job than I had anticipated because it involves a lot of employment law, but luckily we have an employment lawyer, Jessica Sokel, on the Committee who has done a huge amount of work. You can't run an organisation without a committee like this.

I have been involved with a few fundraising events. Many years ago a large concert was organised by Victor Falk and one of the people playing was a teenage Steven Isserlis.

We have always had a big *seder* at home, so I have not often been to the communal one. We squeeze in as many people as we can. High Holydays are always a special occasion, and I love to see the synagogue absolutely packed out.

The LJS has been such a large part of my life, including the important fact that I met my husband, Michael, at the home of Rabbi David and Carole Goldberg. We both enjoy the services as it involves meeting people which is such an important aspect of synagogue life.

I have absorbed many changes in the services over the years. I think it has a lot to do with the fact that my background is partly Orthodox. When my father left the Orthodox synagogue and came to the LJS, he liked the fact that we included more Hebrew because that seemed more familiar to him. I think the changes in the services are part of Liberal Judaism which is about effecting change. What I like is that women have total equality. Everybody sits together, women have equal rights and take part in the service (which is not so in the Orthodox) and there are women rabbis. I am excited to see a large and vibrant KT class and I hope that these young people will stay involved and carry on the traditions of the LJS which are so dear to our hearts.

See photographs 16 (Joan and Eric Abrahams) and 51.

✡

Michael Nathan

Michael Nathan is a lifelong member of the LJS and his grandfather was one of its founding members. He has always been very involved with the synagogue, including chairing the United Charities Fund for forty-five years. He has many memories of the early days of the LJS.

I am a third-generation member of the LJS, my grandfather and great-uncle on my mother's side being founding members of the synagogue. My mother, whose maiden name was Violet Simon, was particularly active and was, I believe, a founding member of the Alumni Society. She was certainly a member at Hill Street and definitely was present at the dedication of the foundation stone at St John's Wood Road.

My father was a member of West London Synagogue and my parents were married there. After that, they joined the LJS and my father was Chairman of Dr Mattuck's committee for refugees in the 1930s. He was also much involved with the formation of the Central British Fund with the Rothschilds, Otto Schiff and others.

My mother died in 1974 when she was seventy-six and my father in 1977 when he was nearing eighty-six. They were both cremated and have rose bushes in their memory at the LJS cemetery at Pound Lane.

Before the war, we lived in Lansdowne Crescent, Holland Park, where I was born, as was my younger brother Peter. It was then quite a popular area for Jewish families with the Walford, Henriques, Karminski and Franklin families, amongst others, all living nearby. I began going to LJS services before the war. It was quite a long walk to St John's Wood Road for a six- or seven-year-old, and the best part of it was always along the canal seeing the barges.

I heard Lily Montagu give sermons, but did not know her very well. I would describe her as a saintly figure. She always sat in the front row wearing a heavy coat with her sister,

Marian, who fell asleep in later life. When Lily Montagu preached, it was very spiritual and special. I also recall Claude Montefiore.

During my childhood Dr Mattuck was the Senior Rabbi. He was a very good preacher and you did not fall asleep during his sermons! He used to wag his finger to emphasise a point. He would have been very good on a soapbox in Hyde Park, since he was very definite in his views as well as being eloquent and a great raconteur. Neither he nor his wife, Edna, completely lost their American accents in spite of many years living in England. In their latter years they had a country retreat in Oxfordshire. They had three children: Naomi, who worked at the BBC, Dorothy, who married Leslie Edgar – later a rabbi at the LJS – and Robert, who had, I believe, a distinguished academic career in America.

Before the war we would often lunch after services on a Saturday at what was then the Tavern Restaurant at Lord's. We always hoped that Dr Mattuck would join us at our table since he was such good company and a close family friend. The Tavern Restaurant was very popular with congregants, a number of whom would also go there for lunch after services.

My mother's parents, Julian and Florence Simon, were very active in the congregation, my grandfather being Treasurer of the synagogue from 1918 until 1946. He was also very involved in the formation of Basil Henriques's Bernhard Baron Settlement, which was a joint venture between the LJS and the West London Synagogue. He encouraged a great many congregants to become involved in the Settlement. I have a copy of the Settlement's first report to the original subscribers.

Florence was, for many years, Treasurer of the Women's Society. My mother helped to run some fundraising events, both for the synagogue and also for the Bernhard Baron Settlement. In the pre-war years the Settlement was, in fact, the synagogue's primary charity.

As regards my religious education, Miss Moos (she was an old friend of my mother) would come to our house once a week and give me an hour's 'teaching'. This was essentially based on biblical stories and involved getting me to make drawings of, for example, David's fight against Goliath, or Moses with the Israelites in the wilderness. As I remember it, Miss Moos had a huge India rubber to rub out my mistakes and was, as others can testify, a great character with a remarkably strong voice even on her 100th birthday. My formal religious education began when I went to boarding school. I had weekly correspondence lessons with Samuel Rich of South London Synagogue and he returned my essays duly marked with corrections and comments. As a result, I had a good grounding in the Old Testament and the Prophets.

Of course, the culmination of my religious education was my Confirmation with thirteen others on Sunday 23 April 1944, St George's Day. It was declared that year to be a Day of National Prayer, so it assumed an even greater significance than it otherwise might have had. This was in the middle of the war and the service sheet was a single sheet of paper due to rationing. It was based on the 1937 LJS prayerbook. We were all asked to write a special prayer to be read out at the service, the three best of which were chosen, including my own. There was also a hymn taken from the hymnal. I had made a note on my chosen prayer that I had sent it to Dr Mattuck for approval, stating that it was written on the train home to where we lived in the country after being inspired by the Passover service, and especially by his sermon on the problem of freedom.

The form of service was very simple and direct, quite different from what it is now and adhering more closely to the principles on which the Liberal Jewish movement was founded. With little Hebrew, and hymns with rousing tunes to involve the congregation, we were stimulated by the poetry of the readings. I knew very little Hebrew at the time of my Confirmation, apart from the *Shema*, and we were not troubled by the use of the word 'Lord' and would have regarded it as insane if anyone had considered it sexist. Sermons too were different in that they were not normally delivered from a script. The eloquence and oratory of Dr Mattuck may have been overdramatic for some, but he was certainly stimulating.

Wartime affected one's preparation for Confirmation. Because of being at boarding school and living some forty miles from London, travel was difficult. However, I was able to come up to London two or three times prior to the great day to meet our teachers and the other members of the Confirmation class. Parties were out of the question. Neither of my mother's brothers was able to be present at the service due to their absence on war service. However, we did have a small family lunch party at my grandparents' flat in Kensington, where Dr and Mrs Mattuck joined us. The main course was roast chicken, then considered to be a great delicacy.

I was very keen to stay involved with the LJS after my Confirmation, but I was shortly called up to join the Navy. I was in one of the last demob groups coming out in 1948. I then joined the Alumni and was on the committee for some years. John Cross was the Chairman when I first joined. He later became Secretary of the synagogue. The society was very active, with many social events such as rambles and dances. Its object was to keep people together as a social organisation rather than being a religious group.

During the 1940s, there was quite a lot of anti-Zionism, encouraged by Dr Mattuck and Basil Henriques and formally expressed through an organisation called the Jewish Fellowship. These anti-Zionist views were entirely based on religious beliefs. It was considered that a theocratic State would, through its policies, debase the fundamental religious tenets of Judaism, which is a view taken today by some ultra-Orthodox Jews who refuse to recognise the State of Israel. I was for a time actively involved as Vice Chairman of the Jewish Fellowship, as were Jane and Nancy Leverson, later Jane Levy and Nancy Caplin.

We had *seder* night at home rather than going out. Usually some cousins of my mother's, the Rubinsteins, joined us. These were distinct from Jenny's family, who were Rubenstein, spelt differently. I do remember going to Communal *Seders*, which were conducted by Dr Mattuck at Lord's (not in the members' section, but in the Tavern upstairs) after the bombing of the synagogue. They were popular, with at least a hundred people attending despite the problems of wartime. The High Holy Day services, some of which I helped to steward, were held at the Friends' Meeting House in Euston Road.

It was about this time that I began going to Stepney one evening each week to help in the Boys' Club at the Bernhard Baron Settlement, usually staying the night there, which gave me much insight into youth work and communal social work. On at least one occasion, I went with the club to camp for a week at High Down near Worthing. This was my first active involvement with a Jewish charity. Soon after this I became the Treasurer of the Association for Jewish Youth and of the Stepney Jewish Club and

Settlement, of which I was later President for seventeen years. I was also the Treasurer for twelve years of what was then the Jewish Board of Guardians, later Jewish Welfare Board and now Jewish Care.

I joined the committee of the synagogue's United Charities Fund, which had been started in about 1929, taking over as Chairman from Leon Rees, who had himself been Chairman for twenty-five years. I remained Chairman for the next forty-five years, so that in the first seventy years of its existence the Fund only had two Chairmen. The object of the Fund was to assist LJS members in making their charitable donations through knowledge of the more deserving causes and allocating funds to the Jewish charities which seemed to be most in need, sometimes a rather difficult task. Occasionally the Fund would receive a substantial legacy from congregants and, on occasion, from completely unknown people. As Chairman, I was responsible, together with the rabbis, for choosing the recipient charities for the synagogue's Day of Atonement appeal.

There have been numerous gifts that my family have made to the synagogue over the years, including a desk in the Rabbi's Robing Room, which was given by my grandparents in commemoration of their diamond wedding. They also gave two chairs that were on the *bimah* in the old building, and my brother and I gave two further chairs in memory of our parents. When my uncle, Arthur Simon, had his 90th birthday, I arranged for a clock from all his nephews and nieces to be erected in the Montefiore Hall. He had no children, but he was a very significant benefactor to the synagogue.

I occasionally help Jenny with the Out and About Club, but I am generally in the background. Jenny and I met at Rabbi David Goldberg's house – very kosher! He was organising a new group of not-so-young unmarried members. I was elected Chairman of this group and Jenny as Secretary so, in a way, we met over the minutes. David was very pleased with himself that he had got an incorrigible bachelor with many girlfriends married off. Our wedding was held at the time of the Miners' Strike (that was in 1984) and David said that if he could get Michael married off, he felt he would have no trouble in settling the strike. Of course, John Rayner married us.

One of the LJS presidents I remember from when I was very, very young was Claude Montefiore. Then came Sir Louis Gluckstein – he was a towering figure. He and my uncle Ronald Simon were joint Treasurers. They used to wear black top hats on *Yom Kippur* and read Jonah. Ronnie (that's Tim Simon's father) was a superb reader. Willie Kessler succeeded Peter Lazarus, who was a distant relation of mine. Willie was a remarkable and very popular President. They all brought different and varied qualities to the job.

We have enjoyed a long association with the LJS and know very many people. My brother, Peter, was confirmed at the same time as Jo Kessler and Ann Kirk. Although neither Jenny nor I sit on the Council, we often get consulted about all manner of things.

See photograph 43.

✡

Karen Newman with Susan Crane

Karen Newman and Susan Crane joined the LJS as a family with their daughter Lily, and her father, Ian. They celebrated their Civil Partnership and twenty-one years of being together, in 2006, at the first same-sex commitment ceremony held at LJS. Since June 2006 Karen has been Chair of the Education Committee.

Susan and I met in 1985 in London. Susan was born in Paris in 1965 and raised in New York. While her mother was Catholic, her father was the son of a Unitarian minister. Susan was a member of the choir in the Congregational church the family attended. Essentially, she had a secular upbringing.

I was born in London in 1958 and had a fairly conventional North London Jewish upbringing within the United Synagogue tradition. Thrice-yearly visits to the synagogue served effectively as a reminder of why I did not visit more frequently in that there was a distinct lack of evidence to suggest that intelligent women with enquiring minds might have a place there. But our home and family represented a celebration of Judaism in various ways, as did regular observance of Friday nights and the key religious holidays that punctuate the year.

Both Susan and I work in the field of international development. We joined LJS in the spring of 2003, together with our daughter Lily, who was then one year old, and Lily's father, who is closer in age to Susan, but who had a similar Jewish upbringing to mine.

My sister is Head of Art at Sherborne School for Girls. There is very little that is Jewish in her life, but she did say, after attending a *Kol Nidre* service at the LJS, that she felt she had been present at a collective act of worship, a feeling she couldn't recall having had at a synagogue before.

I would like to think that I would have found my way to the LJS, but I somehow doubt it. It is more likely that I would have remained paralysed by my inability to bring myself to join a United synagogue, because I would have had to have left my entire family outside the door. Susan's determination to embark on a path that ultimately led to the birth of our daughter Lily, led her to believe that I might be a bit more likely to focus and identify with the venture if the father was Jewish. This led Susan to discover the Jewish Gay and Lesbian Group (JGLG). While I was reasonably secure in both identities, I had never felt the need to manifest both in the same nano-second.

Nevertheless, I agreed to attend a JGLG *Chavurah* service one Friday night. I was totally unprepared for how moving I found the revelation that it was possible to be lesbian/gay and Jewish, and to enjoy and celebrate both as well as each identity. We met Ian at a JGLG weekend in March 2000 and Lily was born in November 2001. An indication that we may have been doing something right occurred while Susan was heavily pregnant with Lily, who was resolutely refusing to reveal on scans whether she was a boy or a girl. Ian made respectful and tentative enquiries as to whether or not we had settled on a name. We said that we were still arguing over boys' names, but that, if it were a girl, she would be called Lily because that was the name of my grandmother who had died a few years earlier and who had been like a grandmother to Susan when she first came to the UK. We then noticed that Ian was quite overcome. It transpired that Lily had been the name of his favourite aunt who had died tragically when quite young. Although we were not members of a synagogue when Lily was born, Rabbi Irit Shillor, who had been at the JGLG weekend when we met Ian, conducted a naming ceremony for Lily when she was four weeks old.

Rabbi Mark Solomon, who, at the time, was Associate Rabbi at the LJS, was the perfect bridge for us to LJS membership. He told us at a JGLG gathering that we would be welcomed as a family at LJS. We therefore joined the synagogue as members in April 2003, partly because we wanted a community to be a constant feature in Lily's life that was accepting of her and her family.

Civil Partnerships for same-sex couples became legal late in 2005. Susan and I decided to enter into this commitment in June 2006, and we were keen to have a spiritual dimension to recognise and celebrate this step. By this time, Lily was an enthusiastic four-year-old in *Gan* class at the LJS Religion School. Rabbi Mark Solomon, who had been one of a few rabbis who had worked hard to secure Liberal Judaism's celebration of same-sex commitment ceremonies, and who had collaborated on Liberal Judaism's 'Covenant of Love' service of commitment for same-sex couples, officiated at our commitment ceremony on 18 June 2006, the first to be held at the LJS. This made the occasion very special for us. Lily, who, until the week previously, had thought that it was her wedding, and that it was she who was getting married, served as the official ring-bearer, while Ian was, of course, our best man. Rabbi Solomon noted the 'seminal' role that Ian played in our lives in his address.

The ceremony was complicated because, as well as being same-sex, it was also mixed-faith. The LJS managed to square that circle with its usual judicious brand of principled flexibility. It was a joyous and deeply meaningful ceremony for us both, enabling us to celebrate and cement our relationship within a Jewish context that both validated and incorporated a deeply meaningful spiritual dimension, while being totally inclusive of Susan.

As well as being the perfect bridge to LJS, Rabbi Solomon also facilitated my transition to Liberal Judaism. This journey began at a time when, to me, a rabbi looked something like Rabbi Mark Solomon. In 2006 I started attending adult education classes regularly – something that happened more or less by accident. I had planned to attend an LJS introductory session on the High Holyday services and found that, after the class finished, there would be an opportunity to set about learning how to read Hebrew properly, no doubt this time by engaging the brain, which I do not recall ever happening during the classes I had attended during my first decade of life. This seemed a particularly appropriate thing to do, since my daughter, aged four, was embarking on a similar task in respect of English. I remember that it also struck me forcibly at the time that, in order to enrol on that course, I didn't even have to go anywhere. All I had to do was not leave.

I came to appreciate how phenomenally lucky we were at LJS to have both Rabbis Alexandra Wright and Mark Solomon. Their teaching styles were different, their commitment total. Each had the capacity to inspire, enthuse and challenge the disparate group of students who showed up in various degrees of exhaustion on cold and wet Tuesday evenings. It turned out that the classes I continued to attend formed part of the Conversion course. No wonder Rabbi Kathleen Middleton thought she must be seeing things on one occasion when she covered one of the sessions, particularly since, by that time, I had become a member of the LJS Council, and Chair of the Education Committee!

By attending the classes I experienced at first hand that 'rabbi' actually means teacher. Teaching adults who know nothing, particularly if they think they know something, without patronising them must be incredibly difficult. Rabbi Alexandra Wright has a genius for enthusing people and inspiring them to do their own thinking about why, whatever the topic under review, is (or could be) relevant for their lives. I remember that, in one session, she was talking about *Tzedakah*, explaining how the root word in Hebrew meant justice. The discussion set me thinking about how different that was to the Latin root for the word (charity) and musing on the patronising *crumbs off the table* aspect of charity that is entirely missing from the Hebrew derivation and concept.

I also remember after one class asking Rabbi Alexandra a question about Lily. The question concerned the possibility of Lily having a *Bat Mitzvah*, so there was clearly no rush for an answer. Since, of Lily's three parents, two are Jewish, but the one who carried her for the first nine months of her existence happened to be the one that isn't, I wondered if Lily would have to do some kind of conversion in order to be eligible for a *Bat Mitzvah*, should she decide that she would like to do that. Rabbi Alexandra answered immediately, saying absolutely not since we were clearly raising her as Jewish.

On an earlier occasion, during a relatively crowded *Kiddush*, Susan and I became separated from Lily, who was about three years old at the time. The whole episode did not last for much more than thirty seconds, but, during that time, Lily had managed to find Rabbi Alexandra, and was quietly holding her hand, obviously having made the astute judgement that that was the best and safest place for her to be until such time as one of her parents might turn up.

Lily started as a pupil of the Religion School when she was three years old. This was when I became a more regular participant at *Shabbat* morning services, it striking me at the time that, given that the LJS was not in the child-care business, not to do so seemed a bit odd. Of course, *Shabbat* mornings are the best time to meet people in the community and I remain grateful to one particular congregant whose encyclopaedic knowledge of girls' educational establishments in London directed me towards a particular school where my daughter has been very happy. I had not known of the school previously. Gratitude takes various forms. In this case it took the form of my agreeing to stand for election as Chair of the Education Committee.

Chairing the Education Committee has been exceptionally rewarding; the professional leadership blends lay and rabbinic skills and energies in pursuit of Jewish learning at all levels and for all ages, while the volunteers on the committee bring a wide range of professional, pedagogical, and parental perspectives to shape educational activities within and beyond the synagogue.

In so many ways, the LJS is itself a celebration of diversity. I do press liaison work for the JGLG and in 2007, we were working with the *Jewish Chronicle* on a feature on being Jewish and Gay. They were looking for suggestions for two rabbis to write contrasting pieces on whether or not homosexuality should be acceptable to Jews. I suggested that they approach Rabbi Alexandra for the more progressive piece, rather than more obvious colleagues who may have been more vulnerable to Mandy Rice-Davies *they would say that, wouldn't they* type of reaction to any opinion they might express. She wrote: 'We should move beyond our era of sexual obsession and learn to cherish the values of faithfulness over fickleness and affection and respect above fleeting gratification. Then perhaps we will see that everything we imagined was under assault – family and fidelity, scholarship and learning, restraint and gentleness – is cherished as dearly by same-sex couples who remain dedicated to a loving and respectful expression of Judaism and who desire to pass it on to the next generation.'

It was terrific to see the *Jewish Chronicle* publish it, and wonderful to be part of a Liberal Jewish community that embraces and celebrates diversity so openly.

✡

Margaret Rigal

Margaret Rigal has been a lifelong member of the LJS, her grandfather having been one of its founding members. Apart from her many memories of the early leaders of the synagogue and of the Women's Society, she also recollects the prominent part that she played in supporting the refuseniks, both through her involvements at the LJS and nationally. For several years she ran the Religion School correspondence course. With her husband, George, she has had a long involvement in the Services and the Social Action Committees.

I am Margaret Rigal, née Lazarus. I was born in November 1932 and am a third-generation Liberal Jew. My grandfather, Samuel Lazarus, was one of the early members of the LJS. My parents were Mary and Kenneth Lazarus. They were both very involved in the synagogue.

My first memory of the synagogue dates back to before the war, to what must have been a *Sukkot* service. I remember being given an apple. I have no idea who gave it to me.

During the war we lived in Bognor Regis. We went down for the summer holidays and stayed on. I went to a small kindergarten. One day there were twenty in the class and the next day there were five, because of the invasion scare. Very shortly after that, the school closed. The local boys' preparatory school, which had evacuated to Wales leaving a very small rump behind, took in sisters of boys who were at the school. So I went there for a good few years, getting a boy's education. That was very helpful because, on the whole, boys were much better taught than girls.

There was no Jewish community, though there were a few Jewish families. We used to join one of them for Orthodox *Seder* Services. The *sedarim* were entirely in Hebrew and meant absolutely nothing to me from the religious point of view, but they were pleasant social occasions.

We sometimes came up for the day to St John's Wood, but I don't remember any High Holyday services before the bombing of the synagogue. After that, I remember going to the Friends' Meeting House, but as I was a complete novice to the services, it was very difficult to make head or tail of them. The Saturday morning services were very small, with an elderly congregation. We were always rushing to get a train back to Bognor and it was fairly chaotic as far as I was concerned. Even after the war, we kept the house at

Bognor so we spent most weekends there. The festival services were always very well attended, especially on the first day of *Pesach*, and I found these more inspiring.

My mother, Mary, was very religious, but not enormously knowledgeable about Judaism. She brought me up to be aware of my Jewish connections. I started taking correspondence lessons with Miss Moos. She really taught me my religion, first by correspondence and then, after we returned to London, she used to come to our house in Pembridge Place in Notting Hill once a week. Eventually, she also taught my mother. We got 'a Miss Moos slant on Liberal Judaism', which was very good. I continued to have Miss Moos teaching me, privately, after my Confirmation. She taught me about Isaiah, a bit of liturgy and a certain amount of Hebrew. She didn't teach me anything about the *Talmud*, but she did give me a sound grounding in Liberal Jewish philosophy. We went through Dr Mattuck's books together. My mother and I both enjoyed the lessons and my father was willing to continue to pay for them. Later I took over Miss Moos's correspondence class and I carried it on under her, Rabbi David Goldstein and then ULPS for the next umpteen years until Jane Kessler took over.

I think that the Lazarus family, throughout their history, has always been involved in setting up and providing synagogues for other people. My father, Kenneth, went to quite a lot of services. I think he was a religious man, but he did not really enjoy long services. He was very, very keen that the services were organised efficiently. He was a member of the Council for as long as I can remember. In those days there was no question of anyone resigning after three or six years. He was a close colleague of Louis Gluckstein. They had been in the Jewish Lads' Brigade together, so had known each other for many years. They worked closely together at the LJS although they didn't always agree on synagogue matters. He was a very active House Committee Chairman. He knew everything and everybody because, in his opinion, the House Committee existed to be a help to all the other committees. Occasionally, on the Day of Atonement or at other times, he used to go round the synagogue, listening to make sure the microphones were working properly.

My mother joined the Women's Society Committee before the war, at a rather younger age than most other women. She always said to me, 'I really don't know why they asked me onto the committee when I was not very active. But it was a great compliment and, so of course, I joined.' During the war, while we were at Bognor, she would always try to time our day trips to London to coincide with a day when there was a committee meeting of the Women's Society. On several occasions I went with her to the meetings and was allowed to sit and listen to them all sitting around the table in the old Mattuck Room. I can clearly remember Mrs Mattuck and Dorothy Edgar. The Chairman was Mrs Dorothy Myer, who was always known as Mrs Horace Myer, although I have since learned that her husband was actually called Horatio. The Secretary was Mrs Elsa Espir, who was a rather prim, elderly lady. Everyone was terribly nice to me. My memory is that they were a most charming, well-mannered group of ladies. I was good at keeping quiet, so I don't think that I was a nuisance to them.

The Committee business on one occasion concerned American servicemen. They were organising some sort of hospitality, a special day when the American servicemen would be invited to come to the synagogue. It seemed to me that there was very little talk about the details, because it was quite obvious that Mrs Mattuck, Dorothy Edgar and one or two of the other ladies were going to do the catering and organisation anyway.

My mother brought in Muriel Samuel to be the Secretary. She was the mother of Charles Samuel, and a great character, far less formal than many. Peggy Lewsen was a very good Chairman. Her father was Major Bernard Davidson, a member of the Council after the war. Peggy was always beautifully groomed and a perfect lady. Dora Wolchover was another Chairman in the early years. She was Welsh and the mother of Lynne Dubin.

I remember Dr Mattuck very well as he was a personal friend of my family. He and his wife would come to dinner at Pembridge Place. Mrs Mattuck was particularly charming to me. She was small, roundish and had very sharp, bright black eyes. She always appeared to be having a wonderful time and she made everybody around her, as far as I was concerned, have a wonderful time too. She was very efficient and fully involved in the synagogue.

Dr Mattuck was extraordinarily dramatic when he was giving sermons – mesmeric. His voice rose and fell, he made gestures and was a very authoritarian sort of figure. I very distinctly remember that when people were discussing the birth of the State of Israel as a national home, he was firmly against it. He went to America and had a very strenuous programme of visiting congregations there to dissuade them from supporting the idea of a national homeland in Israel. He gave a very, very strong sermon about it at the synagogue. He wanted the Jews to be scattered throughout the world so that they would share their message worldwide. He was terrified that, once there was a homeland, there would be troubles and anti-Israel feeling and that the Jews in the Diaspora would become second-class Jews.

I have no memory of how his message was received at the LJS. I doubt that anyone would have argued with him publicly. He was held in the most enormous respect by most people. The atmosphere was quite different in those days. People were far more willing to be admiring and humble in the presence of somebody they thought was an important and great leader. Lily Montagu was equally vehement in her anti-Zionism. I believe that she refused to shake hands with Herbert Richer, who was a Zionist, when he gave a sermon at the LJS in favour of Israel. Lily Montagu was very upset by it.

I knew Lily Montagu reasonably well. She was a remarkable person, quite unlike anyone else that I had known, except for her sister, Marian, who was very like Lily. I also knew her other sister, Mrs Franklin, quite well. We used to go to dances that she gave for her grandchildren, fairly soon after the war, in her house in Bishops Bridge Road in Bayswater.

Miss Lily and Miss Marian lived at the Red Lodge, an enormous house in Palace Court, Bayswater. My parents were very fond of them and used to go there for an occasional Friday night. My father gave us very graphic accounts. The usual fare was two fishcakes. I don't know what went with it. They had a very large dining room, which in the wintertime was very cold. The house obviously had no central heating (none of us had central heating then); there was a single, small, electric fire with one bar.

The two Montagu sisters came regularly to services. Being deaf, both of them had large, old-fashioned hearing aids. They came to a lot of meetings too and the hearing aids always appeared. These went flat down on the table in front of them so that Miss Lily and

Miss Marian could hear what was going on. I can remember, towards the end of her life, Miss Lily giving a sermon and explaining to me afterwards that she now had to wear glasses because she was becoming slightly short-sighted. With some amusement, she compared herself to Marian, who was much deafer than she was, but never needed glasses.

I could chat easily with them because they had known me all my life. Lily was always very nice to me. At one point, towards the end of her life, she held several meetings in her house, to which she invited the people who she believed would carry on Liberal Judaism as she wanted it. George and I were both summoned. By this time congregations were starting up around the fringes of London and Lily was anxious that people were joining these congregations with very little understanding of the basic tenets of Liberal Judaism. She wanted some of us who had gone through the Religion School in her day and who, she felt, understood what Liberal Judaism stood for, to get involved and to try and revitalise the central body.

Miss Lily and Miss Marian also came to the lectures, which were held on Monday evenings in the old library, long before George and I were married. We became engaged in 1953 and from that time on, George came with me. Leslie Edgar gave various courses of lectures, followed by another session, during which we could ask the rabbi anything we wanted. Leslie Edgar was willing to stick his neck out further than anyone else I had ever known. In later days, after his illness, he became a much more nervous individual and I don't think many people remember how outspoken and clear-thinking he was. He was absolutely splendid, a man to whom I would have gone with any kind of problem. I remember while I was a student being upset by seeing some of the malformed babies that were being kept alive for many years. I took this concern to him and he had no hesitation at all in saying that he felt babies who had no appreciation of anything and were obviously uncomfortable or unhappy, should not be kept alive year after year, unless there was a purpose in their continued existence. I don't think many people would have said that. He was a great comfort to me.

I remember when Leslie Edgar came home from Germany where he was serving as an Army chaplain. He gave some wonderful sermons, which were like a breath of fresh air, and we all felt he was 'a man of the future'. I got to know him very well. He taught me for my Confirmation, by correspondence as I was still away in Bognor at the weekends. I think we sent each other long letters most weeks.

Our family came up to the LJS several times before my Confirmation service and there was always great excitement as to what to wear because clothes rationing was still on, so one couldn't have anything new. For the girls it was a question of wearing a plain dress of a length and style suitable for the occasion. The practice of wearing white did not come in until later. Our own children wore white for their Confirmations, which always seemed a very odd Jewish decision. I wore a rust-coloured dress with a rounded collar all the way round.

Mine was a large Confirmation class – sixteen or so I would guess – so there were a lot of people taking part in the service. We each had one passage to read. Some of us also wrote our own prayers and read them. Some read a poem. The Confirmation Service was in the prayerbook. It included Wordsworth's 'Ode to Duty'. As I was going through an anti-

Wordsworth phase, I remember that distinctly. We didn't have a party afterwards, but I went out to lunch, probably to Claridges. I suppose there would have been eight or ten of us.

At that point, the bombed synagogue had not yet been repaired and the Confirmation service was held in the Montefiore Hall, with the Ark on the stage.

I remember the rebuilding. There was some kind of wooden hut next to the synagogue which was used by the youth groups, and disapproved of by Miss Moos. Later, to mark the congregation's Golden Jubilee, a new building – the Montagu Wing – was erected on that site, containing a small synagogue and three classrooms.

I went to St Paul's Girls' School as soon as the war ended. We had Jewish prayers and there was a Jewish Society. It was Orthodox, but not wildly so. We had no Jewish teachers. There were one or two rather elderly members of the staff who complained if we made a noise, because the Jewish service took place at the same time as the general prayers. Once a week we all joined together for a general assembly, which was non-denominational.

St Paul's was very good and kind to us and the school provided *kosher* or vegetarian meals for those who wanted them. Jewish girls opted out of the Religious Education classes, but there was no Jewish alternative. The interesting thing was that Miss Moos came to St Paul's Girls' School, but not to teach the girls. She had become friendly with the Headmistress, Miss Strudwick, and she used to go in and teach her basic Judaism. When I was quite senior, we did have some meetings after school in the Orthodox synagogue in Brook Green. They were run mostly by senior boys as far as I recall, though I don't think they were very successful. I was never one of the 'in' group. They were fairly Orthodox and we weren't.

I then went to Bedford College to study Social Science. I occasionally attended the London University Jewish Society, but didn't enjoy it very much. I really had very little in common with my contemporaries who had been brought up as Orthodox. I was a student until 1953 and then I had a job for a year at the Jewish Welfare Board in the East End. It was in Petticoat Lane, so I picked up quite a few Yiddish words. I did a lot of home visits, mainly alone. There were one or two roads where we would say, 'I am going down Cable Street today, so if you don't hear any more of me...'.

I had already decided I wanted to do social work when I was at school. I was a volunteer at a Settlement called Dame Collett House on Wednesday evenings. During the war the building was like St Paul's Cathedral: bombs landed all around it, leaving it standing in complete isolation. I used to walk back along deserted streets to Stepney Green Station. There were bombed houses on either side, with ruined cellars. We had a couple of after-school clubs. We organised games for the children, who were very poor and uneducated, but they were English rather than from other countries in those days. It gave the children a bit of a break, a social get-together, and they had something to eat and drink.

While I trained as a social worker, I worked for the Family Welfare Association. I was trained by them for a couple of months in the summer and, while I was there, I worked with one or two Jewish ladies who had converted to Christianity, but who still went on going to the Jewish organisations as well, so it was very instructive.

I had a year working with the Jewish Welfare Board during which I learned a lot. I worked mainly in Stepney or Stamford Hill, because, in those days, the Jews who moved out from Stepney went to Stamford Hill. The people were very poor. I used to visit some of them in hospital. They'd had very hard lives. Occasionally I used to visit those who were in hospitals out of London. They were absolutely isolated. In many cases it was a tragic ending to their very hard lives.

During this time I met George and we got married. In those days all our parents gave parties for the young generation and we all met the children of our parents' friends as well as our own friends. It was a very pleasant way for men and women to meet. George is a distant cousin of Elizabeth, the wife of my brother, Peter Lazarus. George and I met in many, many houses; we couldn't get away from each other really. We got married in 1955. Peter married Elizabeth in 1950 in the Montefiore Hall, but by the time George and I were married, the synagogue building had been repaired and was in full use again.

The Monday evening lectures that we went to were also attended by my brother-in-law Lawrence Rigal, who later became a rabbi, and quite a few of our friends. When Abram Spiro came to London in 1954 with the idea of starting a rabbinic training college, he took over the Monday classes. He was an outstanding figure in the scholastic world, so anyone he knew who was passing through London and who had any sort of special knowledge came to his classes as guest speakers and gave their own *spiel*. Afterwards, we would all go back and sit on the floor of Spiro's flat, off the Edgware Road, and have a really good and serious discussion. It was a wonderful, stimulating time. Harry and Rose Jacobi also started to come to the lectures shortly before they got engaged.

Spiro was completely different from anything we had heard before, because he came from an Orthodox background in Poland or Lithuania. He had taught himself English with a gramophone record before going to the United States. His English was entirely unintelligible for the first few hours of listening to him, but you got used to it. As far as I was concerned, he opened up a great many hitherto unknown corners. I still think it was a tragedy for Liberal Judaism that, because of a clash of personalities, he left.

Once some, if not all, of our children were born, I joined the Women's Society Committee. Soon afterwards, in 1966, Eva Feldman became Chairman, succeeding Dora Wolchover. Eva asked me to become Treasurer, taking over from Phyllis Carter. I remained on the Committee for many years, until the Women's Society folded in 1991.

We had a monthly lunch, which was a very good social occasion and, because we had a speaker, also an educational one. In those days the Women's Society did the catering for everything, including the Communal *Seder*, through its Catering Committee. When I first was aware of it, this committee was run by Mrs Magnus, Ruth Ive's mother. The synagogue would say what it wanted and then the ladies would provide it.

When I joined the Women's Society, people paid an annual subscription to belong. Once Eva became Chairman she made an enormous difference to the atmosphere by a decision that *all* women members of the synagogue would be members of the Society, and we asked for a contribution at the beginning of the year. Most of the women did contribute small amounts. We not only had catering and other expenses, we also gave money to charities. All the members of the Women's Society could come to us and suggest causes to support. I remember, for example, that we gave to a charity for people who needed radios at home and to a wonderful small society called Invalids at Home.

An important part of the Women's Society was the Sewing Guild. It was originally set up to make *Torah* mantles using the most wonderful cloth. The names of those involved are embroidered onto a cloth. I remember the cloth used for festival services in the old synagogue and in the Montefiore Hall. It was coloured with beautiful roses on it. To commemorate their Silver Wedding, Luigi (Louis Gluckstein) and his wife, Doreen, donated a beautiful, big white tablecloth, as well as all the matching white embroidered scroll covers that we still use. That was in 1950. I know the year because they were married within days of my parents' wedding in 1925. Claire Alexander took over the Sewing Guild for many years.

My mother was the custodian of the scroll covers and other fabrics, because Mrs Mattuck had said to her, 'Mary, dear, will you look after the scroll covers?' She would go in and iron anything that had become creased, and saw to it that the rabbis' gowns were cleaned when necessary. She looked after the *tallitot* too, but there weren't very many then. I don't think anybody wore a *tallit* other than the rabbis. My mother continued as custodian until she was a very old lady, when I took over.

The Women's Society Sewing Guild also produced garments for the Alice Model Nursery in Stepney. Although the nursery wasn't connected to the synagogue, ladies from the LJS worked there before the war, including Lilian Hill and Esther Rantzen's mother, Kathleen.

In my day, children at the LJS were still expected not to make a sound. If you brought a baby even to a children's service and it gurgled, somebody near you would say 'Shush!' It happened to me at a *Chanukkah* Service. So we didn't bring children to the synagogue much until they started Religion School, which by then was on Saturdays rather than Sundays. I was left at home with the babies.

The children used to come to the festival services. Miss Moos would take them out of the main service and give them a special talk upstairs. They were very happy there, but one of the great difficulties was that, because the synagogue was so full, quite often the children would go straight into the children's service, and when they were brought back after the children's talk they wouldn't know where their parents were sitting. You had to keep an eye open so that you could go out and grab your children when they suddenly appeared.

Our children were lucky to have a number of first-rate teachers: John Rich, the Kirks, the Feldmans and Michael Alpert. They also had David Goldstein, who was very nice and a very good teacher. They were all knowledgeable, civilised educators. But the teaching of Hebrew was difficult and there was a great difference of opinion over the years, including when we were on the Education Committee. First somebody would propose that the children had to learn prayerbook Hebrew; that would be opposed on the grounds that it was more important that they learned about Jewish ethics and beliefs as, in the available time, they were never going to reach a good level of Hebrew anyway, so they might just as well not waste their time. It changed from year to year and I wouldn't say that any of my children learned Hebrew adequately while they were at the Religion School, except for Barry, who was a natural linguist and able to pick it up out of the atmosphere. He stayed on an extra year and took Hebrew O Level.

Looking back, I've known all the rabbis, from Dr Mattuck onward. My father used to say that it was a tradition that the Senior Rabbi argues with the Council and he would have said that while they were all arguing with Dr Mattuck. Leslie Edgar was lovely and easy, although after Dr Mattuck had retired and Leslie Edgar became the Senior Rabbi, he wasn't quite as easy. Louis Gluckstein (or Luigi as he was known) was a very difficult Chairman and President; he and Leslie Edgar disagreed on many matters. As Chairman, Luigi ran the whole show. I had known him all my life – he was 'Uncle Luigi' – but I never did anything of which he disapproved. He continued as President long after he had relinquished the Chairmanship, in which role he was succeeded by Sidney Levine and then by Edward Joseph. Edward Joseph was from a very nice, wealthy family of bankers – he was a good, solid, sensible Chairman.

Chaim Stern and Sidney Brichto both came over from America to work at the LJS as young rabbis. After a few years Sidney moved on to the ULPS. We thought Chaim was outstanding, a wonderful character, thinker and intellectual. We were very upset when he and Louis Gluckstein failed to get on and Chaim returned to America. We were pleased that he and John Rayner continued to work together on writing the ULPS prayerbooks. Chaim made a great contribution during the drafting process.

The LJS has been my only religious home all my life and I hope it goes on from strength to strength.

See photographs 43 and 54.

George Rigal

George Rigal joined the LJS when he married Margaret Lazarus, a third-generation member of the synagogue. Together they were active in the Younger Members' Organisation before George joined the Council and was very active in the Soviet Jewry movement. Dating back to when his children were young he has regularly attended services and was a frequent Ark opener. For many years he has been a prominent member of the Services Committee and of the Social Action Committee. George was one of the first non-professional *shammashim*.

I was born in 1925 into a progressive Jewish family. My grandfather, Lewis Levy, was a Warden of the East London Synagogue and an officer of the United Synagogue. I think he was Overseer of the Poor. He spent much of his time travelling, including to America, France, Germany, and even to Turkey and Jerusalem. When he came back to England in about 1900 he said, 'Well, now I have been to Israel, I only have to keep one day for High Holydays.' This was an indication, I think, of the degree of progressiveness of the Orthodox in those days, which is hard to imagine today. Synagogues like the Hampstead Synagogue were very close to the current Liberal and Reform approach and it was only as a result of the disagreement of half of their members that the Jewish Religious Union (JRU) was formed. The JRU's initial meetings were attended by a number of Orthodox rabbis.

My parents were founder members of the North Western Reform Synagogue when it was in Bridge Lane. I started Religion School classes there in about 1931. Within a few years, the congregation moved to the newly built synagogue in Alyth Gardens, where I was *Bar Mitzvah*. At that time *Bar Mitzvah* was not a social event, but purely a religious ceremony. During that period, we had two rabbis, Rabbi Starrels and Rabbi Perlzweig. I did not know then that they had been rabbis at The Liberal Jewish Synagogue. I was also a member of the 11th Golders Green Scout Group, which was based at Alyth Gardens.

My main memory of that period is about the sermons, but I do recall comments being made about the situation in Germany before 1939. My parents had a young man to dinner who had concentration camp markings on his hand, so they were aware of what was happening there.

In autumn 1939, at the outbreak of war, I entered Highgate School, which had been evacuated to Westward Ho in North Devon. From the very beginning we created a Jewish Society, so that the Jewish boys could meet together at regular intervals on every *Shabbat* and at High Holydays. I had been to religion school classes at Alyth Gardens so, when I went to Highgate, I had a useful background in Hebrew and Judaism. I was very keen to take part in the services, which I did right from the beginning.

At the end of 1943, I volunteered as an Engineering Cadet and in 1945 was commissioned into the Royal Engineers. I spent my Army service in Egypt. I don't think I had any religious development during this period. While I was overseas, my parents moved to Rickmansworth, so our nearest Progressive synagogue was Wembley Liberal. When I came out of the Army, I became a youth leader at the synagogue. The club, 'Two Triangles', was run jointly with Kingsbury United Synagogue for all the Jewish teenagers in that area. We met at the home of a Council member. There was no difficulty at all in working with the Orthodox then. I must say that I was surprised by the way in which their rabbi was regarded. By comparison to Liberal rabbis, he was treated with very little respect.

Sometimes my brother, Lawrence, and I went as visitors to the Alumni Society at the LJS. By comparison to our club, it was a very large and well-run youth club, having all sorts of more advanced and well-organised events. I also represented Wembley at meetings of the Federation of Youth Clubs under the auspices of the Union of Liberal and Progressive Synagogues. During that time I was also the youth representative on Wembley Synagogue Council, so when I came to the LJS, I'd already had previous Council experience.

I joined the LJS as soon as I was engaged to Margaret. We went to the Monday evening lectures regularly, so I became familiar with many of the people at the LJS. My memories of Lily Montagu relate to these Monday evening lectures. She and Miss Marian would come to them and we all sat around a large table in the library. They would plonk their large hearing aid receivers in the middle of the table and point them towards the lecturer so that they didn't miss anything. We also used to go to the group that Miss Lily and her sister formed at their home, Red Lodge, to try and maintain Liberal principles. We all sat around on gilt chairs that were used for dances. Both Miss Lily and Miss Marian were quite large ladies and we all held our breath when they collapsed onto these chairs, because one rather felt that they couldn't possibly be strong enough to take their weight.

We became members of the Younger Members' Organisation (YMO), which organised social events at the LJS. My only memory is of dances, which was about fifty years ago while our children were young.

I used to have to work on Saturdays after the war. It was not until my children were five or six years old that I was able to get to *Shabbat* morning services, and I used to bring our two boys, David and Barry, to the synagogue. Margaret was unable to go as she had to be at home to look after the baby. We always came in by the front doors in those days. Nobody entered by the no. 28 side entrance, as it was cold and draughty. Sometimes services were held in the new, smaller, synagogue built in the 1960s. My memory of that time is of taking the boys up into the balcony of the old synagogue. Very often we sat right at the back so we couldn't be heard. We were then using the Mattuck prayerbook, which I needed to translate into modern English for David and Barry as it was quite archaic. Later on, we used to arrive with the whole family, plus both my mother and mother-in-law, occupying a complete row across one half of the old synagogue, sitting behind Marjorie Moos and Teddy Joseph.

During my life I've had the opportunity to visit other synagogues. My first job was at my mother's shoe factory but when this closed a few years later, I went into the garment business as a buyer. I had to spend about two months each year in the Far East with a considerable amount of travelling to Hong Kong, Taiwan and Korea. There is a synagogue in Hong Kong, *Ohel Leah* in Robinson Road, and I would always arrange that my last appointment on Friday night was in Hong Kong Central. I would then walk in the sunset directly up the peak from Central on the ladder from Queen's Road, in a direct line up to the bustling Chinese quarter and emerge beside the synagogue. At that time, they generally had to wait for enough tourists to arrive to make a *minyan*. As time went on, the Jewish community in Hong Kong grew and then they no longer had that problem.

Again, when I was in Taipei, I would stay at a hotel where they also had a *minyan* on Friday nights. I had a lot of Chinese friends who had a number of Jewish customers. We would sit down to a Chinese meal together and they would say, 'You can't eat that, it's not *kosher.*'

On holiday we have gone to whichever synagogue was within reach, wherever we might happen to be and, as a result, we have been to many interesting synagogues.

When I first started going to services at the LJS, I was constantly being asked to act as Ark opener because, in those days, there were very few male members in the congregation physically able to lift the scrolls. It was not a large congregation then, so I regularly used to do a double act with Mr Klementaski. Louis Steinman was the Beadle at that time who was a law unto himself. He had his 'favourites' and he liked having his 'regulars' open the Ark, so that nothing untoward would occur. From the very beginning, I was on the Services Committee and it was decided that as far as possible, there should always be one lady participating in the Ark opening, so that we had equality of the sexes. It was very difficult to persuade Louis to ask any lady to take part. I constantly had a battle with him and very frequently I would stand with him at the door to ensure that, if possible, we got a lady involved.

The ambience of the service then was very different because *tallitot* were not worn by anybody unless they were going up to open the Ark. *Kippot* were also virtually unknown. However, once John Rayner started to express the opinion that, although hats were perfectly acceptable, they were not a religious object, the wearing of *kippot* came in. Sir Louis Gluckstein traditionally read Jonah wearing a top hat but, out of respect for John Rayner, even he switched to a *kippah*. The wearing of hats by ladies has now dropped off entirely, except for the occasional reader and at the High Holydays. This has made it much easier to see the *bimah*, without the ladies' hats in front of you, but it took a long while for this to happen.

I never knew Rabbi Mattuck. We found Rabbi Leslie Edgar very approachable and a very sympathetic person. Also, as far as I was concerned, he gave very good sermons. Louis Steinman was full of good stories, particularly one about Leslie Edgar who, on hearing that Louis had been in the Guards as a bugler, got him to demonstrate his bugle and bring his busby along so he could see it. Philip Cohen was very interesting because he had journeyed from Orthodoxy to Liberalism and had a rather non-committal approach. When we spoke to him privately he was able to give guidance and decisions which he would have been reluctant to express in front of a full congregation. He was much more outspoken in private than he was in public.

I first knew John Rayner when he came to give sermons to the congregation in Wembley and I also knew Herbert Richer. They were the two bright young men. When John Rayner went to America for his rabbinic studies, Chaim Stern and Sidney Brichto came to the LJS. I remember that we kept a printed copy of one of their sermons, which raised the situation of Soviet Jewry and this was my first introduction to the subject. This must have been in the mid-sixties. I would not normally have kept copies of sermons, but we kept this one because it was so outstanding. Subsequently, I remember David Goldstein giving a sermon about the situation in the Soviet Union. He said that, at that time, people in this country were very afraid of communism and that they should be ashamed if they didn't stand up and give support for Soviet Jewry. He was encouraging people to resist the communist-led ideas and oppose the persecution of Jews in the Soviet Union.

All our children went to the Religion School at the LJS on Saturday mornings. It was very different from how it is now. This was before the days of *Bar Mitzvah*, so there was only Confirmation. The children found many of the teachers very inspiring. John Rich was an excellent teacher and Michael Alpert taught my daughter, Anne, who subsequently has become very Orthodox. I wouldn't necessarily put that down to Michael, but she certainly felt that he had taught her an enormous amount.

When my children were old enough to attend services, I used to organise quizzes for them during the sermons, particularly during the summer holidays. We took the view that you didn't go to synagogue only during term time, so we always took our children during holiday periods as well. The quizzes were to make the sermon times more child-friendly. They weren't just for my children, but for any children in the congregation. They would be announced and I would take the children out. As an incentive for regular attendance, I used to organise cumulative quizzes so the children could carry scores forward from one service to the next. Marjorie Moos would often do something similar during term time, but not during the holidays.

In the old synagogue the library was at the top of a flight of stairs leading from the foyer entrance, and it was not a particularly user-friendly place. When Miss Moos held a class in the library it was as much as anybody dared to do to go in there to try and get a book out.

For many years after I joined the synagogue, there was an overflow service in Porchester Hall for the High Holydays and I was often involved in taking the children's services there. I drafted the older children to take part in the services, and the seniors to assist in leading them. A large number of people went to the overflow services at the Porchester Hall but, after many years, the Council took the view that the extra services were being held mainly for the benefit of non-members. There was plenty of room in the LJS for the existing congregation and we were organising an extra service for people unwilling to pay for their High Holyday tickets. I think they paid much less for tickets at Porchester Hall.

I joined the LJS Council when Peter Lazarus had his first term as Chairman and I was also there during Maxwell Stern's time, which was over the period of the move to the church in Loudoun Road. I was very agreeably surprised to discover how the Council always applied moral considerations in deciding on their actions. I was not a chairman of any committee. I served on the Services Committee from its inception but, at that time, it was not a requirement for every Council member to take on the chairmanship of a committee.

There were, of course, lengthy debates in the period before the rebuilding as to whether we should pull the building down and rebuild it or try to repair it. At that period Trevor Moross was a tremendous leader in the discussions. We made the very good decision that we would utilise the architects in the congregation to help identify which architects to select for the design of the new building. At that time Rita Adler collected views on what the synagogue should be like in the 21st century.

A conscious decision was made when the synagogue was redesigned about the kind of space we wanted. We asked ourselves, 'What are we looking for when we design a new synagogue?' and reached the answer that the Montefiore Hall should look 'more like the King David suite at the Marble Arch Synagogue', which is a room with a relatively low ceiling. The old Montefiore Hall was two storeys high and the effect of lowering the ceiling in the new Montefiore Hall was very marked. If you consider the new synagogue building, we have no rectangular rooms. They are all rather strange shapes, but this gives the immediate effect of a lived-in building rather than an institution, which I think is remarkable. I am not sure if it is still remembered, but we also made an agreement with the architects that we would not make any alterations to the building without consulting them. This was a very good idea, because otherwise you get unnecessary accretions.

While we were at the church in Loudoun Road, the Council used to meet in a very dark and dingy room behind the body of the old church. I suppose it must have been a sort of vestry room. In the church itself, we covered up all the obvious Christian symbols for the purposes of our own services. It was rather chilly. During that period only one marriage took place in the church and that was of my daughter, Mary. The church was totally unsuited for any form of Jewish marriage. There was nowhere for the bride to prepare herself before going into the ceremony, so we had to rig up some curtains. It caused a great deal of hilarity in my own family because we had always told our children that they should not think that we would come to their wedding if they got married in a church.

From the 1970s onwards, Margaret and I were very active in the Soviet Jewry movement and did our best to involve the congregation in its activities. We had met the father of an ex-Soviet prisoner early on and he introduced me to the movement. We wrote letters of appeal, signed by members of the synagogue, whenever various refuseniks were in trouble and we would deliver them to the Soviet Embassy. I can remember walking down the cricket queue at Lord's collecting signatures for petitions. Later on, the LJS Soviet Jewry Group attracted a significant number of people who were not otherwise active in the synagogue. A number of the people involved could be described as 'politicals' and not ones who normally attended services.

The Soviet Jewry Group produced a large number of publications to mark the various festivals, such as a synopsis of the Book of Ruth in Russian for *Shavu'ot* and extracts from *Maccabees*. These were printed off in large numbers and posted to Jews in the Soviet Union. We had enlisted a wide group of supporters who posted things for us. Later, we organised trips to the Soviet Union by various members of the congregation. The LJS membership was wonderful in providing all the necessities such as Hebrew books and various types of food, which were taken to the refuseniks. Whenever we appealed to the congregation, we invariably got support. We went to the Soviet Union on three occasions during the 1970s and various other members of the congregations went at other times.

I generally organised the translations into Russian myself, using Russian books and making photocopies. The biggest thing that we did was to publish a Hebrew-Russian *Haggadah*. Between 80,000 and 100,000 were printed. The concept was that they should each weigh less than 20g, which meant we needed to print them on Bible paper. We arranged for the Oxford University Press to print them and they went out only with the LJS's initials on them: the LJS SJG (the LJS Soviet Jewry Group). The *haggadot* were sent out by many Orthodox congregations all over the world with these initials, with the blessing of the Chief Rabbi. I am sure he would not have approved if the name of The Liberal Jewish Synagogue had been written clearly on them.

Margaret and I have also been involved in the Social Action Group on and off since its beginning. It has always supported the Bayswater Family Centre. We got involved because our doctor, Richard Stone, was active in various social activities and he put us in touch with the Bayswater Centre. His practice was about a hundred yards from it. Living locally, we were able to assist in a variety of ways. The LJS supplied the funding for a computer room for children at the centre who had nowhere to study in the evenings.

The other main piece of work that I have done is on the synagogue's burial records, which I have corrected and computerised. In order to do this, I spent probably two years recording stones in the cemetery and then computerising the records. I have also subsequently computerised the marriage records.

When I look back, one of the great changes was when Louis Steinman left and a team of *shammashim* took over. It made for a very different atmosphere in the synagogue because they all had their different ways of doing things, and therefore we had a much wider variety of people who were given *mitzvot*. Later they were chosen in advance, but it was not until after the beginning of the Services Committee that we had leaflets giving the names of readers and the details of the service. Bob Kirk was responsible for this and for producing the leaflets.

Another change over the fifty years I have been coming to the LJS is the singing. The shape of the old synagogue made it quite impossible to hear other people singing. The choir in those days were concealed in the organ loft above the *bimah*, and however much noise the congregation made when joining in, you couldn't hear it. The acoustics were so poor that you always felt you were on your own, so there was much less congregational participation.

I have always been interested in family history and was a founder member of the Jewish Genealogical Society of Great Britain. I am fortunate in coming from a very cohesive family with close ties to the LJS. The act of producing and circulating a family tree has the effect of maintaining and strengthening the links within the family. It gives a multi-generational picture of the family and shows the effect that a single person can have on succeeding generations to the third or fourth generation, for good or ill. Lack of integrity can alienate children from their Jewish heritage, while sincerity and an intelligent understanding of their religion have the opposite effect. Charity by itself is not enough.

See photographs 53 and 54.

Alex Rosen and Armand Azoulay

Alex Rose and Armand Azoulay joined the LJS ten years ago in 2001. They had a Civil Partnership service at the synagogue in 2006.

Alex Rosen

I was born in December 1925, the second-youngest of seven siblings. Our parents had arrived in London, newly wed, from Antwerp six weeks prior to the outbreak of the Great War in 1914.

Brought up in the East End in an orthodox home, I attended the Jews' Free School until the outbreak of the Second World War, the point at which all our lives changed. My parents had rescued a nine-year-old boy from Germany, who arrived on the *Kindertransporte* to live with us. Within months, my two older brothers, then in their early to mid-twenties, were called up and joined the Royal Air Force. They were both posted to the Middle East war zone. My elder sister was married and her husband was in the Army.

I joined an accounting firm and enrolled at the City of London College to study for the Certified Accountants' exam, passing the intermediate level at eighteen. I was called up into the Army and trained as a Royal Artillery Surveyor, spending the harsh autumn and winter of 1944–45 at the Royal Artillery School on Salisbury Plain. In 1945, with the war in Europe over, I was shipped out to India to join the forces in Burma. Fortunately, when we arrived in Bombay, Japan had surrendered following the dropping of atomic bombs. I remained in India for the next two-and-a-half years.

I was transferred into the Royal Army Education Corps, promoted to Sergeant and within a year, Warrant Officer. I remained in India through the transfer of power, experiencing postings to units in Lucknow, Kanpur, Agra and the Prince's State of Indore, as well as travelling to other parts of the subcontinent. It was later in life that I came to appreciate that this experience was a substitute for going to University.

I encountered no anti-Semitism while I was in the Army. Just prior to my first Passover in India I received a note from the Jewish Chaplain giving the name of a doctor and his wife, who were originally from Germany but had settled in Lucknow. The note suggested that I make contact with them for *Pesach*. I went to the house, where they informed me they no longer kept Jewish festivals or practices. On another occasion, however, when in Bombay over *Rosh Hashanah*, I attended synagogue services and was warmly invited to lunch and dinner with Jewish families.

On demobilisation I returned to accountancy and qualified within a few years. I then gave up the profession. I became Secretary/Accountant to a manufacturing company and five years later the owner successfully sold the business. He asked me to remain with him to help create a finance company. With investment support from two merchant banks, the business emerged in 1963 as a public company called First National Finance Corporation. I remained on the board for a further five years until, in 1968, I decided I needed a break and a new career path.

I joined Goulston Finance Holdings and became their Managing Director, but left the company after two years when they were taken over. I was then invited to join the old-established City investment group, Drayton, to establish a commercial banking operation. I hesitated initially, as I would be the only Jew on the Board alongside people I viewed as being very prestigious, but I was encouraged by the Board members to accept. Three years later Drayton Group was bought by Midland Bank and merged with its merchant bank, Samuel Montagu, where I remained for a further five years.

In 1980 I was approached by the First International Bank of Israel, which wanted to establish a UK subsidiary, and I agreed to take on the task under the chairmanship of Lord Sieff. Within one year the banking license was obtained in the name of FIBI Bank (UK) Ltd. After nine successful years with them I retired at the age of sixty-five.

For many years my private life was overshadowed by my professional responsibilities, but on a visit to Paris in 1973 to attend a friend's birthday party I met Armand Azoulay. We became friends immediately and kept in touch for the next year, spending a few holidays together including a two- week visit to Israel, where we were nearly caught up in the *Yom Kippur* War.

Armand Azoulay

I was born in Morocco in 1937 and as a twelve-year-old spent two years at a school in Jerusalem. My four older siblings had emigrated there following anti-Jewish riots in Morocco at the time of the creation of Israel. On my return home, I continued my schooling and studies in Casablanca. In 1954–55 the anti-Jewish riots re-emerged. The same year, my father, who was the President of our Jewish community, collapsed and died in his business office at the age of fifty-four. He was very highly regarded by the community as both a leader and a philanthropist, especially in the difficult task at that period in organising young, needy children for Youth *Aliyah*.

The family gave up the business and, together with my three sisters and brother. I left Morocco for Paris, where I continued my education. I trained as a typographer and worked as an executive in the field of printing and publications.

I am artistic at heart; I paint and regularly visit galleries and museums. I speak French, Spanish and English and can get by in Hebrew.

In 1974 I joined Alex in London and we have shared a home for the past thirty-six years. My first job in London was with Avon Cosmetics as a typographic designer. After a few years I started an antique business, specialising in Oriental works of art, from Grays Antique Arcade in Mayfair. I continued my painting for a number of years under my good friend and teacher, the late Robert Walls.

When business became more difficult in the late 1990s, I ceased trading and retired. I had an apartment in Antibes for twenty-five years, where we spent many of our holidays. I sold it in 2006. I have family in Paris and in Israel with whom I keep in close contact.

Alex and Armand

In our retirement years, we found our membership of the United Synagogue incompatible with our outlook on life. In particular, we felt that the United Synagogue was moving to a more hardened view of religious practice, where ritual was more important than our understanding of a more humane outlook on daily life. As a result, we decided to join a synagogue with which we would have greater affinity.

We were introduced to the LJS and attended some services. We were welcomed by Rabbi David Goldberg, who encouraged us to apply for membership.

In the last ten years, since becoming members, we have become part of the community. We are regular worshippers almost every *Shabbat*, we participate in regular duties and enjoy the friendship and spirit that is so much part of the synagogue. We have made some very good friends. We entered into our Civil Partnership in February 2006.

Afterword
The LJS in its centenary year

THE LJS CELEBRATED its centenary in 2011 with a range of events which reflected the diversity of make-up and interests of its thriving congregation. The year opened with a Centenary Service, which included all the elements that have been paramount in the community's hundred-year history – music, including a specially commissioned setting of *Mi Chamochah* by Cecilia McDowall; readings taken from the works of its founders and early rabbis; a procession of over one hundred Religion School children, each contributing a single white rose to a floral display on the *bimah,* and the participation in the service of congregants ranging from Ludwig Spiro and Ruth Ive, both in their nineties, to teenagers Jacob Lovick and Sarah Lasher.

> The buzz of excitement and anticipation was evident as soon as the doors were opened at 9 a.m., even to the extent of a queue forming prior to this. This extraordinary atmosphere continued throughout the day and indeed heightened as the day progressed with the enthusiastic involvement of the congregation as a whole ... At the end of the service there was a feeling of self-congratulatory achievement and joy which must have paralleled the feelings of the congregation hundred years ago. In my many years of synagogue membership, I cannot recall such an uplifting atmosphere, even at the opening of the present building.
>
> Michael Nathan[342]

85. *Senior Rabbi, Alexandra Wright, and President Bob Kirk prior to Centenary Service, 5 February 2011. Photograph by Pam Fox. (2011)*

---

[342] Letter to Rabbi Alexandra Wright following the special Centenary Service, February 2011.

86. *Cello concert at the LJS, May 2011, part of centenary celebrations.*
Photograph by Pam Fox. (2011)

Other events included a cello concert, a study day celebrating the life and work of
Rabbi John Rayner, a Midsummer Night's Dance, an interfaith walk, a Religion School
pageant and a *Shabbaton* as a grand finale.

At the beginning of the celebratory year, a Centenary Appeal was launched in memory
of Rabbi John Rayner. Its objectives were to: create a small prayer room that offers a more
intimate space for private worship and ceremonies; update the classrooms with modern
technology, both for the Religion School and adult studies; and improve the ambience of
the communal areas for all users of the building.

Although the centenary celebrations have partly focused on the synagogue's evolution,
encouraged by its rabbis and lay leaders, the congregation has also used the occasion as an
opportunity to re-evaluate what its stands for, reflect on its experience as a community
and to change what needs changing.

This year 5771 the LJS will celebrate its 100th Birthday, our centenary. As a congregation
we ought to use this time to look back with pride on our achievements and accomplishments.
But we must not stop there. We cannot live frozen in the past. Were we to do this we would
become frozen like Lot's Wife who could only look back and therefore became fossilised,
Times change. Communities evolve ... As we look to the future we need open eyes, open
hearts and open minds as we bravely embrace the opportunities for growth and relevance
for tomorrow's member of the LJS.

David Wilfond[343]

---

[343] Sermon by Rabbi David Wilfond at the LJS given on 8 September 2010.

Anniversaries are not just occasions for looking back to see where we have come from; they are opportunities for taking stock and for renewal. And Renewal must be the theme for this coming year 5771, renewal of purpose, and improvement of the facilities we are able to offer.

Bob Kirk[344]

While a range of views exist amongst the congregation on how the synagogue might continue to evolve, there is also a great deal of consensus on important issues, especially the need to seek the views of young people and to cater for their interests, and to retain its external focus and its emphasis on social action and interfaith dialogue. It was therefore with a great deal of pride and optimism that the whole community is looking forward to its next hundred years.

The experiences that I have enjoyed, and friendships that have gone from strength to strength, will never leave me, nor will my truly sincere sense of belonging that I can enjoy being a member of the congregation of the LJS. The buildings might not be the prettiest in the world, and the classrooms might not be the best climate-controlled, but these are all simply part of the charm of this hundred-year-old community. When Lily Montagu, Claude Montefiore and Israel Mattuck, the 'Three Ms' as we tell the students, chatted about the idea of forming a less Orthodox, more welcoming, more inclusive and more egalitarian synagogue, I'm not sure whether they would have predicted what a thriving community it would eventually become. It is something I am proud to belong to, something that I, indeed most of us, have grown up into, and is as much a part of my life as is my school or where I live.

Jacob Lovick (Pt. 3)

We feel the deep, historic significance of having passed our first hundred-year threshold. It's wonderful to have the opportunity to honour those who had the wisdom, courage and determination to create the foundations upon which we base our own principles, and observance. In order to do so, we remind ourselves that as Liberal Jews, 'all bears scrutiny', and that we must resist the all too human temptation to hold fast to that which we know. And now the mantle passes to us – inspired by our founders, its our task to maintain and develop an inspiring, challenging religious, ethical, and spiritual environment in which to continually renew ourselves, and to foster a love and commitment to our community and our Judaism in our children. Soon the task will be theirs.

Harriett Goldenberg

Given the strength of the community, the likelihood is that the synagogue will remain the country's oldest and largest Liberal congregations in a hundred years' time.

---

[344] Bob Kirk, 'A New Year message from our President', *LJS News*, September 2010.

Appendices

Appendix One

Sources of information and material used in the book

Primary Sources

The material used to produce this book has come from many different sources as outlined below:

ULPS interviews

Transcripts of interviews carried out between 1994 and 1995 as part of the *ULPS Oral History Project*. The interviews were carried out by Bryan Diamond, Jon Kaye, Miriam Shire and Clive Winston. Those which have used most are the interviews with:

Rabbi Sidney Brichto

Rabbi John Rayner

Dorothy Edgar

Rosita Rosenberg

Doreen Gluckstein

Maxwell Stern

Marjorie Moos

Where material from these interviews has been used this is referenced in footnotes because the interviews were not commissioned by and are not archived at the LJS.

LJS archival interviews

Carried out over a five-year period by Bryan Diamond and Neil Levitt, and transcribed by Janet Ramsey from the LJS. These interviews included those with:

Rita Adler

Raymon Benedyk

Aileen Davis

Bryan Diamond

Desmond Feldman

Eva Feldman

Hannah Feldman

Denise Franklin

Denis Glaser

Rabbi David Goldberg

Ruth Ive

Ann Kirk

Bob Kirk
Norman Lazarus
Rosemary Lazarus
Neil Levitt
Jill Salmon
Michael Salmon
Barbara Shortt

Some of these interviews were updated and extended for the book.

Additional interviews commissioned for the book

The aim was to obtain a more representative range of interviews, for example, with young people, gay couples, etc. These new interviews were conducted by Bryan Diamond, Neil Levitt, Trixi Blaire, Pam Fox, Vivien Rose and Carolyn Simon. Several of these additional interviews were again transcribed by Janet Ramsey. The additional interviews were with:

Barbara Fidler
Barbara Godfrey
Louise Golding
Elizabeth Lazarus
Trevor Moross
Lee Montague
Jan Roseman
Alex Rosen and Armand Azoulay
Jean Russell
Tim Sandler
Ellen Schmidt
Tamara Schmidt
Martin Slowe
Jocelyne Tobin
Tony Weiss
Walter Wolfgang
Rabbi Alexandra Wright

Some people wrote their own memories having been given an indication of the areas to cover:
Felicity Allen
Cary Berlingieri
Bernie Bulkin
Elaine Feinstein
Michael Hart
Richard and Deborah Lazarus
Jacob Lovick

Carolyn Simon

Tim Simon

Several others provided either a single quote or number memories on specific issues and topics rather than undertaking a full interview:

Prue Baker

Liz Crossick

Diana Da Costa

Jane Finestone

Sally Frankel

Carole Goldberg

Sybil Gottlieb

Jo Kessler

Delia Marmor

Yakov Paul

Jane Pinto

Jacqueline Pinto

Ludwig Spiro

Jane Rayner

Carol Roberts

Vivien Rose

Joan Salter

Anita Schwartz

David Stern

An invitation to submit material for inclusion in the book was inserted in the LJS newsletter and a number of people were invited to make a contribution because of their relevant involvements. As a result of these invitations material was received from:

Trixi Blaire

Rachel Brouwer

Steven Derby

Nicholas Feldman

Lisa Gershon

Harriet Goldenberg

Cathy Heller Jones

Pamela Hershon

Richard Langton

Cathy Lasher

Sharon Lewison

Rabbi Kathleen de Magtige-Middleton

Janet Mills

Karen Newman and Susan Crane

Carol Roberts
Rosita Rosenberg
Ruben Ruiz Daum
Shelley Salter
Jeffrey Spearman
Helga Wolff
Richard Zionts

Material gathered in the following ways is not referenced in footnotes since the material belongs to the LJS.

Transcripts of talks and speeches

Given at various times at LJS events including those given by:
Eric Conrad
Aileen Davis
Diana Gould
Dr Robert Greenberg
Rabbi Harry Jacobi
Rosa Mintz
Marjorie Moos
Rabbi John Rayner
Walter Wolfgang

Copies of these talks and speeches are archived at the LJS but are referenced in footnotes to distinguish them from the interviews listed above.

General and specialist information

I met with a wide range of people to obtain background information on the history of the LJS generally and also on specialist topics covered in the book including:
Edward Cross
Cathy Heller Jones
Jo Kessler
Bob and Ann Kirk
Neil Levitt
Jane Rayner
Margaret and George Rigal
Rosita Rosenberg

None of the above material is referred to in footnotes as it belongs to the LJS.

Interviews in Part Three

The memories of several individuals and couples are reproduced in full in Part Three of the book. A number of criteria were used to determine which memories should be included, notably:

• Interest
• Representativeness (for example, people from different generations, etc.)
• Comprehensiveness.

Where these memories are quoted in Parts One and Two of the book, this is noted after the person's name (Pt. 3).

Other primary sources

Mainly housed in LJS archives, but also in private collections, including:

LJS Annual reports
LJS Newsletters
ULPS/Liberal Judaism Newsletters
Letters and other documents in LJS archive
Newspaper articles (for example, in the *Jewish Chronicle*) and letters printed in newspapers
Memoirs and autobiographies
Sermons and addresses (especially those of Rabbi John Rayner, Rabbi Mattuck and Lily Montagu)
Minutes of LJS Council
Membership lists

Secondary Sources

Tracts and pamphlets
Commemorative leaflets and books
Prayerbooks
ULPS/Liberal Judaism pamphlets on values and beliefs
Books relating to the history of Liberal Judaism
Books relating to the history of Anglo-Jewry
Books relating to historical figures in Liberal Judaism and Anglo-Jewry generally
Books on Jewish beliefs

See Bibliography for full list.

Photographs

The LJS holds an extensive collection of photographs in its archives. However, they are of variable quality and do not cover all aspects of the history of the synagogue. It has not therefore been possible to include photographs of all the major events in the LJS's history, and unfortunately I have not been able to include photographs of everybody I would like to have featured in the book.

Appendix Two

Key dates in the history of the LJS

1899	Lily Montagu article, 'Spiritual Possibilities of Judaism Today,' appeared in the *Jewish Quarterly Review*.
1901	A committee was formed including Dr Claude Montefiore, Dr Israel Abrahams and the Rev. Simeon Singer, named the Jewish Religious Union (JRU).
1902	First meeting of the JRU was held at which Claude Montefiore was elected as President, Lily Montagu as Vice-President. First JRU service was held at the Wharncliffe Rooms, Great Central Hotel on 18 October.
1909	The JRU committee decided to establish a congregation and on 23 June a general meeting voted in favour of this. Claude Montefiore published a pamphlet announcing the intention of the JRU to set up a congregation – 'The Jewish Religious Union – its Principles and its Future', known as 'The Manifesto'.
1910	A disused chapel in Hill Street, off Park Road near Baker Street, was acquired with a seating capacity of 450.
1911	First service was held at Hill Street on Saturday 4 February conducted by Israel Abrahams. Claude Montefiore preached the sermon. In June Rabbi Israel Mattuck visited and appointed the first Minister.
1912	Rabbi Mattuck was inducted on 20 January.
1913	The first Secretary, Michael Duparc and first Beadle, Isaac Nathan, were appointed. The synagogue was registered for marriages and cemetery at Willesden acquired.
1916	The congregation had grown to such an extent that the High Holyday services had to be held at the Bechstein Hall.
1918	On 15 January the Hon. Lily Montagu gave her first sermon to an adult audience. The youth group, the Alumni Society was formed.
1920	Women were allowed to read in the services. The Rev. Maurice Perlzweig was appointed as first Associate Minister.
1923	The congregation sent its first representatives to the Board of Deputies. The Women's Society was formed under the chairmanship of Lady Sassoon.
1924	Members of the synagogue organised a conference of Jews and Christians. Israel Abrahams died in October. The current St John's Wood site was acquired and the building of a new, purpose-built synagogue began.

1925	The consecration of the synagogue took place on 13 September and the Religion School held its first lessons in the new classrooms. The Hebrew Union College conferred the honorary degree of Doctor of Hebrew Law on Rabbi Mattuck.
1926	The first international conference of Liberal and Reform Jews was held at the LJS and the World Union for Progressive Judaism was founded.
1927	The London Society of Jews and Christians was founded Co-Chaired by a rabbi of the LJS and a senior clergyman from either Westminster Abbey or St Paul's Cathedral.
1928	The United Charities Fund was established.
1931	The Rev. Leslie Edgar appointed as an additional Associate Minister.
1933	Rabbi Mattuck set up a club for unemployed men and a Refugee Committee was established. The Younger Members' Organisation was established to cater for the post-Alumni age group.
1935	The LJS was certified by the Board of Deputies as a congregation entitled to conduct marriages.
1937	Rabbi Mattuck celebrated twenty-five years as Senior Minister.
1938	Claude Montefiore died shortly after his 80th birthday.
1940	On Saturday 2 November the synagogue was badly damaged by a bomb.
1944	Sir Louis Gluckstein became President.
1945	Two services were held on 8 May, the Day of National Thanksgiving. On 19 August two services were held to mark the end of the war with Japan.
1946	The Rev. Philip Cohen was appointed Associate Minister.
1947	A special Sabbath peace service was held on 19 April at the request of the World Union for Progressive Judaism. Rabbi Dr Mattuck's book, *The Essentials of Liberal Judaism*, was published.
1948	Rabbi Mattuck became Rabbi Emeritus and Leslie Edgar the Senior Minister. The Communal *Seder* was held in the synagogue for the first time since the bombing.
1951	The main synagogue was reconsecrated.
1954	Rabbi Mattuck died and a special memorial issue of the *Liberal Jewish Monthly* was published. The Hon. Lily Montagu was elected President of the World Union in succession to Rabbi Leo Baeck.
1957	John Rayner joined the ministry of the LJS.
1958	Rabbi Dr Leslie Edgar was conferred the degree of Doctor of Divinity by the Hebrew Union College in the United States. The Rev. Philip Cohen left the LJS after twelve years of service to serve the North-Western Reform Synagogue in Alyth Gardens.
1959	Following unremitting efforts by Sir Louis Gluckstein, the Marriage (Secretaries of Synagogues) Act received Royal Assent.

1961	The Rev. John Rayner succeeded Rabbi Edgar as Senior Minister who became Rabbi Emeritus. Religion School classes were started on Saturdays and study courses were set up for older members.
1963	The Hon Lily Montagu died and a new wing of the synagogue was consecrated in her honour.
1964	The Rev. David Goldstein was appointed Associate Rabbi.
1966	Marjorie Moos retired after forty years of teaching the Religion School, the correspondence class and proselytes.
1967	During the Six Day War the LJS instituted its own Israel Emergency Appeal Fund.
1968	A new prayerbook, *Service of the Heart*, edited by Rabbis John Rayner and Chaim Stern, was introduced.
1969	The Women's Society was reorganised and all women members of the synagogue automatically became members.
1970	An Israel Committee was formed, addressed by the Israeli Ambassador the following year.
1972	The synagogue celebrated its Diamond Jubilee.
1973	The new ULPS prayerbook, *Gate of Repentance*, edited by Rabbis John Rayner and Chaim Stern, was used for the High Holydays.
1974	The Services Committee was set up to provide a forum to review the effectiveness of the synagogue services.
1975	Rabbi Dr David Goldstein left the LJS to take up a research appointment at the British Library. Rabbi David Goldberg joined the LJS.
1976	The category of junior membership was abolished. Full rights and responsibilities were given from the age of sixteen.
1977	The combined ULPS Service held at the LJS celebrated the 75th anniversary of the founding of the Jewish Religious Union.
1978	Malcolm Slowe, a member of the congregation, was the first ULPS member to be elected to the Executive Committee of the Board of Deputies. Peggy Lang House, an Abbeyfield House run by members of the LJS, was opened for seven residents. A Soviet-Jewry Committee was set up.
1979	The President of the congregation, Sir Louis Gluckstein, died.
1980	An interfaith 'tri-alogue', involving a series of meetings between the Central London Mosque, St John's Wood Church and the LJS, was initiated.
1981	Daily evening services were introduced. The Annual General Meeting included a debate on whether the LJS should introduce *Bar* and *Bat Mitzvah*. The Council took the decision to introduce *Bar Mitzvah*, subject to agreement that the young person would continue in the Religion School till confirmation. The murals, depicting the Pilgrimage Festivals, were unveiled by Norman St.John-Stevas.

1982	As a result of the war in Lebanon, the LJS rabbis gave many addresses on their view of current Israeli policies, wrote articles and appeared on television.
1983	Following a report that the building was in need of extensive and expensive repair, recommendations were made for the redevelopment of the Synagogue building.
1984	The Council decided to redevelop the site. Rabbi Dr Leslie Edgar, Minister Emeritus, died.
1986	Rabbi Alexandra Wright became a rabbi at the LJS. The synagogue celebrated the 75th anniversary of its founding.
1987	Maxwell Stern was elected President. Rabbi Dr David Goldstein, former LJS rabbi of the LJS, died.
1988	A farewell service was held and the LJS moved into its temporary home at 152 Loudoun Road. The Religion School moved to 28 Abercorn Place. A rebuilding appeal began. A Steering Committee was set up with to responsibility for all aspects of the new building, as well as the move to Loudoun Road, with a Design and Use Committee to deal with all matters of design and furnishings.
1989	Rabbi John Rayner formally retired and became Rabbi Emeritus. Rabbi Alexandra Wright left the LJS to serve Radlett and Bushey Reform Synagogue.
1990	Rabbi Helen Horn (later Helen Freeman) joined the synagogue as Associate Rabbi. The Women's Society decided to disband at the end of the year.
1991	The first service was held in the new synagogue and a Thanksgiving Service in March. High Holyday services took place in the Montefiore Hall as well as the synagogue.
1992	Rita Adler was the first woman to be elected as Chairman. A progressive women's conference 'The Half Empty Bookcase' was held at the synagogue attracting much interest and publicity. A special service was held to mark the completion of the three-year-long *Bimah* Chair project.
1993	A celebration service was held to mark the final completion of the new building. The multi-faith Bosnian Support Group, actively supported by the synagogue, focused its work on Hrastnik, its adopted refugee camp in Slovenia.
1995	The new prayer book, *Siddur Lev Chadash*, was introduced. The President, Sir Peter Lazarus, died having been elected just a year earlier.
1996	The *Shoah* Memorial, created by Anish Kapoor, was dedicated.
1997	The synagogue was awarded 'The Disability Challenge Award' by Jewish Care.
1999	After nearly ten years at the LJS, Rabbi Freeman left to take up a post at West London Synagogue. Jan Roseman was appointed as the first Director of Education.
2000	Rabbis Mark Solomon and Kathleen de Magtige-Middleton took up posts at the LJS. Willie Kessler was elected President.
2003	The new High Holyday prayerbook, *Ruach Chadashah,* was used for the first time. Liz Crossick was appointed as Community Care Coordinator. The Social Action Committee arranged for the synagogue to be twinned with a Progressive Jewish community in Vinnitsa, the Ukraine.

2004	Rabbi Goldberg was succeeded as Senior Rabbi by Rabbi Alexandra Wright. A special service was held to celebrate the 80th birthday of Rabbi John Rayner. The LJS Nursery School was established under the headship of Caroline Villiers.
2005	Rabbi John Rayner died on 19 September and a special service was held to celebrate his life. An interfaith service took place to commemorate those who were died and were injured on 7/7.
2006	Crystal Clear Services were introduced to provide accessible services for those with a range of disabilities. The synagogue introduced same-sex commitment ceremonies.
2007	Bob Kirk was elected President. Rabbi Mark Solomon officiated at the Westminster Abbey celebration of Advent and *Chanukkah*, the first such event to be held in London.
2011	The synagogue's centenary celebrations commence in February with a special Centenary Service and finish with a *Shabbaton*.

Appendix Three

Leaders of the LJS

Ministers and rabbis

Those listed were appointed to LJS staff. Several others assisted for short periods, including a number of American rabbinic students from the Hebrew Union College, Cincinnati in the late 1950s/early 1960s.

Rabbi Dr Israel Mattuck: Senior Minister 1912–48, Rabbi Emeritus 1948–54

Rev. Maurice Perlzweig: Assistant Minister 1924–38 (also at North London Progressive Synagogue)

Rabbi Solomon Starrels: Assistant Minister 1928–33 (also at West Central Synagogue)

Rabbi Dr Leslie Edgar: Assistant Minister 1938–48, Senior Minister 1948–61 (became Rabbi 1951), Rabbi Emeritus 1961–84

Rabbi Raphael Levine: Assistant Minister 1938–41

Rabbi Jakob Kokotek: Assistant Minister 1941–45

Rev. Philip Cohen: Assistant Minister 1946–58

Rabbi John Rayner: Assistant Minister 1957–61, Senior Minister 1961–89 (became Rabbi 1965), Rabbi Emeritus 1989–2005

Rabbi Herman (Chaim) Stern: Assistant Minister 1962–63, Acting Senior Minister 1963–65

Rabbi Sidney Brichto: Assistant Minister 1962–64

Rabbi Dr David Goldstein: Assistant Minister 1964–75 (became Rabbi 1968)

Rabbi Roger Herst: Assistant Minister 1965–68

Rabbi Alan Mann: Assistant Rabbi 1971–75

Rabbi David Goldberg: Associate Rabbi 1975–2004, Senior Rabbi 1989–2002, Rabbi Emeritus 2002–

Rabbi Alexandra Wright: Associate Rabbi 1986–89, Senior Rabbi 2004–

Rabbi Michael Feinberg: Associate Rabbi 1989–90

Rabbi Helen Freeman: Associate Rabbi 1990–99

Rabbi Mark Solomon: Rabbi 2000–09

Rabbi Kathleen de Magtige-Middleton: Rabbi 2000–07

Rabbi David Wilfond: Rabbi 2010–11

Presidents

Claude Montefiore 1913–38

Col. (later Sir) Louis Gluckstein 1944–79

Maxwell Stern 1987–92
Sir Peter Lazarus 1994–95
Willie Kessler 1999–2006
Bob Kirk 2007–

Vice-Presidents

Lionel Jacob 1920–27
Arthur Joseph 1920–27
Louis Gluckstein 1933–44
Ernest Joseph 1953–56

Chairmen of Council

(Initially the President was also the Chairman of the Council)
Col. (later Sir) Louis Gluckstein 1938–63
Sydney Levine 1963–66
Edward Joseph 1966–72
Sir Peter Lazarus 1972–75
Lewis Levy 1975–80
Maxwell Stern 1981–87
Sir Peter Lazarus 1987–92
Rita Adler 1992–98
Trevor Moross 1998–2002
Timothy Simon 2002–04
Ellen Schmidt 2004–07
Rita Adler 2007–11
Michael Hart 2011–

Honorary Treasurers/Co-Treasurers

Harry Lewis 1910–24
Sidney Mendelssohn 1913–18
Julian Simon* 1918–46
Albert Holt 1926–36
Ernest Joseph 1936–52
Ronald Simon* 1946–66
Edward Joseph 1954–59
Robert Herrman 1959–67

Desmond A Feldman 1966–73
Louis Wolchover 1967–70
Eric Kahn 1971–75
Maxwell Stern 1973–80
Anthony Margo 1975–84
Peter Rossiter 1981–82
William Kessler 1983–87
Julian Tobin 1984–89
Rita Adler 1988–92
Otto (Bob) Beral 1989–98
Bob Kirk 1992–98
Bernard J Bulkin 1998–2001
Tim Simon* 1998–2002
Tony Yablon 2001–08
Ellen Schmidt 2002–04
Michael Hart 2004–07
Barbara Fidler 2007–
Eric Blaire 2008–

*Three generations of Simons

Directors of Education/Head of Religion School

Jan Roseman 1999–10
Dov Softi 2010–

Nursery School Head Teacher

Caroline Villiers 2004–

Secretaries/Directors of Administration

A Lindo Henry: Hon. Sec. 1910–13
Israel Duparc: Secretary 1913–61
Miss Peggy Lang: Organising Secretary 1944–65
John Levinson: Assistant Secretary, 1949–61, Joint Secretary, 1961–67
John Cross: Joint Secretary 1961–66, Secretary 1967–73
Marianne Ghosh: Organising Secretary 1966–67
Raymon Benedyk: Synagogue Secretary 1973–91
Nicki Judah: Administrator, 1991–92

Carol Burns: Organising Secretary 1992–93
Jenny Salter: Administrator 1993–94
David Rigal: Organising Secretary 1994–99
Joyce Whitman: Administrative Director 2000–04
Michael Jacobs: Director of Administration 2005–07
Michael Burman: Director of Administration 2007–11
Caroline Bach: Executive Director 2011–

Choirmasters/Directors of Music

Ivor Warren 1910–48
Israel Hoffman 1948–76
Yakov Paul 1977–96, then Director Emeritus
Cathy Heller Jones 1996–

Glossary

Adon Olam – A hymn of praise.

Aleynu – A prayer used towards the end of synagogue services. It links particularism with the universal mission of Judaism.

Aliyah – Literally 'going up', to be called up to recite the blessings before and after the reading of the *Torah*. Also used to refer to immigration to Israel.

Apocrypha – 'Hidden books'. Those parts in the Septuagint (Greek translation of the Bible) that were added to the original Hebrew text.

Ark (Hebrew: *Aron Ha-Kodesh*) – The cupboard in the synagogue where the scrolls of *Torah* are placed.

Ashkenaz/Ashkenazi – Literally Germany/German, but generally used to describe Jews from Central or Eastern Europe and their pronunciation of Hebrew. See Sephardi.

Aufruf – Literally means 'call up' but is used to refer to calling up on to the *bimah* a couple about to get married.

Bar Mitzvah and *Bat Mitvah* (together *B'nei Mitzvah*) – Literally 'son of the commandment', 'daughter of the commandment' or 'children of the commandment'. Refers to ceremonies to mark the time at which boys/girls become responsible in Jewish law for their actions. The ceremonies for both boys and girls usually take place at the age of thirteen in Progressive synagogues. In Orthodox synagogues, the ceremonies for girls usually take place when they are twelve and are referred to as *Bat Chayil* ('daughters of worth').

Beth Din – Literally 'house of Judgement'. Used to refer to the law court which adjudicates on matters of Jewish law.

Bimah – Literally 'high place'. It actually means the reading desk in a synagogue, but is usually used to describe the platform on which the reading desk stands.

Challah – Plaited bread loaf, sometimes glazed with egg, used to welcome *Shabbat* and festivals

Chanukkah – Literally 'dedication'. The eight-day, mid-winter Festival of Lights commemorating the rededication of the Temple by the Maccabees in 165 BCE.

Chanukkiah – A candleholder with eight branches, often with a ninth for the 'servant' (*shamash* q.v.) candle that is used to light the other candles. It is used for celebrating the eight days of *Chanukkah* (q.v.).

Chassid – Member of the Jewish sect which follow the teachings of the eighteenth-century *Chassidic* movement.

Chavurah (plural *chavurot*) – Literally 'a group of friends'. Used to refer to informal gatherings with a meal, discussion, study and prayer.

Cheder – Literally 'room', but generally used to refer to a school for younger Jewish children.

The Chief Rabbi – The Senior Rabbi of the United Synagogue (q.v.) and claiming some authority over other Orthodox Jews in this country and in Commonwealth countries, but representing the entire Jewish community to the outside world.

Chumash – Literally 'Five'. A book containing the weekly readings in synagogue, laid out with the *Pentateuch* reading (q.v.) followed by the *Haftarah* (q.v.) for each week.

Chuppah – The wedding canopy used at Jewish weddings

Day of Atonement – *Yom Kippur* (q.v.).

Day of Memorial – *Rosh Hashanah* (q.v.).

Diaspora – Collective word for Jewish people living outside the land of Israel.

Erev Shabbat – The eve of Sabbath which commences at sunset on a Friday evening.

Federation of Synagogues – A group of Orthodox Synagogues joined in one organisation, set up by Lily Montagu's father, Baron Swaythling. Originally composed of Russian and Polish Jews. Now more to the right of the United Synagogue.

Get – Jewish divorce document.

Habonim – Zionist cultural youth movement.

Haftarah – The reading from the Prophets that follows the *Torah* (q.v.) reading on *Shabbat* (q.v.) and festivals.

Haggadah (plural *haggadot*) – Literally 'telling'. The prayerbook used at the *seder* (q.v.) meal on the eve of Passover (*Pesach* q.v.) telling the story of the Exodus from Egypt.

Halachah – Literally 'the way of going'. Rabbinic law based on the interpretation of biblical and later texts and commentaries.

Hebrew Union College – The American rabbinic seminary for Reform (Liberal/Progressive) Jews. There are four campuses: Cincinnati, New York, Los Angeles and Jerusalem.

High Holyday services – Services for the Jewish New Year (*Rosh Hashanah* q.v.) and the Day of Atonement (*Yom Kippur* q.v.).

Ivrit – Modern Hebrew spoken in Israel.

Jewish Board of Guardians – Original name for the Jewish Welfare Board (q.v.).

Jewish Care – The umbrella Jewish organisation concerned with welfare work.

Jewish Welfare Board – The former name of Jewish Care (q.v.).

Jews' College – Established to train men to be ministers in Orthodox Synagogues in Britain. Now renamed London School of Jewish Studies.

Kabbalat Torah – Literally 'acceptance of the *Torah*'. Liberal Jewish service of confirmation for young people aged fifteen/sixteen. Once it was the only rite of passage in Liberal Jewish synagogues.

Kaddish – An Aramaic prayer of praise of God. This has come to be associated with funerals and mourning.

Kashrut – The set of Jewish dietary laws. Food in accord with *halachah* (q.v.) is termed kosher in English, from the Ashkenazi (q.v.) pronunciation of the Hebrew term *kashér* meaning 'fit' (in this context, fit for consumption by Jews according to traditional Jewish law),

Ketubbah – Jewish marriage contract.

Kiddush – Blessings to sanctify *Shabbat* (q.v.) or festival with wine and bread. Can also be used to refer to other food served to accompany these blessings.

Kindertransport (plural *Kindertransporte*) – Also Refugee Children Movement (or RCM) is the name given to the rescue mission that took place nine months prior to the outbreak of the Second World War. The United Kingdom took in nearly 10,000 predominantly Jewish children from Nazi Germany, Austria, Czechoslovakia, Poland and the Free City of Danzig. The children were placed in British foster homes, hostels, and farms. Most of the rescued children survived the war. A small number were reunited with parents who had either spent the war in hiding or survived the Nazi camps, but the majority, after the war, found their parents had been killed.

Kippah (plural *kippot*) – Skullcap. Also referred to as *cappel* or *yarmulke*.

Kol Nidre – An Aramaic declaration of the nullity of unfulfilled vows to God recited in a synagogue before the beginning of the evening service on every *Yom Kippur* (q.v.), the Day of Atonement (q.v.).

Liberal Judaism – One of the two forms of Progressive Judaism found in the United Kingdom, the other being Reform Judaism (q.v.). Liberal Judaism, which developed at the beginning of the twentieth century is less conservative than UK Reform Judaism.

Machzor – The prayer book for *Rosh Hashanah* (q.v.) and *Yom Kippur* (q.v.).

Matzah (plural *matzot*) – Unleavened bread eaten at *Pesach* (q.v.).

Messiah – 'Anointed One'. The anointed messenger of God, whom Jews in the past believed would come at the end of days.

Mitzvah (plural *mitzvot*) – A commandment. Also used colloquially to mean a good deed or an honour, such as being called up to make a scroll reading in a synagogue.

Ner tamid – 'Perpetual light', always kept burning above the Ark in a synagogue.

Omer – Measure of wheat. Title given to the seven-week period between *Pesach* (q.v.) and *Shavu'ot* (q.v.).

Oneg Shabbat – Literally 'joy of Sabbath', informal Sabbath (or Friday evening) gathering of Jews in a synagogue or private home to express outwardly the happiness inherent in the Sabbath holiday. Usually refreshments are provided to complement the congenial atmosphere which are followed by some kind of talk, discussion or other form of entertainment.

Orthodox – A term introduced in the nineteenth century to describe traditional Jews or Judaism to distinguish them from Reform Judaism which appeared at the same time. The term Orthodox was taken from Christianity, and is not strictly accurate as it describes belief, while in Judaism it is generally used to describe practice.

Passover – See Pesach.

Pentecost – See *Shavu'ot*.

Pentateuch – 'Five books' (Greek). The first five books of the Bible: Genesis, Exodus, Leviticus, Numbers and Deuteronomy.

Pesach – Passover, the festival that celebrates the freedom gained with the Exodus from Egypt.

Pilgrimage Festivals – *Pesach*, *Shavu'ot* and *Sukkot* (all q.v.), so-called because scripture required people to travel to the Temple to offer sacrifice.

Progressive – A form of Judaism that teaches progressive revelation. Originally used to include both Liberal and Reform, but now mostly associated with the Liberal movement.

Purim – Literally 'lots'. Minor festival remembering the events described in the book of Esther, telling how the Jews were saved from persecution.

Purim spiel – 'Purim play' (Yiddish). A comic or satirical piece performed or written at *Purim*.

Purim (q.v.) *Megillah* – The scroll telling of the story of Esther read at *Purim*.

Reform Judaism – A form of Progressive Judaism which is generally more traditional in its practices than Liberal Judaism.

Refuseniks – Name given to Russian Jews refused permission by the State to emigrate (to Israel) and, mostly, deprived of their original livelihood. (The description is currently being used to indicate Israelis who refuse to serve in the army in the occupied territories.)

Rosh Chodesh – Literally 'head of the month'. The first day of the new moon in the Jewish calendar.

Rosh Hashanah – Literally 'head of the year'. Jewish New Year's Day, the first of the High Holydays.

Sanctuary – That part of the synagogue building used for worship.

Seder – 'Order'. The name of the service for the first night of Passover, which takes place in Jewish homes, using symbolic foods. (Orthodox Jews outside of Israel observe two nights.)

Selichot – Jewish penitential poems and prayers, especially those said in the period leading up to the High Holydays (q.v.), and on fast days. The Thirteen Attributes of God are a central theme throughout the prayers. The *Selichot* service is usually held late at night on the *Shabbat* before the High Holydays (q.v.).

Sephardi – 'Spanish'. Used to describe Jews who come from the countries around the Mediterranean. Today generally extended to those Jews from Islamic countries. Also refers to their pronunciation of Hebrew.

Shabbat – Sabbath. From sunset on Friday until sunset on Saturday.

Shamash (plural *shammashim*) – Salaried sexton in a Jewish synagogue whose duties now generally include secretarial work and assistance to the cantor, or *chazan,* who directs the public service. At the LJS the duties of the *shamash* are carried out on a voluntary basis by a rota of synagogue members.

Shavu'ot – Literally 'weeks'. The festival celebrating the giving of God's revelation to the Children of Israel.

Shiur – A study session or a lesson on any *Torah* (q.v.) topic.

Sho'ah – Literally 'destruction'. Hebrew name for the Nazi Holocaust.

Shofar – Literally 'ram's horn'. Shaped into a musical instrument and blown on *Rosh Hashanah* (q.v.).

Siddur – Literally 'ordered'. The prayerbook for daily and Sabbath services.

Siddur Lev Chadash – 'Prayerbook new heart' (Ezekiel 36: 26). Published by ULPS in 1995.

Simchat Torah – Literally 'rejoicing or joy of the *Torah*'. The festival celebrating the end of the cycle of scroll readings and the beginning of the new cycle. The festival occurs at the end of *Sukkot* (q.v.).

Sukkot – 'Tabernacles' (singular, *sukkah*). The seven-day autumn harvest festival when temporary structures are built, in which some Jews eat and sleep.

Tabernacles – See *Sukkot.*

Tallit (plural *tallitot*) – A fringed garment used as a prayer shawl, see Numbers 15:37ff.

Talmud – The name of two compilations of rabbinic discussions and decisions which date from roughly third to fifth century CE. Where no adjective is used, then it refers to the Babylonian *Talmud*. The alternative is the Jerusalem *Talmud.*

Tikkun Leyl Shavuot – A special service and all-night study session for *Shavu'ot* (q.v.).

Tisha B'Av – The ninth of the Hebrew month of Av. It is a day of fasting, commemorating the destruction of the Temple.

Torah – Variously defined as the Pentateuch (q.v.), the Law, or better, as the revelation of God's teaching to the Children of Israel.

Tu bi Sh'vat – Fifteenth of *Shevat*. The New Year for trees.

United Synagogue – A confederation of a number of Orthodox Synagogues in Britain, founded 1870. Today its members are probably the least observant of those claiming to be so. Seventy per cent of Anglo-Jews who belong to synagogues are in the United Synagogue.

Yeshivah – A place of study for younger Jewish men where they study the *Talmud.*

Yom ha-Atzma'ut – Israel Independence Day.

Yom ha-Sho'ah – A special service to commemorate the Holocaust.

Yom Kippur – 'Day of Atonement'. A day of fasting when Jews seek forgiveness from God for wrongdoing.

Bibliography

General bibliography

Abrahams, I, *Notes on Singers Prayer Book* (London, 1912)

Abrahams, I, and Montefiore, C G, *Aspects of Judaism* (London, 1895)

Anon., *Jewish Addresses Delivered at The Services of the J.R.U. 1902–3* (London, 1904)

Anon., (Magnus, C.L) *E.M.J., The Man and His Work* (London, 1962)

Apple, R, *The Hampstead Synagogue 1892–1967* (London, 1967)

Bayme, S, 'Claude Montefiore, Lily Montagu and the origins of the Jewish Religious Union', *Transactions of the Jewish Historical Society* vol. xxvii (1982)

Bermant, C, *Troubled Eden: An Anatomy of British Jewry* (London, 1969)

—— *The Cousinhood* (London, 1971)

The Bernhard Baron St George's Jewish Settlement, *Fiftieth Anniversary Review 1914–1964* (London, 1964)

Cohen, L, *Some Recollections of Claude Goldsmid Montefiore* (London, 1940)

Conrad, E, *Lily H. Montagu Prophet of a Living Judaism* (New York, 1953)

—— *In Memory of Lily H. Montagu* (London, 1967)

Edgar, L, *Some Memories of My Ministry* (London, 1985)

Goldberg D J, and Rayner, J D, *The Jewish People, their history and religion* (London 1987)

Goodman, Arnold, *Tell Them I'm On My Way* (London, 1993).

Henriques, B L Q, *Indiscretions of A Warden* (London, 1937)

—— *Fratres, Club Boys in Uniform* (London, 1951)

Hertz, J H, *The New Paths, Whither Do They Lead?* (London, 1926)

Hooker B, *Facts and Fallacies about Liberal Judaism* (London 1961, revised 1972)

—— *A Manual of Judaism.* (London 1962)

Jacobs, L, *We have reason to believe.* (London 1957)

Kershen, A J, and Romain, J A, *Tradition and Change* (London, 1995)

Kessler, E, ed., *A Reader of Early Liberal Judaism: Writings of Israel Abrahams, Claude Montefiore, Lily Montagu and Israel Mattuck* (London and Portland, OR, 2004)

Langdon, H, 'Living Judaism', *Journal of the RSGB* (November 1972)

Lazarus, O, *Liberal Judaism and its Standpoint* (London, 1947)

Levin, S L, *A Century of Anglo-Jewish Life* (London, 1970)

Levy, N G, *The West Central Story and its Founders* (London, 1968)

Lipman, V D, *Social History of the Jews in England 1850–1950* (London, 1954)

—— 'The Rise of Jewish Suburbia', *Transactions of the Jewish Historical Society* vol. xxi (1968)

Loewe, L L, *Basil Henriques: A Portrait* (London, 1976)

Mattuck, I I, *The Essentials of Liberal Judaism* (London, 1947)

Montagu, L H, 'Spiritual Possibilities of Judaism Today', *The Jewish Quarterly Review,* vol. xi no. 42 (1899)

—— *Out of Zion Shall the Law Go Forth* (London, 1917)

—— *The Jewish Religious Union and its Beginnings* (London, 1927)

—— *The Faith of a Jewish Woman* (London, 1943)

—— *My Club and I* (London, 1954)

—— *Samuel Montagu First Lord Swaythling* (London, undated)

Montefiore, C G, *The Bible for Home Reading,* 2 vols. (London, 1896 and 1899)

—— *Liberal Judaism* (London, 1903)

—— *Judaism, Unitarianism and Theism* (London, 1908)

—— *The Jewish Religious Union, Its Principles and Its Future* (London, 1909 and 1918).

—— *A Laudation of Judaism* (London, 1910)

—— *Outlines of Liberal Judaism* (London, 1912)

—— *Liberal Judaism and Nationalism* (London, 1917)

—— *The Dangers of Zionism* (London, 1918)

—— *Race, Nation, Religion and the Jews* (London, 1918)

Montefiore, C G, and Henriques, B L Q, *The English Jew and His Religion* (London, 1918)

Montefiore, C G, and Perlzweig, M L, *Why the Jewish Religious Union Can Be, and Justifiably is 'Neutral' as regards Zionism* (London, 1935)

Neuberger, J, *On Being Jewish* (London, 1995)

Picciotto, J, *Sketches of Anglo-Jewish History* (London, 1956)

Rayner, J D, *The Practices of Liberal Judaism* (London, 1958)

—— *Progressive Judaism, Zionism and the State of Israel* (London, 1983)

—— *An Understanding of Judaism* (London 1997)

—— *Jewish Religious Law; A Progressive Perspective* (London 1998)

—— *A Jewish Understanding of the World* (London 1998)

—— *Before I Forget* (1999)

—— 'Non-Conformism in Anglo-Jewry', *Jewish Quarterly* (Winter 1999/2000)

Rayner, J D, and Hooker, B, *Judaism for Today* (London, 1978)

Renton, P, *The Lost Synagogues of London* (London, 2000)

Rich, S, *South London Story* (London, 1954)

Rigal, L A, *A Brief History of The West Central Liberal Synagogue* (London, 1978)

—— *The Story of a Synagogue, 1919–1996* (London, 1996)

Rigal, L A, and Rosenberg, R, *Liberal Judaism: The First Hundred Years,* (Liberal Judaism, 2004)

Schindler, H, 'Reminiscences of FLPJYG', *Golden Jubilee – 50 Years of Youth in Words and Pictures* (ULPS, December 1997).

Sheridan, S, and Rothschild, S, *Taking up the Timbrel* (London, 2000)

Teacher, V, 'Reminiscences of FLPJYG', *Golden Jubilee – 50 Years of Youth in Words and Pictures* (ULPS, December 1997)

Umansky, E, *Lily Montagu and the Advancement of Liberal Judaism* (New York and Toronto, 1983)

—— *Lily Montagu: Sermons, Addresses, Letters and Prayers* (New York and Toronto, 1985)

World Union for Progressive Judaism, *International Conference of Liberal Jews, London, 1926* (London, 1926)

World Union for Progressive Judaism, *First Conference of the World Union for Liberal Judaism* (Berlin, 1928)

Younger Members' Organisation and the Alumni Society of the LJS, *The First Fifty Years* (London, 1950)

Younger Members' Organisation of The Liberal Jewish Synagogue, 'The Years Between 1911–1951' (London, 1951)

Prayerbooks

Gate of Repentance, Editors: Rabbi John Rayner and Rabbi Chaim Stern (ULPS, 1973)

Liberal Jewish Prayer Book, 3 vols. (1923–26)

Passover Haggadah (ULPS, 1962 and 1968)

Passover Haggadah (ULPS, 1981)

A Selection of Prayers, Psalms and Other Scriptural Passages and Hymns for use at the services of the Jewish Religious Union, London (London, 1902)

A Selection of Prayers, Psalms and Other Scriptural Passages and Hymns for use at the services of the Jewish Religious Union, London (London, 1903)

Service of the Heart, Editors: Rabbi John D Rayner and Rabbi Chaim Stern (ULPS, 1967)

Services and Prayers for Jewish Homes (LJS, 1918)

Siddur Lev Chadash, Editors: Rabbi John D Rayner and Rabbi Chaim Stern (ULPS, 1995)

Index